# Que's Using Enable™

Walter R. Bruce III

*Revised for Version 4.0 by*

Lisa G. Bunton
Gary Farkas
Leslie M. Kreizman
Jodi L. Schroth

*Que's Using Enable*™

Library of Congress Catalog No: 90-64402

ISBN: 0-88022-701-X

94  93  92  91    4  3  2  1

Interpretation of the printing code: the rightmost double-digit number is the year of the book's printing; the rightmost single-digit number, the number of the book's printing. For example, a printing code of 91-1 shows that the first printing of the book occurred in 1991.

Screen reproductions in this book were created with Collage Plus from Inner Media, Inc., Hollis, NH.

*Que's Using Enable*™ is based on Enable/OA™ Version 4.0 and also can be used with Versions OA, BP, 2.15, and 2.0.

---

*Publisher:* Lloyd J. Short

*Associate Publisher:* Karen A. Bluestein

*Acquisitions Editor:* Tim Ryan

*Project Development Manager:* Mary Bednarek

*Managing Editor:* Paul Boger

*Book Designer:* Scott Cook

*Production Team:* Hilary Adams, Claudia Bell, Jeanne Clark, Sandy Grieshop, Betty Kish, Phil Kitchel, Bob LaRoche, Sarah Leatherman, Anne Owen, Julie Pavey, Louise Shinault, Bruce Steed, Suzanne Tully, Johnna VanHoose, Christine Young

**Product Director**
Walter R. Bruce III

**Production Editor**
Diane L. Steele

**Editors**
Frances R. Huber
Barbara K. Koenig

**Technical Editors**
Janet Healey and
the Technical Support Staff
at Enable Software, Inc.

**Editorial Assistant**
Patty Brooks

*Composed in Garamond and
Macmillan by Que Corporation*

**Walter R. Bruce III** is the author of Que's *Using Enable/OA, Using Paradox 3, Using DataEase, Using PROCOMM PLUS, Using PC Tools Deluxe,* and *Using Carbon Copy Plus.* He has written several instructional texts for intermediate and advanced workshops on using popular micro-computer software packages. He also has led workshops for government and private industry clients from coast to coast. Mr. Bruce is a licensed attorney who practiced for three years in North Carolina and six years in the United States Air Force.

**Gary Farkas** is vice-president of F&T Computer Services in Schenectady, New York. He has more than six years of experience with Enable as an author of software applications, a trainer for beginners and programmers, and a developer of many of the current Enable functions and features. Mr. Farkas is a graduate of the State University of Albany; his education is in programming, mathematics, and education.

**Lisa G. Bunton**, **Leslie M. Kreizman**, and **Jodi L. Schroth** are senior instructors/consultants with N. J. Naclerio and Associates, Inc., an Enable Software Authorized Training Center in Springfield, Virginia, and Harrisburg, Pennsylvania.

Lisa Bunton began her career with Naclerio and Associates in 1987; she currently is the manager of the Naclerio Harrisburg office. She has presented more than 750 days of Enable training to private and government clients across the country. Ms. Bunton is a graduate of Pennsylvania State University at Harrisburg with a degree in Information Systems.

Leslie Kreizman has been associated with Enable since its initial release in 1985. She was involved with one of the firm's first large training contracts for the Pennsylvania Department of Environmental Resources, and she recently initiated the "train-the-trainer" program for in-house personnel. Ms. Kreizman is a graduate of the University of North Carolina at Chapel Hill with a degree in Communications.

Jodi Schroth has been teaching and consulting in Enable since 1979. She has worked primarily with the Pennsylvania Department of Environmental Resources, the Defense Logistics Agency, and the U.S. Army Corp of Engineers. Her expertise is in making difficult concepts understandable and in preparing training manuals. Ms. Schroth is a graduate of Elizabethtown College, Elizabethtown, Pennsylvania, with a degree in Computer Science and Mathematics.

For more information about consulting, training, on-site seminars, or support materials from N. J. Naclerio and Associates, Inc., contact

N. J. Naclerio and Associates, Inc.
7830 Backlick Road, Suite 403
Springfield, VA 22150
703-451-7557

# TRADEMARK
# ACKNOWLEDGMENTS

Que Corporation has made every effort to supply trademark information about company names, products, and services mentioned in this book. Trademarks indicated below were derived from various sources. Que Corporation cannot attest to the accuracy of this information.

Associated Press is a registered trademark of Associated Press. AT&T is a registered trademark of AT&T. BYTE is a registered trademark of McGraw-Hill, Inc. BYTE Information Exchange (BIX) is a service mark of McGraw-Hill, Inc. Color 400 is a trademark of Sigma Design, Inc. CompuServe is a registered trademark of CompuServe Incorporated. CONDOR3 is a trademark of Condor DBMS Services, Inc. Cordata is a trademark of Cordata Technologies, Inc. Crosstalk is a registered trademark of Digital Communications, Inc. dBASE II, dBASE III PLUS, dBASE IV, MultiMate, and MultiPlan are registered trademarks and MultiMate Advantage II is a trademark of Ashton-Tate Corporation. Enable and Enable/OA are trademarks of Enable Software, Inc. Epson is a registered trademark of Seiko Epson Corporation. GEM is a trademark of Digital Research, Inc. GEnie is a service mark of General Electric Corporation. Harvard Graphics is a registered trademark of Software Publishing Corporation. Hayes and Hayes Smartcom II are registered trademarks of Hayes Microcomputer Products, Inc. Hewlett-Packard Vectra and Hewlett-Packard are registered trademarks of Hewlett-Packard Company. IBM, Personal Computer AT, and PS/2 are registered trademarks and Personal Computer XT is a trademark of International Business Machines Corporation. Leading Edge Model D and Leading Edge are registered trademarks of Leading Edge Products, Inc. Lotus, 1-2-3, and VisiCalc are registered trademarks of Lotus Development Corporation. Mace Utilities is a registered trademark of Paul Mace Software, Inc. MacPaint is a registered trademark of Apple Computer, Inc. MCI and MCI Mail are registered trademarks of MCI Telecommunications Corporation. MS-DOS, Microsoft Word, and Microsoft Excel are registered trademarks and Windows is a trademark of Microsoft Corporation. NEC APC is a registered trademark of NEC Corporation. NewsNet is a registered trademark of NewsNet, Inc. Norton Utilities is a registered trademark of Symantec Corporation. PC-File III is a trademark of ButtonWare, Inc. and of Jim Button. PC Magazine is a registered trademark of Ziff Communications Co. PC Paintbrush is a registered trademark of ZSoft Corporation. PCTools is a trademark of Central Point Software. PeachText is a registered trademark of PeachTree Software, Inc. Perspective and Perspective Junior are trademarks of Three D Graphics, Inc. PROCOMM PLUS is a registered trademark of DATASTORM TECHNOLOGIES, Inc. Prodigy is a registered trademark of Prodigy Systems. The Source is a service mark of Source Telecomputing Corporation, a subsidiary of The Reader's Digest Association, Inc. SuperCalc is a registered trademark of Computer Associates International, Inc. TANDY Deluxe Graphics Display Adapter and Tandy are registered trademarks of Tandy Corporation. Telenet is a registered trademark of Telenet Communications Corporation. Tymnet is a registered trademark of Tymnet, Inc. Uninet is a registered trademark of Uninet. UNIX is a registered trademark of AT&T. WordPerfect is a registered trademark of WordPerfect Corporation. Zenith is a registered trademark of Zenith Electronics Corporation.

# ACKNOWLEDGMENTS

T hanks to the following individuals for their invaluable help in bringing this book together:

Janet Healey and her staff at Enable Software, Inc. for the technical review of the book.

Diane Steele, Fran Huber, and Barbara Koenig, Que's editorial team on this book, for their dedication and hard work on this seemingly endless project.

—W.B.

# CONTENTS AT A GLANCE

## II   The Master Control Module

## IV   The Spreadsheet Module

# V   The Database Management Module

# VI   The Graphics Module

# VII The Telecommunications Module

# Introduction

---

Enable/OA Version 4.0 is perhaps the most comprehensive, all-inclusive software package available for an IBM-compatible personal computer.

With *Que's Using Enable,* you easily can become a versatile user of the feature-rich modules that make up Enable/OA Version 4.0. You learn to use the Master Control, word processing, spreadsheet, database management (DBMS), graphics, and telecommunications modules.

You may be surprised at the breadth and depth of this program and the ease with which you can learn it. Even if you are a computer novice, with Enable and this book you may discover you have become a seasoned PC user.

## History of Enable

Enable is produced by

Enable Software, Inc.
313 Ushers Road
Northway Ten Executive Park
Ballston Lake, NY 12019-1519

Several of the founders of Enable Software previously built and sold Bibliographic Retrieval Services (BRS), a successful software company specializing in mainframe and minicomputer information management systems. They formed Enable Software, Inc. (formerly The Software Group) in 1982 to produce software that approaches the power and flexibility of much larger systems while maintaining the accessibility, familiarity, and compatibility of PC-based systems.

As with all other major PC-based software developers, Enable Software, Inc. has released Enable in several versions. The first version of Enable, Version 1.0, was released in November, 1984. Since then, Enable Software has released for commercial distribution: Version 1.1, Version 2.0, Version 2.15, Enable/OA, and, most recently, Enable/OA Version 4.0. In addition, the company has released several customized versions, such as Enable/BP, for institutional clients such as the Internal Revenue Service and the Department of Defense, and a special version for value-added retailers (VARs). This book covers the essential features of all versions of Enable released at the time of this writing.

# New in Enable/OA Version 4.0

Enable/OA Version 4.0 includes many features that earlier versions of Enable do not have. Table I.1 summarizes the most important new features of each of Enable's modules.

**Table I.1**
**New Features with Enable/OA Version 4.0**

| Module | New Features |
| --- | --- |
| Master Control Module | Multiple Operating System Support: DOS, UNIX (SCO 3.2) <br> X Windowing System <br> Complete Mouse Support <br> Clipboard <br> Hypertext: Full Documentation On-line <br> User-Selectable Interface: Enable/OA Version 4.0, Enable/OA Version 3.0, Enable Version 2.15 <br> Utilities: Pop-up Calculator, Pop-up Clock, Card File, Calendar, Telephone Book |
| Word Processing | Page Preview Mode <br> Font Support <br> Snaking and Side-by-Side Columns <br> Collapsible Outline <br> Find and Replace Attributes and Format Codes <br> Paragraph Numbering |

| Module | New Features |
|---|---|
| | Line Numbering |
| | Link to Spreadsheet and Graphic Data, Update by Command |
| | Document History: Author, Version |
| | Foreign Dictionary Support |
| Spreadsheet | Numerous new functions |
| | Landscape Printing |
| | Hidden Columns, Levels, or Cells |
| | Cell Notes |
| | Undo |
| | Find and Replace: Text, Within Formulas |
| | Cell Colors by Criteria: Highlighted, Linked, Less than X, @NA, @ERR, Labels, Annotated, Protected, Changed by last Recalc, Negative or 0 value, All other cells |
| | Interruptible Recalculation |
| Database Management | Data Dictionary |
| | User Assisted Import of text files (ASCII, Enable WP) |
| | New Procedural Language Commands: .clrmouse, .setmouse, .mshiftl, .mshiftr, .color, .sql |
| | Floating Point Data Type |
| | Report Debugger |
| | Print reports up to 255 characters |
| | ANSI Level 1 SQL |
| | Array Structure |
| | Memo Field Functions |
| Graphics | New Graph Types: Organizational Charts, Text and Bar/Line Graph, Step Graph, Horizontal Bar |
| | Symbol Library |
| | Perspective Junior |
| Telecommunications | New Protocols: 1K-Xmodem, CompuServ B+, CRC-Xmodem, Ymodem-Batch |
| | New Terminal Emulations: ANSI (X3.64-79), VT220, VT320 |

# Integrated versus Stand-Alone Software

PC-based programs that focus on providing extensive capability to do only one of the major functions of PC-based software, such as word processing, spreadsheets (calculation-intensive models), databases (processing large amounts of information), presentation graphics, or telecommunications, are called *stand-alone* programs. Enable is an *integrated* program because it combines the functions of each of these software types into one program and provides the means to move data easily from any one of these modules to another.

Buying an integrated program such as Enable has some distinct advantages over buying several stand-alone programs:

- *Purchase price.* Enable costs about the same as any one of the most popular word processing, spreadsheet, or database programs.

- *Ease of learning.* The user interfaces of most popular programs are inconsistent with each other, creating difficulty in mastering all of these programs; however, Enable's menus, command syntax, and screen layout are consistent for all of its modules.

- *Data integration.* Although most popular programs provide some method for moving data from one program to another, the process is often cumbersome. In this area, integrated programs are particularly effective. With Enable, you even can run another program in an on-screen "window" and move data between Enable and another program. You can perform this task as easily as you move data between Enable's modules.

The popular stand-alone programs still offers some advantages:

- *Third-party support.* Supply-and-demand market forces attract other companies to provide add-on and add-in programs, utilities, and accessories designed to work with a best-selling stand-alone program.

- *Power.* Generally, the most powerful stand-alone programs provide added features that may be of interest to advanced users and system integrators; however, Enable compares favorably with most stand-alone programs. The program even has some powerful features that the stand-alone programs can duplicate only through extensive programming, if at all.

Enable provides the basic functions of 1-2-3, dBASE IV, WordPerfect, and PROCOMM PLUS, and also includes some impressive presentation graphics. Enable also can read 1-2-3, dBASE, and WordPerfect files, and files created by many other programs.

# What You Should Have

You can use Enable/OA Version 4.0 on any IBM PC, XT, AT, PS/2, or 100-percent compatible computer with one 5 1/4-inch or 3 1/2-inch disk drive and a hard disk.

The system should have MS-DOS or PC DOS 3.1 (or later), or UNIX. The system should have the following minimum configurations for the operating environment:

- 640K RAM with DOS
- 6M RAM with UNIX

To use all of Enable's features, your system should include the following:

- Graphics display capability
- Text printer
- Graphics-capable printer (plotters are also supported)
- Modem

For information about installing Enable and using start-up parameters and commands, refer to Appendix A, "Installing and Getting Started with Enable."

# Who Should Read This Book?

*Que's Using Enable* is an asset to both new and experienced Enable users, not taking the place of the documentation that comes with Enable/OA Version 4.0, but rather supplementing and complementing it. Enable is so robust, with hundreds of important features in every module, that learning the program can seem overwhelming without a guide. This book is your guide, leading the way with numerous hints, suggestions, and examples of the best ways to get the most from Enable.

This book serves two major functions:

- Provides an overall guide to the fundamental features of each of the program's six modules: the Master Control, word processing, spreadsheet, database management, graphics, and telecommunications.

- Introduces and explains the new features of Enable/OA Version 4.0.

# What Is in This Book?

You can read the chapters of *Que's Using Enable* in the same manner you use Enable: word processing to database management, database management to spreadsheet, spreadsheet to graphics, graphics back to word processing, and so on. The book is divided into seven parts. Each part begins with a quick-start lesson. If you are new to Enable, use these lessons as introductions. After you feel comfortable with the basics, you can use the chapters in each part to accomplish your work faster and more easily.

The major parts of the book are as follows:

### I. An Overview of Enable

This part provides a first look at Enable's six modules. Read these chapters to get a better idea of Enable's overall structure.

### II. The Master Control Module

As its name implies, the Master Control Module (MCM) is the cohesive force that binds the other five modules into a whole. Enable Software informally refers to MCM as "Corporate Staff." These chapters describe how to use the MCM to manage files, to use Enable's powerful windowing and multitasking environment, and to store keystrokes as macros.

### III. The Word Processing Module

The list of Enable's word processing features has grown longer with each new release. The first chapters in this part explore the fundamental word processing features, such as entering text, moving the cursor, performing simple editing, and setting margins. The remaining chapters in Part III explain how to use advanced word processing features, such as sort, automatic hyphenation, and linking spreadsheet and graphics data.

### IV. The Spreadsheet Module

The chapters in this part of the book also divide the basic features and advanced features. By first using the fundamental features, new spreadsheet users become familiar with the terms and concepts peculiar to spreadsheet programs. The advanced chapters explain many of the features that give spreadsheets their amazing power and flexibility, including Enable's built-in functions, linking, and in-cell macros.

### V. The Database Management Module

Word processing and, to some extent, spreadsheets are fairly obvious extensions of work you already do on paper. Switching to do this work on the PC is fairly natural because you work on the electronic equivalent of paper. Entering and manipulating data in a database is not as intuitive for most people. This part of the book first presents each of the fundamental steps necessary to define and build a database, to edit and manipulate the data, and to print a report from the data. Enable's more powerful database features follow, including using several database files at once and creating powerful customized input forms and reports. The final chapter discusses the DBMS procedural language, an advanced topic.

### VI. The Graphics Module

Enable has the capability of extracting data from either a spreadsheet file or a DBMS file to create graphs. The first chapter in this part describes how to use either data source to generate each of the six types of graphs. The second chapter presents the amazing capabilities of Perspective Junior, Enable's three-dimensional graphics program.

### VII. The Telecommunications Module

Probably the least understood and most underused module in Enable is telecommunications. This chapter presents the fundamentals of this module, introducing new telecommunicators to the necessary terms and typical uses for this technology. The chapter then describes the basics of Enable telecommunications.

This book also includes two appendixes:

Appendix A, "Installing and Getting Started with Enable," is a guide to getting started with Enable. This appendix explains how to install the program on your computer and how properly to configure Enable to suit your needs.

Appendix B, "Customizing Enable: Profiles," explains how to customize Enable's numerous features by creating collections of option settings called profiles.

# Conventions Used in This Book

Enable uses menus extensively. With few exceptions, you can accomplish every feature and task through a series of menu choices. Usually, you select the menu and choose the menu item by pressing the key for the first letter. For clarity, *Que's Using Enable* indicates menu selections as follows:

Use_System Word_Processing Create

This sequence, for creating a new word processing file, means to press the keys U, W, and C in succession. If a command has more than one word, an underscore connects the words in this book—the underscores do not appear on-screen. To assist you in learning these commands, many of the commands are mnemonics: the keys you press are the first letters of the commands' names.

Sometimes more than one menu choice begins with the same letter. In those cases, the menu indicates one of the options by highlighting a letter other than the first letter. For example, to check spelling while in a word processing file, press these keys:

F10 Tools Spell_Check

In addition to its menus, Enable has an extensive set of F9 commands— commands that bypass the menus. You can use the F9 commands to bypass the menus; however, you must know the correct sequence of keystrokes. Usually, F9 commands use fewer keystrokes than their menu counterparts. For example, the F9 command for saving a word processing file and continuing to edit is as follows:

F9 Save Edit

This means you press the keys F9, S, and E in succession.

Occasionally, you need to press two keys at the same time, such as when you use the Alt, Ctrl, or Shift key in a key combination. In this book, the two keys are joined by a hyphen (-). Thus, Alt-Home means to hold down the Alt key and press the Home key. Keys are written as they appear on the IBM keyboard.

Words that are variable or optional and words that are terms used for the first time are printed in *italic typeface*. Screen messages and prompts are printed in a `special typeface`. Information you are asked to type is printed in **boldface**. Words printed in uppercase letters include range names, modes, macros, and cell references.

*Que's Using Enable* helps you learn to use Enable, regardless of the version you own; however, the text and figures assume that Enable/OA Version 4.0 is the current standard. Features new in Enable/OA 4.0 are specially marked by an icon in the margin. Files, macros, and procedural language programs created with earlier versions of Enable are compatible with Enable/OA 4.0 without requiring any special steps, but the reverse is not true.

Margin icons and boxed text mark Notes, Tips, and Cautions. A Note provides brief, additional information relating to the topic in the surrounding text. A Tip is an insight that can help you more fully realize and benefit from the features of Enable. A Caution warns you about the potential negative consequences of a an operation or action.

Enable's word processing and spreadsheet modules provide an option for saving your work in a format that is compatible with earlier Enable versions, but the DBMS module does not have a direct conversion method. You can accomplish the same result by saving the file in dBASE II format.

Now that you have an idea of what to expect in this book, use it to guide you to a better awareness and understanding of the impressive ease, flexibility, and power of Enable.

# Part I

# An Overview of Enable

---
Includes
---

**Quick Start I: Starting and Quitting Enable**

**Using Enable's Modules**

**Understanding the Keyboard and Enable's Screens, Menus, and Keyboard Commands**

# Quick Start I

# Starting and Qutting Enable

For each of the seven parts of this book, you find a quick-start lesson to help you "break the ice"; you can try out some of Enable's most fundamental features without having to do a lot of reading. This first lesson explains how to start and quit Enable. Turn to the beginning of each of the other parts in the book for a quick-start lesson on Enable's individual applications, or *modules*.

If you have not yet installed Enable, turn to Appendix A for tips on the best installation method. Appendix B discusses various configuration (*profile*) choices, but you may want to use Enable as it is configured "right out of the box" until you become comfortable with the program. Then use Appendix B to explore the various profile settings. The instructions in the remainder of this lesson assume that you have installed Enable properly on your computer's hard disk.

## Starting Enable

To start Enable, do the following:

1.  To create a directory on your hard disk drive C (for example, MYDATA) to hold the working files you create with Enable, type the following command from the C:\ prompt:

**MD\MYDATA**

and then press Enter. This command establishes a directory called MYDATA in which you can store your data.

2. Assuming that you installed Enable in the \EN400 directory, you type the following command to go to the Enable program directory:

   **CD\EN400**

3. To start Enable on a DOS system, type

   **ENABLE (,,,,C:\MYDATA)**

   Enable displays its sign-on screen, as shown in figure QSI.1.

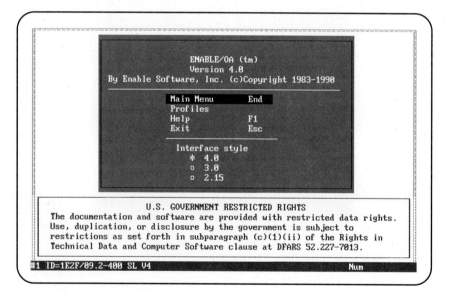

*Fig. QSI.1. Enable's sign-on screen.*

4. Press the End key to start Enable. Enable displays the Main Menu (see fig. QSI.2).

You access each of Enable's modules—word processing, spreadsheet, database management (DBMS), graphics, and telecommunications—from the Main Menu, as you do many of the Master Control Module's (MCM) features. Turn to the respective quick-start lessons to learn how to create word processing, spreadsheet, DBMS, and graphics files, and how to read and send electronic mail by using Enable's telecommunications module.

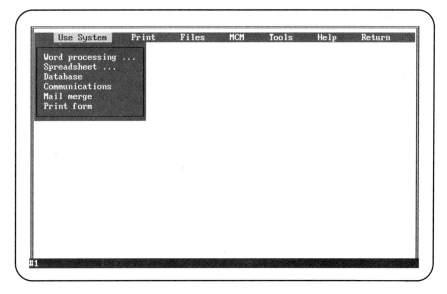

*Fig. QSI.2. Enable's Main Menu.*

# Quitting Enable

To quit Enable from the Main Menu, press

**Return Return_to_OpSys**

Enable returns the screen to the operating system prompt.

# 1

# Using Enable's Modules

This chapter gives you a broad overview of Enable. In addition to the Master Control Module, Enable has five modules, each of which is the equivalent of one of the major business applications—word processing, spreadsheet, database, graphics, and telecommunications. Read this chapter quickly to get an idea of what the program and each of its modules can do, and to see how each module relates to the other modules and to the whole program. This discussion is not meant to be exhaustive but to whet your appetite.

To understand clearly how Enable can work for you, you must recognize Enable's modular design. Enable accomplishes each major application—word processing, spreadsheet, database management, graphics, and telecommunications—through a separate *module* that appears to stand on its own. Indeed, each module compares favorably, feature for feature, with even the most powerful and sophisticated stand-alone PC programs. Enable, however, is not five stand-alone programs but one tightly knit program; each module is accessed and managed by a sixth module, called the *Master Control Module* or *MCM*.

## The Master Control Module

The MCM is Enable's own operating system. Through the MCM, you can open up to eight separate windows to perform up to eight separate tasks.

For example, you can have two word processing windows, a spreadsheet, and a print task active at the same time. The MCM enables you to print while you are editing your word processing document. The MCM also manages all data going into, out of, and between Enable's applications modules.

You can think of Enable as star-shaped, with the five applications modules radiating from the MCM at the center (see fig. 1.1). All external data goes in and comes out through the MCM, which also can pass data internally from one module to another. Suppose that you are working on a report in a word processing file, for example; you decide that you need to include a table of numbers you already have created as a spreadsheet. If you first open the spreadsheet file (a second point on the star) and then perform an interwindow copy (moving data between points on the star), you can place the table in the report without retyping the table. The MCM can manage up to eight separate tasks at once and can easily pass data between several word processing files, several spreadsheets, and so on.

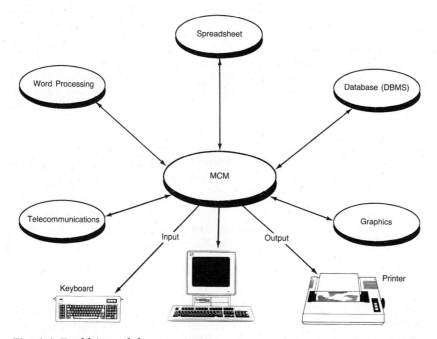

***Fig. 1.1.*** *Enable's modular structure.*

The Master Control Module also manages all Enable files. Through the MCM, you can list, copy, rename, and delete all Enable files. In fact, you can use the MCM to manage all DOS files, regardless of which program created them. Enable/OA has an enhanced set of file management utilities that include the capacity to change DOS file attributes as well as protect a file with a password. When you use these extended utilities, you can make and delete directories, change volume labels, and assign a new default data path.

Part II, "The Master Control Module," covers in detail the MCM and its special features.

# The Word Processing Module

Although Enable's word processing module is only one of five applications modules, the word processing module is in the same league as popular corporate word processing programs such as WordPerfect and Microsoft Word. The list of features goes on, but the most important improvements added in Enable/OA Version 4.0 follow:

- Page preview mode

- Search and replace attributes

- Paragraph numbering

- Line numbering

- Spelling checker for single words

- "Warm-link" to spreadsheet data

- "Warm-link" to graphics data

- Landscape printing available for most printers (rather than only laser printers)

These new capabilities top off a word processing program that already was full-featured, document-oriented, and menu- and command-driven. The word processing module features a final mode and, in version 4.0, offers a page preview option that shows you exactly what your document will look like when you print it (see fig. 1.2). The Enable word processing module has plenty of advanced features, including a spelling checker, hanging indention, columns, numeric tabs, headers and footers, outline processing, index and table of contents generation, mail merge, and box drawing. The word processing module has direct access to all the math functions available in Enable's spreadsheet and DBMS modules, including the capability to add columns of numbers. Part III, "The Word Processing Module," discusses both the basic and advanced uses of the word processing module.

```
┌═C:\4ODATA\SAMPLE.WPF══════════════════════════════════════F1O═┐

   Sample Header                                           Page 1

   Although Enable is not a true WYSIWYG word processor

          1.  It can display text on the screen as it will appear in print
              through page preview
                  o This text is in italic.
                  o This text is in boldface.
                  o This text is underlined.
                  o This text is boldfaced and underlined.
                  o This text is subscript: H₂O.
                  o This text is superscript: πr².

          2.  Headers, footers, page numbers, page breaks, footnotes, etc.,
              can be previewed in Final Mode.


 F1O,PgUp,PgDn,Home,Ctrl/Home,Ctrl/End,F2nG,Ctrl/Brk              Page    1
```

*Fig. 1.2. The page preview feature in the word processing module.*

# The Spreadsheet Module

Enable's spreadsheet module compares well with popular stand-alone spreadsheets such as Lotus 1-2-3, Excel, and SuperCalc.

 Enable/OA Version 4.0 has added several significant features to the spreadsheet module, including the following:

- Find and replace commands for text and formulas

- Cell notation

- Cell colors

- Command undo

- Hide cells

- Pull-down menus (see fig. 1.3)

Part IV of this book covers the spreadsheet module. In Part IV, you learn about the basic features of spreadsheets. You also learn to use spreadsheet functions and spreadsheet macros.

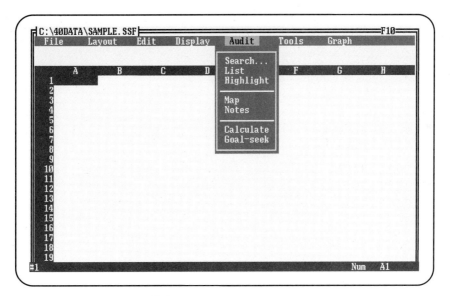

**Fig. 1.3.** *A spreadsheet pull-down menu.*

# The Database Module

Enable's database module is designed primarily as a menu-driven database management system. Enable's database module (DBMS), however, has the capability to access, display, and change data from any number of database files at once, and it can merge two database files to create a third. The DBMS even can update data in several files from the same input form.

Enable also provides a powerful procedural language that you can use to generate customized reports from multiple files as well as directly manipulate data in files on the disk. You access DBMS commands from a menu (see fig. 1.4), and the syntax of the various commands is clear and consistent. Because database programs are conceptually different from the way most people work, they are not easy to learn. Few people are as organized as a DBMS forces them to be. As database programs go, however, Enable is accessible, and you don't need a degree in programming to master the DBMS module.

New features in Enable/OA 4.0's database include the following:

- ANSI Level 1 SQL

- Floating point data type

- Better memo field functions

- Better color control in procedural language

- Several new procedural language commands

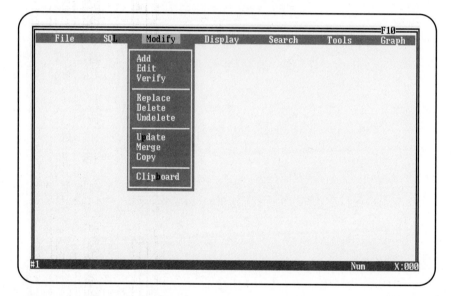

*Fig. 1.4. A DBMS pull-down menu.*

Because initial database definition is completely menu-driven, you can define fields quickly and easily (see figs. 1.5 through 1.7). Error checking and validation options also are available. Text fields can be up to 254 characters long. Enable provides memo fields as a means to store variable-sized text data for a record. You edit memo fields with Enable's word processing module and store them in a separate file. Your database can include as many records as your disk can hold.

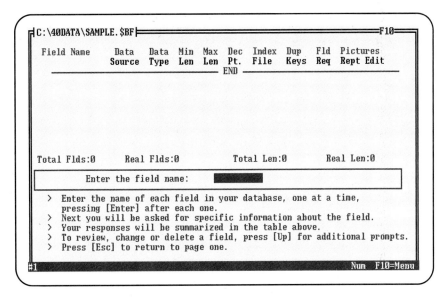

*Fig. 1.5. The initial Field Definition screen.*

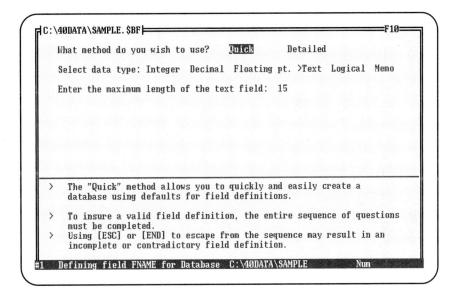

*Fig. 1.6. The Quick Field Definition screen.*

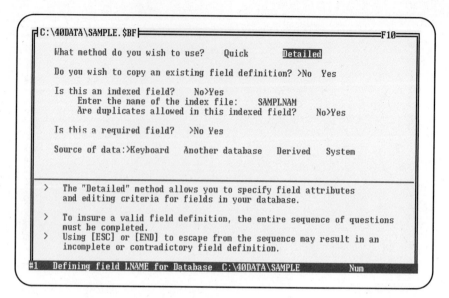

**Fig. 1.7.** *The Detailed Field Definition screen.*

You enter data using one of two forms: an automatically generated fill-in-the-blank input form (see fig. 1.8) or a custom input form that you design using a word processing screen and a "put-it-here" screen-painting technique, where you place your cursor in the position of the desired field and press a command to enter the data (see fig. 1.9). Some processing options are available in the custom form, including advanced features such as the capability to include default data and have the data copied to the next screen. Enable also inserts system-supplied data, such as the date or time, into appropriately defined fields and handles both calculated fields and fields looked up from another database.

Enable's DBMS includes a feature called *Query By Example* (*QBE*). Through QBE, even a new user can search a database like an expert by entering sample data in the blanks on an input form. Enable finds the record or records that match these criteria and displays the information one record at a time until you find the information you want.

A significant feature of Enable/OA is full-file compatibility with dBASE III Plus, including memo fields. Enable can create, use, and update memo fields while maintaining complete dBASE III Plus file compatibility.

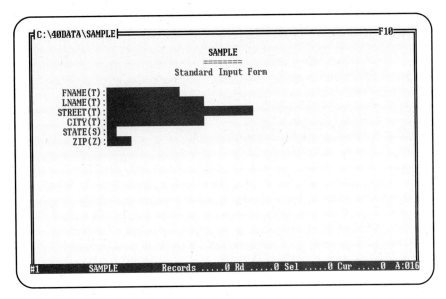

**Fig. 1.8.** *A Standard Input Form.*

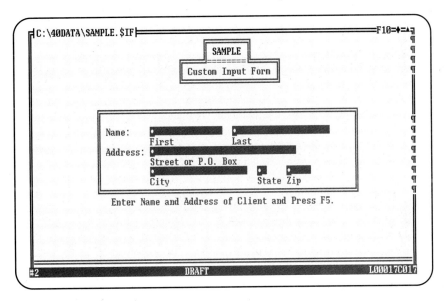

**Fig. 1.9.** *A Custom Input Form.*

The goal of most database projects is to produce output, usually on paper. Enable provides several options. If you simply need the data printed in columns—even if you want the data sorted with grand totals, subtotals, and sub-subtotals—the default columnar report form is sufficient. To create noncolumnar reports or to include data from more than one database file at once, you can use the procedural language, although you may have to do some programming. Enable also can generate a report to disk so that you can edit the report as a word processing file.

Part V covers Enable's database management module. Chapter 13 covers the basics of designing, building, displaying, editing, and printing a database file. Chapter 14 discusses the more powerful features of Enable's DBMS, including commands that deal with two related database files at once. Chapter 15 introduces you to the basics of Enable's DBMS procedural language.

# The Graphics Module

Enable's graphics module, presented in Part VI, uses the numbers from a spreadsheet or a DBMS file to create graphs. The graphics module can use up to eight data groups to create nine different types of high-resolution graphs: two-dimensional vertical bar graphs, two-dimensional stacked-bar graphs, three-dimensional vertical or stacked-bar graphs, standard and exploded pie graphs, line graphs, X-Y graphs, and open-high-low-close graphs for stock quotations (see figs. 1.10 and 1.11). If you are using an EGA or VGA monitor, you can display the graph in high-resolution color.

In its earlier versions, Enable had an outstanding array of graphics features. In 1987, Enable Software enhanced this part of the program for Version 2.0 by adding the award-winning graphics package Perspective (see fig. 1.12). Enable/OA also includes a version of Perspective that displays the two- and three-dimensional graphics in color.

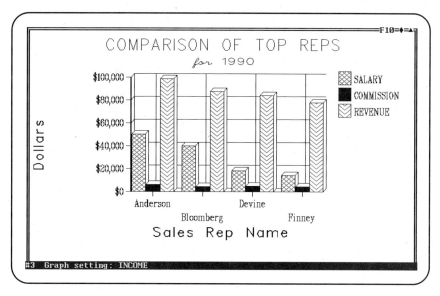

**Fig. 1.10.** *A vertical bar graph.*

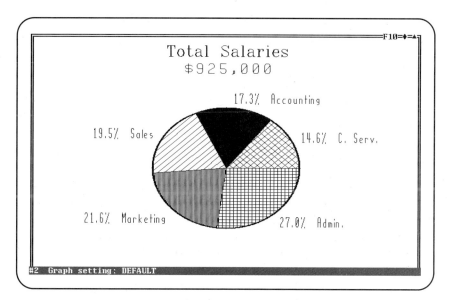

**Fig. 1.11.** *A standard pie graph.*

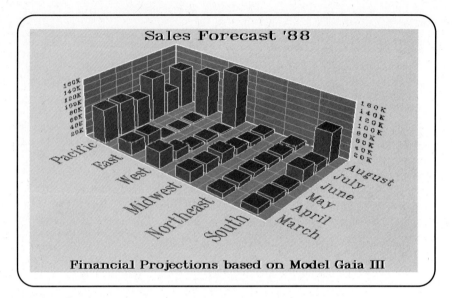

**Fig. 1.12.** *A Perspective Junior three-dimensional bar graph.*

# The Telecommunications Module

Enable's telecommunications module (*TP*—for *teleprocessing*), like the other modules, is full-featured and easy to use. In many ways, the telecommunications module's features are comparable to those features of popular programs such as Crosstalk XVI and Smartcom II. TP is designed for use with Hayes-compatible modems that use the AT command set, but you also can configure Enable/OA for other command sets.

TP initiates a telecommunications session in three different ways: Quick-Connect, Use Setup, and Perform Script (see fig. 1.13). The last two methods enable you to preset the communication parameters (such as baud rate, parity, phone number, and passwords), and the first method enables you to select the parameters each time you start a TP session. The most powerful connect method, Perform Script, is similar to the DBMS procedural language; it enables you to program routine tasks or makes it possible for novices to use the telecommunications module. The Perform Script feature is beyond the scope of this book.

Whichever connect method you choose, you can use Enable to communicate over the telephone lines with other PCs and PC bulletin boards, with public networks such as Telenet or Tymnet, or with electronic information and mail services such as The Source, CompuServe, GEnie, or MCI Mail. Part VII of this book discusses telecommunicating with Enable.

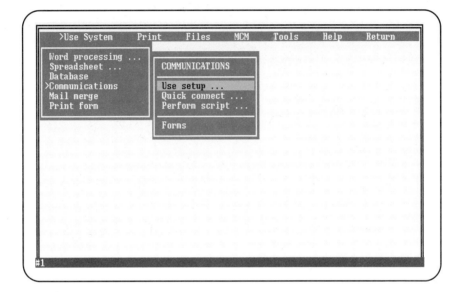

**Fig. 1.13.** *The Telecommunications options menu.*

# Summary

This chapter gives you an overview of Enable and its six modules—five applications modules plus the Master Control Module. Now that you have a better idea of the program's capabilities, you can decide more easily which section of the book you want to read next. If you are new to Enable, try the quick-start lessons at the beginning of each part before you go through the chapter that explains fundamental concepts and features. If you're an experienced Enable user, skim the "basics" chapters for explanations of new features and then read the advanced chapters more carefully.

Obviously, you cannot read this book in one sitting. Take your time and really explore Enable as you go along. Use the book as a guide, and you will find that Enable is a helpful tool. Keep Enable's modular structure in mind, regardless of the module you may be using. The program's real power, when compared with the countless other excellent programs available, is in its capability to switch painlessly from one window to another. If you learn to take full advantage of this "cutting edge" technology, you will never go back to stand-alone programs.

**2**

# Understanding the Keyboard and Enable's Screens, Menus, and Keyboard Commands

E nable is one of the most sophisticated programs available for the PC. It seems to do everything you want a microcomputer to do, and more. Because Enable is so sophisticated, its designers have tried to make learning the program as easy as possible by supplying the program's modules with carefully designed screen prompts and menus that lead a new user through the different options for each command. This chapter discusses how to use these screens and menus most effectively.

Using screen prompts and menus is an excellent way to learn a program because the prompts and menus act as signposts to guide you through features you may not otherwise use. Enable's pull-down menus are popular because they enable you to begin using the program immediately; you can read the menu choices on-screen to decide your next step. Thus, you can spend more time at the keyboard getting used to the program and less time reading the documentation.

After you become familiar with the program, however, menus can become annoying, especially for touch typists, who are trained not to look at the screen, and users who no longer need the pull-down menus. Consequently, the programmers of Enable/OA 4.0 accommodate users who don't need menus by providing keyboard commands, such as F9 commands and other function key commands, that duplicate the effect of nearly every menu selection, often with fewer keystrokes. Some important features and short-cuts—such as boldface and underlined text and cursor-movement commands—can be performed only with keyboard commands. Therefore, this chapter also describes in a general way the categories of keyboard commands, and gives you some tips on when and how best to use them.

# Using the Keyboard

You can use Enable with any PC or compatible keyboard, regardless of the arrangement of the keys. The numeric keypad on the original PC and AT keyboards serves two functions. After you press the Num Lock key once, the keypad keys enter numbers. After you press the Num Lock key again, these keys become cursor-movement keys (Home, End, PgUp, PgDn, Up arrow, Down arrow, Left arrow, and Right arrow). The enhanced keyboard provides an extra set of cursor-movement keys so that you can leave Num Lock turned on all the time (see fig. 2.1). *Note:* In the spreadsheet and database modules these keys move the pointer and are referred to as the *direction keys*.

Most of the keys are labeled clearly on all three IBM keyboards, but the meaning of a few keys, especially on the PC and AT keyboards, may be unclear. First, each keyboard has either 10 or 12 shaded keys labeled F1 through F10 or F12. Enable does not use F11 and F12 but extensively uses all the others. You use these shaded keys, called *function keys*, to perform certain keyboard commands. Function keys do not add text to the screen. Because the effects of the function keys vary from module to module, refer to the appropriate part of this book for more information on function keys.

Your keyboard may have a number of other shaded keys labeled with special symbols depicting each key's function. A few other keys are labeled with abbreviations. Table 2.1 translates these keys.

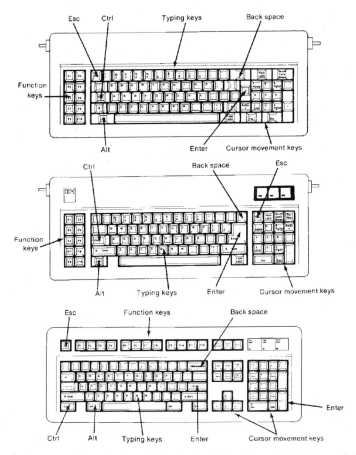

**Fig. 2.1.** *The original PC keyboard (top); the AT keyboard (center); and the enhanced keyboard (bottom).*

## Table 2.1
## Keyboard Labels

| Keyboard Label | Meaning |
| --- | --- |
| ↵ | Enter |
| ← | Left arrow |
| → | Right arrow |
| ↑ | Up arrow |
| ↓ | Down arrow |

*continued*

**Table 2.1** (*continued*)

| Keyboard Label | Meaning |
|---|---|
| ← | Backspace |
| → | Tab |
| ↑ | Shift |
| Esc | Escape |
| Alt | Alternate |
| Ctrl | Control |
| PrtSc | Print screen |
| Ins | Insert |
| Del | Delete |

# Using Enable's Screens

Mastering the command syntax is often the most difficult part of learning early computer programs. Are you using the correct command? Is this parameter valid? Are the parameters listed in the correct order? Should they be separated by commas or just spaces? To eliminate this problem, Enable often prompts you to answer various questions, many times providing a list of valid responses. The program then uses your response to perform the appropriate function.

## Using the Sign-On Screen

After you start Enable, you first encounter the Sign-On screen (see fig. 2.2). Normally, you press the End key to accept the default profiles and go to Enable's Main Menu. You also can choose a profile, read the help screen, or change the interface style. To change any of these options, you can use your cursor-movement keys to highlight the desired option, and then press Enter; you can press the key displayed to the right of the option; or you can use your mouse to click that option.

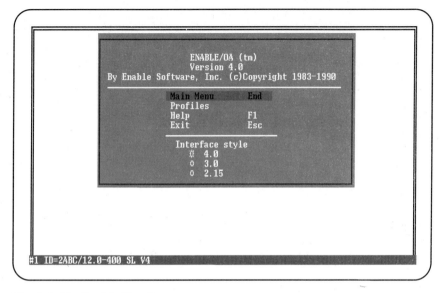

**Fig. 2.2.** *The Enable Sign-On screen.*

The first option, Main_Menu, enables you to accept the default profile and the 4.0 interface style by pressing End.

The next option, Profiles, enables you to choose a *profile*. A profile is a collection of options (usually called *defaults*) that you have made about your hardware (printer, plotter, and modem), your monitor type, and several options available for each module. For example, you can determine how many keystrokes activate auto-save in both word processing and spreadsheet documents. Enable comes with several built-in profiles, such as DEFAULT, which you use if you have a monochrome system, and COLOR, which you use if you have a color monitor. You can modify both of these defaults, which are supplied only as examples.

If you bypass the Profiles option by pressing the End key at the Sign-On screen, Enable automatically uses the DEFAULT profile. To choose another profile or to create or revise a profile, press the down-arrow key once to highlight Profiles, and press Enter. Enable displays a list of options from which you choose to select, create, or revise a profile. Creating and changing profiles is explained in Appendix B.

The third option, Help, provides assistance with the Sign-On screen. To access Help, press F1.

Exit, the fourth option, enables you to return to the operating system without entering Enable. Press Esc to exit.

 Interface_style, the final option, is a new option in Enable/OA 4.0. This option enables you to choose the menu style you would like to use for this session of Enable. If you have been using Enable Version 2.15, you press Use_System Word_Processing Revise and enter the file name to revise a file. If you press **U W R** in the 4.0 interface style, however, you inadvertently enter R as your file name.

Because Enable's new interface style may cause such problems for users of earlier versions, the program enables you to choose the menu style you want to use: 4.0 interface style, which is the default; 3.0 interface style, which is equivalent to Enable/OA (Version 3.0); or 2.15 interface style. Figure 2.3 shows Enable's Main Menu in 4.0 interface style. To choose a different interface style, press the down-arrow key until the desired interface style is highlighted, and press Enter. The cursor returns to the first option, Main Menu.

A following section in this chapter, "Using Menus," discusses the interface styles in more detail.

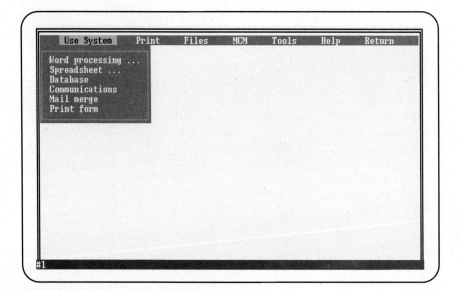

***Fig. 2.3.*** *The Main Menu in 4.0 interface style.*

# Using Other Screens

Enable has many other screens, like the Sign-On screen, that require you to enter information before you continue to work. These screens display *dialog boxes*, so named because they transmit and request information from you. For example, you use the Page Form screen (see fig. 2.4) to describe your page layout. Each time you need to print a file, you can change each of these settings. You find dialog boxes throughout the word processing and spreadsheet modules when you issue commands such as find and replace, copy, graphics, and printing.

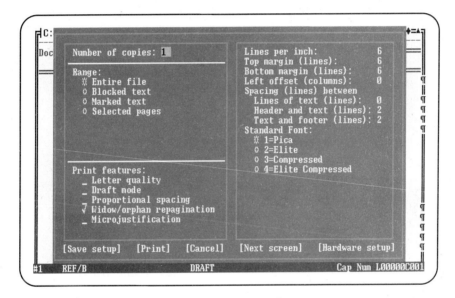

*Fig. 2.4. The Page Form screen.*

The database module also uses screens, such as the Quick Field Definition screen (see fig. 2.5), to ask you questions. In these screens, each line presents a single question and provides several options. The bottom third of the screen provides help on the current option. To choose an option, either use the cursor-movement keys to highlight the desired option and then press Enter, or press the key that corresponds to the first character of that option. You usually find this type of screen in the telecommunications and database modules and in the profile section.

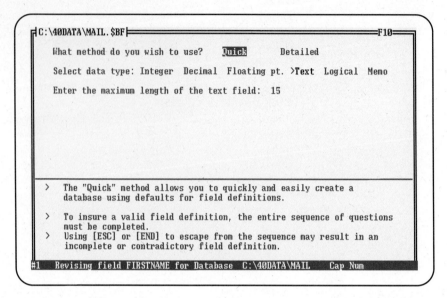

```
┌C:\40DATA\MAIL.$BF┌════════════════════════════════════════════F10═┐
│                                                                  │
│   What method do you wish to use?    Quick       Detailed        │
│                                                                  │
│   Select data type: Integer  Decimal  Floating pt. >Text  Logical  Memo │
│                                                                  │
│   Enter the maximum length of the text field:  15               │
│                                                                  │
│                                                                  │
│                                                                  │
│                                                                  │
│  ────────────────────────────────────────────────────────────  │
│   >    The "Quick" method allows you to quickly and easily create a │
│        database using defaults for field definitions.            │
│                                                                  │
│   >    To insure a valid field definition, the entire sequence of questions │
│        must be completed.                                        │
│   >    Using [ESC] or [END] to escape from the sequence may result in an │
│        incomplete or contradictory field definition.             │
│ #1   Revising field FIRSTNAME for Database  C:\40DATA\MAIL    Cap Num │
└──────────────────────────────────────────────────────────────────┘
```

***Fig. 2.5.*** *The Quick Field Definition screen.*

# Using Menus

Enable includes an extensive system of menus. Nearly everything in Enable can be done by making a series of menu choices.

As mentioned previously in this chapter, Enable/OA 4.0 has a new feature that enables you to choose the menu style you want to use. If you are an experienced Enable user who doesn't want to use Enable's new menus, you can choose the 3.0 or 2.15 interface style. If you are a novice Enable user, you can choose an interface style that matches your experience.

The following sections discuss the interfaces you may choose.

## Using the 4.0 Interface Style

The main difference between the 4.0 interface style and the other interface styles is that all the menus in the 4.0 interface style are pull-down menus. While in the Main Menu, you can use the left- and right-arrow keys to pull down other menus that list more selections. The Print menu shown in figure 2.6 is one of the pull-down menus from the Main Menu.

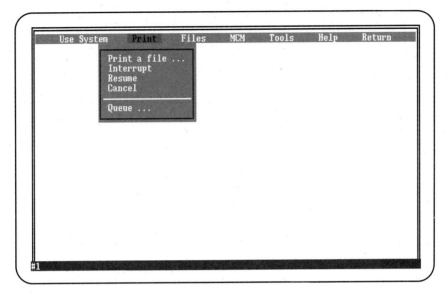

**Fig. 2.6.** *The Main Menu's pull-down Print menu.*

Each module has a Top Line menu with its own, individual pull-down menus. Each module's Top Line menu basically has the same options. Figures 2.7–2.9 show the Top Line menus in Enable's word processing, spreadsheet, and database (DBMS) modules.

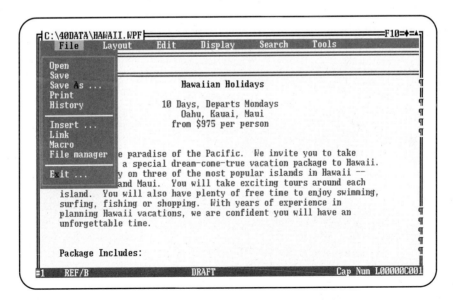

**Fig. 2.7.** *The word processing Top Line menu.*

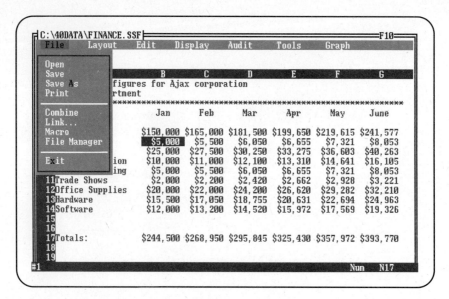

*Fig. 2.8. The spreadsheet Top Line menu.*

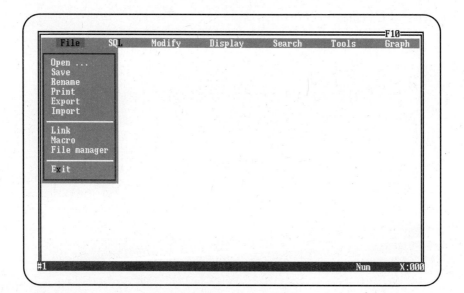

*Fig. 2.9. The DBMS Top Line menu.*

Another type of menu used in Enable/OA Version 4.0 is a *dialog box*, in which you enter additional information to operate a menu option. For example, when you ask Enable to perform a find and replace function, the program displays the Find and Replace Text dialog box (see fig. 2.10) so that you can enter the text to find, the text to replace, where to perform the search, and how many times to check the section of text. Use the up- and down-arrow keys or the Tab key to choose the options in the dialog box. Choose Accept and press Enter to record the dialog box data; choose Cancel to abort the operation.

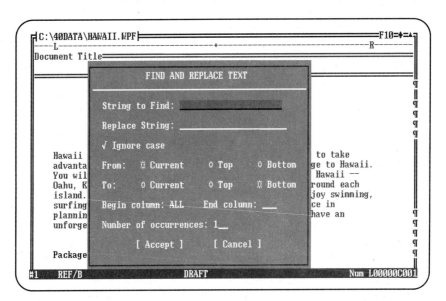

*Fig. 2.10. The word processing Find and Replace Text dialog box.*

Some dialog boxes contain lists of options from which you can choose only one option. The options in such lists are called *buttons*. To turn on a button, move the cursor to the option you want and press Enter. When you turn on a button, Enable turns off the previously chosen button. In the Find and Replace Text dialog box, for example, on the From: line, the Current button is on and the Top and Bottom buttons are off (again see fig. 2.10).

# Using Other Interface Styles

You already may be familiar with an earlier version of Enable and may want to continue using its menu style. Earlier versions of Enable do not use pull-down menus or dialog boxes.

NOTE

If you wrote macros in an earlier version, you must select that version's interface style to use the macros in Enable/OA Version 4.0. You must rewrite macros written in Versions 2.15 or 3.0 if you want to use them in 4.0 interface style.

Figure 2.11 shows the 3.0 interface style Main Menu, and figures 2.12–2.14 show the 3.0 interface style Top Line menus in the word processing and spreadsheet modules and the comparable Interact menu in the database management modules.

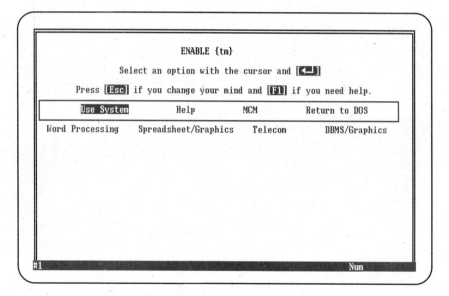

*Fig. 2.11. The Main Menu in 3.0 interface style.*

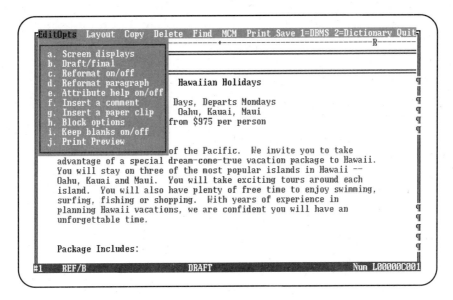

**Fig. 2.12.** *The word processing Top Line menu in 3.0 interface style.*

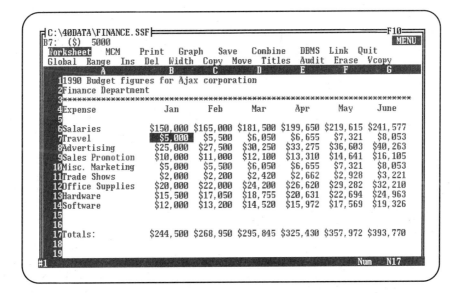

**Fig. 2.13.** *The spreadsheet Top Line menu in 3.0 interface style.*

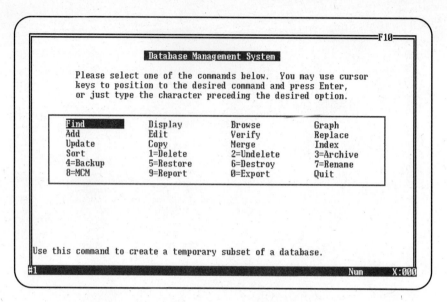

**Fig. 2.14.** *The DBMS Interact menu in 3.0 interface style.*

To learn about each module's menu options, turn to the part of the book that discusses the relevant Enable module. Refer to Part II for a discussion of the Master Control Module (MCM), Part III for instructions on working with word processing files, Part IV for spreadsheet information, Part V for database (DBMS) management, Part VI for graphics instruction, and Part VII for a discussion of telecommunications. Appendix A explains how to access the tutorial.

# Using Keyboard Commands

As explained previously in this chapter, you can use both menus and keyboard commands to operate Enable. Beginners usually find Enable easier to learn if they use the menus to operate the program because so many keyboard commands are available. Eventually, however, if you wean yourself from the menus and use keyboard commands, you will find Enable extremely flexible.

Keyboard commands do not always require fewer keystrokes than using menus; however, because keyboard commands bypass menu display, they are almost always faster than using menus to operate Enable. Keyboard commands also enable you to repeat a command easily. You can press F9 F9, for example, to repeat an F9 command, and you can press F2 F2 to repeat a Goto command.

Not all of Enable's operations can be performed through the menus. You must use keyboard commands to perform certain functions, such as applying print attributes to text in the word processing and spreadsheet modules.

> Keep in mind that menus and keyboard commands do not mix. You cannot execute a keyboard command when Enable is displaying a menu.

Because learning Enable's keyboard commands increases your productivity, this book stresses that you use keyboard commands instead of menus, which are designed for learning, not speed.

# Using Common Function Key Commands

Enable makes full use of function keys F1 through F10. Using function keys is always quicker and easier than using any other method for performing tasks. For example, using menus to copy a block of text that already is marked (highlighted) in the word processing module requires the following keystrokes:

> **F10**
> **Edit**
> **Copy**
> **Object**
> **From**
> **Accept**

You can accomplish the same action when you move the cursor to the place in the text where you want the block copied and then press F8.

The developers of Enable/OA 4.0 have attempted to make the use of the function keys as consistent as possible from one module to another. Seven of the ten keys perform the same or similar functions in each module. Using these seven keys in each module involves special nuances that are discussed in the relevant chapters of this book. Table 2.2 broadly defines these commands. The other three function keys—F4, F5, and F6—have different meanings in each module, primarily due to the different purposes of the modules. Refer to the discussions of the individual modules for descriptions of these keys' uses.

**Table 2.2**
**Function Key Commands**

| Function Key | Description |
| --- | --- |
| F1 | Displays the help feature's table of contents |
| Alt-F1 | Displays a list of function key commands |
| F2 | Performs Goto commands |
| Alt-F2 | Quick print |
| Ctrl-F2 | Cancel printing |
| Shift-F2 | Priority print (if Print Queue option is on) |
| F3 | Inserts a line |
| Alt-F3 | Deletes a line |
| F7 | Select text |
| Alt-F7 | Unselect text |
| F8 | Copies |
| Alt-F8 | Moves |
| F9 | Performs F9 commands |
| Alt-F9 | Performs system macros |
| F10 | Displays Top Line menu |
| Alt-F10 | Displays Save menu |
| Ctrl-F10 | Displays keyboard-selected user-defined menu |
| Shift-F10 | Displays default user-defined menu |

# Using F9 Commands

No matter what software package you use, you always want to find the quickest way to perform a command, which usually means avoiding the Top Line menus. Nearly every command that you can issue through Enable's word processing, database, or telecommunications Top Line menus also can be issued with *F9 commands*. These commands are called F9 commands because the F9 key is the first key you press to access the command. Menus do not prompt you through the commands. After you press F9, Enable displays in the *status line* a list of letters and numbers separated by commas. This list shows the next available keystrokes but does not indicate what the choices represent. Figure 2.15 shows the status line in word processing after you press the F9 key.

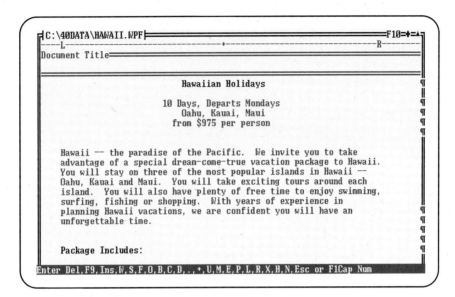

**Fig. 2.15.** *The F9 command list in the word processing status line.*

After you press one of the displayed options, Enable either executes the command or displays another list of keystroke choices. For example, after you press F9 D (in sequence, not as a key combination), Enable displays all the word processing files on the default directory (see fig. 2.16). To make these commands easier to remember, the keys you press are often *mnemonic* (assigned to help your memory). The command just described, for example, is F9 Directory; however, the status line lists only the letter D, not the entire word Directory.

As with Enable's menu commands, some F9 commands take as many as four keystrokes. If the first keystroke after the F9 key does not complete the command, another list of options appears in the status line. You then press one of the listed keys. For example, to save a word processing file and continue editing, you press F9 **Save Edit**. Pressing F9 brings up one list of options, and choosing Save brings up a second list, which includes the Edit option. Choosing Edit returns you to the original screen.

Each of Enable's modules has its own set of F9 commands, and a few (such as F9 S E) can be used in several modules. Enable/OA 4.0 includes so many of these commands (approximately 80 in word processing) that memorizing them is nearly impossible. When you get tired of using menus, experiment with the equivalent F9 commands. You soon will acquire a preference for some of them, and, without even trying, commit them to memory.

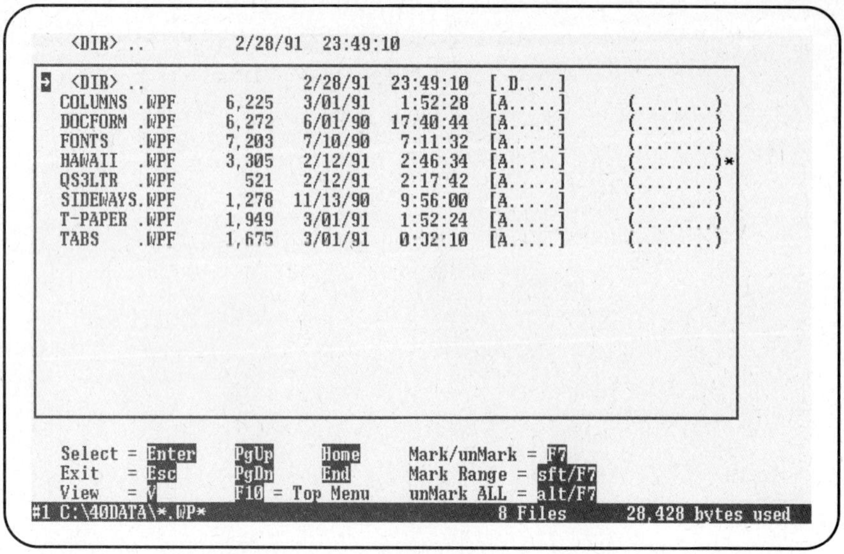

```
 <DIR> ..        2/28/91  23:49:10

 <DIR> ..                 2/28/91  23:49:10  [.D....]
 COLUMNS .WPF     6,225    3/01/91   1:52:28  [A.....]      (........)
 DOCFORM .WPF     6,272    6/01/90  17:40:44  [A.....]      (........)
 FONTS   .WPF     7,203    7/10/90   7:11:32  [A.....]      (........)
 HAWAII  .WPF     3,305    2/12/91   2:46:34  [A.....]      (........)*
 QS3LTR  .WPF       521    2/12/91   2:17:42  [A.....]      (........)
 SIDEWAYS.WPF     1,278   11/13/90   9:56:00  [A.....]      (........)
 T-PAPER .WPF     1,949    3/01/91   1:52:24  [A.....]      (........)
 TABS    .WPF     1,675    3/01/91   0:32:10  [A.....]      (........)




     Select = Enter    PgUp    Home     Mark/unMark = F7
     Exit   = Esc      PgDn    End      Mark Range  = sft/F7
     View   = V        F10 = Top Menu   unMark ALL  = alt/F7
 #1 C:\40DATA\*.WP*                          8 Files      28,428 bytes used
```

*Fig. 2.16. A word processing directory.*

One significant advantage of using F9 commands becomes clear when you
need to use the same command more than once in sequence. For example,
in a word processing window you can switch from *draft mode* to *final mode*
by pressing F9 **O**n/Off **D**raft. You typically use draft mode (see fig. 2.17)
when editing because no formatting is displayed; you use final mode (see
fig. 2.18) to see how the document will look when printed, with headers,
footers, footnotes, and so on. This command (F9 O D) is a *toggle switch*
(back and forth between two modes) that switches your screen from draft
mode to final mode, and back to draft mode. You usually switch back to draft
mode after changing to final mode, and if no other F9 commands have been
issued since you pressed F9 O D, you can press F9 F9 to execute the
command a second time.

F9 commands execute somewhat faster than their menu-command counterparts, even when both methods require the same number of keystrokes,
because Enable does not display menus when you use F9 commands.
Specific F9 commands are discussed in the chapters that cover the Enable
modules.

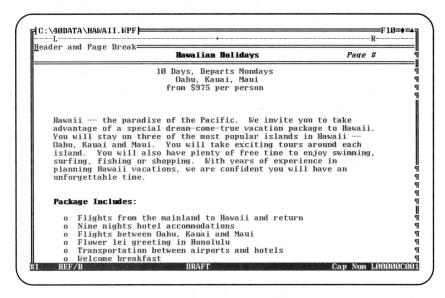

**Fig. 2.17.** *A word processing screen in draft mode.*

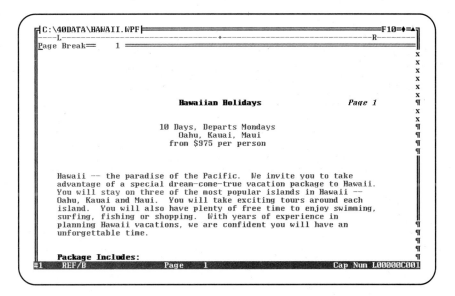

**Fig. 2.18.** *A word processing screen in final mode.*

# Using the Cursor, Pointer, and Goto Commands

Most users want to be able to move quickly within their documents, spreadsheets, and databases. In Enable, you use different methods of cursor movement, depending on which module you are using. When you use Enable's database, you control the cursor with the up-, down-, left-, and right-arrow keys and the Home, End, Tab, PgUp, and PgDn keys. In Enable's spreadsheet, you quickly can control the cursor, called the *cell pointer*, by pressing F2 and entering the cell address to which you want to go. In word processing, however, you use a series of Goto commands, accessed with the F2 key, to move quickly within a document. You operate F2 commands the same way you operate F9 commands; after pressing F2, you choose from a series of characters displayed on the status line. See the discussions of the individual modules for more information about these commands.

# Using Keystroke Commands

To perform certain commands, you use keystroke commands, usually pressing Alt, Ctrl, or Shift in combination with another key (key combinations).

In Enable's word processing module, for example, you use keystroke commands to underline text. You can underline text as you type or underline existing text by turning on the underline attribute. You press Alt-U to turn on the underline attribute. A lowercase u appears in the status line, indicating that the attribute is active. Any text you type is underlined. You also can underline existing text through one or more keystroke commands, such as Ctrl-C to underline a character or Ctrl-W to underline a word.

As another example of using keystroke commands, you press Shift-F7 to display simultaneously a graph and underlying spreadsheet data in the spreadsheet module (see fig. 2.19). The keystroke commands available in each of Enable's modules are listed and explained in the appropriate chapters of this book.

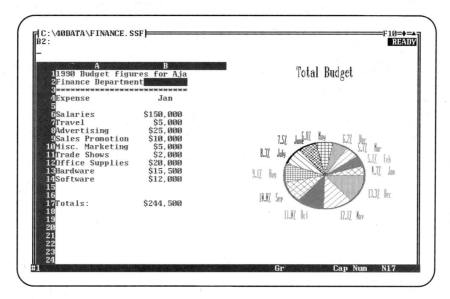

***Fig. 2.19.** Simultaneous display of graphics and spreadsheet.*

# Summary

This chapter covers Enable's user interface—the keyboard, screens, menus, and keyboard commands. You can use the chapter as a quick reference for the basic uses of Enable's commands. Now you are ready to learn about Enable's Master Control Module.

# Part II

# The Master Control Module

## Includes

**Quick Start II: Using the Master Control Module**

**Understanding the Master Control Module**

**Using the Master Control Module's
Advanced Features**

# Quick Start II

# Using the Master Control Module

This lesson is the second of seven quick-start lessons in this book. The design of this lesson gives you a taste of what the Master Control Module can do for you—copy a file from one disk or directory to another, open both a word processing file and a spreadsheet file at the same time, or copy information from one open file to another.

The instructions in this lesson assume you already have installed and started Enable properly, so that Enable displays the Main Menu. If you do not have the Main Menu on-screen, refer to Appendix A and Quick Start I for information on getting started.

## Copying a File from Directory to Directory

To copy a file from directory to directory, do the following:

1. From the Main Menu in window #1 (the window should show #1 in the bottom left corner of the screen), to display a list of all the files stored in your Enable data directory, MYDATA, press

   **Files All**

   Enable displays the Directory of Files screen, which lists the names of all files in your data directory (see fig. QSII.1). Notice the status line; Enable displays C:\MYDATA\*.* to describe which directory it is displaying.

```
   <DIR> ..          6/19/91   0:10:18

  <DIR> ..                      6/19/91    0:10:18   [.D.....]
  1QSMEMO .WPF          890    6/05/91   15:57:10   [A.....]    (........)
  ABSFUNC .SSF        1,536    4/03/91   11:31:06   [A.....]    (........)
  BOXES   .WPF          752    3/17/91   18:37:52   [A.....]    (........)
  CHOOSE  .SSF          512    5/13/91   12:46:06   [A.....]    (........)
  COLORS  .SSF          512    6/03/91   11:54:46   [A.....]    (........)
  DBMSDEF .$RF        5,632    8/03/90   11:46:44   [A.....]    (........)
  DEMOWORD.WPF        8,403    6/05/91   17:39:54   [A.....]    (........)
  DOCFORM .WPF        6,301    6/05/91   17:40:30   [A.....]    (........)
  ELECT1  .WPF        1,745    3/18/91    2:03:00   [A.....]    (........)
  FILEDIR .WPF        2,330    3/17/91   23:27:24   [A.....]    (........)
  FINANCE .$BF        5,120    1/14/90   21:48:32   [A.....]    (........)
  FINANCE .$IF        3,584    1/14/90   20:54:52   [A.....]    (........)
  FINANCE .DBF        1,024    4/03/91   10:21:24   [A.....]    (........)
  FINANCE .SSF        7,168    3/17/91   16:56:18   [A.....]    (........)
  FINEMPID.NDX        1,024    1/13/90   18:37:40   [A.....]    (........)
  FINFUNC .SSF          512    5/13/91   10:46:44   [A.....]    (........)


  Select = Enter    PgUp       Home      Mark/unMark = F7
  Exit   = Esc      PgDn       End       Mark Range  = sft/F7
  View   = V        F10 = Top Menu       unMark ALL  = alt/F7
#1 C:\MYDATA\*.*                              80 Files     204,734 bytes used
```

**Fig. QSII.1.** *The Directory of Files screen displaying the directory MYDATA.*

You must copy a spreadsheet file and a word processing file onto
your data directory so that you have two files with which to work.
The original Enable disks you installed contain two tutorial files
you can copy. The remaining instructions in this section assume
you installed these tutorial files on your hard disk. If the files are
not on your hard disk, follow the instructions in Appendix A,
"Installing and Starting Enable."

2. To change the Directory of Files screen to the directory containing
   the files you need to copy, press

   F10 File List_new_path

   At the prompt, type **C:\ENTUT**, the directory that contains the tutorial files, and press Enter.

   Enable displays a new Directory of Files screen consisting of all the
   Enable tutorial files. The status line displays the directory name
   C:\ENTUT.

3. The first file you copy is a spreadsheet called A.SSF. Use the arrow
   keys to move the highlighted arrow, referred to as the *pointer*, to
   A.SSF.

To copy the file to your data directory, MYDATA, where the file is easier to use, press F7 to mark the file, and then press

F10 **Mark Copy_marked_files**

Enable displays the Copy Marked Files screen. Type C:\**MYDATA**, the destination directory name. Press Enter to confirm your choice and to copy the file A.SSF from ENTUT to MYDATA.

After copying the file, Enable redisplays the Directory of Files screen, still showing the directory C:\ENTUT.

4.  Use the procedures in step 3 to copy the second file, a word processing file called HAWAII.WPF, from the directory C:\ENTUT to C:\MYDATA.

5.  After you copy the file HAWAII.WPF, check to make sure you correctly copied both tutorial files to C:\MYDATA by pressing

F10 **File List_new_path**

Type C:\**MYDATA** and press Enter. Notice that the Directory of Files screen now lists the files A.SSF and HAWAII.WPF in the data directory. You successfully have copied both files from your tutorial directory, ENTUT, to your data directory, MYDATA.

6.  Press Esc to return to the Main Menu.

# Opening Two Files at Once

To open two files at once, do the following:

1.  Open the word processing file HAWAII.WPF in window #1. Enable always puts the first file you open into window #1. To open HAWAII.WPF and display it on-screen, press ·

    Use_System **Word_processing**

    Type **HAWAII** and press Enter. Enable displays the word processing file HAWAII. Notice the #1 at the left end of the status line, where Enable always displays the current window number. You must open a second window to display the second file, A.SSF.

2.  To open a second window, press Alt-Home.

Enable displays a new Main Menu that looks exactly like the preceding one, with the exception that the status line displays #2 for the window number. The word processing file HAWAII remains open; Enable opens window #2 "on top of" window #1. This procedure is like removing a file folder from your filing cabinet and placing it on top of the already open file folders on your desk.

3. To open A.SSF in window #2, press

    Use_System **S**preadsheet

Type **A** and then press Enter. Enable displays the spreadsheet A.SSF (see fig. QSII.2).

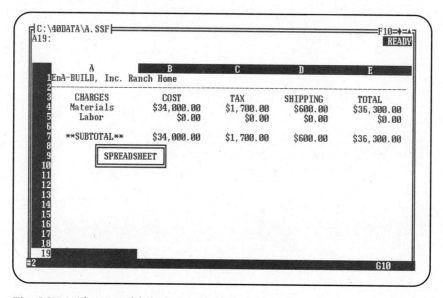

*Fig. QSII.2. The spreadsheet A.SSF in window #2.*

4. Press Alt-up arrow to switch back to window #1.

You can switch back and forth between the two windows by pressing Alt-up arrow to move backward one window and Alt-down arrow to move forward one window. Now you are ready to copy data from window to window, which you learn to do in the following section.

# Copying Data from Window to Window

1. If you are not in window #1, press Alt-up arrow to switch to window #1. Place the cursor at the end of the file HAWAII, where you are going to copy the spreadsheet data. Press PgDn to move the cursor quickly, or press Ctrl-End to move the cursor directly to the end of the file (see fig. QSII.3). Make sure that the cursor is well below the existing text.

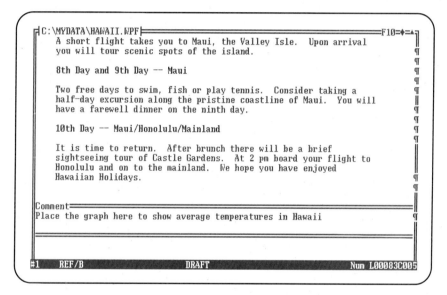

```
C:\MYDATA\HAWAII.WPF                                          F10=♦=▲
    A short flight takes you to Maui, the Valley Isle.  Upon arrival
    you will tour scenic spots of the island.                        ¶
                                                                     ¶
    8th Day and 9th Day -- Maui                                      ¶
                                                                     ¶
    Two free days to swim, fish or play tennis.  Consider taking a   ¶
    half-day excursion along the pristine coastline of Maui.  You will ‖
    have a farewell dinner on the ninth day.                         ¶
                                                                     ¶
    10th Day -- Maui/Honolulu/Mainland                               ¶
                                                                     ¶
    It is time to return.  After brunch there will be a brief         ‖
    sightseeing tour of Castle Gardens.  At 2 pm board your flight to
    Honolulu and on to the mainland.  We hope you have enjoyed
    Hawaiian Holidays.                                               ¶
                                                                     ¶
Comment
Place the graph here to show average temperatures in Hawaii         ¶


#1   REF/B                    DRAFT                      Num L0083C005
```

*Fig. QSII.3. The word processing file HAWAII.WPF in window #1.*

2. Press Alt-F5 to begin the copy procedure.

Enable displays the Interwindow Copy Options screen (see fig. QSII.4). Notice that Enable asks for the number of the window from which you want to copy. You started in window #1, HAWAII.WPF, and you want to copy the spreadsheet data from window #2.

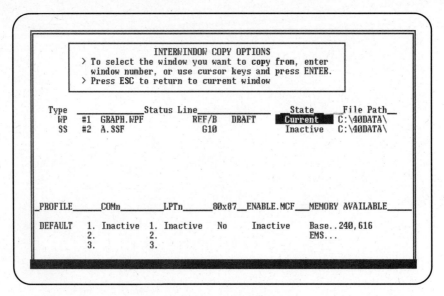

**Fig. QSII.4.** *The Interwindow Copy Options screen.*

3. Type **2** to specify that you want to copy data from window #2. Enable displays window #2 and the message

   ```
   Enter range to include in document
   ```

   Because you want to copy all of the spreadsheet data, press Enter to accept the default answer, ALL. Enable immediately copies all of the spreadsheet data to the location of the cursor in the word processing window and displays window #1 (see fig. QSII.5). If you cannot see the spreadsheet because your cursor already is at the bottom of your screen, use the down-arrow key to move down through the file.

4. To save HAWAII.WPF to the disk, press

   F10 **F**ile **S**ave

5. To close window #1, press

   F10 **F**ile **E**xit

6. To close window #2, press

   F10 **F**ile **E**xit

   Enable displays the Main Menu in window #1, where the lesson began.

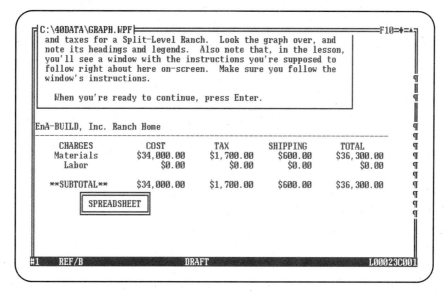

*Fig. QSII.5. Spreadsheet data copied into a word processing file.*

# 3

# Understanding the Master Control Module

A s explained in Chapter 1, "Using Enable's Modules," the Master Control Module (MCM) controls the flow of information to and from the other modules and takes care of much of the overhead common to all the modules. The MCM is referred to internally by Enable Software as the "Corporate Staff." Window functions, help functions, and file management functions discussed in this chapter are among the functions of the MCM. Study this chapter one section at a time. Try each technique under real working conditions before you continue. Only when you have mastered these skills can you use Enable to its full potential.

## Using Enable's Windows

Working in multiple windows on your computer may seem foreign to you at first. Consider, though, how you work at your desk. You may have several files out at once. As your work continues, you open more files, referring to one and then to another and then back to the first. You can work with Enable in the same natural way. You don't have to close the report file you are editing and run another program just to look at the monthly budget spreadsheet. With Enable, you simply open another window and access the budget file. Your report remains open where you left it, and you can press a few keys to return to the report. You even can "paste" the budget into the report.

The window metaphor is an apt one. Your computer screen acts like a window into the data in each file, displaying only a screen of characters at a time. If this term confuses you, remember that each file you open must be in its own window; in Enable you can open up to eight windows (files) at a time, and you can switch easily between windows.

## Opening a Window

If you have used one of Enable's modules, you already know that one way to open a window is through the Main Menu at start-up. The first file you open each time you use Enable is always in window #1. Enable displays the number of the current window on the left side of the *status line* (the bottom line of the display). Figure 3.1 shows a word processing file opened from the initial Main Menu, in window #1.

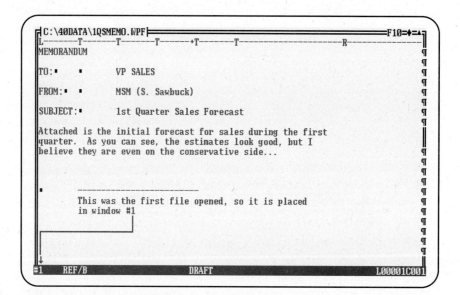

**Fig. 3.1.** *A word processing file in window #1.*

To open a new window from within an open window, press the key combination Alt-Home. If you start in window #1, you can use this command to open a second Main Menu, with #2 in the status line (see fig. 3.2).

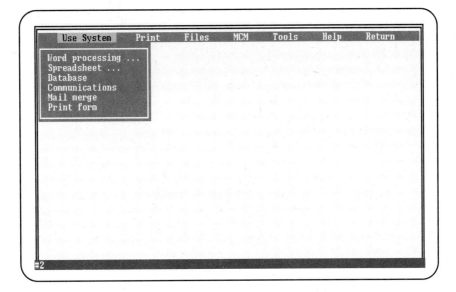

*Fig. 3.2. The Main Menu in window #2.*

Enable offers alternative ways to open windows. To open a window using the F9 command, from any Enable module you can press

F9 **Window Open**

If you prefer to use Enable's menus to open a window, follow these guidelines:

1. From within any application, press F10 **Tools Window Open**.

2. From the new Main Menu, open the next file in the usual way; for example, to open the spreadsheet file WIDGETS.SSF (the sales forecast of Hyperion Widget Corporation) in window #2, press Use_System **Spreadsheet**

3. Type the name of the spreadsheet, in this case **WIDGETS**, or, for Enable/OA 4.0, use the down arrow to highlight WIDGETS.SSF; then press Enter. Enable displays a screen similar to the screen shown in figure 3.3.

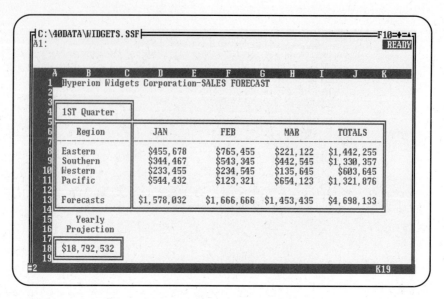

*Fig. 3.3. A spreadsheet in window #2.*

You can open eight windows this way and access any combination of files. The window number always appears on the left side of the status line.

# Switching between Windows

When you have only two windows open, you can press Alt-up arrow or Alt-down arrow to switch from one window to another. If you have several windows open, press Alt-up arrow to move to the window with the next higher number—from window #1 to window #2, to window #3, and so on. If you are in the highest number window, press Alt-up arrow to move to window #1. The key combination Alt-down arrow moves to windows in descending numeric order—window #3, to #2, to #1, and back to #3.

If you use the Alt-arrow key commands from any window, you eventually will reach any other window. If you have several windows open, however, you can use an F9 command to switch to a specific window. To go to any other open window, press

F9 **Window G**oto

Enable displays the Window Status Options screen, as shown in figure 3.4. Press the number of the window in which you want to work, or highlight the status line of the window and press Enter. The window appears on-screen.

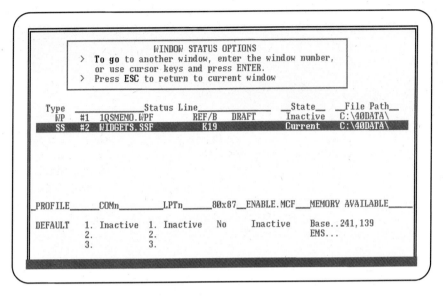

**Fig. 3.4.** *The Window Status Options screen.*

If you know the window number, you can use the F9 command with the window number added to the command. For example, to go to window #3, press

    F9 **Window 3 Goto**

**TIP**

# Closing a Window

Just as Enable opens a window each time you open a file, a window closes whenever you close a file. In Enable, the phrases "Close the window," "Close the file," and "Quit from the file" mean the same thing.

The Exit command in Enable's menus closes the window and thus the file. This command, however, can be tedious to use. The most efficient way to close a window is to press Alt-End. This rule has two exceptions; when you quit from Communications Setups and from Profiles, you must choose Exit from the menu.

The word processing and spreadsheet applications of Enable/OA 4.0 have a "Smart-Save" feature. When you look at a file and do not make any changes, you can press Alt-End to close the window. If you do make changes to a file, however, when you close the window, a dialog box appears with the message

```
Save Changes to: filename [Yes] [No] [Cancel]
```

To save the file, press **Y** or Enter. If you want to ignore the changes, press **N**. To cancel your request to close the window, press **C**.

# Getting Help

When you need help to learn the new software package or employ an option you seldom use, in addition to this book you can refer to the documentation and the Quick Reference Guide that come with Enable/OA 4.0. In addition, the MCM provides an on-line help function to assist you.

## Understanding Hypertext

The help function in Enable/OA 4.0 is known as *Hypertext*. In Hypertext, the actual documentation is on-line. Hypertext is organized in the same way as your Enable documentation—in several books divided into articles. Each book has its own table of contents and alphabetical index. To access the help function, press F1. Enable displays the table of contents for the current module, as shown in figure 3.5. To read any article, move your cursor to the article name, for example, Word Processing - Introduction, and then press Enter.

The top line of the new screen shows the article name. The scroll bar on the right shows the relative position of the current screen within the article (see fig. 3.6). Press the plus sign (+) to see the next article in the table of contents and the minus sign (–) to see the preceding article.

Notice in figure 3.6 that the word Creating is highlighted. If you press Enter, you see a related article on creating a file (see fig. 3.7). Press Esc to return to the original article; press the Tab key to see other references.

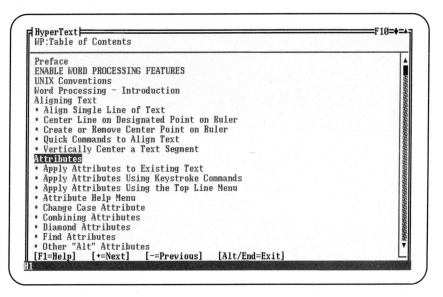

**Fig. 3.5.** *The Hypertext Table of Contents for word processing.*

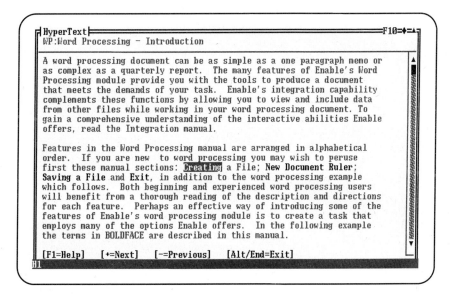

**Fig. 3.6.** *An article in Hypertext.*

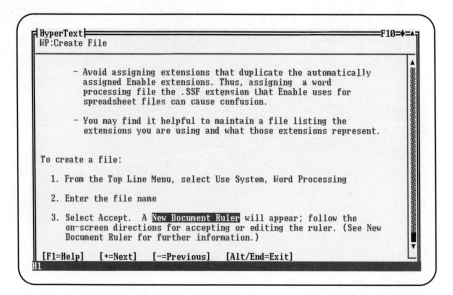

*Fig. 3.7. The Create File article in Hypertext.*

# Using the Hypertext Index

When you look at software documentation, you usually refer first to the index, not the table of contents. You can do the same in Hypertext. To change to the index, press

    **F10 Context Index**

Enable displays the index with the cursor on

    `Word Processing - Alphabetical Index.`

To move quickly through the index, press the first letter of the topic about which you want to read. For example, to read the article about headers, press **H**. The cursor goes to the first topic under the letter H—`Hanging Indent.` Use the cursor-movement keys to move to the article you want to read, and press Enter.

# Changing Books

When you read articles in Hypertext, you sometimes need to change books. For example, if you are reading the article in the Database Book about derived fields, and then want to see a list of available functions, you need to switch to the System Integration Book. To change books in Hypertext, press

F10 **B**ooks System_Integration

# Seeing Help Window and Current Window Simultaneously

You can use the window-sizing commands to see the help window and the current window at the same time. Use the F9 commands to shrink the windows. To shrink the Hypertext window, press

F9 **W**indow **L**ocate_and_size **S**hrink

Press the up arrow several times to place the help window at the top of the screen. Notice that the original word processing document is still on-screen. You now need to use the same commands to shrink and move the word processing window so that you can see both windows (see fig. 3.8).

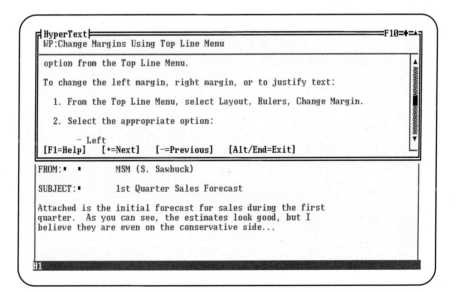

**Fig. 3.8.** *Two windows displayed simultaneously.*

Hypertext is a powerful tool that you can use to browse quickly through the documentation and often to read parts of the documentation you otherwise would not read. For example, while you are reading an article on headers, you may choose to read the related article on page numbering. Refer to Hypertext frequently to enhance your use of Enable.

# Using the File Manager

No matter what PC program you use, you need to create, use, change, and delete files on your computer's disks. Enable/OA 4.0 handles these file management chores through the MCM. In fact, Enable has so many useful file management utilities that the program rivals some of the popular stand-alone DOS shells.

When you start using Enable to create word processing files, spreadsheet files, database files, and so on, be aware of where Enable stores these files. Just as you manage paper-based information by placing related documents in labeled file folders and then placing the folders behind dividers in labeled file drawers, Enable/OA and Enable/OA 4.0 manage data files on your computer by storing them in appropriately labeled directories and subdirectories on your disks. (Pre-Enable/OA versions do not handle multiple directory levels.) Refer to Appendix A, "Installing and Starting Enable," for details on how to install and run Enable so that it can store the files you create in the correct directories.

After you become familiar with Enable and are ready to manage files on a more advanced level, explore the following sections on renaming files, copying files to other disks, destroying files to make room for others, and so on.

Before you learn about these basic file management commands, you should be aware of the special file-naming conventions that Enable follows.

## Using File Names in Enable

Enable can create many types of files, including word processing, spreadsheet, and database files. Unless you override the program, Enable automatically adds a special three-letter code, or extension, to each file name. Because this code denotes the particular file type, you can distinguish between similarly named files in the same directory. Table 3.1 lists the Enable extensions and their corresponding file types. The table also includes several special file names that you should reserve for the purposes indicated. The rule for you to follow with file name extensions is to let Enable do all the work. You need to know what the extensions mean; however, when you perform the file management commands explained in the sections that follow, be careful not to change the extensions that Enable assigns.

### Table 3.1
### Extensions for Enable File Names

| Extension | File Type |
|---|---|
| *System Files* | |
| .TSG | Enable program file |
| .$PR | Profile |
| .MCM | System-wide macro |
| MCM.MNU | Default MCM menu |
| x.MNU | Named system-wide menu |
| .COM or.EXE | Executable DOS file |
| .BAT | Batch file |
| x.MC | Named MCM menu |
| | |
| *Word Processing Files* | |
| .WPF | Word processing document |
| .WPP | Print file* |
| .WP@ | Automatic document save file |
| .WTA | Table of authority file |
| .WPI | Word processing index file |
| .WPT | Table of contents file |
| .WPM | Word processing macro |
| WP.MNU | Default word processing menu |
| x.WP | Named word processing menu |
| .DOC | Required extension for using MultiMate and PeachText files |
| | |
| *Spreadsheet Files* | |
| .SSF | Spreadsheet file |
| .SSP | Print file* |
| .SSM | Spreadsheet macro |

*continued*

**Table 3.1** (*continued*)

| Extension | File Type |
| --- | --- |
| SS.MNU | Default spreadsheet menu |
| x.SM | Named spreadsheet menu |
| .ASC | Extension for files saved in ASCII format |
| .CAL | Extension for files saved in SuperCalc 3 Release 2 format |
| .WKS | Extension for files saved in 1-2-3 Release 1A format |
| .WK1 | Extension for files saved in 1-2-3 Release 2 format |
| .DIF | Extension for files saved in DIF format |
| *DBMS Files* | |
| .DBF | Database file |
| .$BF | Database definition |
| .DBT | Memo field file |
| .NDX | Database index |
| .$IF | Input form |
| .$RF | Report form |
| .UTF | Update transfer form |
| .CTF | Copy transfer form |
| .MTF | Merge transfer form |
| .SS | Select set |
| .SSn | Internal record-processing file |
| .ERR | Error select set |
| .ARC | Database archive file |
| .@@@ | Database backup file |
| .DEF | Database definition used as a database |
| .DBM | DBMS macro |
| DB.MNU | Default DBMS menu |
| x.DB | Named DBMS menu |
| .DAT | Required extension for Condor 3 file import |
| WINDOWn.m | Window import file |

| Extension | File Type |
|---|---|
| *Graphics Files* | |
| PRINTPLOT.GRP | Print or plot file |
| SETTINGn.GRS | Current graph setting (temporary) |
| .GRM | Graphics macro |
| .GRF | DBMS graph setting file |
| .FNT | Graphics font file |
| *Telecommunications Files* | |
| .$TP | Telecommunications setup |
| .TPF | Disk capture file or file received by file transfer |
| .TPU | Unattended file transfer form |
| .TPT | Terminal mapping table |
| .TPK | Keyboard mapping table |
| .WPF | Memory capture file; also word processing version of transfer form and mapping table |
| .TPM | Telecommunications macro |
| TP.MNU | Default telecommunications menu |
| x.TP | Named telecommunications menu |
| *Gadget Files* | |
| .CLF | Calendar file[*] |
| .CDF | Card File/Telephone Book[*] |

[*]These files are temporary; Enable deletes the files after printing.

If you work with many files, pay special attention to the name you give each file that you create. You can use a particular file name only once in each directory. Enable's use of file name extensions gives you some flexibility here because Enable treats two files with the same name but different extensions as two different file names. You can have a word processing file named MYFILE as well as a spreadsheet named MYFILE because Enable adds the extension WPF to the name of the first file and SSF to the name of the second. In other words, you really have two files:

MYFILE.WPF

MYFILE.SSF

# Accessing the File Manager Screen

DOS shell programs are popular because they can assist you in necessary file management without requiring that you work directly in the operating system. Enable's File Manager is similar to a DOS shell program and surprisingly powerful.

You can access the MCM's File Manager screen in the following ways:

- From the Main Menu, choose **Files**; then choose from the following options for the type of file you want to list:

     **All**
     **Word_processing**
     **Spreadsheet**
     **Database**
     **Communications**
     **Macro**
     **Menu_generator**
     **SQL**

     For example, if you choose **Word_processing**, Enable displays a File Manager screen similar to the screen in figure 3.9. Notice that the directory lists only word processing files, and all the file name extensions are WPF.

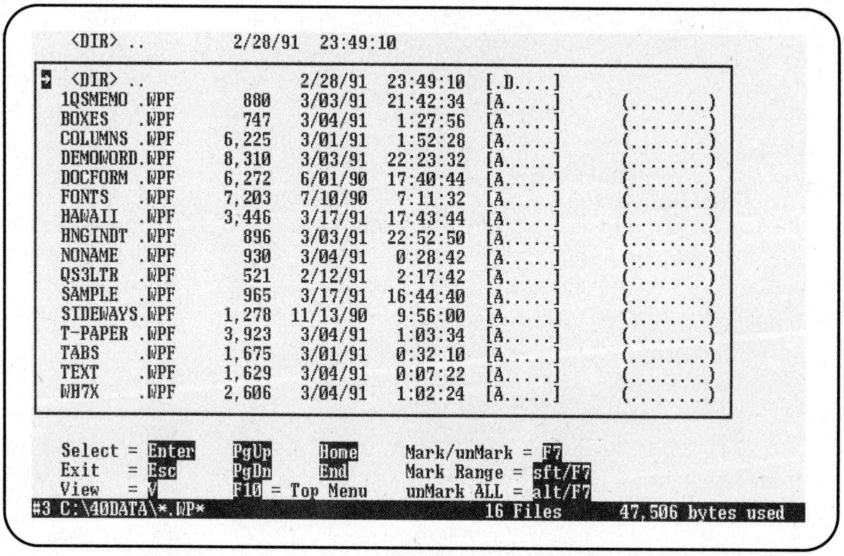

```
    <DIR> ..        2/28/91  23:49:10

  <DIR> ..                  2/28/91  23:49:10  [.D....]
    1QSMEMO .WPF       880   3/03/91  21:42:34  [A.....]     (........)
    BOXES   .WPF       747   3/04/91   1:27:56  [A.....]     (........)
    COLUMNS .WPF     6,225   3/01/91   1:52:28  [A.....]     (........)
    DEMOWORD.WPF     8,310   3/03/91  22:23:32  [A.....]     (........)
    DOCFORM .WPF     6,272   6/01/90  17:40:44  [A.....]     (........)
    FONTS   .WPF     7,203   7/10/90   7:11:32  [A.....]     (........)
    HAWAII  .WPF     3,446   3/17/91  17:43:44  [A.....]     (........)
    HNGINDT .WPF       896   3/03/91  22:52:50  [A.....]     (........)
    NONAME  .WPF       930   3/04/91   0:28:42  [A.....]     (........)
    QS3LTR  .WPF       521   2/12/91   2:17:42  [A.....]     (........)
    SAMPLE  .WPF       965   3/17/91  16:44:40  [A.....]     (........)
    SIDEWAYS.WPF     1,278  11/13/90   9:56:00  [A.....]     (........)
    T-PAPER .WPF     3,923   3/04/91   1:03:34  [A.....]     (........)
    TABS    .WPF     1,675   3/01/91   0:32:10  [A.....]     (........)
    TEXT    .WPF     1,629   3/04/91   0:07:22  [A.....]     (........)
    WH7X    .WPF     2,606   3/04/91   1:02:24  [A.....]     (........)


    Select = Enter   PgUp    Home     Mark/unMark = F7
    Exit   = Esc     PgDn    End      Mark Range = sft/F7
    View   = V       F10 = Top Menu   unMark ALL = alt/F7
 #3 C:\40DATA\*.WP*                          16 Files      47,506 bytes used
```

**Fig. 3.9.** *The word processing File Manager screen under DOS.*

- Press the question mark (?) at any file name prompt. For example, from the Main Menu, choose Use_System **S**preadsheet **?** and then press Enter. The File Manager screen lists all spreadsheet files.

- Each applications module has a File Manager option under the File option in the Top Line menu. To access the File Manager, press

    **F10 File File_manager**

  or use the F9 command

    **F9 Directory**

# Understanding the File Manager Screen

The pointer in the File Manager screen is an arrow to the left of the target file. Use the cursor-movement keys—the up-, down-, left-, and right-arrow keys and the PgUp, PgDn, Home, and End keys—to move the pointer around the directory. When you first display the Directory screen, the pointer is at the top.

Figure 3.9 shows a sample File Manager screen under DOS. The top line of the screen, or *information display area*, includes the name of the file or directory indicated by the pointer, as well as the date and time the file was last changed. The bottom line of the screen displays the current drive and directory, which were the default drive and directory at the time you opened the window. The bottom line also displays the number of files listed and the amount of disk space the files occupy.

Below the information display area you see the list of files. The size of each file, the date and time of the last change to the file, current file attributes, and special directory codes appear to the right of each file's name. The list of commands available to you is below the file list. Table 3.2 lists the special codes used in the File Manager screen and the code meanings.

**Table 3.2**
**File Manager Screen**
**Meaning of Special Codes**

| Special Code | Meaning |
| --- | --- |
| *Code* | |
| <DIR> dirname | Directory named DIRNAME |
| <DIR> .. | Parent directory |
| <VOL> volname | Volume named VOLNAME |
| *File Attribute* | |
| [A.....] | Archive attribute set |
| [.D....] | Directory attribute set |
| [..V...] | Volume attribute set |
| [...S..] | System attribute set |
| [....H.] | Hidden attribute set |
| [.....R] | Read-only attribute set |
| *Special Code* | |
| {m.......} | File previously marked |
| {.c......} | File previously copied |
| {..s.....} | File skipped during copy |
| {...*....} | Text found during TextScan |
| {....t...} | Text not found during TextScan |
| {.....r..} | File renamed by copy |
| {......a.} | File whose archive bit was reset (DOS only) |
| {........}* | File is active in another window |

Figure 3.10 shows the File Manager screen under UNIX. This screen is the only screen within Enable that is different in the two environments (DOS and UNIX). Within these screens, all the same options are available.

Below the information display area, you see the list of files and, below that list, a list of commands. File permissions; the number of current links; the owner name; the group name; and the size, date, and time of the last change to the file appear to the left of the file's name.

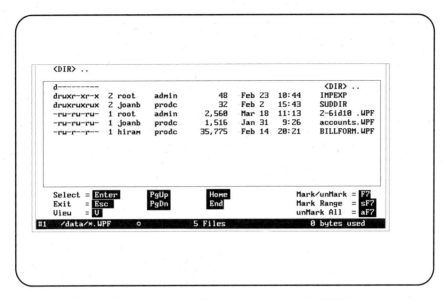

*Fig 3.10. The word processing File Manager screen under UNIX.*

# Using the Directory and File Management Commands

The next sections of this chapter explain how to use Enable's File Manager screen to perform the following directory and file management functions:

- Set passwords
- Change Enable's data directory
- Make and remove directories
- Mark and unmark files
- Copy files
- Destroy files
- Rename files
- View files
- Scan files
- Sort files

For most options on the File Manager menu, you can press the first letter of the option without using the menu (see table 3.3).

**Table 3.3**
**Keyboard Shortcuts for File Manager Menu**

| Keystroke | Option |
| --- | --- |
| F | Find next mark |
| W | Wildcard marking |
| A | Attribute options |
| L | List new path/pattern |
| S | Sort directory |
| T | TextScan marked files |
| V | View file |
| O | Oldmark options |
| C | Copy marked files |
| D | Destroy marked files |
| R | Rename marked files |
| P | Assign password |
| Q | Display path aliases |
| – | Reverse all marks |

# Assigning, Changing, and Removing a Password

With Enable/OA and Enable/OA 4.0, you can add a level of security to your files that the operating system alone does not provide. After you add a password to a file in Enable, no one can access the file without first entering the password. This feature is not intended to be foolproof protection, however, and should be only one aspect of a more comprehensive file-security program if you work with sensitive data.

The password feature works only with files saved in Enable/OA and Enable/OA 4.0 format. If you attempt to password-protect an incompatible file, Enable responds with the message

```
Unable to set password on designated file.
```

To add password protection to a file you created with an earlier version of Enable or with another program, first retrieve the file and then save it in Enable/OA or Enable/OA 4.0 format. Then you can add a password to the new version of the file. The new file, however, no longer is compatible with the original program.

**TIP**

Enable does not provide you with a method to remove a password that you have forgotten. Consequently, be careful to choose a password that you can remember. The best practice is to password-protect a file only after you have made a backup copy without a password to another disk. If the data is sensitive, lock up the copy. Don't forget to remove the password temporarily before you make subsequent backup copies.

To add a password from the File Manager screen, move the pointer to the target file and press

F10 **File Password**

At the prompt, type in the password of up to five characters, and then press Enter.

When you retrieve the file, the following prompt displays in the status line:

`Enter password. [Alt-F3] erase, [RET] accept, [ESC] exit. file.ext -----`

As you type the password, asterisks (*) replace the hyphens (-----), but the password itself does not appear. If you enter the correct password, Enable continues as usual; if not, Enable displays the following error box:

`Incorrect password supplied. [OK]`

When you press Enter, the initial prompt returns; you have two additional chances to enter the correct password. After three unsuccessful password attempts, Enable aborts the operation and you must choose another file.

If you assign passwords to your files for security reasons, you should change the passwords periodically. The procedure is the same as for assigning a password, but Enable prompts you to enter the old password before you can assign a new one. To remove all password protection, at the `Enter a new password` prompt, press Enter without entering a new password.

# Assigning a New Default Drive/ Directory for a Window

During the start-up procedure (described in Appendix A, "Installing and Starting Enable"), you specify the drive and directory you want to use for data files, usually a separate directory on your hard disk. The start-up procedure establishes the *default* drive and directory. When you display the File Manager screen, the default drive appears in the bottom left corner of the screen.

You occasionally need to reassign the default drive and directory for the window in which you are working. Use the procedure described next. If you want to reassign the defaults for the current window and all windows that you subsequently open, but you don't want to restart Enable, refer to the section "Assigning a New Enable Data Path" in this chapter.

To reassign the default drive and/or directory for the current window, press the following from the File Manager screen:

F10 **D**irectory **A**ssign_default_for_window

Enable displays the Extended Directory Utility Menu Screen, with the current window default listed at the top of the screen and the prompt

```
Enter the new default path for this window.
```

at the bottom. At this prompt, enter the drive and directory of the new data path. Enable treats the new drive and directory as the default until you close this window. In other words, if you are working in a spreadsheet in this window, and you display the File Manager screen, you see files only from the newly assigned drive and directory and not the files from the drive and directory specified with the start-up command. After you close this window, however, the default returns to the one designated by the start-up command.

> If you are selecting a database file and you change the directory, make sure that you change the default directory. Otherwise, Enable may not find default input and report forms, and linked database files.

## Assigning a New Enable Data Path

Suppose that you need to change the directory for all windows that you subsequently open. The procedure for this task is very similar to the procedure described in the preceding section.

To reassign the default drive and/or directory for all subsequent windows, from the File Manager screen press

F10 **D**irectory **A**ssign_Enable_data_path

Enable displays the Extended Directory Utility Menu Screen, with the current window default at the top of the screen and the prompt

```
Enter the new ENABLE data path.
```

at the bottom of the screen. At the prompt, enter the drive and directory of the new data path. Unless you repeat this command, Enable treats the new drive and directory as the default. This command does not affect current windows. If you are working in a database in window 1 and then change the Enable data path in window 2, all files in window 1 are still from the data directory of that window. After you close window 1, however, the default switches to the one designated by the new Enable data path.

# Using Aliases

Enable/OA 4.0 supports multiple levels of directories. You can use the File List_new_path command, discussed in the section "Listing a New Path and Pattern" to display the file names in a second (or third or fourth, and so on) level directory, often called a *subdirectory* or *path*—C:\40DATA\WPFILES, for example. Enable/OA 4.0 automatically assigns an *alias* to this subdirectory name. You can use the alias in place of the much longer path name. Enable assigns the alias +001 to the first multilevel path it uses. To display the list of assigned aliases, from the File Manager screen, press

F10 **Directory Display_path_aliases**

Assume that earlier in the current Enable session you accessed the C:\40DATA\WPFILES subdirectory, represented on the screen in figure 3.11. Subdirectories that you subsequently use in an Enable session receive aliases in sequence: +002, +003, +004, and so on. Enable wipes clean the alias list and begins numbering at +001 when you begin your next Enable session.

If you later decide to edit a word processing file in the C:\40DATA\WPFILES subdirectory, from the Main Menu you can press

Use_System **Word_processing**

and then type \\**+001**\\**?** and press Enter. You see a screen similar to the one shown in figure 3.12. Aliases save you from always having to type a long multilevel path to access files in a subdirectory.

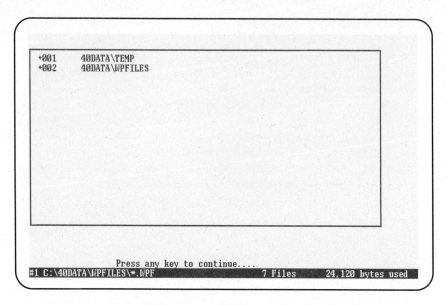

*Fig. 3.11. Aliases assigned to subdirectories.*

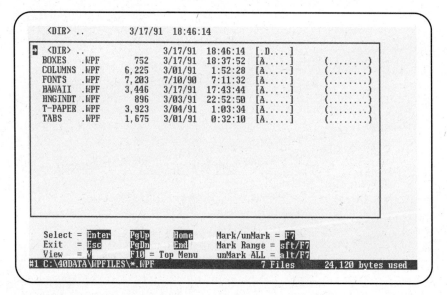

*Fig. 3.12. A directory of word processing files called up by an alias.*

# Making and Removing Directories

When you perform hard disk management, you sometimes have to make or remove a directory. To choose one of these options from the File Manager screen, press

F10 **Directory**

Then, to make a directory, press

**Make_directory**

Enable displays the prompt Enter directory path to be created. Type the complete directory path name. To create a directory named EN3FILS2 on your hard disk, for example, type the path name **C:\EN3FILS2**, and press Enter.

To remove a directory, press

F10 **Directory**

Then press

**R**emove_directory

Enable displays the prompt Enter directory path to be REMOVED. Type the complete directory path name. To remove a directory named EN3FILS2 from your hard disk, for example, type the path name **C:\EN3FILS2** and press Enter. Note that Enable can remove a directory only if it contains no files or subdirectories. If your directory contains other files or sub-directories, you must remove them before you can remove the current directory.

# Marking and Unmarking File Names

You must indicate which file or files you want a file command to operate on before Enable can complete the command. Through the File Manager screen, use Enable's F7 marking key to mark files (see Chapter 6, "Using Word Processing Advanced Features," and Chapter 14, "Using Database Management System Power Features," for discussions of marking with the F7 key). Enable displays marked files in reverse video and with the special code *m* (see fig. 3.13). Use the F7 key as a toggle switch to mark and then unmark one file name at a time. You can mark a group or groups of file names by pressing Shift-F7 at the first and last file names of the group of files. Press Alt-F7 to remove all file marking. You can reverse all marks—unmark all marked files and mark all unmarked files—by pressing the hyphen (-) key.

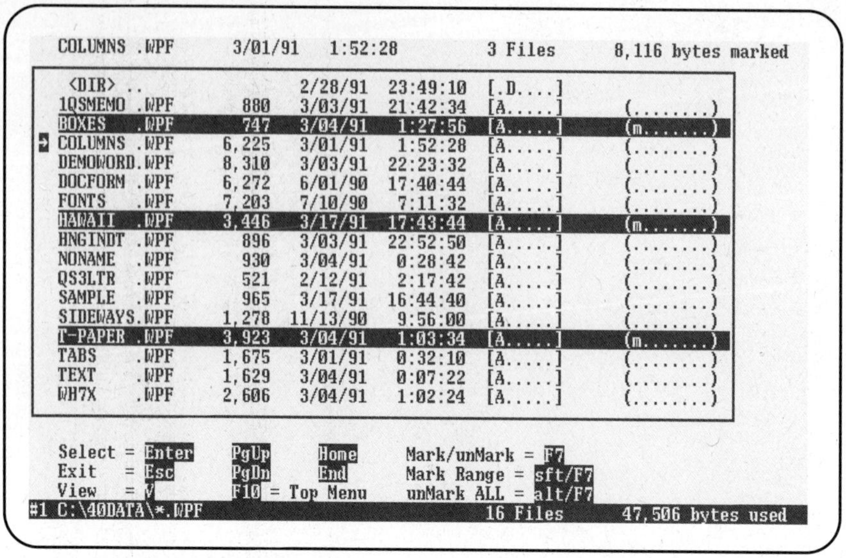

```
COLUMNS .WPF      3/01/91  1:52:28        3 Files      8,116 bytes marked

   <DIR> ..                 2/28/91  23:49:10  [.D....]
   1QSMEMO .WPF      880    3/03/91  21:42:34  [A.....]      (........)
   BOXES   .WPF      747    3/04/91   1:27:56  [A.....]      (m.......)
   COLUMNS .WPF    6,225    3/01/91   1:52:28  [A.....]      (........)
   DEMOWORD.WPF    8,310    3/03/91  22:23:32  [A.....]      (........)
   DOCFORM .WPF    6,272    6/01/90  17:40:44  [A.....]      (........)
   FONTS   .WPF    7,203    7/10/90   7:11:32  [A.....]      (........)
   HAWAII  .WPF    3,446    3/17/91  17:43:44  [A.....]      (m.......)
   HNGINDT .WPF      896    3/03/91  22:52:50  [A.....]      (........)
   NONAME  .WPF      930    3/04/91   0:28:42  [A.....]      (........)
   QS3LTR  .WPF      521    2/12/91   2:17:42  [A.....]      (........)
   SAMPLE  .WPF      965    3/17/91  16:44:40  [A.....]      (........)
   SIDEWAYS.WPF    1,278   11/13/90   9:56:00  [A.....]      (........)
   T-PAPER .WPF    3,923    3/04/91   1:03:34  [A.....]      (m.......)
   TABS    .WPF    1,675    3/01/91   0:32:10  [A.....]      (........)
   TEXT    .WPF    1,629    3/04/91   0:07:22  [A.....]      (........)
   WH7X    .WPF    2,606    3/04/91   1:02:24  [A.....]      (........)


   Select = Enter   PgUp    Home      Mark/unMark  = F7
   Exit   = Esc     PgDn    End       Mark Range   = sft/F7
   View   = V       F10 = Top Menu    unMark ALL   = alt/F7
#1 C:\40DATA\*.WPF                              16 Files     47,506 bytes used
```

**Fig. 3.13.** *The File Manager screen displaying marked and unmarked files.*

You also can use wild-card characters to specify the files you want to mark. From the File Manager screen, press

F10 **Mark Wildcard_marking**

Type the search pattern in the blank line above the prompt

```
Mark which files (wildcards acceptable)?
```

An asterisk (*) represents any number of characters, and each question mark (?) represents one character.

If the directory contains several marked file names, Enable moves the pointer to the next marked file name each time you press

F10 **Mark Find_next_mark**

Now that you know how to mark files, you can learn in the following section to use the commands that you need for file management.

# Copying Marked Files

Sometimes you need to copy files between directories and/or disks. You may want to copy more than one file at a time or only files that have been updated since you last made a copy. Through Enable's File Manager screen these tasks are simple.

First, use the methods discussed in the preceding section to mark the file(s) you want to copy. Then press

F10 **Mark Copy_marked_files**

Enable displays the Copy Marked Files menu (see fig. 3.14). The source drive and directory already appear on-screen. Enable immediately prompts you for a destination path (Enable/OA and Enable/OA 4.0 support multilevel directories). In the blank line above the drive/directory prompt, type the drive, directory, and subdirectory, if applicable, where you want to copy the file(s)—even if they are the same as the source drive and directory. Press Enter. Your screen should look like the one in figure 3.15.

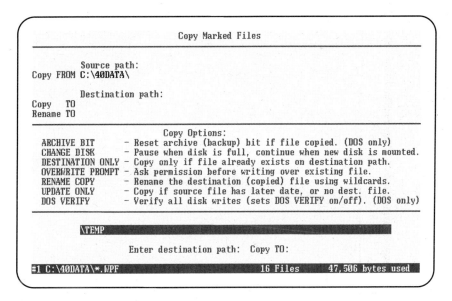

```
                           Copy Marked Files
_____

              Source path:
Copy FROM C:\40DATA\

              Destination path:
Copy   TO
Rename TO
_____
                         Copy Options:
   ARCHIVE BIT        - Reset archive (backup) bit if file copied. (DOS only)
   CHANGE DISK        - Pause when disk is full, continue when new disk is mounted.
   DESTINATION ONLY   - Copy only if file already exists on destination path.
   OVERWRITE PROMPT   - Ask permission before writing over existing file.
   RENAME COPY        - Rename the destination (copied) file using wildcards.
   UPDATE ONLY        - Copy if source file has later date, or no dest. file.
   DOS VERIFY         - Verify all disk writes (sets DOS VERIFY on/off). (DOS only)
_____

      \TEMP

          Enter destination path:  Copy TO:
_____
#1 C:\40DATA\*.WPF                        16 Files        47,506 bytes used
```

***Fig. 3.14.*** *The Copy Marked Files screen.*

Enable offers you several copy options. The following options toggle on and off when you press the letter in brackets to the left of the option on-screen:

- **Archive_bit.** Press **A** for Enable to reset (remove) the archive bit. DOS's BACKUP and XCOPY use the archive bit to determine whether or not the file has been backed up since it was created or last changed. ***Note:*** This option does not apply in UNIX.

- **Change_disk.** Press **C** for Enable to display a warning message when the destination disk becomes full while you are copying files. Enable skips files that it cannot copy completely onto the destination disk. Enable copies these skipped files only after you replace the destination disk and press Enter. *Note:* This option does not apply in UNIX.

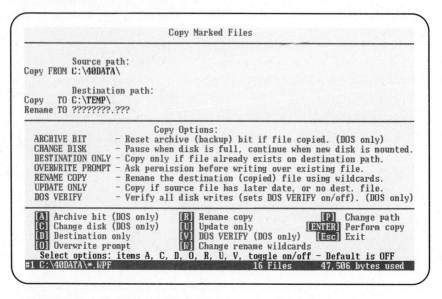

                            Copy Marked Files

            Source path:
Copy FROM C:\40DATA\

            Destination path:
Copy  TO C:\TEMP\
Rename TO ????????.???

                          Copy Options:
    ARCHIVE BIT       - Reset archive (backup) bit if file copied. (DOS only)
    CHANGE DISK       - Pause when disk is full, continue when new disk is mounted.
    DESTINATION ONLY  - Copy only if file already exists on destination path.
    OVERWRITE PROMPT  - Ask permission before writing over existing file.
    RENAME COPY       - Rename the destination (copied) file using wildcards.
    UPDATE ONLY       - Copy if source file has later date, or no dest. file.
    DOS VERIFY        - Verify all disk writes (sets DOS VERIFY on/off). (DOS only)

    [A] Archive bit (DOS only)    [R] Rename copy           [P]  Change path
    [C] Change disk (DOS only)    [U] Update only          [ENTER] Perform copy
    [D] Destination only          [V] DOS VERIFY (DOS only) [Esc] Exit
    [O] Overwrite prompt          [W] Change rename wildcards
    Select options: items A, C, D, O, R, U, V, toggle on/off - Default is OFF
#1 C:\40DATA\*.WPF                        16 Files        47,506 bytes used

*Fig. 3.15. The Copy Marked Files screen with the Copy Options list.*

- **Destination_only.** Press **D** for Enable to copy only files that exist on both the source disk and the destination disk. Enable places a letter *c* to the right of the file size on the File Manager screen for all files that it copies. The name of any marked file that Enable does not copy because the file didn't already exist on the destination disk remains highlighted.

- **Overwrite_prompt.** Press **O** for Enable to require that you confirm **Yes** or **No** for each copy that will overwrite an existing file in the destination path.

- **Rename_copy.** Press **R** for Enable to rename the files while copying. If the source and destination paths are the same, you must use this option. You also must use Change_rename_wildcards so that this command works.

- **Update_only.** Press **U** for Enable to copy only files that either do not yet exist on the destination disk or have a later date and time. The letter *c* indicates a successful copy, but here Enable uses the letter *s* to denote a skipped file.

- DOS_VERIFY_FLAG. Press **V** to toggle DOS VERIFY FLAG on and off. This DOS feature verifies that Enable copied properly and can read each file written to the disk. DOS VERIFY FLAG is a good safety feature but slows down copying. *Note:* This option does not apply in UNIX.

The Copy Marked Files menu lists two more options that do not toggle on and off:

- **W** Change_rename_wildcards. Whenever you use the Rename_copy option, you can also press **W** and use wild cards (* and/or ?) to indicate how to change the name(s) of the files you are copying.

- **P** Change_path. Press **P** when you want to indicate a destination path for a file(s) different from the one you chose initially.

## Destroying Marked Files

After you use the Destroy_marked_files command to destroy files, the files are gone forever. File recovery programs, such as Norton Utilities, Mace Utilities, and PC Tools, are available to recover files that you have destroyed by mistake; however, in practice you should think of these programs as insurance against catastrophe, not as routine utilities. Don't destroy a file unless you really do not need it anymore. When in doubt, copy a file to a floppy diskette and file it away in the back of your disk box for safekeeping.

After you mark the files you intend to destroy, press the following from the File Manager screen:

F10 **Mark Destroy_marked_files Yes Delete**

You can abort at the first prompt by pressing **N** (for No) or at the second prompt by pressing any key except **D**. If you cancel the Destroy command, the file names remain marked.

Enable does not permit you to destroy certain files: program-related files with the TSG extension, read-only files, and files that are open or are in use (marked in the File Manager screen by an asterisk to the right of the special codes list). The Destroy command skips these files.

TIP

# Renaming and Moving Marked Files

Sometimes you need to rename files. The Rename_marked_files command is a useful utility for moving—as opposed to copying—a single file or many files at once to another directory. *Note:* The directory and the files must be on the same physical disk. To move files to another disk, you first must copy the files, then delete the originals.

To rename or move several marked files, press the following from the File Manager screen:

F10 **M**ark **R**ename_marked_files

Enable prompts you to

`Enter new PATH`

or

`Press (Enter) to keep current path.`

Type the new directory path to move the files; press Enter to rename files. Enable displays the path and a blank line below the path for a new name or wild-card pattern. To rename one file, type the new name and press Enter. To rename several files, enter an appropriate wild-card pattern, following DOS conventions (* represents any number of characters and ? represents one character).

Suppose that, for example, you have just converted several ASCII (American Standard Code for Information Interchange) text files to Enable's word processing format, but the file names still have the ASC extension. To change all the extensions to WPF at once, use **W**ildcard_marking to mark the ASC files and press **R**ename_marked_files. Then press Enter at the `PATH` prompt. At the `new name` prompt, type *.**wpf** and press Enter again. The converted files now have the appropriate file name extension for Enable word processing files.

Suppose that your Enable data directory is cluttered with files, and you decide to move some files to a new directory, C:\EN3FILS2. Using normal DOS commands, you need to copy the files to the new directory and then delete the files from the old directory. If no convenient wild-card pattern is available to select the entire group of files, you may have to use two commands for each file you move. With Enable, however, in the File Manager screen you mark all the files you want to move; then press

F10 **M**ark **R**ename_marked_files

At the PATH prompt, type **c:\en3fils2** (assuming that you have first created the new directory; see the section "Making and Removing Directories" in this chapter). Press Enter. At the `new name` prompt, type *.* and press Enter.

# Listing a New Path and Pattern

When Enable first displays the File Manager screen, the files list from the start-up data disk and directory. The path name, number of files, and bytes used appear in the status line (bottom line) of the screen (see fig. 3.16). You can change to another directory by moving the pointer to the directory name and pressing Enter or by using the File List_new_path command. To change to another disk from the File Manager screen, however, you can only use the following command:

F10 **File List_new_path**

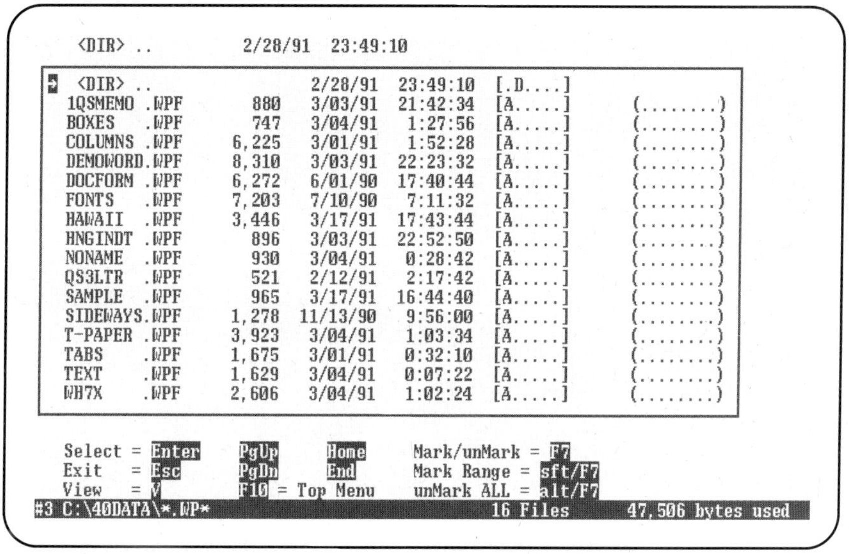

```
    <DIR> ..        2/28/91  23:49:10

▶  <DIR> ..                 2/28/91  23:49:10  [.D....]
   1QSMEMO .WPF      880     3/03/91  21:42:34  [A.....]    (........)
   BOXES   .WPF      747     3/04/91   1:27:56  [A.....]    (........)
   COLUMNS .WPF    6,225     3/01/91   1:52:28  [A.....]    (........)
   DEMOWORD.WPF    8,310     3/03/91  22:23:32  [A.....]    (........)
   DOCFORM .WPF    6,272     6/01/90  17:40:44  [A.....]    (........)
   FONTS   .WPF    7,203     7/10/90   7:11:32  [A.....]    (........)
   HAWAII  .WPF    3,446     3/17/91  17:43:44  [A.....]    (........)
   HNGINDT .WPF      896     3/03/91  22:52:50  [A.....]    (........)
   NONAME  .WPF      930     3/04/91   0:28:42  [A.....]    (........)
   QS3LTR  .WPF      521     2/12/91   2:17:42  [A.....]    (........)
   SAMPLE  .WPF      965     3/17/91  16:44:40  [A.....]    (........)
   SIDEWAYS.WPF    1,278    11/13/90   9:56:00  [A.....]    (........)
   T-PAPER .WPF    3,923     3/04/91   1:03:34  [A.....]    (........)
   TABS    .WPF    1,675     3/01/91   0:32:10  [A.....]    (........)
   TEXT    .WPF    1,629     3/04/91   0:07:22  [A.....]    (........)
   WH7X    .WPF    2,606     3/04/91   1:02:24  [A.....]    (........)


   Select = Enter   PgUp     Home     Mark/unMark = F7
   Exit   = Esc     PgDn     End      Mark Range  = sft/F7
   View   = V        F10 = Top Menu   unMark ALL  = alt/F7
#3 C:\40DATA\*.WP*                          16 Files     47,506 bytes used
```

*Fig. 3.16. The word processing File Manager screen under DOS*

Enable displays a blank line in which you can type, and the following three prompts:

Enter new directory path only (keep current wild card pattern).

Enter new wild card pattern only (keep current directory path).

Enter new directory path including wild card pattern.

As the first prompt indicates, you can type a path (a new drive, directory, or drive and directory) without typing a new wild-card (search) pattern; Enable displays the file names that meet the old search pattern in the new disk/ directory. To display matching file names in the current drive and directory, type a new wild-card pattern without indicating a path. To change both the path and the search pattern, type both in the blank line. Remember to press Enter following the option you choose.

# Viewing Files

Like several other File Manager functions, the View function serves a dual purpose. You can use this function to move between directories on the same disk and to look at word processing and ASCII files without opening a word processing window. (You even can look at the contents of binary files, but for most users, binary files are about as easy to read as hieroglyphics!)

**TIP**

If your Enable data directory is on a hard disk, you notice that the first listed file is <DIR>.., unless your disk has a volume name that displays first. The two dots (..) designate the parent directory of the current directory. Place the pointer at this file and press **V** or Enter. You probably will move to the *root* directory, unless the current directory has a parent directory. From the root directory, you can move to another *branch* of the *directory tree*.

For example, you can move to your Enable program directory, C:\EN400, by moving the pointer to that name and pressing **V** (or Enter) again. When you navigate your computer's hard disk in this manner, you can better understand its organization. Take your time; if you get lost, press the Esc key twice to return to your work.

You also can use the View_file/directory command to view the contents of a word processing or ASCII file, which is useful when you are looking for a particular document but aren't sure of its name. Move the pointer to a file name and press

**View_file/directory**

If the file is an Enable word processing file or an ASCII file, Enable immediately displays the file's contents. Enable also displays the contents of other types of files, but in binary format. Remember that you cannot edit the information displayed without first opening a word processing window. The purpose of the View_file/directory option is to give you a quick look.

The View option can make finding a lost file easy, especially when you use it with the TextScan option described in the next section.

# Using TextScan

The TextScan option, when teamed with the View option, can help you quickly find a certain file that you know exists but you cannot locate. Suppose that at 5:00 p.m. on Friday afternoon, your boss wants to see a copy of the WIDGETCO memo you wrote last month concerning the Hyperion Widget Corporation. You remember the memo, but you cannot remember exactly what you called the file. Enable's TextScan function can help.

Display the File Manager screen; then mark every file that you think may be the one you want and press

   F10 **Mark** TextScan_marked_files

Enable displays the prompt

   `Enter text string to scan for in marked files.`

Type the target text, **widgetco**, as shown in figure 3.17. Then press Enter. Enable quickly scans through each marked file looking for *widgetco*.

```
 WH7X    .WPF    3/04/91   1:02:24        9 Files    23,398 bytes marked

   <DIR> ..               2/28/91  23:49:10  [.D....]
 1QSMEMO .WPF       890   3/17/91  18:38:04  [A.....]      (m.......)
 BOXES   .WPF       752   3/17/91  18:37:52  [A.....]      (m.......)
 COLUMNS .WPF     6,225   3/01/91   1:52:28  [A.....]      (........)
 DEMOWORD.WPF     8,310   3/03/91  22:23:32  [A.....]      (........)
 DOCFORM .WPF     6,272   6/01/90  17:40:44  [A.....]      (m.......)
 FONTS   .WPF     7,203   7/10/90   7:11:32  [A.....]      (m.......)
 HAWAII  .WPF     3,446   3/17/91  17:43:44  [A.....]      (........)
 HNGINDT .WPF       896   3/03/91  22:52:50  [A.....]      (........)
 NONAME  .WPF       930   3/04/91   0:28:42  [A.....]      (m.......)
 QS3LTR  .WPF       521   2/12/91   2:17:42  [A.....]      (........)
 SAMPLE  .WPF       965   3/17/91  16:44:40  [A.....]      (........)
 SIDEWAYS.WPF     1,278  11/13/90   9:56:00  [A.....]      (m.......)
 T-PAPER .WPF     3,923   3/04/91   1:03:34  [A.....]      (m.......)
 TABS    .WPF     1,675   3/01/91   0:32:10  [A.....]      (........)
 TEXT    .WPF     1,629   3/04/91   0:07:22  [A.....]      (m.......)
 WH7X    .WPF     2,606   3/04/91   1:02:24  [A.....]      (........)

        WIDGETCO
        Enter text string to scan for in marked files:
           (The text scan is not case sensitive)
        Press [Esc] to exit without scanning
#1 C:\40DATA\*.WPF                         16 Files    47,521 bytes used
```

*Fig. 3.17. Files marked for a TextScan search.*

Any file that contains the target text string remains highlighted and has an asterisk in the special codes area. Scanned files that do not contain the text string are no longer highlighted and have a *t* (for TextScan completed) in the special codes area (see fig. 3.18).

```
1QSMEMO .WPF     3/17/91  18:38:04      4 Files      4,251 bytes marked

   <DIR> ..                  2/28/91  23:49:10  [.D....]
➔ 1QSMEMO .WPF        890   3/17/91  18:38:04  [A.....]      (m..*....)
   BOXES   .WPF        752   3/17/91  18:37:52  [A.....]      (m..*....)
   COLUMNS .WPF      6,225   3/01/91   1:52:28  [A.....]      (m...t...)
   DEMOWORD.WPF      8,310   3/03/91  22:23:32  [A.....]      (m...t...)
   DOCFORM .WPF      6,272   6/01/90  17:40:44  [A.....]      (m...t...)
   FONTS   .WPF      7,203   7/10/90   7:11:32  [A.....]      (m...t...)
   HAWAII  .WPF      3,446   3/17/91  17:43:44  [A.....]      (m...t...)
   HNGINDT .WPF        896   3/03/91  22:52:50  [A.....]      (m...t...)
   NONAME  .WPF        930   3/04/91   0:28:42  [A.....]      (m...t...)
   QS3LTR  .WPF        521   2/12/91   2:17:42  [A.....]      (m...t...)
   SAMPLE  .WPF        974   3/17/91  18:39:18  [A.....]      (m..*....)
   SIDEWAYS.WPF      1,278  11/13/90   9:56:00  [A.....]      (m...t...)
   T-PAPER .WPF      3,923   3/04/91   1:03:34  [A.....]      (m...t...)
   TABS    .WPF      1,675   3/01/91   0:32:10  [A.....]      (m...t...)
   TEXT    .WPF      1,638   3/17/91  18:39:32  [A.....]      (m..*....)
   WH7X    .WPF      2,606   3/04/91   1:02:24  [A.....]      (m...t...)


   Select = Enter    PgUp    Home     Mark/unMark = F7
   Exit   = Esc      PgDn    End      Mark Range  = sft/F7
   View   = V        F10 = Top Menu   unMark ALL  = alt/F7
#1 C:\40DATA\*.WPF                          16 Files      47,539 bytes used
```

**Fig. 3.18.** *A list of files after a TextScan search.*

You use TextScan to find the files that contain the word *WIDGETCO*. Use View to find the correct file. For example, with the pointer on the first marked file, press

    **View_file**

If this file is not the correct one, press Esc to return to the File Manager screen. To move to and view the next marked file, press

    **Find_next_mark View_file**

Repeat the preceding command until you find the correct file.

Enable's TextScan feature is useful to everyone who creates many files on a hard disk without routinely cataloging them. When you use TextScan with the View option, the feature may well become one of your favorite tools.

# Sorting the Directory

The File Manager screen normally displays file names in ascending alphanumeric order. Enable/OA 4.0 gives you a choice of several other sorting orders as well. To choose a sorting order from the File Manager screen, press

F10 **F**ile **S**ort_directory

Enable prompts you for Forward or Reverse order. After you choose the order, a third menu lists the following sort choices:

- *Sort by date/time*. Press **D** to sort the file names by the date and time the files were last changed (see fig. 3.19).

- *Sort by extension*. Press **E** to sort the directory first by the file extensions, and next by the file name (see fig. 3.20).

- *Sort by file name*. Press **N** (for normal) to sort only by file name. This option is the default or normal sorted order (see fig. 3.21).

- *Sort by file size*. Press **S** to sort the file names in file size order (see fig. 3.22).

- *Unsorted*. Press **U** to see the file names in an unsorted list—the physical order of the disk directory (see fig. 3.23).

```
    <DIR> ..        2/28/91  23:49:10

  <DIR> ..                  2/28/91  23:49:10  [.D....]
  A       .CDF        705   3/17/91  18:10:30  [A.....]     (........)
  A       .CLF        577   3/17/91  18:09:52  [A.....]     (........)
  A       .NDX      1,024   3/17/91  18:09:26  [A.....]     (........)
  M       .MC         698   3/17/91  18:08:00  [A.....]     (........)
  HAWAII  .WPF      3,446   3/17/91  17:43:44  [A.....]     (........)
  FINANCE .SSF      7,168   3/17/91  16:56:18  [A.....]     (........)
  SAMPLE  .WPF        965   3/17/91  16:44:40  [A.....]     (........)
  SALES   .SSF      2,048   3/04/91   5:38:54  [A.....]     (........)
  WNCH10  .GAF     12,060   3/04/91   5:38:16  [A.....]     (........)
  SIMPTEXT.SSF      2,048   3/04/91   5:08:30  [A.....]     (........)
  SIMPSTAT.SSF      2,048   3/04/91   4:34:40  [A.....]     (........)
  TRIGSIMP.SSF      2,560   3/04/91   4:28:28  [A.....]     (........)
  MATHSIM .SSF      3,072   3/04/91   4:28:24  [A.....]     (........)
  RANGES  .SSF      1,536   3/04/91   3:37:18  [A.....]     (........)
  WIDGETS .SSF      2,560   3/04/91   3:11:44  [A.....]     (........)
  QS4BUDGT.SSF      1,024   3/04/91   2:31:04  [A.....]     (........)


  Select = Enter    PgUp      Home      Mark/unMark = F7
  Exit   = Esc      PgDn      End       Mark Range  = sft/F7
  View   = V        F10 = Top Menu      unMark ALL  = alt/F7
#1 C:\40DATA\*.*                              52 Files      150,267 bytes used
```

*Fig. 3.19. File names sorted by date and time.*

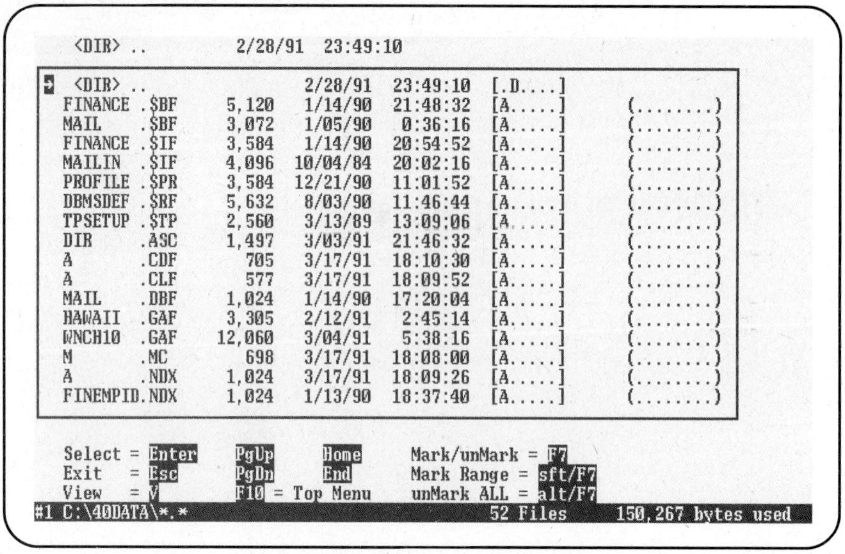

```
   <DIR> ..        2/28/91  23:49:10

   <DIR> ..                 2/28/91  23:49:10  [.D....]
   FINANCE .$BF      5,120   1/14/90  21:48:32  [A.....]      (........)
   MAIL    .$BF      3,072   1/05/90   0:36:16  [A.....]      (........)
   FINANCE .$IF      3,584   1/14/90  20:54:52  [A.....]      (........)
   MAILIN  .$IF      4,096  10/04/84  20:02:16  [A.....]      (........)
   PROFILE .$PR      3,584  12/21/90  11:01:52  [A.....]      (........)
   DBMSDEF .$RF      5,632   8/03/90  11:46:44  [A.....]      (........)
   TPSETUP .$TP      2,560   3/13/89  13:09:06  [A.....]      (........)
   DIR     .ASC      1,497   3/03/91  21:46:32  [A.....]      (........)
   A       .CDF        705   3/17/91  18:10:30  [A.....]      (........)
   A       .CLF        577   3/17/91  18:09:52  [A.....]      (........)
   MAIL    .DBF      1,024   1/14/90  17:20:04  [A.....]      (........)
   HAWAII  .GAF      3,305   2/12/91   2:45:14  [A.....]      (........)
   WNCH10  .GAF     12,060   3/04/91   5:38:16  [A.....]      (........)
   M       .MC         698   3/17/91  18:08:00  [A.....]      (........)
   A       .NDX      1,024   3/17/91  18:09:26  [A.....]      (........)
   FINEMPID.NDX      1,024   1/13/90  18:37:40  [A.....]      (........)

   Select = Enter    PgUp    Home       Mark/unMark = F7
   Exit   = Esc      PgDn    End        Mark Range  = sft/F7
   View   = V        F10 = Top Menu     unMark ALL  = alt/F7
#1 C:\40DATA\*.*                        52 Files    150,267 bytes used
```

**Fig. 3.20.** *File names sorted by file name extension.*

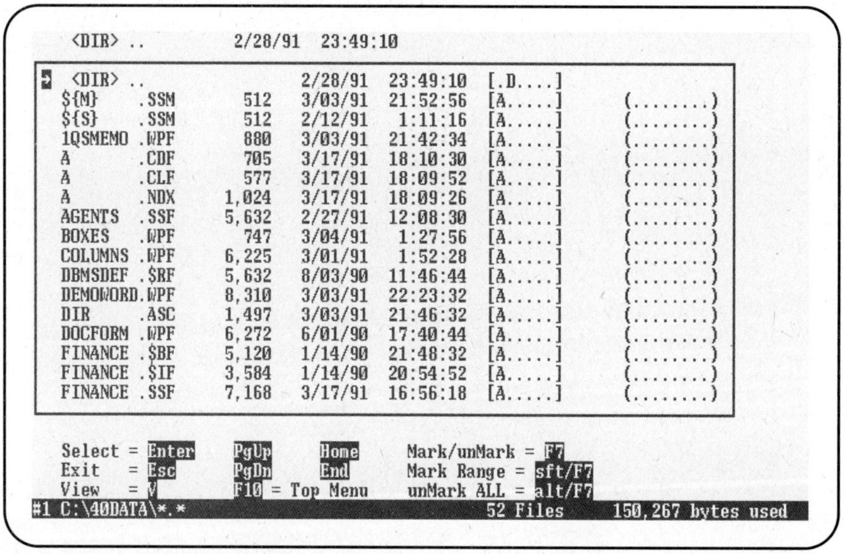

```
   <DIR> ..        2/28/91  23:49:10

   <DIR> ..                 2/28/91  23:49:10  [.D....]
   ${M}    .SSM        512   3/03/91  21:52:56  [A.....]      (........)
   ${S}    .SSM        512   2/12/91   1:11:16  [A.....]      (........)
   1QSMEMO .WPF        880   3/03/91  21:42:34  [A.....]      (........)
   A       .CDF        705   3/17/91  18:10:30  [A.....]      (........)
   A       .CLF        577   3/17/91  18:09:52  [A.....]      (........)
   A       .NDX      1,024   3/17/91  18:09:26  [A.....]      (........)
   AGENTS  .SSF      5,632   2/27/91  12:08:30  [A.....]      (........)
   BOXES   .WPF        747   3/04/91   1:27:56  [A.....]      (........)
   COLUMNS .WPF      6,225   3/01/91   1:52:28  [A.....]      (........)
   DBMSDEF .$RF      5,632   8/03/90  11:46:44  [A.....]      (........)
   DEMOWORD.WPF      8,310   3/03/91  22:23:32  [A.....]      (........)
   DIR     .ASC      1,497   3/03/91  21:46:32  [A.....]      (........)
   DOCFORM .WPF      6,272   6/01/90  17:40:44  [A.....]      (........)
   FINANCE .$BF      5,120   1/14/90  21:48:32  [A.....]      (........)
   FINANCE .$IF      3,584   1/14/90  20:54:52  [A.....]      (........)
   FINANCE .SSF      7,168   3/17/91  16:56:18  [A.....]      (........)

   Select = Enter    PgUp    Home       Mark/unMark = F7
   Exit   = Esc      PgDn    End        Mark Range  = sft/F7
   View   = V        F10 = Top Menu     unMark ALL  = alt/F7
#1 C:\40DATA\*.*                        52 Files    150,267 bytes used
```

**Fig. 3.21.** *Normal sort order by file name.*

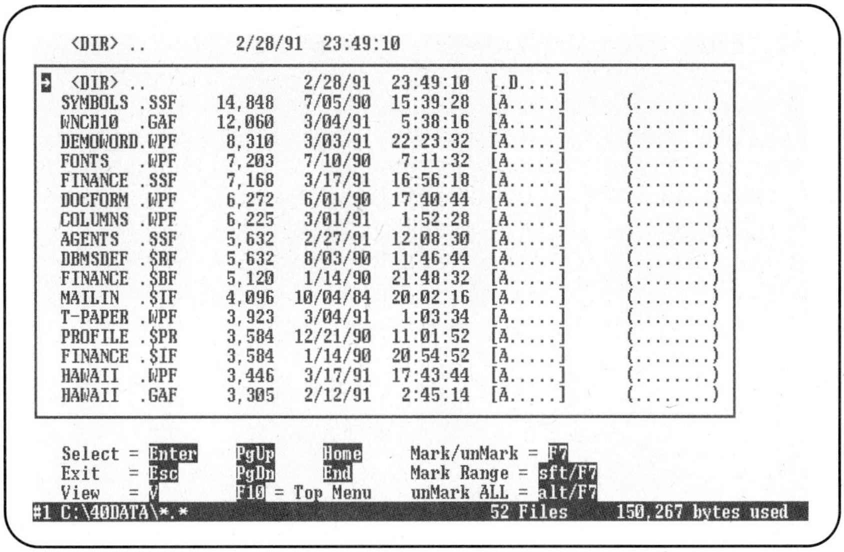

```
   <DIR> ..        2/28/91  23:49:10

   <DIR> ..                 2/28/91  23:49:10  [.D.....]
   SYMBOLS  .SSF    14,848   7/05/90  15:39:28  [A.....]    (........)
   WNCH10   .GAF    12,060   3/04/91   5:38:16  [A.....]    (........)
   DEMOWORD.WPF      8,310   3/03/91  22:23:32  [A.....]    (........)
   FONTS    .WPF     7,203   7/10/90   7:11:32  [A.....]    (........)
   FINANCE  .SSF     7,168   3/17/91  16:56:18  [A.....]    (........)
   DOCFORM  .WPF     6,272   6/01/90  17:40:44  [A.....]    (........)
   COLUMNS  .WPF     6,225   3/01/91   1:52:28  [A.....]    (........)
   AGENTS   .SSF     5,632   2/27/91  12:08:30  [A.....]    (........)
   DBMSDEF  .$RF     5,632   8/03/90  11:46:44  [A.....]    (........)
   FINANCE  .$BF     5,120   1/14/90  21:48:32  [A.....]    (........)
   MAILIN   .$IF     4,096  10/04/84  20:02:16  [A.....]    (........)
   T-PAPER  .WPF     3,923   3/04/91   1:03:34  [A.....]    (........)
   PROFILE  .$PR     3,584  12/21/90  11:01:52  [A.....]    (........)
   FINANCE  .$IF     3,584   1/14/90  20:54:52  [A.....]    (........)
   HAWAII   .WPF     3,446   3/17/91  17:43:44  [A.....]    (........)
   HAWAII   .GAF     3,305   2/12/91   2:45:14  [A.....]    (........)


   Select = Enter   PgUp     Home      Mark/unMark = F7
   Exit   = Esc     PgDn     End       Mark Range  = sft/F7
   View   = V       F10 = Top Menu     unMark ALL  = alt/F7
#1 C:\40DATA\*.*                          52 Files     150,267 bytes used
```

**Fig. 3.22.** *File names sorted by file size.*

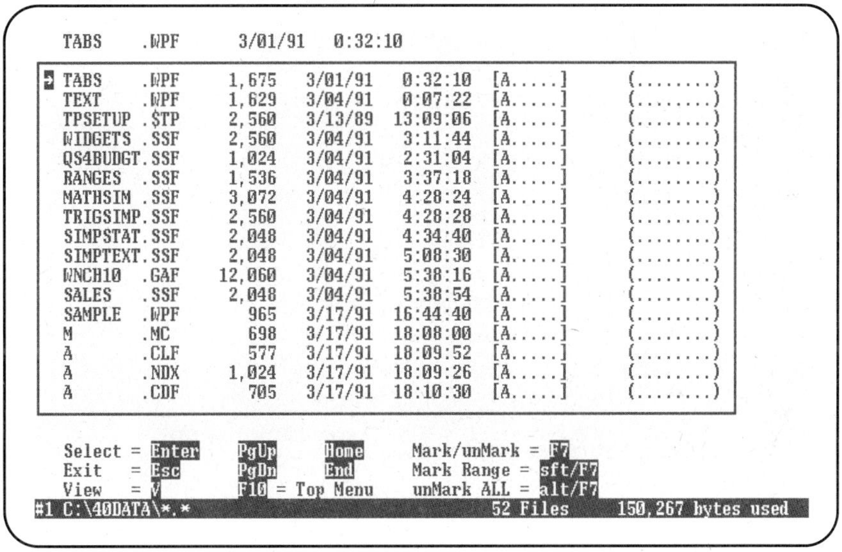

```
   TABS     .WPF    3/01/91   0:32:10

   TABS     .WPF     1,675   3/01/91   0:32:10  [A....]    (........)
   TEXT     .WPF     1,629   3/04/91   0:07:22  [A....]    (........)
   TPSETUP  .$TP     2,560   3/13/89  13:09:06  [A....]    (........)
   WIDGETS  .SSF     2,560   3/04/91   3:11:44  [A....]    (........)
   QS4BUDGT.SSF      1,024   3/04/91   2:31:04  [A....]    (........)
   RANGES   .SSF     1,536   3/04/91   3:37:18  [A....]    (........)
   MATHSIM  .SSF     3,072   3/04/91   4:28:24  [A....]    (........)
   TRIGSIMP.SSF      2,560   3/04/91   4:28:28  [A....]    (........)
   SIMPSTAT.SSF      2,048   3/04/91   4:34:40  [A....]    (........)
   SIMPTEXT.SSF      2,048   3/04/91   5:08:30  [A....]    (........)
   WNCH10   .GAF    12,060   3/04/91   5:38:16  [A....]    (........)
   SALES    .SSF     2,048   3/04/91   5:38:54  [A....]    (........)
   SAMPLE   .WPF       965   3/17/91  16:44:40  [A....]    (........)
   M        .MC        698   3/17/91  18:08:00  [A....]    (........)
   A        .CLF       577   3/17/91  18:09:52  [A....]    (........)
   A        .NDX     1,024   3/17/91  18:09:26  [A....]    (........)
   A        .CDF       705   3/17/91  18:10:30  [A....]    (........)


   Select = Enter   PgUp     Home      Mark/unMark = F7
   Exit   = Esc     PgDn     End       Mark Range  = sft/F7
   View   = V       F10 = Top Menu     unMark ALL  = alt/F7
#1 C:\40DATA\*.*                          52 Files     150,267 bytes used
```

**Fig. 3.23.** *Unsorted file names.*

# Using Advanced Options

The following sections discuss the operating system window, which you can use to leave Enable/OA and access your operating system. The MCM has several more options, including Attribute options and Oldmark options. These two options display screens from which you can manipulate certain file parameters called, respectively, *attributes* and *oldmarks*. Other options include Locate_file(s) and Visual_map_of_drive under the Disk_utilities. You can use the Locate_files option to search an entire drive for a particular file name, including one with wild cards. The Visual_map_of_drive option enables you to look at the usage of your disk space. These features can be useful to the experienced user, but detailed explanations of them are beyond the scope of this book. See your Enable/OA 4.0 documentation for these options.

## Using the Operating System Window

One command available through the Main Menu is MCM OpSys_window. This command opens a special kind of window called the *operating system window*. This command loads a second copy of the *operating system command interpreter* and displays the *operating system command line*. Many other programs have a similar feature, which sometimes is called a *system window* or *shell window*. With the operating system window, you can use your operating system without first having to save all your open files and leave Enable.

Because Enable/OA 4.0 covers most operating system operations through the commands in the File Manager screen, you may see no reason to access the operating system directly. The operating system window, however, has some special properties. For example, you can move to and from this window as easily as you can move between other Enable/OA 4.0 windows. Thus you can use Enable as a window environment for running other programs (although small ones) while you are running Enable.

## Setting Up Your Computer for the Operating System Window

To use the operating system window (or *DOS window*, if your operating system is DOS), your Enable startup command must include a memory-allocation parameter (see Appendix A, "Installing and Starting Enable").

The amount of random-access memory (RAM) you need to allocate depends on the total RAM available in your computer and what you want to do in the operating system window. The operating system window must have enough room left at least for a second copy of COMMAND.COM, the command interpreter. In DOS, this is about 40K. You do not need to do this in UNIX.

In DOS, you also need to add a DEVICE command to your system configuration file, CONFIG.SYS. This command loads a special screen driver into memory so that your computer can shrink and move the DOS window (see Appendix A). If you are using a hard disk system, add the following line:

**DEVICE=C:\EN400\ANSITSG.SYS**

Make sure that you have configured your system properly and have reserved enough memory for the DOS window. Then go to the next section for information about using the DOS window.

## Copying from the DOS Window

The following example describes the procedure for copying from the DOS window to a word processing file.

Suppose that you want to create a word processing file that contains a list of the files in your data disk or directory. First, open a word processing file, FILEDIR.WPF, to hold the list of files. Then open a DOS window by pressing

Alt-Home **MCM O**pSys_window

When Enable displays the operating system prompt, you are in the operating system window. For this example, you are in DOS.

Next, issue the DOS command to display the directory listing. You can get an alphabetically sorted list that pauses at the end of each screen of file names by typing the following commands:

**DIR ¦ SORT ¦ MORE**

For this command to work, the files SORT.EXE and MORE.COM must be on your disk where DOS can find them. Using the vertical bar is called *piping*, which causes the output of the first command to be used as input for the second command.

The list of data files appears on-screen. If the directory contains too many files to appear on-screen at once, DOS displays the message

—More—

at the bottom of the screen, as in figure 3.24.

```
      56 File(s)    5144576 bytes free
Directory of  C:\40DATA
Volume in drive C is GARF'S 386
Volume Serial Number is 293D-1AF6
${M}      SSM       512 03-03-91    9:52p
${S}      SSM       512 02-12-91    1:11a
.              <DIR>     02-28-91   11:49p
..             <DIR>     02-28-91   11:49p
1QSMEMO   WPF       890 03-17-91    6:38p
A         CDF       705 03-17-91    6:10p
A         CLF       577 03-17-91    6:09p
A         NDX      1024 03-17-91    6:09p
AGENTS    SSF      5632 02-27-91   12:08p
BOXES     WPF       752 03-17-91    6:37p
COLUMNS   WPF      6225 03-01-91    1:52a
DBMSDEF   $RF      5632 08-03-90   11:46a
DEMOWORD  WPF      8310 03-03-91   10:23p
DIR       ASC      1497 03-03-91    9:46p
DOCFORM   WPF      6272 06-01-90    5:40p
FINANCE   $BF      5120 01-14-90    9:48p
FINANCE   $IF      3584 01-14-90    8:54p
FINANCE   SSF      7168 03-17-91    4:56p
-- More --
```

**Fig. 3.24.** *A result of the DOS command, DIR | SORT | MORE.*

**TIP**

If you want to print the directory listing without creating a copy as a word processing file, issue the DOS commands

**DIR | SORT | PRN**

Before you press a key to see the next screen, press Alt-up arrow to return to the Enable word processing window. Follow the copy procedure explained in the section, "Copying Data between Windows," in Chapter 4.

Position the cursor in the upper left corner of the word processing window, where you want to copy the file list, and press Alt-F5 to display the Interwindow Copy Options screen (see fig. 3.25).

Press **2**, the number of the DOS window (operating system window); Enable displays the window. At first, the DOS window appears the same; nothing indicates that a copy is in progress. Now press the cursor-movement keys—the arrow keys, PgUp, PgDn, Home, and End—that move the cursor around the window. These cursor-movement keys have the following effect during an interwindow copy:

| *Cursor-Movement Key* | *Effect* |
| --- | --- |
| Arrow keys | Move the cursor in the direction of the arrow |
| Home | Move to the upper left corner of the DOS window |
| PgUp | Move to the upper right corner of the DOS window |
| End | Move to the lower left corner of the DOS window |
| PgDn | Move to the lower right corner of the DOS window |

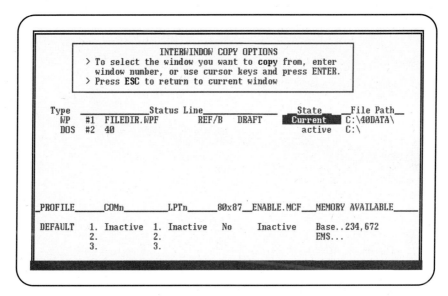

**Fig. 3.25.** *The Interwindow Copy Options screen.*

Press Home to move to the upper left corner of the screen, and use the arrow keys to position the cursor on the first character of the first file name. Press F7 to begin marking the list.

You are not concerned about the time the files were created, but you do want your file catalog to show the last revision dates. To mark a column to include the date but not the time, use the arrow keys to move the cursor to the last character in the date column, and press Shift-F7. The block of text is highlighted, or blocked, as shown in figure 3.26. (When you press F7 at the beginning and end of the block of text, you highlight the full screen width.)

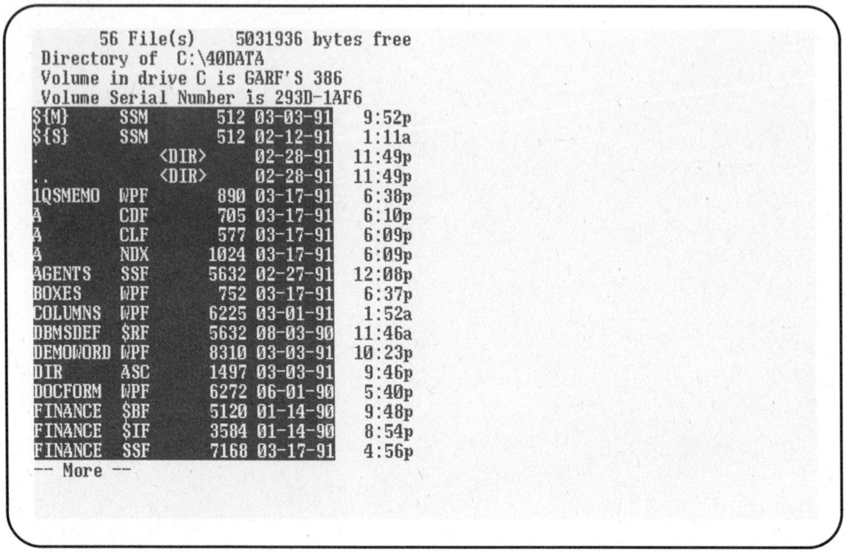

```
        56 File(s)    5031936 bytes free
   Directory of  C:\40DATA
   Volume in drive C is GARF'S 386
   Volume Serial Number is 293D-1AF6
$(M)      SSM        512 03-03-91    9:52p
$(S)      SSM        512 02-12-91    1:11a
.        <DIR>           02-28-91   11:49p
..       <DIR>           02-28-91   11:49p
1QSMEMO   WPF        890 03-17-91    6:38p
A         CDF        705 03-17-91    6:10p
A         CLF        577 03-17-91    6:09p
A         NDX       1024 03-17-91    6:09p
AGENTS    SSF       5632 02-27-91   12:08p
BOXES     WPF        752 03-17-91    6:37p
COLUMNS   WPF       6225 03-01-91    1:52a
DBMSDEF   $RF       5632 08-03-90   11:46a
DEMOWORD  WPF       8310 03-03-91   10:23p
DIR       ASC       1497 03-03-91    9:46p
DOCFORM   WPF       6272 06-01-90    5:40p
FINANCE   $BF       5120 01-14-90    9:48p
FINANCE   $IF       3584 01-14-90    8:54p
FINANCE   SSF       7168 03-17-91    4:56p
-- More --
```

*Fig. 3.26. Marked columns in the DOS window (operating system window).*

Press Alt-F5 to complete the copy process. You now have a word processing file that contains a sorted list of the files in your data directory (or at least the first full screen), including the date of the last revision of each file (see fig. 3.27). Press Alt-up arrow to return to the DOS window. If the -More- prompt is displayed, press any key to list the next group of files. Then repeat the preceding steps to copy this list to FILEDIR.WPF.

This example demonstrates copying from the DOS window to a word processing window; you can use the same basic procedure to copy from any DOS program into DBMS. You also can copy from a word processing window or a DBMS window into the DOS window. The steps for this Enable-to-DOS copying are the same as the steps for copying within word processing.

```
┌C:\40DATA\FILEDIR.WPF════════════════════════════════════════════F10=◆=▲┐
L────────T──────────T──────────T──────────T───────+T──────────────────────R
$(M)      SSM          512 03-03-91
$(S)      SSM          512 02-12-91
.                <DIR>     02-28-91
..               <DIR>     02-28-91
1QSMEMO   WPF          890 03-17-91
A         CDF          705 03-17-91
A         CLF          577 03-17-91
A         NDX         1024 03-17-91
AGENTS    SSF         5632 02-27-91
BOXES     WPF          752 03-17-91
COLUMNS   WPF         6225 03-01-91
DBMSDEF   $RF         5632 08-03-90
DEMOWORD  WPF         8310 03-03-91
DIR       ASC          880 03-17-91
DOCFORM   WPF         6272 06-01-90
FINANCE   $BF         5120 01-14-90
FINANCE   $IF         3584 01-14-90
FINANCE   SSF         7168 03-17-91
FINEMPID  NDX         1024 01-13-90
FINLAST   NDX         1024 01-13-90
FINST     NDX         1024 01-13-90
FONTS     WPF         7203 07-10-90
#1     /B                DRAFT                          L00000C001
```

*Fig. 3.27. A file catalog in FILEDIR.WPF.*

# Using Native and Nonnative Modes

In addition to working at the DOS command line, you can run most DOS programs in the DOS window if you previously reserved enough memory. Problems can arise, however, if the *native program* (DOS program other than Enable) uses any of the same key combinations as Enable's window-related commands.

To ensure that all keystrokes perform their native functions in the non-Enable program, press Alt-backspace to toggle on the *native mode*. Press Alt-backspace again to return the key combinations to their *nonnative functions* (that is, Enable functions).

While in *nonnative mode* (Enable mode), the Enable window-related commands are as follows:

- F10. This command brings up a Top Line menu consisting of two choices: Windows and Quit (see fig. 3.26). Choose **Windows** to display the menu Open, close, and switch windows. Choose **Quit** to close the window and return to Enable.

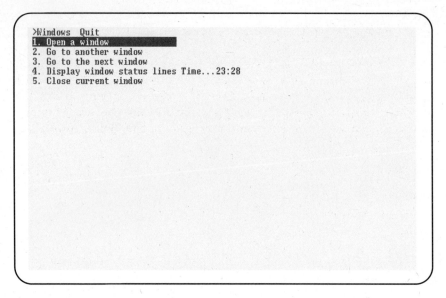

```
>Windows  Quit
1. Open a window
2. Go to another window
3. Go to the next window
4. Display window status lines Time...23:28
5. Close current window
```

**Fig. 3.28.** *The operating system window Top Line menu.*

The Quit command can play havoc if you are still in a program, rather than at the DOS command line. You always should leave programs through the normal method, and not through F10 Quit.

- Alt-Home. This command opens a new Enable window.

- Alt-End. This command closes the window and returns you to Enable. You also can type **exit** yourself at the DOS command line and press Enter. If you are not at the command line when you press Alt-End, the effect varies depending on the program you are running.

You always should return to the operating system prompt before closing the operating system window. If you don't exit programs in the normal way, you may loose your data.

- Alt-5. (*Note:* Press **5** on the numeric keypad.) This command invokes the location and sizing mode, enabling you to size and move the screen as with Enable windows. This command works only if you have loaded the ANSITSG.SYS driver.

# Summary

The functions of the Master Control Module and the commands discussed in this chapter can help you in your daily work with Enable. Make an effort to use these commands at least once before you continue to the next chapter; when you later encounter a situation where you really need a particular command, the command may come to mind more quickly.

# 4

# Using the Master Control Module's Advanced Features

This chapter introduces two features that help alleviate task repetition and keystroke drudgery: *macros* and Enable's window capabilities.

## Using Macros

In Enable, a *macro* is a stored list of keystrokes that you can retrieve to execute a series of commands by pressing a few keys. You can perform a long series of keystrokes just by issuing the macro command. You can record Enable's macros while you enter them, which is like leaving your VCR running during the Super Bowl so that you can play back the videotape later. You should record as macros any keystrokes you often repeat. The next time you need those keystrokes, the macro can do all the work.

Enable's *macros* can do more than simply repeat your keystrokes. Special macro commands, entered through a full-screen macro editor, can add such features as pauses, status-line prompts, and pop-up menus created with Enable's menu generator. Not all of these advanced features are within the scope of this book; however, the following sections describe most of the available macro commands.

# Recording a Macro

With Enable, you can record your keystrokes as you execute them and store them in a file called a *macro file*. Enable creates the file, names it, and saves it on the disk for you, when you use the following procedure:

1. To begin recording keystrokes, from the Enable screen or menu where you intend to use the macro, press

   Alt-F9 \ (the backslash key)

   Your screen does not change yet.

2. Name the macro by pressing a key. Do not use Esc, the backslash key (\), the equal sign (=), the minus sign (–), PgUp, PgDn, the arrow keys, or End; these keys are not valid macro names.

   The key you press becomes the name of the macro. The message MAC (all uppercase) appears in the status line, indicating that the macro recorder is active. This indicator is the only sign that the procedure is working. If you don't see the message MAC in the status line, repeat steps 1 and 2. *Note:* Make sure that you use the backslash key (\) and not the slash key (/).

3. Press the keys and commands you want to record the way you normally press them to perform the procedure. If keystrokes invoke a command that uses the status line, the message MAC disappears; however, the macro recorder is still working and remains activated until you turn it off.

4. To stop the macro recorder, press

   Alt-F9 End

   The message MAC no longer appears in the status line, and you may notice that your disk read/write light comes on as Enable saves the macro to disk.

# Running a Macro

Playing back the recorded keystrokes is even easier than recording them. Just press Alt-F9, and then press the key you assigned as the macro's name. To run a macro recorded under the S key, press

   Alt-F9 **S**

All keystrokes (including errors) function as if you were sitting at the keyboard pressing the keys again. To indicate that a macro is running (and that your computer doesn't have a mind of its own), the word `mac` (all lowercase) appears in the status line until the macro is finished. To stop a macro before it is finished, press Ctrl-Break.

The possible uses for macros are almost endless, as the following example demonstrates.

One common spreadsheet practice—whether you are working on a household budget, tracking monthly sales figures, or projecting production costs—is to put figures in columns labeled with the months of the year. Although you must enter the numbers yourself, entering the column headings is a good job for a macro. To create a simple macro named *M* (for *M*onths) that enters the twelve month names in adjacent cells, complete the following steps:

1. Open any spreadsheet. (For this purpose you can use a spreadsheet named BUDGET.SSF. Don't save BUDGET.SSF when you finish. See Chapter 9, "Understanding Spreadsheet Basics," for spreadsheet basics.) With the cell pointer in a blank row, press

   Alt-F9 \ (the backslash key)  **M**

   The word `MAC` appears in the status line to indicate that the macro recorder is recording, as in figure 4.1.

2. Type the names of the twelve months, pressing the right-arrow key after each label (except December). After you type **December**, press the down-arrow key once, and then the left-arrow key eleven times until the cell pointer is in cell A2 (below `January`), as in figure 4.1.

3. To turn off the recorder, press

   Alt-F9 End

4. Test the macro. Place the pointer in a blank row and press

   Alt-F9 **M**

   Enable enters the twelve month names in twelve adjacent columns, and the cell pointer returns to the cell below `January`.

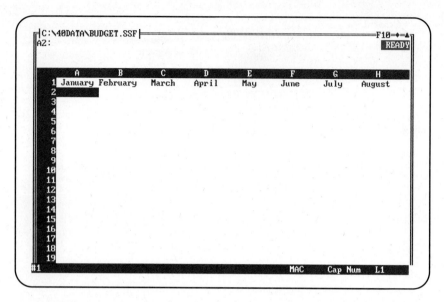

**Fig. 4.1.** *The macro-recording MAC message in a spreadsheet status line.*

After you record and test the macro, you can use it in any spreadsheet, but you must use it only from a spreadsheet. Although you can create macros in any Enable module and in nearly any screen, use them only from the module and screen in which you create them so that you are working in the same environment at the start of the macro. If you record the macro in a word processing screen, run the macro only from another word processing screen. If you record the macro at the Main Menu, run it only from the Main Menu.

When Enable saves a macro, it names the macro according to the module in which you record the macro. Table 4.1 shows the conventions Enable uses for naming macro files. The macro described in this section has the file name ${M}.SSM and works only in a spreadsheet. You can have a macro named M in each of Enable's other modules as well, because Enable gives each macro a unique file name extension on the disk.

**Table 4.1**
**System-Macro Naming Conventions**

| File Name (x is the macro name) | Created in Module |
| --- | --- |
| ${x}.WPM | Word Processing |
| ${x}.SSM | Spreadsheet |

| File Name (x is the macro name) | Created in Module |
|---|---|
| ${x}.DBM | DBMS |
| ${x}.GRM | Graphics |
| ${x}.TPM | Telecommunications |
| ${x}.MCM | Master Control Module |

TIP

To avoid trouble, use the following "unwritten rules" or guidelines to record a macro:

1. Before you start recording, check the File Manager screen to make sure that no macro is associated already with the desired keys; Enable does not warn you that you are about to replace an existing macro.

2. When you choose from a menu, always press the appropriate letter or number of each option rather than use the point method. If the menu pointer is in a different location when you play back the macro, it chooses the wrong option.

3. Whenever possible, start recording the macro without any menu selected. For example, to record a macro from the Main Menu, start at the top line. Don't choose Use_System, and then turn on the recorder. Similarly, record macros in word processing and spreadsheet windows from the working screens rather than from the Top Line menu. If you play back the macro from a different menu, the macro does not perform the intended task.

4. Type the file or field names at the appropriate prompts. Do not use the File Manager screen to choose file names or the PgDn method (in DBMS, see Chapter 13, "Understanding Database Management System Basics") to choose field names. If you add or delete files or fields after you create the macro, without the typed name, the macro may not choose the correct file or field.

   Of course, these are guidelines and all unwritten rules can be broken; however, work outside the guidelines only if you have a good reason, and be sure to remember the potential hazards.

# Editing a Macro

Enable provides a full-screen macro editor that looks and acts like Enable's word processing module, except that the macro editor saves files in a special macro format rather than a word processing format.

To edit a macro file, you need to understand the codes that Enable uses in macros. Character keys are obvious. A character that can be displayed on-screen by pressing a key (such as letters and numbers) can be used in a macro to represent itself. The letter *a* in a macro enters an *a* when the macro executes.

Some keys, such as function keys, do not normally display a character on-screen; some Enable commands require that you press two keys at once. Enable uses special codes in macros to mean "Press the F1 key," or "Hold Alt and press the F2 key," and so on. Table 4.2 lists the codes for these keys and for combination keystrokes. You can use the macro editor to add any of these keystrokes to a macro. For example, to instruct a macro to press the F1 key, type the macro code **{F1}**, typing all four characters in sequence.

**Table 4.2**
**Macro-Command Equivalents of Keyboard Commands**

| Keyboard Command | Macro Equivalent |
|---|---|
| F1 | {F1} |
| F2 | {F2} |
| F3 | {F3} |
| F4 | {F4} |
| F5 | {F5} |
| F6 | {F6} |
| F7 | {F7} |
| F8 | {F8} |
| F9 | {F9} |
| F10 | {F10} |
| Esc | {Esc} |
| Tab | {Tab} |
| Home | {Home} |
| Up arrow | {Up} |
| Left arrow | {Left} |
| Right arrow | {Right} |
| Down arrow | {Down} |

| Keyboard Command | Macro Equivalent |
|---|---|
| PgUp | {PgUp} |
| PgDn | {PgDn} |
| End | {End} |
| Ins | {Ins} |
| Del | {Del} |
| Backspace | {Bs} |
| Enter | ~ |
| Ctrl-Enter | {LF} |
| { | {{} |
| } | {}} |
| ~ | {~} |
| Alt-X | {&X} |
| Ctrl-X | {^X} |
| Shift-X | {!X} |
| Alt-up arrow | {NextW} or {&Up} |
| Alt-down arrow | {PrevW} or {&Down} |
| Alt-End | {CloseW} or {&End} |
| Alt-Home | {OpenW} or {&Home} |

You also can use the macro editor to enter the special macro commands, which cannot be recorded. These commands are listed in table 4.3. The "Using Macro Programming Commands" section in this chapter describes the most common of these commands. You can enter these commands in upper- or lowercase.

**Table 4.3**
**Macro Programming Commands**

| Command | While Recording | Function |
|---|---|---|
| *Error condition functions* | | |
| {If Error}*commands* | | If error, perform commands |
| {Else}*more commands* | | Else, perform more commands |

*continued*

**Table 4.3** (*continued*)

| Command | While Recording | Function |
|---|---|---|
| {Endif} | End of If/ | Else commands |
| *Menu functions* | | |
| {DoMenu}*name~* | | Display the named menu |
| {Menu}*name~* | | Make the named menu the default menu |
| {Do Macro}*name~* | | Run the named macro |
| {*n*X}*k* | | Repeat keystroke *k n* times, where *k* is any valid keystroke and *n* is a whole number |
| {Beep} | | Sound tone |
| *Status line functions* | | |
| {Send}(S)*message~* | | Send the message to the status line |
| {Send}(R) | | Restore the status line |
| {Voff} | | Freeze the screen display |
| {Von} | | Restore the screen display |
| {?} | Ctrl-I Enter | Wait to accept input until Enter is pressed |
| {^F9}*k* | Ctrl-F9 *k* | Wait to accept input until *k* is pressed, where *k* is any valid keystroke |
| {Wait} | Ctrl-[hyphen] | Wait for any key, and send "Press any key" to status line |
| {Pause} | | Timed pause (one second) |
| *Window functions* | | |
| {Wname}*name~* | | Name current window |
| {GotoW}*name~* | | Go to named window |
| *Operating System Function* | | |
| {OS}*program* | | Perform a named program |

> You can use the macro editor to create a macro from scratch, but this method involves a great deal of work and easily can create mistakes. A more reasonable approach is to record as much of the macro as possible, and then use the editor to add special commands.

**TIP**

To edit a macro to correct mistakes or enter special macro commands, first press Alt-Home to open a new window. Then press

      **Tools Macro Edit**

Using the naming conventions in table 4.1, select the appropriate macro. The M macro recorded example in this chapter is shown in figure 4.2.

```
┤C:\40DATA\$(M).SSM├──────────────────────────F10=◆=▲┐
January{Right}
February{Right}
March{Right}
Ar{Bs}
pril{Right}
May{Right}
June{Right}
July{Right}
August{Right}
September{Right}
October{Right}
November{Right}              ▮
December{Right}
{Down}
{11x}{Left}




#2                    DRAFT              Cap Num L00001C001
```

***Fig. 4.2.** The macro $\{M\}.SSM.*

You can edit a displayed macro the same way you edit a word processing file. To make changes, use normal word processing commands (however, you do not have a ruler line). Ignore the paragraph symbols that may appear at the right side of the screen. Although this symbol represents a hard carriage return in word processing, it does not affect the macro's execution.

The macro in figure 4.2 contains a typing error corrected during recording (refer to the fourth line of fig. 4.2). When the macro runs, it corrects the typing error, but this correction creates unneeded keystrokes. You can correct the original error in the macro editor, thus cleaning up the macro. You also can add internal comments or documentation to remind you of the macro's purpose. Begin the line of documentation with two semicolons (;;)—the comment does not affect the macro's operation. When you use special macro programming commands, internal documentation of the macro is even more important. A corrected macro ${M}.SSM, enhanced with special commands and internal documentation, is shown in figure 4.3. The special macro commands are discussed in the following sections.

```
C:\40DATA\${M}.SSM                                           F10=✦=▲
;;
;;----------------------------------------------------------------
;; Ask the user to position the pointer and press Enter.
{Send}(S) Position the pointer and press Enter~
{?}
;;----------------------------------------------------------------
;; Freeze the video.
{Voff}
;;----------------------------------------------------------------
;; Enter the month headings and return the pointer one cell below January.
JANUARY{Right}
FEBRUARY{Right}
MARCH{Right}
APRIL{Right}
MAY{Right}
JUNE{Right}
JULY{Right}
AUGUST{Right}
SEPTEMBER{Right}
OCTOBER{Right}
NOVEMBER{Right}
DECEMBER{Down}
{11X}{Left}
#1                          DRAFT                 Num L00002C001
```

*Fig. 4.3. The macro ${M}.SSM with added comments and special commands.*

**TIP**

To view a description of the macro from the File Manager screen, include the description as a one-line comment (preceded by two semicolons) in the first line of the macro. Then you can use the View command to preview the contents of a macro without opening a macro editing window. Refer to Chapter 3, "Understanding the Master Control Module," for a discussion of this screen and command. Otherwise, you usually should leave the first line of the macro screen blank. These practices don't affect the macro's operation, but they make inserting lines at the top of the file easier.

# Using Macro Programming Commands

When you get used to recording keystrokes in macros for later use, you begin to recognize the possibilities that macros offer. You may discover that you don't want a macro to operate the same way every time. Enable has several macro commands you can use to control a macro's operation. The Enable/OA documentation calls these commands *macro programming commands* or *special macro commands*. These commands, listed in table 4.3, are used most often in Enable's macros, but you can use them also in the special spreadsheet macros discussed in Chapter 11, "Using Spreadsheet Advanced Features."

Enable provides several ways to make a macro pause so that you can enter information, move the cursor, or read a message before going on. In addition to the pause commands, other commonly used macro programming commands include {Beep}, {Voff}, {Von}, {Wname}, {GotoW}, {Send}(S) and {Send}(R). The following sections explain the uses of these commands.

## Using the Pause Commands

You can use four kinds of pause commands in Enable macros, depending on the length of the pause.

| Command | Length of Pause |
| --- | --- |
| {?} | Until you press Enter |
| {Wait} | Until you press any key |
| {^F9} | Until you press a specific key |
| {2X}{Pause} | For a predetermined time |

To cause a macro to pause until you press Enter—usually so that you can enter data—type the following command in the macro with the macro editor:

    {?}

To make Enable insert this pause command while you record the macro, press Ctrl-I; then press Enter. This pause command appears on the fourth line in figure 4.3.

When you use the macro ${M}.SSM, you can move the cell pointer to the cell in which you want *January* to appear, and then press Enter. The macro begins to type the column headings in that spot.

To insert a pause that lasts until you press any key, enter the {**Wait**} command in the macro, or press Ctrl-- (Ctrl-hyphen) during recording. (Use the white minus key; the gray minus key does not perform this function.) You can use this kind of pause to give the user time to read an on-screen message and press a key to continue the macro.

Because the Enter key often has an effect of its own in an Enable module, you may want to use some other key as the "trigger" that causes the macro to continue after a pause. Insert {^F9} and a character key to stop the macro until you press the character key. You can record this code, as shown in table 4.3, but doing so is sometimes difficult. The better practice is to use the macro editor to type the code.

**TIP**

When you use the {^F9} command, the key that makes the macro continue actually executes. To avoid this potential problem, you may want to specify a key such as {!F8} (Shift-F8) as the key the macro waits for, because this function key command has no effect in most of Enable's modules. Be sure that you know what the key you are waiting for does, and make sure that, if necessary, you "undo" that action.

In the macro file, you can enter the following command:

   {^F9}{!F8}

When the macro pauses, press Shift-F8 to continue.

Sometimes you need the macro to pause only a few seconds, so that you can read some part of the screen or decide whether you should stop the macro with Ctrl-Break. Insert timed pauses into your macro with the {Pause} command. You can enter this command only through the macro editor, not during recording. Whenever the macro reaches a {Pause} command in the sequence of keystrokes, the macro waits one second, and then continues. To create a longer pause, precede {Pause} with a number and an X within braces. For example, type {**5X**}{**Pause**} for a five-second pause, or {**10X**}{**Pause**} for a ten-second pause.

# Using the {Beep} Command

A {Beep} command in a macro sounds a tone through the computer's speaker. You can use this tone to alert the user to specific parts of the macro.

> To sound two beeps, type **{BEEP}{PAUSE}{BEEP}**. If you type **{2X}{BEEP}**, the resulting beeps sound like one beep.

TIP

# Using the {Voff} and {Von} Commands

The {Voff} command prevents Enable from continually updating the display as it executes the macro's keystrokes. Without the {Voff} command, when Enable runs a complex macro, it revises the screen rapidly over and over. This distraction can be annoying. Use the {Voff} command within a macro to freeze the screen. The keystrokes and commands in the macro sequence continue to execute, but the changes do not appear on-screen. Another advantage of using the {Voff} command is that macros run faster when the computer doesn't have to display the results of each command.

You can use the {Von} command to resume normal screen display at the end of a section of the macro that involves repeated screen changes or when the macro requires user input. You do not need a {Von} command for every {Voff} command. Normal screen display automatically resumes if the macro terminates for any reason between a {Voff} and {Von} command. A command that requires user interaction, such as {?}, also forces the screen on. For these and other more technical reasons, the better practice is to use {Von} only if the screen fails to display on its own at the appropriate places.

> You do not need a {Von} command for every {Voff} command. Use {Von} only if the screen fails to display on its own. Adding too many {Von} commands to a macro can cause problems, such as disrupting the next {Voff} command.

CAUTION

The ${M}.SSM macro, shown in figure 4.3, uses the {Voff} command to freeze the video while the macro enters the month names. This freezing also speeds the macro's execution. If you have an AT or compatible system, the difference probably isn't noticeable because these systems execute the macro so quickly anyway.

## Using the {Wname}*name~* and {GotoW}*name~* Commands

When Enable encounters the {Wname}name~ command in a macro, it gives the current window the name you typed before the tilde (~). The window keeps the assigned name until you close or rename it (with another {Wname} command). This capability is useful because window numbers may vary each time you execute the macro. A macro that always goes to a particular window number would therefore not always work.

You can use up to 14 characters in the window name. This command is case-sensitive; the window's name must be entered exactly the same way wherever it appears in the macro. After you use a particular name, you must clear the name before you can use it again. Clear any name assigned to the current window by typing

    **{Wname}~**

You can make a macro move to a particular named window by using the {GotoW}name~ command. This command displays the named window (named by a {Wname} command) without forcing you to specify the window number. Then the macro can continue to execute its commands.

> If the window you name in the {GotoW}name~ command doesn't exist, Enable does not display an error message; Enable continues to execute the remaining macro commands in the current window.

## Using the {Send}(S) and {Send}(R) Commands

Virtually all PC programs at some time use an attention-getting tone or beep to alert you to a mistake or warn that you need to take some significant action. Enable uses these tones often, usually to notify you that a message is in the status line. You can use the {Beep} command, discussed in the section "Using the {Beep} Command" in this chapter, in the same way if you place it before a {Send}(S) command.

Use the {Send}(S) command to place a text message in the current window's status line. The syntax is

> **{Send}(S)***message~*

where *message* is a text string less than 70 characters long. This command displays the specified message in the status line until some other message replaces it, until Enable encounters a {Send}(R) command, or until Enable updates the status line on its own. The {Send}(R) command restores the status line to normal; the command normally is not necessary.

---

The {Send}(S) macro command is a convenient way to prompt the user to act, for example, to enter data or press a certain key, especially when the command is used with {Beep}. The {Beep} and {Send}(S) commands almost always should precede any pause command that requires some action by the user.

**TIP**

---

# Using Advanced Window Features

In Chapter 2, "Understanding the Keyboard and Enable's Screens, Menus and Keyboard Commands," you learn to open, close, and switch windows. In addition to these options, you can size and move windows and have multiple windows open at once. The following two sections discuss these options.

## Opening Multiple Windows

As with paper files, you normally work on one computer file at a time, even though you may have several open. Looking at more than one spreadsheet or contract side-by-side is sometimes helpful. With Enable's windowing capabilities, you can have several files open on the screen at the same time. You can arrange windows so that eight can appear on-screen at once. The following example shows how to display multiple windows at the same time.

Suppose that you are preparing a memo to accompany this quarter's sales forecast for the Hyperion Widget Corporation (HWC). You want to see the forecast and the memo at the same time on the screen, because you don't have a printout of either document, and you may make some changes to the files.

First, open window #1, the memo file (see fig. 4.4), then open window #2, the spreadsheet file (see fig. 4.5). At this point, both windows are open and available; however, you want to see both windows on-screen together.

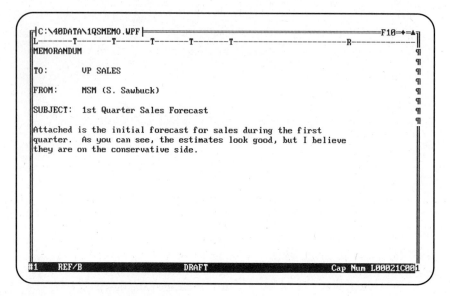

*Fig. 4.4. A memo in window #1.*

# Shrinking and Moving Windows

To see both windows at the same time, you need to shrink and move the two open windows. To display the forecast in the top half of the screen and the memo in the bottom half, do the following:

1. Press Alt-up arrow to move back to window #1, the memo file (refer to fig. 4.4). To shrink this window to the bottom half of the screen, press

   F9 Window Location_and_Size Shrink

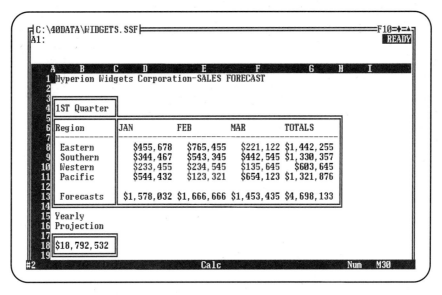

*Fig. 4.5. A spreadsheet in window #2.*

2. Press the down arrow key 12 times to move the top edge of the window about halfway down the screen.

3. Press Esc to accept the new screen size. You now can see the memo in the bottom half of the screen and part of the spreadsheet window in the background (see fig. 4.6), but if you switch to window #2, the memo disappears. You want both windows to stay on-screen.

4. To adjust the spreadsheet window, switch to window #2 by pressing Alt-up arrow, and shrink the window to the top half of the screen by pressing the following command:

   F9 **Window Location_and_Size Shrink**

5. Press the up-arrow key 12 times to move the bottom edge of the window about halfway up the screen.

6. Press Esc to accept the new screen size.

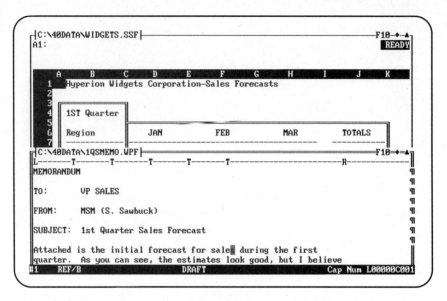

*Fig. 4.6. Window #1 in the bottom half of the screen, with window #2 in the background.*

The spreadsheet is now in the top half of the screen, and the memo is visible again in the bottom half. Switching windows now moves the cursor from one half of the screen to the other. Each half of the screen is independent of the other half. You can scroll, make changes, and print in either window as if that window filled the whole screen. You can switch between windows with Alt-up arrow and Alt-down arrow. If you lose track of the window you are in, find the cursor or simply look at the status line that always displays the window number. A double line surrounds the current window (see fig. 4.7).

Several commands, including Shrink, are available from the Locate and Size menu (see fig. 4.8). To display the options, press

F9 **W**indow **L**ocation_and_Size

Then press Esc after you perform any of the following tasks:

- *Shrink*. In shrink mode, the arrow keys shrink the window borders until you press another command key. The up arrow moves the bottom edge of the window up; the down arrow moves the top edge down; the right arrow moves the left edge to the right; the left arrow moves the right edge to the left. Pressing **R**apid causes the window to shrink proportionally on all sides.

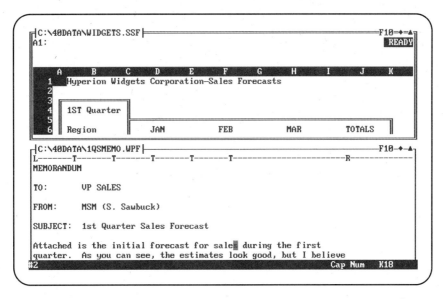

*Fig. 4.7. Window #1 in the bottom half of the screen and active window #2 in the top half.*

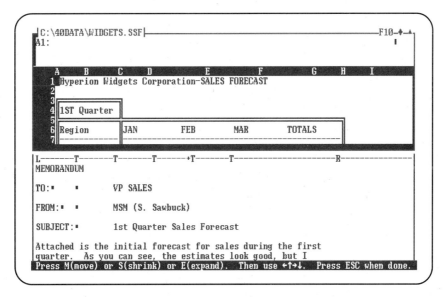

*Fig. 4.8. Commands available from the Locate and Size menu in the status line.*

- *Expand*. In expand mode, the arrow keys expand the window borders until you press another command key. The up arrow moves the top edge of the window up; the down arrow moves the bottom edge down; the right arrow moves the right edge to the right; the left arrow moves the left edge to the left. Pressing **R**apid causes the window to expand proportionally on all sides. Expand is the opposite of Shrink.

- *Move*. Move mode operates only if the window is less than full size. Until you press one of the other command keys, the arrow keys move the entire window in the direction of the arrow.

After you size the window, you can toggle between this size and full size. To return to full size, press

F9 Window **Z**oom

To shrink the window again, simply press

F9 Window **P**revious_Size

## Copying Data between Windows

The term *integration* has come to have many meanings. One definition is the capability to share data among different applications. For example, you may want to include spreadsheet information in a monthly memo. You can copy the data between the files to avoid the tedious and difficult task of re-creating the spreadsheet data in the memo.

With Enable, you don't have to re-create numbers, data, and graphs to use them in another file. You easily can copy data between disk files—from window to window, from disk file to window, or from disk file to disk file. You determine the method by the module in which you created the file and the module to which you want to copy the data. You can copy data easily in the following directions:

- *Spreadsheet to spreadsheet*—copy from window to window or from disk file to window

- *Spreadsheet to word processing*—copy from window to window

- *Spreadsheet to DBMS*—copy from window to window or from disk file to window

- *DBMS to DBMS*—copy from disk file to disk file

- *DBMS to word processing*—copy from window to window

- *DBMS to spreadsheet*—copy from window to window

- *Graphics to word processing*—copy from window to window

- *Word processing to word processing*—copy from window to window or from disk file to window

- *Word processing to spreadsheet*—copy from window to window

- *Word processing to DBMS*—copy from window to window or from disk file to window

- *Word processing to telecommunications*—copy from window to window

- *Word processing (telecommunications captured data) to word processing*—copy from window to window or from disk file to window

Most of these options involve copying data from one window to another. To do a window-to-window copy in Enable, complete the following basic steps:

1. Display the original data in one window and the destination file in another window.

2. Position your cursor (or cell pointer in a spreadsheet) at the location you want the copied data to begin (the destination).

3. Start the copy procedure by pressing the function key command Alt-F5. The Interwindow Copy Options screen appears, listing the open windows and their file information (see fig. 4.9).

4. At the Interwindow Copy Options screen, press the number of the window to copy from (the source window).

5. Mark the text, spreadsheet range, or data you want to copy.

6. Complete the copy procedure by pressing Alt-F5.

The specific procedures vary somewhat from these general steps, depending on the modules. Enable provides many on-screen prompts that tell you what to do at each step.

A new feature in Enable/OA 4.0 is the capability to use data from different modules within other modules, automatically. For example, if you don't have enough memory to load both your word processing file and spreadsheet to perform a copy, you simply can ask for the spreadsheet at the word processing prompt, transfer the data, and continue to work on your word processing document. In addition, you can type a database name at the spreadsheet prompt. *Note:* When you ask for a file from a different module, be sure to include the file extension (SSF, DBF, and so on).

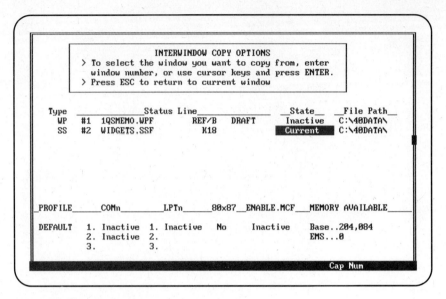

**Fig. 4.9.** *The Interwindow Copy Options screen.*

# Summary

In this chapter, you learn several advanced master control module features, like macros, viewing multiple windows, and copying data between windows. Although these features at first may seem complicated for you to use, take the time to understand them; the more you know about the MCM, the more efficiently you can work with Enable.

# Part III

# The Word Processing Module

## Includes

**Quick Start III: Creating a Word Processing File**

**Understanding Word Processing Basics**

**Using Word Processing Advanced Features**

**Using Formatting Features**

**Using Word Processing Power Features**

# Quick Start III

# Creating a Word Processing File

As with the previous quick-start lessons, this lesson quickly introduces you to the topics that this part of the book explains. Without having to do much reading, you receive a better idea of what to expect in Part III, "The Word Processing Module." In this lesson, you open a word processing file, type a simple letter, and print the letter. You also learn how to save the file to disk storage and remove the file from the screen. Keep in mind that the purpose of this lesson is only to get you started. The following four chapters explain Enable's extensive word processing functions in much more detail.

The assumption in this lesson is that you properly have installed and started Enable so that your screen displays the Main Menu. If not, refer to Appendix A and Quick Start I for information on how to get started.

## Typing a Letter

You are going to type a letter in a word processing file you name QS3LTR.WPF. The root file name stands for Quick Start III Letter. The part of the file name that follows the dot (.) is the *file name extension*. Enable automatically assigns the extension WPF, which stands for Word Processing File. You can find a discussion of file names and file name extensions in Chapter 3, "Understanding the Master Control Module."

To create and name a word processing file, and then set the margins and tabs, follow these steps:

1. From the Main Menu, choose

   Use_System **Word**_Processing

   Then type **QS3LTR** as the file name and press Enter.

   Enable displays the word processing screen and prompts you either to set the margins and tabs or to press Enter to accept the margins and tabs the way they are (see fig. QSIII.1). Enable displays these settings on the *ruler line*, the top line of the word processing screen. You are going to set the ruler line with margins at columns 11 and 75 and tabs at columns 16, 21, 26, and 51.

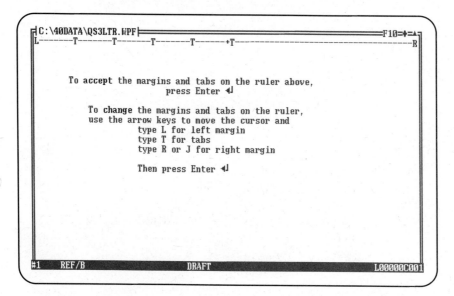

```
C:\40DATA\QS3LTR.WPF                                          F10=↕=▲
L-------T-------T-------T-------T-----+T--------------------------R




          To accept the margins and tabs on the ruler above,
                           press Enter ↵

              To change the margins and tabs on the ruler,
              use the arrow keys to move the cursor and
                      type L for left margin
                      type T for tabs
                      type R or J for right margin

                      Then press Enter ↵






#1    REF/B                     DRAFT                     L00000C001
```

*Fig. QSIII.1. On-screen prompts to set the ruler line in a word processing file.*

2. Use the space bar to move the *cursor* (the blinking underscore character at the top of the screen) to column 11. You can tell which column (and line) your cursor is in by looking at the *line/column counter* in the bottom right corner of the screen. Initially, you see the number L00000C001, which means the cursor is at line 0 and column 1. As you use the space bar to move the cursor, the counter changes.

3. After you move the cursor to column 11, press **L** (for left margin). Enable displays L on the ruler line and establishes the left margin at column 11. Do not press Enter yet.

4. Move the cursor to column 16 and press **T** (for tab). Enable displays T on the ruler line and establishes a tab setting at column 16. In the same way, set tabs at columns 21, 26, and 51.

5. Move the cursor to column 75, and press **R** to set the right margin. Enable displays R on the ruler line at column 75. Press Enter. Enable displays the completed ruler line with your new settings (see fig. QSIII.2).

```
C:\40DATA\QS3LTR.WPF                                              F10=↕=↔=↕
        L----T----T----T------------------+-------T-----------------------R---
        L----T----T----T------------------+-------T-----------------------R---








#1    REF/B                          DRAFT                          L00000C011
```

*Fig. QSIII.2. A completed ruler line in a word processing line.*

Depending on your profile settings (see Appendix B), Enable may place your cursor between two double lines, called the *title area*. To establish a title page, Enable prints and vertically centers on the first page of your document anything you type in the title area. If Enable displays the title area, use the arrow keys to move the cursor below the bottom double line, leaving the title area blank, because you do not need a title page for this quick-start lesson.

To begin typing your letter, you first type the return address as follows:

6. Press Tab four times to move the cursor to the tab setting at column 51.

7. Type the following return address, pressing Enter at the end of every line, and pressing Tab four times at the beginning of the second line:

   **7306 Westridge Drive**
   **Springfield, VA 22150**

8. Leave a blank line after the return address by pressing Enter a second time, and then type the code **%DATE** directly below the return address. This special *automatic date* code inserts the current system date in the letter. Your screen should resemble the screen shown in figure QSIII.3. At the end of the %DATE code, press Enter twice to create two blank lines.

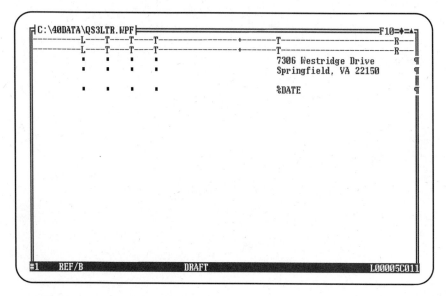

*Fig. QSIII.3. The automatic date feature.*

Now you are ready to type the body of the letter. If you make mistakes, you can use the Backspace key to move the cursor to the left, erasing characters as you go, or you can use the left-arrow key to move the cursor backward without erasing text and press Del to erase the character at the cursor's location. Typing a character on top of another character simply overwrites the existing character. You can, however, turn on *insert mode* by pressing the Ins key once. In insert mode, the cursor becomes a blinking block instead of a blinking underscore. While Enable is in insert mode, typing on top of another character pushes the existing character—and everything else in the paragraph—to the right. To turn off insert mode, press Ins again.

As you type the following letter, press Enter only where indicated by <Enter> and press Tab where indicated by <Tab>. Note that your margins are set somewhat differently than the margins shown in the following letter; therefore, each line of text in your letter may be different than the following lines:

**Springfield Gazette**<Enter>
**P.O. Box 21987**<Enter>
**Springfield, VA 22150**<Enter>
<Enter>
**Dear Aunt Bessie,**<Enter>
<Enter>
**I read your advice to "Mr. Lonely," published in last Friday's paper. He was having a terrible time communicating with the opposite sex, and so do I. He said he is devilishly handsome, a "rad" dresser, and drives a red BMW, but just can't muster the courage to tell the woman he loves how he feels. Well, we sound like twins, except I drive a black BMX.**<Enter>
<Enter>
**You advised Mr. L to let his actions speak louder than words, especially since, like me, his words just couldn't seem to make it past his lips. You suggested that perhaps a dozen roses and a bottle of Chanel No. 5 would say more than clever banter ever could.**<Enter>
<Enter>
**Well, I followed your advice today. But when my French teacher, the most beautiful woman I have ever seen, opened the flowers and perfume, she just laughed and said, "How sweet," and then she gave me a C on my homework.**<Enter>
<Enter>
**You owe me $50.89!**<Enter>
<Enter>
<Tab><Tab><Tab><Tab>**Sincerely,**<Enter>
<Enter>
<Enter>
<Enter>
<Tab><Tab><Tab><Tab>**Busted & Brokenhearted**<Enter>

When you finish, your letter should look similar to the one in figure QSIII.4.

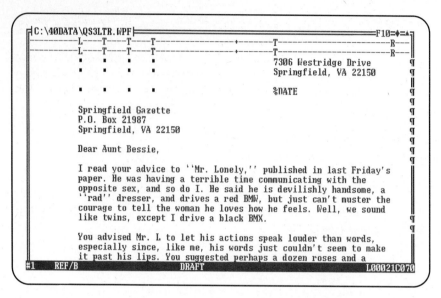

**Fig. QSIII.4.** *The first part of a finished word processing document on-screen.*

# Printing the Letter

Now that you have completed your letter, you can print it. First you must specify the printer you use, which you should have done when you installed Enable. (See the section, "Choosing a Printer," in Chapter 5 for a discussion of how to specify your printer.) The following steps explain how to print a word processing file:

1. Make sure you turn on your printer and load your printer with paper.

2. With the letter displayed on-screen, press Alt-F2.

   Alt-F2 commands Enable to print the file. Notice that Enable prints the current date where you typed %DATE.

# Saving the Letter and Quitting

Enable has placed everything you have typed in temporary memory (*random-access memory*, or RAM). If you think you may want to change or refer to your letter later, you should save the file to more permanent storage.

To save the letter to your current data directory, press

> F10 **File S**ave

or

> Alt-F10

Enable saves the letter to your data directory as a word processing file with the file name QS3LTR.WPF.

Because you are finished with this letter and have saved it for future use, you can remove the letter from the screen. To quit from the file and exit word processing, press

> F10 **File E**xit

or

> Alt-End

Enable returns you to the Main Menu.

# 5

# Understanding Word Processing Basics

Just 15 years ago, word processing systems of any kind were a rarity. The speed with which personal computers have taken over the majority of word processing tasks in the office is amazing. The popularity of the personal computer for producing letters and documents is so great that many word processing programs are available. So many programs are available that magazine editors and others to whom the public often turns for advice are forced to sort the programs into neat, digestible groups: professional, corporate, personal, scientific, and so on.

Where does Enable fit into this scheme? Enable's word processing module compares to popular word processing programs in any category. Early integrated programs typically require users to sacrifice advanced features for versatility and, in some cases, provide minimal word processing capability. From Enable's initial release, however, the power of its word processing module always has set Enable apart from other integrated packages.

Enable's word processing module has become better and more powerful with each revision. Enable/OA 4.0 has so many impressive features that you will have trouble thinking of one that Enable lacks. Although its word processing module does not yet qualify as a desktop publishing program, Enable comes close to that description with its enhanced support for laser printer fonts and capability to import custom graphics.

This chapter introduces the fundamentals of word processing with Enable. If you already are experienced with Enable, you can skip this chapter and go on to Chapter 6, "Using Word Processing Advanced Features." If you are a seasoned word processing operator but are new to Enable, you may want first to skim this chapter quickly before going on to the next chapter to learn about Enable's more powerful word processing features. On the other hand, if you are new to both Enable and word processing, begin with this chapter.

The first section of this chapter explains how to open, save, quit, and retrieve Enable word processing files. The remainder of the chapter explains the fundamentals of editing and printing a document.

# Creating, Saving, and Retrieving a Word Processing File

Whenever you work on a computer and want to manipulate, store, and retrieve data, you must work with the electronic version of paper files. These electronic blocks of information are called *files*. Generally, then, when you speak of a document that you create with Enable's word processing module, you call it a *word processing file*. If electronic files are to give you the same flexibility as paper files, you should be able to create, modify, and destroy the files as the need arises. The first portion of this chapter focuses on these subjects.

## Creating a Word Processing File

After you install and configure Enable, and then sign on, you probably are eager to create your first document. Before you can begin typing, though, you must open a file in which to put your document.

When you create a document on paper, you pull out a piece of blank paper, lay it on your desk, and begin to write on it. You may or may not have a file folder that eventually will be the destination of this document. You even may decide to toss the document into the trash can without ever using it for anything. Creating a document with Enable is similar to creating one on paper. Your PC's memory, or RAM (random-access memory), is much like the blank paper. When you begin, RAM is completely empty. The difference is that Enable requires you to specify a "file folder" (a *file*) for your new document before you can start typing, even though you can discard the document without ever placing it in this file.

Because each document has its own file, you consider the document and its file to be one and the same item. Enable also opens a separate window for each document/file you open. In Enable word processing, then, the terms *file*, *document*, and *window* are nearly synonymous.

To open a blank screen for typing and, at the same time, designate a file name that you intend to use when you store the document on the data disk, choose from the Main Menu

Use_System **W**ord_Processing

Enable displays the Open File dialog box, which prompts you to give your new file a name (see fig. 5.1). Type a file name, using no more than eight characters. The file name actually can have as many as 11 characters: a maximum of eight to the left of a dot (.) and three to the right. The portion of the file name to the right of the dot is the file name *extension*. If you do not add an extension, Enable automatically assigns the extension WPF to all word processing files. (Table 3.1 in Chapter 3, "Understanding the Master Control Module," lists other automatically assigned file name extensions.) Unless you have a good reason to assign an extension to the file name, let Enable assign it for you. After you type the file name, press Enter.

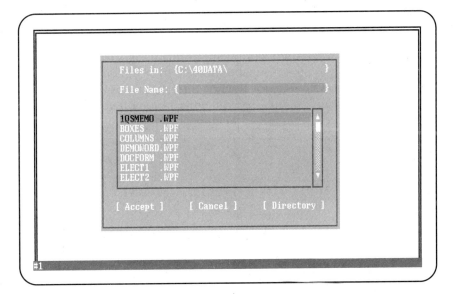

**Fig. 5.1.** *The Open File dialog box.*

Next, you must specify ruler settings for your new document. The following section discusses changing the ruler settings.

# Changing Settings on the Word Processing Ruler

After you give your new file a name, Enable displays a new word processing screen. At the top of this screen is a *ruler*. When you open a word processing document for the first time, Enable gives you an opportunity to change the margins and tab settings on this ruler (see fig. 5.2). If you don't make any changes, Enable uses the settings established in the *profile* (see Appendix B for a discussion of profiles).

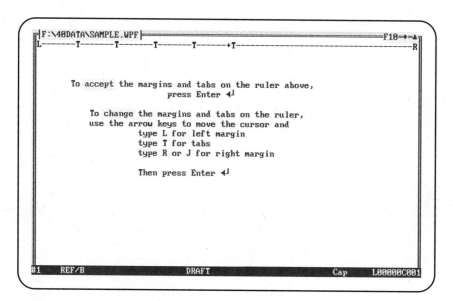

**Fig. 5.2.** *The initial ruler prompt.*

After you make any desired changes or decide not to make changes, press Enter. Enable displays the new ruler at the top of the document (see fig. 5.3). Depending on your profile settings for displaying rulers, Enable displays two, one, or no rulers at the top of your screen. If you choose to display the current ruler at the top of your screen, Enable displays only one ruler. If you choose also to display the ruler within the text, Enable displays a second ruler directly below the first ruler. You can insert additional ruler lines while you work in the document; this initial ruler line establishes the margin and tab settings from the top of the document to the next ruler line you insert.

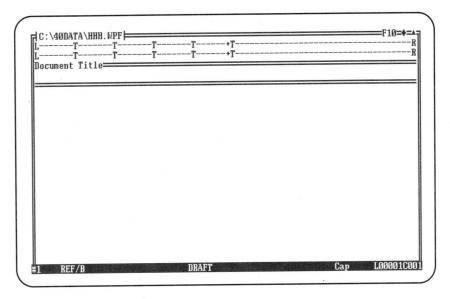

*Fig. 5.3. A new word processing document.*

To set the margins at the initial ruler prompt, press the appropriate code: **L** for left margin, **R** for right margin, and **J** for justified right margin. When you press L, R, or J, Enable displays the corresponding letter on the ruler. Only one L, R, or J can appear on the ruler at one time. If you type L, for example, on the ruler, Enable erases the L from its previous position and places it in its new position.

Press **T** to set a tab. Enable's tab stops work the same way as tab stops work on a typewriter. Pressing the Tab key enables you quickly to move the cursor a fixed number of blank characters in your document. You can erase a default tab setting by moving your cursor to a T on the ruler and either pressing the space bar or typing a hyphen (-). Enable also has several special tab codes that are discussed in the following chapter, "Using Word Processing Advanced Features."

Enable indicates the center point between the left and right margins with a plus sign on the ruler. To set this point to the right or left of its current position, move the cursor to the desired center position, and press the plus (**+**) key.

# Using or Disabling the Document Title Feature

After you accept the ruler settings, Enable places your cursor below two double lines, called the *document title area*. Enable displays the document title area at the top of your screen, below the ruler, unless you previously turned off the document title feature in your Enable profile settings (see Appendix B). Any text that you type in the document title area prints on the first page of the document as your title page; the text automatically centers top to bottom when it prints.

To disable the document title feature, place the cursor on the top double line and press Alt-F3. If you leave the title area blank without disabling the document title feature, you may get a blank page at the beginning of your document when you print it, depending on how you set up your page and print forms. (You can learn about setting up these forms in "Printing: The Basics," in this chapter.)

The word processing profile settings, discussed in Appendix B, include a choice that enables you to prevent the document title area from appearing every time you open a new document.

You receive a fringe benefit when you use the document title feature—even if you never print the title page. Enable creates and maintains a special *file summary* for each word processing file (see fig. 5.4). The file summary feature provides a convenient way to maintain a short description of each document. To open the File Summary screen, press F10 **File History View**. Enable displays the date the file originally was created, the date it last was revised, and the approximate number of words, lines, and pages in the file. Enable also displays the first 57 characters that you typed on the first line in the document title area as the document title.

Using the document title feature offers you an additional benefit. This feature can serve as a file management utility and can save you a great deal of time when you are trying to locate a special file but cannot remember its name. When you activate the View feature from the Directory of Files screen (described in Chapter 3, "Understanding the Master Control Module"), Enable first displays the document title. You can use the document title feature as a narrative description of the document that you can view from the directory, even if you never want to print your title page. (The print menus, discussed further in this chapter, include an option that suppresses printing of a title page.)

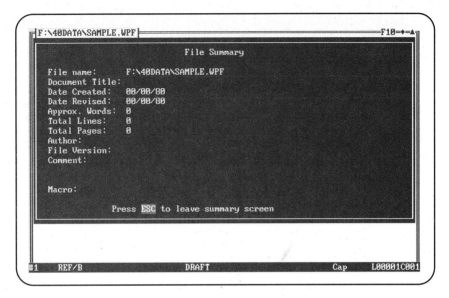

*Fig. 5.4. The File Summary screen.*

# Learning about the Status Line

Enable displays the *status line* at the bottom of the word processing screen. The #1 at the left end of the status line refers to the current window number, which can range from 1 to 8. All Enable windows that you open display a similar status line. The status line displays the state of the following word processing features:

- *Automatic reformat.* When the automatic reformat feature is turned on, Enable displays the message REF near the left end of the status line. This feature causes words that would otherwise extend beyond the right margin to wrap to the next line while you type the text (see the section "Entering Text" in this chapter for a discussion of Enable's word wrap feature). This reformatting feature also automatically closes any gaps that are left in a paragraph after you delete letters or words. Automatic reformat always operates from the position of the cursor to the end of the paragraph (marked by the paragraph symbol at the right edge of the screen) and not from the cursor to the beginning of the paragraph. To toggle automatic reformat on or off, press

   F9 **On/off Automatic Reformat**

- *Retain blanks while reformatting.* When this feature is on, the message /B is in the status line. Whenever Enable reformats the entire first line of an indented paragraph, which usually occurs when you insert a ruler or move or copy the paragraph, the program has to decide whether to retain the blank spaces that are at the beginning of the line. These spaces are generated by pressing either the space bar or the right-arrow key. Enable retains the blank spaces when this feature is on. If you disable the retain blanks feature, the blank spaces disappear during automatic reformatting. *Note:* This feature does not affect the blank spaces between words.

  To toggle this feature off or on, press

      F9 **On/off Automatic Blanks_retain**

- *Draft mode and final mode.* Normally, you do the majority of your work in *draft mode*, indicated by the message DRAFT in the status line (again see fig. 5.4). Draft is the more flexible mode and is convenient when you enter and edit text. Draft mode, however, does not display features such as page breaks, headers, footers, and page numbers exactly as they appear when printed. To preview the document as it appears when printed (showing page breaks and so on), you can switch the screen to *final mode.* The final mode displays the message Page, followed by the number of the page currently on-screen (see fig. 5.5). To toggle between draft and final mode, press

      F9 **On/off Draft/Final**

For a more detailed discussion of draft and final modes, see the section "Using the Draft and Final Modes" in this chapter.

- *Caps Lock.* After you press the Caps Lock key, Enable displays the message Cap in the status line and locks the keyboard in caps lock mode. When you turn on caps lock mode, you can enter uppercase letters without pressing the Shift key. This feature is not completely analogous to the Shift Lock key on a typewriter because the Caps Lock key affects only the letter keys. To type the dollar sign ($) symbol while in caps lock mode, you must hold the Shift key while you press the 4 key.

- *Num Lock.* After you press the Num Lock key, Enable displays the message Num in the status line and locks the keyboard in number lock mode. When you turn on number lock mode, you disable the cursor-movement keys on the numeric keypad so that you can use these keys to type numbers rather than to move the cursor. (If you have the IBM Enhanced Keyboard, you have an additional set of cursor-movement keys that num lock mode does not affect.)

- *The line/column counter.* The far right side of the status line in a new word processing file displays the message

    ```
    L00000C001
    ```

    This message, the line/column counter, indicates that the cursor is positioned at line 0 and column 1 of the file. The line/column counter keeps track of the cursor's position as you move it around the screen while you type or use the cursor-movement keys. The counter displays the current line number to the right of the L and the column number to the right of the C.

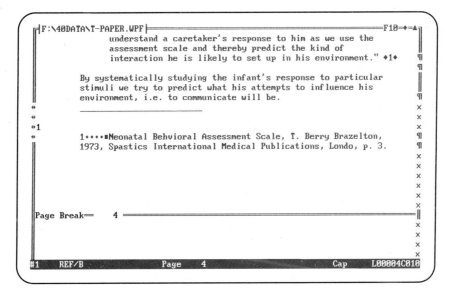

**Fig. 5.5.** *A word processing document in final mode.*

# Saving a Word Processing File

As explained at the beginning of this chapter, text that you type on-screen initially goes into RAM. To have text available for later use, it must be stored to a disk. You can type a document and print it without ever saving the typed text to disk, but if you delete that text, it is gone forever. RAM is volatile, actually existing in tiny computer chips inside your computer. When you delete text from the screen, Enable tells RAM to erase that text from its memory banks. When you turn off your computer, everything in RAM is lost. As the safer practice, you should save any word processing file that you create.

To save a word processing file to disk, press F10 while the file displays on the screen; Enable displays the word processing Top Line menu (see fig. 5.6). Then press

File Save

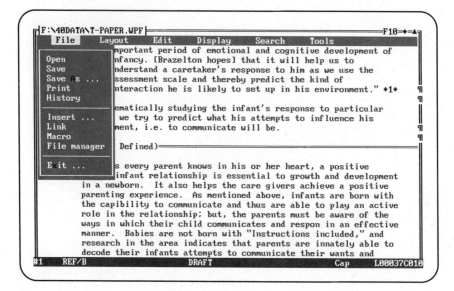

*Fig. 5.6. The word processing Top Line menu.*

Enable permanently saves the entire file on your data disk (and directory, if you are using a hard disk). After you save your file, you can continue to edit the text; your screen does not change after you save a file. If you make changes to the document, save the file again before you quit. The second and subsequent times you save a file, the new copy replaces the old one on the disk.

Other keystrokes duplicate the menu method of saving a file. To save a file in Enable word processing format, the F9 command F9 Save Edit saves the entire file to the data disk or directory, and you can continue to edit. Also, the function key command Alt-F10 saves the file and enables you to continue editing.

# Using the Save As Options

Sometimes you may not want to save the entire file you are working on, or you may want to save it in another format. For these reasons, Enable offers Save As options. To use different options when you save a file, press F10 to display the word processing Top Line menu. To choose the option Save_As, press

File Save_As

Enable displays the Open File dialog box (see fig. 5.7).

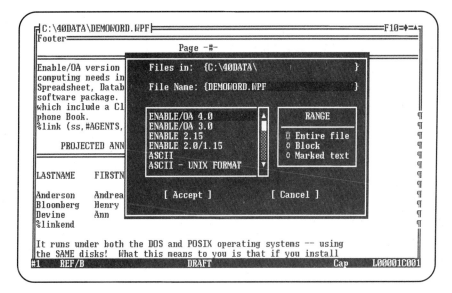

**Fig. 5.7.** *The Open File dialog box.*

Enable displays the following three options in the Open File dialog box:

1. *File_Name.* The cursor initially rests on the file name prompt. If you want to save the current file with a new name, simply type the new file name here. If you want to change the directory, press the up-arrow key to move the cursor to the Files_in prompt. Type the name of the new disk drive or path name.

2. *File Format.* After you specify a new file name, you can choose the format in which you want to save the file. If you choose a format that requires a default extension, Enable automatically adds the

required extension to the new file name. For example, Multimate uses the extension DOC; thus, if you choose the format for Multimate or Multimate Advantage II, Enable gives your file name the extension DOC. To choose a format, use the arrow keys to highlight the format you want, and then press Enter.

3. *RANGE.* This option enables you to save all the text that has been typed into RAM (the default choice) or only part of the text. Sometimes you do not want to save the entire file; therefore, you can save a range of text—either blocked text or marked text. You learn more about blocked and marked text in Chapter 6, "Using Word Processing Advanced Features."

After you make the appropriate choices to these three options of the dialog box, choose Accept to save the file as you specified. Then you can continue to edit the current file.

You can use F9 key commands to save files. Table 5.1 lists these commands. You may find that one of these F9 commands is more convenient than its menu counterpart.

**Table 5.1**
**F9 Save Commands**

| *F9 Command* | *Save Option* |
| --- | --- |
| F9 **Save Edit** | Saves file and returns to same file |
| F9 **Save Home** | Saves file and returns to Main Menu |
| F9 **Save Create** | Saves file and prompts you for the name of the next file you want to create |
| F9 **Save Revise** | Saves file and prompts you for the name of the next file you want to edit |
| F9 **Save End** | Saves file and exits Enable |
| F9 **Save New_name** | Saves file in Enable format with a new name |
| F9 **Save ASCII** | Saves file in ASCII format. Then choose one of the following options to specify the text you want to save in ASCII format: **Displayed_file, New_name, Marked_text,** or **Block.** |
| F9 **Save Marked_text** | Saves marked text with a new name |
| F9 **Save Block** | Saves block of text with a new name |

# Quitting a File

Several of the Save options discussed in the preceding table save the file to disk storage and return you to the Main Menu. Otherwise, you must use the following procedure to quit the file.

To quit a word processing file, press

> **F10 File Exit**

or

> **Alt-End**

A new feature of Enable/OA 4.0 is Smart Save. If you quit a word processing file without first saving it, Enable displays the message

```
Save Changes to:FILENAME
[Yes] [No] [Cancel]
```

Choose **Yes** to save and quit the file, **No** to quit the file without saving, and **Cancel** to return to your file without saving.

> Because the document resides in RAM until you perform a save, if anything happens to your document while you are editing it, you can quit without saving, and none of those changes actually takes effect. The file, however, is only as good as your last save. Thus, saving frequently and whenever you try a new feature on an important file is a good habit.

TIP

# Retrieving a Word Processing File

If you want to review an existing word processing file, choose from the Main Menu

> **Use_System Word_Processing**

After Enable displays the Open File dialog box, type the name of the file you want to retrieve, and press Enter. To display all the word processing files on your data disk or directory, press **?** at the File_Name prompt, and press Enter. To choose the file you want to edit, use the arrow keys to highlight the desired file name, and press Enter.

# Entering and Editing Text: The Basics

This portion of the chapter covers the basics of entering, modifying, and deleting text in a word processing file. After you master these fundamentals, you can move on to the more advanced features covered in Chapter 6, "Using Word Processing Advanced Features."

## Entering Text

Typing with Enable initially is no different from typing with a typewriter. Pressing a key on your computer keyboard or on your typewriter keyboard essentially produces the same result: a character prints on the page. The only difference is that the page you work with when you use a computer is an electronic page—your screen.

One big advantage of using a word processing program over a typewriter is its *word wrap* feature. With traditional styles of typewriters, if you forget to press the carriage return key when you get close to the right margin, you keep typing on the same line, past the margin and right off the edge of the paper. Enable is smarter than these typewriters. When a word exceeds the right margin, Enable automatically pushes that word to the next line. The word "wraps" to the next line, virtually eliminating the need for a carriage return key.

In the following circumstances, you do need to press the computer's carriage return key, or Enter key:

- *At the end of a paragraph.* Enable has several important features that can be applied to an entire paragraph. You use the Enter key to tell Enable where each paragraph ends. When you press the Enter key, Enable places a paragraph symbol at the right edge of the screen in the same line. Also, the cursor jumps down to the beginning of the next line, just like the effect of a typewriter carriage return.

- *For a blank line.* To insert a blank line that is protected from being lost during automatic reformatting, press the Enter key. This procedure places a paragraph symbol at the right edge of the screen.

- *To prevent automatic reformatting.* When you type text in columns (without using the special columnar margin settings) or use the box-drawing character set to construct diagrams, you don't want the automatic reformat feature to scramble the screen whenever you decide to delete a character or word. Press Enter at the end of every line you want to "lock" against automatic reformatting. The paragraph symbol at the right edge of the screen prevents word wrapping and reformatting beyond the end of that line in the document.

To delete a paragraph symbol entered by mistake, move your cursor to the line containing the paragraph symbol, press F9 Del, and then press Enter. This procedure removes the paragraph symbol that is on the same line as the cursor and automatically reformats the remaining text to the next paragraph symbol.

# Using the Typeover and Insert Modes

A second advantage of using a word processing program rather than a typewriter is the capability to make changes easily to existing text. By default, Enable is in *typeover mode*, which enables you to correct existing text by overwriting it. In typeover mode, any character you type replaces the character at which the cursor is located.

Many word processing programs are by default in *insert mode* rather than typeover mode. In insert mode, any character you type pushes the character at the cursor's location to the right and inserts the new character. You can turn on Enable's insert mode by pressing the Ins key.

Press the Ins key to toggle back and forth between typeover mode and insert mode. You easily can tell when you're in insert mode because the cursor changes shape, becoming a full character in height.

To erase a character, you can press the Del key, press the space bar while the cursor is resting on the character, or "back" over it with the Backspace key. Using these few features and the typing skills you already have, you can produce almost any document.

**TIP**

If you prefer to type in insert mode, you initially may be disappointed with the effect of the Backspace key in Enable's word processing module. With most word processing programs that have an insert mode, pressing the Backspace key erases both the character and the space to the left of the cursor, which gives the appearance of "pulling" to the left any text to the right of the cursor. Enable's Backspace key, however, erases only the characters, not the spaces consumed by those characters; therefore, you must use the Del key to delete the blank spaces that remain.

If you type in insert mode and frequently use the Backspace key to correct or revise text, large strings of blank spaces extend to the right of your cursor. To eliminate this inconvenience, set the profile System Options setting for operation of the Backspace key to choice number 4. (See "Setting System Options" in Appendix B to learn how to eliminate this inconvenience.)

## Inserting a Blank Line

To insert a blank line in the middle of existing text, place the cursor on the line above where you want to insert the blank line, and press F3. If you want to keep this blank line from being lost during automatic reformatting, remember to press Enter, which places the paragraph symbol in the right edge of the screen.

## Aligning Text

With Enable, you can align text one line at a time. You can center a line of text, align it along the right margin (flush right), or align it along the left margin (flush left).

## Centering Text

Enable's automatic centering feature enables you to center text, one line at a time, at the ruler's plus (+) mark. To center a line of text, position the cursor on the line you want to center, and press Alt-F4. If you change the text, you must return the cursor to the line you modified and press Alt-F4 again to reformat the line with your changes.

## Aligning Text Flush Right

To align a line of text so that it is flush with the right margin, position the cursor on the line you want to align. Press

Ctrl-]

## Aligning Text Flush Left

To align a line of text flush left, place the cursor on the line you want to align and press

Ctrl-[

# Using the Draft and Final Modes

The default editing mode in Enable's word processing module is draft mode. When you type text in draft mode, Enable does not display text that extends beyond the bottom of a page, and it doesn't display the headers, footers, footnotes, and so on, as they will appear on the printed page. Enable displays the message DRAFT in the status line when you are in draft mode (see fig. 5.8).

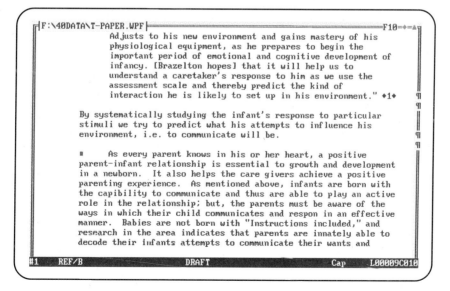

*Fig. 5.8. A word processing file in draft mode.*

Final mode, primarily, enables you to view the document as it will print. Enable waits to insert automatic page breaks until you ask for this final mode so that it continuously does not have to adjust the page breaks on the screen while you edit your document. Inserting or deleting a line somewhere in the middle of a long document takes significantly longer in final mode than in draft mode because Enable must reformat the page breaks.

To toggle the display to final mode, press

F9 **On**/off **D**raft/final

In final mode, Enable inserts numbered page breaks to separate each page when documents are greater than one page in length (see fig. 5.9). At the top and bottom of each page, Enable displays blank lines with x at the right edge of the screen. These lines represent the top and bottom margins that Enable inserts when you print the document. Enable also displays headers, footers, and other special features (discussed in Chapter 6) when in final mode. The status line displays the current page number, which represents the page number that Enable will print, based on the current print form settings. See "Using the Page Form" further in this chapter for a discussion of these settings.

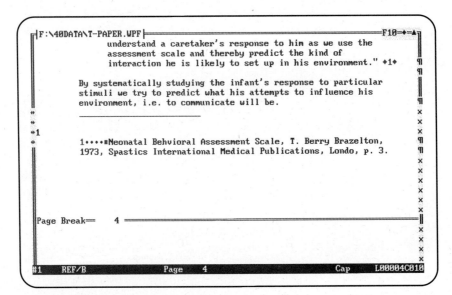

*Fig. 5.9. A word processing file in final mode.*

Editing in final mode is not good practice because Enable always updates the page breaks, which significantly interrupts your editing. Enable displays the message BUSY on the right side of the status line while it recalculates page breaks. You cannot edit your document while Enable is busy. Edit in draft mode, but keep in mind that page breaks continue to change until you print or until you display the file in final mode.

TIP

## Defining Your Own Page Breaks

Enable does a good job of inserting page breaks, and it prevents *orphans* and *widows* from being abandoned on a page; the program does not break a page so that fewer than two lines of a paragraph are left alone immediately above (orphan) or below (widow) the page break. Sometimes, however, Enable does not insert page breaks where you need them. In these cases, you can insert a *user-defined* page break, also called a *hard* or *forced* page break, which causes your document always to break at the location you specify. To insert a user-defined page break, position your cursor anywhere in the line immediately above where you want the page break to occur, and press

   F9 **Ins Marker P**age_break

Enable inserts a double line across the page, just below where the cursor was when you executed the command. On the line is the message Page Break (User Defined) (see fig. 5.10). The cursor moves to the first space on the first line that follows the page break. After you insert a page break, toggle the screen to final mode to see what changes, if any, were caused by your page breaks.

In a long document, inserting user-defined page breaks has a ripple effect throughout the file. If you insert a page break in a file to maintain a format, and later insert another page break prior to the first one, you may find pages within your document that are only several lines long. Always insert page breaks near the top of the document first, and then work your way down through the ensuing pages.

TIP

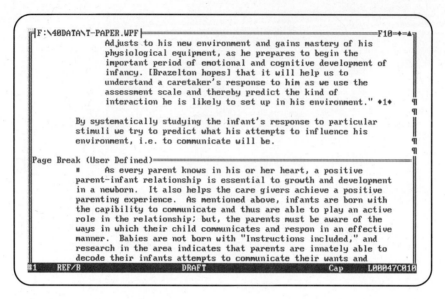

**Fig. 5.10.** *A user-defined page break.*

# Using Cursor-Movement Keys and Goto Commands

Chapters 3 and 4 detail how to open, size, and switch between Enable's windows. Probably of more immediate interest to you now is learning to move quickly within individual windows. Using the cursor-movement keys and the Goto commands, discussed in this section, you quickly can move around within your document—from word to word, sentence to sentence, page to page, and beginning to end.

You already know that you can use the arrow keys to move the cursor around the document screen. When you move the cursor to the bottom edge of the screen, the text scrolls up as you continue to press the down-arrow key, or "scroll" down through the document. Pressing the up-arrow key to move the cursor to the top edge of the screen has the opposite effect—scrolling up through the document.

You can move more quickly through your document by using the other standard cursor-movement keys: PgUp, PgDn, Home, and End. You must use some of these keys in combination with the Ctrl key. Table 5.2 lists the cursor-movement keys you use in word processing.

**Table 5.2**
**Word Processing Cursor-Movement Keys**

| Cursor-Movement Key | New Cursor Location |
|---|---|
| PgUp | Half screen up |
| Ctrl-PgUp | Full screen up |
| PgDn | Half screen down |
| Ctrl-PgDn | Full screen down |
| Home | Top of screen |
| Ctrl-Home | Top of file |
| End | Bottom of screen |
| Ctrl-End | Bottom of file |
| Ctrl-→ | Beginning of following word |
| Ctrl-← | Beginning of preceding word |

TIP

With the exception of Home and End, if you precede a cursor-movement key (up arrow, down arrow, PgUp, or PgDn) with the system macro function key command Alt-F9, Enable executes the cursor-movement keystroke over and over again until you press Ctrl-Break to stop. This feature provides a nice *auto-scroll* capability, if you remember how to turn it off.

The cursor-movement keys described in the preceding section are fine if you are working in a relatively small document; however, scrolling through a long document, one line or screen at a time, to get to a specific section can be tedious. Enable, therefore, includes a set of *Goto commands* that facilitate fast navigation throughout even the longest file.

The F2 function key is the *Goto key* in the word processing module (and in the spreadsheet module, as well). The Goto key operates in a manner similar to the F9 key. When you press F2, you see a list of letters, each representing a different command, in the status line (see fig. 5.11).

Because Enable does not display a menu to prompt you to a correct second keystroke, most of the Goto commands are mnemonic. Also, as with the F9 commands, when you press F2 twice in succession, Enable repeats the last Goto command that you executed. Table 5.3 lists the Goto commands.

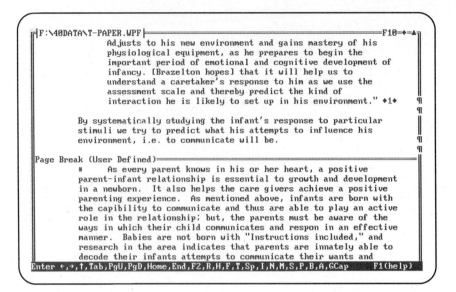

*Fig. 5.11. The Goto command options in the word processing status line.*

**Table 5.3**
**Word Processing Goto Commands**

| *Goto Command* | *New Cursor Location* |
| --- | --- |
| F2 → | Last character on the line. A profile option enables you to choose whether you want the cursor to stop at the last character or go on to the next space. |
| F2 ← | First character on the line. |
| F2 Tab | Left margin. Executing this Goto command a second time moves the cursor to the right margin. Executing this command a third time moves the cursor back to the left, and so on. |
| F2 Sentence | End of the sentence. This command looks for punctuation that is appropriate at the end of a sentence and places the cursor there. |
| F2 ↑ Sentence | Beginning of the sentence. |

| *Goto Command* | *New Cursor Location* |
|---|---|
| F2 **Paragraph** | End of the paragraph. Enable looks for the paragraph symbol as indication of the end of a paragraph. |
| F2 ↑ **Paragraph** | Beginning of the paragraph. |
| F2 Home | Beginning of the page. Enable moves the cursor to the line following the preceding page break. |
| F2 End | End of the page. |
| F2 *n* PgDn | The *n*th page break, down.* |
| F2 *n* PgUp | The *n*th page break, up.* |
| F2 *n* Space bar | The *n*th column of the current line.* |
| F2 **Goto** *n* | The *n*th page.* Use only in final mode. |

*Where *n* is a positive whole number.

A number of other Goto commands enable you to move to and between special features such as *paper clips*, *comments*, headers, and footers. These commands and features are discussed in Chapter 6, "Using Word Processing Advanced Features."

# Deleting Text

In addition to deleting one character at a time from the screen (with the space bar, Backspace key, or Del key), you quickly can delete large quantities of text with Enable. Enable places the text that you last deleted into a holding area, usually called a *buffer*. Until you replace the buffer's contents with other deleted text, you can retrieve the contents currently in the buffer by using one of several undelete commands. You can use menu methods, function key command methods, and F9 command methods to delete and undelete text.

## Accessing the DELETE Menu

You can use the word processing Top Line menu to access the DELETE menu (see fig. 5.12). Press

F10 **Edit Delete**

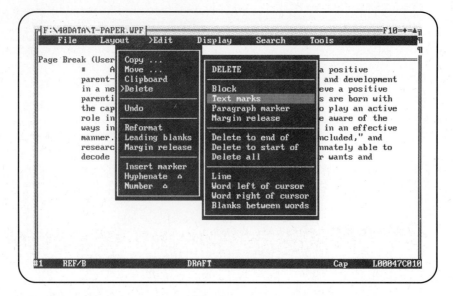

*Fig. 5.12. The word processing DELETE menu.*

The DELETE menu enables you to delete blocked text (blocked with the F7 key), marked text (marked with Alt-M), paragraph markers, and margin release markers. You also can delete all text from the cursor's location to the end of a sentence, paragraph, page, file, or line, and from the cursor's location to the start of a page or file. Finally, you can delete all the text in your file, a line, the word to the left or right of the cursor, and the blanks between words. Before you choose any of the commands from the DELETE menu, you first must position the cursor where you want to make the deletion.

## Deleting a Word

To delete the entire word at the cursor's location, press F4. If the cursor is not on a word, F4 deletes the first word to the right of the cursor. After deleting the word, Enable brings the word following the deleted word to the location of the cursor.

You can use the following F9 command to undelete the last word you deleted with F4. First place the cursor where you want Enable to reinsert the deleted word, then press

    F9 Undo

Enable reinserts the deleted word at the cursor's position.

The F9 Undo feature actually copies the last text deleted and restores it to your document. If you use the F4 command to delete a word, then delete more text before you decide to undelete the word, you cannot restore the word because the buffer holds only the text that was last deleted.

You can use F4 and F9 Undo in tandem to move a word quickly around in a sentence or paragraph.

## Deleting a Line

To delete the line at the cursor's location, press Alt-F3. This command is versatile; you can use it to delete headers, footers, footnotes, document titles, and so on. To restore the last line deleted with this command, press F9 Undo. Enable reinserts into your document the previously deleted line, just above the cursor. This method is sometimes convenient when you want to move a line from one spot in your document to another.

## Using the F9 Delete Commands

Table 5.4 lists the largest group of delete commands—the F9 delete commands. These commands are grouped according to the text they delete.

**Table 5.4**
**Word Processing F9 Delete Commands**

| Command | Text Deleted |
| --- | --- |
| F9 Del Backspace | To the left of cursor |
| F9 Del Space bar | To the right of cursor |
| F9 Del Del | On both sides of cursor |
| *Word* | |
| F9 Del ← | To the left of cursor |
| F9 Del → | To the right of cursor |

*continued*

**Table 5.4** *(continued)*

| *Command* | *Text Deleted* |
|---|---|
| *Line* | |
| F9 Del L | Entire line |
| F9 Del ↓ | From cursor to the right margin |
| *Sentence* | |
| F9 Del S | From cursor to end of sentence |
| F9 Del ↑ S | From cursor to beginning of sentence |
| *Paragraph* | |
| F9 Del P | From cursor to paragraph symbol |
| F9 Del ↑ P | From cursor to preceding paragraph symbol |
| F9 Del Enter | Paragraph symbol |
| *Screen* | |
| F9 Del Home | From cursor to top of screen |
| F9 Del End | From cursor to bottom of screen |
| *Page* | |
| F9 Del PgUp | From cursor to preceding page break |
| F9 Del PgDn | From cursor to following page break |
| *File* | |
| F9 Del Ctrl-Home | From cursor to beginning of the file |
| F9 Del Ctrl-End | From cursor to end of file |
| F9 Del B | Blocked text |
| F9 Del M T | Text marking |
| F9 Del M P | Automatic page breaks |
| F9 Del M C | All paper clips |

You can turn on a profile setting that requires Enable to request your confirmation before deleting any blocked text or text that is longer than one line (see Appendix B, "Using Profiles to Customize Enable," to change profile options). Enable requires only an additional keystroke (press **Y** for Yes) as confirmation for the requested deletion—a small price to pay for this added security.

To minimize accidental deletions, block the text you want to delete; then delete the block. If you use this method, the text you plan to delete is clearly highlighted before it is destroyed forever. If the wrong text is highlighted, you may be more likely to notice the error in time to stop the deletion. Blocked text is discussed in Chapter 6, "Using Word Processing Advanced Features."

TIP

# Printing: The Basics

After you create a document, you probably want to see it in print. Enable's *quick print* feature enables you to print the document that is on-screen by pressing Alt-F2. (Make sure that the printer is on-line, has paper, and has a good ribbon.) Enable prints the entire contents of your document.

Sometimes, though, you may not want to print the entire file, or you may want to modify the print parameters chosen when the profile was created. With Enable, you have many printing options, including the options to print specified parts of a file and to modify the print parameters. In this section, you learn about your printing options, accessed through the PRINT menu.

## Accessing the PRINT Menu

To access the many print options, press

F10 **File Print**

Enable displays the PRINT menu (see fig. 5.13).

## Choosing a Printer

When you installed Enable, you also indicated the individual printer you expect to use most, which set this printer as the default printer. You can change the default printer to one of the other printers you specified when installing the program. The printer you choose remains active until you choose another printer. To choose one of the other installed printers to print your file, press

F10 **File Print Hardware**

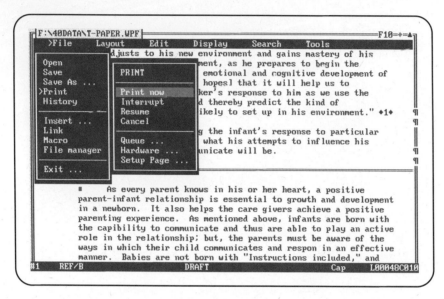

*Fig. 5.13. The word processing PRINT menu.*

Figure 5.14 shows the Print Hardware menu. If you want to change the current printer, simply move your cursor up or down to highlight the desired printer, and press Enter. If you have a mouse, you can use the list's scroll bar to move rapidly through the list, and then click the printer you want.

After you choose a printer, you can change the following settings:

- *Verify_connection*. This option verifies the connection to your printer. If Enable tries to print a file, and the printer doesn't respond, the program displays an error message. With most laser printers, however, printing a file takes longer than Enable expects, thus causing an unnecessary error. If you receive a printer fault error and the printer is printing, simply turn off Verify_connection.

- *Unidirectional*. This feature prevents the printer from printing in both directions, but it also slows down output. Use this feature only with dot-matrix printers and only if you have problems with vertical lines looking crooked.

- *Continuous_form*. If you use continuous paper, turn on this option. If you use single sheets, turn off this option so that Enable stops after each page and asks you to press Enter before the next page is printed to give you time to insert a new sheet of paper.

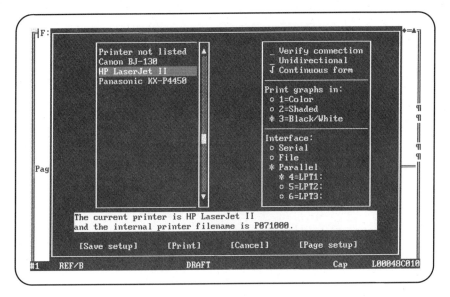

*Fig. 5.14. The Print Hardware menu.*

- *Print_graphs_in*. This feature enables you to specify how to print your graphs. Choose the option that best matches your printer. If your printer does not support color, choose either Shaded or Black/White.

- *Interface*. This feature tells Enable where your printer is. To determine which option you need, check the back of your computer and see if the printer cable is attached to the serial or parallel ports. Most PC printers are parallel printers. If you use a serial printer, check the printer manual for the appropriate settings. You should not need to change this option setting unless you choose a different printer in the printer list.

  - *Parallel.* If you choose Parallel, you must select the port to which your printer is connected: LPT1, LPT2, or LPT3. You should not have to change this option unless you use Enable on a network or have multiple printers connected to a single computer.

  - *Serial.* If you choose Serial, you must set five serial printer parameters (see fig. 5.15.). To confirm your choices, press Enter or choose Accept. Be sure that you consult your printer manual for the correct settings.

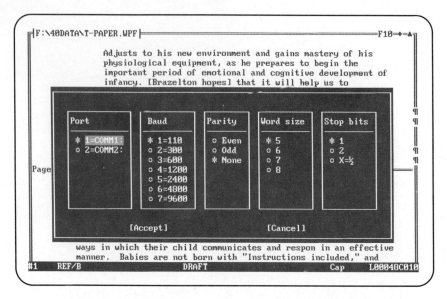

**Fig. 5.15.** *The Printer Serial Interface menu.*

- *File.* This option creates a file that you later can print in DOS by typing the following command at the DOS prompt:

  **COPY WPFILE.PPD LPT1:**

> **NOTE**
>
> If you choose the File option, the file has the same root file name as your word processing file with the extension PPD.

After you make changes to the Print Hardware menu, choose one of the following four options displayed at the bottom of the menu:

- *Save_Setup* saves your changes for the next time you print this file.

- *Print* immediately prints the file according to the options you specified.

- *Cancel* returns you to your word processing document without saving the options.

- *Page_Setup* enables you to set other options, discussed in the following section.

# Using the Page Form

The Page Form contains options that enable you to set up the pages in your document to fully customize your print job. Figure 5.16 shows the first of two screens of options. To access the Page Form, press

F10 **File Print Setup_Page**

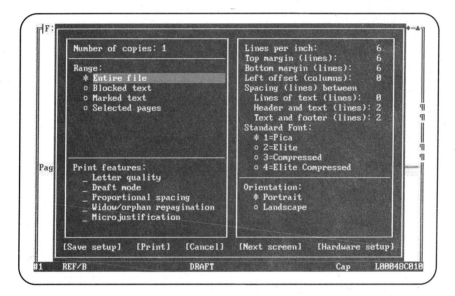

**Fig. 5.16.** *The first Page Form screen.*

In the first Page Form screen, you can make changes to the following settings:

- *Number_of_copies*. Type the number of copies you want Enable to print. Enable completely prints one copy before starting to print the next copy.

- *Range*. The following range options enable you to specify how much of the file you want to print.

  ° Choose *Entire_file* to print the entire document.

  ° Choose *Selected_pages* to indicate specific pages that you want to print. You can indicate one or more ranges of pages. To print pages 2 through 5, for example, type **2-5**. To print pages 1 through 3 and 7 through 9, type **1-3,7-9**.

>   ° With Enable/OA 4.0, you have two new range options available: the *Blocked_text* option to print blocked text and the *Marked_text* option to print marked text. (You learn how to block and mark text in the following chapter.)

- *Print_features*. The following print features affect the way Enable prints your file. Check your printer manual or Enable's manual "Printing with Enable" to determine whether your printer can use these options.

  - ° *Letter_quality*. This feature enables you to improve the quality of the text characters printed from a dot-matrix printer. If your printer doesn't support the letter-quality feature, Enable substitutes the double-strike feature in its place. The double-strike feature strikes all characters twice to make them darker, but printing is much slower.

  - ° *Draft_mode*. To print the document exactly as it appears on-screen in draft mode (without headers, footers, footnotes, automatic dating, and so on), choose this option. This option produces a printed document similar to the product you get when you use Shift-PrtSc—printing *exactly* what appears on-screen. **Note:** Your printer has a draft mode and a final mode similar to the draft and final modes on-screen. The screen default mode is draft; the printer default mode is final.

  - ° *Proportional_spacing*. This feature enables you to use a special proportional printing feature available on many printers. Proportional spacing allocates character widths that are proportional to character shapes so that all characters do not have equal widths.

  - ° *Widow/orphan_repagination*. Choose this option to prevent one line of a multiple-line paragraph from appearing alone at the top (widow) or bottom (orphan) of a page. Enable automatically adjusts page breaks to prevent widows and orphans.

  - ° *Microjustification*. If you want Enable to use the microspaces between letters to right-justify text, turn on Microjustification. This option may cause dot-matrix printers to print very slowly.

- *Lines_per_inch*. By default, Enable prints six lines per inch, vertically, on the page. You seldom, if ever, need to change this parameter.

- *Top_margin_(lines)*. Expressed in lines, with this option you can specify the amount of blank space you want Enable to leave at the top of each page. By default, the top margin is six lines, which is equal to one inch.

- *Bottom_margin_(lines)*. Expressed in lines, with this option you can specify the amount of blank space you want Enable to leave at the bottom of each page. The default bottom margin is six lines.

- *Left_offset_(columns)*. Expressed in tenths (1/10) of an inch, this option enables you to insert columns of space between your left margin and the edge of the page. If your left margin is set at column 1, for example, and you want the file to print one inch from the left edge of the paper, you must set the left offset to 10.

- *Spacing_between_Lines_of_text_(lines)*. The number at this prompt indicates the number of additional blank lines you want to place between lines of text. You enter a 1, for example, to choose double spacing.

- *Spacing_between_Header_and_text_(lines)*. When you include a header (discussed in Chapter 6), Enable inserts between the header and the text the number of lines that you specify. Even without a header, Enable still leaves this many blank lines in addition to the top margin, before printing any text.

- *Spacing_between_Text_and_footer_(lines)*. As with the preceding option, Enable inserts between the text and the footer (discussed in Chapter 6) the number of lines that you specify.

- *Standard_Font*. The font choices refer to the horizontal spacing, or *pitch*, of the characters that you print. ***Note:*** If you use a daisywheel printer, remember to use the correct daisywheel.

    ° *Pica* is 10 characters per inch.

    ° *Elite* is 12 characters per inch.

    ° *Compressed* ranges from 15 to 17 characters per inch, depending on your printer.

    ° *Elite Compressed* ranges from 18 to 20 characters per inch.

- *Orientation*. This option enables you to choose the printing orientation you want: Portrait or Landscape. (If your printer is not capable of printing in landscape mode, Enable does not display the option Orientation.) Many laser printers can print in either portrait mode (vertical) or landscape mode (horizontal). These modes affect the length and width of each page.

    ° Choose *Portrait*, the default mode, to print on 8 1/2- by-11-inch paper.

° New in Enable/OA 4.0 is a feature called *Landscape* that enables you to print sideways on both laser printers and dot-matrix printers.

**TIP**

If you choose Landscape, be sure that you change the paper size settings to reflect the size of the printed page. For example, when you print in portrait mode (the default), the paper length is 11 inches and the width is 8.5 inches; however, in landscape mode, the length is 8.5 inches and the width is 11 inches.

The second Page Form screen (see fig. 5.17) displays the following options:

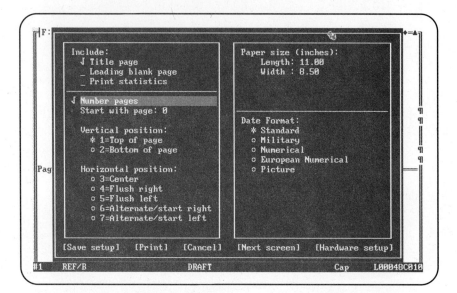

*Fig. 5.17. The second Page Form screen.*

- *Title_page*. Turn on this option if you want to print the title page.

- *Leading_blank_page*. If you turn on this option, Enable ejects a blank page before printing each new document.

- *Print_statistics*. This feature adds a "trailer" page to the end of the document and is convenient for identifying each file printed on a shared printer. The statistics on this page include the file summary information displayed when you choose F10 **File History View**.

*Number_pages*. This option is one of two methods for numbering pages. If you choose this option, you must then choose the horizontal and vertical position of the numbers. In Enable/OA 4.0, you can alternate the location of the page numbers, as in a book. To alternate page numbers, you must choose whether you want the page numbering to begin on the right page or the left page.

- *Length*. With this option, you specify in inches the length of the paper on which you print. The default length is 11 inches.

- *Width*. With this option, you specify in inches the width of the paper on which you print. The default width is 8 inches.

- *Date_Format*. If you use Enable's automatic date feature, you can use this setting to control the format of the date. Choose from the following established settings:

  - *Standard*, the default setting, entirely spells out the date, such as July 15, 1992.

  - *Military* prints the date in the format Day, Month, Year, such as 15 July 1992.

  - *Numerical* prints only digits for the date, such as 7/15/92.

  - *European_Numerical* prints digits for the date in the format Day, Month, Year, such as 15/7/92.

  - *Picture* prints the date in the format you specify.

> If you make changes to any of the Print Form or Page Form settings and want to use these new settings the next time you print your file, be sure that you save your file, even if you haven't made any other changes. If you do not save the file, the settings remain the same as they were before you changed them.

**TIP**

# Using Enable's Print Queue

If you want to print several files or different versions of the same file without waiting for the previous file to finish printing, use the *print queue* feature of Enable/OA 4.0. If you activate this feature, every time you command Enable to print a file, the program adds the file to its print queue, a file that contains a list of files that you want to print. Enable prints the file after it prints all previously added files.

Normally you never need to access the print queue itself; however, you can access it if you manually want to add files to the queue. Follow the instructions in the following section, "Editing the Print Queue," to manually add files to the queue.

To activate the print queue, press

F10 **File** **Print** **Queue**

Enable displays the ENABLE QUEUE FILE menu (see fig. 5.18). Choose

Use_ENABLE_print_queue

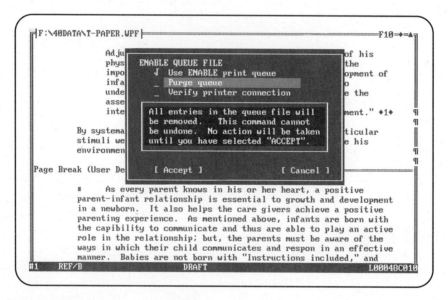

**Fig. 5.18.** *The ENABLE QUEUE FILE menu.*

Before you decide to use the print queue, you need to understand its side effects. First, whenever you use the print queue to print a file, Enable creates a print file—your file name with the extension @##, where ## is the sequential number Enable assigns. Then, Enable updates the print queue to include this file. Enable prints the files in the order you send them to the print queue. After printing each file, Enable automatically removes the file from the queue.

If you want the file in which you currently are working to print before the other files in the print queue, you can override the order of the print queue by pressing Shift-F2 instead of Alt-F2 (the quick print command). Enable places this file at the beginning of the print queue so that it prints after Enable completes the current printing job.

## Editing the Print Queue

Enable's print queue actually is a word processing file. The file name is PRINTQ.TSG. (If you use Enable on a network, the file name is PRINTQXX.TSG, where XX is your two-character user identification.) You can use Enable's word processing features to access and edit this file. To edit the file PRINTQ.TSG, from the Main Menu, press

Use_System Word_Processing

and type **PRINTQ.TSG** in the Open File dialog as the name of the file you want to open. Enable displays a list of all the files in the print queue.

If you decide not to print a file already in the print queue, position the cursor on the line containing the file name and press Alt-F3 to delete the line. After you delete the file from the print queue, press Alt-F10 to save the revised print queue file.

## Purging the Print Queue

If Enable does not print a file completely—for example, if the printer runs out of paper or is off-line—the file remains in the print queue. Thus, the next time you print a file, Enable first prints the original file that did not print completely. To purge the print queue, choose **P**urge_queue from the ENABLE QUEUE FILE menu (again see fig. 5.18). Enable clears all previous files.

If you try to print a document with the Alt-F2 function key command and nothing happens, do not execute the command again. First make sure your printer is plugged in and on-line. Check to see whether your printer cable firmly connects the printer to the computer. Also make sure your printer is supplied with a ribbon and paper. Any one of these problems can prevent your printer from printing. If you press Alt-F2 over and over again before you find and fix the problem, the next time you use the print queue to print a document, Enable prints the document once for every time you pressed Alt-F2.

## Canceling Printing

If you ever want to stop a print job in midstream, press Ctrl-F2. Enable displays a message in the status line to indicate that the printing will stop when the buffer is empty (referring to your printer buffer). Because the computer sends information to the printer much faster than the printer can print, all printers have a special, built-in RAM buffer that receives a block of text for printing and tells the computer not to send another block until receiving a command to continue.

**TIP**

> When you tell Enable to stop printing, the program probably has sent a lot more text to the printer than has been printed. Because Enable can refrain only from sending more text to the printer, the printing continues until the printer's RAM is empty. Turn off the printer to stop this printing.

# Summary

This chapter presents the fundamentals of using Enable to create and edit a document, save it to disk, retrieve it, and print it. Using the techniques in this chapter, you easily can produce most documents and correspondence that you may need at home and even at the office. Enable has many other features, however, that you can use to enhance the editing process; these features include spelling check, search and replace, and cut and paste. Become comfortable with the features presented in this chapter, and then learn about these other features in Chapter 6, "Using Word Processing Advanced Features."

# 6

# Using
# Word Processing
# Advanced Features

**M**any people buy a computer program for its most innovative advanced features, and then use only a handful of basic tools. The unused features aren't extravagant; users just don't learn how to operate them fully. If you take the time to learn how to use Enable's advanced word processing features, you may be surprised at how quickly they become "trusted tools" you pull out of the toolbox daily.

This chapter does not explain in detail all of Enable's advanced word processing features, but discusses those features that are significantly helpful to most users. To get the most out of Enable's advanced capabilities, read this chapter thoroughly and work through the example tasks. If you haven't looked at the preceding chapter and used Enable to create some documents, you may want to look at Chapter 5, "Understanding Word Processing Basics," before going on.

The word processing features discussed in this chapter help you fine-tune your document after you type it on-screen. You rarely write a first draft exactly the same as your eventual final document. This chapter explains how easily you can move, rearrange, find, and correct text in Enable. This chapter also explains how to use Enable's powerful sort feature, the spelling checker, the thesaurus, and the automatic hyphenation feature.

# Working with Blocks of Text and Marked Text

Have you ever finished a letter, and then wished you had said the last sentence first, the second sentence last, and the first sentence not at all, but just didn't have the time to rewrite the whole letter? Or maybe your job involves preparing documents for others who often change their minds. You can use several features in Enable to rearrange text you have already typed, without having to rework the entire document.

Enable offers three methods for moving text on-screen: the block method, the blocked column method, and the marking method. The first two methods require that all the text you want to use be together in a block— thus the term *block methods*. With the third method, you can use separate sections of text that can be located throughout a document.

You usually copy or move text within one document, but occasionally you want to copy text between two open word processing files or from a file on disk to an open file. The following sections discuss copying and moving blocked text, blocked columns, and marked text within a single file and between files.

## Blocking Linear and Columnar Text

Enable calls a continuous section of text a *block*. A *linear block* is in paragraph format; in figure 6.1, the highlighted text is a linear block. Another type of block is the *columnar block*. In figure 6.2, the highlighted text is a columnar block, because it includes text only within columns 14 and 21 of the document. The difference is important, because the results of moving and copying text are different for each type of block. The method for highlighting each is also different.

Working with blocks of text is useful when you are editing a word processing document. For instance, you can copy, move, and delete sentences, paragraphs, or entire sections with only a few keystrokes. Highlighting blocks is also an essential step in copying text from one Enable file to another through the use of windows.

To indicate you want to work with a linear block of text, position the cursor at the first letter of that block and press F7. The letter changes to reverse video (highlighted). Move the cursor to the end of the block of text, and again press F7. Enable highlights the entire block, as in figure 6.1.

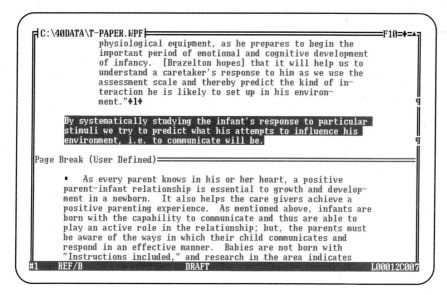

**Fig. 6.1.** *A linear block of text.*

```
F:\40DATA\FILEDIR.WPF                                    F10=◆=▲
DBMSDEF   $RF    5632   8-03-90  11:46a
HAWAII    WPF    3305   2-12-91   2:46a
SYMBOLS   SSF   14848   7-05-90   3:39p
COLUMNS   WPF    6196   6-08-90   5:39p
DOCFORM   WPF    6272   6-01-90   5:40p
FONTS     WPF    7203   7-10-90   7:11a
SIDEWAYS  WPF    1278  11-13-90   9:56a
LABEL     TSG    1377  10-12-88  10:16a
LETTER    TSG    1144  10-12-88  10:14a
SLETTER   TSG    2048   1-05-90   4:50p
MAIL      $BF    3072   1-05-90  12:36a
MAIL      DBF    1024   1-14-90   5:20p
MAILIN    $IF    4096  10-04-84   8:02p
FINANCE   $BF    5120   1-14-90   9:48p
FINANCE   $IF    3584   1-14-90   8:54p
FINANCE   SSF    7168   1-14-90   6:49p
FINEMPID  NDX    1024   1-13-90   6:37p
FINLAST   NDX    1024   1-13-90   6:37p
FINST     NDX    1024   1-13-90   6:37p
PROFILE   $PR    3584  12-21-90  11:01a
TPSETUP   $TP    2560   3-13-89   1:09p
$(S)      SSM     512   2-12-91   1:11a
$(M)      SSM     512   2-12-91   1:07a
#1      /B                DRAFT              Cap   L00019C021
```

**Fig. 6.2.** *A columnar block of text.*

To create a block from the current position to the last character on the current line, place the cursor on the first character and press F7 F7.

To create a block of several lines, you can press F7 on the first character, and then move your cursor to the left margin of the line below the last line and press F7.

You work with a columnar block when you have columns of text, such as a table. To indicate you want to work with a columnar block of text, position the cursor at the first letter of that block and press F7. The letter under the cursor changes to reverse video (highlighted). Then move the cursor to the end of the block of text and press Shift-F7. Enable highlights the entire block, as in figure 6.2.

An alternative way to indicate a blocked column is to position the cursor at the top left corner of the column and press F9 F7.

Next, use the cursor keys to move the cursor to the bottom right corner of the text to be blocked and press Enter. The highlighting follows as you move the cursor. This method is similar to "pointing out" a range of cells in the spreadsheet module.

To clear any text that is marked, press Alt-F7.

## Moving and Copying Blocks of Text within a File

To move the blocked text or columnar blocks to another location in the document, place the cursor at the new location and press Alt-F8. Enable deletes the text from its original location and inserts it at the cursor. All existing text starting at the cursor moves to the right and down.

Enable beeps to indicate that it cannot move a block of text to a new location on the same line as any of the blocked text, using the usual procedure. To move blocked text to a new location that includes part of the original location, issue the following command to delete the block:

F9 Del **Block Yes**

This command removes the blocked text and places it in a section of memory called a *buffer*. *Note:* You need to answer Yes only if you have chosen the profile option that requests confirmation of deletions. Position the cursor where you want to insert the text and undelete by using the Undo command as follows:

F9 Undo

Enable pulls the original block of text out of the buffer and inserts it on-screen in the new location.

TIP

To copy blocked text to another place in the document without moving the original block of text, place the cursor where you want the new copy to begin, and press F8. Enable inserts a copy of the blocked text into the document beginning at the cursor; the original blocked text remains in the original location.

F8 issues the Copy command and Alt-F8 issues the Move command in Enable's spreadsheet module as well as in the word processing module.

NOTE

## Moving and Copying Blocked Columns within a File

To move blocked columns elsewhere in the same document, move the cursor to the desired location and press Alt-F8. Enable removes the text from its original location and inserts it at the cursor.

All original text starting at the cursor moves to the right and down. In a blocked column move, Enable does not wrap text from one line to another as it does in a regular block move, but keeps the format of the moved column. If a row does not have enough room for the text that you are inserting, Enable displays a caution box with the following message:

```
CAUTION! Right margin not wide enough.
```

and offers you the options Truncate and Expand (see fig. 6.3).

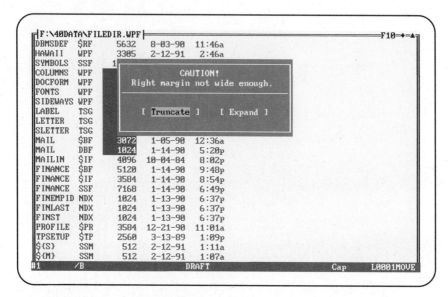

*Fig. 6.3.* A caution box warning that the right margin is not wide enough.

If you choose **Expand**, Enable extends the right margin, up to column 160, as far as necessary to accommodate the new text. If you choose **Truncate**, Enable deletes all text that extends beyond the right margin.

**TIP**

Moving a column to a location that partially overlaps the original column location can have unpredictable results. Refer to the preceding Tip for the delete/undelete alternative for moving blocked text. Moving columns of text by deleting and undeleting works especially well when the source and destination locations overlap.

To copy the blocked column to another position in the same document without moving the original text, place the cursor where you want the new copy to begin and press F8. If the margins are not wide enough to accept the column you are copying, Enable again displays the Caution box.

# Moving and Copying Marked Text within a File

Sometimes you need to copy or move text that is not in a linear block or a column. For instance, you may want to select several words from a paragraph to construct a summary, as shown in figure 6.4. The marked words in figure 6.4 were highlighted by pressing Alt-M.

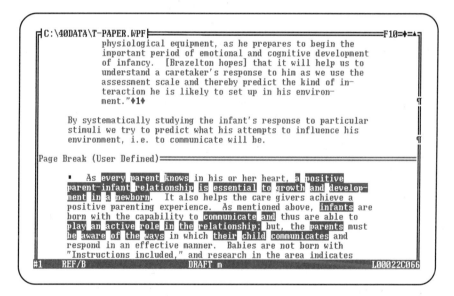

*Fig. 6.4. Text marked for copying or moving.*

Press Alt-M to turn on the marked text attribute (see Chapter 7, "Using Formatting Features," for more information on attributes). When you activate this attribute, Enable places the letter *m* in the status line, after the draft/final mode indicator (see fig. 6.4). When the attribute is on, all text that you type will have the attribute. Press Alt-M again to turn off the marking attribute.

To mark text, place the cursor at the first character you want to mark and use one of the Ctrl-key combinations shown in table 6.1 to apply the attribute. You also can remove the mark attribute with these keystrokes. Check the status of the attribute in the status line before using these keystrokes. You can mark as little or as much of the text as you want to copy or move.

**Table 6.1**
**Ctrl-Key Combinations To Apply or Remove Marked Text Attribute**

| *Apply to* | *Key Combination* |
|------------|-------------------|
| Character | Ctrl-C |
| Word | Ctrl-W |
| Line | Ctrl-L |
| Sentence | Ctrl-S |
| Paragraph | Ctrl-P |
| Page | Ctrl-G |
| Blocked text | Ctrl-B |

After you mark the text, you can move it to another location in the document by positioning the cursor in the new location and pressing

F10 **Edit Move Marked_text**

Enable inserts all the marked text at the cursor and removes the marking.

To copy marked text to another location in the file, position the cursor where you want the copied text to begin, and press

F10 **Edit Copy Marked_text**

When you copy the marked text, Enable does not remove the marking. To remove all marking in the file at one time, press

F9 **Del Marked Text**

This command removes the highlighting but does not delete the text that was marked. Enable has no command to delete all marked text at once. To remove the marking from just some of the text, use the normalize attribute (described in Chapter 7).

# Copying Text between Windows

Sections in Chapters 2 and 4 introduce you to interwindow copying. This section explains how to copy blocked and marked text from one window to another. This operation is much easier in Enable than in some word processing programs because you can keep both files open at once. *Note:* Enable can only *copy* text between windows; you cannot *move* text between windows.

## Copying Blocked Text between Windows

To copy a block or a blocked column of text from one open word processing window (the *source window*) to another open window (the *destination window*), first mark the destination, and then mark the text you want to copy. The destination window can be another word processing window, a spreadsheet window, a database window, or a telecommunications window.

Position the cursor in the destination window where you want to insert the text. Press Alt-F5 to display the Interwindow Copy Options screen (see fig. 6.5).

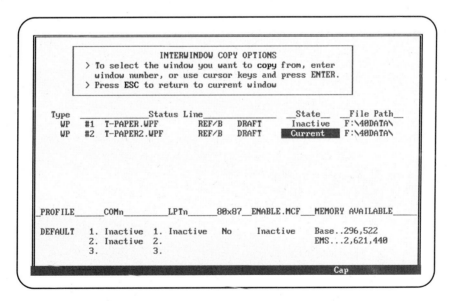

**Fig. 6.5.** *The Interwindow Copy Options screen.*

Press the number of the source window; the Interwindow Copy Options screen disappears and the cursor jumps to the source window. Enable displays the message `Block text then copy` in the status line (see fig. 6.6).

Use either the F7 F7 or the F7 Shift-F7 method described in the section "Blocking Linear and Columnar Text" to highlight the block or column you want to copy to the destination window. Figure 6.6 shows a portion of a paragraph, blocked and ready to copy.

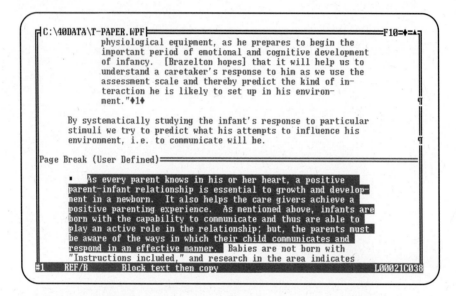

*Fig. 6.6. Source window with blocked text for interwindow copying.*

Finally, press Alt-F5 to finish the copy. Enable copies the blocked text from the source window to the cursor location in the destination window.

## Copying Marked Text between Windows

Copying marked text from one open word processing window to another open word processing window is similar to copying marked text within one window.

In the destination window, press

F10 **Edit Copy**

Enable prompts you to `Position cursor and press ENTER`. At this point, move your cursor to the place where you want the marked text to appear, and press Enter. Enable displays the copy screen. Press

      **Marked_text Another Accept**

As with a block copy, Enable displays the Interwindow Copy Options screen (refer to fig. 6.5). Press the number of the source window. The cursor moves to the source window, and Enable displays the message

    `Block text then copy`

in the status line. Mark the text you want to copy with the mark attribute, described in the section "Moving and Copying Marked Text within a File" in this chapter (see fig 6.7).

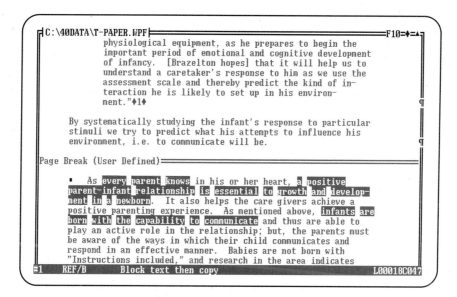

**Fig. 6.7.** *Marked text ready for interwindow copying.*

Press Alt-F5 to complete the copy. Enable copies the marked text to the destination window. The text appears in the same order as in the source window. Figure 6.8 shows the copied block of text shown in figure 6.6 and the copied marked text shown in figure 6.7.

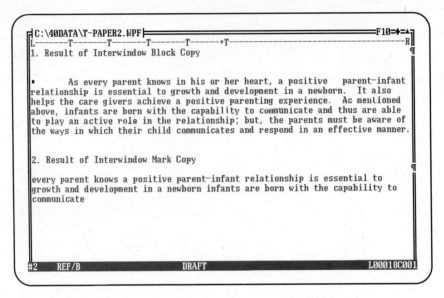

*Fig. 6.8. Results of interwindow block copy and interwindow mark copy.*

# Finding and Replacing Text

A common feature in good word processing programs is a text search capability. In fact, sometimes word processing programs are compared by how quickly they can find a certain word at the end of a long file. However, you can use a search capability to do many more things, including the following:

- Find a repeating word or phrase that you need to edit. In a book, for example, if you add a figure at the beginning of a chapter, you need to change all subsequent figure numbers. You can use Enable to search for the word *fig.* or *figure*, and then edit the figure numbers as Enable finds each occurrence.

- Find a specific section of a long file. When you edit a long file, you often think of something you need to change but don't know where to find it in the file. You can use Enable's search feature to find a word you know occurs in the area of the document you want to edit.

- Find and replace a word that occurs several times in a file. Enable's search feature has a versatile replace option you can use to replace a word or phrase with some other word or phrase. This feature can be especially useful when you want to save time by using text you originally typed for another purpose. If the older file refers to something that doesn't apply in the new file, you can use Enable to replace the inaccurate references.

- Find and mark text for later review or editing. In Enable, you can find text and mark it without making any permanent change. You can return to that text at another time and decide which changes to make in the marked text.

## Finding Text

To search for a word or string of words in a word processing file without replacing them, press

F9 **Find Text**

Enable displays the dialog box shown in figure 6.9.

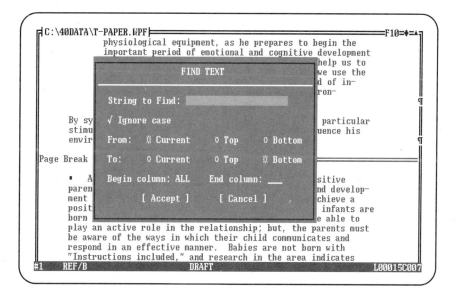

**Fig. 6.9.** *The Find Text dialog box.*

You have the option to choose the following settings:

- *String_to_Find*. At the prompt, type any alphanumeric text (letters and numbers) you want Enable to find and press Enter. This text is the *search string*.

- *Ignore_case*. Turn on this option if you want the search to find the text, regardless of case. For example, if you turn on this option and search for the word *costs*, Enable stops at all occurrences of either *Costs* or *costs*. If you leave this option off, Enable finds only the exact match, *costs*.

- *From*. By default, Enable starts the search from the current cursor position. Enable also can search from the top or bottom of the file; choose Current, Top, or Bottom.

- *To*. The end point of the search can be the top or bottom of the file, or the current cursor position. The default choice is Bottom. If you start the search at the bottom, however, you may want to search to the cursor; in that case, choose Current. To search from the cursor to the top of the file, choose Top.

- *Begin_column* and *End_column*. You usually want Enable to search the file from margin to margin—in other words, all columns of characters in the document. Thus, the default choice is to search all columns; simply press Enter at the two Column prompts. Occasionally, however, you may want to search in a restricted number of columns of text. To do so, type the starting column number (the current column number is displayed on the right side of the status line) at the Begin_column prompt, and the ending column number at the End_column prompt.

When finding text, Enable stops at the first occurrence of the text. If you want to edit this text, Enable is in normal edit mode for you to resume editing. To find the next occurrence of the text string, press F5. Enable tells you with a beep that the document has no more matching search strings in the direction of the search.

## Finding and Replacing Text

In Enable, you can replace text that occurs several times throughout the document with a new text string. Press

F9 **Find** **Replace**

Enable displays the Find and Replace Text dialog box, shown in figure 6.10.

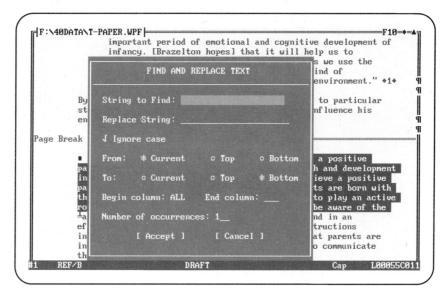

*Fig. 6.10. The Find and Replace Text dialog box.*

**TIP**

When replacing text, Enable does not adjust the case of the letters to fit the sentence. If the text you are replacing occurs sometimes in uppercase and sometimes in lowercase, you should conduct a find and replace operation for each variation of the search string.

All the options available in the find search are available in the find and replace search. In addition, you enter the *replacement string* (the text string you want to substitute for the search string) and the number of occurrences to replace.

To find the next occurrence of the search string without replacing it, press F5. You then can press F6 to replace the search string with the new text. With this two-step procedure, you can examine the search string in context before you replace it.

To replace the next occurrence of the search string without inspecting it, press F6 (rather than F5 and then F6). Enable finds and replaces the next occurrence of the search string in one step.

You also can make global replacements. Sometimes you know you want to edit every occurrence of a word or phrase the same way. To make a global replacement, enter ALL at the `Number of occurrences` prompt in the dialog box (see figure 6.10).

**CAUTION**

> Perform a separate find and replace operation for each variation of a search string in your document. Enable does not make adjustments for upper- and lowercase, plurals, or verb tense to match the words it replaces.

## Finding and Marking Text

You occasionally may want to mark text quickly for later reference. To find text and mark it with the mark attribute, press

    F9 **Find** **Mark**

Enter the search string and choose the appropriate search options, as described in the preceding sections. After Enable marks the search string, you can later edit the file at your own pace.

## Using Wild Cards

Using several different forms of a word can cause problems when you want to find a word, because you may not remember the exact form you used. In addition, sometimes you may search for a person's name in your document and forget how to spell the name. To help solve these problems, Enable has two wild-card characters that you can use to search for variations of the same root word.

The dollar sign ($) wild card represents up to nine characters and can be put in a search string at the beginning or end or both, but not in the middle.

To search for all words beginning with a certain root word, at the

```
String to Find
```

prompt type the root string followed by a dollar sign ($). For example, if you want to find all variations of the word *infant* in the file T-PAPER.WPF, shown in figure 6.11, enter **infant$**. With this search string, Enable finds occurrences of *infant*, *infants*, and *infantile*—but not *infancy*. If you also need to locate *infancy*, the search string should be *infan$*.

Similarly, you can search for all words that end with the same letters by beginning the search pattern with the wild card. To find both *verbal* and *nonverbal*, use the search string *$verbal*.

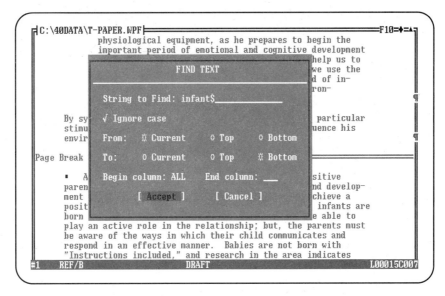

*Fig. 6.11. The Find Text dialog box for a wild card search.*

The second wild-card character is the question mark (?). This character takes the place of only one character in a search pattern. You can use the question mark (?) at the beginning, at the end, or in the middle of a search string.

You usually use the question mark to narrow the search pattern somewhat. For example, to search the file T-PAPER.WPF for *infants* but not *infantile*, type **infant?**. You can use more than one question mark in a search string to take the place of a corresponding number of characters. Thus, *infan??* finds *infants* and *infancy*, but not *infant* or *infantile*.

You can find more variations by using the dollar sign followed by a number. The search string *infan$2* finds all words beginning with *infan* and ending with zero, one, or two other characters. This search string finds *infant*. On the other hand, *infan??* finds only words that begin with the string *infan* and end with two other letters. Because the word *infant* does not match this pattern, the search does not find it.

# Sorting in Word Processing

The Enable/OA word processing module has a sort feature you can use to rearrange a document by sorting lines and even paragraphs of text. You can best understand this feature through an example. Use the FILEDIR.WPF (the file you used in Chapter 4 to copy a file-name listing into a word processing file) for a demonstration of the line sorting feature of the word processing module.

# Sorting Lines of Text

To sort lines of text, the text first must be arranged in columns, like information in reports often is. Sorting lines is not the same as moving columns, however. When you sort lines, you change the order of the entries for all columns. For example, you may decide you want the file-name list, FILEDIR.WPF (see fig. 6.12), in order by the file extensions, rather than by the root file names.

```
┌─ C:\40DATA\FILEDIR.WPF ════════════════════════════════════ F10=♦=▲┐
│ FONTS     WPF     7203 07-10-90                                      │
│ HAWAII    GAF     3305 02-12-91                                      │
│ HAWAII    WPF     3446 03-17-91                                      │
│ HNGINDT   WPF      896 03-03-91                                      │
│ LABEL     TSG     1377 10-12-88                                      │
│ LETTER    TSG     1144 10-12-88                                      │
│ M         MC       698 03-17-91                                      │
│ MAIL      $BF     3072 01-05-90                                      │
│ MAIL      DBF     1024 01-14-90                                      │
│ MAILIN    $IF     4096 10-04-84                                      │
│ MATHSIM   SSF     3072 03-04-91                                      │
│ NONAME    SSF      512 02-12-91                                      │
│ NONAME    WPF      930 03-04-91                                      │
│ NTEGAF    LOG      140 03-17-91                                      │
│ PROFILE   $PR     3584 12-21-90                                      │
│ QS3LTR    WPF      521 02-12-91                                      │
│ QS4BUDGT  SSF     1024 03-04-91                                      │
│ RANGES    SSF     1536 03-04-91                                      │
│ SALES     SSF     2048 03-04-91                                      │
│ SAMPLE    WPF      974 03-17-91                                      │
│ SIDEWAYS  WPF     1278 11-13-90                                      │
│ SIMPSTAT  SSF     2048 03-04-91                                      │
│ SIMPTEXT  SSF     2048 03-04-91                                      │
│ #1    REF/B                 DRAFT                    L00044C001      │
└─────────────────────────────────────────────────────────────────────┘
```

*Fig. 6.12. The file directory FILEDIR.WPF in order by root file names.*

Field start and field length are the two factors that determine which text is to be sorted. You can think of the term field as equivalent to the term column. The FILEDIR.WPF file, shown in figure 6.12, has four columns, or fields.

The sort in FILEDIR.WPF is by file name. To rearrange the rows and place them in order by the file name extension, press

F10 **T**ools **S**ort **D**efine_keys

Enable displays the dialog box shown in figure 6.13, with the following choices:

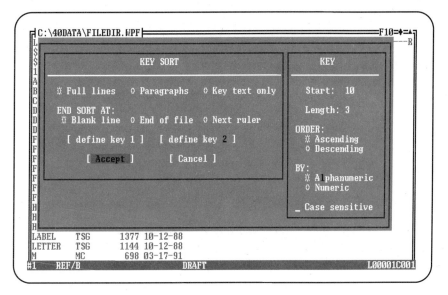

**Fig. 6.13.** *The Key Sort dialog box.*

- *Sort Type.* You can sort by Full_lines or by Paragraphs, or by Key_text_only. For this example choose Full_lines.

- *END_SORT_AT.* Use this option to select how much text you want to sort. You can sort to the next blank line, to the end of the file, or to the next ruler.

- *Define_key_1.* Use this option to enter the following key information:

  ° *Start* (of key word). Enter the column of the first character of the key word.

  ° *Length* (of key word). The length of a field is the number of spaces from the tab stop that begins the field to the next tab stop. You must tell Enable the number of characters in the key-word field to consider during the sort. The default length is 10, but Enable can sort fields up to 160 characters long.

  ° *Order.* Enable sorts either in Ascending (*a* to *z* and 0 to 9) or Descending order. Enable sorts all uppercase letters before lowercase letters when the sort is ascending.

○ *By*. You can choose to have Enable sort alphanumeric or numeric text. If you choose numeric, Enable does not sort any nonnumeric text; you therefore should choose this option only if you are sorting a column of numbers.

○ *Case_sensitive*. If you choose this option, Enable sorts uppercase letters before lowercase letters. For example, Andrew sorts before alien, even though "al" normally sorts before "an" in ascending order.

- *Define_key_2*. Choose this option to enter secondary key information, using the same options as key 1. Enable sorts on key 2 whenever two key 1 values are the same; you can think of key 2 as a "tie-breaker."

In the example, the sort is by line, in ascending order, from the top of the file, with key 1 starting on 10 and having a key length of 3, and with key 2 starting on 1 and having a key length of 8. Figure 6.14 shows the file name list, sorted by extension.

```
C:\40DATA\FILEDIR.WPF                                    F10=◆=▲
L────────T────────T────────T────────T────────+T────────────R
FINANCE   $BF      5120 01-14-90
MAIL      $BF      3072 01-05-90
FINANCE   $IF      3584 01-14-90
MAILIN    $IF      4096 10-04-84
PROFILE   $PR      3584 12-21-90
DBMSDEF   $RF      5632 08-03-90
TPSETUP   $TP      2560 03-13-89
MAIL      DBF      1024 01-14-90
HAWAII    GAF      3305 02-12-91
M         MC        698 03-17-91
FINEMPID  NDX      1024 01-13-90
FINLAST   NDX      1024 01-13-90
FINST     NDX      1024 01-13-90
AGENTS    SSF      5632 02-27-91
FINANCE   SSF      7168 03-17-91
MATHSIM   SSF      3072 03-04-91
NONAME    SSF       512 02-12-91
QS4BUDGT  SSF      1024 03-04-91
RANGES    SSF      1536 03-04-91
SALES     SSF      2048 03-04-91
SIMPSTAT  SSF      2048 03-04-91
SIMPTEXT  SSF      2048 03-04-91
#1    REF/B               DRAFT                     L00001C001
```

*Fig. 6.14. FILEDIR.WPF sorted by file name extension.*

To sort the list of file names shown in figure 6.14 in descending order by file size, press

F10 **T**ools **S**ort **D**efine_keys

Fill in the options as described in the preceding example, but change key 1 to start at 17 and make the field length 7. The sort is in descending order, numeric, and not case-sensitive. Figure 6.15 shows the result of this sort.

```
C:\40DATA\FILEDIR.WPF                                        F10=↕=▲
L--------T--------T--------T--------T------+T--------------------------R
SYMBOLS   SSF     14848 07-05-90
DEMOWORD  WPF      8310 03-03-91
FONTS     WPF      7203 07-10-90
FINANCE   SSF      7168 03-17-91
DOCFORM   WPF      6272 06-01-90
COLUMNS   WPF      6225 03-01-91
DBMSDEF   $RF      5632 08-03-90
AGENTS    SSF      5632 02-27-91
FINANCE   $BF      5120 01-14-90
MAILIN    $IF      4096 10-04-84
T-PAPER   WPF      3923 03-04-91
PROFILE   $PR      3584 12-21-90
FINANCE   $IF      3584 01-14-90
HAWAII    WPF      3446 03-17-91
HAWAII    GAF      3305 02-12-91
MATHSIM   SSF      3072 03-04-91
MAIL      $BF      3072 01-05-90
WIDGETS   SSF      2560 03-04-91
TRIGSIMP  SSF      2560 03-04-91
TPSETUP   $TP      2560 03-13-89
SIMPTEXT  SSF      2048 03-04-91
SIMPSTAT  SSF      2048 03-04-91
#1    REF/B                   DRAFT                          L00022C001
```

**Fig. 6.15.** *FILEDIR.WPF sorted in descending order by file size.*

# Sorting Paragraphs

For the sort feature, a *paragraph* is any text or spaces between two paragraph symbols. Enable can sort using entire paragraphs as the keyword field. For Enable to sort correctly, your file should have no blank lines between paragraphs. This feature is most useful for reordering several text paragraphs at once.

To rearrange a file, you can number the paragraphs in the new order, as shown in figure 6.16, and sort the paragraphs by the new numbers (see fig. 6.17) by pressing

F10 **T**ools **S**ort **D**efine_keys

Then press Enter. Choose Paragraph and Accept.

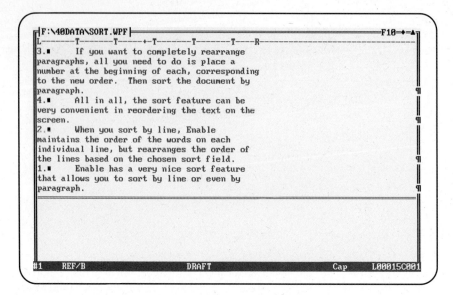

*Fig. 6.16. Paragraphs numbered in a new order.*

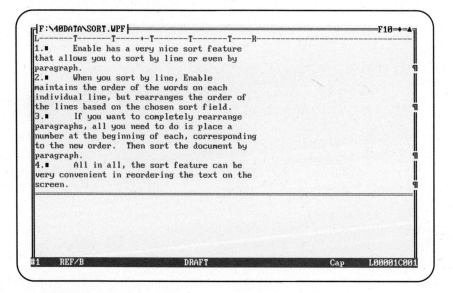

*Fig. 6.17. SORT.WPF with paragraphs in the new order.*

# Using the Dictionary Features

No matter how many times you proofread a report, often you can overlook a misspelled word or two. With Enable's word processing module, that need never happen again. You can use Enable/Check, Enable's built-in spelling checker, to check spelling in a word processing document.

If you use legal, medical, or other unique jargon in your writing, you can use Enable/OA's special legal, medical, and multiple-user dictionaries, which include many new words.

To use Enable/Check, press

F9 **E**xpert **C**heck **T**otal_file

Enable displays the Spell Check dialog box, as shown in figure 6.18. If you accept the default options, Enable starts the spelling check from the top of the file, uses the standard Proximity/Merriam-Webster Linguibase master dictionary and any user-created dictionary found in the normal Enable data directory, and stops at word duplications.

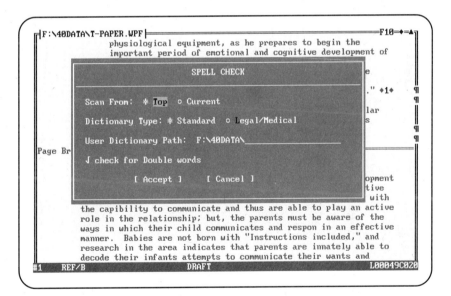

***Fig. 6.18.*** *The Spell Check dialog box.*

The available Spell Check dialog box options are as follows:

- *Scan_From*. Normally Enable checks for misspelled and duplicated words from the Top of the file. If you previously checked part of the file, you can choose to start the check from the Current cursor position.

- *Dictionary_Type*. Check most documents against Enable's normal standard dictionary; however, if your file contains legal or medical terminology, you can choose one of the specialized professional dictionaries.

- *User_Dictionary_Path*. If more than one person routinely uses your computer, you each can have a separate Enable/Check user-created dictionary. Indicate the drive and directory of the user-created dictionary you want Enable to use. If Enable does not find a word in the master dictionary, it looks for the word in this dictionary.

- *Check_for_Double_words*. Unless you deselect this option, Enable stops when a word appears more than once in a row (such as the the). Whenever it stops at such a probable error, Enable asks you whether to remove or ignore the word duplication.

After you accept the default options or choose from the preceding choices, Enable begins checking the spelling in the document. When Enable finds an unfamiliar word, it stops and gives you the following choices, shown in figure 6.19:

- *0. Enter Replacement*. Choose this option if you want to type the correct spelling of the word. *Note:* Because Enable doesn't check the replacement against its dictionaries, be sure you don't misspell the replacement.

- *1. Choose Replacement*. Choose this option to cause Enable to search its built-in dictionary for a probable correct spelling, and then search any user-created dictionary. Enable then suggests as many as ten replacements (see fig. 6.20). You also have the option to replace all occurrences of this misspelling with the replacement word.

- *2. Ignore EVERY Occurrence*. Choose this option if you know that the word is spelled correctly, but you don't want to add it to your user-created dictionary. For example, you may not want to add a proper name to your user-created dictionary, but you don't want Enable to stop at every occurrence.

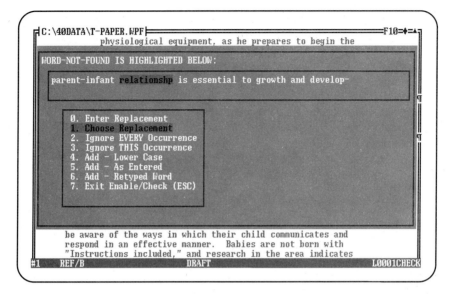

**Fig. 6.19.** *Spelling check options.*

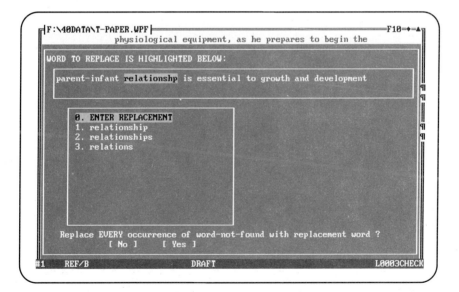

**Fig. 6.20.** *Suggested replacements for a misspelled word.*

- *3. Ignore THIS Occurrence*. Choose this option if you know that the word is spelled correctly, and you want to skip this occurrence without adding it to your user-created dictionary.

- *4. Add - Lower Case*. Choose this option to add, in lowercase, correctly spelled words that aren't part of Enable's dictionary and that can be used properly in upper- or lowercase.

- *5. Add - As Entered*. Choose this option to add, as entered, words that must be in all uppercase, such as acronyms (DOS), or words with certain letters in uppercase, such as proper names."

- *6. Add - Retyped Word*. Choose this option if you want to retype the word and add it to your user-created dictionary.

- *7. Exit Enable/Check*. Choose this option to quit the spelling check before you reach the end of the file.

Keep in mind that Enable can identify most misspelled words, but it cannot read. If you use the wrong word but spell it correctly, Enable won't catch the mistake. Don't give up proofreading your work just because Enable checks your spelling for you.

When Enable/Check stops at duplicated words, it displays the menu shown in figure 6.21. The Word Duplication menu offers you the following three choices:

- *1. Delete Duplication*

- *2. Ignore Error*

- *3. Exit Enable/Check (ESC)*

When you complete or exit the spelling check, Enable displays the Enable/Check Summary screen (see fig. 6.22). This screen shows a count of the words checked, the duplicated words, the words Enable could not find, the corrections made, and the words added to the user-created dictionary. Press Esc to leave this screen.

After you check the spelling in your document, remember to save the document to disk. If Enable/Check made any corrections, it made them on-screen only and not on the disk. Just as you should save after any editing, save the changes made during the spelling check, or you lose them when you clear the file from the screen.

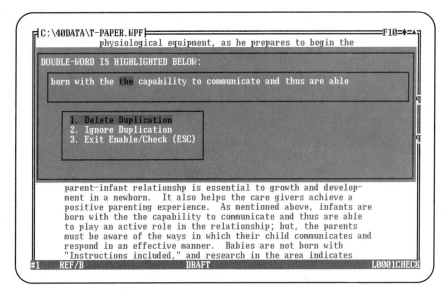

*Fig. 6.21. The Word Duplication menu.*

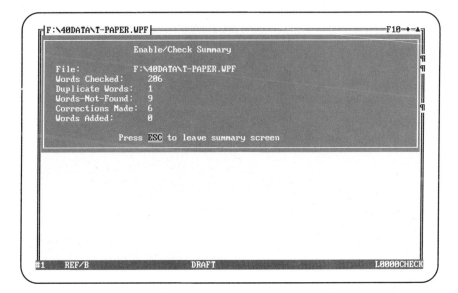

*Fig. 6.22. The Enable/Check Summary screen.*

In Enable/OA 4.0, you can use Enable/Check to check the spelling of a single word or to run a spelling check in blocked text or marked text. Press

F9 Expert Spell_Check Word

# Maintaining the User-Created Dictionary

Whatever your profession or avocation, you use words in writing or correspondence that are not in Enable's built-in dictionary. The preceding section on Enable/Check describes how you can add these words to a special user-created dictionary that supplements the built-in dictionary.

What do you do if you have a long list of unique terms and you don't want to wait for Enable/Check to add them one at a time? If you added a misspelled word to the user-created dictionary, how can you correct the error? In Enable, you can add, edit, or delete words within the user-created dictionary.

To display the current user-created dictionary, you must be at Enable's Main Menu. Then choose

Tools Dictionary

Enable displays the dialog box shown in figure 6.23, with the following options:

- *Type.* Enter the type of dictionary. If you have installed a foreign language dictionary, you may choose the proper language.

- *User Dictionary Path.* You can keep more than one user-created dictionary, each in a different directory. Usually you have only one such dictionary, stored in the default data directory. If so, press Enter. If you have not added any words to the user-created dictionary, Enable displays a blank word processing screen. Otherwise, Enable displays a list such as the one shown in figure 6.24.

You can type new words into your dictionary, like any word processing screen. Begin all the words at the left margin and remember to press the Enter key after each word. Notice that the automatic reformat feature is off. If you want to delete a word from the user-created dictionary, move the cursor to the line with the word, and press Alt-F3.

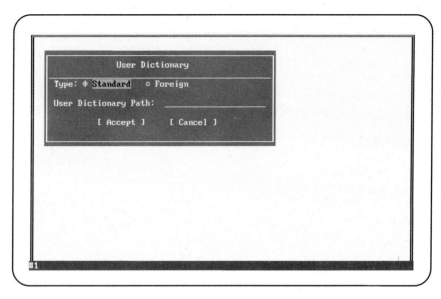

**Fig. 6.23.** *The User Dictionary dialog box.*

```
┌─┤F:\40DATA\USERDI__.TSG├────────────────────────────F10=◆=▲─┐
│L────────T────────T────────T────────T───────+T──────────────R│
│add                                                          ¶│
│do                                                           ¶│
│database                                                     ¶│
│gosub                                                        ¶│
│body                                                         ¶│
│position                                                     ¶│
│else                                                         ¶│
│screenpos                                                    ¶│
│subroutines                                                  ¶│
│elseif                                                       ¶│
│if                                                           ¶│
│endcase                                                      ¶│
│endif                                                        ¶│
│endwhile                                                     ¶│
│intro                                                        ¶│
│Enable                                                       ¶│
│while                                                        ¶│
│let                                                          ¶│
│label                                                        ¶│
│case                                                         ¶│
│conclusion                                                   ¶│
│color                                                        ¶│
│#1      /B              DRAFT              Cap      L00002C001 │
└──────────────────────────────────────────────────────────────┘
```

**Fig. 6.24.** *A user-created dictionary.*

To use a list of words from another word processing file, use the interwindow copy procedure explained in the section "Copying Text between Windows" to copy the list into this file.

After you make any additions, deletions, or corrections, save the file as you do any word processing file. Press

Alt-F10

Press Alt-End to quit the dictionary file.

## Using the Thesaurus

Enable/OA has a built-in *thesaurus* that displays a list of words with meanings similar to the chosen word. Writers find that this feature is a real benefit. To look up the meaning of the word at the cursor, simply press

F9 **Expert Thesaurus**

Enable gives you a list of possible definitions for the word. Press the number next to the best definition for this context, and Enable's thesaurus displays three lists of words: synonyms, related words, and contrasting words. The following prompt that displays at the bottom of the pop-up screen explains the process:

```
Use cursor keys to select a word; Press ENTER to lookup
selected word, INSERT to insert into document, ESC to
pick another definition.
```

## Using Automatic Hyphenation

Enable/OA has a built-in right-justification feature that adds spaces to create an even right margin. Many people, however, don't care for the odd spacing between words that results. Another way to straighten the right margin somewhat is to hyphenate words that otherwise drop down to the next line, thereby using as many spaces as possible on each line. Enable/OA has an automatic hyphenation feature that you can use as you type the text or after you type it. The latter method is probably the most efficient for most users.

Enable/OA includes automatic hyphenation as a feature of the ruler, which establishes the margins and tab settings. Enable/OA inserts hyphens according to the built-in Proximity/Merriam-Webster Linguibase dictionary.

To force Enable/OA to insert hyphens automatically, define a hyphenation zone in the ruler as follows:

1. Position the cursor on the line below the current ruler, and press Alt-F6 to insert a new ruler line for modification.

2. Press the right-arrow key or the Tab key to move the cursor to the right margin.

3. Press the left-arrow key to move about five spaces to the left of the right margin.

4. Press either **z** or **Z** and press Enter.

As soon as you press Enter, Enable begins to reformat all text from this ruler to the next ruler or to the end of the file. If possible, Enable hyphenates any words that extend across this zone. Words that begin to the right of this zone and go past the right margin, wrap to the next line.

If you press the lowercase letter **z**, Enable hyphenates all words without your assistance, according to the built-in dictionary. If you use **Z**, Enable still hyphenates most words without your assistance, but if it cannot tell where to hyphenate a word, Enable displays a prompt in the status line similar to the one shown in figure 6.25, asking for your help. (The word may not be in the text on-screen.) Brackets ([ ]) surround the part of the word that extends beyond the right margin. The hyphen displays in a suggested position but usually is before the word, meaning that Enable does not hyphenate this word unless you show it how.

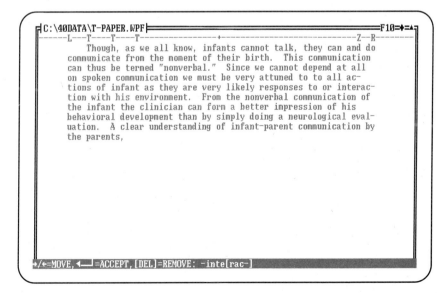

**Fig. 6.25.** *A file with a prompt for hyphenation in the status line.*

Use the right- and left-arrow keys to move the hyphen to the correct position, and then press Enter. To force the entire word to the next line without hyphenating it, press the Del key.

**TIP**

Enable/Check does not accept hyphenated words; it stops at each one, displaying the message, Word-Not-Found. To avoid this message, add the hyphenation after you check the spelling of your document. You really don't need to worry about a straight right margin until you are ready to print your final version.

If you need to check the spelling again after you add the hyphenation zone to the ruler, just redo the ruler, deleting the Z; Enable deletes the hyphenation. Check the spelling, and then replace the hyphenation zone.

# Summary

In this chapter, you see how Enable's power editing features can help save you time in creating a document. Use as many as these features as you can, and you learn to appreciate the power of a word processing program.

# Using Formatting Features

C hapter 5, "Understanding Word Processing Basics," and Chapter 6, "Using Word Processing Advanced Features," explain how to enter text and then copy it, move it, search for it, sort it, and correct it. This chapter discusses the format, or layout, of the text—margins, tabs, columns, line spacing, print settings, and text attributes—rather than the content of the text.

## Using Rulers

With Enable's word processing module, you can create multiple rulers, each with different margins and tabs. You can establish a default ruler in the system profile, and you also can insert a custom ruler anywhere in the document. Enable uses the ruler to set character alignment and newspaper-style columns. In this section, you learn how to use Enable's rulers and how to use the codes on the rulers to set margins and tabs.

### Inserting and Changing Rulers

Enable offers four ways to insert and change rulers:

- Modify the initial default ruler. Whenever you open a new word processing file, Enable prompts you either to accept or to change the margins and tabs on the default ruler (see fig. 7.1). Enable sets the tabs and margins on the default ruler according to the ruler settings in the current system profile. (See Appendix B, "Using Profiles to Customize Enable," to change the default settings of this ruler.) You press Enter or Esc to accept the default ruler, but if you want to use different margin settings, change the ruler and press Enter.

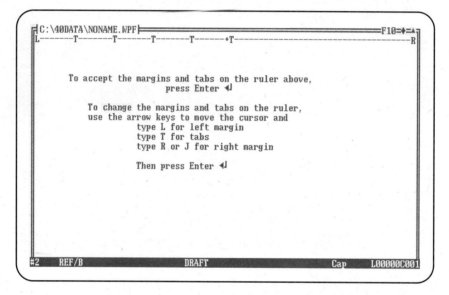

**Fig. 7.1.** *The new ruler prompt.*

- Change the current ruler. To modify the *current ruler* (the ruler for the text that you currently are editing), position the cursor on the ruler and press Alt-F6. Enable places your cursor on the first character of the ruler line. Make your changes, and press Enter. Enable reformats all existing and new text according to the settings of this new, modified ruler, from this location to the following ruler. The following sections, "Setting Margins" and "Setting Tabs," discuss faster ways to change the current ruler.

- Insert a copy of the current ruler. If you are making changes to a section of text, you may want to insert a copy of the current ruler to protect the rest of the document from being reformatted according to the new ruler. To make a copy of the current ruler, position the cursor where you want to insert the new ruler, and press Alt-F6. Make any changes and press Enter. Enable formats all new and existing text down to the next ruler according to these settings.

- Insert a copy of the default ruler. To insert a default ruler rather than the current ruler, position the cursor on the line below where you want to insert the ruler, and press

    F10 **Layout Rulers Default**

    Enable displays the message `Position cursor and press Enter`. Because you already have positioned the cursor, press Enter. Enable then inserts a default ruler. Make any changes, and press Enter to confirm your adjustments.

## Setting Margins

To set or change the left or right margin, use one of the methods listed in "Inserting and Changing Rulers" to access the ruler. Then press any of the following codes in the ruler:

| Code | Margin |
| --- | --- |
| L | To set the left margin |
| R | To set the right margin |
| J | To set a *justified* (evenly aligned) right margin |

You can press any of these keys as often as you want because they do not take effect until you press Enter; however, each time you press one of these keys, Enable removes any previously set margin on the corresponding side of the ruler. Thus, you never have more than one R or L on the ruler. You also never have both a J and an R on the ruler at the same time.

You can use a quick method to change either margin, without even using one of the ruler insertion methods. Position the cursor in the column where you want the new margin to begin, and press one of the following keystroke commands:

| Keystroke Command | Margin |
| --- | --- |
| Alt-L | To set a new left margin |
| Alt-R | To set a new right margin |
| Alt-J | To set a new justified right margin |

If the cursor is on the ruler when you issue the keystroke command, Enable modifies the current ruler. If the cursor is within the text when you issue the keystroke command, Enable inserts a new ruler. The new margin settings apply to all new and existing text that follows this ruler.

## Temporary Margins

To set a temporary margin for an entire paragraph, move the cursor to the column where you want to locate the temporary margin and press Alt-H. Then type the paragraph. After you press Enter, the left margin returns to the one set on the ruler.

## Hanging Indents

You often may want to emphasize or set apart text by indenting it several spaces from the left margin. Although you can insert a new ruler for each indented paragraph, Enable has a more convenient feature, a *hanging indent*, which indents the second and following lines of a paragraph.

To create a hanging indent five spaces from the left margin, type the first five letters of the paragraph, and then press Alt-H to set a temporary left margin. As you type the rest of the paragraph, Enable wraps text in the second and subsequent lines of the paragraph to the temporary margin (see fig. 7.2). When you press Enter, the left margin returns to the position set on the ruler.

> When you create a hanging indent by setting a temporary left margin, you must press Enter to return the left margin to the position that is set on the ruler. If you move your cursor to a new location in your document before you press Enter, the temporary left margin remains active.

# Setting Tabs

Typists often set tab stops where they need to type address blocks, signature blocks, and columns of text. Tab settings on typewriters can align columns along only the left edge of the column; however, you may want to align columns along the right edge of the column or, if you want to align numbers, on a decimal point.

When you press the Tab key, Enable stores a tab character in that position in the text. One of the profile options enables you to display this tab character on-screen. The character appears as a block-shaped character each time you press the Tab key (see fig. 7.3). Whether or not you display this character, it exists in the file and causes the text that follows this character to start at the next available tab stop. You automatically can adjust text, therefore, by moving, adding, and deleting tab stop characters.

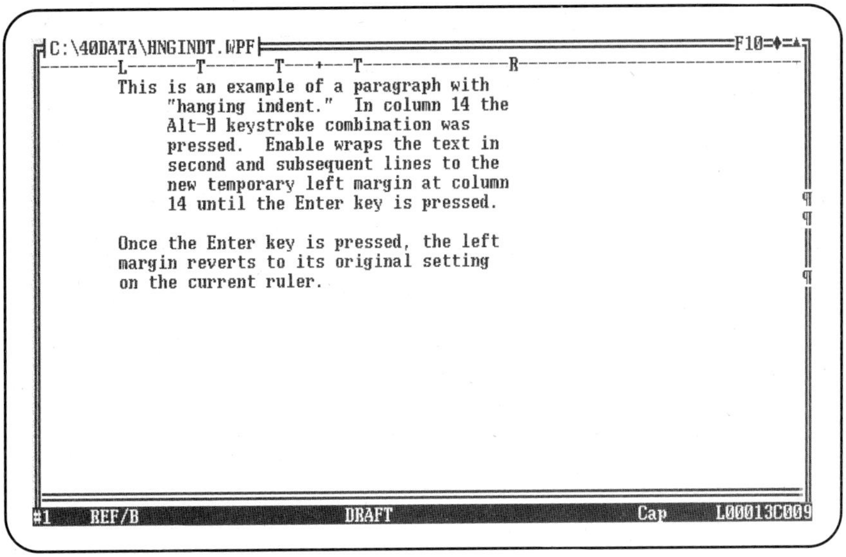

```
 C:\40DATA\HNGINDT.WPF                                    F10=◆=▲
      L------T------T----+---T------------R------
         This is an example of a paragraph with
         "hanging indent."  In column 14 the
         Alt-H keystroke combination was
         pressed.  Enable wraps the text in
         second and subsequent lines to the
         new temporary left margin at column
         14 until the Enter key is pressed.               ¶
                                                          ¶
         Once the Enter key is pressed, the left
         margin reverts to its original setting
         on the current ruler.                            ¶




#1    REF/B                   DRAFT              Cap    L00013C009
```

**Fig. 7.2.** *A hanging indent.*

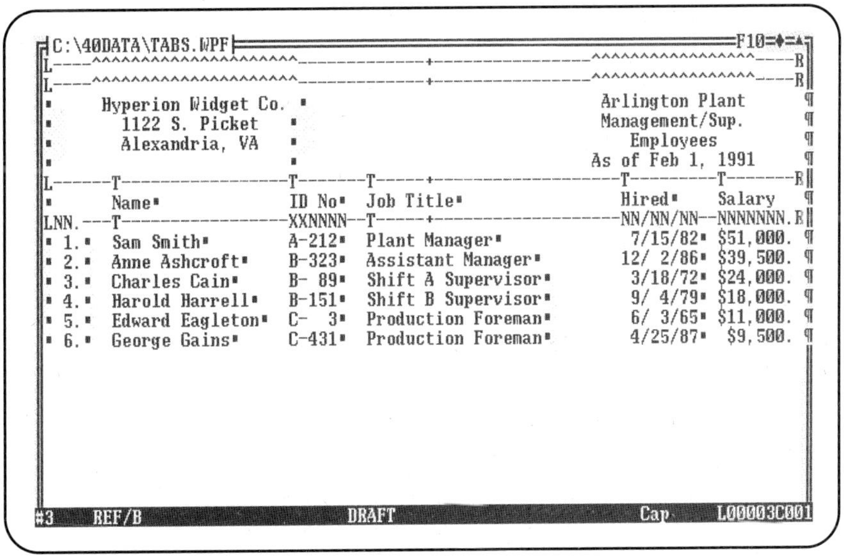

```
 C:\40DATA\TABS.WPF                                       F10=◆=▲
L  ^^^^^^^^^^^^^^^^^^^^^^^^^_____+_____   ^^^^^^^^^^^^^^^^_____R
L  ^^^^^^^^^^^^^^^^^^^^^^^^^_____+_____   ^^^^^^^^^^^^^^^^_____R
  ■      Hyperion Widget Co. ■                     Arlington Plant    ¶
  ■        1122 S. Picket      ■                   Management/Sup.    ¶
  ■        Alexandria, VA      ■                   Employees          ¶
  ■                            ■                   As of Feb 1, 1991  ¶
L------T-----------------T------T-----+----------T---------T-----R
  ■     Name■           ID No■  Job Title■        Hired■   Salary■  ¶
LNN.---T-----------------XXNNNN-T-----+----------NN/NN/NN--NNNNNNN.R
  ■  1. ■  Sam Smith■         A-212■  Plant Manager■        7/15/82■ $51,000. ¶
  ■  2. ■  Anne Ashcroft■     B-323■  Assistant Manager■   12/ 2/86■ $39,500. ¶
  ■  3. ■  Charles Cain■      B- 89■  Shift A Supervisor■   3/18/72■ $24,000. ¶
  ■  4. ■  Harold Harrell■    B-151■  Shift B Supervisor■   9/ 4/79■ $18,000. ¶
  ■  5. ■  Edward Eagleton■   C-  3■  Production Foreman■    6/ 3/65■ $11,000. ¶
  ■  6. ■  George Gains■      C-431■  Production Foreman■   4/25/87■  $9,500. ¶




#3    REF/B                   DRAFT              Cap    L00003C001
```

**Fig. 7.3.** *Tab settings.*

One benefit of Enable's tab character is that you can insert tabs after you have typed the text. When you press the Tab key in insert mode, all existing text in the line moves one tab to the right. Conversely, if you delete a tab character, any text that follows it moves back one tab to the left.

Enable provides not only the traditional tab stop but also several tab stop options that allow other types of text alignment. Enable even has a special tab setting for centering text. To set or change the tab settings, use one of the methods listed in the section "Inserting and Changing Rulers" to access the ruler. You can use the following codes on the ruler line:

- Press **T** to set a normal tab stop. To set a tab that is like the tab on a traditional typewriter, press **T** on the ruler line or Alt-T within the text. While you type your document, press the Tab key to jump the cursor to the next tab stop or, if no more tab stops are on that line, to the right margin. Columns aligned with this tab are left-aligned. Press Shift-Tab to move the cursor to the left, one tab stop at a time.

- Press **P** to set automatic paragraph indentation. First place the cursor on the ruler line in the column where you want each paragraph to indent from the left margin. Press **P** on the ruler line to set the initial tab setting, called the *auto-indentation tab*, for each new paragraph. The ruler shows the character (¶). Every time you press Enter, Enable automatically indents the new paragraph by aligning the cursor under the (¶) on the ruler line. Figure 7.4 shows an example of the auto-indentation tab.

- Press ^ to set a *centering tab*. Use the caret (^) to create on the ruler line an area that centers text. Normally you center text by pressing Alt-F4, which centers the entire line. To create a separate area in which you want centered text, type carets on the ruler line to specify the location and width of the area of centered text. To use the feature in a document, press Tab until the cursor is in the caret area, and then type the text you want to center. As you type, Enable centers the text beneath the carets (again see fig. 7.3, which shows two centering tab areas).

- Press **N** to set a numeric tab. To right-align a column of numbers at a decimal point, press N for each possible digit in a column of numbers plus one more N for the decimal place (even if you don't type a decimal). To use this tab setting in a document, press the Tab key until the cursor is beneath the rightmost N. Then type the number. Enable lines up the number as if the rightmost N is a decimal point by "backing up" to the left of the decimal as you type numbers.

After you type a decimal point, Enable moves any numbers you type to the right of the decimal point; thus, any decimal point you type lines up under the rightmost N. Any text you type jumps to the right of the numeric tab area, except the following characters (again see fig. 7.3):

( [ { + $ # ' "

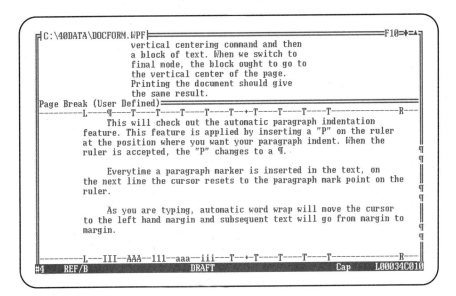

*Fig. 7.4. The auto-indentation tab.*

- Press **X** to set an alphanumeric tab. Press X for each possible letter or number in a column. This type of tab right-aligns text at the rightmost X, instead of left-aligning it like a normal tab aligns text at the T.

- Press any of the following keys to set alignment tabs:

. ; : | / \ ) } ]

Alignment tabs right justify characters until you press the alignment symbol; then the text you type follows the alignment symbol. To set the alignment tab, insert one of them after an N or an X. The column titled Hired in figure 7.3 shows the slash (/) used in this manner.

# Using Columns

With Enable's column feature, you can create text columns within your word processing file. These columns can be either newspaper-style *snaking columns* or independent *side-by-side columns*. Enable automatically splits snaking columns to fill the page; side-by-side columns are independent and do not continue into the next column. While in draft mode, Enable does not split the text into two columns. You must switch to final mode to view the columns side by side.

## Snaking Columns

To create a newspaper-style word processing file, you need to use the snaking column feature. To create a snaking column, press

> F10 Layout Columns **Define_column_ruler**

Position the cursor at the start of the snaking columns, and press Enter. Enable displays the SNAKING COLUMNS dialog box (see fig. 7.5), which enables you to change the options that follow:

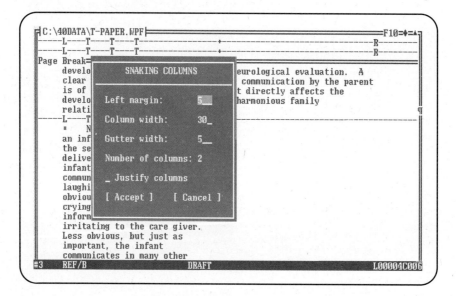

*Fig. 7.5. The SNAKING COLUMNS dialog box.*

- *Left_margin.* Enter the left margin for the snaking columns.

- *Column_width.* Enter the character width of each column. Note that each column will be of equal width.

- *Gutter_width.* Enter the number of character spaces you want between each set of columns.

- *Number_of_columns.* Enter the number of columns you want across the page.

- *Justify_columns.* If you want each column to have a right-justified margin, press Enter; otherwise, press Tab to continue.

After you choose Accept to confirm the snaking columns options, Enable inserts a new ruler. Figure 7.6 shows in draft mode a ruler created for two columns, and figure 7.7 shows the result in final mode. On the ruler line, the L represents the left margin of the first column, the R represents the right margin of the first column, and the C represents the left margin of the second column.

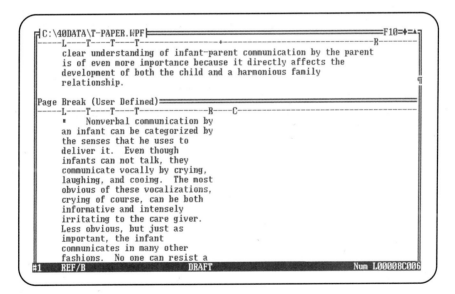

**Fig.** *7.6. Columns in draft mode.*

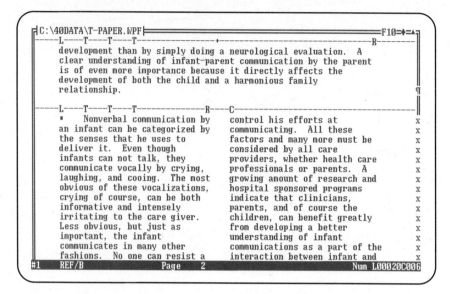

*Fig. 7.7. Columns in final mode.*

# Side-By-Side Columns

Side-by-side columns enable you to have independent columns that do not "snake" within a word processing file. Unlike snaking columns, which are all the same width, side-by-side columns can be any width. Side-by-side columns work well for lists (see fig. 7.8). Although you can achieve the same result with tabs, side-by-side columns enable you to type multiple lines without worrying about reformatting each line. To define side-by-side columns, you must insert a special multiple-column ruler.

To create a multiple-column ruler, move your cursor to the location at which you want the side-by-side columns to begin, and press Alt-F6 to insert a new ruler. With your cursor on the ruler, press L to set the left margin and R to set the right margin (J for justified) of the first column. Then, without pressing Enter, press F3 to set the left margin of the second column. Enable displays the characters ö2 on the ruler. Press R or J to set the right margin of the second column. Continue this procedure until you define all the columns you want. If you want to change the position of a left or right margin, use the Ins and Del keys to move the margins before you press Enter. After you press Enter, Enable inserts the new ruler and automatically generates the first section of field breaks (see fig. 7.9).

```
╓═C:\40DATA\COLUMNS.WPF════════════════════════════════════F10=◆=▲═╖
║       This is a document which demonstrates side by side columns and
║       columns with justified text.  There have been 5 columns set on
║       this ruler and sample information typed into each field. In order
║       to see what it will look like, invoke Final mode (F9 O D) or, if
║       you have a printer connected to your machine, print it out (F10 F
║       P P).
║
║L───────+──────R───ö2─────────────────────r───ö3──────r───ö4──r──ö5──r────║
║Name              Address                  Phone      Sch.   Gr.       x
║                                                                       x
║Joseph Adams      5 Main Street, Albany    439-2286   HS2    11        x
║                  Apartment 3B                                         x
║                                                                       x
║Marie Vecchio     32 Elm Street, San Diego 452-5296   HS1    9         x
║                  Suite 200                                            x
║                                                                       x
║Alec Czerny       49 Maple Ave., New Orleans 452-4391 ES3    3         x
║                                                                       x
║Jean Baker        123 State Street, Dallas 439-2080   ES3    5         x
║                                                                       x
║Lawrence Grady    21 Elm Street, Chicago   432-5147   MS2    7         x
║                  Apartment 2A                                         x
║                                                                       x
╟─────────────────────────────────────────────────────────────────────────╢
║#1    REF/B              Page    1                    Cap    L00034C001
╙───────────────────────────────────────────────────────────────────────────╜
```

*Fig. 7.8. Side-by-side columns.*

Depending on the use of the current ruler, you may want to use the default ruler to set up side-by-side columns. For example, if you use the ruler for snaking columns and it has C's on it, you must clear all the C's before you can press F3 and enter a field break.

**TIP**

When you use side-by-side columns, Enable contains the text for each column in a *field break*. The margins for each field break are governed by corresponding sections on the ruler line. In figure 7.9, for example, Field Break #1 corresponds to the space between L and R on the ruler line, Field Break #2 corresponds to the space between ö2 and r, and so on. Enable reformats text in each field break according its margins. Before typing, be sure your cursor is in the correct field break.

To insert a new section of field breaks, press

**F10** Layout Columns Item_break_insert

Position the cursor where you want to insert the new field break section, and press Enter. Enable inserts a new section of field breaks (see fig. 7.10).

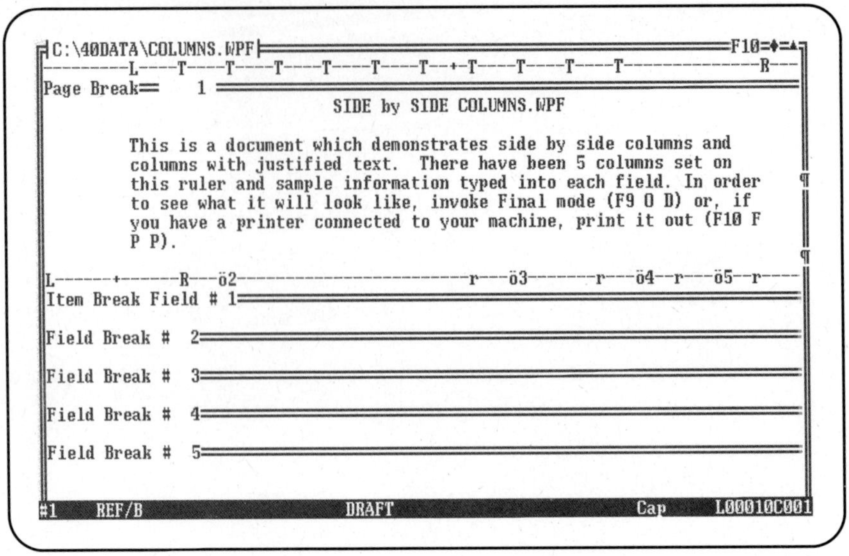

**Fig. 7.9.** *Side-by-side column field breaks.*

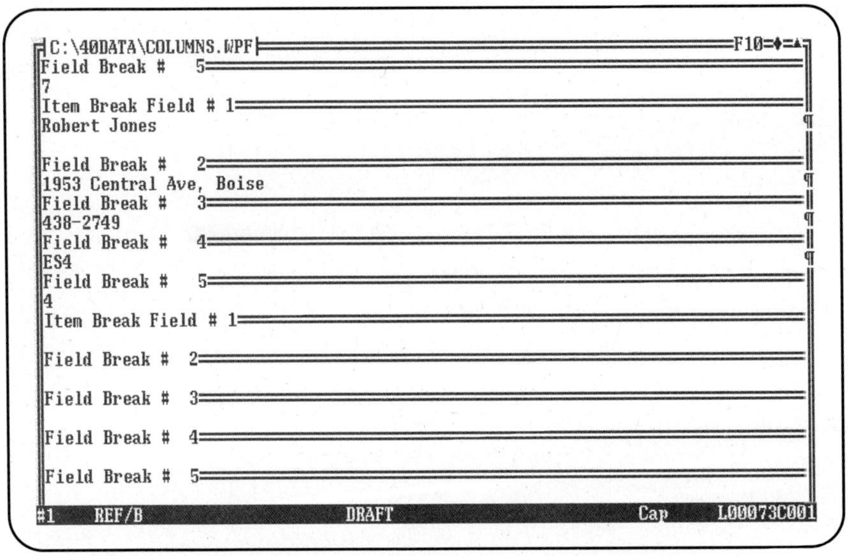

**Fig. 7.10.** *Multiple field break sections.*

## User-Defined Column Breaks

Because you may not always like the location of the column breaks automatically determined by Enable, you may want to insert your own column breaks, called *user-defined column breaks*. This feature enables you to indicate where you want the next column to begin. To insert a user-defined column break, press F10 Layout Columns Column_break_insert. Then, position your cursor on the line above where you want to insert the column break, and press Enter. Figure 7.11 shows a user-defined column break indicator. *Note:* You can only use this feature on snaking columns.

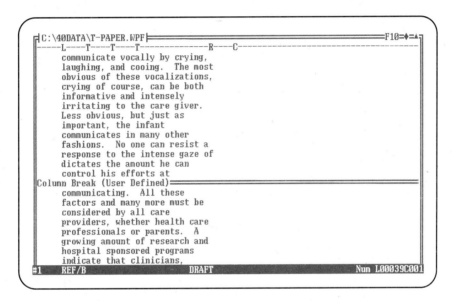

*Fig. 7.11. A user-defined column break.*

# Using Text Attributes

With the advent of laser printers and desktop publishing, you find available many interesting *text enhancements*, such as special typeset-like fonts and numerous type sizes. Most word processing programs provide a method of applying text enhancements such as underlining and boldfacing. Enable provides a wide variety of text enhancements, or *attributes*, but it is not a true desktop publishing program.

In Enable/OA 4.0, you access all text attributes from the Top Line menu. To access these attributes, press

   F10 Layout Character

Enable displays the Character dialog box (see fig. 7.12).

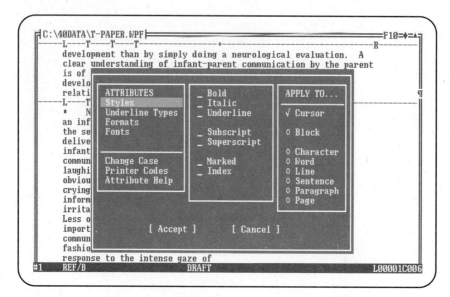

*Fig. 7.12. The Character dialog box.*

Enable places its text attributes into the following categories: Styles, Formats, and Fonts. These categories are discussed in the following sections.

A fourth category from the Character dialog box, Underline_Types, enables you to specify the type of underlining, single or double, you want Enable to use when you underline text. To select an underline type, choose Underline_Types from the Character dialog box, and press Enter. Then choose either Single_Underline or Double_Underline. Enable prompts you to position the cursor where you want to activate the underlining type you specified. Press Enter to confirm your choice. You now must apply the underlining style to your text to see the results of the underlining type you specified (see the following section, "Using and Applying Style Attributes," to learn how to underline text).

# Using and Applying Style Attributes

The category of attributes that is used most often is Styles. The basic difference between style attributes and the other attributes is that you can see the style attributes on-screen, if you have the proper display card and monitor. You can see the other attributes only in page preview mode (discussed in Chapter 8, "Using Word Processing Power Features") or after you print the document.

Style attributes include Bold, Italic, Underline, Subscript, Superscript, Marked, and Index. You can apply these enhancements while you type text, or you can return to previously typed text and apply the enhancements later. Each attribute operates like a toggle switch. (This book discusses marked text in Chapter 6, "Using Word Processing Advanced Features," and discusses indexes in Chapter 8, "Using Word Processing Power Features.")

To select an attribute, place your cursor on the desired attribute and press Enter. Enable places a check mark next to each option you choose (see fig. 7.13).

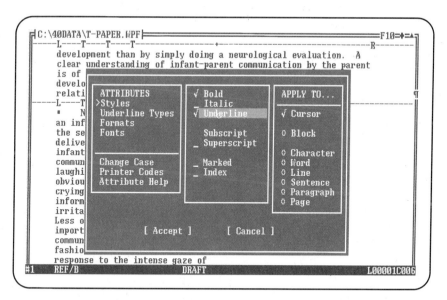

**Fig. 7.13.** *The style options from the Character dialog box.*

> The Character dialog box is standardized. Enable displays options that your printer may not support. When applying style and font attributes, your final authority should be your Enable manual "Printing with Enable," which lists the attributes that each printer supports.

After you choose the style attributes you want, you must either apply them to existing text or apply them to text as you type it. If you want to apply these attributes as you type, simply select Cursor in the APPLY TO section of the dialog box. Otherwise, choose one of the appropriate options from the Character dialog box. You also can use one of the Ctrl-key combinations listed in table 7.1.

**Table 7.1**
**Style Attribute Applications**

| Key Combination | Apply to |
| --- | --- |
| Ctrl-C | Character |
| Ctrl-W | Word |
| Ctrl-L | Line |
| Ctrl-S | Sentence |
| Ctrl-P | Paragraph |
| Ctrl-G | Page |
| Ctrl-B | Blocked text |

If you want to bypass the menu, you can use keystrokes to toggle the style attributes on and off. Enable indicates in the status line the name of each toggle switch that you turn on.

Table 7.2 lists the style attributes and the keystrokes that toggle them on and off.

**Table 7.2**
**Text Attribute Keystroke Commands**

| Attribute | Keystroke | Status Line Indicator |
| --- | --- | --- |
| Bold | Alt-B | b |
| Italic | Alt-I | i |
| Underline | Alt-U | u |
| Subscript | Alt-V | v |

| Attribute | Keystroke | Status Line Indicator |
|-----------|-----------|-----------------------|
| Superscript | Alt-A | a |
| Marked Text | Alt-M | m |
| Index | Alt-X | x |
| Normal | Alt-N | None (removes attributes) |
| Show | Alt-S | Shows appropriate code (shows current attribute) characters in uppercase letters on status line |

Alt-N removes all attributes; thus, you quickly can remove all attributes and then reapply the ones you want to keep.

You can combine the style attributes in almost any combination, except for the following:

superscript-subscript
subscript-underline
subscript-underline-index

As long as Enable displays an attribute code in the status line, any text you type assumes that attribute. To apply the indicated attribute to existing text, position the cursor where the attribute should begin, and press the appropriate Ctrl-key combination, such as Ctrl-S to apply the style to the sentence on which your cursor is positioned. Enable applies the indicated attribute to the portion of text you specify.

## Using and Applying Format Attributes: Diamond Characters

Formats, another category of text attributes in the Character dialog box (see fig. 7.14), does not show its effects on-screen. You can see the effects only when you print the file or when you view the file in page preview mode (see "Using Page Preview" in Chapter 8). The different Format options enable you to change the way text is printed. For example, Compressed prints 15-17 characters per inch, Elite prints 12 characters per inch, and Quality prints characters that simulate those produced by a high-quality typewriter.

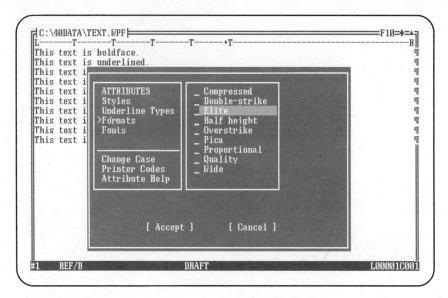

*Fig. 7.14. The format options from the Character dialog box.*

On-screen, Enable depicts attributes from the Formats category differently than it depicts attributes from the Styles category. Like style attributes, format attributes are toggled on and off, either from the menu or with an Alt-key combination; however, rather than displaying a letter code in the status line to indicate that you have turned on a format attribute, Enable inserts a highlighted *diamond character* and letter at the position of the cursor when you turn on the format attribute. During printing, the first occurrence of a particular diamond character sends a command to the printer to turn on that enhancement. The printer continues printing in this mode until it encounters that particular kind of diamond character a second time, which turns off the enhancement. Therefore, you always should insert these diamond characters in pairs (see fig. 7.15). *Note:* You cannot suppress the display of diamond characters.

Most of these attributes concern the characters per inch (cpi) of the printed document. Table 7.3 lists Enable's diamond characters and the keystrokes that toggle them on and off.

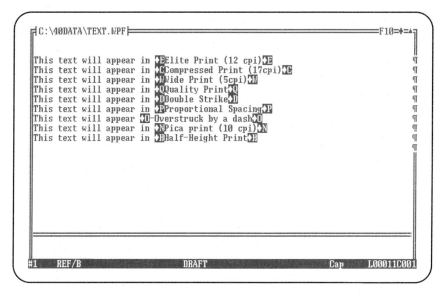

**Fig. 7.15.** Examples of diamond-character attributes.

## Table 7.3
### Format Attributes

| Keystroke | Attribute | Meaning |
|---|---|---|
| Alt-C | Compressed | Prints 15-17 cpi, depending on your printer |
| Alt-D | Double-strike | Shadow prints (strikes characters twice) |
| Alt-E | Elite | Prints 12 cpi |
| Alt-O | Overstrike | Prints one character on top of another |
| Alt-P | Proportional | Adjusts space between characters |
| Alt-Q | Quality | Prints a near-letter-quality font |
| Alt-W | Wide | Prints 5 cpi |

*Available only through the menus:*

| | | |
|---|---|---|
| | Pica | Prints 10 cpi |
| | Half_height | Prints characters at half the normal height |

**NOTE** Press Alt-O to toggle on overstrike print, and press the overstrike character (often a slash or a hyphen). Then type the text you want to overstrike, and press Alt-O again. Enable overstrikes all the text between the overstrike codes with the first character you pressed.

You remove a format attribute simply by deleting the diamond-character pair from the screen as you would delete any other character. Be sure to delete both the diamond character and the character immediately following it.

**TIP** Whether you can use the diamond-character enhancements together depends on the capabilities of your printer. See your Enable manual, "Printing with Enable," for a full description of your printer's capabilities.

If you have problems getting combinations of these features to work with your printer, you can use embedded *control codes*, special printer commands discussed in your printer manual. You can use control codes to access any enhancement your printer can accommodate.

Using the tab character in text with one of these attributes may produce improper tab alignment. To prevent this problem, Enable provides special, embedded *%TABS commands* (see table 7.4) so that the program can make provision for the attribute when formatting tabs during printing. Type the appropriate command in the leftmost column on a separate line above the attribute. For proportional spacing, type **%TABS ON** above and **%TABS OFF** below the proportionally spaced text, causing Enable to align the text at the tab stops.

**Table 7.4**
**%TABS Commands**

| Attribute | Command |
| --- | --- |
| Compressed | %TABS COMP |
| Double-strike | %TABS DOUBLE |
| Elite | %TABS ELITE |
| Proportional | %TABS ON/OFF |
| Quality | %TABS QUAL |

# Using and Applying Font Attributes: Heart Characters

The final category of text attributes in the Character dialog box is Fonts, a new feature of Enable/OA Version 4.0, which involves the use of special fonts. When you insert a font, that font is active until you insert a different font. To access the many fonts available, choose Fonts in the Character dialog box (see figure 7.16). After you choose the font and point size that you want, Enable inserts within the text a highlighted *heart character* and a symbol, which together command the printer to turn on the font that you specified. Be sure to turn off the font when you are finished with it by choosing the default font. Figure 7.17 shows some examples of fonts.

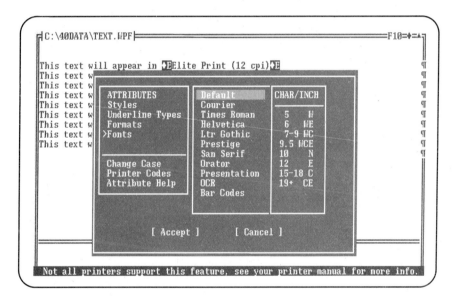

*Fig. 7.16. The font options from the Character dialog box.*

Use a font only if your printer supports it. For the most part, you must have a laser printer to use fonts. See your Enable manual "Printing with Enable" to determine the fonts your printer supports.

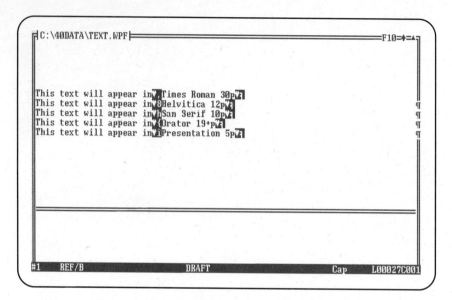

**Fig. 7.17.** *Examples of font attributes.*

# Determining Which Attributes Have Been Applied

Whether you actually can see on-screen the attributes you apply to your text largely depends on your monitor and display card. Because a color monitor normally cannot display text enhancements on-screen, Enable indicates the attributes by changing the color of the text to denote a particular attribute or a combination of attributes. You can customize these colors in the system profile. Monochrome monitors display some enhancements—underline and bold, for example—but not all of them.

An alternative to the graphics mode is the Show option, which enables you to determine which attributes are applied to existing text. Enable doesn't display a letter in the status line to indicate that you turned on the Show option. This option simply provides an easy method of determining which attributes are applied to existing text, even if your system cannot display the attributes. To discover which attributes are applied to existing text, press Alt-S. Then move the cursor to the text you want to check. The status line displays in uppercase letters the codes that indicate the applied attributes.

**TIP**

Enable displays most enhancements on-screen if you have a graphics-capable display card and monitor. You first must switch the screen to graphics mode; then press F10 **D**isplay **V**ideo_mode **G**raphics.

Depending on your monitor, you may see bold, underlining, italic, superscript, and subscript on-screen. Index entries appear in reverse video. If you switch also to final mode (F9 O D), the document appears on-screen much like it actually prints. Figure 7.18 shows how several attributes appear in graphics mode on a VGA monitor. Because graphics mode is a high-resolution mode, it slowly revises the screen and is not efficient for normal editing; however, this mode does seem to work well on laptop computers with LCD screens. Be sure to check your printer manual to learn whether your printer supports all the available text attributes.

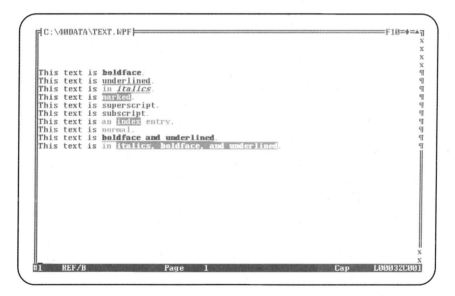

***Fig. 7.18.*** *Text attributes in graphics mode.*

# Setting Line Spacing

Enable offers two ways to set line spacing: through a setting on the Page Form screen or through a line-spacing marker. The former method is more convenient for temporary line-spacing changes, such as printing a double-spaced draft. For permanent line-spacing changes and for changing line spacing several times in a document, use line-spacing markers.

To set line spacing through the Page Form screens, press F10 **File Print Setup_Page**. Enable displays the first Page Form screen (see fig. 7.19). To print the document with single spacing, make sure that the Lines_per_inch choice is set to 6; then set the Line_of_text choice to 0, which inserts no blank lines in the text. For each blank line you want inserted between lines of text, add 1 to this setting. For example, entering a 1 adds one blank line, causing double spacing, and entering a 2 adds two blank lines, causing triple spacing.

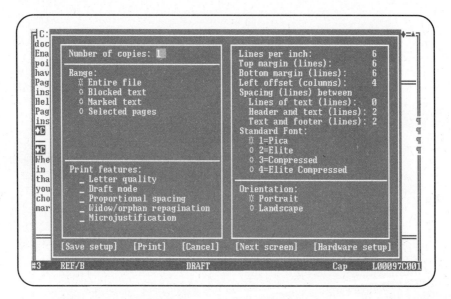

**Fig. 7.19.** *The first Page Form screen.*

To set line spacing through a line-spacing marker, press F9 **Ins Spacing**. Enable displays the Set Line Spacing dialog box. At the prompt, type the number that corresponds to the line spacing you want: **2** for double spacing, **3** for triple spacing, and so on. When you press Enter to accept the line spacing, Enable inserts a line spacing marker that indicates the line spacing you chose. The new spacing applies from the marker to the end of the file, or to the next line-spacing marker, whichever occurs first.

> Line-spacing changes do not appear on-screen in final mode unless you set line spacing through line-spacing markers. Changes you make to line-spacing settings in the Page Form screen do not appear on-screen in final mode.

TIP

# Using Headers and Footers

Enable has a header and footer feature that can save you a lot of time when you format lengthy documents. A *header* is text that appears at the top of each page in a document, and a *footer* is text that appears at the bottom of each page. Without this feature, you must type text such as titles and page numbers again and again. Enable has several capabilities associated with headers and footers, including *automatic page numbering*.

To insert a header anywhere in your document, position the cursor at the top of the text where you want the header to appear. Press F9 Ins Header. Enable displays a header entry space (see fig. 7.20), which is between the Header_and_Page_Break line and the double line below it.

> Notice that the header entry space reads, Header and Page Break. Enable automatically inserts a page break with each new header. If you leave a blank line at the top of the file, above the header entry space, you get a blank page when you print the file. You also get an extra blank page if you insert the header so that it immediately follows a user-defined page break.

CAUTION

Enable positions the cursor in the header entry space, below the H in Header. Type your header text just as you type normal text. Use the cursor keys to move the cursor out of the header entry space when you finish.

Insert a footer in the same manner. First, position the cursor on the page where the footer should begin. Then press F9 Ins Footer. Enable displays a footer entry space (see fig. 7.21). Type the desired footer text in the entry space. Press an arrow key to return to your document.

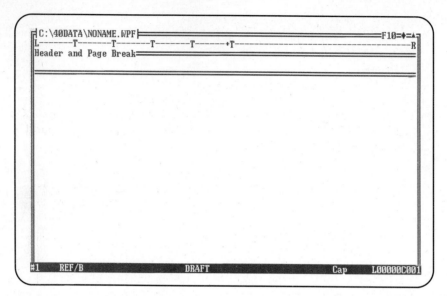

*Fig. 7.20. The header entry space.*

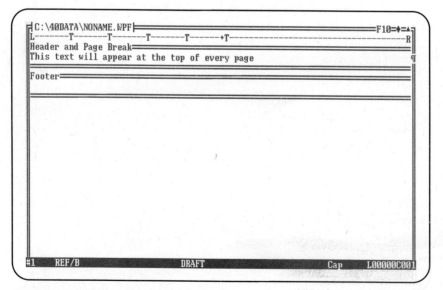

*Fig. 7.21. The footer entry space.*

# Using Page Numbers in Headers and Footers

Enable's print options offer a nice page numbering feature, but numbering pages in a header or footer is a more flexible method. To issue automatic page numbering in a header or footer entry space, press the pound sign (**#**). You can precede this symbol with the word Page (**Page #**) or surround it with hyphens (**-#-**).

To begin page numbering at a certain page, use the syntax *#=n* where *n* is a positive integer. Thus, if you want 47 as the page number of your file's first page, type **#=47** into either a header or footer entry space at the top of the file.

# Using Rulers in Headers and Footers

Headers and footers use the ruler preceding them; because they are generally placed at the top of the document, headers and footers normally use the beginning ruler. To set a different margin or tab setting in a header or footer, position the cursor on the top line of the entry space—the `Header and Page Break` or `Footer` line—and press Alt-F6 to insert a ruler line for your modifications. This command changes the setting for the header or footer, but does not affect the regular text.

Make the changes you want to the ruler, and press Enter. This new ruler controls the margins, tabs, and other settings for any other entry spaces of the same type in the document. In other words, the first header's ruler controls the margins, tabs, and other settings for all other headers, and the first footer's ruler controls the ruler settings for all other footers.

# Using Alternating Headers and Footers

With Enable you can insert one header or footer on every odd-numbered page and a different one on every even-numbered page. Simply include both headers or footers in the same entry space, one above the other, and separate them with the command %ALT. This command must begin in column 1 (see fig. 7.22). Enable displays the first header or footer—the one above %ALT—on the page on which you inserted the entry space, such as page 1, and on every other following page, such as pages 3, 5, 7, 9, and 11. Enable displays the second entry—the one below %ALT—on each of the other pages, such as 2, 4, 6, 8, and 10.

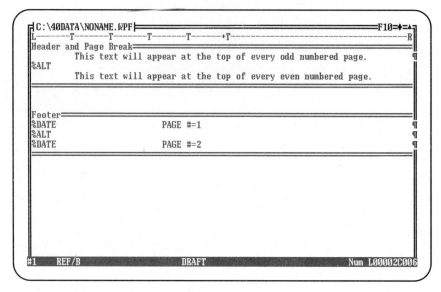

**Fig. 7.22.** *Alternating headers and footers.*

# Using Dates in Headers and Footers

You may want the current system date to appear at the top or bottom of every page. To include the date, simply type **%DATE** in the appropriate area of the header or footer entry space. Enable displays the date according to the format you set in the Page Form screen. To set the date format, press F10 **File Print Setup_Page**, and press PgDn to display the second Page Form screen (see fig. 7.23). In the Date_Format area, choose the format you want. If you accept the default option, Standard, Enable spells out the month rather than expressing it with a figure—for example, September 12, 1991.

Each document can have only one date format.

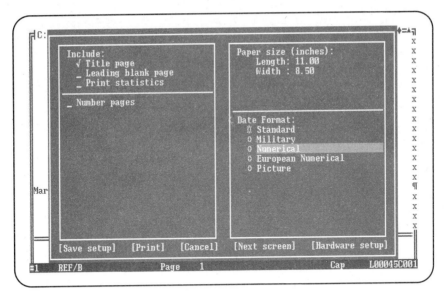

*Fig. 7.23. The second Page Form screen.*

Figure 7.24 shows the effect of the header and footer of figure 7.22.

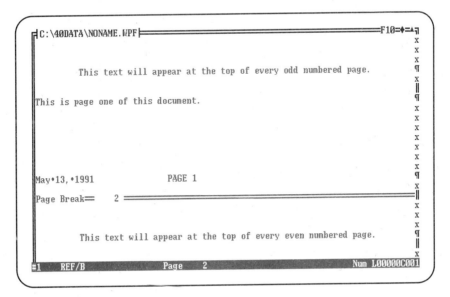

*Fig. 7.24. Alternating footers with dates.*

# Using Goto Commands with Headers and Footers

You can use headers and footers to quickly move the cursor within a document. Table 7.5 lists Goto commands that use headers and footers for moving quickly through the file.

**Table 7.5**
**Header and Footer Goto Commands**

| *Goto Command* | *Moves Cursor to* |
| --- | --- |
| F2 **Header** | Following header |
| F2 *n* **Header** | Following *n*th header |
| F2 ↑ **Header** | Preceding header |
| F2 ↑ *n* **Header** | Preceding *n*th header |
| F2 **Footer** | Following footer |
| F2 *n* Footer | Following *n*th footer |
| F2 ↑ *Footer* | Preceding footer |
| F2 ↑ *n* Footer | Preceding *n*th footer |

# Deleting Headers and Footers

Delete a header or footer with the line-delete keystroke command, Alt-F3. First, position the cursor on the top double line of the header or footer entry space, and then press Alt-F3. Enable deletes the entire entry space.

TIP

Enable initially places a deleted header or footer in a buffer, as it does with any deletion. You can reinsert a deleted header or footer with the undo command, F9 Undo, as long as the deleted header or footer is still in the buffer—that is, as long as you have not made another deletion in the meantime.

# Using Footnotes

One of the strongest features of Enable, when compared with popular stand-alone word processing programs, is its footnoting capability. Enable has significant footnote formatting flexibility, which means you most likely can create footnotes that suit your needs.

## Inserting Footnotes

To insert a footnote anywhere in the text (except in headers, footers, or document titles), position the cursor where you want the footnote reference number to appear, and press

F9 Ins Next Footnote

Enable inserts two diamond characters with a number between them (see fig. 7.25). Enable assigns this number, called the *reference number*, in the order in which you create the footnotes, not in the order in which they appear in the text. Notice that in figure 7.25 footnote reference number 5 precedes reference number 4. When you print the file, however, Enable prints the footnotes in the correct order in the text. With one of Enable's footnote layout options, you can command the program to automatically resequence the footnote reference numbers as you insert them, so that the number order on-screen matches the order in which the footnotes print (see "Using Footnote Layout Options" in this chapter).

On the line below the footnote reference number, Enable inserts a footnote entry space, which is similar to a header or footer entry space, with an additional option of setting multiple rulers. You can press Alt-F6 to insert additional rulers within a footnote (see previous section "Using Rulers" in this chapter). Unlike a header or footer ruler, a footnote ruler affects only that footnote.

Type the footnote text in the entry space, beginning at the left margin. When you print the document, Enable automatically inserts five spaces, called the *footnote symbol entry space*, to the left of the footnote text, depending on the layout you choose. Enable prints the footnote number (or character) in this space, or you can use the footnote layout options (see the following section, "Using Footnote Layout Options") to choose your own set of footnote symbols or numbers to insert. Press the up- or down-arrow key to leave the footnote entry space. Enable wraps multiple-line text in the footnote entry space.

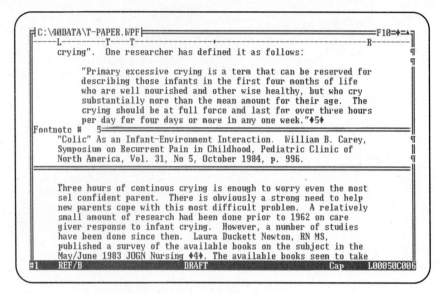

```
┌┤C:\40DATA\T-PAPER.WPF╞═══════════════════════════════════════╤F10═◆═▲╕
│───L─────────T────T─────────────────◆────────────────────R──────────│
│  crying".  One researcher has defined it as follows:              ¶│
│                                                                   ¶│
│        "Primary excessive crying is a term that can be reserved for│
│        describing those infants in the first four months of life  │
│        who are well nourished and other wise healthy, but who cry │
│        substantially more than the mean amount for their age.  The│
│        crying should be at full force and last for over three hours│
│        per day for four days or more in any one week."◆5◆          │
│├Footnote #    5╞══════════════════════════════════════════════════│
│        "Colic" As an Infant-Environment Interaction.  William B. Carey,  ¶│
│        Symposium on Recurrent Pain in Childhood, Pediatric Clinic of ‖│
│        North America, Vol. 31, No 5, October 1984, p. 996.         ¶│
│                                                                    │
│────────────────────────────────────────────────────────────────────│
│        Three hours of continous crying is enough to worry even the most│
│        sel confident parent.  There is obviously a strong need to help│
│        new parents cope with this most difficult problem.  A relatively│
│        small amount of research had been done prior to 1962 on care│
│        giver response to infant crying.  However, a number of studies│
│        have been done since then.  Laura Duckett Newton, RN MS,    │
│        published a survey of the available books on the subject in the│
│        May/June 1983 JOGN Nursing ◆4◆. The available books seem to take│
│#1    REF/B              DRAFT                    Cap        L0005 0C006│
└────────────────────────────────────────────────────────────────────┘
```

*Fig. 7.25. A footnote inserted into a document.*

Enable moves all of the footnote entry spaces to the top of your document when you change from draft mode to final mode and back to draft mode, or when you save, close, and retrieve your document.

To delete a footnote, you need to delete both the reference number (press Del) and the footnote entry space (press Alt-F3).

# Using Footnote Layout Options

Enable includes an extensive number of footnote layout options to enable you to specify exactly how you want your footnotes to appear. In the system profile, you set these options according to your typical work (see Appendix B), but you also can adjust them for the current document by pressing F10 Layout Footnotes Modify_form. Enable displays a series of three screens. The bottom third portion of each screen contains information about the option on which your cursor is positioned. Use your up- and down-arrow keys to move among the following options:

- *Location.* You can set footnotes to print at the bottom of the page or at the end of the document.

- *Blank lines.* These two options enable you to insert blank lines between the divider line and footnotes and between footnotes.

- *Minimum number of lines.* You can specify the minimum number of lines of normal text that you want to appear on each page, in case a footnote continues onto another page.

- *Divider line.* Use this option to indicate the character that you want Enable to repeat at the bottom of the text to create a divider line between the text and the footnotes. You can specify the repeat count of this character; however, Enable repeats this character no more than 30 times. The hard hyphen character (Alt-[hyphen]) usually produces the neatest divider line. You also can specify the column in which you want the divider line to begin.

- *Footnote symbol style.* Indicate whether the footnote symbols should be numbers or characters. If you choose characters, you must type a list of characters in the order in which you want them assigned. If you choose numbers, you also must indicate whether to restart the numbering sequence at the beginning of each page or to continue it throughout the document.

- *Footnote symbol position.* Use this option to start the footnote symbol entry space at some point left or right of the left margin. Enter L, L-$n$, or L+$n$, where $n$ is the number of columns to the left or right, respectively, of the left margin.

- *Footnote symbol justification.* Use this option to set the position of the footnote character (left, right, or centered) within the five-character footnote symbol entry space.

- *Footnote symbol placement style.* This option affects only numeric symbols and offers three placement styles: superscripted in text and footnote, underscored and followed by slash, or superscripted in text and followed by a period in the footnote.

- *Resequence reference numbers.* This option renumbers reference numbers as you insert footnotes so that you can view the numbers on-screen in the order in which they appear when printed rather than the order in which you insert them.

- *Footnote continuation message.* Indicate the content and position of the message (up to 80 characters) to appear at the bottom of the footnote space if a footnote continues onto the next page.

- *Message at start of a continued footnote.* Indicate the content and position of the message to appear at the start of a continued footnote. To insert a blank line before the footnote, add a tilde (~) to the end of the message.

# Displaying and Printing Footnotes

Footnotes appear on-screen in final mode, but Enable does not display them exactly as it prints them. The footnote numbers or characters do not appear in the text; the reference numbers continue to appear instead. The footnote numbers appear in the footnote space. The reference numbers also appear in the footnote space, at the left edge of the word processing screen. If you choose the option to resequence the reference numbers, Enable resequences them in final mode.

The best way to explain this feature is with an example. Figure 7.26 shows the same footnote as figure 7.25, except that the screen shown in figure 7.26 is in final mode and contains renumbered footnotes. In figure 7.25, the footnote displayed is the fifth one added to the file—notice that the footnote reference number is 5. When you display the file in final mode, however, Enable changes the reference number to 4 (see fig. 7.26) because the footnote is the fourth one in the file.

When you print the file, Enable changes this footnote reference number to 1 because the numbering sequence style is set to restart at the beginning of each page, and this footnote is the first one on the page. Enable also prints the number 1 in the text, following the quotation. The next time you display this document in draft mode, the footnote reference number will be 4, if the footnote form question "Resequence draft footnote reference numbers in final form" is set to Yes. If the question is set to No, the footnotes do not resequence—the reference number will be 5.

Any time you print a page that contains a footnote, Enable prints its corresponding footnote text at the bottom of the page. If all of the footnote text does not fit on that page, Enable prints the remaining text at the bottom of the following page.

**TIP**

Enable can handle up to 1,900 footnotes per file. If you want to start with a footnote number other than 1, precede the first footnote with the embedded command

%FNUM *n*

where *n* is the footnote number that you want to appear first. Do not use more than four digits for your footnote numbers. If you create a long document, such as a manuscript, in multiple word processing files, you can insert up to 9,999 footnotes.

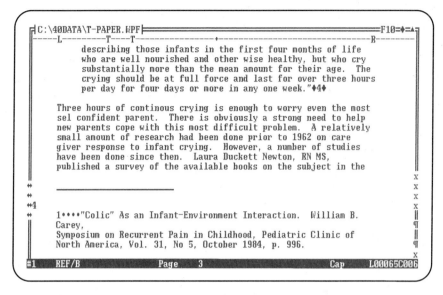

**Fig. 7.26.** *A footnote in final mode.*

# Using Special Characters

With Enable, you can create many special characters in your document, if your printer supports such characters. You access these special characters through the following character sets:

- *Box-drawing character set.* This set includes the characters shown in figure 7.27. To access box-drawing characters, press

  F9 **On**/Off **Characters Box_drawing_set**

- *Greek character set.* This set includes the characters shown in figure 7.28. To access the Greek character set, press

  F9 **On**/Off **Characters Greek**

- *Miscellaneous (special) character set.* This set includes the characters shown in figure 7.29. To access the miscellaneous character set, press

  F9 **On**/Off **Characters Special**

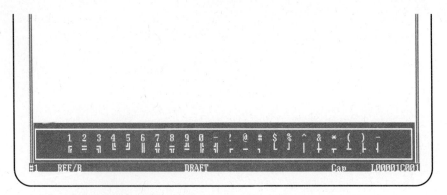

***Fig. 7.27.*** *The box-drawing character set.*

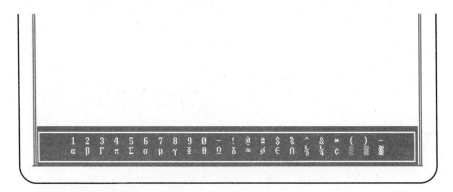

***Fig. 7.28.*** *The Greek character set.*

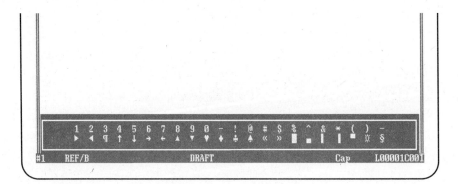

***Fig. 7.29.*** *The miscellaneous character set.*

- *First foreign character set.* This set includes the characters shown in figure 7.30. To access the first foreign character set, press

  F9 **On**/**Off** **C**haracters **F**oreign

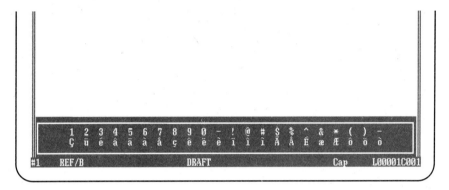

*Fig. 7.30. The first foreign character set.*

- *Second foreign character set.* This set includes the characters shown in figure 7.31. To access the second foreign character set, press

  F9 **On**/**Off** **C**haracters **T**wo

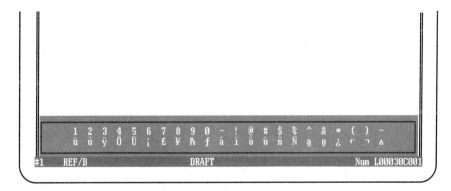

*Fig. 7.31. The second foreign character set.*

The character set you choose appears in a box at the bottom of the screen (see fig. 7.32). Each key listed in the top row of this box creates the character listed below it. *Note:* Keep in mind that not all printers support Enable's special characters.

To turn off any of the special character sets, press

F9 **On/off** Characters **Off**

To display the em-dash character (—), press Alt-[hyphen] twice.

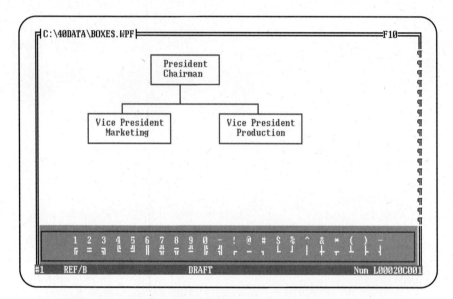

*Fig. 7.32. The box-drawing character set.*

With a new feature in Enable/OA 4.0 you can now draw single- and double-line boxes using the numeric keypad arrow keys, with Num Lock *on*. (Press and hold the Shift key to suspend drawing with the arrow keys and move the cursor to a new location.) To access this feature, press F10 **Layout**, and choose either **S**ingle_cursor_draw or **D**ouble_cursor_draw. You then can draw boxes, like the ones shown in figure 7.32, with your cursor. Enable automatically uses the correct characters to draw corners and other intersections.

To exit the cursor line-draw mode, press Esc.

# 8

# Using
# Word Processing
# Power Features

The word processing features discussed in this chapter are powerful shortcuts that make otherwise tedious and repetitive tasks easy to do. These features are not absolutely necessary, but they often appear prominently in advertisements of popular word processing programs.

## Using Page Preview

In Chapter 5, "Understanding Word Processing Basics," you learn that when you go to the final mode in Enable's word processing module, the text on-screen has the same format as the printed text. Final mode, however, is an effective tool for seeing page formatting, only. To see *exactly* how a document will print, with all the fonts and graphs, you need to use the page preview feature now available in Enable/OA 4.0.

> Because the page preview feature shows you how a document prints, be sure to select a printer before you go to page preview mode (refer to the section "Choosing a Printer" in Chapter 5).

To use page preview, press

F10 **D**isplay **P**age_Preview

Enable then displays the Page Preview menu, as shown in figure 8.1.

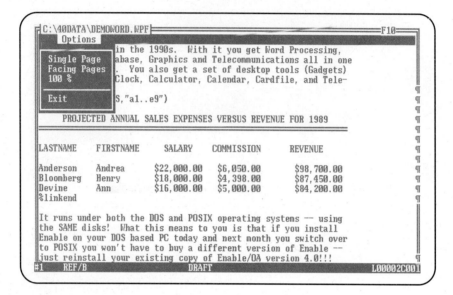

```
┌─C:\40DATA\DEMOWORD.WPF══════════════════════════════════F10═┐
│ ┌──────────┐                                                │
│ │ Options  │  in the 1990s.  With it you get Word Processing,│
│ ├──────────┤  abase, Graphics and Telecommunications all in one│
│ │Single Page│ .  You also get a set of desktop tools (Gadgets)│
│ │Facing Pages│ Clock, Calculator, Calendar, Cardfile, and Tele-│
│ │100 %     │                                                 │
│ ├──────────┤  S,"a1..e9")                                   ¶│
│ │Exit      │                                                ¶│
│ └──────────┘                                                ¶│
│       PROJECTED ANNUAL SALES EXPENSES VERSUS REVENUE FOR 1989 ¶│
│                                                             ¶│
│                                                             ¶│
│ LASTNAME    FIRSTNAME    SALARY     COMMISSION    REVENUE   ¶│
│                                                             ¶│
│ Anderson    Andrea      $22,000.00  $6,050.00    $98,700.00 ¶│
│ Bloomberg   Henry       $18,000.00  $4,398.00    $87,450.00 ¶│
│ Devine      Ann         $16,000.00  $5,000.00    $84,200.00 ¶│
│ %linkend                                                    ¶│
│                                                             ¶│
│ It runs under both the DOS and POSIX operating systems -- using│
│ the SAME disks!  What this means to you is that if you install│
│ Enable on your DOS based PC today and next month you switch over│
│ to POSIX you won't have to buy a different version of Enable --│
│ just reinstall your existing copy of Enable/OA version 4.0!!! ¶│
│#1    REF/B                  DRAFT                  L00002C001│
└─────────────────────────────────────────────────────────────┘
```

*Fig. 8.1. The Page Preview menu.*

Choose from the following options on the Page Preview menu:

- *Single Page.* Use this option to view each page individually on-screen (see fig. 8.2).

- *Facing Pages.* With this option, you can view facing pages simultaneously. Even-numbered pages appear on the left side of the screen (see fig. 8.3).

- *100%.* Choose this option to view a single page in the actual size of the printed version (see fig. 8.4).

- *Exit.* Press **X** to resume editing your document.

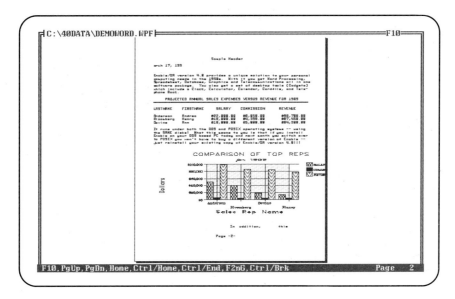

**Fig. 8.2.** *Page Preview mode—Single Page.*

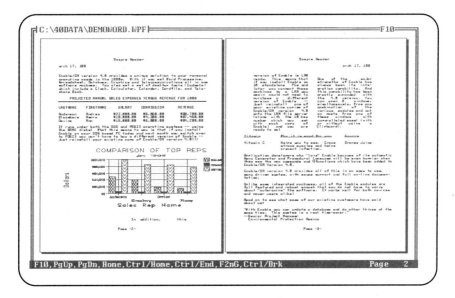

**Fig. 8.3.** *Page Preview mode—Facing Pages.*

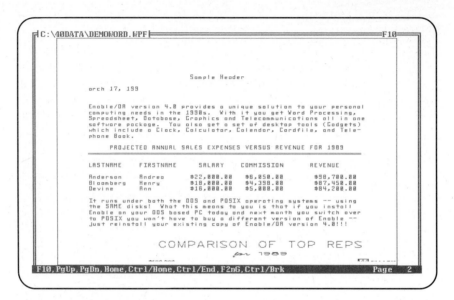

*Fig. 8.4. Page Preview mode—100%.*

While a document displays on-screen in page preview mode, you can use only the keys listed in table 8.1.

**Table 8.1**
**Page Preview Keys**

| Keystroke | Function |
| --- | --- |
| PgDn | Move to the next page. |
| PgUp | Move to the preceding page. |
| Home | Move to the top of the current page (use in 100% mode). |
| Ctrl-Home | Move to the first page of the document. |
| Ctrl-End | Move to the last page of the document. |
| F2 *n* G | Move to page *n* of your document. |
| F10 | Access the Page Preview menu. |

# Numbering Paragraphs

Enable/OA 4.0 has an automatic paragraph numbering feature, which is useful if you create legal documents and official documents, such as organizational constitutions. You can use this feature to number up to seven levels or subsections. Figures 8.5 and 8.6 show a document with levels of numbered paragraphs in draft mode and final mode.

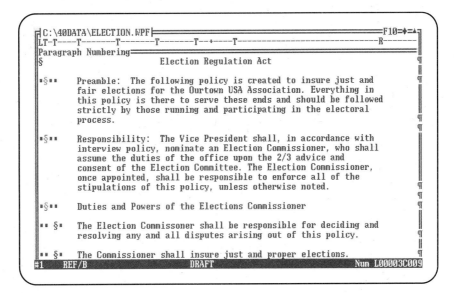

*Fig. 8.5. Numbered paragraphs in draft mode.*

Paragraph numbering involves two steps: the first step is to insert a paragraph symbol (¶) into the margin of your document; the second step is to create a paragraph numbering style form. To insert the paragraph symbol, move your cursor to the correct line and position it below the correct tab character; then press

F9 **N**umber_Symbol

The paragraph symbol appears in the margin. This character is for display only; you cannot rest your cursor on it. To delete a paragraph numbering symbol, position your cursor anywhere on the line, and press F9 **N** again; Enable removes the symbol.

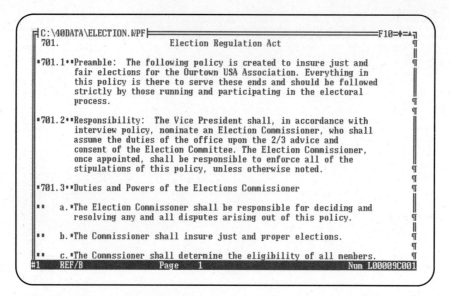

```
┌─C:\40DATA\ELECTION.WPF════════════════════════════════════════════F10=◆=▲┐
│ 701.                        Election Regulation Act                     ¶
│                                                                         ║
│ ▪701.1▪▪Preamble:  The following policy is created to insure just and   ¶
│         fair elections for the Ourtown USA Association. Everything in   ║
│         this policy is there to serve these ends and should be followed ║
│         strictly by those running and participating in the electoral   ║
│         process.                                                        ¶
│                                                                         ¶
│ ▪701.2▪▪Responsibility:  The Vice President shall, in accordance with   ¶
│         interview policy, nominate an Election Commissioner, who shall  ║
│         assume the duties of the office upon the 2/3 advice and         ║
│         consent of the Election Committee. The Election Commissioner,   ║
│         once appointed, shall be responsible to enforce all of the      ║
│         stipulations of this policy, unless otherwise noted.            ¶
│                                                                         ¶
│ ▪701.3▪▪Duties and Powers of the Elections Commissioner                 ¶
│                                                                         ║
│ ▪ ▪   a.▪The Election Commissoner shall be responsible for deciding and ¶
│         resolving any and all disputes arising out of this policy.      ¶
│                                                                         ║
│ ▪ ▪   b.▪The Commissioner shall insure just and proper elections.       ¶
│                                                                         ¶
│ ▪ ▪   c.▪The Commssioner shall determine the eligibility of all members.¶
├#1    REF/B              Page    1                    Num L00009C001─────┘
```

*Fig. 8.6. Numbered paragraphs in final mode.*

**NOTE:** After you change your document from draft to final mode, the paragraph numbers remain in place. If you insert or remove numbering symbols, Enable automatically renumbers the paragraphs.

Next, you create a paragraph numbering style form, which stores information about the numbering style and sequencing options. You can use as many forms as you want in a document. A sample form is shown in figure 8.7. To access the form, press

> F10 **T**ools **P**aragraph_Numbering **M**odify_form

In figure 8.7, the level refers to the offset of the left margin. The left margin is level 1, the first tab is level 2, the second tab is level 3, and so on, up to seven levels. You can move your cursor among the columns labeled `Style`, `End Char.`, and `Legal` for each level. As you move your cursor, the options for each are displayed on-screen in a box.

For each level, you can choose from the following:

- *Style*. Choose the numbering style. Using the on-screen codes, you can choose

    1 Numeric (Arabic numbers)

    2 Upper Case Alpha

    3 Lower Case

    4 Upper Case Roman

    5 Lower Case Roman

- *End Character*. Choose the character to immediately follow the paragraph number (or letter). Using the codes found on-screen, you can choose

    A Period

    B Space

    C Closing Parenthesis

    D Between Parentheses

    E None

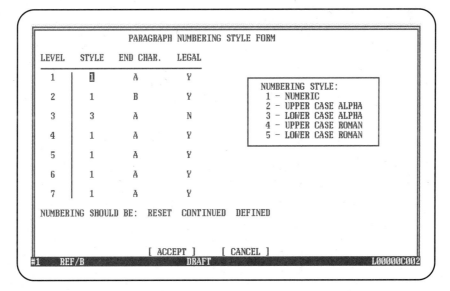

**Fig. 8.7.** *Paragraph Numbering Style Form.*

- *Legal*. If you choose yes, the numbers for lower levels also include the numbers for higher levels. For example, in figure 8.6, if you choose Yes, the number for the second level will be *701.1*; if you choose No, the number for the second level will be *.1*. Numbers for level three, however, just show the appropriate character for level three.

After you make choices for the preceding options, you can decide how to set the numbering for the level. To define the initial value for a level, select DEFINED. Otherwise, if the current form is not the first paragraph numbering style form in your document, select RESET to start numbering at 1, or select CONTINUED to use the next available numbers.

If you select DEFINED, you see the following prompt:

```
Define Number: 1.1.1.1.1.1.1.
```

Each period separates one level from the next. To set the starting number for any level, insert the number for that level. In the preceding example, because you want to start at 701 in level 1, edit this prompt as follows:

```
701.1.1.1.1.1.1.
```

# Numbering Lines

Line numbering is a new feature that enables you to print line numbers in your document. This feature includes the following options: print line numbers before or after the line (the left or right margin), indicate the distance between the number and the margin, indicate the starting value at each page, indicate the starting line number, indicate the increment between each line, number blank lines, and number footnote lines. To access line numbering, press

F10 **Tools** Line_Numbering

You see the dialog box shown in figure 8.8. Because line numbering occurs only during print, you must use page preview to see the effect of numbering. Figure 8.9 shows a sample document with line numbering in page preview mode.

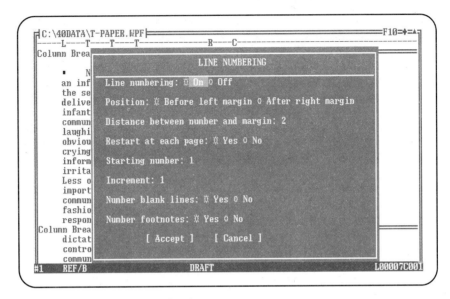

**Fig. 8.8.** Line Numbering dialog box.

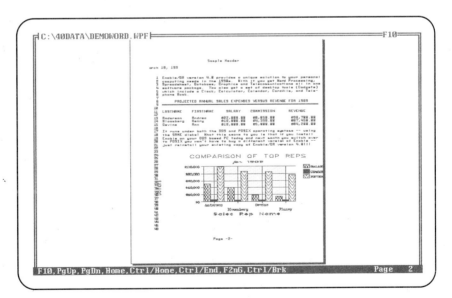

**Fig. 8.9.** Line Numbering in page preview mode.

# Using Shorthand

If you repeatedly use a particular word or phrase in a document, Enable's shorthand feature should interest you. With this feature, you can substitute a question mark (?) and a single character, or up to eight alphanumeric characters, for a phrase or word. When you type your document, you type in the shorthand representation wherever you want the phrase to occur. For example, in figure 8.10, ?E stands for "Elections Commissioner." During compilation, Enable/OA inserts the words "Elections Commissioner" wherever ?E appears in the document. This feature is case-sensitive; ?E is not equivalent to ?e.

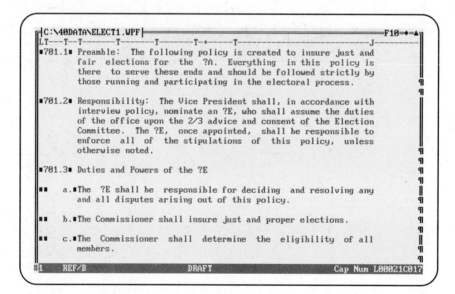

**Fig. 8.10.** *Shorthand within a document.*

To tell Enable what each shorthand abbreviation means, you insert a shorthand entry space in the document any time before compilation. To insert a shorthand space, press

　　　F10 Tools Shorthand Insert

Enable prompts you to position the cursor and press Enter. After you press Enter, Enable inserts a shorthand entry space in your document. Within this space, you may enter as many shorthand entries as you need. To enter an entry, type a question mark (?), immediately followed by the abbreviation and a space. Next, type in the desired text, which can be one word or several lines. Although you can define multiple shorthand entry spaces, when you save your document, Enable combines them all into one shorthand entry space. See figure 8.11 for a sample shorthand entry space.

If you want to use your shorthand entry space in more than one document, create a word processing document that holds just the shorthand entry space. You then can use the F9 command F9 Ins **D** to include this file in each document.

**TIP**

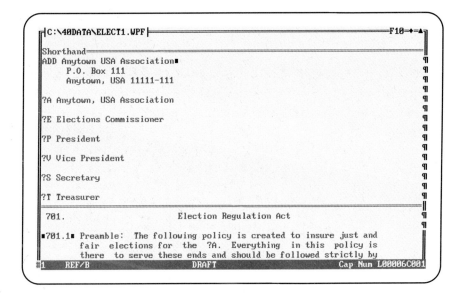

```
┌─┤C:\40DATA\ELECT1.WPF├═══════════════════════════════════════════F10═◆═▲┐
║                                                                          ║
║╞Shorthand═══════════════════════════════════════════════════════════════
║ADD Anytown USA Association■                                             ¶
║        P.O. Box 111                                                     ¶
║        Anytown, USA 11111-111                                           ¶
║                                                                         ¶
║?A Anytown, USA Association                                              ¶
║                                                                         ¶
║?E Elections Commissioner                                                ¶
║                                                                         ¶
║?P President                                                             ¶
║                                                                         ¶
║?V Vice President                                                        ¶
║                                                                         ¶
║?S Secretary                                                             ¶
║                                                                         ¶
║?T Treasurer                                                             ¶
║╞════════════════════════════════════════════════════════════════════════
║  701.                        Election Regulation Act                    ¶
║                                                                         ¶
║ ■701.1■ Preamble:  The following policy is created to insure just and   ¶
║         fair  elections  for  the  ?A.  Everything  in this  policy is
║         there  to serve these ends and should be followed strictly by
│#1    REF/B                   DRAFT                      Cap Num L00006C001
```

*Fig. 8.11. Shorthand entry space.*

After you create your shorthand entry space, you need to *compile* the shorthand, that is, to expand the abbreviations. Figure 8.12 shows the document in figure 8.10 after Enable has compiled the shorthand.

To compile the shorthand, press

> F10 **T**ools Shorthand Compile

Enable checks the entire document for shorthand entries and expands each one. Note that after you compile the shorthand, you cannot change what the shorthand means. You can compile a document as often as you want, if you make any changes.

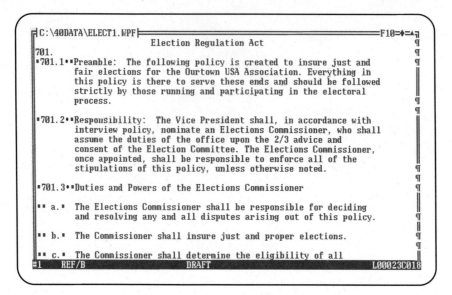

**Fig. 8.12.** *A document with shorthand compiled.*

# Creating a Table of Contents

When you create a large document, you may want to provide readers with an accurate table of contents. Compiling the table by hand can become a tedious chore, especially if you reedit or reorganize the document after you create the table. Enable has a relatively easy-to-use capability for generating a table of contents. This feature also can be useful to generate an outline.

Compiling a table of contents in the word processing module involves two basic steps: creating the individual table entries, and then compiling the table. You can choose several options to customize the appearance of the entries, including adding an outline format with sequence numbers.

To create a table of contents entry, move the cursor to the beginning of the section and press

F9 Ins **T**able_of_Contents_Entry

Enable displays a table of contents (TOC) entry space, similar to the short-hand entry space (see fig. 8.13). If you do not intend to use outline-style section numbering, leave column 1 blank and type the table of contents heading in the entry space. You can type any text in the TOC entry space, beginning in column 2. Press an arrow key to leave the entry space.

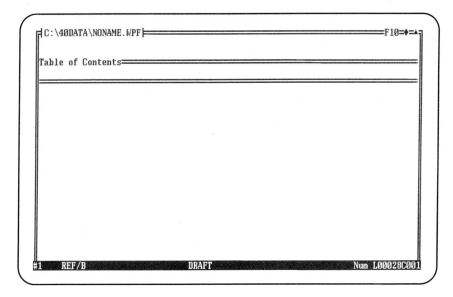

*Fig. 8.13. A table of contents entry space.*

In Enable, you can arrange TOC headings in outline form. To use the outline-style TOC feature, press one of the characters listed in the following table in column 1 of the TOC entry space. The table lists the heading levels from highest (the entire unit) to lowest (a minor section).

| Level | Letter |
| --- | --- |
| Unit | U |
| Chapter | C |
| Section | S |
| Minor section | M |

If you do not specify an outline level for a heading, Enable assigns the TOC entry to the unit level.

To determine which numbering style to use for the TOC, press

F10 **T**ools Table_of_**C**ontents **M**odify

Enable displays a screen in which you can modify the numbering style for each heading level (see fig. 8.14). First, specify whether the TOC entries should be printed as headings in the text itself. In this way, you can avoid typing the same heading twice: once in the text and once in the entry space.

You then can select the numbering styles for the four outline levels. For example, you can choose *I* for the unit level, *A* for the chapter level, *a* for the section level, and *i* for the minor section level. The default number style for TOC headings results in a minor section heading as follows:

```
II.B.a.iii. Sample Table of Contents Heading............5
```

This method works best if you use Arabic numerals for all outline levels (for example, a minor section numbered 2.2.1.3). As an alternate style, you can select `Optional outline style; end mark only` so that only the number of the appropriate section level appears. The sample minor section heading then looks as follows:

```
iii. Sample Table of Contents Heading..................5
```

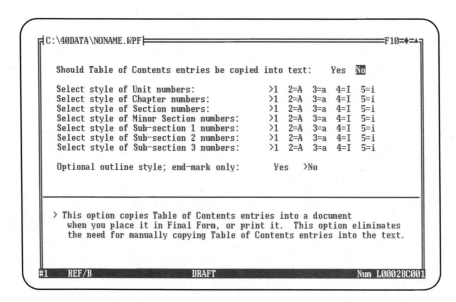

*Fig. 8.14. The table of contents format option table.*

After you define the TOC entries, you can instruct Enable to compile the TOC. Press

**F9 Compile Table_of_Contents**

Enable asks

```
Do you want periods between the
entry and the page number?
   Yes No Cancel
```

Choose **Yes**, **No**, or **Cancel**. Enable displays a default ruler with a justified right margin. Accept or change the margin settings, and press Enter.

Enable creates a separate word processing file with the same file name but with the file extension WPT; Enable compiles the TOC into this file. You can print this file in three ways: separately, using the %Include embedded command, or by copying it into the current document.

# Compiling an Index

Enable's index generator is another powerful feature of interest if you create large documents that you later need to reference or cross-reference.

You can use two methods to create an index entry. To index specific words as they appear in the text, apply the index attribute (Alt-X) to those words (refer to the text attributes sections in Chapter 7, "Using Formatting Features"). If you want some other wording to appear in the index, press

F9 Ins Index_Entry_Area

Enable creates an index entry space in the text where the referenced text occurs. Type the index entry in this space. To create subentries in the index, type the main entry, a semicolon, and then the subentry in the index entry space. Subentries appear in the index in alphabetical order, indented below the main entry.

To delete an entry space, press Alt-F3.

To compile an index, press

F9 **Compile Index**

Enable asks

```
Do you want periods between the
entry and the page number?
  Yes No Cancel
```

Choose **Yes**, **No**, or **Cancel**. Enable displays a default ruler with a justified right margin. Accept or change the margin settings and press Enter.

Like a table of contents, Enable creates an index as a separate word processing file with the same name but with the file extension WPI. You can print this file in three ways: separately, using the %Include embedded command, or by copying it into the current document.

# Creating an Outline

Although the table of contents feature provides an outline generator, this feature is not the program's primary outline resource. Enable has another, more convenient outline feature. When you use this feature, you create a special ruler on which you specify the numbering style and column location of the outline levels. The outline feature works best when the only purpose of the document you use it in is to be an outline; the outline feature does not work as well when the outline file contains other text. This file is actually a normal word processing file with a special ruler line at the top.

To create an outline ruler, position the cursor on the first line of the outline, and press Alt-F6. Enable displays a ruler for you to modify. Use the following codes on the ruler:

- *I* for uppercase Roman numerals

- *A* for uppercase letters

- *1* for Arabic numerals

- *a* for lowercase letters

- *i* for lowercase Roman numerals

These codes work similarly to numeric and alphanumeric tabs, discussed in Chapter 7, "Using Formatting Features." Include a period in the ruler wherever you want one to occur in outline numbers. If your outline numbers are to be more than one digit long (for example, III, or 12), repeat the appropriate symbols on the ruler. For example, if you are using Roman numerals for the first outline level and expect to have nine first-level sections, type **IIII** in the ruler, to provide space for the longest outline number, *VIII*. A typical outline ruler can appear as follows:

```
—IIII.—A.—11.—a.—iiii.————————————————R
```

To type an outline entry, use the Tab key to move the cursor to the appropriate outline level and press the pound sign (#). Leave at least two spaces to allow for double-digit levels; then type the text. Use the hanging indent feature (Alt-H) if you don't want lines to wrap all the way to the left margin (see Chapter 7, "Using Formatting Features"). In final mode and when you print, Enable translates the pound signs into the desired outline numbers or letters. Because Enable automatically handles the numbering and lettering sequence, if you later insert another entry, Enable renumbers all subsequent entries in the document.

# Using Comments and Paper Clips

The comment and the paper clip features are especially useful if you often revise documents.

A *comment* is text that appears in the file but does not print. You most often use comments to place a note in the file that does not need to appear in the printout. A typical comment is a revision note that explains when and why you made a certain change. Another comment may be a reminder to insert additional information at a certain point in the file.

To insert a comment at the cursor, press

F9 Ins **Note Comment**

Enable displays a comment entry area. Type the comment in this area. Use the arrow keys to move out of this entry space.

If you want to print a comment that you created with the comment feature, you must print the document in draft mode. See Chapter 5, "Understanding Word Processing Basics," for more detailed information on printing.

TIP

A *paper clip* marks a location in the electronic file, just as a metal paper clip does in a paper file. To insert a paper clip at the cursor, press

F9 Ins **Marker** *n* **Clip**

where *n* is the number (an integer less than 10,000) of the paper clip you want to insert. At the cursor, a double line appears with the label

```
Paper Clip # n
```

where *n* is the number you typed.

You can use paper clips and comments as signposts in Goto commands. Table 8.2 lists several Goto commands that move the cursor to paper clips or comments.

**Table 8.2**
**Enable Comment and Paper Clip Goto Commands**

| Goto Command | Moves the Cursor to |
|---|---|
| F2 **Next** Comment | Next comment down from the current cursor position |
| F2 *n* Next Comment | The *n*th comment down from the current cursor position |
| F2 up arrow Next Comment | Next comment above the current cursor position |
| F2 up arrow *n* Next Comment | The *n*th comment above the current cursor position |
| F2 Marker Clip | Next paper clip down from the current cursor position |
| F2 *n* Marker Clip | Paper clip number *n* |

# Using the Math Features

Enable's word processing module has a built-in calculator and the capability to add a column of numbers.

To use the calculator, simply type a mathematical expression with any of these operators:

| Operator | Operation |
|---|---|
| + | Add |
| – | Subtract |
| * | Multiply |
| / | Divide |
| ** | Raise to a power |

Enclose the calculations you want done first in parentheses. You also can use the special built-in functions listed in chapter 14 of Enable's integration documentation. To calculate the equation, position the cursor just to the right of the equation and press

F9 **+**

Enable replaces the equation with the resulting number, rounded to two decimal places.

Enable also has a convenient capability to add a column of numbers on-screen. First, block the column of numbers with one of the methods discussed in Chapter 6, "Using Word Processing Advanced Features." Position the cursor where you want the total to appear and press

F9 **Math +**

Enable adds the numbers in the block and inserts the total at the cursor, rounded to two decimal places. For example, in Chapter 4, "Using the Master Control Module's Advanced Features," you create a word processing file from a directory. If you want to know how much disk space the files occupy, you can ask Enable to add up the column. To find the average size of a file, copy the total disk space number to the bottom of the column (see fig. 8.15). Divide that number by the number of lines in the document (the number of files in your list).

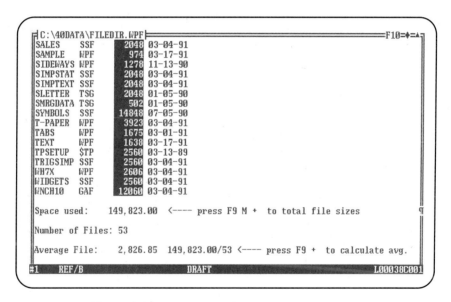

```
C:\40DATA\FILEDIR.WPF                                        F10=◆=▲
SALES     SSF       2048 03-04-91
SAMPLE    WPF        974 03-17-91
SIDEWAYS  WPF       1278 11-13-90
SIMPSTAT  SSF       2048 03-04-91
SIMPTEXT  SSF       2048 03-04-91
SLETTER   TSG       2048 01-05-90
SMRGDATA  TSG        502 01-05-90
SYMBOLS   SSF      14848 07-05-90
T-PAPER   WPF       3923 03-04-91
TABS      WPF       1675 03-01-91
TEXT      WPF       1638 03-17-91
TPSETUP   $TP       2560 03-13-89
TRIGSIMP  SSF       2560 03-04-91
WH7X      WPF       2606 03-04-91
WIDGETS   SSF       2560 03-04-91
WNCH10    GAF      12060 03-04-91

Space used:     149,823.00  <---- press F9 M +  to total file sizes

Number of Files: 53

Average File:     2,826.85  149,823.00/53 <---- press F9 +  to calculate avg.
#1    REF/B                    DRAFT                        L00038C001
```

*Fig. 8.15. Enable math functions in word processing.*

The Pop-up Calculator is a new feature of Enable/OA 4.0. To access the calculator, press Alt-+ (press + from the extended keypad). Enable displays the calculator, as shown in figure 8.16. The function keys represent the available functions; press Tab to change the functions. To end a session, press Alt-End.

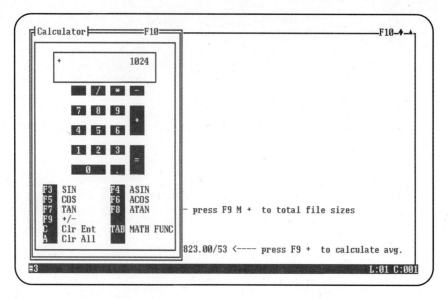

*Fig. 8.16. Enable's Pop-Up Calculator.*

# Importing Graphic Files

You can use graphics files from other software packages in your Enable/OA 4.0 word processing file. For example, suppose that you want to include a PC Paintbrush, MacPaint or Harvard Graphics file in your document. To import these files, open your document and press

F9 Ins **D**ocument

At the file prompt, enter the name of your graphics file and press Enter. Because a graphics file is not a standard Enable word processing file, Enable displays a list and asks you to specify the type of file. The last choice in the list is Graph. Choose Graph; a choice of graphics files appears on-screen. If your file is a PC Paintbrush or MacPaint file, choose the appropriate option. To import Harvard Graphics files and files from other packages such as CAD/CAM packages or Perspective, you first have to use the IBM Plotter 6180 to create a plot file. Enable then can recognize and import the file.

# Using File Linking

You easily can incorporate data from spreadsheets and graphs into your word processing documents. If your original data changes, however, you need not perform an interwindow copy to change your document. Enable/OA 4.0 includes a new feature, *file linking* (sometimes called *warm linking* in other packages), which makes the incorporation of changing data worry-free. File linking enables you to update your word processing file to access automatically the most current data from the spreadsheet or graph. You use the %Link command to activate this feature.

## Linking Spreadsheet Data

Figure 8.17 shows a word processing file with a %Link command before you activate a link. The %Link command takes several arguments:

%link(ss,*#file*,"*range*")

where ss indicates that the following link is from a spreadsheet file, *#file* refers to the physical disk file you want to link, and *range* refers to the specific range you want to link. The range can be either a range name or a physical range. The command %Linkend shows the link process where to stop inserting data.

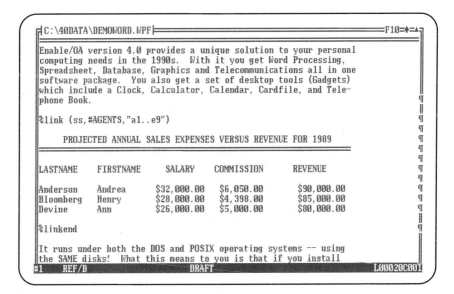

*Fig. 8.17. Spreadsheet linking before update.*

If you update a link, Enable deletes all data between the beginning and end of a link and inserts the new range with the most recent data. Figure 8.18 shows the document in figure 8.17 after the link update.

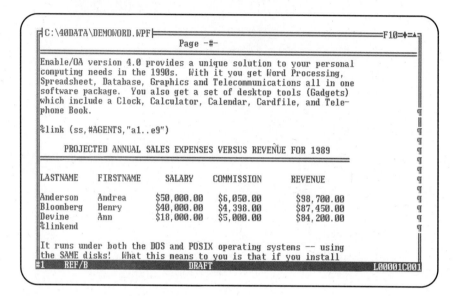

**Fig. 8.18.** *Spreadsheet linking after update.*

# Linking Graph Data

You also can use the %Link command to link with graphs in spreadsheet files. You need to perform an interwindow copy the first time you incorporate the graph into the word processing document (see Chapter 4, "Using the Master Control Module's Advanced Features"). After you incorporate the graph, add the %Link command to the comment area added above the graph. The syntax for the graph linking command is as follows:

%Link(gr,*#file*,"*setting*")

where gr indicates that the following link data is from a graph, *#file* refers to the spreadsheet where the graph setting is stored, and *setting* refers to the setting name within the spreadsheet file.

When you update the link, Enable moves the most recent graph into the graph area. Even if the new graph is a different kind of graph, the graph in your document reflects the change. Figure 8.19 shows a graph linking statement.

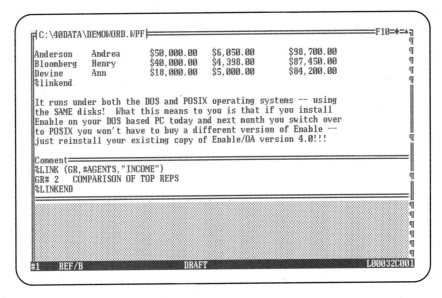

*Fig. 8.19. Graph linking statement.*

# Updating Links

To update the current links, press

F10 **File Link**

Enable offers you two choices: one update or all updates. If you want to update a single link, spreadsheet or graph, choose **One_update**. Enable prompts you to position your cursor and press Enter. Enable locates the next %Link command in your document and prompts

```
Press any key to update
```

Press any key to update the link, or press Esc to skip this link.

If you want to update all links, choose **All_updates**. Enable stops on each %LINK command and prompts `Press any key to update`. Press any key to update the link. If you press Esc, Enable stops on the next link and again issues the prompt. Respond to the prompt and continue this process until you have updated all links.

# Summary

This chapter describes some powerful features of Enable's word processing module. Although some may seem difficult if you are a beginner, as your Enable experience increases, so will your need for these powerful features. Use as many of the features as you can in your daily work. You may be surprised at the number of powerful word processing tools that Enable offers.

# Part IV

# The Spreadsheet Module

## Includes

# Quick Start IV

# Creating a Simple Spreadsheet

---

This quick-start lesson gives you an opportunity to create a simple spreadsheet with text, numbers, and formulas. You also learn how to print the spreadsheet, save and quit the file, and return to Enable's Main Menu. Like the other quick-start lessons, this one is intended to help you "break the ice." If you never have used a spreadsheet program, this lesson serves as a quick orientation.

To start the lesson, you already should have installed and started Enable properly. Your screen should show Enable's Main Menu. If it does not, refer to Appendix A and Quick Start I for information on getting started.

## Creating a Spreadsheet File

In this section, you create a spreadsheet file named QS4BUDGT.SSF. The portion of the file name before the dot (.) stands for Quick Start Lesson 4 Budget. Enable automatically assigns the file name extension SSF, which stands for Spreadsheet File.

To create the file, give it a name, and start constructing a simple family budget, follow these steps:

1. From the Main Menu, choose

   Use_System Spreadsheet

2. Type **QS4BUDGT** and press Enter. Enable displays a new spreadsheet (see fig. QSIV.1). Enable places the cursor on the second line from the top of the screen, called the *edit line*. As you type characters, Enable initially displays them in the edit line.

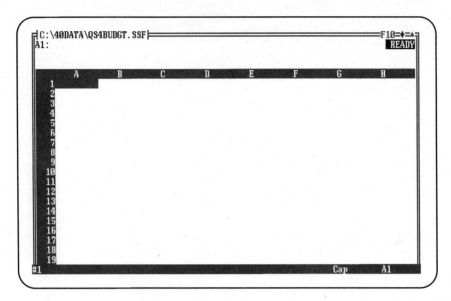

*Fig. QSIV.1. New spreadsheet QS4BUDGT.SSF.*

3. To place a title in your spreadsheet, type **Family Budget** and press Enter. As you type, Enable displays the text in the edit line. After you press Enter, Enable displays the text in a *cell*, the intersection of a row and column. You refer to a cell by its *cell address*, which identifies its location in the spreadsheet by its row and column. If a cell's address is C5, for example, the cell is located in column C, row 5. Enable enters the words Family Budget into cell A1. Because the cell is only nine characters wide by default, the text you enter into the cell "spills over" into the next cell, B1.

Enable displays the cell address in the top left corner on-screen and displays the text `Family Budget` to the right of this address. This top line is the *information line* and shows the contents of the current cell, which is highlighted (see fig. QSIV.2). This highlight, a reverse-video block (light blue if you have a color screen), is called the *cell pointer*. In the spreadsheet module, you use the cursor-movement keys (arrow keys, PgUp, PgDn, Tab, Home, and End) to move the cell pointer within the spreadsheet.

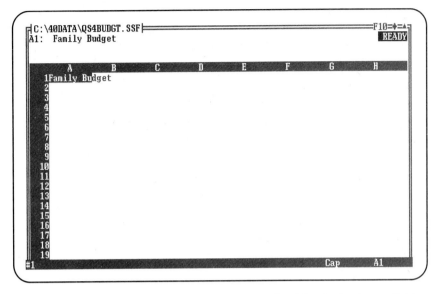

```
C:\40DATA\QS4BUDGT.SSF                                    F10=+=▲
A1:  Family Budget                                         READY

        A     B      C      D      E      F      G      H
    1Family Budget
    2
    3
    4
    5
    6
    7
    8
    9
   10
   11
   12
   13
   14
   15
   16
   17
   18
   19
                                              Cap        A1
```

**Fig. QSIV.2.** *QS4BUDGT.SSF spreadsheet with text* `Family Budget` *in cell A1.*

Now you learn to move the cell pointer to other cells to enter additional text.

4. Press the down-arrow key twice. The cell pointer moves down to cell A3.

5. To place a column heading in your spreadsheet, type **Income** and press Enter. Enable centers the word Income in cell A3. The program automatically centers text that is not as wide as the cell.

6. Without moving the cell pointer, type the same word again, but this time precede it with a less-than symbol (<):

   **<Income**

7. Press Enter. Enable overwrites the prior entry with the new entry. This time, however, Enable left-justifies the word Income. Using the less-than symbol as the first character in a text entry causes Enable to left-justify the entire entry (see fig. QSIV.3).

8. Type the following names in cells A4 through A6, respectively, and leave two spaces between the less-than symbol and each name to indent the names (again see fig. QSIV.3). As you type the characters, Enable displays LABEL in a reverse-video block at the upper right corner on-screen. (After you finish, Enable returns to ready mode.) This block is called the *mode indicator*. The LABEL mode indicates that the current cell will contain text.

Remember to press the down-arrow key after you type each name:

&lt; **Joe**
&lt; **Sarah**
&lt; **Harry**

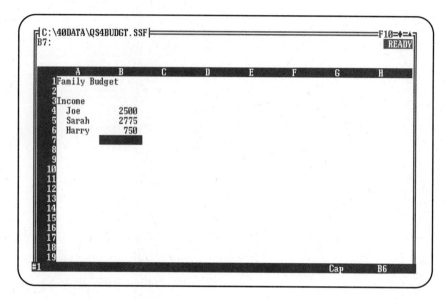

**Fig. QSIV.3.** *Left-justified spreadsheet text entry.*

9. Move the cell pointer to cell B4. Type **2500** and press Enter. Enable displays this number in cell B4. Notice that the program always reserves one space at the right end of the cell. Also notice that, as you type the number, Enable displays VALUE in the mode indicator.

10. Type the following values in cells B5 and B6, respectively (again see fig. QSIV.3):

   **2775**
   **750**

11. Enter a line in cell B7, to mark the end of the income figures, by typing a backslash (\) followed by a hyphen (-). The backslash is a "repeat" command that causes the hyphen to repeat across the width of the cell (see fig. QSIV.4).

12. To cause Enable to add the numbers in cells B4 through B6 and place the result in cell B8, type the following characters into cell B8:

    **+B4+B5+B6**

    As you type this formula, Enable displays VALUE in the mode indicator. The formula tells Enable to add the contents of cells B4, B5, and B6.

13. Press Enter. Enable adds the three numbers and displays the answer, 6025, in cell B8 (see fig. QSIV.4).

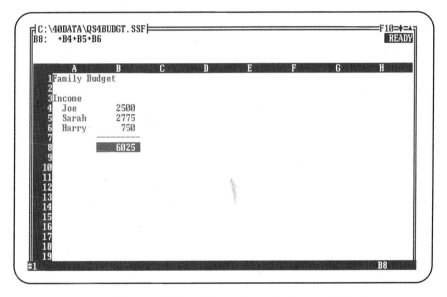

*Fig. QSIV.4. Spreadsheet with formula used to calculate total family income.*

14. Use the arrow keys to move the cell pointer to A10. Type labels (text) into cells A10 through A16. Be sure to indent each label, except Expenses, two spaces.

Instead of pressing Enter and then the down-arrow key after you type each label, just press the down-arrow key.

TIP

Enter the following labels into cells A10 through A16, respectively:

&lt;**Expenses**
  &lt;  **Rent**
  &lt;  **Food**
  &lt;  **Utils**
  &lt;  **Car**
  &lt;  **Fun**
  &lt;  **Miscl**

15. Enter the following values into cells B11 through B16, respectively:

    **1300**
    **500**
    **350**
    **650**
    **400**
    **600**

16. Use the backslash and hyphen to enter a line in cell B17.

With Enable, you can use special, built-in formulas, called *functions*. A function provides an easy way to enter formulas that are too complicated to put into a single calculation. Enable supplies more than 100 functions, many of them discussed in Chapter 10, "Using Spreadsheet Functions," and Chapter 12, "Using 3D Spreadsheets."

The following steps explain how to use a function to calculate the sum of the numbers in cells B11 through B16.

17. With the cell pointer in cell B18, type the following function:

    **@SUM(B11..B16)**

    This function tells Enable to calculate the sum of the cells in the range B11 through B16. Compare this function to the formula in step 12. Press Enter to display in cell B18 the result of this function (see fig. QSIV.5).

18. Enter the label &lt;**Save** in cell A20, and the following formula into cell B20:

    **+B8-B18**

Enable subtracts the total expenses from the total income and displays the result (see fig. QSIV.6) in cell B20.

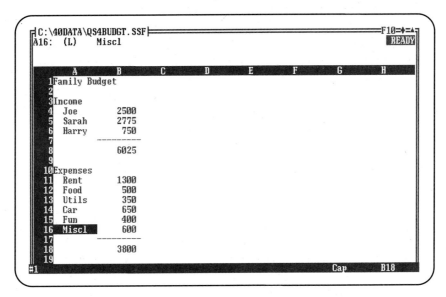

*Fig. QSIV.5. Spreadsheet with the function @SUM used to calculate total family expenses.*

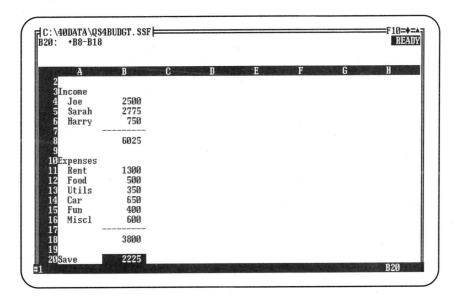

*Fig. QSIV.6. The completed family budget.*

The family budget doesn't look quite right. Because the numbers represent money, they should have dollar signs and commas.

To format all the numbers in the spreadsheet as currency, press

F10 **L**ayout **G**lobal **F**ormat

Then type a dollar sign ($), press 0, and press Enter. Enable displays all the numbers in the spreadsheet with dollar signs. Numbers greater than $999 also have commas (see fig. QSIV.7).

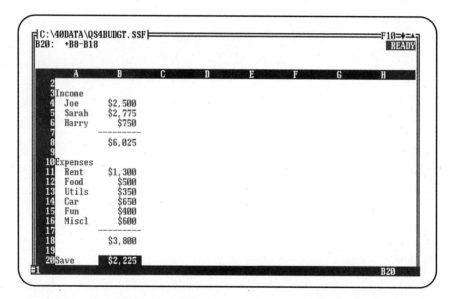

*Fig. QSIV.7. The completed family budget with currency value formatting.*

# Printing the Spreadsheet

Now you are ready to print your spreadsheet. Make sure that your printer is turned on, connected, on-line, and loaded with paper. Then press Alt-F2.

After you press Alt-F2, which activates Enable's *Quick Print* feature, the program prints your entire spreadsheet.

# Saving the Spreadsheet and Quitting

To save the file, quit, and return to the Main Menu, do the following:

1. Press Alt-F10 to save the current spreadsheet.

2. Press Alt-End to return to Enable's Main Menu, where you began.

# 9

# Understanding Spreadsheet Basics

**Y**ou probably have used spreadsheets most of your life. A spreadsheet, after all, is nothing more than a column or columns of numbers on which you perform mathematical operations. Any time you compute your taxes, balance your checkbook, or estimate the effects of different mortgage rates on your monthly payment, you use a spreadsheet. If you are new to microcomputers, however, your work with "spreadsheets" has been manual. You jotted down the numbers on a piece of paper and figured the results with your calculator or in your head.

The larger and more complex these "manual" spreadsheets become, the harder they are to manage. Electronic spreadsheets assist you with spreadsheet management by performing the necessary repetitive tasks for you. With electronic spreadsheets, the computer carries out the calculations so that you can concentrate on analyzing and interpreting the results. Imagine, for example, a complex financial model with dozens of formulas, each depending on a single variable. You can change the variable. The spreadsheet instantly recalculates all your formulas, saving you the time you may have spent reentering data with a calculator.

Suppose that you use a spreadsheet with hundreds of cells, and the value of each cell depends on the same rate. If you enter the tax rate into each formula that depends on the rate, the resulting spreadsheet is useful only while that tax rate remains in effect. If, however, you place the tax rate in a separate cell and include references to that cell in the formulas, the spreadsheet is useful no matter how the tax rate changes. In fact, the same spreadsheet becomes a perfect tool for making projections; you can use it to measure the effects of different tax rates on a complete set of figures. To perform this task, simply place the new tax rate in the appropriate cell and watch the spreadsheet recalculate.

The capacity to recalculate quickly is the power that makes the spreadsheet such an incredible tool. This power is not limited to the business world. Picture a beleaguered high school teacher trying to calculate end-of-term grades for 180 students. If the student grades and formulas are stored in a spreadsheet rather than a traditional grade book, the teacher can calculate the final grades with a keystroke and can respond quickly when a student asks, "What do I have to get on the final to pass?"

# Understanding the Spreadsheet Screen

As with all Enable modules, you begin working in a spreadsheet at the Main menu. To access the Main menu, press

Use_System Spreadsheet

Enable prompts you to enter a name for your new spreadsheet. Type any valid Enable file name, and then press the Enter key. You see a blank spreadsheet (see fig. 9.1).

The column headings, letters A through H, appear across the screen. You enter your data in the *columns* below these headings. These 8 on-screen columns are only a portion of the 1,024 columns actually available on the Enable spreadsheet.

To display other columns on the spreadsheet, try the following exercise. First, make sure that the Num Lock key on your keyboard is inactive; then hold down the right-arrow key. Notice that when you hold down the key without releasing it, the spreadsheet scrolls past column Z to columns AA, AB, AC, and so on. This format continues all the way to column AMJ—1,024 columns to the right of your starting point.

Enable also offers you many more than the 20 *rows* you see in figure 9.1. When you press and hold down the down-arrow key, you can scroll down 9,999 rows. A faster way to get to the bottom of the spreadsheet, however, is to press End-down arrow.

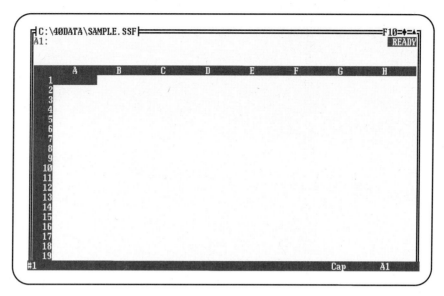

**Fig. 9.1.** *A blank spreadsheet.*

The intersections of these rows and columns are called *cells*; you enter data directly into these cells. Each cell is identified by a *cell address* consisting of the column letter and row number of the cell. The cell address of the intersection of column G and row 12, for example, is G12; the intersection of column R and row 212 is addressed R212. Enable's 9,999 rows and 1,024 columns provide you 10,238,976 cells to use with your spreadsheet. Of course, you probably will not fill them all; however, if you want to use all the possible cells, you can because Enable/OA supports LIM/EMS 4.0.

If you experimented with moving around in the spreadsheet, press the Home key once. Enable redisplays the starting screen, columns A through H and rows 1 through 20. A reverse video block fills cell A1. This block is called the *cell pointer*—the on-screen locator that functions like the cursor in the word processing module. The position of the cell pointer indicates the cell that is ready to receive data. The address of the cell that contains the cell pointer is the *current cell indicator* (in this example, A1). The current cell indicator always appears in the upper left corner of the *information display area* above the spreadsheet, except when Enable displays the Top Line menu (see fig. 9.2).

At the bottom of the screen is the *status line*, which displays the window number on the far left side and the address of the *highest cell* used in the spreadsheet. The highest cell used is the occupied cell with the largest row number and rightmost column name. When the *deepest cell* (the cell with the highest row number) is in a column other than the rightmost column, the intersection of the rightmost column with the deepest row used anywhere in the spreadsheet becomes the highest cell (see fig. 9.3).

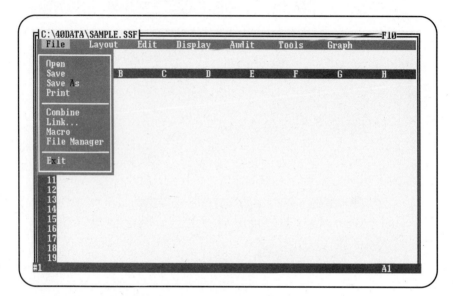

**Fig. 9.2.** *The spreadsheet pull-down menu.*

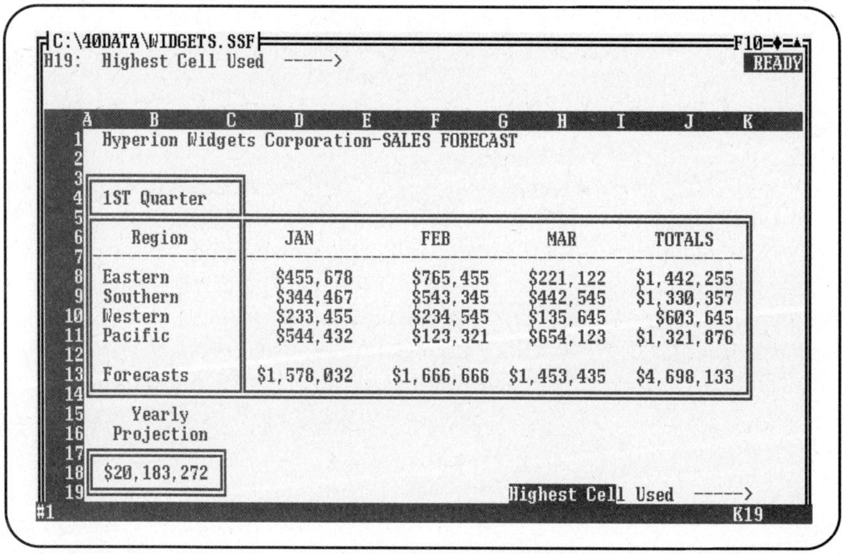

**Fig. 9.3.** *The window number and address of the highest cell used displayed on the status line.*

# Entering Data into a Cell

Although spreadsheets are used primarily for "crunching" numbers, you type a great deal of text into spreadsheets as well, to make them understandable. In the spreadsheet module, Enable treats the numbers you enter much differently from the text; numbers are called *values* and strings of text are called *labels*.

## Entering Numbers: Values

In the spreadsheet module, Enable assumes that any cell entry that begins with any of the numbers *0 through 9* or any of the characters @ + − . *$ (* is a value. To work with the numbers, first, do the following exercise:

In a blank spreadsheet, type a three-digit number with the cell pointer at cell A1. Before you press Enter, notice two things. First, the numbers you type appear directly below the current cell indicator in the information display area, not in the cell itself. This line is the *edit line*. Enable does not transfer the entry from the edit line to the cell until you press Enter or one of the direction keys (right arrow, left arrow, and so on). See figure 9.4.

The natural tendency of many first-time spreadsheet users is to use the left-arrow key to correct typing errors. Break this habit immediately! Use the Backspace key instead. When you press the left-arrow key to make a correction, you actually enter the incorrect data into the current cell and move the pointer one cell to the left.

Another natural tendency you need to resist is the urge to enter dollar signs and commas with the numbers for financial calculations. In the Enable spreadsheet, dollar signs have a special purpose, unrelated to currency, and you never use commas when you enter a value. You can, however, cause values to appear on-screen like currency by using the Format command, discussed in the section "Using the Currency Formatting Option" in this chapter.

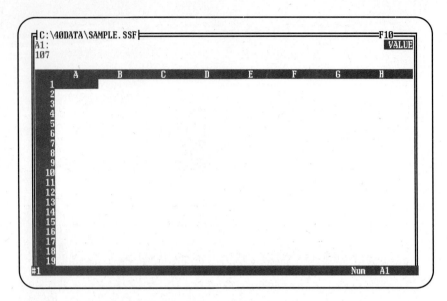

*Fig. 9.4. A value in the edit line of a spreadsheet.*

Second, notice the box in the upper right corner of the screen—the *mode indicator*. Before you type anything, the mode indicator displays READY. As you type a number, the indicator displays VALUE. The mode indicator always indicates the current activity in your spreadsheet, whether you are entering text or numbers, carrying out a command, working with a menu, or doing other tasks. The mode indicator is a useful tool for your spreadsheet. Make sure that you check the mode regularly, particularly if Enable does not respond as you expect. You may find that you are doing one task in a spreadsheet while your computer is set to do another.

Table 9.1 lists the Mode Indicator messages.

**Table 9.1**
**Enable's Mode Indicator Messages**

| Message | Meaning |
|---------|---------|
| BUSY | Currently processing a requested action; please wait. |
| CMENU | Displaying a user-defined menu. |
| COMM | Processing a command. |
| DBMS | Copying DBMS records. |
| EDIT | Permitting modification to input. |
| GRAPH | Creating a graph. |

| Message | Meaning |
|---------|---------|
| LABEL | User is entering a label. |
| MENU | Displaying the Top Line menu. |
| POINT | User is pointing out a range or formula. |
| VALUE | User is entering a value, formula, or function. |
| READY | Waiting for the next command or entry.[*] |

[*]The READY message may display as:

| | |
|---------|---------|
| +READY | The interruptible calculation feature is active. |
| *READY | A macro is active. |
| #READY | Both the interruptible calculation and a macro are active. |

If you haven't succumbed to the temptation already, press the Enter key now. The mode indicator changes to READY, indicating that Enable is ready to accept your data. The three-digit number you entered has disappeared from the edit line; the number now appears to the right of the cell address in the information display area. In addition, the number itself now appears in the A1 cell (see fig. 9.5).

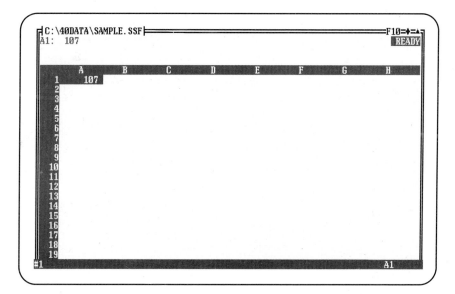

**Fig. 9.5.** *A value entry.*

Press the down-arrow key once. The current cell indicator tells you that you are in cell A2. Type another three-digit number; once again, don't press Enter. Notice that the mode indicator reads VALUE. When you press the down-arrow key again, the second number appears in the cell A2 in the spreadsheet. The pointer moves down to the next cell. This alternative to pressing Enter works with all the direction keys (the four arrows, Home, End, PgUp, and PgDn).

You may notice that Enable places values in what appears as the right-justified position in the cell. Actually, the last available space at the right side of the cell is left blank so that numbers in adjacent cells do not run together. This alignment is different from the default alignment for labels, discussed in the next section. But before you go on to that section, move the cell pointer to an empty cell, type **123456789**, and then press Enter. Because this number is too long to display in the eight available spaces of a cell, Enable automatically displays it in scientific format: 1.23E+08. This format means 1.23 times 10 to the 8th power.

## Entering Text: Labels

A cell entry is a label when it begins with any character other than the characters + − . $ or the numbers 0 through 9. As you type your name, for example, into a cell, Enable's mode indicator displays the word LABEL. Type a label of only three or four characters. Instead of right-justifying, Enable normally centers the label.

To change the alignment of a label entry, use one of the following characters:

| Alignment Character | Cell Alignment |
| --- | --- |
| < | Left |
| > | Right |
| ^ | Center |

**TIP**

When you begin a value entry with one of the alignment characters, Enable automatically converts the entry to a label.

Now type a longer label—at least 10 characters. If the cell to the immediate right of the current cell is not occupied, the label longer than 8 characters continues to display through the cells to the right until stopped by a cell that contains a value. Labels actually can be up to 240 characters long.

You can create any ASCII code that your printer can print by simultaneously holding down the Alt key and pressing in sequence the numbers in the decimal code for the character. Use the number keys on the number pad and the decimal code listed in Appendix B of the "Integration" section of Enable's documentation. For example, you can display the box-drawing upper left corner character in a cell by holding Alt while pressing the 2, 1, and 8 keys (decimal code 218). You can also apply the text attributes described in Chapter 7, "Using Formatting Features," to spreadsheet labels.

TIP

To create a line in a cell—a line, for example, that separates a column of numbers from the total of those numbers—type the following label:

    \-

The backslash is a "repeat" key when it is the first character in a cell. The backslash causes any character(s) following it to repeat across the cell, regardless of cell width.

# Editing a Cell

After you enter either a value or label into a cell, you may decide to change or delete the value or label. Move the cell pointer to the cell that you want to edit, and then press F4.

F4 is the edit key. Notice that the mode indicator displays EDIT, and the current cell entry is in the edit line. Because the direction keys now move the cursor in the edit line, rather than the cell pointer in the spreadsheet itself, the keys operate more like they do in the word processing module: the left- or right-arrow key moves the cursor one character at a time in the expected direction, the End key moves the cursor all the way to the right end of the current entry, and the Home key moves the cursor all the way to the left end of the current entry. You also can use the Ins and Del keys to edit the entry, and use the Esc key to abort the edit without making any changes. The Esc key aborts the edit only if you do not press Enter first.

# Entering a Formula

The power of any spreadsheet resides in its *formulas*. A spreadsheet formula defines the relationship between two or more values in a specific cell.

Without formulas, you have nothing more effective than a big sheet of paper. Formulas provide you with the capability to change a parameter in even the most complex financial model and immediately see the effect. An operation that used to take business students, accountants, and budget analysts hours or even days to recalculate is done now in the blink of an eye.

Spreadsheet formulas look much like normal math formulas. A spreadsheet, in fact, can be used as a glorified electronic calculator. Therefore, when you type $3+4-2$ you receive the expected answer: 5.

Spreadsheet formulas are most useful when you substitute cell addresses for numbers in the formulas. For example, suppose that you type the following formula:

**+A3+A4−A2**

Enable looks at the contents of the referenced cells and uses those numbers to do the calculations required by the formula. The result of the formula in this example depends on the values of the cells A2, A3, and A4. Changing the value of one or more of these cells changes the answer to the formula. Compare the formulas in the information display areas, the values of the cells A2, A3, and A4, and the results in cell A6 in figures 9.6 and 9.7.

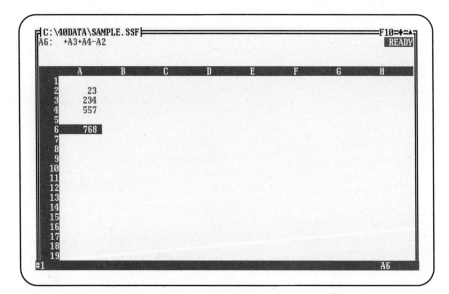

*Fig. 9.6. The result of a simple formula in the Enable spreadsheet.*

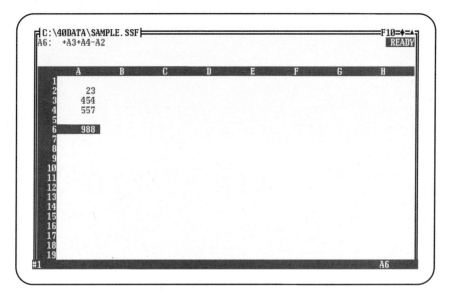

**Fig. 9.7.** *A simple formula in the Enable Spreadsheet.*

Compare the result of the new value for cell A3 to figure 9.6.

> When the first character in a formula would normally tell Enable
> that the entry is a label, you must begin the formula with the plus
> sign (+). All formulas must be values, not labels.

CAUTION

# Using Operators in Formulas

All formulas contain *operators* that indicate the relationships between the
values. Operators are the symbols that indicate the arithmetic operation,
such as addition, subtraction, multiplication, and division. You can think of
a formula as a mathematical sentence: the values are nouns and the
operators are verbs. Operators specify the actions (the mathematical operations) you want to perform.

The following list of Enable's mathematical operators are familiar to you:

| Symbol | Operation |
|--------|-----------|
| ** | Exponentiation |
| * | Multiplication |
| / | Division |
| + | Addition |
| − | Subtraction |

Using these operators, to enter $4^6$ in Enable format, type **4\*\*6**, or to divide the value of cell A6 by 3, type **+A6/3**.

The order of operations determines how Enable groups the values and operators in a formula to arrive at an answer. You can have very different answers depending on how you read the following formula:

+A6+36/2*3

Suppose that cell A6 holds the value 17. If you simply read the formula left to right, you add 17 and 36, which equals 53; then you divide by 2, which equals 26.5, and multiply by 3 for a total of 79.5. However, when Enable evaluates this formula as written, the result is 71.

Why? Enable does mathematical calculations based on three "rules" for the order of operations. The first rule is the following standard order of precedence:

1. Exponentiation

2. Negative number assignment

3. Multiplication and division

4. Addition and subtraction

For example, in the formula +A6+36/2, Enable first divides 36 by 2 (division is the higher operator in the order of precedence), which equals 18; then Enable adds (addition is the lower operator in the order of precedence) 18 to 17 (the value of cell A6) and the result is 35.

The second rule is that in a formula consisting of equivalent operators such as multiplication and division, which are equal in the order of precedence, Enable uses the standard order of left to right. In the formula +A6+36/2*3, therefore, Enable first divides 36 by 2 (division is the higher operator in the order of precedence and the first in the order of left to right), which equals 18; then Enable multiplies (in this formula, multiplication is the higher operator in the order of precedence and second in the order of left to right) the result by 3 to equal 54. Finally, Enable adds (addition is the lower operator in the order of precedence) 17 to 54, which equals 71.

Enable's third rule for the order of operations is that any operation in parentheses is calculated first. For example, suppose that you rewrite your formula as +A6+36/(2*3). Enable first multiplies (the operator in the parentheses) 2 by 3, which equals 6; then Enable divides (of the remaining operators, division is the higher operator in the order of precedence) 36 by 6 to equal 6; finally Enable adds (of the operators outside the parentheses, addition is the lower operator in the order of precedence) 6 to 17 (the value of cell A6). The result is yet another value: 23. *Note:* If a formula contains more than one set of parentheses, Enable treats each set as a separate formula. If a formula contains nested parentheses, for example, +A6+36/(2*(2+3)), the formula in the innermost parentheses is calculated first.

> Pay close attention to the order of operations. A misplaced set of parentheses or a carelessly designed formula can result in a spreadsheet that yields reasonable-looking answers which are entirely incorrect.

# Using the Point Method to Enter a Formula

One of the most useful skills for you to master when building spreadsheets is the *point method*. To create a formula, you can point to the cells that contain the values you want to use in the formula. In the Widget spreadsheet shown in figure 9.8, to create a formula for the yearly projection (cell B18) that is equal to four times the amount of a quarterly forecast (cell J13), enter the formula 4*J13 in cell B18. To create this formula, follow these steps:

1. Move the cell pointer into cell B18, the cell you want to contain the answer.

2. Press the number 4, and then press the asterisk (*). Do not type the address of the cell that contains the first quarter total.

3. Use the arrow keys to point to the cell that is the next reference in the formula—cell J13. Watch the information display area; the formula changes as you move the cell pointer, and the mode indicator displays POINT. When the pointer is in cell J13, press Enter.

*Note:* In this example, you can type the cell address directly into the formula as easily as you can point to the cell; however, if the cell you need is not on the current screen, or if the formula is lengthy, the point method can prove to be more accurate.

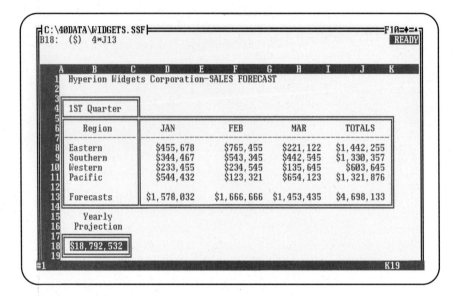

**Fig. 9.8.** *A formula created with the point method.*

# Using Functions and Ranges in Formulas

Thus far, you have worked with simple formulas in which each cell necessary to calculate an answer has been explicitly referenced in the formula. If this method were the only way to create a formula, to add just a short column of numbers would require a great deal of typing or pointing. The more efficient method to create a long formula is to use a *function*—a built-in logical or mathematical operation into which you can enter appropriate values. Within a function you can use a *range*—a rectangular group of contiguous cells in a spreadsheet.

# Using the Basic Rules of Spreadsheet Functions

Spreadsheet functions generally conform to the standard syntax

@NAME(ARGUMENT)

Enable has only a few exceptions to the following basic rules of spreadsheet functions:

- The first element is the *at sign (@)*. This character tells Enable that the characters which follow represent a built-in formula. Recall from an earlier section in this chapter that this symbol is one of the valid characters for beginning a value cell entry in a spreadsheet.

- The second element, which follows the at sign, is the *NAME* of the function.

- The third element, which follows the function name, is one or more *ARGUMENTS*. The arguments—values and sometimes labels—are the parameters used to perform the built-in calculation and must be enclosed in a set of parentheses. Arguments can be a range of cells, a list of cells, a list of values, or some combination of these three alternatives. The following are valid arguments with the @SUM function:

  ◦ Range of cells: @SUM(A1..A5)

  ◦ List of values: @SUM(2,3,9)

  ◦ Combination: @SUM(G7,4,F3..F6)

The few exceptions to these rules fall into two categories: string operators and functions without arguments. A few functions that don't begin with the @ symbol really are operators. Examples of operators are +, −, *, and *string concatenate operators* R, R+, R−, which you use to join strings. The other group of exceptions are functions that are constants. For example, in Enable, the function @PI represents the mathematical constant *pi* (3.141592653589794). These functions are exceptions to the syntax rules because they take no argument.

# Using Ranges

In the preceding examples for spreadsheet functions, the first argument is (A1..A5), referring to cells A1, A2, A3, A4, and A5. In the argument, these five cells are expressed as a range. When you use a range in a function or with a command, the function or command operates on all the cells in the range. The effect is the same as if you enter each cell individually.

Remember that a range of cells must be rectangular in shape and consist of contiguous cells. Valid ranges include a single cell, part of a column, part of a row, and a block that spans several columns and several rows (see fig 9.9).

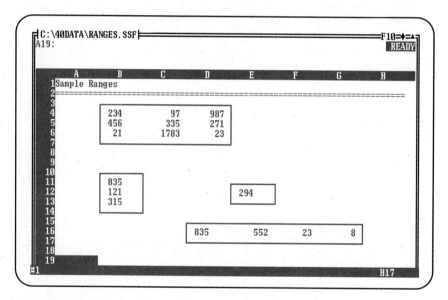

*Fig. 9.9. Sample ranges.*

To identify a range in a function or command you create a *range expression* by listing the diagonal coordinates (the upper left cell and the lower right cell) of the block of cells, separated by two periods. The range expression for all the cells from A6 through A17 and across through B17, for example, would be A6..B17.

# Using Basic Spreadsheet Commands

Although formulas are probably the tools you will use most often in a spreadsheet, they can operate only upon the cells. You can use commands, however, to manipulate the entire spreadsheet. For example, suppose that you want to copy or move a range, change the width of a column, save the spreadsheet, or analyze the spreadsheet. Enable provides you with a large arsenal of commands for managing spreadsheets. The following sections introduce you to the most basic commands; Chapter 11, "Using Spreadsheet Advanced Features," discusses more advanced commands.

Enable groups its spreadsheet commands into six menu categories: Edit commands, Layout commands (which are divided into Global commands and Range commands), Display commands, Audit commands, File commands, and Tools commands (see Chapter 11 for a discussion of Tools).

## Using Edit Commands

Edit commands affect the spreadsheet itself rather than the labels and values that the spreadsheet contains. You can use these commands to copy and move cells, insert and delete rows and columns, erase cells, undo your last command, and perform other useful tasks.

To choose an Edit command, press

F10 **Edit**

You see a pull-down menu that displays the twelve Edit options (see fig. 9.10). To choose a command, press the highlighted letter of the command, or the first letter of the command with no highlighted letter. Depending on your choice, a new menu may appear on-screen. The following sections discuss four Edit commands you use most often: Insert, Delete, Undo, and Erase. Chapter 11, "Using Spreadsheet Advanced Features," discusses more Edit commands.

## Using the Insert Command

Use the Insert command to add new rows or columns to an existing spreadsheet. (You can also use the Insert command to insert levels and blocks; levels are discussed in Chapter 11, "Using Spreadsheet Advanced Features," however, a discussion of blocks is beyond the scope of this book.)

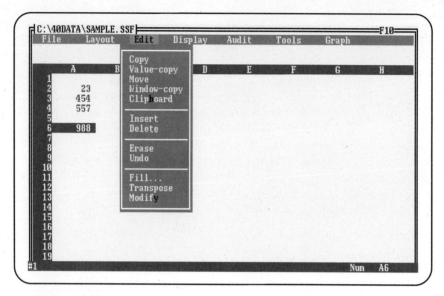

*Fig. 9.10. The Edit command menu.*

Before you choose the Insert command, make sure that you place the cell pointer where you want the new row(s) or column(s) to appear. When you insert a new column, all columns from the point of insertion move to the right. When you insert a row, all rows from the point of insertion move down the specified number of rows. Therefore, to insert a new column, place the pointer on the column you want to have on the *right* of your inserted column. To insert a new row, place the pointer on the row you want to have *below* the new row.

After you place the cell pointer at the correct position in the spreadsheet, to insert a row or column, press

F10 **Edit Insert**

Enable displays the Insert menu to the right of the Edit menu (see fig. 9.11). Choose Row or Column. Enable displays a third menu that offers you the choice to use the Insert command on this level or all levels. (Each spreadsheet consists of 32 pages or levels; each level resembles a standard 9999-row and 1028-column worksheet.) For purposes of this basic instruction, choose This level, and then press Enter. Enable then asks how many rows or columns you want to insert. Type the number and press Enter.

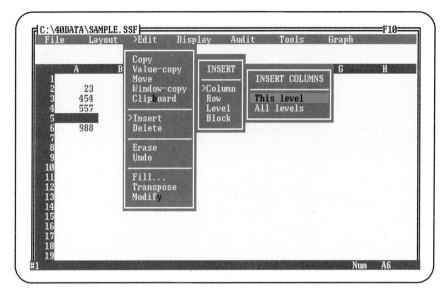

*Fig. 9.11. The Insert Columns menus.*

Remember that all columns from the point of insertion move to the right, and all rows from the point of insertion move down. Any formulas with ranges interrupted by the insertion of new columns or rows readjust to account for the new row or column. If a formula in cell B9 reads @SUM(B3..B7), for example, and you insert a new row at B5, the formula automatically changes to @SUM(B3..B8).

This adjustment for inserted columns and rows applies only to *ranges* in formulas. If you express the original formula as +B3+B4+B5+B6+B7, for example, and you insert a row at B5, the resulting formula is +B3+B4+B6+B7+B8; B5 is not included.

In addition, if you insert a row or column at the very *end* of the range so that you add the new row or column *outside* the range, the formula does not adjust automatically to include the new row or column in the range. Unfortunately, this situation often occurs quite naturally when you insert a new row into a column of numbers you are adding. In the example @SUM(B3..B7, if you insert the row at the bottom of the column just before the formula (creating a new row 8), the formula does not adjust to include the new row.

One way to avoid this potentially disastrous situation, at least when you're *adding* the numbers in the range, is to include a *total line* in the original range. In the example, to place a line in cell B8, use the *repeat character (\)*

and the *hard hyphen (Alt-hyphen)*. (If you reference a label in a formula, Enable treats the label as if it has the value 0; you therefore can include a label, the total line in this example, without affecting the sum. *Note:* Be careful that you do not reference a label in a formula that may be adversely affected. For instance, @AVG=@SUM/@COUNT—if you reference a label in a formula that includes @AVG, the @SUM is unaffected, but the result of @COUNT is 1 too many. The original formula to add the range of numbers in cells B3 through B7 then becomes @SUM(B3..B8). Now, even if you insert a new row 8, the range adjusts properly and the formula is @SUM(B3..B9).

An alternative way to insert rows (but not columns) is to place the pointer on a row you want to delete and press Alt-F3. Then indicate the range and press Enter.

## Using the Delete Command

The Delete command works much like the Insert command, but in reverse. You can delete a row, column, level, block, or multiple rows or columns at once. To delete a row or column, place the pointer on the desired row or column and press

F10 **Edit Delete**

Enable displays the Delete menu to the right of the Edit menu, from which you can choose to delete a row, column, level, or block (see fig. 9.12). Choose **R**ow or **C**olumn. Enable displays a pull-down menu from which you can choose to delete a column or row in this level or all levels. For purposes of this basic instruction, choose This level, and then press Enter. Enable then asks for the range of rows or columns you want to delete. Specify the range of cells that spans the appropriate columns or rows, and press Enter.

**TIP**

Use the point method to specify the range so that you can see the range highlighted, and check the accuracy of your command before you delete.

If you delete a column, all columns to the *right* of the insertion point move left. If you delete a row, all columns *below* the insertion point move up. Enable adjusts all ranges (and only ranges) in formulas to account for the deletions.

An alternative way to delete rows (but not columns) is to place the pointer on a row you want to delete and press Alt-F3. Then indicate the range and press Enter.

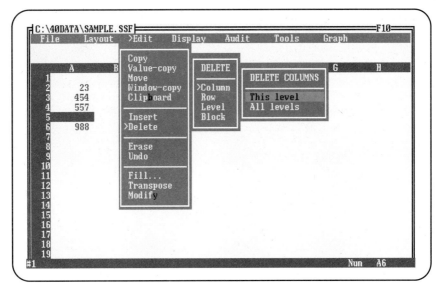

***Fig. 9.12.*** *The Delete Columns menus.*

## Using the Undo Command

The Undo command is a new feature in the Enable/OA 4.0 Spreadsheet module. Use the Undo command if you delete more columns or rows than you need to delete, or if you need to restore the preceding value of a cell. To choose the Undo command, press

>F10 **Edit Undo**

or press

>F9 **U**

Enable restores any spreadsheet information changed by the last command. ***Note:*** Enable can restore only up to the last command. If you make a mistake, undo it immediately.

Because the Undo command takes more memory, it may not be turned on in your spreadsheet. Before you can use the Undo command, be sure that you turn it on. To check the status of Undo, press F10 **Tools Defaults** to display the Spreadsheet Environment screen. Activate the Undo command, if necessary. You also can set this feature in Profile.

# Using the Erase Command

You can use the Erase command to erase either a range or your entire spreadsheet. To choose the Erase command, press

**F10 Edit Erase**

From the succeeding menu, choose **R**ange or **S**preadsheet (see fig. 9.13).

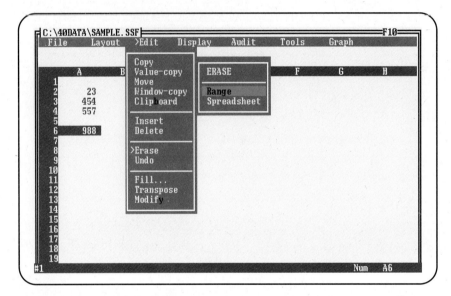

**Fig. 9.13.** *The Erase Range menu options.*

If you choose **R**ange, Enable asks you for the range to erase. Use the point method to be sure that you erase the desired range. If you choose **S**preadsheet, Enable asks you to verify that you want to erase the spreadsheet. If you answer **Y**es to the prompt, Enable deletes your entire spreadsheet in an instant.

> The Erase command is final; you cannot recover an erased spreadsheet; therefore you should save your spreadsheet before you issue the Erase command.

# Using Range Commands

Range commands affect individual ranges of your spreadsheet. To access the Range commands (see fig. 9.14), press

F10 **L**ayout **R**ange

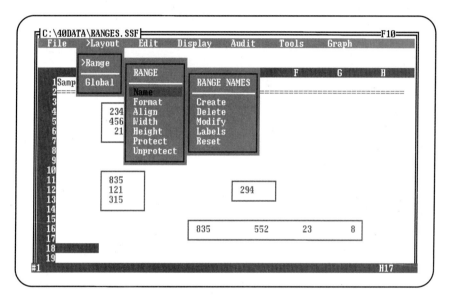

*Fig. 9.14. The Range menu.*

The following sections discuss the Range Format, Align, Name, Height, and Width commands; see Chapter 11 for a discussion of Protect and Unprotect.

## Formatting a Range

Even though you enter all values in your spreadsheet in the same format, you may want them to appear differently on-screen. If you know a particular range always has integer values, or you want a range always to appear in currency format, you can use the Range Format command to format the range. With the Range Format command, you can display and print the values in your spreadsheet in 10 different ways: with a fixed number of decimal places, as integers, as currency, with commas, as percentages, as dates, as time, in scientific notation, in general format, and as plus or minus signs (see fig. 9.15).

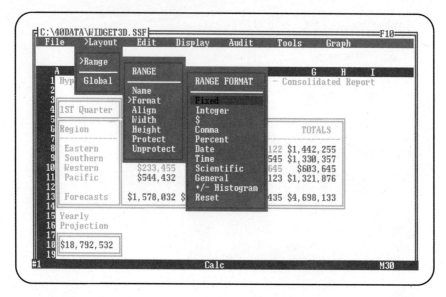

**Fig. 9.15.** *Format options.*

To format a range, press

F10 **Layout R**ange **F**ormat

Enable displays a menu of formatting options, which are discussed in the following sections. After you select an option, Enable prompts you for a range to format. Type in the range or use the point method to highlight it.

Changing the format of spreadsheet values does not affect the way Enable uses the values in internal calculations. The format affects only the way the value looks on-screen and prints. A value of 7.5 appears as 8 if the format is set to display all values in the range as integers. *Note:* Enable always displays the actual number you enter in the current cell (up to 14 decimal places) next to the cell indicator in the information display area—without regard to the range format command.

## Using the Fixed Formatting Option

Use the Fixed formatting option to display your data on-screen in a fixed number of decimal places up to 14 places. Enable rounds any further decimal places upward if the value is 5 or greater. If you format the number 45.496 to 2 places, for example, the number 45.50 appears on-screen and in print.

To choose Fixed formatting, press

F10 **Layout Range** Format **Fixed**

You see the prompt `Enter number of decimal places (0..14)`. Type the number you want and press Enter. Enable then prompts you to `Enter range to format:`; enter the range and press Enter.

## Using the Integer Formatting Option

The Integer formatting option displays all values in the range as integers (numbers without decimal places). This option rounds numbers to the nearest integer; for example, 34.34 appears as 34, but 34.74 appears as 35.

To choose Integer formatting, press

F10 **Layout Range** Format **Integer**

At the prompt, specify the range, and press Enter.

## Using the Currency ($) Formatting Option

The Currency ($) formatting option displays all values in the range in dollars-and-cents format. A dollar sign ($) precedes the values, and Enable marks every third place to the left of the decimal with a comma. You can display the value with 0 to 14 decimal places. For example, the number 1456.65478 displayed in Currency format with 2 decimal places appears as $1,456.65.

To choose Currency formatting, press

F10 **Layout Range** Format **$**

Enable prompts `Enter number of decimal places (0-14)`. Type your choice and press Enter. At the prompt `Enter range to format:`, enter the range and press Enter.

## Using the Comma Formatting Option

The Comma formatting option is exactly like the Currency option but without the dollar sign; Enable marks every third place to the left of the decimal with a comma.

To choose Comma formatting, press

F10 **Layout Range** Format **Comma**

The prompts are familiar: `Enter number of decimal places (0-14)`; type your choice and press Enter. At `Enter range to format`: specify the range and press Enter.

## Using the Percent Formatting Option

The Percent formatting option displays values as percentages with a percent sign (%). For example, the value 0.2322 formatted with the Percent option with two decimal places appears as 23.22%.

To choose Percent formatting, press

F10 **Layout Range Format Percent**

Enable prompts you to `Enter number of decimal places (0-14)`. Type the number and press Enter. When you see the range prompt, specify the range and press Enter.

## Using the Date Formatting Option

To represent a date in an Enable spreadsheet, you use a special number, sometimes referred to as a *serial date number*, which is the number of days that have elapsed since December 31, 1899. The number 1, for example, represents January 1, 1900. You can use several special functions to calculate the serial date number. For example, type the following formula in a blank cell of your spreadsheet:

**@DATE(89,3,9)**

Enable returns the number 32575, the serial date number for March 9, 1989. Use the Date formatting option to make this number look like the date that it represents. With this approach to dates, you can do arithmetic with a serial date number, and then have Enable convert the result into a date format on-screen.

Thirteen different date formats are available. Figure 9.16 shows all the different formatting options for the serial date number 32516. The mini-table that follows explains what each date formatting character in figure 9.16 means.

| Character | Meaning |
|-----------|---------|
| DD | Day of the month in digits |
| DDD | Day of the year |
| MM | Month of the year in digits |
| MON | Three-character abbreviation for the month |
| MONTH | Full month name |
| YY | Two-digit year |
| YYYY | Full four-digit year |

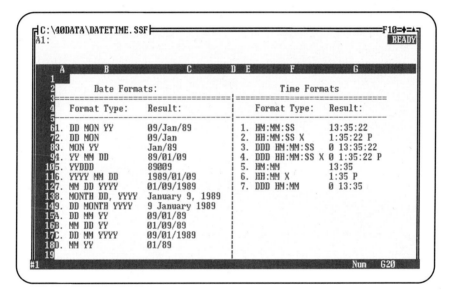

**Fig. 9.16.** *Date and time formats.*

*Note:* The only format in figure 9.16 that may require some explanation is YYDDD. The result, 89009, tells you that January 9, 1989, is the ninth day of the 89th year of the century. This format is known as the *Julian date.* Enable's calendar goes through the year 2499.

To choose Date formatting, press

F10 **L**ayout **R**ange **F**ormat **D**ate

Enable displays a list of date formatting options, as shown in figure 9.17. Choose a Date format from this list.

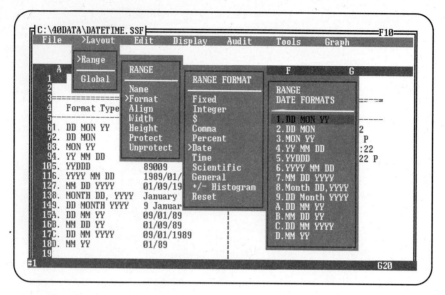

**Fig. 9.17.** *Date formatting options.*

At the prompt, `Enter range to format:`, specify the range and press Enter.

## Using the Time Formatting Option

Just as the serial date number represents the number of days elapsed since December 31, 1899, the *serial time number* represents the number of seconds elapsed since midnight. As with dates, Enable has a number of special functions that return elapsed seconds. Use the Time formatting option to convert elapsed seconds to time.

You can use the Time formatting option to display *time integers*—serial time numbers—in seven formats, as shown in figure 9.16. The table that follows explains what each character in figure 9.16 represents.

| *Character* | *Meaning* |
|---|---|
| HM | Military Hours (24 hours). |
| HH | Regular Hours (12 Hours). |
| MM | Minutes. |
| SS | Seconds. |
| X | A or P for a.m. or p.m. |
| DDD | Number of days—for elapsed time. |

Formats 1, 2, 5, and 6 in figure 9.16 are fairly simple. To use the @TIME function on 1:35:22 p.m., for example, you write the formula

@TIME(13,35,22)

Enable returns the serial time number 48922. In the two time formats, this number appears as follows:

Military time:    13:35:22

Standard time:  1:35:22 P

Notice the P for p.m. at the end of the standard time display.

The two elapsed-time formats (4 and 7 in figure 9.16) simply add a parameter for days. Enable converts elapsed seconds to days, hours, minutes, and seconds.

To choose Time formatting, press

F10 **Layout Range Format Time**

Then choose one of the seven time formats from the menu (see fig. 9.18).

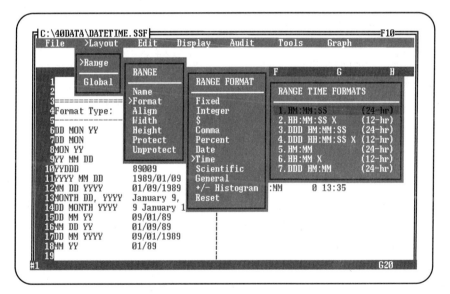

**Fig. 9.18.** *Time formats.*

Enable now prompts you to `Enter range to format:`; specify the range and press Enter.

## Using the Scientific Formatting Option

When you use the Scientific formatting option, Enable expresses numbers in scientific notation—as a decimal number between 1 and 10 multiplied by a power of 10. In this format, the letter E (for *exponent*) separates the decimal portion and the exponent of 10. Enable rounds the decimal portion to the number of decimal places you designate. For example, if you choose three decimal places rather than the default of two, 7678.234510 becomes 7.678E+03

Read this number as "7.678 times 10 to the third power."

To choose Scientific formatting, press

> F10 **Layout** **Range** **Format** **Scientific**

Enable displays the prompt

> `Enter number of decimal places (0..14):`

Type a number from 0 to 14 and press Enter. At the prompt

> `Enter range to format:`

specify the range and press Enter.

## Using the General Formatting Option

The General formatting option is the default in an Enable spreadsheet. Values appear on-screen exactly the way you type them. Decimals do not necessarily line up when numbers appear in a column.

To choose the General formatting option, press

> F10 **Layout** **Range** **Format** **General**

and press Enter. At the prompt, `Enter range to format:`, specify the range, and then press Enter.

## Using the Plus/Minus (+/–) Formatting Option

Plus/Minus (+/–) formatting has been around since the days of VisiCalc, the first electronic spreadsheet. The Plus/Minus formatting option displays a *histogram* that represents the value in each cell in a range. (If a cell in the range contains the value 41, for example, Enable displays 41 plus signs in that cell. If the cell contains the value –6, Enable displays six minus signs.) The histogram, however, is somewhat crude and is no match for Enable's graphics capabilities.

To format a range in Plus/Minus format, first use the Layout Range Width command, discussed in the section "Using the Range Width Command," to make the cells wide enough to display your histogram. Then press

F10 **Layout Range Format +/–**

and specify the range.

Because you can have a total of only 72 characters displayed in a given cell, the Plus/Minus option is somewhat limited. Be sure that you make your column display wide enough to accommodate all your histogram bars. If you want values greater than +72 or –72 to appear, you need to scale the values by dividing by a factor of 10.

TIP

## Resetting the Format

Use the Format Reset option to remove any applied formatting from a range. When you reset a formatted range, Enable removes the current range format and returns the range to the current global format setting.

To reset a formatted range, press

F10 **Layout Range Format Reset**

Enable prompts you to `Enter range to format:`; specify the range and press Enter.

# Aligning a Range

Within any cell, data can be left-justified, right-justified, or centered. Use the Layout Range Align command to change the alignment of data within a cell.

To align a range, press

F10 **Layout Range Align**

Enable displays a menu from which you choose to left-justify, right-justify, center, or reset the range. The default setting for labels is Centered; the default setting for values is Right (right-justified). If you choose Reset, the range returns to the system default or the current global settings.

After you choose an option from the four menu choices, Enable prompts you to enter the range you want to align. Type or point to the range and press Enter.

**TIP**

You also can use the three alignment characters, the less-than (<) sign, greater-than (>) sign, and caret (^), to align a particular cell. When a cell entry begins with an alignment character, Enable performs a range alignment on that cell.

To align a single cell after the contents have been entered, position the pointer to the cell and press one of the following key combinations:

Ctrl-[ for left alignment

Ctrl-] for right alignment

Alt-F4 for center alignment

## Naming a Range

Range Name, one of the most useful commands in Enable's Spreadsheet module, makes your work with ranges considerably easier. You can use the Range Name commands to substitute plain English names for range coordinates. In other words, instead of referring to the January sales range in figure 9.19 as D8..D11, you can refer to the range as JAN. You can use the range name anywhere you ordinarily use range coordinates. @SUM(JAN), for example, is the same as @SUM(D8..D11).

To choose the Range Name command, press

F10 **L**ayout **R**ange **N**ame

Enable displays a menu with the following five options:

**C**reate **D**elete **M**odify **L**abels **R**eset

- Choose **C**reate to create a new named range. Enable prompts you to enter the name. Type a name, which can be up to 15 characters long. Don't include any spaces or special characters.

  After you press Enter, Enable prompts you to enter the range. Type or point to the range coordinates and press Enter. Then name another range or press Esc to leave the menu.

- Choose **D**elete to eliminate a named range from your spreadsheet. After you choose the Delete option, Enable prompts you to enter the name of the range to delete. Type the name of the named range and press Enter. Then delete another range name or press Esc to leave the menu.

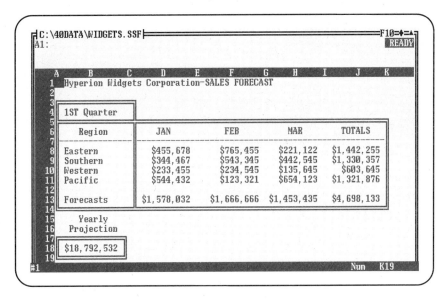

*Fig. 9.19.* *The WIDGET.SSF spreadsheet.*

- Choose **M**odify to modify an existing named range. When Enable prompts you to enter the name of a range, type an existing range name. Enable displays the current range to the right of the prompt Enter new range. Make any changes and press Enter and Esc.

- Choose **L**abels for a quick method of labeling a range of adjacent single-cell ranges.

- Choose **R**eset to eliminate all named ranges from your spreadsheet.

## Using the Range Height Command

You may sometimes need to add more height to certain rows in your spreadsheet. To emphasize the heading of the WIDGETS spreadsheet in figure 9.19, for example, you can add more height to row 1. Figure 9.20 shows the WIDGETS spreadsheet where row 1 has a height of 3 (rows). Notice that Enable adds the extra space on the border above the number 1.

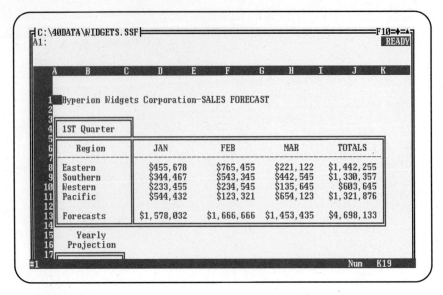

*Fig. 9.20. WIDGETS.SSF spreadsheet with extra height in row 1.*

To change the height of a row, first move your cursor to the desired row, then press

F10 **L**ayout **R**ange **H**eight

Enable offers the following two options:

**S**et   **R**eset

Choose **S**et to change the height of the current row. Enable displays the following prompt:

```
Enter row height (1-15):
```

Type the appropriate number and press Enter.

Choose **R**eset to change height of the current row back to 1.

## Using the Range Width Command

Use the Range Width Command primarily for two purposes: to widen a column to accommodate a longer result, and to narrow a column to hide it from view. With the Range Width command, you can change the width of a column to anything between 0 and 72 characters. If, when you execute a formula, a string of asterisks appears in your result column, the column is too narrow to hold your result.

To change the width of a column, place the pointer on the desired column, then press

F10 **L**ayout **R**ange **W**idth

Enable offers the following two options:

**S**et   **R**eset

Choose **S**et to select a new column width. Enable prompts you to enter a width between 0 and 72 characters. Type the new column width or use the right- and left-arrow keys to increase or decrease the current width setting; then press Enter. If your new column is wide enough, the asterisks disappear, and Enable displays your result.

You can use the Range Width command and choose a column width of zero to hide a column; the column disappears from the screen, although it remains in your computer's memory. Figure 9.21 shows the WIDGETS spreadsheet where column F has been hidden with the Range Width command.

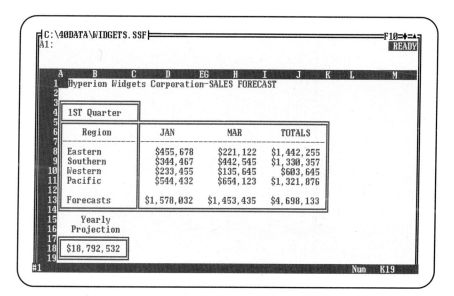

*Fig. 9.21. A spreadsheet with a hidden column.*

# Using Global Commands

In addition to the format, alignment, and width range commands discussed in the preceding sections, Enable provides global commands for changing the format, alignment, and column widths for your entire spreadsheet.

> If you change the global format after you have set range formats for particular ranges in your spreadsheet, the global format affects only the unformatted cells and not the formatted ranges.

To access the Global commands, press

      F10 **L**ayout **G**lobal

Enable displays the Global menu (see fig. 9.22).

```
C:\4ODATA\WIDGETS.SSF                                          F10
  File    >Layout    Edit    Display    Audit    Tools    Graph

          Range
  A       >Global    GLOBAL      E         F          G      H      I
1 Hyp                           on-SALES FORECAST
2                     Format
3                     Align
4 1ST Quarter         Width
5                     Protect
6 Region              Unprotect  EB        MAR        TOTALS
7
8 Eastern             $455,678  $765,455  $221,122  $1,442,255
9 Southern            $344,467  $543,345  $442,545  $1,330,357
10 Western            $233,455  $234,545  $135,645    $603,645
11 Pacific            $544,432  $123,321  $654,123  $1,321,876
12
13 Forecasts          $1,578,032 $1,666,666 $1,453,435 $4,698,133
14
15 Yearly
16 Projection
17
18 $18,792,532
19
#1                              Calc                          M30
```

***Fig. 9.22.** The Global menu.*

The following sections discuss the Global Format, Align, and Width commands; see Chapter 11 for a discussion of the more advanced global commands (Protect and Unprotect) available in Enable's Spreadsheet module.

# Setting a Global Format

In the section "Formatting a Range," you learned to format specific ranges.
You also can set a default for the entire spreadsheet. To do this, you set a
global format.

To set a global format, press

F10 **Layout Global Format**

Choose the desired format. Refer to figure 9.23 for a list of the available
formats and to the discussion of range formatting for descriptions of each
of these format options.

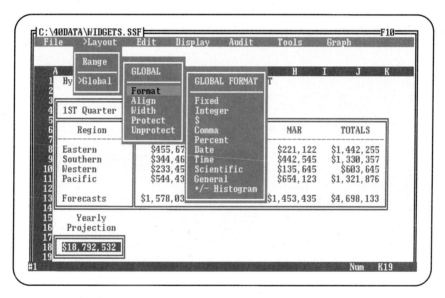

**Fig. 9.23.** *The Global Format options.*

# Setting Global Alignment

You can use the Global Align command to change Enable's default align-
ments for labels (centered) and values (right-justified). To change the
alignment of labels and values in your spreadsheet, choose

F10 **Layout Global Align**

Choose from the subsequent menus whether you want to align values or
labels, and then whether you want left-, right-, or center-justification.

## Using the Global Width Command

You can use the Global Width command to set a standard column width of 1 to 72 characters for your spreadsheet. To set the column width, press

F10 **Layout Global Width**

Enable prompts you to `Enter global column width (1..72)`. You can type the column width or use the right- and left-arrow keys to widen or narrow the columns until they suit your needs. The left-arrow key will decrease the width by one column width; the right arrow increases the column width by one character. Then press Enter.

# Using Display Commands

The Display commands affect the way your spreadsheet appears on-screen. You can use Display commands to set titles, split the screen, hide portions of your spreadsheet, and change the mode of the screen.

## Using the Display Titles Command

When you work with a spreadsheet, you often find yourself scrolling so far down or to the right that you scroll your column or row header labels off the screen. If you cannot remember what data goes in which column, you can use the Display Titles command to "freeze" specified rows and columns on-screen while you scroll to others.

Before you choose the Display Titles command, you must place the pointer directly below the rows or directly to the right of the columns you want to freeze. After you position the pointer, press

F10 **Display Titles**

The screen displays the menu shown in figure 9.24, with the following four options:

- *Horizontal.* Press **H** to freeze only the row(s) above the pointer.

- *Vertical.* Press **V** to freeze only the column(s) to the left of the pointer.

- *Both.* Press **B** to freeze the row(s) above the pointer and the column(s) to the left of the pointer.

- *Clear.* Press **C** to cancel the freeze.

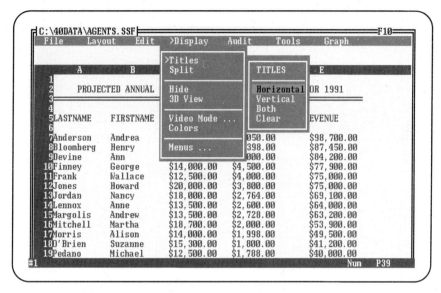

**Fig. 9.24.** *The Display Titles options.*

In tabular spreadsheets, such as FINANCE.SSF, shown in figure 9.25, you often will want to keep a reference row and column frozen. In this spreadsheet, column A and rows 1 through 5 are frozen. Note that columns B through I are not hidden. When you scroll to the right, past column I, you still can see column A, as shown in figure 9.25.

Keep in mind that you cannot place your pointer on frozen titles. The frozen rows and columns remain inaccessible until you clear the freeze.

## Using the Display Hide Command

Sometimes you may need to *hide* a column or a cell. Suppose that your spreadsheet has a column for each month. During any given month, however, you want to view only the current month's column. You can use the Hide command to hide the other eleven columns from view. A hidden column or cell is still available to use in formulas. Figure 9.26 shows the spreadsheet WIDGETS.SSF with columns D through G hidden.

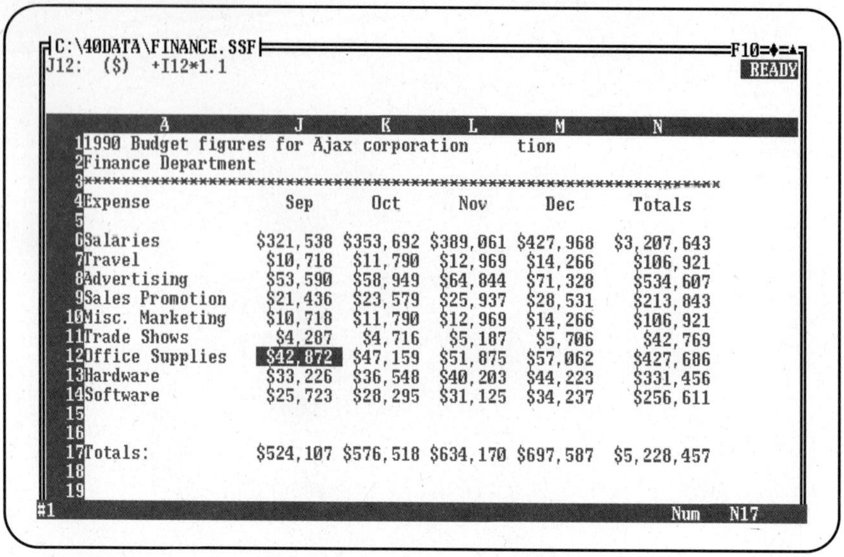

```
┌C:\40DATA\FINANCE.SSF┠━━━━━━━━━━━━━━━━━━━━━━━━━F10=◆=▲┐
 J12:  ($)  +I12*1.1                                        READY

        A           J        K        L        M        N
  1 1990 Budget figures for Ajax corporation      tion
  2 Finance Department
  3 ******************************************************************×
  4 Expense         Sep      Oct      Nov      Dec      Totals
  5
  6 Salaries     $321,538 $353,692 $389,061 $427,968  $3,207,643
  7 Travel        $10,718  $11,790  $12,969  $14,266    $106,921
  8 Advertising   $53,590  $58,949  $64,844  $71,328    $534,607
  9 Sales Promotion $21,436 $23,579 $25,937  $28,531    $213,843
 10 Misc. Marketing $10,718 $11,790 $12,969  $14,266    $106,921
 11 Trade Shows    $4,287   $4,716   $5,187   $5,706     $42,769
 12 Office Supplies $42,872 $47,159 $51,875  $57,062    $427,686
 13 Hardware      $33,226  $36,548  $40,203  $44,223    $331,456
 14 Software      $25,723  $28,295  $31,125  $34,237    $256,611
 15
 16
 17 Totals:      $524,107 $576,518 $634,170 $697,587  $5,228,457
 18
 19
#1                                               Num    N17
```

*Fig. 9.25. A spreadsheet with horizontal titles frozen.*

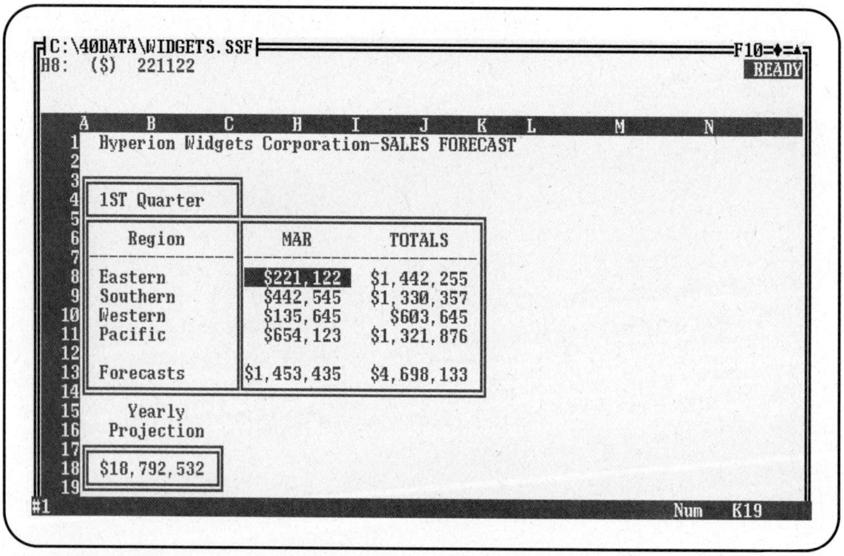

```
┌C:\40DATA\WIDGETS.SSF┠━━━━━━━━━━━━━━━━━━━━━━━━━F10=◆=▲┐
 H8:  ($)  221122                                          READY

   A   B       C     H      I      J      K     L    M       N
  1   Hyperion Widgets Corporation-SALES FORECAST
  2
  3
  4   1ST Quarter
  5
  6      Region        MAR       TOTALS
  7
  8   Eastern       $221,122   $1,442,255
  9   Southern      $442,545   $1,330,357
 10   Western       $135,645     $603,645
 11   Pacific       $654,123   $1,321,876
 12
 13   Forecasts    $1,453,435  $4,698,133
 14
 15      Yearly
 16     Projection
 17
 18   $18,792,532
 19
#1                                               Num    K19
```

*Fig. 9.26. The WIDGETS spreadsheet with hidden columns.*

To hide a column or a cell, first move your cursor to the column or cell you want to hide. Then press

F10 **Display Hide**

The screen displays the menu shown in figure 9.27. Choose **C**olumn or **C**ell under Hide_current. If you choose **C**olumn, the current column disappears. If you choose **C**ell, Enable prompts Enter range to hide:. Use the point method to highlight the desired range. After you hide the cells, the range appears empty, and the cell information area contains the message

    ***HIDDEN CELL.

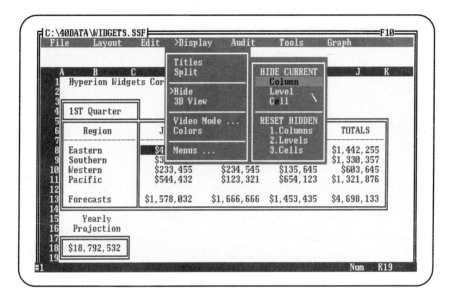

**Fig. 9.27.** *The Hide options.*

Hidden cells or columns are still accessible; you can type in them and use them in formulas. The formula +C3 in any other cell shows the contents of hidden cell C3. Use the Unhide command to redisplay the hidden columns or cells.

To reset a hidden column or cell, press

    F10 **Display Hide**

Enable displays the menu shown in figure 9.27. If you choose **1.**Columns under Reset_hidden, Enable prompts:

    Enter range that includes columns or levels to be reset:

Enable's default setting for the Reset Hidden command is to unhide all columns or levels; however, you can select a particular column by entering any cell within that column. For example, to unhide column D, enter the range **D1..D1**. If the adjacent columns are not hidden, then you can use the point method to select the range.

If you choose **3**.Cells under Reset_Hidden, Enable prompts:

```
Enter range to unhide:
```

Again, Enable's default is to unhide all ranges, but you can enter a particular range. (Press Enter to unhide all ranges.)

# Using Audit Commands

Enable's Audit feature offers several analysis tools which you can use to "audit" your spreadsheet. For example, you may want to know the location of all the formulas, what range names you used, what cells depend on others, and where you used cells in other formulas. The following sections cover the List and Search features, which you can use to print a list of your formulas and range names and to search your spreadsheet, including the formulas. See Chapter 11 for a discussion of more advanced Audit commands.

## Listing Formulas

The more formulas your spreadsheet contains, the more difficult it becomes to read. If a formula contains more than 78 characters, you cannot see the entire formula in the cell information area. To make your spreadsheets easy to manage, you can create printouts of all the formulas within your spreadsheet using the List Formula option. To list your formulas, press

  F10 **Audit List**

Then choose either **Formulas_Id-order** or **Formulas_Calc-order** from the pull-down menu (see fig. 9.28). If you choose Id_order, Enable displays all formulas starting with column A, then column B, and so on, to the last formula. If you choose Calc_order (see fig. 9.29), Enable displays the formulas in the order that Enable calculates the spreadsheet. If you choose Calc-order, you can specify a range for the formulas. Then choose to send your output to the screen, the printer, or an Enable format file. If you choose Enable_format_file, enter a file name. Enable creates a new word processing file with the default extension SSP. Figure 9.29 shows the formulas from the WIDGETS spreadsheet.

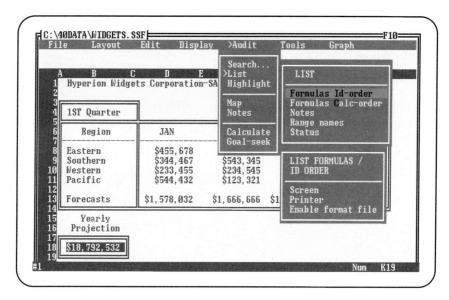

**Fig. 9.28.** *The List options.*

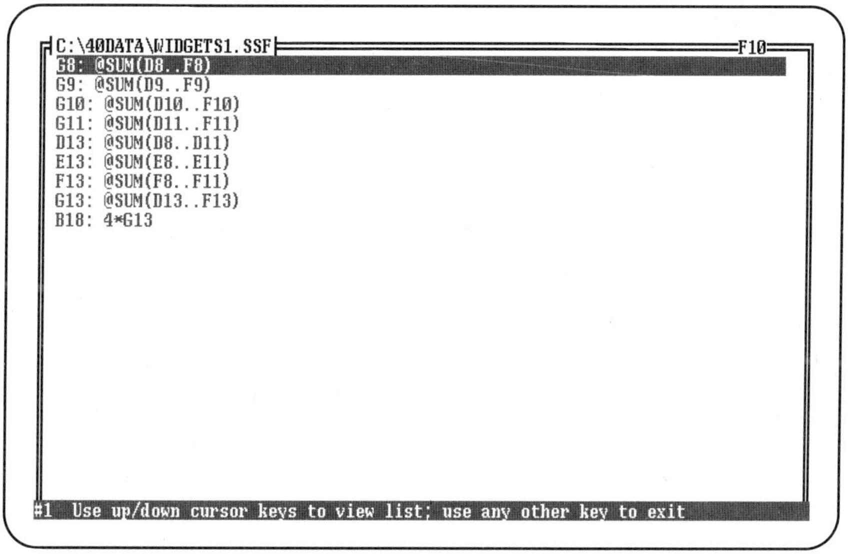

**Fig. 9.29.** *Listed formulas in Calc_order from the WIDGETS spreadsheet.*

**TIP**

When you create elaborate spreadsheets, you may create a *circular reference*—a formula that depends on itself for its answer. A simple example of a circular reference is cell D3 with the formula +D3+1. Most circular references are much more complicated, however, and can take a long time to find. If you use the Calc-order option, you can follow the path Enable takes to calculate all formulas.

## Listing Range Names

As you use more spreadsheets, you create more range names. You may want to keep a list of your range names as well as your formulas. To list your range names, press

> F10 Audit List Range_Names

As with the List Formulas option discussed in the preceding section, you can send the output from the List Range_Names command to the screen, the printer, or an Enable format file. You can use an additional option, Table, to place two columns, the range name and its range, inside the spreadsheet.

## Using Search Commands

The Search command is a new feature in the Enable/OA 4.0 Spreadsheet module. You can use the Search command to perform a find-and-replace search within the spreadsheet, and you can search the value of a cell or its actual contents. To perform a search within the spreadsheet, press

> F10 Audit Search

You see the dialog box shown in figure 9.30.

The search dialog box offers the following choices:

- *Data to find.* Enter the data that you want to find. If you do not want the search to be case-sensitive, choose Ignore_Case.

- *Options.* Choose Find_only if you want only to find the data, or choose Find/Replace if you want to replace the data with other data.

- *Replace_with.* If you choose Find/Replace, enter the new data in this space.

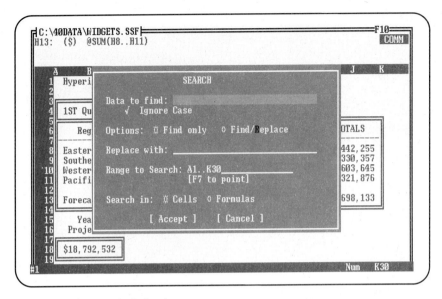

*Fig. 9.30. The Search dialog box.*

- *Range_to_Search.* Enter the range you want to search, or press F7 to use the point method to select your range. The default range is the entire spreadsheet.

- *Search_in.* Choose Cells or Formulas. Choose Cells if you want to search either the text of a cell or its value. Choose Formulas if you want the search to find only a value that is part of a formula.

After you fill in the options, choose Accept. The cursor moves to the first cell that meets the criteria. An error box appears if Enable cannot find a match. If Enable finds a match, you can press F4 to edit that cell, F2 to continue the search, or Escape to cancel the search.

# Using the Print Command

You can use the Print command to print your spreadsheet easily and with flexibility.

To print your spreadsheet, press

F10 **File Print**

Enable displays a menu of options similar to those options discussed in Chapter 5, "Understanding Word Processing Basics." One option, Design_sheet, gives you print options for the spreadsheet. Choose Design_sheet, and you see the Spreadsheet Print Options dialog box, shown in figure 9.31.

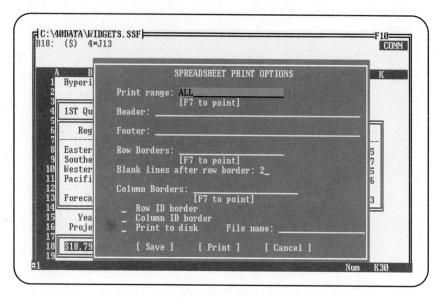

*Fig. 9.31. The Spreadsheet Print Options dialog box.*

The Spreadsheet Print Options dialog box offers you the following choices:

- *Print_range.* Use the Print_range option to specify the portion of your spreadsheet you want to print. You can press F7 to use the point method for highlighting the desired range.

- *Header.* Choose the Header option to place a one-line header at the top of every page of your printed spreadsheet. Type the header text and press Enter.

- *Footer.* The Footer option works in the same way as the Header option except that, if you choose Footer, the line of text you enter appears on the bottom of every printed page.

- *Row_Borders.* When Enable prints a spreadsheet that is longer or wider than a single printed page, the column and row headings do not carry over to the additional pages. You can use the Row_Borders option to designate a particular range of rows to appear above your data on every page of your printed spreadsheet. To specify the row border, enter the range or press F7 to point to the range.

- *Blank_Lines_after_row_border.* Enter the number of lines you want to appear between the border and the first row of data.

- *Column_Borders.* Just as row borders appear above the data on every page, column borders appear to the left of each row on every page. To specify the column border, enter the range or press F7 to point to the range.

If your spreadsheet is too long to fit on one page, and you want the column headings to appear on each page of overflow, choose Row_Borders. When Enable prompts you to enter the range, choose the rows that contain your column headings. If your spreadsheet is too wide to fit on one page, and you want the row headings to appear on each page of overflow, choose Column_Borders. When Enable prompts you to enter the range, choose the column that contains your row titles.

- *Row_ID_border.* Choose this option if you want the row number to appear to the left of each row.

- *Column_ID_border.* Choose this option if you want the column letter to appear above each column.

If you want to print the spreadsheet exactly as it appears on screen, choose both the Row_ID_border option and the Column_ID_border option.

- *Print_to_disk.* Choose this option to produce a disk file rather than to print the file directly to the printer. The disk file name has a default extension of SSP. Choose the Print_to_disk option if you want to preview or touch up your spreadsheet before you actually produce the printout.

## Using the Save Command

To save your spreadsheet to disk, press

F10 **File Save**

Enable saves the entire spreadsheet with the current name. To change the name, to save in a different format, or to save just a range, press

F10 **File Save_As**

Enable displays the dialog box shown in figure 9.32.

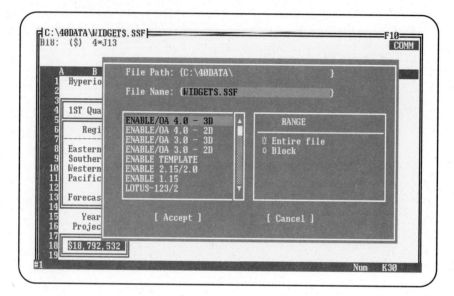

**Fig. 9.32.** *The Save_As dialog box.*

The Save_As dialog box offers the following choices:

- *File_Name.* Enter the name of the file you want to save.

- Choose from the box on the left the format in which you want to save the spreadsheet. For example, choose Lotus-123/2 to save in Lotus format.

TIP

You can save a template file in Enable/OA 4.0. The Enable_Template option is helpful if you often use the same basic spreadsheet and want to clear the data before using the spreadsheet again. After you design a spreadsheet, you can choose this option; Enable retains all formulas in a template file with the default extension SST.

- *Range.* Choose Entire_file or Block. If you choose Block, Enable prompts you for the range. Use the point method to highlight the range you want to save.

After you choose your options, choose Accept. If you decide not to save, choose Cancel. If you previously saved this same spreadsheet, Enable asks whether you want to replace the version on disk with the version on-screen. If you do not want to replace the version on disk, press Esc to cancel the save. If you do want to replace the version on disk, choose Yes, and Enable saves the current version.

To save the current spreadsheet with the same name in Enable/OA 4.0 format, simply press Alt-F10.

# Using the Copy Command

Your Enable spreadsheets are likely to have many columns and rows—possibly dozens or more. Suppose that you want to sum 12 columns of sales figures—one column for each month. You need not type a separate formula at the end of each column.

The sample spreadsheet in figure 9.33 shows the first six months' sales figures. Cell B9 contains a formula for calculating the total sales for January: @SUM(B3..B7).

| | A | B | C | D | E | F | G | H |
|---|---|---|---|---|---|---|---|---|
| 1 | SALESREP | Jan | Feb | Mar | Apr | May | Jun | |
| 2 | | | | | | | | |
| 3 | Brown | 2454 | 2876 | 3358 | 2648 | 1999 | 3567 | |
| 4 | Jeffries | 2335 | 2558 | 1879 | 2311 | 3109 | 3359 | |
| 5 | Holloway | 3311 | 3567 | 3244 | 3754 | 2980 | 4195 | |
| 6 | Steele | 5432 | 4908 | 4852 | 5338 | 4775 | 5279 | |
| 7 | Baker | 4343 | 3873 | 3922 | 4277 | 4598 | 4324 | |
| 8 | | | | | | | | |
| 9 | Total | 17875 | | | | | | |

*Fig. 9.33. A spreadsheet with sales figures for the first six months.*

To re-create the formula in cell B9 in the other columns of row 9, you can choose the Enable Copy command, which is basic to spreadsheet operations. To copy a range, press

F10 **Edit Copy**

Enable displays the prompt

```
Enter FROM range
```

Next to this prompt, the program lists the single-cell range address of your current cell. If B9 is not your current cell, use the direction keys to move your cell pointer to B9. Because you want to copy only the single cell B9, make sure that B9..B9 appears at the prompt, and then press Enter.

Enable then displays the prompt

```
Enter range to copy TO
```

The program again lists the coordinates of the current cell. Because you want to copy the formula in B9 to the cells at the bottom of columns C through G, first move the cell pointer to cell C9. To *anchor* the beginning point of the range to which you want to copy, press the period (.). Point to the end of the range—G9. When the cell pointer is on G9 and the TO range displays C9..G9, press Enter. Enable immediately displays a sum at the bottom of each column.

**TIP**

> You can use the F8 key to perform a copy. Place your cursor in the cell that you want to copy, and press F8. Enable displays the usual copy prompts.

## Relative Cell References

In the preceding example, if you move the pointer to cell C9 and read the formula in the information display, the formula in cell C9 reads @SUM(C3..C7), even though the formula you copied—@SUM(B3..B7)—references cells B3 through B7. When you copy the formula in cell B9 to the other columns, what you really want to do is sum up all the numbers in each respective column. This process, where the cell addresses change during the copy operation, is a *relative copy*. The default for the copy command is to use *relative addressing* with any cell references. In other words, the formula in cell B9 that you copy to the other columns actually means: sum up the cells above the current pointer, starting 6 cells directly above the current cell, and ending 2 cells directly above the current cell.

# Absolute Cell References

Although you usually want formulas to contain *relative cell references*, sometimes you want to refer to a cell in a formula by the original cell address; even if you copy the formula you do not want the cell address to change. For example, the spreadsheet in figure 9.33 contains the sales figures for each sales representative for the first six months. To determine the commission for each representative based on the same commission rate for all representatives, you need one cell that contains the commission rate. In figure 9.34, cell A12 contains the commission rate; column H contains the commission that each sales representative earned.

```
C:\40DATA\SALES.SSF                                    F10=◆=▲
H3:   $A$12*@SUM(B3..G3)                                  READY

          A         B        C        D        E        F        G        H
    1 SALESREP    Jan      Feb      Mar      Apr      May      Jun     COMM.
    2
    3 Brown       2454     2876     3358     2648     1999     3567    1690.2
    4 Jeffries    2335     2558     1879     2311     3109     3359    1555.1
    5 Holloway    3311     3567     3244     3754     2980     4195    2105.1
    6 Steele      5432     4908     4852     5338     4775     5279    3058.4
    7 Baker       4343     3873     3922     4277     4598     4324    2533.7
    8
    9 Total      17875    17782    17255    18328    17461    20724   10942.5
   10
   11 Commission
   12      10%
   13
   14
   15
   16
   17
   18
   19
  #1                                                              H12
```

*Fig. 9.34. A spreadsheet with the commission rate in cell A12.*

When you change the commission rate, you easily can update the spreadsheet, even if you have many sales representatives. If cell H3 contains the formula +A12 * @SUM(B3..G3), and you copy H3 to H4, H4 then contains the formula +A13 * @SUM(B4..G4); this formula returns the wrong answer, because cell A13 is blank. In this case, you need to make the reference (in the formula) to cell A12 constant, or *absolute*.

To make a cell reference absolute, use the $ in the cell reference. A complete absolute reference (both row and column) looks like $A$12. Use $A12 to force the column to be absolute; use A$12 to force only the row to be absolute. Your reference can be relative, absolute, or a combination of the two, depending on your needs.

# Summary

This chapter introduces you to the calculating world of spreadsheets. By learning how to enter data and formulas into a spreadsheet, you can design powerful worksheets that perform complicated calculations. Now that you have looked at spreadsheet basics, remember that your spreadsheet always gives you the answers to the questions you ask, therefore, asking the questions correctly is critical. Always suspect your spreadsheets until you test them thoroughly, and don't sacrifice your own reasoning to your computer.

# 10

# Using Spreadsheet Functions

C hapter 9, "Understanding Spreadsheet Basics," introduces you to some basic features of Enable's spreadsheet module. Whether you are working with your first spreadsheet or are an expert, you probably need to work with several types of calculations. Enable supplies many different types of calculations, known as functions. The first section of this chapter introduces you to some of Enable's simple functions; later sections in the chapter cover more advanced functions.

Many of Enable's functions can be useful to you on a daily basis. This chapter discusses these functions fully and gives some examples that show you how to use them. If you are a beginning user, you may want to review Chapter 9.

> Enable's functions are not useful only in the spreadsheet module. You can use most of the functions in the DBMS module to do calculations, both in defining a calculated field and in creating reports. You also can use many of the functions in the word processing module with the math function (F9 +). The Enable documentation lists the available functions for each module; the functions work in essentially the same way in each module.

For convenience, this chapter divides the functions into groups: mathematical, statistical, and text (or string). The discussion of each function gives the name of the function, an example that shows proper syntax, and an explanation. In many cases, you also find suggested uses for the function.

# Using Basic Spreadsheet Functions

Functions can be broken down into several groups. Most users already are familiar with the basic functions. For example, the @SUM function adds numbers, the @SQRT function finds the square root of a number, and the @LEN function determines the length of a string. This section discusses these and more basic functions.

## Using Mathematical Functions

Use the following functions to perform mathematical operations. Of all the functions, the mathematical functions are the most basic. These are the functions you spent your school days memorizing. This section includes functions that calculate absolute value, square root, logarithms, and so on.

### @ABS

*Example:* @ABS(−25) = 25

The @ABS function calculates the absolute value of a number. The function leaves positive numbers unchanged but converts negative numbers to positive numbers. You usually use absolute value to determine the difference between a number and some target number.

For example, the manager of Big Bargain Food Warehouse has equal concern about whether a cashier's till is over or under the register tape. In the spreadsheet shown in figure 10.1, the number in each cell in the Difference column results from subtracting the register tape amount from the corresponding amount of cash remaining in the till at the end of the cashier's shift. The Absolute Difference column applies the @ABS function to the same formula. Compare the respective column totals.

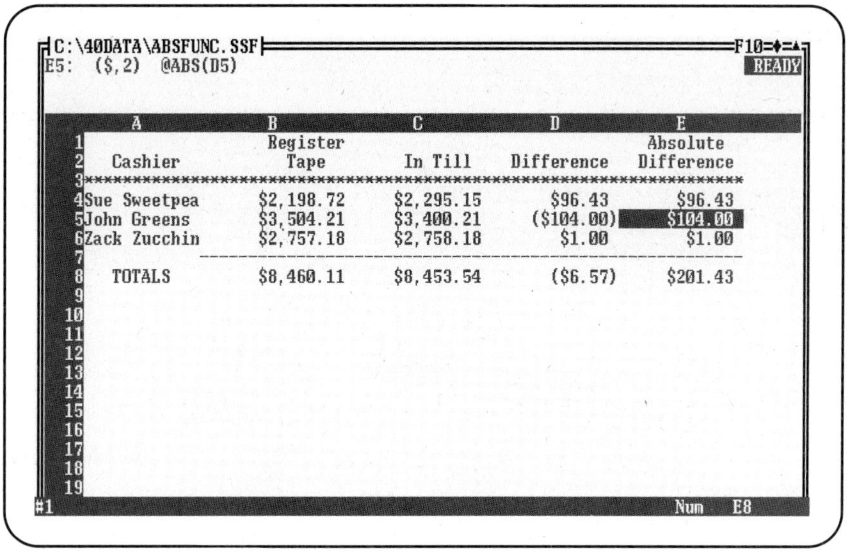

```
┌─C:\40DATA\ABSFUNC.SSF───────────────────────────────F10=◆=▲┐
│E5:  ($,2)  @ABS(D5)                                        READY
│
│        A            B            C            D            E
│ 1                Register                              Absolute
│ 2    Cashier        Tape      In Till    Difference   Difference
│ 3*********************************************************************
│ 4Sue Sweetpea   $2,198.72   $2,295.15      $96.43       $96.43
│ 5John Greens    $3,504.21   $3,400.21    ($104.00)      $104.00
│ 6Zack Zucchin   $2,757.18   $2,758.18       $1.00        $1.00
│ 7              ─────────────────────────────────────────────────
│ 8    TOTALS     $8,460.11   $8,453.54      ($6.57)      $201.43
│ 9
│10
│11
│12
│13
│14
│15
│16
│17
│18
│19
│#1                                              Num     E8
```

**Fig. 10.1.** *The @ABS function.*

## @E

*Example:* @E = 2.7182818284590

The @E function finds the natural number e, which is the base of natural logarithms. This function requires no argument.

## @EXP

*Example:* @EXP(2)= 7.3890560989306

The @EXP function returns e raised to the power of the number in parentheses. This function is the inverse of @NLOG.

@EXP(0) = 1

@EXP(5) = 54.598150033142

@EXP(11)= 59874.141715204

@EXP(−4)= 0.018315638888734

# @EXP10

*Example:* @EXP10(2) = 100

The @EXP10 function returns 10 raised to the power of the number in parentheses.

    @EXP10(3) = 1000

    @EXP10(−3) = 0.001

# @INT

*Example:* @INT(7.8) = 7

The @INT function truncates any fractional portion of a number and, thereby, returns an integer.

Enable gives you several ways to format numbers so that they appear as integers on-screen. For example, you can format a cell that contains the number 123.499 as either Integer or Fixed with zero decimal places (see "Formatting a Range" in Chapter 9), and the number appears as 123. The number 356.511 formatted in the same way appears as 357. Note, however, that if you change the displayed format with Integer or Fixed, Enable does not change the value itself; Enable still uses the complete number in its internal calculations.

The @INT function, on the other hand, creates a new value by truncating the number or omitting any part of the number that comes after the decimal point. Enable uses the result both internally and on-screen.

    @INT(3.2) = 3

    @INT(−4.923) = −4

Compare the result of the @INT function to the effect of @ROUND (see the discussion of @ROUND in this chapter).

# @LOG

*Example:* @LOG(10) = 1

@LOG returns the base 10 logarithm of the number in parentheses.

The argument must be greater than zero; otherwise, Enable displays an error, represented by **ERR**. (See "Logical Functions" in this chapter for more information on @ERR.)

@LOG(100)= 2

@LOG(75) = 1.8750612633917

# @MOD

*Example:* @MOD(7,3)= 1

The *modulus*—the value returned by the @MOD function—is the remainder after Enable divides the first argument by the second. This function is useful when you work with nondecimal-based weights and measurements.

For example, you want to ship the items whose weights, in pounds and ounces, appear in figure 10.2. Suppose that the shipping fee is $3 per pound and 22 cents per ounce for any fraction of a pound.

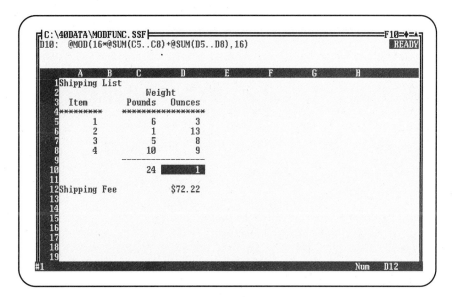

*Fig. 10.2. The @MOD function.*

To determine the number of full pounds, use the following formula in cell C10:

@INT((16*@SUM(C5..C8)+ @SUM(D5..D8))/16)

This formula first divides the total number of ounces by 16; the formula then uses the @INT function to truncate any fraction of a pound.

Next, use @MOD to determine whether any ounces are left over. Cell D10 contains the following formula:

@MOD((16 * @SUM(C5..C8)+ @SUM(D5..D8)),16)

Use the following formula in cell D12 to determine the shipping fee:

(3*C10)+(0.22*D10)

# @NLOG (synonym @LN)

*Example:* @NLOG(35)= 3.5553480614894

The @NLOG function returns the natural logarithm (log base e) of the number in parentheses. The @NLOG function is the inverse of @EXP. The argument must be a number greater than zero.

@NLOG(@E)= 0.99999999999995 (equivalent to 1)

@NLOG(1) = 0

@NLOG(14)= 2.6390573296151

# @RAND (synonyms @RAN and @RANDOM)

*Example:* @RAND

The @RAND function generates a random number between 0 and 1.0 and takes no argument. Multiply @RAND by a constant to increase or decrease the range over which the numbers vary without affecting the starting point. Add a constant to @RAND to move the starting point without affecting the size of the range. You can combine the two methods to change both the starting point and the range of the random numbers @RAND generates.

10 * @RAND varies from 0 to 10.0.

10 + @RAND varies from 10 to 11.0.

10 + (10 * @RAND) varies from 10 to 20.

10 * (10 + @RAND) varies from 100 to 110.

# @ROUND

*Example:* @ROUND(5.23854,3) = 5.239

The @ROUND function returns the first argument rounded to the number of decimal places specified in the second argument. If the second argument is negative, then the @ROUND function rounds the first argument to the nearest value of 10 raised to that exponent. Like @INT, @ROUND changes the appearance of a value on-screen, and Enable uses the rounded number in its internal calculations.

If the value in cell A1 of a spreadsheet is 3359.5416, then the following expressions are true:

@ROUND(A1,0) = 3360

@ROUND(A1,1) = 3359.5

@ROUND(A1,2) = 3359.54

@ROUND(A1,3) = 3359.542

@ROUND(A1,4) = 3359.5416

@ROUND(A1,−1) = 3360

@ROUND(A1,−2) = 3400

@ROUND(A1,−3) = 3000

Figure 10.3 illustrates the different effects of @INT and @ROUND (with zero decimal places) when applied to the same numbers.

Notice that the totals from columns B and D are the same; in both cases, Enable used the original numbers in internal calculations. On the other hand, the total in column F is lower than the original because Enable used truncated numbers in the calculation. The total in column G is higher because Enable used rounded numbers to calculate the sum.

Compare the operation of @ROUND to that of @UROUND, also discussed in this chapter.

# @SIGN

*Example:* @SIGN(−34) = −1

The @SIGN function returns the number 1 when the argument is a positive value, and the number −1 when the argument is a negative value.

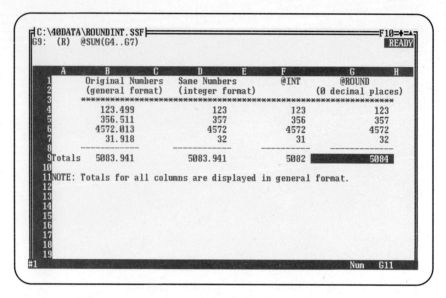

**Fig. 10.3.** *The @ROUND and @INT functions.*

# @SQRT

*Example:* @SQRT(9) = 3

The @SQRT function returns the square root of the number in parentheses. The argument must be greater than zero; otherwise, ERR results.

# @TRUNC

*Example:* @TRUNC(22.56,1) = 22.5

The @TRUNC function truncates from the first argument all digits past the number of decimal places indicated in the second argument. If the second argument is negative, this function truncates the first argument that many digits before the decimal place. The @TRUNC function does not round the remaining digits either up or down. Compare the effect of @TRUNC in the following examples to the examples listed in the discussion of @ROUND.

If the value in cell A1 of a spreadsheet is 3359.5416, then the following expressions are true:

@TRUNC(A1,0) = 3359

@TRUNC(A1,1) = 3359.5

@TRUNC(A1,2) = 3359.54

@TRUNC(A1,3) = 3359.541

@TRUNC(A1,4) = 3359.5416

@TRUNC(A1,–1)= 3350

@TRUNC(A1,–2)= 3300

@TRUNC(A1,–3)= 3000

# @UROUND

*Example:* @UROUND(5.2385,3)= 5.238

*Example:* @UROUND(5.23851,3)= 5.239

@UROUND, the unbiased round function, returns the first argument rounded to the number of decimal places specified in the second argument. However, the function performs in a manner designed to eliminate possible bias (inaccuracy) that may otherwise result from the use of rounded numbers in calculations. The operation of @UROUND is identical to that of @ROUND except for a special case: whenever only one digit is to the right of the specified decimal places, and that digit equals 5, this function always rounds the last digit to the nearest *even number*. In the first example, because the fourth decimal place contains the digit 5, @UROUND rounds the third decimal place to the nearest even number. In the second example, because more than one digit is to the right of the third decimal place, @UROUND works exactly like @ROUND and rounds up to 5.239.

The following examples further demonstrate the effect of @UROUND:

@UROUND(5.2375,3) = 5.238

@UROUND(5.23751,3)= 5.238

# Using Statistical Functions

Statistical functions, like mathematical functions, are already familiar to many users. Use the functions in this group to perform statistical analysis, such as calculating the average, standard deviation, high value, low value, and so on.

## @AVG

*Example:* @AVG(B3..B11)

The @AVG function calculates the arithmetic mean average of a group of values. The argument can be a list of values, a list of cell references that contain values, or a range. See the discussion of @STD for an example of the use of the @AVG function.

$$@AVG(3,5,2,8) = (3 + 5 + 2 + 8)/4 = 18/4 = 4.5$$

## @AVGPRD

*Example:* @AVGPRD(A1..A8,B1..B8)

The @AVGPRD function calculates the average of the products of two lists of values. In the example, A1 is multiplied by B1, A2 by B2, and so on, and the resulting products are averaged.

## @COUNT

*Example:* @COUNT(G15..G65)

The @COUNT function determines how many nonempty cells are in the list or range of cells specified in the argument.

$$@COUNT(3,5,2,8) = 4$$

## @MAX

*Example:* @MAX(H3..H20)

The @MAX function returns the maximum value in the argument. See the discussion of @STD for an example of the use of the @MAX function.

$$@MAX(3,5,2,8) = 8$$

# @MIN

*Example:* @MIN(H3..H20)

The @MIN function returns the minimum value in the argument. See the discussion of @STD for an example of the use of the @MIN function.

@MIN(3,5,2,8) = 2

# @STD

*Example:* @STD(B4..B17)

The @STD function returns the standard deviation of its argument. You can use this statistic to determine how much certain data varies from the average. Along with the average, maximum, and minimum values, you often use standard deviation to evaluate the statistical significance of data you have collected.

Suppose that Ms. Doss, a sixth-grade teacher, wants to "curve" the grading of a 30-question math test. The test scores, as well as several statistics derived from the scores, appear in figure 10.4.

```
┌─C:\40DATA\STATFUNC.SSF════════════════════════════F10=◆=▲┐
│H11:  (F,3)  @STD(B4..B17)                            READY │
│                                                             │
│        A        B      C     D     E      F      G      H    │
│ 1  Math Test Scores and Grades        Statistics and        │
│ 2 (Maximum possible score = 30)        Grade Scale          │
│ 3********************************** ************************* │
│ 4 Bernie      24     P                                       │
│ 5 Mac         18     P         Highest Score (@MAX)      30  │
│ 6 Fred        13     F                                       │
│ 7 Jennifer    30     A         Lowest Score (@MIN)       13  │
│ 8 Wendy       22     P                                       │
│ 9 Cal         21     P         Average Score (@AVG)   20.643 │
│10 Val         21     P                                       │
│11 Charlie     19     P         Standard Deviation (@STD) 4.529 │
│12 Phillipe    17     P                                       │
│13 Bill        17     P         Passing Grade (P)       16.113 │
│14 Buffy       27     G                                       │
│15 Star        15     F         Good (G)                25.172 │
│16 Debbie      20     P                                       │
│17 Steve       25     P         Excellent (A)           29.702 │
│18                                                            │
│19                                                            │
│#1                                              Num    J18   │
└─────────────────────────────────────────────────────────────┘
```

*Fig. 10.4. Statistical functions used to determine a grading scale.*

Assuming that the test scores exhibit a normal or "bell curve" distribution, Ms. Doss defines a passing score (P) as the average score minus one standard deviation: 16.113. A good score (G) is at least one standard deviation more than the average: 25.172. To receive an excellent score (A), a student must receive the average plus two standard deviations: 29.702.

# @SUM

*Example:* @SUM(A1..A10)

The @SUM function adds the values listed in the argument. @SUM is one of the most frequently used functions in Enable.

You can use @SUM to total long columns of numbers. If you decide to add a row to the column, be careful to insert the row within the existing range—at any row between 2 and 11 (inclusive) in the example (see fig. 10.5). Otherwise, Enable does not include the new row in the sum unless you edit the formula. To avoid this potential pitfall, always include a "total line" as the last cell in the range, as shown in figure 10.5.

In figure 10.5, Enable automatically includes a row you insert at the total line (row 11). The formula adjusts automatically and becomes @SUM(A1..A12).

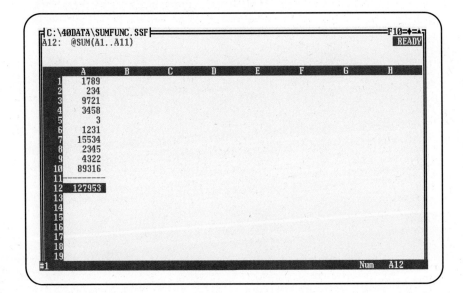

*Fig. 10.5. The @SUM function.*

## @SUMPRD

*Example:* @SUMPRD(A1..A5,B1..B5)

The @SUMPRD function calculates the sum of the products of two lists of values. In the example, A1 is multiplied by B1, A2 by B2, and so on. The five products are then added together.

## @VAR

*Example:* @VAR(H1..H20)

The @VAR function calculates the *variance*, equal to the standard deviation squared, of its argument. Use the variance to measure the variation from the average of the data you have collected.

# Using String Functions

Enable has a variety of functions that manipulate text strings rather than perform calculations with numbers. The term *string* means the same thing as *label*: data that is not a value (number).

The first three string functions covered in this section are the only functions that do not begin with the @ symbol. Use them to combine two or more strings to create a longer string.

## &

*Example:* +H23 & H24

The & function combines the labels in cells H23 and H24. If H23 contains the label *STEVE*, and H24 the label *GRAND*, this expression returns *STEVEGRAND*. If the first argument contains any trailing blanks, the & function inserts them between the two strings (although this situation rarely occurs in the spreadsheet module).

## &–

*Example:* +H23 &– H24

The &– function combines the labels in cells H23 and H24, leaving no more than one space between them. If H23 contains the label *STEVE* (with at least one trailing blank), and H24 contains the label *GRAND*, this expression returns *STEVE GRAND*. You seldom need this function in the spreadsheet module because Enable normally does not create trailing blanks in labels.

# &+

*Example:* +H23 &+ H24

The &+ function combines the labels in cells H23 and H24, leaving exactly one space between them. If H23 contains the label *STEVE*, and H24 contains the label *GRAND*, this expression returns *STEVE GRAND* . In other words, this function adds a space between the two text strings.

# @LEN

*Example:* @LEN(D2)

The @LEN function returns the length of the character string in D2.

@LEN("ABCD") = 4

See the discussion of @UC for an example of the use of the @LEN function.

# @REPEAT

*Example:* @REPEAT("*",10) = *********

@REPEAT, as its name implies, returns the first argument repeated the number of times specified in the second argument.

# @SUBSTR, @LEFT, and @RIGHT

*Example:* @SUBSTR(D2,1,4)   @LEFT(D2,4)   @RIGHT(D2,7)

The @SUBSTR function retrieves a group of characters from a text string. The first argument is the text string; the second argument is the starting position of the characters you want to extract; and the third argument is the number of characters you want to extract. For example, if D2 contains the name *John Johnson*, the @SUBSTR function returns the string *John*. This string begins at the first character and is four characters long.

The functions @LEFT and @RIGHT are specialized versions of @SUBSTR. The @LEFT function always retrieves the leftmost specified number of characters. The @RIGHT function always retrieves the rightmost specified number of characters. In the examples, if D2 is *John Johnson*, then the @LEFT function returns *John*, and the @RIGHT function returns *Johnson*.

# @TRIM

*Example:* @TRIM("ABC ") = ABC

The @TRIM function removes trailing spaces from the end of a string. For example, in figure 10.6, the @TRIM function removes trailing blanks so that the comma immediately follows the city name.

```
┌C:\40DATA\TRIMFUNC.SSF├─────────────────────────────F10=◆=▲┐
│G9:  @TRIM(C9)&", "&D9                                 READY │
│                                                             │
│       A      B      C      D      E      F      G      H   ◆ │
│ 1                                                           │
│ 2First  Last                                                │
│ 3Name   Name   City   State         Name   City, State      │
│ 4══════════════════════════════════════════════════════════│
│ 5John   Jones  New York NY          John Jones  New York, NY │
│ 6                                                           │
│ 7Sue    Smith  Gary   IN            Sue Smith   Gary, IN     │
│ 8                                                           │
│ 9Larry  Larson Boise  ID            Larry Larson Boise, ID   │
│10                                                           │
│11Jane   Doe    Albany NY            Jane Doe    Albany, NY   │
│12                                                           │
│13                                                           │
│14                                                           │
│15                                                           │
│16                                                           │
│17                                                           │
│18                                                           │
│19                                                           │
│#1                                              Num   H17    │
└─────────────────────────────────────────────────────────────┘
```

**Fig. 10.6.** *The @TRIM function.*

# @UC, @LC, and @PROPER

*Example:* @UC("upper") = UPPER
@LC("LOWER") = lower
@PROPER("PROPER") = Proper

The @UC function changes lowercase text to uppercase, and @LC changes uppercase to lowercase. Figure 10.7 demonstrates how several string functions can convert a first and last name into proper format—uppercase first letters and lowercase for all other letters in the name. @PROPER does the entire operation with one function.

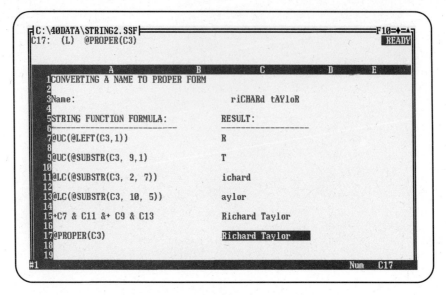

*Fig. 10.7. The @UC, @LC, and @PROPER functions.*

# Using Logical Functions

You use logical functions to create conditional formulas—formulas that give Enable alternative courses of action to take depending on the status of specified conditions in the spreadsheet.

## @ALPHA

*Example:* @ALPHA(H7)

@ALPHA is logically true and has a value of 1 whenever the argument contains only letters. In the example, if cell H7 contains the text "Sales", then @ALPHA returns the value 1. On the other hand, if H7 contains nonalphabetic characters (such as "Sales Group 1"), @ALPHA returns a zero.

# @AND

*Example:* @AND(3<4,6>5,7=7) = 1

The @AND function has the logical value 1 or 0, meaning true or false. The function returns a true value only if all arguments have a logical value of true. The following examples assume that cell K21 has the value 25:

@AND(2*K21<51,K21>0) = 1

@AND(K21<=20,22/K21>1) = 0

In the database module, use @AND instead of AND, and place the expression which is most likely false first. The @AND function stops evaluating its arguments once a false condition is found; the AND logical operator must evaluate all its arguments before it determines an answer.

TIP

# @ERR

*Example:* @ERR

The @ERR function can indicate an error condition in the spreadsheet. You usually use this function as an argument in an @IF function formula. For example, in a company whose highest paid employee makes $150,000, an entry greater than that amount in a column of salaries is an error. The following formula checks the cell C3 for that problem and displays either ERR (if an error exists) or OK (if no error exists):

@IF(C3>150000,@ERR,"OK")

Enable also displays ERR in a cell when the cell contains a formula using another cell whose value is ERR, or a formula that contains an illegal operation (dividing by 0 is illegal because it has no logical answer).

If a cell's value is ERR, it can create a *ripple effect* through the spreadsheet. Many formulas, which may be valid, become @ERR because of one incorrect cell. If this ripple effect is not the result you want, then consider combining @IF with @ISERR to trap the ERR.

# @EXACT

*Example:* @EXACT(B7,"PAID")

The @EXACT function has a value of either 1 or 0 (logically true or false). Use @EXACT to determine whether the string content of a cell is exactly the same as another given string. This function enables you to create tests with the @IF function using any text you want as a "trigger" for some action. This function is case-sensitive. The example shown is true if B7 is the text string "PAID" but false if B7 is any other string (including "paid").

# @EXIST

*Example:* @EXIST("FILENAME")

Use @EXIST to determine whether a particular file exists on the disk. This function has a value of 1 (true) when the file exists, and 0 (false) when it doesn't. Specify the entire file name in double quotation marks. Also include the path (for example, C:\ENFILES2\MYSS.SSF) when you want to look for a file that is not in the default data directory.

# @FALSE (also @NO)

*Example:* @FALSE

The @FALSE function uses no argument and always returns the logical value 0, or false. Although you can use the number 0 to indicate a false condition, @FALSE has the advantage of being self-documenting. The function clearly indicates that you mean a logical value rather than simply the number 0.

# @IF

*Example:* @IF(SALE>250000, 1000, 0)

@IF is one of the most powerful functions available in the Enable spreadsheet because it provides a mechanism by which the computer can "make decisions." When the condition in the first argument is true, the value in the second argument is placed in the cell; otherwise, the value in the third argument is placed in the cell. In the example, a bonus of $1,000 is given to anyone whose sale is greater than $250,000. Otherwise, no bonus is given.

The third argument, which specifies a second value, is optional. If this argument is not specified, and the condition evaluates as false, then nothing is returned by the function.

Using @IF, @TRUE, and @FALSE together can provide a convenient method for tallying the number of times a condition is met. In the example shown in figure 10.8, Wally's World of Wheels has set a weekly sales goal of $50,000. With the total sales for week 1 is in cell B7, the following formula returns 0 if the sales goal has not been met and 1 if it has been met:

@IF(B7<50000, @FALSE, @TRUE)

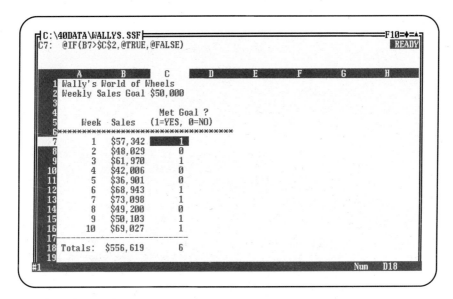

**Fig. 10.8.** *An example of the @IF, @TRUE, and @FALSE Functions.*

At the end of 10 weeks, Wally can count the number of weeks in which the goal was reached by adding the 1's and 0's in column C.

By nesting @IF functions, multiple decisions can be accomplished in one expression. Suppose that Wally pays a bonus of $1,000 to the sales manager for meeting the weekly sales goal depicted in figure 10.8. Suppose also that Wally adds an extra $500 if this is the second or subsequent week in a row that this goal is met. The bonus for week 10 returns uses the following formula:

@IF(C16=1,@IF(C15=1,1500,1000),0)

With this formula, Wally pays the $1,500 bonus only if the following two conditions are met:

1. The sales manager meets the goal in week 10 (C16=1).

2. The sales manager also met the goal in week 9 (C15=1).

Wally pays a bonus of $1,000 if the following two conditions are met:

1. The sales manager meets the goal in week 10 (C16=1).

2. The sales manager did not meet the goal in week 9 (C15=0).

If the sales manager does not meet the goal in week 10 (C16=0), he receives no bonus.

# @ISBLANK

*Example:* @ISBLANK(C13)

Use the @ISBLANK function to determine whether a particular cell is blank. The function returns the number 1 (true) when the cell is blank, and 0 (false) when the cell contains a label, formula, or value. In the example, @ISBLANK(C13) has the value 0 as long as the cell C13 contains a label, formula, or value. Otherwise, the function has the value 1. Compare @ISBLANK with @ISEMPTY.

# @ISEMPTY

*Example:* @ISEMPTY(C13)

Use the @ISEMPTY function to determine whether a particular cell is empty. The difference between @ISEMPTY and @ISBLANK is that while a cell may be blank—does not contain data—it may be formatted. A formatted cell, or a cell with alignment set, is not considered empty.

# @ISERR

*Example:* @ISERR(A26)

The sample @ISERR function checks for an error condition (@ERR) in cell A26. The function returns the number 1 (true) if an error is found and 0 (false) if the specified cell has no error condition.

You can use this function with the @IF function to prevent (or "trap") ERR messages resulting from division by zero throughout the spreadsheet.

# @ISLABEL

*Example:* @ISLABEL(C13)

Use the @ISLABEL function to determine whether a particular cell contains a label. This function returns the number 1 (true) when the cell contains a label and 0 (false) when it does not.

# @ISNA

*Example:* @ISNA(G1)

@ISNA returns a 1 (true) when the specified cell contains the value @NA (data not available). Otherwise, the function returns the value 0. Refer to the section on @NA for more information.

# @ISNUM

*Example:* @ISNUM(F3)

@ISNUM returns 1 (true) when the specified cell contains either a value, or a formula that evaluates to a value. Otherwise, the function returns the value 0.

# @ISREF

*Example:* @ISREF(D10)

The @ISREF function tests for the REF message (reference to another spreadsheet) in the cell specified in the argument. (See the discussion of @LINK in Chapter 11, "Using Spreadsheet Advanced Features.") This function has a value of 1 (true) when the message REF occurs and 0 (false) when it does not.

# @NA

*Example:* @NA

Use the @NA function when certain data is not yet available for you to enter, and you don't want to leave the cell blank. If other cells depend on this cell for their value, they also display NA.

## @NOT

*Example:* @NOT(3<4) = 0

The @NOT function reverses the logical true/false state of the argument. Thus, true statements return 0, and false statements return 1.

## @NUMERIC

*Example:* @NUMERIC("1234546") = 1

or

@NUMERIC("(555) 123-4546") = 0

@NUMERIC has the value 1 (true) when its argument contains only numeric characters and 0 when its argument contains any nonnumeric character.

## @OR

*Example:* @OR(3<4,4<3) = 1

The @OR function returns 1 (true) if any one of the expressions listed as arguments is a true expression. This function returns 0 (false) only if all the arguments are false.

In the database module, use @OR instead of or, and place the expression which is most likely true first. The @OR function stops evaluating its arguments once it finds a true condition; the OR logical operator must evaluate all its arguments before it determines an answer.

## @TRUE (also @YES)

*Example:* @TRUE

@TRUE always has the value 1, or true. This function has no argument. Even though you could (with less typing) use the number 1 to indicate a true condition, using @TRUE is clearer because it plainly represents a logical condition rather than a numeric value.

# Using Advanced Spreadsheet Functions

Spreadsheet functions are the real key to understanding spreadsheets; most users find plenty of uses for the simple functions. The advanced functions discussed in the following sections can enhance your spreadsheet use significantly—date, financial, statistical, string, trigonometric, and lookup functions. Through the use of these functions, what you may think of as complicated tasks can become easy. These functions are available in the database module as well.

## Using Date Functions

Enable provides several functions to display and manipulate dates. To perform date arithmetic, however, Enable first must convert each date to a number. This number, called a date serial number, represents the number of days from December 31, 1899. To Enable, this number is a value that can be used in calculations. You must use either a Global Format command or a Range Format command to change the display to a date format; otherwise, Enable displays the date as a number.

### @TODAY

*Example:* @TODAY

The @TODAY function simply returns today's serial date number. For this function to work properly, the system clock must be set to the correct date. The $@TODAY function requires no argument.

### @DATE – format 1

*Example:* @DATE(76,12,31) = 28124

or

@DATE("76/12/31") = 28124

The @DATE function returns a serial date number representing the number of days since December 31, 1899. Using a date format displays the appropriate date.

## @DATE – format 2

*Example:* @DATE(28124) = 76/12/31

@DATE is a unique function because, based on its argument, the result can be a text date or a date serial number. In format 1, supplying the date results in a date serial number as an answer. However, with a date serial number as an argument, the result is a text date.

You use this form of the @DATE function in conjunction with other date functions, because the other functions supply the date serial number as an answer. To convert this answer to a usable date without formatting the cells first, use a final @DATE function. For example, a single formula to calculate three weeks from today is as follows:

> @DATE(@TODAY + 21)

The following example uses a serial date number as the argument to return a string (label) in the form YY/MM/DD:

> @DATE(32455) = 88/11/09

Figure 10.9 illustrates the @DATE function used to return the serial date number for October 24, 1963, in cell B7. When formatted in a date format (D,1) the same number displays as a date in cell D7. @TODAY is used in cell B5. Because @DATE returns a number in cell D7, as does @TODAY, the formula shown in figure 10.10 (cell B13) can calculate age. Use the @YEAR function to convert to full years, because you don't count years of age until the anniversary date (birth date). Use a similar formula—@YEAR(B5-B9)—(as in cell C15) to calculate the number of whole years worked.

## @DATE$

*Example:* @DATE$(28124) = December 31, 1976

The @DATE$ function returns the date as a string (label), fully spelled out, in the form month, day, (four-digit) year. The result of the @DATE$ function appears in column F of figure 10.10 to display the dates as strings.

## @DAY

*Example:* @DAY(31041)=26

The @DAY function returns the day of the month (a value) on which a date will occur. The argument is a serial date number.

In figure 10.11, John Johnson had to prepay interest from the date of the loan, 14-August-88, until the end of the month. The bank and the borrower have agreed (for the purpose of calculating the interest) that all months have 30 days. The formula in H7 uses the @DAY function in figuring the prepaid interest.

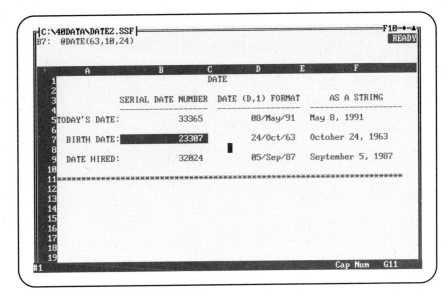

*Fig. 10.9. The serial date number of October 24, 1963.*

## @WEEKDAY

*Example:* @WEEKDAY(23653) = 0

The @WEEKDAY function returns the number (value) of the day of the week for the date represented by the serial date number argument.

(0 = Sunday) (0 to 6, 0=Sunday and 6= Saturday)

## @WEEKDAY$

*Example:* @WEEKDAY$(23653) = Sunday

The @WEEKDAY$ function returns the day of the week—a string, fully spelled out—for the date represented by the serial date number argument.

Using the @WEEKDAY$ and the @DATE$ together can fully spell out any date. For example

@WEEKDAY$(@TODAY)&+@DATE$(@TODAY) = Wednesday May 3, 1991

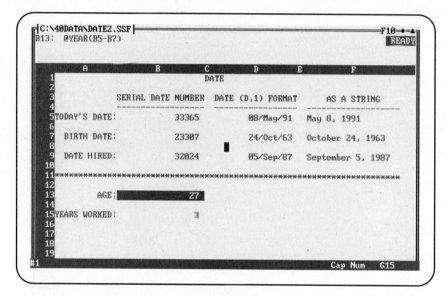

*Fig 10.10. Serial date numbers in calculations.*

## @MONTH

*Example:* @MONTH(23653) = 10

The @MONTH function returns a number from 1 to 12, which represents the month of a serial date number. For example, the month of the serial date number 23653 is 10, or October.

## @MONTH$

*Example:* @MONTH$(23653) = October

The @MONTH$ function is the same as @MONTH except that @MONTH$ returns the name of the month—a string, fully spelled out. In the spreadsheet illustrated in figure 10.11, the loan officer can use the @MONTH$ function in cell B18, along with date arithmetic and the date from cell H6, to determine the month when the first payment is due. Because the month name is a string, the & functions can be used to concatenate the string into the sentence.

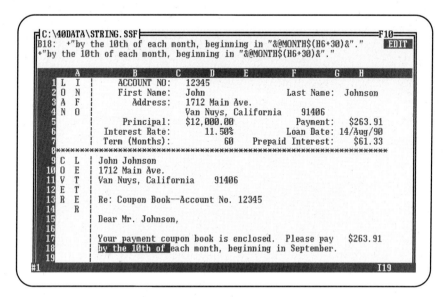

**Fig. 10.11.** *@MONTH in an equation.*

# @YEAR

*Example:* @YEAR(23653) = 64

The @YEAR function returns the last two digits (value) of the year for the date represented by the serial date number argument. In figure 10.10 the @YEAR function calculates the number of years since a specific date.

# @YEAR$

*Example:* @YEAR$(23653) = 1964

The @YEAR$ function returns the four-digit year (string) for the date represented by the serial date number argument.

## @ADDMONTH (synonym @ADDM)

*Example:* @ADDMONTH(32498,3) = 32588

The @ADDMONTH function determines the date of a given number of months from a starting date. In other words, Enable calculates the serial date number *n* months from a certain date. In the example, if you want to know three months from December 22, 1988 (32498), then the @ADDMONTH function returns the serial date number for March 22, 1989 (32588). Use one of the DATE formats to display this number as a date on-screen. The use of this function ensures that you always get the desired number of months. For example, @ADDMONTH(@DATE("91/01/31"), 1) = 33296, the equivalent of 91/02/28.

## @END_MONTH

*Example:* @END_MONTH(32455) = 32476

The @END_MONTH function returns the serial date number of the last day of the month in which the date represented by the argument occurs.

## @JULIAN

*Example:* @JULIAN(32455) = 88314

The @JULIAN function returns the Julian date (value) in the form of two-digit years and three-digit days. In the example, the serial date number represents the 314th day of 1988, or 88314.

# Using Time Functions

With Enable's time functions, you can manipulate and perform calculations with the time of day. Enable converts time designations to the number of seconds since midnight—the *serial time number*—and displays this number as time in conjunction with the appropriate Global or Range format option selection.

# @ETIME

*Example:* @ETIME(32063,1800,32064,2009) = 86609

The @ETIME function returns the elapsed time—the number of seconds (value) between the beginning date and time and the end date and time. The first and third arguments are serial date numbers, and the second and fourth arguments are serial time numbers.

The spreadsheet shown in figure 10.12 calculates the duration of an airplane flight. With the @TIME function Enable places the respective estimated and actual departure and arrival times in cells E4, E7, G4, and G7. The @ETIME function then calculates the duration of the flight. Notice that the @TIME function subtracted three hours from the arrival time to account for the difference between Pacific and Eastern Standard Time.

```
┌C:\40DATA\TIME.SSF                                          ═F10═♦═▲┐
│G11:  (T,7)  @ETIME($C$4,G4,$C$7,G7-@TIME(3,0,0))            READY │
│                                                                   │
│       A       B        C      D       E      F      G       H     │
│   1                                                               │
│   2                 Date           Estimated    Actual            │
│   3               ─────────        ─────────    ─────────         │
│   4 Time of Departure  24/Nov/87      8:45 P     9:05 P           │
│   5 (Pacific Time)                                                │
│   6                                                               │
│   7 Time of Arrival    25/Nov/87      7:23 A     7:32 A           │
│   8 (Eastern Standard Time)                                       │
│   9                                                               │
│  10                                                               │
│  11 Duration of Flight                0 7:38     0 7:27           │
│  12                                                               │
│  13                                                               │
│  14                                                               │
│  15                                                               │
│  16                                                               │
│  17                                                               │
│  18                                                               │
│  19                                                               │
│#2                                                  Num   G11      │
└───────────────────────────────────────────────────────────────────┘
```

*Fig. 10.12. An example of the @ETIME Function.*

# @HOUR

*Example:* @HOUR(2009) = 0

The @HOUR function returns the hour represented by the time serial number. The value is between 0 and 23, where 0 is midnight.

# @MINUTE

*Example:* @MINUTE(2009) = 33

The @MINUTE function returns the minutes represented by the time serial number. The value is between 0 and 59.

# @NOW

*Example:* @NOW

The @NOW function returns the current time serial number—the number of seconds since midnight (00:00:00). The system clock must be set correctly to enable this function to work properly. The @NOW function requires no argument.

# @SECOND

*Example:* @SECOND(2009) = 29

The @SECOND function returns the seconds represented by the time serial number. The value is between 0 and 59.

# @TIME

*Example:* @TIME(13,45,15) = 49515

or

@TIME("13:45:15") = 49515

The @TIME function returns the time expressed in number of seconds. The time is calculated from hours (value), minutes (value <= 59), and seconds (value <= 59). Refer to the discussion of @ETIME for an example of using the @TIME function.

The @TIME function also can return the time of day (label) in the form HH:MM:SS by using a serial time number as the argument:

@TIME(49515) = 13:45:15

## @TIME$

*Example:* @TIME$(49515) = 13:45:15

The @TIME$ function returns the elapsed time (label) in days, hours, minutes, and seconds (DD HH:MM:SS). The elapsed time is computed from the number of seconds (value).

# Using Financial Functions

These functions represent sophisticated formulas used to answer questions that commonly arise when evaluating financial and investment opportunities.

## @CTERM

*Example:* @CTERM(.095,3500,2500) = 3.71

Use this function to calculate the number of compounding terms required to reach a specific future value. The first argument is the fixed rate of return, the second argument is the expected future value, and the third argument is the initial investment (present value). In the example, the annual interest rate is 9.5%, the initial investment is $2,500, and the desired return is $3,500. The answer, 3.71 (rounded to two decimal places), means that 3.71 years are necessary to reach a balance of $3,500, with the interest compounded yearly.

## @FV

*Example:* @FV(500,.0075,24) = $13,094.24

The @FV function returns the future value of an investment accumulated by regular equal payments at a given rate of return and after a set number of payments. The three arguments represent payment, rate, and term, respectively. In the example (see fig. 10.13), 12 monthly payments of $500 each to an investment fund that pays 9 percent interest per year (0.75 percent per month), yields $13,094.24 at the end of 2 years.

Keep in mind that the time unit of all three arguments must match. Note that the formula in cell B6 of figure 10.13 makes appropriate adjustments so that the payment, rate, and term parameters all use one month as the unit of time.

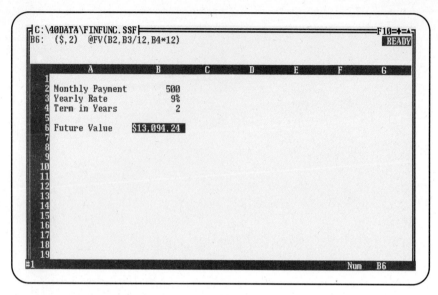

*Fig. 10.13. An example of the @FV function.*

# @IRR

*Example:* @IRR(A4,F1..F5)

The @IRR function calculates the internal rate of return, which is the profit you expect an investment to earn. You must provide a best estimate of the rate (between 0% and 100%), and then specify a range of cells in the spreadsheet that contains the original investment (for example, a loan) as a negative number and a series of positive numbers that represent payments on the investment (loan). The syntax for the function is as follows:

@IRR (*estimated rate of return,range containing payments*)

The amount of each payment can vary, but payments must be at equal intervals. To make the formula work, the series must list the negative value (cash outflow—the investment), and then the positive values (cash inflow).

Figure 10.14 illustrates the use of the function. Enable calculates the actual discount rate that equates the present value of the cash outflow, $10,000 in cell F1, with the present value of the series of inflow listed in F2 through F5.

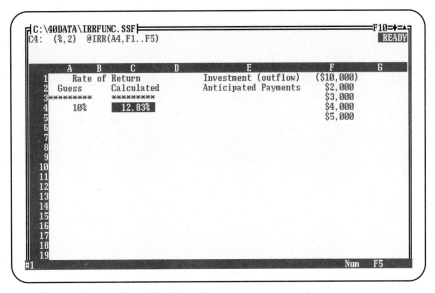

**Fig. 10.14.** *An example of the @IRR function.*

# @NPV

*Example:* @NPV(0.1,A1..A5)

The @NPV function calculates the net present value of an investment when you expect a series of unequal payments (cash inflow) at regular intervals. The first argument is the going discount rate (the rate of return you can expect to receive on other similar investments). The second argument is a range of cells that contain the expected payments, in chronological order. You can use this function to compare the value of one investment with the value of other similar investments.

If the cash flows depicted in figure 10.15 can be obtained for an initial investment of less than $30,925, then the investment is better than the currently available 12-month CDs.

# @PMT

*Example:* @PMT(B5,B6/12,B7*12)

The @PMT function calculates the loan payment per unit of time, assuming a certain initial loan principal, interest rate, and term.

The syntax for the function is as follows:

@PMT(*principal,interest,term*)

Figure 10.16 shows an example of how you can use @PMT to calculate monthly home loan payments. Notice that the unit of time for all three arguments must be the same (one month in fig. 10.16).

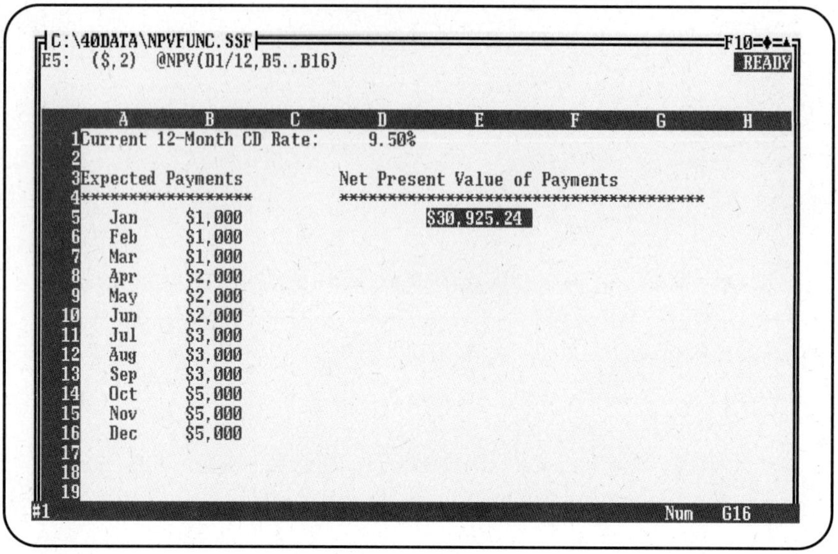

```
C:\40DATA\NPVFUNC.SSF                                    F10=♦=▲
E5:  ($,2)  @NPV(D1/12,B5..B16)                           READY

       A        B        C        D        E        F        G        H
 1 Current 12-Month CD Rate:     9.50%
 2
 3 Expected Payments              Net Present Value of Payments
 4 ********************           *******************************************
 5    Jan    $1,000                    $30,925.24
 6    Feb    $1,000
 7    Mar    $1,000
 8    Apr    $2,000
 9    May    $2,000
10    Jun    $2,000
11    Jul    $3,000
12    Aug    $3,000
13    Sep    $3,000
14    Oct    $5,000
15    Nov    $5,000
16    Dec    $5,000
17
18
19
#1                                                        Num      G16
```

**Fig. 10.15.** *An example of the @NPV function.*

# @PV

*Example:* @PV(950.00,0.1025/12,30*12) = $106,014.80

The @PV function calculates the present value of an investment that returns a fixed amount per period at a set rate of return. This function is the inverse of @PMT. The syntax for the function is as follows:

@PV(*payment,interest,term*)

For example, if you can afford a monthly mortgage payment of $950.00, and the currently available interest rate on a 30-year loan is 10.25%, then the formula in the example determines the principal amount you can borrow.

Figure 10.16 also shows use of the @PV function to determine the loan principal when given the payment, interest rate, and loan term. The formula in cell F11 is @PV(B11,B12/12,B13*12).

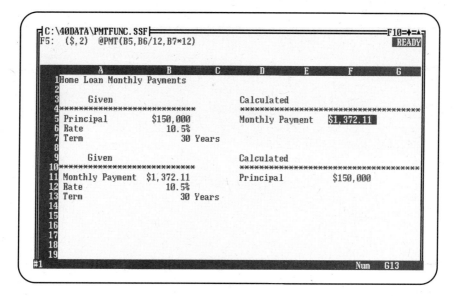

**Fig. 10.16.** *An example of the @PMT function.*

# @RATE

*Example:* @RATE(200000,100000,8) = 9.05%

This function determines the rate at which an investment must grow to reach a given value, assuming an initial investment and term. The syntax is as follows:

@RATE(*future value,present value,term*)

In the example, an initial investment of $100,000 grows to a value of $200,000 in 8 years if the rate of return is 9.05% per year.

# @TERM

*Example:* @TERM(25,.085/12,3000) = 87.15697

This function is the inverse of the @FV function. Assuming you have a goal you want to reach by investing a set amount every period, how long does it take to reach that goal? The syntax for this function is as follows:

@TERM(*payment,interest rate,future value*)

In the example, 88 payments are necessary to exceed the $3,000 goal, assuming you make $25 payments each month and the yearly interest rate is 8.5%.

# Using Statistical Functions

Use each function in this group to perform a statistical analysis.

> The following three functions are unique, in the fact that the cell they are in does not have a value; they actually place a value in another range of cells. The cell that contains the formula appears blank, and the resultant cells appear as though their numbers have been entered manually. Thus, you should exercise great care when developing a spreadsheet that contains these formulas, as you can innocently corrupt both the formula and the results.

## @CUMSUM

*Example:* @CUMSUM(C4..C17,D4..D17)

The @CUMSUM function calculates the cumulative sum of the values in the first range and places the result in the second range. In the example, @CUMSUM adds C4 to zero and puts the total in D4; then the function adds C4..C5 and puts that total in D5; and so on.

As shown in figure 10.17, @CUMSUM is perfect for calculating a running balance for a checking account.

## @PCT

*Example:* @PCT(A1..D1,A2..D2)

@PCT calculates the percentage of the sum (of all the cells in the first range) that the value in each cell of the first range represents and places the result (expressed as a decimal fraction) in the corresponding cell of the second range. Suppose, for example, that your spreadsheet contains the values 2, 8, 6, and 4 in the range A1..D1, and that you have entered the following formula in A3:

    $@PCT(A1..D1,A2..D2)

Range A2..D2 now contains the values .1, .4, .3, and .2. The sum of the values in range A1..D1 is 20. The value in cell A1 is 1/10 of 20, and A2 therefore contains .1. The value in cell A2 is 8, which is 4/10 of 20, and B2 therefore contains the value .4.

Borrowing an example from politics, suppose that the local pollster asks local residents which of the leading four candidates they favor for city council. The results appear in figure 10.18. Using the @PCT function, the pollster can determine the relative popularity of the candidates.

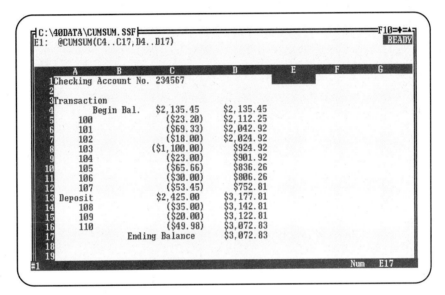

**Fig. 10.17.** *An example of the @CUMSUM function.*

# @CUMPCT

*Example:* @CUMPCT(C6..C18,E6..E18)

The @CUMPCT function calculates the cumulative percentage of the values in the range of the first argument and places the result in the range of the second argument. In the example, range E6..E18 contains values derived from values in range C6..C18. Each value in the source range (the first argument) adds to the preceding values in the range; the result, expressed as a percentage of the total of all values in the source range, is placed in the corresponding cell in the target range (the second argument).

When the @CUMPCT function applies to votes cast on election day, as shown in figure 10.19, a table displays the percentage of the total vote cast by the end of each hour. This information may be valuable to election authorities and news agencies.

```
┌─C:\40DATA\PCTFUNC.SSF├──────────────────────────F10=+=▲─┐
│B1:    @PCT(B5..B9,D5..D9)                          READY │
│                                                          │
│        ▐       A      │   B   │  C  │   D   │ E  │ F │ G  │
│       1 Pollie's Poll                                    │
│       2              Preferred      Preference           │
│       3    Candidate     by         Perecentage          │
│       4**************************************************│
│       5 Alice Allright    85            34%              │
│       6 Terence Rubberstamp 32          13%              │
│       7 Larry Leftwing    18             7%              │
│       8 Al Most           82            33%              │
│       9 Undecided         35            14%              │
│      10              ─────────────                       │
│      11 Total People Polled 252                          │
│      12                                                  │
│      13                                                  │
│      14                                                  │
│      15                                                  │
│      16                                                  │
│      17                                                  │
│      18                                                  │
│      19                                                  │
│#1                                       Num    D11       │
└──────────────────────────────────────────────────────────┘
```

**Fig. 10.18.** *An example of the @PCT function.*

# Using String Functions

Sometimes, you may find it necessary to perform operations on text data. Remember that some basic string functions were discussed earlier in this chapter.

## @CHAR and @CODE

*Example:* @CHAR(232) = @CODE("text string") = 116

The @CHAR function returns the ASCII character that corresponds to the decimal code specified in the argument. The Enable spreadsheet documentation includes a complete list of available ASCII codes. Valid values for @CHAR are from 1 to 239.

The @CODE function is the opposite of the @CHAR function. @CODE returns the decimal ASCII code of the first character in the text string argument. The @CODE example returns 116, because that number is the decimal ASCII code for the lowercase *t*.

```
C:\40DATA\CUMPCT.SSF                                    F10=◆=▲
C1:   @CUMPCT(C6..C18,E6..E18)                          READY

              A         B      C      D      E       F      G      H
 1 Election Results
 2                             Votes Cast
 3                             Total     Cumulative
 4 Time of Votes             (thousands)  Precentage
 5 ********************      ***************************
 6   7 to  8 am                  2        1.54%
 7   8 to  9 am                 10        9.23%
 8   9 to 10 am                  8       15.38%
 9  10 to 11 am                  6       20.00%
10  11 to 12 pm                 11       28.46%
11  12 to  1 pm                 15       40.00%
12   1 to  2 pm                  4       43.08%
13   2 to  3 pm                  5       46.92%
14   3 to  4 pm                  8       53.08%
15   4 to  5 pm                 16       65.38%
16   5 to  6 pm                 20       80.77%
17   6 to  7 pm                 21       96.92%
18   7 to  8 pm                  4      100.00%
19
#1                                                Num    F18
```

*Fig. 10.19. An example of the @CUMPCT function.*

# @DEC and @HEX

*Example:* @DEC("E8") = 232 @HEX(232) = 0E8H

These functions also are opposites. @DEC converts a string containing a hexadecimal number to its decimal equivalent; its result is a value. The @HEX function has the opposite effect, converting a decimal number into a hexadecimal string. These functions are most useful to programmers, because computers work in hexadecimal.

# @NUM and @STRING

*Example:* @NUM("375") = 375 @STRING(8) = 8

The @NUM function converts string data to a numeric value; the @STRING function converts a numeric value to string data. Note that the @STRING function always leaves one trailing blank.

If you attempt to convert nonnumeric data with either @NUM or @STRING, @ERR will result. You may want to use the @IF, @ISNUM, @NUMERIC, and @NA functions to test for these conditions first. For example, you can use formulas as follow:

@IF(@ISNUM(C3), @STRING(C3), @NA)

@IF(@NUMERIC(C4), @NUM(C4), 0)

## @LTRIM

*Example:* @LTRIM("ABCD") = ABCD

@LTRIM is a function used to remove leading blanks, as opposed to @TRIM, which removes trailing blanks. Used together, you can remove all blanks from any text string.

## @MATCH

*Example:* @MATCH("alphabet","bet",1) = 6

The @MATCH function returns a number indicating where the string "bet" begins within the string "alphabet". In the example, the string "bet" begins at the sixth position in the string "alphabet". A common use of @MATCH is to find the first occurrence of a blank in a string, to determine the end of the current word. You can use the optional last option of this function to choose a starting position within the string to start the search. For example, @MATCH("alphabet","a") = 1, while @MATCH("alphabet","a",2) = 5. Figure 10.20 shows several examples of @MATCH.

NOTE

@MATCH is case-sensitive, thus @MATCH("a","A") = 0.

## @REPLACE

*Example:* @REPLACE("minicomputer",0,4,"micro") = microcomputer

This function is equivalent to the search-and-replace function in the word processing module. The first argument is the string you want to search. The second argument indicates the position of the first character you want to remove, with zero as the first character. The third argument specifies how many characters you want removed. The fourth argument provides a replacement string. If the replacement string is longer than the third argument, then Enable adds enough space to insert the new text.

Figure 10.21 shows some more examples of @REPLACE.

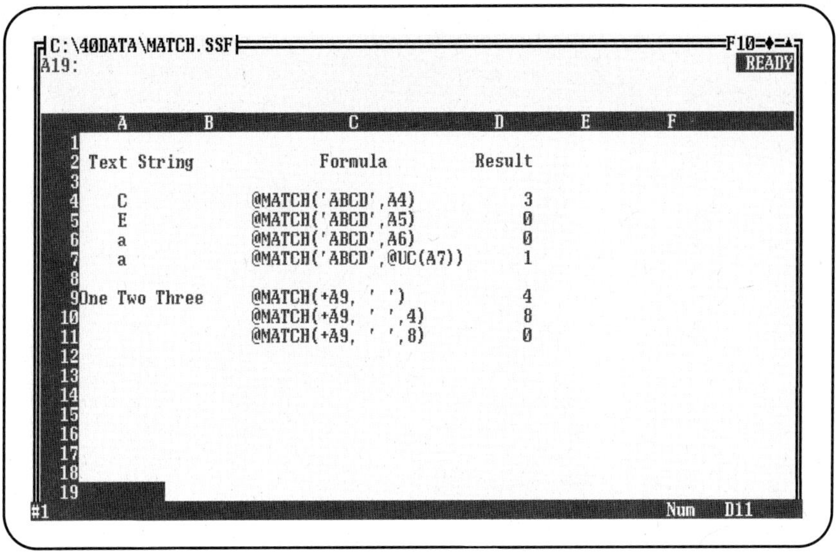

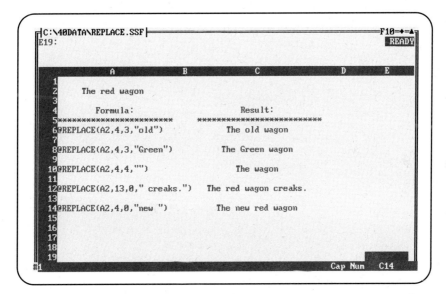

**Fig. 10.20.** *Several examples of the @MATCH function.*

**Fig. 10.21.** *Several examples of the @REPLACE function.*

## @STRING

*Example:* @STRING(8) = "8 "

The @STRING function converts a numeric value to a string. Note that after the conversion one trailing blank remains. Use this function mainly to create string data from numerics. For example,

>   @STRING(8) & 'Dollars' = "8 Dollars"

# Using Trigonometric Functions

You can use trigonometric functions in very complicated mathematical expressions that are beyond the scope of this book. However, you can successfully put these functions to good use without becoming overly technical. First you need to review some basic principles of trigonometry.

A right triangle is a triangle with one 90-degree angle. Given an angle and the length of a side of a right triangle, you can use @SIN, @COS, and @TAN to find the length of the other sides. Similarly, if given two sides, you can use @ATAN, @ACOS, and @ASIN to find the angles. Because you must express all angles to Enable in radians, you also use the new function @RADIAN to convert degrees to radians and @DEGREE to convert radians to degrees.

## @ACOS

*Example:* @ACOS(0.5) = 1.0472

The @ACOS function calculates the arc cosine of its argument. @ACOS, the inverse of @COS, returns the angle in radians whose cosine is the argument.

>   @ACOS(1) = 0
>
>   @ACOS(0) = 1.5707963267949 or @PI/2
>
>   @ACOS(–1) = 3.1415926535897 or @PI

## @ASIN

*Example:* @ASIN(0.5) = 0.5236

The @ASIN function calculates the arc sine of its argument. @ASIN, the inverse of @SIN, returns the angle in radians whose sine is the argument.

Suppose that a road crew needs to know the grade, expressed as an angle <CFT4><NE>0<RV1>–<EL1>, of a road that rises 10 feet in vertical altitude in a 150-foot span.

To find the solution, use one of the basic trigonometric axioms:

sin <CFT4><NE>0<RV1>–<EL1> = opposite / hypotenuse = 10 feet / 150 feet

Therefore, @ASIN(10/150) = <CFT4><NE>0<RV1>–<EL1> in radians.

Applying the conversion function @DEGREE (to convert radians to degrees), the crew can find the grade of the road by using the following formula:

@DEGREE(@ASIN(10/150))

Figure 10.22 shows how to use the @ASIN function in this example.

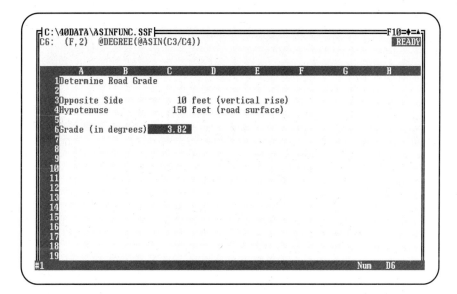

*Fig. 10.22. The @ASIN function.*

# @ATAN

*Example:* @ATAN(1) = 0.78539816339744

The @ATAN function calculates the arc tangent of its argument. The inverse of @TAN, @ATAN returns the angle in radians whose tangent is the argument. This function does not distinguish angles in the third and fourth quadrants from angles in the first two quadrants that have the same tangent.

@ATAN(–1) = –0.78539816339744

# @ATAN2

*Example:* @ATAN2(1,1) = 0.78539816339744

The @ATAN2 function calculates the four-quadrant arc tangent of its argument. With this function, Enable can solve trigonometric problems in any of the four quadrants of the Cartesian coordinate system. The function returns the angle in radians whose tangent is the second argument divided by the first argument. Therefore, when given the sides adjacent to, and opposite to, an angle of a right triangle, the following expressions return the size of the angle in radians:

@ATAN2(length of adjacent side, length of opposite side)

@ATAN2(1,–1) = –0.78539816339744

@ATAN2(–1,–1) = –2.3561944901923

@ATAN2(–1,1) = 2.3561944901923

# @COS

*Example:* @COS(13) = 0.907446

The @COS function finds the cosine of its argument. The argument must be expressed in radians.

Suppose that a team of surveyors knows that the distance between points A and B is 500 feet, and that the angle <CFT4><NE>0<RV1>– is 23 degrees.

The distance between points A and C, which the surveyors call X, encompasses an impassable thicket. The surveyors can determine X by using the following equations:

cos = adjacent side / hypotenuse

cos 23 degrees = 500 feet / X

X = 500/cos 23 degrees

Using the @COS function and the conversion function @RADIAN, the appropriate Enable formula is the following:

500/@COS(@RADIAN(23))

Figure 10.23 illustrates the use of the @COS function in this example. Refer to the discussion of the @TAN function for the formula needed to determine the length of the opposite side (cell B12).

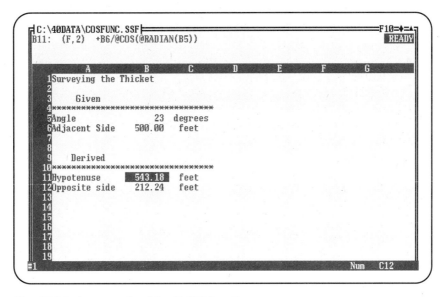

**Fig. 10.23.** *An example of the @COS function.*

# @DEGREE

*Example:* @DEGREE(@PI/2) = 90

The @DEGREE function converts a radian argument into degrees. The @DEGREE function is the inverse of @RADIAN. Because most trigonometric functions return radian answers, you must apply the @DEGREE function to obtain the number of degrees. Figure 10.22 shows the use of @DEGREE to obtain a result from the @ASIN function.

The following examples are uses of @DEGREE:

@DEGREE(0) = 0

@DEGREE(.5235987) = 30

@DEGREE(@RADIAN(47.5)) = 47.5

## @PI

*Example:* @PI = 3.141592653589794

The @PI function returns the value of *pi*.

## @RADIAN

*Example:* @RADIAN(45) = .7865398

The @RADIAN function converts a degree argument into radians. @RADIAN is the inverse of @DEGREE. Because most trigonometric functions require their arguments to be in radians, you need to use the @RADIAN function to convert degrees to radians.

Figure 10.23 shows the use of @RADIAN as an argument for the @COS function.

The following examples are uses of @RADIAN:

@RADIAN(180) = 3.141592653589794 = *pi*

@RADIAN(@DEGREE(@PI/2)) = 1.5707963267949 = @PI/2

## @SIN

*Example:* @SIN(1) = 0.8414709848079

The @SIN function finds the sine of its argument. The argument represents an angle and must be expressed in radians. You can use $@SIN to solve problems in which you know an angle of a right triangle and either the length of the hypotenuse or the length of the side opposite the known angle. The following examples are uses of @SIN:

@SIN(@RADIAN(90)) = 1

@SIN(@RADIAN(180)) = 0

@SIN(@RADIAN(270)) = −1

## @TAN

@TAN(1) = 1.5574077246549

The @TAN function calculates the tangent of its argument. The argument is an angle and must be expressed in radians. If the angle is an odd multiple of 90 degrees (1/2 pi radians), then @TAN returns a huge negative number.

@TAN(@RADIAN(45)) = 0.99999999999999

@TAN(@RADIAN(90)) = –295857988165680.00

Consider again the surveying crew mentioned in the discussion of @COS. The surveyors can calculate the length of the side opposite the angle using this trigonometric equation:

tan = opposite side / adjacent side

By substituting the available information into this equation, the surveyors obtain the formula for cell B12 of figure 10.23:

@TAN(@RADIAN(B5)) * B6

# Using Selection Functions

Selection functions find specific values from lists and tables in the spreadsheet.

## @CHOOSE

*Example:* @CHOOSE(C3,D2,D3,D4,D5,D6,D7)

The @CHOOSE function specifies a position in the list or range specified in the subsequent arguments. Suppose that cell C3 contains the value 3, and cells D2 through D7 contain the values 1, 5, 8, 11, 15, and 18 (see fig. 10.24). Enable considers 1 to be at offset zero, 5 to be at offset 1, 8 to be at offset 2, and so on. Therefore, the example returns the value 11, which is at offset 3.

## @HLOOKUP AND @VLOOKUP

*Example:* @HLOOKUP(37500, A8..A21,1) AND @VLOOKUP(37500,A8..C12,1)

The @HLOOKUP and @VLOOKUP functions retrieve values from a look-up table. @VLOOKUP "looks up" data arranged in vertical columns—thus the name VLOOKUP. @HLOOKUP operates in the same way, but arranges the data in the table in horizontal rows instead of columns.

The first argument, called a key value, must be a number. The first column of the table, called the comparison or key column, is the second argument. This column must contain a list of numbers in ascending order. The other columns in the table contain values or sometimes text. The location of each entry in these subsequent columns depends on the location of a corresponding identifying entry in the key column.

The last argument indicates an offset from the key column; the key column itself has an offset of 0. In the preceding example, the function searches for the largest value in the key column that does not exceed the key value, 37500. Then, the function returns the corresponding value (or text) in the same row, which is one column away.

An income tax table is a perfect example of a look-up table. Figure 10.25 shows a Schedule X Federal Income Tax rate table for single taxpayers. J. Paycheck's taxable income ($18,525) is the key value, and column A is the key column because it contains the various tax brackets. With the help of the @VLOOKUP function, J. Paycheck can calculate his taxes using the following formulas:

Cell I10: @VLOOKUP(I8,A8..C12,1)

Cell I11: +I8–@VLOOKUP(I8,A8..C12,0)

Cell I12: @VLOOKUP(I8,A8..C12,2)

Cell I14: +I10+I11*I12

## @LOOKUP

*Example:* @LOOKUP(I8,A8..B12)

The @LOOKUP function is a compact version of @HLOOKUP and @VLOOKUP. The range must be two rows of values or two columns of values. Enable automatically determines whether to do a vertical lookup or horizontal lookup and assumes an offset of 1. Otherwise, this function operates like @VLOOKUP and @HLOOKUP.

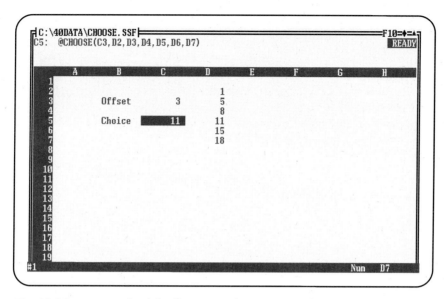

**Fig. 10.24.** *An example of the @CHOOSE function.*

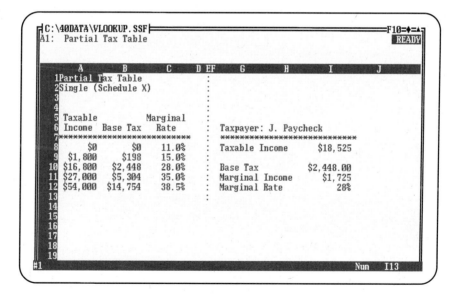

**Fig. 10.25.** *Examples of the @VLOOKUP function.*

## @INDEX

*Example:* @INDEX(A8..C12,1,2)

This function returns a value identified by specifying coordinates in a range. The first column of the range is offset zero, the second column is offset 1, and so on. Similarly, the first row in the range is row offset zero, the second row is offset 1, and so on. In the example, the value in the second column of the range and third row of the range returns the value in cell B10. Applying the same formula to the VLOOKUP spreadsheet shown in figure 10.25 returns the value $2,448.

# Using Special Functions

Several of the functions in this group are most useful in macros. They return such information as the location of the cell pointer, the contents of the cell that the pointer is in, and the network user ID code.

## @COLS, @ROWS, and @LEVELS

*Example:* @COLS(B3..G3)=6
     @ROWS(B3..B7)=5
     @LEVELS(A:B3..C:G3)=2

@COLS returns the number of columns in the range specified in the argument. @ROWS returns the number of rows in the specified range. Finally, @LEVELS returns the number of levels in the specified range. Refer to Chapter 13, "Using 3-D Spreadsheets," for a detailed discussion of levels. These functions provide handy ways to quickly determine the size of a named range.

## @CURCOL, @CURROW, @CURLEVEL, @CURPOS, and @CURVAL

These functions do not take an argument. @CURCOL returns a value that corresponds to the current column (at the pointer), where 1 means column A, 2 means column B, and so on. @CURROW is the function for determining the current row and also returns a value. @CURLEVEL returns a value that corresponds to the current level (at the pointer) where 1 means level A, 2 means level B, and so on. The @CURPOS function returns a text string that is the cell address of the pointer. For example, cell A1 returns "A1". @CURVAL returns the value of the cell where the pointer is positioned.

Use these five functions only in macros.

## @ID

*Example:* @ID(1,2)

This function returns your network user ID code.

> In version 4.0, the 1 and 2 in the above expression have no meaning, but must be used. To use the @ID function, you literally type **@ID(1,2)**.

## @LASTERR

The @LASTERR function has no arguments and returns the error number of the last system error.

# Summary

This chapter presents an overview of Enable's built-in functions—basic and advanced. Because most functions are available within both the spreadsheet and database modules, you can save yourself many hours if you fully understand all the functions available. You can realize the full potential of these functions only by incorporating them into as much of your spreadsheet and database work as possible.

# 11

# Using Spreadsheet Advanced Features

After studying the introduction to spreadsheets in Chapter 9, "Understanding Spreadsheet Basics," you have a good sense of what spreadsheets can do for you. If you are comfortable with the material in Chapter 9 or you are an experienced spreadsheet user, you are ready to apply this chapter's material on Enable's advanced and new spreadsheet features.

The chapter first looks at the spreadsheet protection applied with Global and Range commands. Then the text discusses some Edit commands, including the Data-Fill command, the Modify command, and the Transpose command. From there, the chapter examines the new Display-Colors command and then the Audit commands, paying particular attention to Map Mode, Notes, and the Highlight commands. Following Audit commands, the chapter discusses Goal-seeking and several recalculation options. Next, the chapter examines spreadsheet tools, including the Sort command, and the new Spreadsheet Defaults command. This chapter also covers the Combine command and Linking spreadsheets, and ends with an in-depth look of Spreadsheet's In-Cell Macros.

## Protecting Cell Formulas

As any professional data processor knows, data security is one of the prime concerns of a computer installation. Unfortunately, MS-DOS-based PCs offer you no way to protect your data. The original designers seem to have reasoned that because the PC was to be a single-user machine, the user would not need to protect data from other people. In fact, PC security does not seem to have been a concern at all in the original design.

The business world's acceptance and use of the spreadsheet as a basic tool, however, has established the need for protection. Spreadsheets often hold sensitive data and elaborate formulas and cell relationships that take weeks to develop and debug. A single accidental—or deliberate—change in a single cell may lead to incorrect assumptions, invalid numbers, and general hysteria. Ideally, you should protect your spreadsheets from sabotage and accident—from unauthorized users and from clumsy operators.

If you are a new spreadsheet user, you may wonder when you should protect a spreadsheet and what parts of it you should protect. Although no absolute rule answers that question, in general, you should protect anything you don't need to change—including data, labels, and formulas. In fact, if you have an important spreadsheet, make a copy of the file and put it away somewhere. Where data security is concerned, caution is a virtue.

Because users on a network often share access to file directories, Enable Software includes password protection in its LAN version of Enable. Enable/OA also includes this feature. Chapter 3, "Understanding the Master Control Module," discusses password protection. Enable also provides excellent protection against accidental spreadsheet modification through the Protection commands, which prevent a user from accidentally changing cell contents. Saboteurs, however, may not be deterred.

## Choosing the Style of Protection

You can establish spreadsheet protection in one of the following ways:

- Protect individual ranges from change and leave the rest of the spreadsheet available for data entry (Enable's native default protection).

- Protect the entire spreadsheet and leave specific ranges unprotected (1-2-3-style protection).

You make the choice when you set up your profile (see Appendix B, "Using Profiles to Customize Enable"). When you see the various profile options, choose

   **7.** Spreadsheet

Enable prompts

```
Protect all cells in spreadsheet?
```

You must respond either **Yes** or **No**. If you choose **Yes**, you get the 1-2-3 option—protect all cells in the spreadsheet when you execute the Global Protection command. If you want particular ranges to be unprotected, you must establish each of them individually with the Range Unprotect command.

You may prefer to choose the **No** option. Lotus's way of doing things is somewhat complex, particularly if you have a large spreadsheet with only a few ranges worth protecting. Even if you are a 1-2-3 veteran, you probably will find Enable's protection scheme quite logical.

# Understanding the Protection Commands

When you set protection, you use both Global and Range commands. To turn on protection, press

> F10 **L**ayout **G**lobal **P**rotect

This command activates protection on all cells in the spreadsheet. Notice the `Prot` indicator in the status line when you turn on this feature. To protect a range of cells so that the cells cannot be changed, you also must use the command

> F10 **L**ayout **R**ange **P**rotect

Then, indicate the range you want to protect. After you use this command, you cannot change anything in the protected cells, but you still can modify the rest of the spreadsheet. If you try to make changes in a protected cell, Enable beeps and displays the Protected Cell error box.

To remove protection from specific cells, press

> F10 **L**ayout **R**ange **U**nprotect

Again, indicate the range. With this command, you can remove protection from a specific range while keeping protection in others.

Finally, you can deactivate protection altogether by pressing

> F10 **L**ayout **G**lobal **U**nprotect

After you deactivate protection, *all* protection disappears, although you still can set range protection for particular ranges.

# Using Advanced Editing Commands

To aid in the addition or modification of spreadsheet data, Enable has three advanced commands: Fill, Modify, and Transpose. You will find these commands useful if you need to enter a large list of sequential data, alter the contents of existing data by a constant factor, or change data that was entered one way (vertically or horizontally) to its opposite.

## Using the Fill Command

Enable's Fill command doesn't get much attention but is quite useful. The command does exactly what its name implies: it automatically fills data ranges and can save you from a dreary bout of typing. In Enable/OA 4.0, you also can use this command to fill a range with dates.

The Fill command fills a specified range with sequential data. That capability may not sound significant at first, but think of all the applications in which you need to use sequential numbers. Bank check numbers, for example, usually are sequential, as are dates in a mortgage amortization. Using Fill can make any data entry for such uses much easier.

Suppose, for example, that you want to enter a column of sequential numbers, 1 through 200. Position the cell pointer where you want the column to start, and press

F10 **Edit Fill**...

In the range prompt, enter a range of 200 cells, such as A1..J20.

A dialog box appears (see fig. 11.1). Enable prompts you to enter the range. In response, type or point to a range of 199 cells.

Enable then prompts you for the units to be used. You have a choice of numbers and various date components (Days, Weeks, Weekdays, Months, and Years). To choose the numbers units, highlight the option and press Enter. An asterisk (*) appears next to the option. (If you choose one of the date options, Enable then prompts you for a date format. Again, highlight the choice and press Enter.)

Next, Enable prompts you for a start value, a step value, and a stop value. For the start value, enter the number **1**. For the step value, enter **1**, and **199** as the stop value. Press the Tab key to move to the Accept space. As soon as you press Enter on Accept, Enable does the data fill and enters the 190 numbers for you. The numbers in figure 11.2 were entered using the Fill command to fill the range A1..J20.

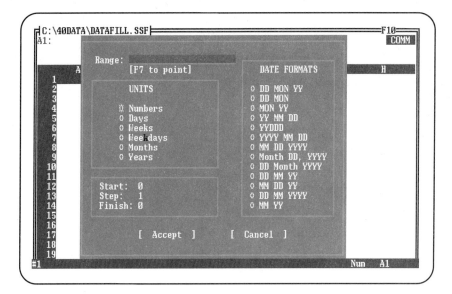

**Fig. 11.1.** *The Fill Dialog Box.*

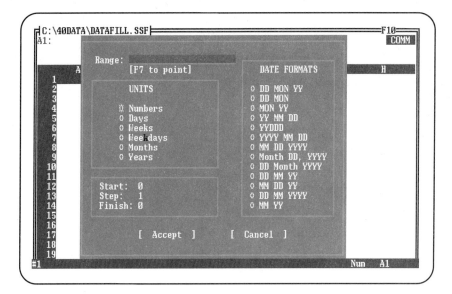

**Fig. 11.2.** *Numbers entered with the Fill command.*

You can use the Fill command to create a column of sequential numbers, and then use interwindow copy to copy the column to a word processing document. In this way, you can avoid typing numbers down the side of a page.

## Using the Modify Command

The Modify command, another original Enable contribution to spreadsheets, is similar to the Fill command. With Modify, you can add, subtract, multiply, or divide—by a constant—all the cells in a given range.

To invoke the option, press

**F10 Edit Modify**

The first menu gives you the choice to add, subtract, multiply, or divide. After you make your choice, Enable prompts `Enter range`. Enter or point to the range to modify, and then press Enter. Enable then prompts you to

`Enter adjustment value`

Type a constant, and press Enter. The range recalculates immediately, based on the operation you requested and the constant's value. Figure 11.3 displays the spreadsheet shown in figure 11.2 after Data-Fill Modify multiplies all values by the constant 3.

## Using the Transpose Command

While designing your spreadsheet, you sometimes need to switch, or transpose, the rows and columns. You can use Enable's Transpose command to take a vertical range of cells and rearrange them horizontally, and vice versa.

Suppose, for example, that you have created a spreadsheet that lists the names of salespeople at the top, as shown in figure 11.4. As you continue your spreadsheet design, however, you realize that your spreadsheet is more effective if you list the names in column A (see fig. 11.5).

```
┌─C:\40DATA\DATAFILL.SSF═══════════════════════════════F10=◆=▲─┐
│A1:   3                                                  READY │
│                                                               │
│       A        B        C        D        E        F        G        H    │
│  1       3       63      123      183      243      303      363      423  │
│  2       6       66      126      186      246      306      366      426  │
│  3       9       69      129      189      249      309      369      429  │
│  4      12       72      132      192      252      312      372      432  │
│  5      15       75      135      195      255      315      375      435  │
│  6      18       78      138      198      258      318      378      438  │
│  7      21       81      141      201      261      321      381      441  │
│  8      24       84      144      204      264      324      384      444  │
│  9      27       87      147      207      267      327      387      447  │
│ 10      30       90      150      210      270      330      390      450  │
│ 11      33       93      153      213      273      333      393      453  │
│ 12      36       96      156      216      276      336      396      456  │
│ 13      39       99      159      219      279      339      399      459  │
│ 14      42      102      162      222      282      342      402      462  │
│ 15      45      105      165      225      285      345      405      465  │
│ 16      48      108      168      228      288      348      408      468  │
│ 17      51      111      171      231      291      351      411      471  │
│ 18      54      114      174      234      294      354      414      474  │
│ 19      57      117      177      237      297      357      417      477  │
│#1                                                    Num   J20│
└───────────────────────────────────────────────────────────────┘
```

**Fig. 11.3.** *A spreadsheet after use of the Modify command.*

To invoke the Transpose command, press

F10 Edit **Transpose**

Enable first prompts `Enter FROM range`. Type or point to the range you want to move, and press Enter. Enable then prompts

`Enter TO range starting cell`

Type or point to the left coordinate of the range, and press Enter. The range to move from disappears from its original position and reappears starting at the new coordinate.

Although you sometimes may want to place the new cells on top of the old cells, you cannot use the Transpose command to overlap the old cells with the new (with the exception of the cell at the top left corner of the spreadsheet). Instead, use a blank range as the new range; then, after you have transposed the data to the new location, copy the data to the place you originally wanted it to go.

NOTE

All formula references to transposed cells change to reflect the move. For example, if your original formula was @SUM(A1..A6) and the range A1..A6 is transposed to begin at cell B23, the formula adjusts to read @SUM(B23..G23).

TIP

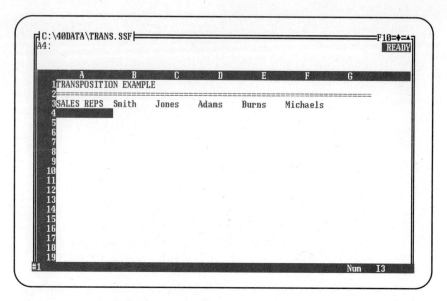

*Fig. 11.4. A spreadsheet before application of the Transpose command.*

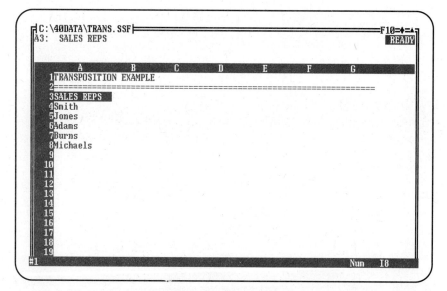

*Fig. 11.5. A spreadsheet after application of the Transpose command.*

# Changing the Display Colors

When you use a spreadsheet, you may want to know quickly whether any values are negative or less than a given value, whether any cells are protected, which cells have notes, which cells are highlighted, and which cells were changed by the last recalculation. In Enable/OA 4.0, the spreadsheet has added colors so that you can specify different colors to correspond to these conditions.

To invoke the Display Colors command, press

F10 **D**isplay Colors

Enable then displays a menu with the following options:

- *Settings:* Use this option to select the colors for each possible condition. Figure 11.6 shows a sample Settings box. To choose a color, move your cursor to the desired cell type, and press Enter. Enable then displays a color palette with sample background and character colors, as shown in figure 11.7. Move your cursor to the desired color combination, and press Enter. Notice that as you move your cursor from square to square in the color palette, the word text changes colors to match. After you choose a color, the C in the Settings box to the left of each cell type reflects the change.

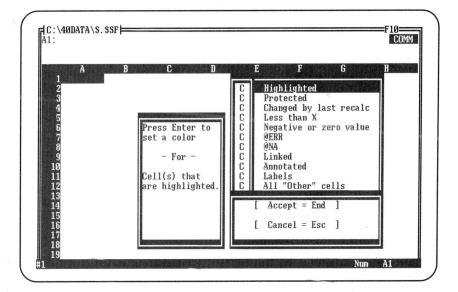

*Fig. 11.6. The Display Colors Setting dialog box.*

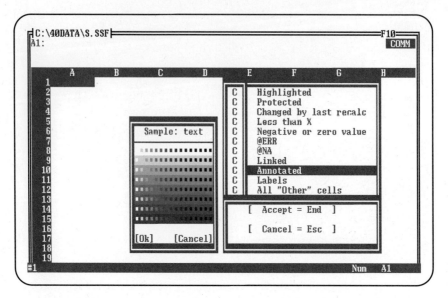

**Fig. 11.7.** *The color palette in the Display-Colors Setting dialog box.*

- *Range.* You can use the range option to specify these colors for a range; you therefore can have different color schemes in different parts of your spreadsheet. When you select range, Enable prompts:

```
Enter range for color display:
```

Enter the desired range, or press Enter to accept Enable's default of ALL.

- *Number.* In the settings section, use the option Less_than_X to define *x*. After you choose this option, Enable gives you the following prompt:

```
Enter value for 'Less than X' color option:
```

Respond to this prompt with the desired value.

Figure 11.8 shows a sample spreadsheet with colors set (although in this book, the colored sections appear as gray or black areas). In this example, the Less_than_X value is 300,000.

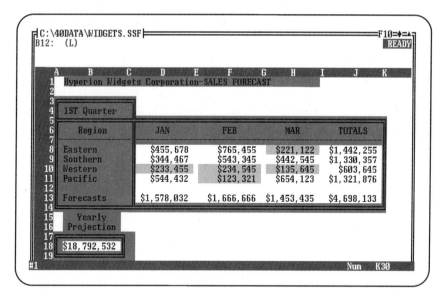

**Fig. 11.8.** *A sample spreadsheet with Colors.*

# Using Advanced Audit Commands

Chapter 9, "Understanding Spreadsheet Basics," introduces you to some basic Audit commands. Enable/OA, however, offers many more Audit, or debugging, commands. This section covers map mode, notes, the Highlight Command, goal seeking, and recalculation options.

## Using the Map Command

One of the biggest drawbacks to using spreadsheets is the credibility they give to numeric data that may be totally in error. As the creator of a spreadsheet, you have a duty to make sure that the spreadsheet does what it should do.

The Map command is a helpful tool for this purpose. This feature quickly shows you which cells contain labels (text), which cells contain values (numbers), and which cells contain formulas. Because labels and formulas can look like numbers, sometimes this information is not readily apparent when you look at the screen.

To use the Map feature, press

F10 **Audit Map Set**

Enable displays the spreadsheet in an unusual way. Double quotation marks (") replace every label; a pound symbol (#) replaces every value; a plus sign (+) replaces every formula (or function). Figure 11.9 shows a "mapped" version of the Hyperion Widget spreadsheet.

Notice that the cell information area still displays the current contents of the cell. All spreadsheet commands are available in Map mode.

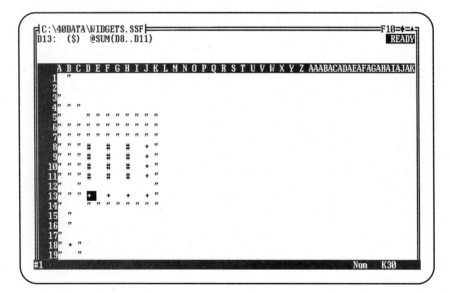

*Fig. 11.9. The Widgets spreadsheet in map mode.*

**TIP**

Use Map mode when you use commands (such as Format, Align, and Name) that cover large ranges. Because the spreadsheet is condensed, you can move your cell pointer more quickly in this mode.

To return to normal spreadsheet display, press

> F10 **Audit Map Clear**

# Using the Notes Command

Within a spreadsheet, you often have long, involved formulas, or data, the source of which is hard to remember. With Enable/OA 4.0, you can store a text note along with any cell. For example, you can add a note to cell F11 in the Widgets spreadsheet (see fig. 11.10) to explain the drastic drop in sales.

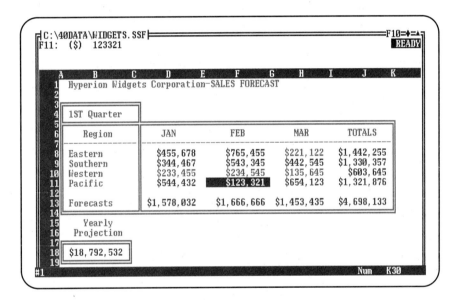

**Fig. 11.10.** *The Widgets spreadsheet.*

To insert a note in the spreadsheet, press

> F10 **Audit Notes**

Enable displays a note area at the top of the screen, as shown in figure 11.11. Type the text of your note, and press F10 for the Notes menu, which gives you the option to **Save, Cancel, Edit,** or **Delete** the note.

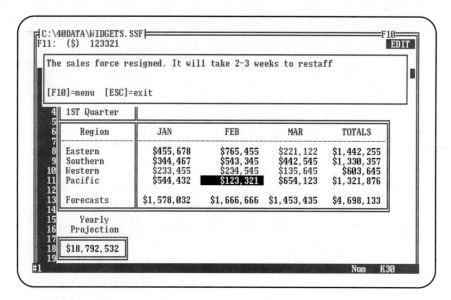

*Fig. 11.11. A note area at the top of a screen.*

After you attach a note to a cell, a note symbol appears in the cell information display area (see fig. 11.12).

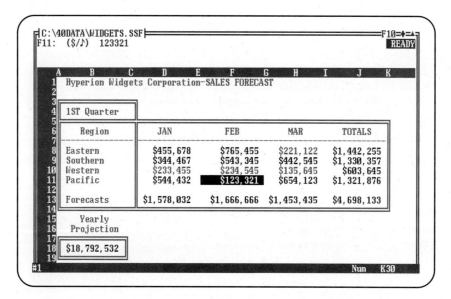

*Fig. 11.12. The cell information display area with an associated note.*

# Using the Highlight Command

Another useful debugging tool is the Highlight command, which you can use to see relationships among the cells in your spreadsheet. Sometimes you may change or erase a cell without realizing that your change causes many other cells that don't appear on this screen to become invalid. With the Highlight command, if cell A1 changes, you can see which other cells are affected. To invoke the Highlight command, press

F10 **Audit Highlight**

Enable displays the Highlight menu, which has three options: Referenced_Cells, Consolidated_Formulas, and Dependent_Cells.

## Using the Referenced Cells Command

Use the Referenced_Cells command to see which cells are needed to determine the result of a given cell. For example, in the Widgets spreadsheet, cell J13 has the formula @SUM(D13..H13) as in figure 11.10. Therefore, the cells D13 through H13 are referenced in cell J13.

When you choose Referenced_Cells from the highlight menu, Enable prompts

```
Highlight cells related to:
```

Enter the cell address, or move your cell pointer to the desired cell, and press Enter. Enable then moves the pointer to the first referenced cell and displays the number of related cells on the status line, as shown in figure 11.13. You can move your pointer around the spreadsheet and view the referenced cells, or you can press F2 so that Enable moves your pointer. After you view the cells, press Escape to enter another cell. Press Escape again to return to your spreadsheet.

## Using the Dependent Cells Command

Use the Dependent_Cells option to see which cells will change if you change a given cell. Under Dependent_Cells, you can choose **Direct** or **All**. Direct dependence means that a given cell actually is used in a formula in another cell. **All** shows you *any* cells affected if you change this cell. For example, in the Widgets spreadsheet, only cells J8 and D13 are directly dependent upon cell D8. However, if you select **All**, cells J13 and B18 are included also.

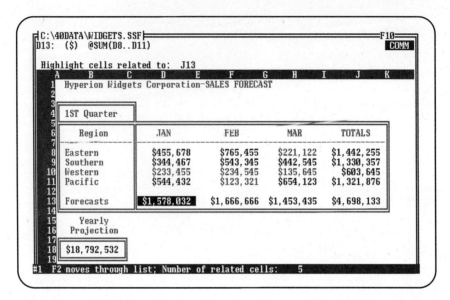

*Fig. 11.13. The cells referenced by cell J13.*

## Using Consolidated Formulas

In Enable/OA, copying formulas is more efficient than typing them in every cell. For example, in the Widgets spreadsheet, cells J8 through J11 have similar formulas. If you type the @SUM function in each cell, Enable does not know that these formulas are really the same, with a different row. Thus, as a final audit, you may want to see if Enable has consolidated a column or row of formulas correctly. When you select the Consolidated formulas option, use the F2 key to move around your spreadsheet. If a cell that should have been created using a copy is not highlighted, then you should perform the copy.

## Using the Goal-Seek Command

Perhaps the most original feature of the Enable spreadsheet is the Goal-seek command, which takes advantage of Enable's method of recalculating only cells affected by a change. You can think of this command as the "what-if" command, because you can use it to determine quickly the results of a formula based on several factors. With Goal-seek, you can increment or decrement a cell, manually or automatically, until another cell that depends on that cell reaches a specified value.

Suppose, for example, that as the sales manager from Hyperion Widgets, you want to determine how large a sales increase is necessary to boost next quarter's sales at Hyperion Widgets up to $5,000,000 from the current $4,698,133 (see fig. 11.14). You already have an established method for making the projection. All the cells in column I recalculate when you change the projected increase figure in D4. You can enter figures arbitrarily in D4 until you hit $5,000,000 in cell I13, but that is inefficient. Instead, press

F10 **Audit Goal-seek Automatic**

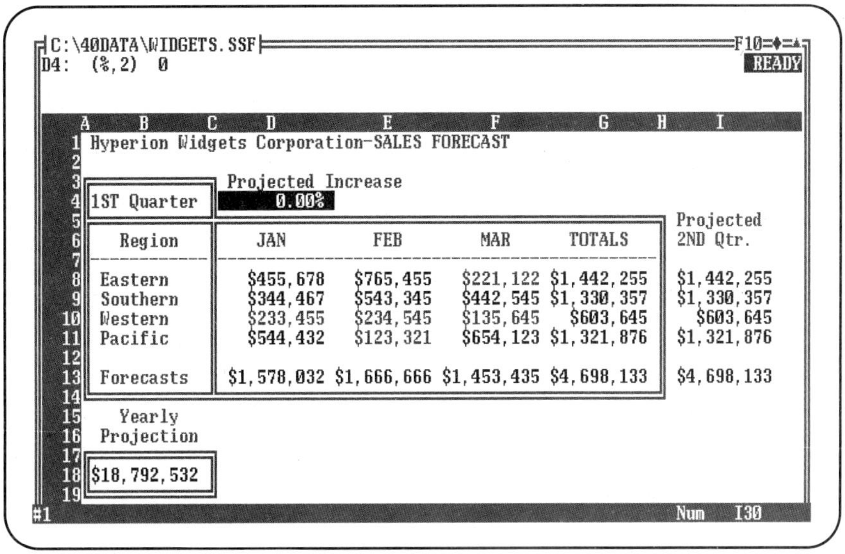
C:\40DATA\WIDGETS.SSF
F10
D4: (%,2) 0
READY
A B C D E F G H I
1 Hyperion Widgets Corporation-SALES FORECAST
3 Projected Increase
4 1ST Quarter 0.00%
Projected 2ND Qtr.
Region JAN FEB MAR TOTALS
Eastern $455,678 $765,455 $221,122 $1,442,255 $1,442,255
Southern $344,467 $543,345 $442,545 $1,330,357 $1,330,357
Western $233,455 $234,545 $135,645 $603,645 $603,645
Pacific $544,432 $123,321 $654,123 $1,321,876 $1,321,876
Forecasts $1,578,032 $1,666,666 $1,453,435 $4,698,133 $4,698,133
Yearly Projection
$18,792,532
#1
Num I30

***Fig. 11.14.*** *A spreadsheet for calculating a projected 2nd quarter sales total.*

Enable first prompts, `Enter cell to be adjusted`. Enter **D4**, the cell holding the percentage. Then Enable prompts, `Enter adjustment value`. Enter an incremental value by which to change D4—for example, .25% or **.0025**.

Enable displays the next prompt, `Enter target cell`. Enter **I13**, the cell that you want to hold the $5,000,000 value for which you are looking. Finally, Enable prompts `Enter completion value`. Here you type **5000000** (without commas, of course).

When you press Enter, Enable begins to increment cell D4 by .0025 until the value in I13 exactly matches or just passes 5,000,000 by one iteration. When 100 iterations have been calculated, Enable displays a message that gives you the option to cancel the request or continue. You can see the result in figure 11.15. A 21% sales increase results in sales of $5,001,007.

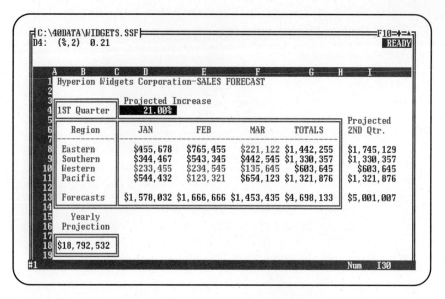

**Fig. 11.15.** *Results of using the Audit Goal-seek command.*

When you use the Goal-seek command, start with a larger adjustment value. When you get close, perform the automatic step recalculation again with a smaller adjustment value. This approach optimizes time and accuracy.

# Using Automatic and Manual Calculation

Another option under Audit is the Calculate option (see fig. 11.16). This option determines whether Enable recalculates the spreadsheet every time you make a change to a cell (**Automatic**), or whether the user must request that the calculation be done (**Manual**). Although Enable uses a sparse recalculation method, which means only cells affected by the current cell are recalculated, in a big spreadsheet, many formulas may be dependent on a column. While you are entering data, you may want the spreadsheet to recalculate after every entry; in that case, use the default setting, **Automatic**.

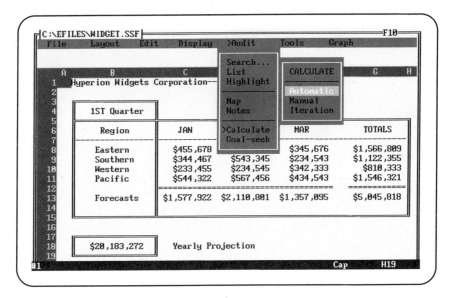

**Fig. 11.16.** *The Calculate menu.*

With **A**utomatic recalculation (the default), Enable automatically recalculates any cells affected by a change you make to the spreadsheet.

The **M**anual option turns off automatic recalculation. You then can enter data into any number of cells without affecting the results of any related formulas. To invoke manual recalculation, press

    F10 **A**udit **C**alculate **M**anual

After you enter your data, the word `Calc` appears in the Status Line of any cells affected by that cell. You can invoke recalculation manually by pressing the F5 key. All the formulas affected by the new cell entries recalculate. Remember, however, that after you use F5 to recalculate manually, you need to reset the program to change back to automatic recalculation. Recalculation remains manual until you again press

    F10 **A**udit **C**alculate **A**utomatic

Even when recalculation is set to Manual, pressing Ctrl-F5 always recalculates every formula in your spreadsheet.

TIP

The Iteration option is the least understood of the three Calculate options. Iteration, the repeated recalculation of a formula, comes into play in cases of *circular references*—when a cell containing a formula is itself referenced in that formula.

In most cases, circular references are errors. Beginners often create circular reference errors by copying formulas from one cell to an adjacent range. The user may make the mistake of copying the sum formula into part of the range being summed. In most spreadsheets, circular references are very difficult to track down. Enable's Highlight command (see "Using the Highlight Command" in this chapter), which highlights all cells that reference a particular cell, makes discovering circular references somewhat easier.

On rare occasions, you deliberately use circular references. Consider the following typical situation. A salesman earns a bonus based on the amount of profit generated by a sale. However, you must consider the bonus itself as part of the overhead and subtract it from the gross sale to help calculate the profit (see fig. 11.17).

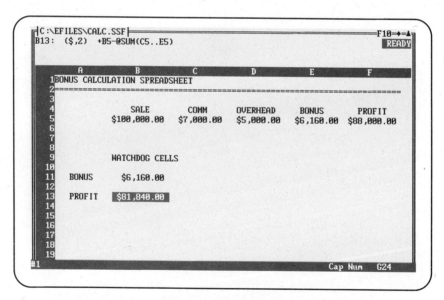

*Fig. 11.17. A spreadsheet with a circular reference.*

You can calculate this problem with the Iteration command. You calculate the salesman's bonus as 7% of the profit (+F5*.07). You calculate the profit as the gross sales figure minus the sum of commission, overhead, and bonus: +B5–@SUM(C5..E5). With one iteration, the bonus calculates as $6,160.00, and the net profit as $88,000.00. This profit figure is incorrect. How do you know? Cells B11 and B13 are used as "watchdogs." Cell B11 holds the current value of the bonus, a reference to E5. The bonus is calculated to four places. Cell B13 contains the formula to calculate the profit with the current bonus. The formula in that cell subtracts the current value of the bonus and the constant costs of the commission and overhead from the sale price: +B5–@SUM(C5..E5).

To solve this calculation problem, you have two options: you can recalculate the values manually until you see no more changes in the Profit and Bonus cells; or you can use the following commands:

F10 **A**udit **C**alculate **I**teration

After you use these commands, you set the Iteration value. Start with ten iterations. Then, one press of the F5 key gives you all ten iterations. Remember that, if you choose this latter route, you first have to reenter the formulas. The Iteration procedure works only when you have set it *before* you enter the formulas. To find out whether you need more iterations, press F5 again. If you have no more changes in the related cells, the process is complete.

# Using Spreadsheet Tools

Enable's spreadsheet includes several tools that you may find helpful. This section discusses two particularly useful tools: Sort and Defaults. Use Sort to order your spreadsheet according to certain criteria. Use Defaults to reset locally some options that were set in the profile.

## Using the Sort Command

*Sorting* is the process of placing data values in alphabetical or numerical order. Practically every spreadsheet user wants to sort numbers at some time. For example, a business manager may want to sort sales in highest-to-lowest order; a teacher may want to sort randomly recorded student names and grades in order by student name; and a storekeeper may want to sort inventory costs by stock number. With Enable, you can sort not only in the traditional ascending or descending sort orders, but also in row-based or column-based sorting order.

To choose the Sort command, press

F10 **Tools** **S**ort

Enable displays the Sort dialog box with the following options (see fig. 11.18):

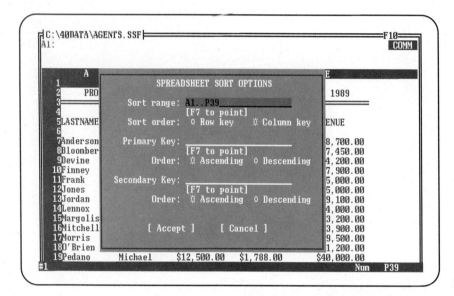

```
╔C:\40DATA\AGENTS.SSF══════════════════════════════════════F10═╗
║A1:                                                     ║COMM║
║                                                            ║
║    ┌──────A──────────────────────────────────────────E──────┐
║   1│                                                        │
║   2│   PRO          SPREADSHEET SORT OPTIONS        1989     │
║   3│                                                         │
║   4│          Sort range: A1..P39_____                    │
║  5LASTNAME│               [F7 to point]            ENUE      │
║   6│          Sort order: ◇ Row key    ▨ Column key          │
║  7Anderson│                                         8,700.00 │
║  8Bloomber│  Primary Key: _____           7,450.00 │
║  9Devine  │               [F7 to point]            4,200.00 │
║ 10Finney  │      Order: ▨ Ascending  ◇ Descending  7,900.00 │
║ 11Frank   │                                         5,000.00 │
║ 12Jones   │Secondary Key: _____           5,000.00 │
║ 13Jordan  │               [F7 to point]            9,100.00 │
║ 14Lennox  │      Order: ▨ Ascending  ◇ Descending  4,000.00 │
║ 15Margolis│                                         3,200.00 │
║ 16Mitchell│                                         3,900.00 │
║ 17Morris  │       [ Accept ]      [ Cancel ]        9,500.00 │
║ 18O'Brien │                                         1,200.00 │
║ 19Pedano   Michael   $12,500.00   $1,788.00   $40,000.00    │
║#1                                              Num    P39   ║
╚════════════════════════════════════════════════════════════╝
```

**Fig. 11.18.** *The Sort dialog box.*

- *Sort_range.* Use this option to select the range you want to sort. Type in, or press F7 to point to, the entire range that you want to sort, and then press Enter. When you specify the sort range, remember that you must give Enable the entire range of cells to be rearranged by the sort process. For example, in the spreadsheet shown in figure 11.19, suppose that you specify the sort range as C7..E19, and you want to sort by the revenue. Enable sorts the numeric cells, but not the names in columns A and B; this sort returns highly misleading results.

**TIP**

Remember to include any data you want to sort that lies beyond the screen. Omitting data is an especially common mistake when you point to the sort range.

```
┌─C:\40DATA\AGENTS.SSF────────────────────────────────────F10=◆=▲┐
│A1:                                                         READY │
│                                                                  │
│        A         B         C          D          E        F    G │
│ 1                                                                │
│ 2       PROJECTED ANNUAL SALES EXPENSES VERSUS REVENUE FOR 1992  │
│ 3                                                                │
│ 4                                                                │
│ 5 LASTNAME   FIRSTNAME   SALARY    COMMISSION   REVENUE    BRANCH │
│ 6                                                                │
│ 7 Anderson   Andrea    $50,000.00  $6,050.00   $98,700.00   4   1│
│ 8 Bloomberg  Henry     $40,000.00  $4,398.00   $87,450.00   3   2│
│ 9 Devine     Ann       $18,000.00  $5,000.00   $84,200.00   1   3│
│10 Finney     George    $14,000.00  $4,500.00   $77,900.00   2   4│
│11 Frank      Wallace   $12,500.00  $4,000.00   $75,000.00   1   5│
│12 Jones      Howard    $20,000.00  $3,800.00   $75,000.00   2   6│
│13 Jordan     Nancy     $18,000.00  $2,764.00   $69,100.00   2   7│
│14 Lennox     Anne      $13,500.00  $2,600.00   $64,000.00   4   8│
│15 Margolis   Andrew    $13,500.00  $2,728.00   $63,200.00   4   9│
│16 Mitchell   Martha    $18,700.00  $2,000.00   $53,900.00   5  10│
│17 Morris     Alison    $14,000.00  $1,998.00   $49,500.00   5  11│
│18 O'Brien    Suzanne   $15,300.00  $1,800.00   $41,200.00   5  12│
│19 Pedano     Michael   $12,500.00  $1,788.00   $40,000.00   5  13│
│#1                                                     Num   P39 │
└──────────────────────────────────────────────────────────────────┘
```

*Fig. 11.19. A sample spreadsheet to be sorted.*

Notice that when you invoke the Sort command, Enable offers you a default sort range that includes all the cells from A1 to the highest cell used. After you enter a new sort range, Enable uses the new range until you change it or close the spreadsheet.

- *Sort_order: Row_key or Column_key*. After you type or point to the range, you must decide how you want the data sorted. You can sort in two ways: by Column_key or by Row_key. A column sort is the default; if you are setting up your sort for the first time, or if the last sort you chose was column-based, you need not choose the Column_key option now. You need to choose Column_key only if your preceding sort was row-based.

    If you want a row-based sort, you must choose Row_key. Even if your sort range includes cells from only a single row, Enable attempts to sort the range by columns unless you specify otherwise.

- *Primary_Key*. Use this option to choose the primary key by which to sort. Selecting a sort key simply identifies which rows or columns contain the data by which to sort your range. For example, look again at figure 11.19. If you want to sort the range A7..E19, you can do so in a number of different ways. You can sort the entire range in alphabetical order by last name; in that case, any cell in the range A7..A19 can be your sort key. If you want to sort by revenue, any cell in E7..E19 can be your sort key.

In response to this prompt, you simply can enter a single cell within the sort range. Use F7 to place your pointer on any cell in the range you are using as the sort key, and press Enter. Remember that you must not use the label heading the row or column as the sort-key identifying cell.

- *Order. Ascending or Descending.* In an ascending sort, Enable sorts numbers from lowest to highest, and letters in alphabetical order. In a descending sort, Enable does the reverse.

  Enable sorts cell contents according to their ASCII values. Therefore, in an ascending sort, Enable sorts negative values before positive ones and all uppercase letters before lowercase ones.

- *Secondary_Key.* Use this option to perform a *nested sort*—a sort with a second level of sorting within the first level.

  For example, consider the spreadsheet shown in figure 11.19. Suppose that you want the agents sorted by the branch and then in alphabetical order by last name. Take the primary key from the Branch column, and the secondary key from the Agent column.

After entering each of these options, press Accept to perform the sort. Figure 11.20 shows the dialog box entries necessary to perform this sort, and figure 11.21 shows the result of this nested sort.

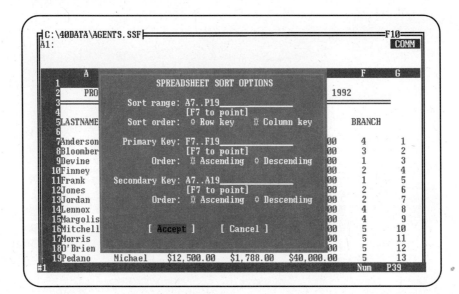

**Fig. 11.20.** *A sample Sort dialog box.*

```
┌─C:\40DATA\AGENTS.SSF┤═══════════════════════════════════════════F10=◆=▲┐
│A1:                                                               READY│
│                                                                      │
│        A         B          C          D          E          F     G │
│    1                                                                 │
│    2  PROJECTED ANNUAL SALES EXPENSES VERSUS REVENUE FOR 1992        │
│    3                                                                 │
│    4                                                                 │
│    5 LASTNAME  FIRSTNAME   SALARY   COMMISSION   REVENUE    BRANCH    │
│    6                                                                 │
│    7 Devine    Ann       $18,000.00  $5,000.00  $84,200.00    1     3 │
│    8 Frank     Wallace   $12,500.00  $4,000.00  $75,000.00    1     5 │
│    9 Finney    George    $14,000.00  $4,500.00  $77,900.00    2     4 │
│   10 Jones     Howard    $20,000.00  $3,800.00  $75,000.00    2     6 │
│   11 Jordan    Nancy     $18,000.00  $2,764.00  $69,100.00    2     7 │
│   12 Bloomberg Henry     $40,000.00  $4,398.00  $87,450.00    3     2 │
│   13 Anderson  Andrea    $50,000.00  $6,050.00  $98,700.00    4     1 │
│   14 Lennox    Anne      $13,500.00  $2,600.00  $64,000.00    4     8 │
│   15 Margolis  Andrew    $13,500.00  $2,728.00  $63,200.00    4     9 │
│   16 Mitchell  Martha    $18,700.00  $2,000.00  $53,900.00    5    10 │
│   17 Morris    Alison    $14,000.00  $1,998.00  $49,500.00    5    11 │
│   18 O'Brien   Suzanne   $15,300.00  $1,800.00  $41,200.00    5    12 │
│   19 Pedano    Michael   $12,500.00  $1,788.00  $40,000.00    5    13 │
│ #1                                                        Num   P39  │
└──────────────────────────────────────────────────────────────────────┘
```

**Fig. 11.21.** *The sorted spreadsheet AGENTS.SSF.*

> Notice that column G in the spreadsheet shown in figures 11.19 and 11.20 is initially a sequential list of whole numbers. This column was created with the Fill command, discussed in a previous section of this chapter. Include a column like this one in the sort range; then you easily can put the data back in the original order by doing another sort with this column as the primary key.

TIP

# Changing Defaults

A new feature in Enable/OA 4.0 is the capability to save certain default values in your spreadsheet. You may want to change your profile options (discussed in Appendix B) but only in a particular spreadsheet. Defaults, such as suppressing zeroes, displaying cell colors, centering numeric data on the decimal point, and so on, are available. To access the defaults options, press

F10 **T**ools **D**efaults

Enable displays the Spreadsheet Environment dialog box. Figure 11.22 shows all the available options. If you save these defaults, they remain in affect only for this spreadsheet. If you change the defaults, but don't save the spreadsheet itself, the defaults are not active the next time you edit the spreadsheet.

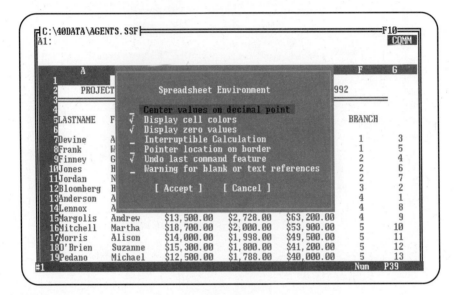

***Fig. 11.22.** The Defaults Spreadsheet Environment dialog box.*

# Using Multiple Spreadsheets

To work efficiently, you sometimes need to combine several spreadsheets. For example, if several departments need to enter budget information, you may not want to pass a single spreadsheet around to all departments. When the budgets are due, you want each department to have its own physical spreadsheet. This practice is even more practical if several separate offices are involved. The finance department, however, needs to see the budget as a whole. Enable/OA offers two options to solve this problem: the File Combine command, and spreadsheet linking. The following section looks at both options.

## Using the Combine Command

Use Enable's Combine command to combine information from two spreadsheets. With the Combine command, you can copy data from one spreadsheet into another. The spreadsheet you want to copy from can be on disk or in memory. In addition, you can add or subtract values from a range in one spreadsheet to or from a range in another. Combine does *not* link spreadsheets (*combining* makes one spreadsheet from multiple spreadsheets; *linking* connects two spreadsheets while maintaining them separately).

To invoke the Combine command, first place the pointer where you want the data from the other spreadsheet combined. Press

F10 **File Combine**

Enable then displays a menu that asks whether you want to Copy, Add, or Subtract from another spreadsheet (see fig. 11.23). Figure 11.24 shows two spreadsheets, in the top and bottom of the screen, to be combined. You don't need to display both files together to combine them, but you can see the result more clearly this way.

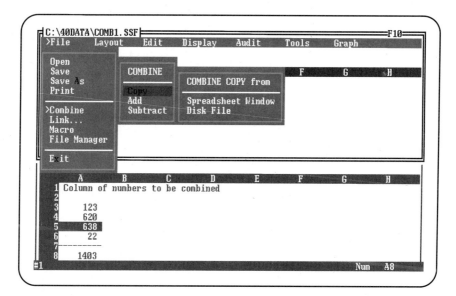

*Fig. 11.23. The Combine menu.*

Choose Copy to replace the contents in the target range with the contents of the range you are copying from the other spreadsheet. If you are copying a range containing a formula, Enable copies the formula—not the result of the formula.

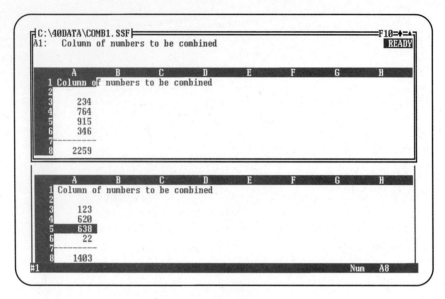

*Fig. 11.24. Two spreadsheets to be combined.*

The Add option adds the values in the FROM range to the TO range. This option works properly only if both ranges contain the same number of values in the same relative positions. The Subtract option subtracts the values in the FROM range from the values in the TO range.

Whether you select Copy, Add, or Subtract, Enable responds by displaying a menu that asks whether the file from which you want to combine is on disk or in a window in memory (see fig. 11.23). The following two sections explain the difference between these two options.

## Using Combine Disk_File

If you choose the Disk_File option, Enable prompts `Enter file name`. Respond with the proper file name, and press Enter. Enable then responds with the prompt

```
Enter range to combine FROM
```

The default response `ALL` follows the prompt. Choosing this option causes the entire spreadsheet in the other file to be combined. Normally, you should combine a spreadsheet directly from the disk only if you are sure of the proper range, because you have no way to look at the spreadsheet to determine the range.

After you type the range and press Enter, Enable prompts

```
Enter TO range starting cell
```

This starting cell should match the relative position of the upper left corner of the spreadsheet range you are copying, adding, or subtracting from the other file. Your cell pointer should be there already; if not, type or point to the appropriate response, and again press Enter.

## Using Combine Spreadsheet_Window

If you choose Spreadsheet_Window, Enable displays the Interwindow Copy Options screen (see fig. 11.25). To combine from an open spreadsheet window, choose the number of the window that holds the appropriate file. For example, in figure 11.24, the file COMB2.SSF from window #2 will be added to the file COMB1.SSF, which is in window #1. Enable displays the other window, and prompts Enter range to combine FROM.

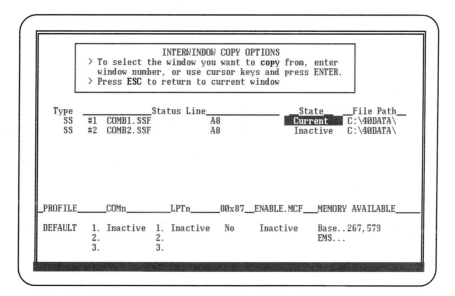

*Fig. 11.25. The Interwindow Copy Options screen.*

Again, the program lists the default ALL. Type or point to the range you want, and then press Enter. This time, Enable does accept range names. After you enter the FROM range, Enable again displays the TO window, now with the prompt

```
Enter TO range starting cell
```

Type or point to the cell address, and then press Enter. The Combine operation executes immediately. Figure 11.26 shows the result of using Combine to add the entire file COMB2.SSF, in the bottom of the screen, to COMB1.SSF, in the top of the screen, beginning at cell A1. Notice that the formula in cell A8 of COMB1.SSF is not affected.

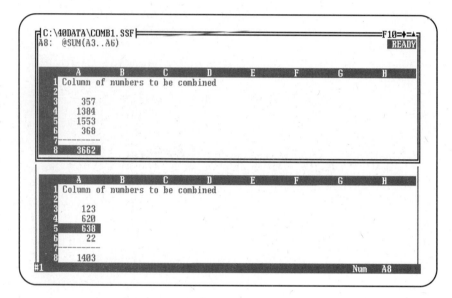

**Fig. 11.26.** *The result of Combine Add.*

In addition, you can use the keystroke command Alt-F5, as in the word processing module, for an interwindow copy between spreadsheets—the equivalent of Combine Copy from another window.

**NOTE**

If you choose Disk_File rather than Spreadsheet_Window, and the desired spreadsheet is open in another window, the combine reflects the spreadsheet only as of the last time you saved it. The same thing is true on a network, if the spreadsheet is open on another user's machine.

# Linking Spreadsheets

Enable/OA can link spreadsheets stored on disk to a spreadsheet that is active on-screen. You can use this feature when nonlinkable spreadsheets have outgrown practical limits. In versions of Enable prior to Enable/OA, all dependent formulas had to appear on the same spreadsheet as the values on which they were based. Through spreadsheet linking, however, Enable/OA has the capability to keep formulas and values separate. Many benefits result, but probably the most obvious one is the end of giant, unfathomable spreadsheets. Linking is accomplished through functions discussed in this section.

# Using the @LINK Function

The @LINK function is the tool that forges the link between two spreadsheets. This function works only when the spreadsheet that contains it, called the *dependent spreadsheet*, is on-screen. Just as important, the spreadsheet to which @LINK will link the current spreadsheet, referred to as the *supporting spreadsheet*, must be stored in the current data directory.

If you use @LINK often, you may need to increase the number of files specified in the FILES line of your CONFIG.SYS file. See Appendix A, "Installing and Starting Enable," for information about this file.

TIP

The syntax for the @LINK command is

@LINK(#*filename*,"*string*")

The pound sign (#) is necessary before the file name of the supporting spreadsheet. You do not have to include the SSF file extension; Enable adds it for you. The "*string*" indicated in the syntax should be replaced by a cell address, a cell range, or a range name. The string specifies the cell(s) to be retrieved from the supporting spreadsheet. The quotation marks are necessary but can be single (right) quotation marks. Use this function as if the cell, range, or range name were actually in the dependent spreadsheet.

Figure 11.27 shows an example of a @LINK function. In this example, a corporate sales forecast has been compiled based on regional forecasts in supporting spreadsheets. One of these regional forecasts is the spreadsheet named PACIFIC.SSF. Because the total January sales forecast for the Pacific Region is found in cell D13 of the PACIFIC spreadsheet, the appropriate formula to retrieve the total is

@LINK(#PACIFIC,"D13")

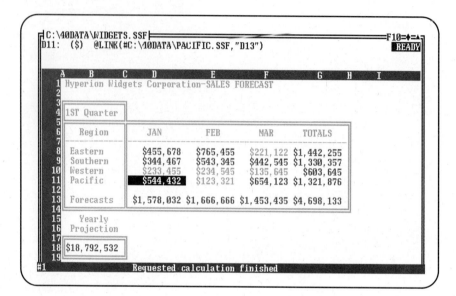

*Fig. 11.27. The @LINK function.*

After you enter this formula and press Enter, Enable displays the prompt

```
Activate this external link? Yes No
```

To activate immediately the link to the supporting file, press **Yes**.

If, however, the supporting file does not yet exist, or for some other reason you don't want the link activated, you can choose **No**. In that case, Enable displays REF in the cell to indicate that a reference to another spreadsheet exists in the cell but has not been activated. Another message, REF, appears if you try to activate a link to a spreadsheet that does not yet exist.

NOTE

Regardless of the range you give the function, only one cell is put into the current cell. The value is the first cell referenced in the range. Thus, if you had a range name, or a range that contains more than one cell, be aware that only the top right cell is used. See the discussion of @EXTCOPY in this section to copy multiple cells at once.

To see a list of spreadsheet files currently linked to your spreadsheet, press

F10 **File Link**

Enable displays a screen similar to figure 11.28.

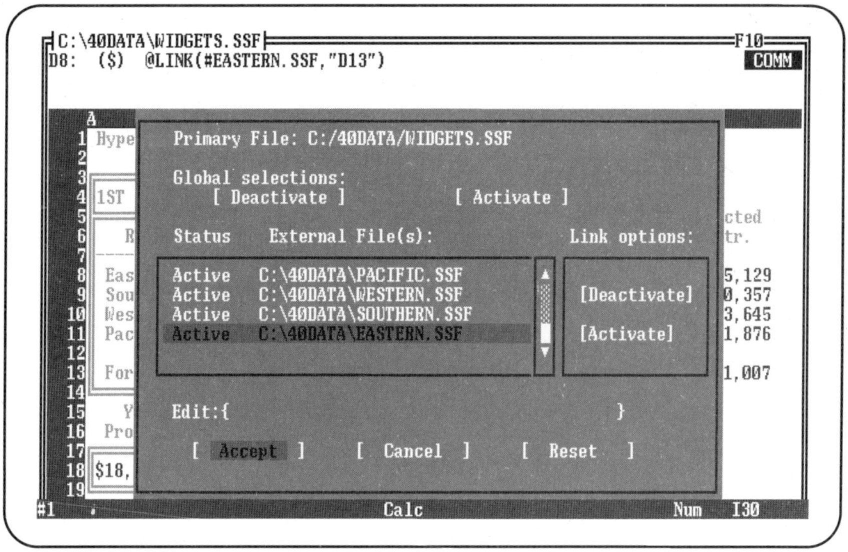

**Fig. 11.28.** *A Link Options screen.*

The WIDGET spreadsheet depends on four regional forecasts: EASTERN.SSF, SOUTHERN.SSF, WESTERN.SSF, and PACIFIC.SSF. The screen shown in figure 11.28 indicates that they all are linked actively to WIDGET. You can use this screen to activate and deactivate links together or one at a time.

## Using the @RNGSTR Function

The @RNGSTR (range string) function gives you a way to create relative references in an @LINK formula. Use this function when you want to be able to copy an @LINK formula to another cell in the dependent spreadsheet and you want cell and range references to adjust automatically. To use @RNGSTR, use the following syntax:

@LINK(#PACIFIC,@RNGSTR(D13..D13))

The preceding formula is equal to the @LINK formula in cell D11 of the WIDGET spreadsheet shown in figure 11.27. The difference is that you can copy the formula to columns E and F when you also use the @RNGSTR function. Notice that the argument must be a range and is not enclosed in quotation marks.

## Using the @EXTCOPY Function

In the spreadsheet shown in figure 11.27, you may want to have the whole row from the PACIFIC sprcadsheet linked at once. Because @LINK only links a single cell, you need a function to link multiple cells. @EXTCOPY does just that. The syntax is as follows:

@EXTCOPY(@LINK(#PACIFIC,"D13..G13"),D11..G11)

The @LINK( ) function actually creates the link to the external spreadsheet. In this case, the range is significant; Enable copies this range into the current spreadsheet. The second argument, D11..G11, is the target range, or the range where you want to place the data. Figure 11.29 shows an updated WIDGETS spreadsheet just before the @EXTCOPY formula in cell D11 is used.

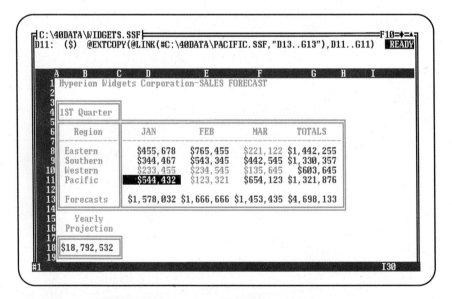

*Fig. 11.29. The WIDGETS Spreadsheet with @EXTCOPY.*

# Using Spreadsheet In-Cell Macros

In addition to the system macros, which you can create in any module, Enable also has macros exclusively for use in spreadsheets. These spreadsheet macros serve two purposes: they enable you to create macros specifically for individual spreadsheets, and they offer you nearly complete compatibility with 1-2-3. (***Note:*** Enable does not support the macro commands of 1-2-3 Release 2.) To create and use spreadsheet macros, you must understand Enable's spreadsheet module.

Enter spreadsheet macros in vertically adjoining cells of a spreadsheet (see fig. 11.30). Execution of a macro begins in the uppermost cell of the cells containing the macro, and continues from left to right within the cell. When no more keystrokes are found in a cell, Enable moves down to the cell below for further keystrokes—from cell A1, to A2, to A3. Execution stops when Enable reaches a blank cell.

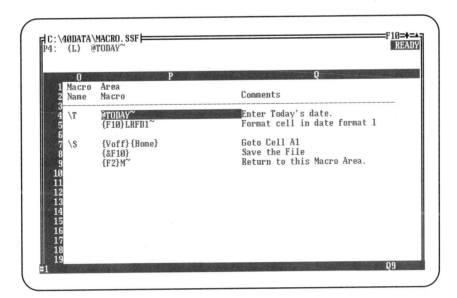

***Fig. 11.30.*** *Spreadsheet macros in an macro area.*

# Creating and Naming Macros

To create a spreadsheet macro, you need to follow two steps:

1. Type the macro codes into the cell(s).

2. Assign a range name to the beginning cell of the macro, using the spreadsheet's F10 **L**ayout **R**ange **N**ame **C**reate command.

Unlike system macros, for spreadsheet macros you cannot use the macro recorder to record the keystrokes you want repeated later. Instead, you must type the keystrokes into the spreadsheet cell(s). The process is similar to using the macro editor described in Chapter 4, "Using the Master Control Module's Advanced Features." You can use the same system macro codes shown in tables 4.2 and 4.3 in spreadsheet macros as well. You do not use the macro editor, however, to create or change a spreadsheet macro. You work entirely in the spreadsheet.

The safest place to create macros in a spreadsheet is to the right and below any other spreadsheet data. This area is less likely to be affected by changes to other portions of the spreadsheet. Set up a special area, like the area shown in figure 11.30, to hold all macros. One column should be reserved for macro names, one for the macros themselves, and another for comments and documentation. Give the top left cell of this area an easy-to-remember range name. In the spreadsheet shown in figure 11.30, cell O1 has the range name *M* for *Macro*.

Use the left-alignment character as the first character in each macro cell. This trick causes Enable to treat as a label any entry that may otherwise look like a value. The entry shown in cell P4 in figure 11.30 can not be entered successfully without one of the alignment characters, because Enable tries to place the system date in the cell. Left alignment is used simply because it looks the best.

After you type the desired codes into the cell(s), you need to give the first cell in the macro a unique range name. The range name must consist of the backslash (\) followed by a letter or number. The backslash in the name indicates to Enable that this range is a spreadsheet macro. Enable reserves the macro range name \0 for special use; any macro by this name executes automatically every time you retrieve the spreadsheet.

To name a macro, position the cell pointer on the first cell of the macro and press

F10 **Layout Range Name Create**

Type the range name (for example, \T or \S), press Enter, and then press Esc.

To see a list of the current range names, press

F9 **List Names**

## Running Spreadsheet In-Cell Macros

You invoke a spreadsheet in-cell macro in much the same way that you invoke a system macro. To execute a spreadsheet macro, simply press Shift-F9 and then the letter or number used to name the macro. For example, to execute a spreadsheet macro that begins in a cell range named \A, press

Shift-F9 **A**

## Using Spreadsheet In-Cell Macro Programming Commands

To maintain macro compatibility, Enable's spreadsheet in-cell macros can execute several macro programming commands that are identical to commands in 1-2-3 Release 1A. Enable uses these commands—for spreadsheet macros only—to make decisions, do subroutines, send messages, solicit input, and display user-created menus. This section briefly describes all the spreadsheet programming macro commands, although detailed discussion is beyond the scope of this book.

The /XI command is the spreadsheet macro's "if statement." /XI tests to see whether a stated condition in a cell is true or false, and then carries out an action based on the conclusion. The syntax for the command is

/XI*condition~action*

To use the command, enter in a macro cell the /XI label, the test condition, a tilde (~), and then an action. Do not include any spaces in the command.

The /XG command is the spreadsheet macro equivalent of the Goto command found in many programming languages. The syntax for the command is

/XG*cell~*

/XG transfers execution of the macro to the range beginning with the cell named in the command.

The /XC and /XR commands are the macro equivalents of BASIC's GOSUB and RETURN subroutine commands. A subroutine branches a program to a specific location—usually the start of a separate operation. At the end of that operation is a command to return the program to the statement just after the one that launched the subroutine.

The syntaxes for the /XC and /XR spreadsheet macro commands are

> /XC*cell~*

and

> /XR

/XC, the macro subroutine command, transfers the macro program to the stated cell. Enable/OA executes the commands in that cell and the cells below until it encounters an /XR command or a blank cell. The macro then returns to the keystroke immediately after the first /XC.

The /XL and /XN commands are excellent for data entry. You can use each command to display a prompt in the information display. When the user types a response to the prompt, the command places that information in the specified cell. Only one difference exists between the two commands: /XL takes only label data; /XN takes only values.

These spreadsheet macro commands take the following syntaxes:

> /XL*message~cell~*

and

> /XN*message~cell~*

Enable/OA also has the capability to "trap" the Esc key with the /XL and /XN commands. In case the user presses the Esc key rather than some valid response, add the appropriate action on the same line as the /XL or /XN command. The syntaxes then become

> /XL*message~cell~*contingent action on Esc

and

> /XN*message~cell~*contingent action on Esc

The /XE command evaluates an expression and places the result in a specified cell. The syntax for this command is

/XE*expression~cell~*

The /XQ command causes the macro to stop and return control to the user. This command is often used with the /XI command to instruct the program to stop the macro if the specified condition is true. The syntax for /XQ is simply /XQ.

You can use the /XM macro command to create a menu that looks and acts like Enable/OA's standard spreadsheet menus. Each menu choice has two parts: the name of the choice and submenus or a brief description below the choice. When you press an arrow key to highlight a different menu selection, the message changes to reflect the new selection. For a user-created menu, eight options is the maximum. You can create the same type of menu using the /XM command in a spreadsheet macro. Enable/OA has added an Esc code option to this command as well.

## Creating a Macro Library

Enable/OA has the capability to use macros that have been saved in another file on the disk. With this feature, you can create a spreadsheet whose primary purpose is to store macros: a *macro library*. Using a macro library involves a special spreadsheet function, @MACRO.

Use the @MACRO function to extract macros from a spreadsheet on the disk. Just place an @MACRO command in any spreadsheet where you need to use the macro. The syntax of the command is

@MACRO(#*filename*,"display *cell*,execute *cell*")

Design the macro area in the dependent spreadsheet (the on-screen spreadsheet that extracts a macro from the library) the same way as a nonlibrary spreadsheet, with a Name column, a Macro column, and a Comments column. Type the name you want to use for this macro in the Name column. Use the @MACRO function in the Macro column. Don't forget to put some documentation in the Comments column. Figure 11.31 shows one method of using the @MACRO function. Notice that because the macro name in the library is also a range name, the macro name is used to retrieve a display cell and an execute cell for the macro without your having to remember the cell address in the MACROS.SSF spreadsheet.

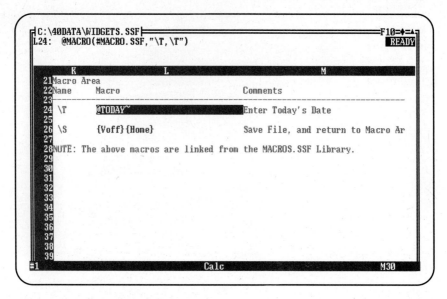

*Fig. 11.31. A Sample @MACRO Function.*

# Summary

In this chapter, you learn that Enable includes a powerful and capable spreadsheet. With the combination of all the commands, functions, and macros, Enable has enough tools to meet the needs of any spreadsheet user.

# 12

# Using 3D
# Spreadsheets

T his chapter describes how to create, change the view of, and use ranges in a 3D spreadsheet. You also learn how to use 3D spreadsheet commands, print and save a 3D spreadsheet, and use several functions specifically designed for 3D spreadsheets.

## Creating a 3D Spreadsheet

You create a 3D spreadsheet the same way you create a standard two-dimensional spreadsheet (refer to "Understanding the Spreadsheet Screen" in Chapter 9). From the Main Menu, press

Use_System Spreadsheet

After Enable prompts you for a file name, type a valid Enable file name and press Enter. Enable displays a blank spreadsheet. Figure 12.1 shows a new spreadsheet named WIDGET3D.SSF. The cell pointer rests in cell A1, as indicated by the pointer location reference A1 in the information display area (the upper left corner on-screen).

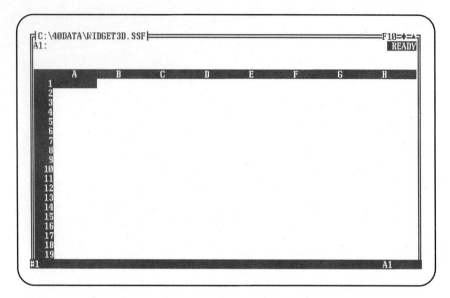

*Fig. 12.1. A new spreadsheet with the cell pointer in cell A1.*

To activate the 3D spreadsheet features, press Ctrl-PgDn. Enable impercep-
tibly converts the spreadsheet to three dimensions and moves the cell
pointer to cell A1 of level B, denoted by the legend B:A1 in the information
display area (see fig. 12.2). Press Ctrl-PgUp to move the pointer back to cell
A1 of level A.

The 3D spreadsheet now has 32 levels, labeled A through AF. The original
spreadsheet is level A. Subsequent levels are B, C, D, E, and so on. If you
think of a spreadsheet as an accountant's columnar worksheet, a 3D
spreadsheet is a 32-page pad of columnar worksheets. All 32 pages make up
the 3D spreadsheet.

Use Ctrl-PgDn and Ctrl-PgUp to move between levels. Ctrl-PgDn moves the
cell pointer to a lower level; Ctrl-PgUp moves it to a higher level.

# Changing the View

After you activate the third dimension in an Enable spreadsheet, the
program displays only one level—level B (again see fig. 12.2). You may want
to see multiple levels in the same spreadsheet screen. Enable provides two
ways for you to see multiple levels at the same time: the 3D-View method and
the split-screen method. The program also enables you to hide multiple
levels. In this section, you learn how to use these features.

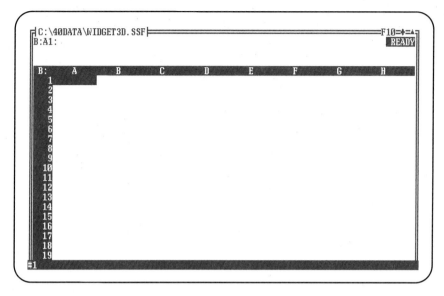

*Fig. 12.2. The 3D spreadsheet WIDGET3D.SSF, with the cell pointer in cell B:A1.*

# Toggling the 3D View

To display three levels at the same time, press

> F10 **D**isplay **3**D_View

or

> F9 **3**D

Enable displays rows 1-5 of three levels (see fig. 12.3). This spreadsheet view is 3D View.

To toggle off 3D View, execute the same series of keystrokes you used to toggle on the view. Enable returns the screen to the two-dimensional view.

While the spreadsheet screen is in 3D View, press F6 to cycle the cell pointer among the three levels that are on-screen. For example, when levels A, B, and C display and the cell pointer is in level A, press F6 to move the pointer to the same cell address in level B. Press F6 again to move the pointer to level C, and again to move the pointer back to level A.

Press Ctrl-PgDn and Ctrl-PgUp to shift the 3D View down or up by one level. Ctrl-PgDn shifts the view down a level (A/B/C to B/C/D, respectively). Ctrl-PgUp moves to a higher level (A/B/C to AF/A/B, and AF/A/B to AE/AF/A, respectively).

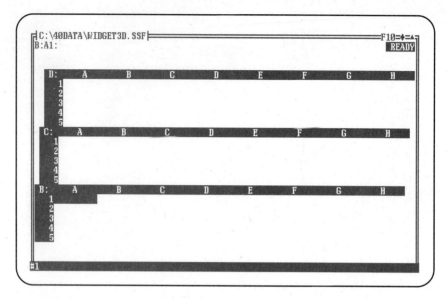

**Fig. 12.3.** *The 3D spreadsheet WIDGET3D.SSF in 3D View, showing levels B, C, and D.*

To move the pointer within a 3D spreadsheet, you can use the directional keys available in a 2D spreadsheet. Press Ctrl-Home to move the pointer to cell A1 in the top nonhidden level, which is A:A1 whenever level A is not hidden (refer to "Hiding Levels from View," further in this chapter, to learn about hidden and nonhidden levels). Ctrl-End moves the pointer to the last cell containing data in the lowest level that contains data.

You can move the pointer directly to a specific cell in the 3D spreadsheet. Press F2. Enable prompts you to

```
Enter address to go to:
```

Type the address of the target cell, including the level, and press Enter. Enable positions the pointer in the target cell. To move the pointer to cell R15 in level D, for example, press F2, type **d:r15**, and press Enter.

Although the pointer is never in more than one level at a time, all three levels always are synchronized. As you move the pointer to a column or row, the program scrolls all three levels to display the target cell address in all levels. For example, if you move the cell pointer in the WIDGET3D.SSF spreadsheet from cell A:A1 to A:Q1, Enable scrolls the screen so that it displays cell Q1 in all levels (see fig. 12.4).

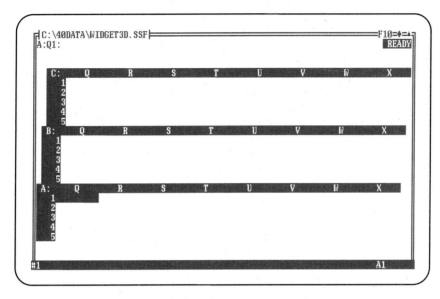

*Fig. 12.4. Synchronized scrolling of all levels.*

# Splitting the Screen

In addition to the two- and three-dimensional views, you can split a 3D spreadsheet screen vertically or horizontally, just as you split a standard 2D spreadsheet. After Enable splits the screen, you can press Ctrl-PgDn or Ctrl-PgUp to see a different level of the spreadsheet in each half of the screen. *Note:* To split a 3D spreadsheet while in 3D View, you must return to the standard two-dimensional view.

You can display level A of a 3D spreadsheet on the left half of the screen and level B on the right half of the screen. First, display level A in the standard two-dimensional view, with the pointer in cell A:A1. Move the cell pointer to the column where you want the split to occur, and press F10 Display Split **Vertical** or F9 Window **Vertical** to split the screen vertically. (To clear a split screen, press F10 Display Split Clear or F9 Window **X**.)

Enable positions the pointer in column D on the left half of the screen. Press F6 to jump the pointer to the right side of the screen. Press Ctrl-PgDn to display level B in the right half of the screen. Press Home to move the cursor to cell B:A1. Figure 12.5 shows the 3D spreadsheet WIDGET3D.SSF with level A on the left side of the screen and level B on the right side of the screen.

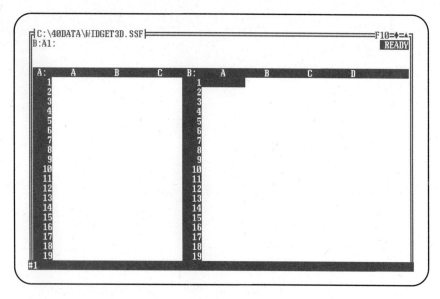

**Fig. 12.5.** *A vertically split screen displaying two levels.*

After you split the spreadsheet screen, press Ctrl-PgDn to display a lower level of the 3D spreadsheet in the half of the screen containing the pointer. Press Ctrl-PgUp to display a higher level of the spreadsheet in the half of the screen containing the pointer, such as from A to AF or AF to AE.

By vertically splitting the screen, you can display any two levels of the spreadsheet side by side in the same screen. By horizontally splitting the screen, you can display one level above another.

Compare a horizontally split screen to the 3D View. A horizontally split screen enables you to display any two levels, one above the other, without having to hide a level (see the following section, "Hiding Levels from View").

Vertical and horizontal scrolling is synchronized in 3D View, but only horizontal scrolling is synchronized when you use the horizontal split-screen method to display two levels of a 3D view (horizontal scrolling can be unsynchronized).

# Hiding Levels from View

Just as the program enables you to hide one or more spreadsheet columns from view (refer to "Using Range Commands" in Chapter 9), you also can hide one or more spreadsheet levels from view.

Position the pointer in the level you want to hide from view, and press

> F10 **Display Hide Level**

Enable removes from view the level containing the pointer.

For example, to hide level B in the spreadsheet WIDGET3D.SSF (again see fig. 12.3), press F6 until the pointer is in level B, and press

> F10 **Display Hide Level**

Enable removes level B from view, displaying only levels A, C, and D (see fig. 12.6).

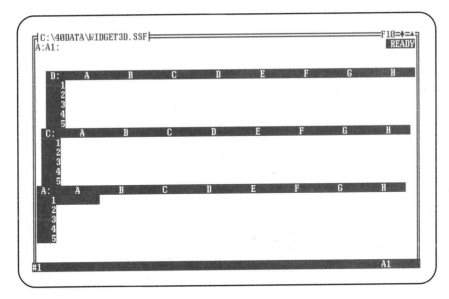

**Fig. 12.6.** *The spreadsheet WIDGET3D.SSF after hiding level B.*

You can use this method to hide up to 29 levels of a 3D spreadsheet. Enable does not print hidden levels.

TIP

To redisplay a hidden level, press

> F10 **Display Hide 2.**Levels

Enable then prompts you to enter the range of levels you want to reset (redisplay). The default answer is ALL. To redisplay all hidden levels, press Enter. To redisplay one or more contiguous hidden levels, type a range that includes the level or levels you want to redisplay (refer to the following section for instructions on specifying a range), and press Enter. Enable redisplays the specified levels.

# Using 3D Ranges

As explained in "Using Functions and Ranges in Formulas" in Chapter 9, a *range* in a 2D spreadsheet is any contiguous block of cells. When you use 3D spreadsheets, you can extend this concept one step further.

## Using Cubic Ranges

A range in a 3D spreadsheet can include cells in more than one level. A 3D range, or a *cubic range*, is a contiguous block of cells covering one or more contiguous levels. A cubic range creates a rectangular box. When using a range in a formula or in response to an Enable prompt, you identify the range by listing its diagonal coordinates, separated by two periods. The following examples all are valid cubic ranges:

> A:A3..C:A3
> C:C3..F:C5
> B:E3..C:G4
> D:I4..G:K4
> A:D8..A:D12

When Enable prompts you to enter a range, you can type the cubic range, listing its diagonal coordinates separated by two dots, or you can use the point method (see "Using the Copy Command" in Chapter 9). If you use the point method to specify a cubic range, press Ctrl-PgDn and Ctrl-PgUp to move between levels.

For example, you may want to copy the data from the cubic range C:C3..F:C5 to the cubic range G:A1..J:A3. Press

> F10 **Edit Copy**

Enable prompts you to enter the FROM range. You can type the range **C:C3..F:C5** and press Enter, or you can use the point method. To use the point method, move the cell pointer to the beginning cell, C:C3, and press the period key (.) to anchor the range. Press the down-arrow key twice to move the cell pointer to cell C:C5. Then press Ctrl-PgDn three times to move the cell pointer to the last cell in the range, F:C5. Press Enter.

Enable then prompts you to enter the TO range. Type **G:A1** or use the direction keys to move the pointer to cell G:A1. Press Enter. Enable copies the contents of the cells in the cubic range C:C3..F:C5 to a range of the same shape that begins at cell G:A1, which is the cubic range G:A1..J:A3.

# Using Named Ranges and Relative Level References

You can assign a name to a cubic range using the same procedure you use to assign a name to a 2D range. You then can use the range name in place of the cubic range in formulas and in response to Enable prompts.

One of the ways to use a range name is with the F2 key. When you quickly want to move the cell pointer to the first cell in a range, press F2 and type the range name as the target address. Press Enter. If the target address is a cubic range, Enable moves the cell pointer to the first cell in the first level of the specified range.

For example, you can assign the name JAN to the range A:D7..A:D11 in the spreadsheet WIDGET3D.SSF (see fig. 12.7). If you want to move the pointer to cell A:D7, press F2, type **JAN**, and press Enter. Even if the cell pointer is in another level of the spreadsheet when you execute the command, Enable moves the pointer to cell A:D7.

When you work in a 3D spreadsheet, you also can use a special *relative level reference* when you specify a range name. Suppose, for example, that the pointer is in level B (see fig. 12.8). Although you assigned the range JAN in level A, you want to move the pointer to the top of the column of numbers below the heading JAN in level B. Press F2, type **!JAN**, and press Enter. Enable moves the pointer to cell B:D7. Even though you assigned the range JAN in level A, the exclamation point that precedes the range name causes Enable to move the pointer to the beginning of the range D7..D11 (cell B:D7) in the level containing the pointer (level B).

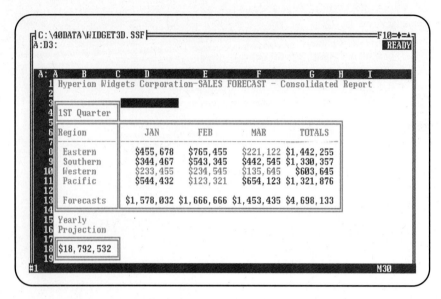

**Fig. 12.7.** *The spreadsheet WIDGET3D.SSF.*

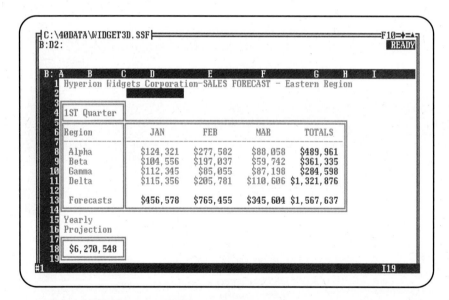

**Fig. 12.8.** *Level B of the spreadsheet WIDGET3D.SSF.*

The relative level reference feature is effective only when the named range includes cells from a single level. When the named range includes cells from multiple levels (a cubic range), pressing F2 moves the cell pointer to the first cell of the specified cubic range, whether or not you precede the range name with an exclamation point.

# Using Spreadsheet Commands in 3D Spreadsheets

Most Enable spreadsheet commands work in a 3D spreadsheet the same way they work in a 2D spreadsheet. A few commands, however, are available only in a 3D spreadsheet, and several commands operate on all levels at once. This section discusses how to use commands in a 3D spreadsheet.

## Using Insert and Delete Commands

In a 2D spreadsheet, the **Edit Insert** command enables you to add rows and columns to the spreadsheet (refer to "Using the Insert Command" in Chapter 9). You use the same command to insert columns and rows in a 3D spreadsheet. When you use this command in a 3D spreadsheet, however, Enable prompts you to specify whether you want to insert rows or columns in only the current level (the one containing the pointer) or in all levels.

Similarly, to delete a column or a row, press

F10 **Edit Delete**

and specify whether you want to delete a **R**ow or a **C**olumn. Enable prompts you to specify whether you want the deletion in only the current level or in all levels.

When you work in a 3D spreadsheet, you can insert a level. To insert a level, position the cell pointer in the level that you want to come *after* the new level, and press

F10 **Edit Insert Level**

Enable inserts a blank worksheet in front of the level containing the pointer and renames all worksheets at higher levels. If you want to insert a new level in between levels A and B, for example, position the pointer in level B and execute the **Edit Insert Level** command. The original level B becomes level C; level C becomes level D; and so on. The new level, a blank worksheet, becomes level B.

When you work in a 3D spreadsheet, you also can delete a level. Position the cursor in the level you want to delete and press

> F10 **Edit Delete Level Yes**

> When you delete a level, Enable also deletes all data in that level.

# Using Spreadsheet Commands

Several spreadsheet commands act upon all levels of your 3D spreadsheet (see Chapter 9 and Chapter 11 for a discussion of when and how to use Spreadsheet commands). The **Layout Range Width** command that enables you to adjust the width of individual spreadsheet columns affects the target column in all levels. A column in a 3D spreadsheet always is the same width in each level of the spreadsheet. For example, if you adjust column F in level C to a width of 15, Enable also adjusts column F to a width of 15 in levels A through level AF.

In addition to the **Layout Range Width** command, the commands **Display Titles**, **Audit**, and **Erase Spreadsheet** operate on all levels of the spreadsheet at once. The **Edit Copy** and **Edit Vcopy** commands operate on two-dimensional ranges and cubic ranges in the same manner. Using the **Edit Move** command, you can move a two-dimensional range of cells within a single level or from one level to another, but you cannot use the command to move a cubic range of cells.

The **Data Transpose** command enables you to transpose a row to a column or a column to a row (refer to "Using the Transpose Command" in Chapter 11). In a 3D spreadsheet, the Transpose command enables you also to move a column or row to another level of the spreadsheet when you transpose it from a column to a row or from a row to a column. You cannot transpose a cubic range.

# Using Layout Global Commands

The Layout Global commands—Format, Alignment, Width, Protection, and Unprotection—apply to all levels of a 3D spreadsheet (refer to "Using Global Commands" in Chapter 9 for more information on how to use these commands).

A 3D spreadsheet often contains a similar layout in each level. For example, level B in WIDGET3D.SSF displays the sales of Hyperion Widgets' Eastern region's four districts (again see fig. 12.8). Level A displays the Hyperion Widgets Corporation's first quarter sales projections for the four sales regions: Eastern, Southern, Western, and Pacific (again see fig. 12.7). For this reason, you can use the Layout Global commands to modify each level of your spreadsheet at once.

# Using Layout Range Commands

Most of the Layout Range commands (refer to "Using Range Commands" in Chapter 9) can operate on a cubic range. You can apply the Layout Range commands—Name, Format, Alignment, Width, Height, Protect, and Unprotect—to a two-dimensional cell range or to a cubic range.

For example, to erase the cubic range B:I1..GLK3, press

> F10 **Edit Erase Range**

Enable prompts you to Enter range to erase. Type the cubic range **B:I1..G:K3**, or use the point method to specify the range. Press Enter; Enable erases contents from all the cells in the cubic range.

The Tools Sort command can sort only values in a range of cells in the current level (refer to "Using the Sort Command" in Chapter 11).

# Printing 3D Spreadsheets

When you print a 3D spreadsheet, Enable treats each level as a separate spreadsheet. The program prints all of level A, then all of level B, and so on. Enable always starts a new level on a new page. To print the entire 3D spreadsheet, press Alt-F2 or

> F10 **File Print Print_Now**

Enable defines the default print range by the *highest cell used* in any level (refer to "Understanding the Spreadsheet Screen" in Chapter 9 for a discussion of the highest cell used). Enable indicates the highest cell used in each level by displaying its cell address at the right end of the status line. Enable prints the same range in every nonhidden level containing data. Unless every level is laid out in the same way, use two-dimensional print ranges to individually print each level of a 3D spreadsheet.

The status line in level B of WIDGET3D.SSF (again see fig. 12.8) indicates I19 as the highest cell used in level B. Assuming that no other level of WIDGET3D.SSF has a highest cell used that is higher than I19, the default print range for WIDGET.SSF is A1..I19. When you instruct Enable to print the entire spreadsheet, the program prints the range A:A1..A:I19, then prints the range B:A1..B:I19, and then prints the range C:A1..C:I19, and so on, until Enable prints all nonhidden levels containing data. Even if a level contains only a single entry in one cell, Enable prints the entire range A1..I19, which can result in the printing of numerous blank pages if some of the levels contain no entries.

To print a specific range, press

F10 File **Print Design_sheet**

At the prompt Print range, type the range (two-dimensional or cubic), and press End.

Press Alt-F2 or press

F10 File **Print Print_Now**

All other Print commands, including Header, Footer, List_Formulas, Row_Borders, and Column_Borders, operate in the same manner as they operate in a 2D spreadsheet (refer to "Using the Print Command" in Chapter 9).

# Saving 3D Spreadsheets

Enable provides three ways of saving a 3D spreadsheet. By default, the program saves all levels of a 3D spreadsheet to a single file. You also can save a portion of a 3D spreadsheet to a separate file, and you can save a level to a separate 2D spreadsheet file.

# Saving a 3D Spreadsheet to a Single File

Using the same procedure you use to save a 2D spreadsheet (see "Using the Save Command" in Chapter 9), you can save a 3D spreadsheet, including all of its levels, to one file. Press

F10 **File Save**

You also can use the quick command Alt-F10. By default, Enable saves the spreadsheet in 3D format. If you want to change the spreadsheet file name, you can specify a new file name from the Save As dialog box (see the following section).

# Saving a Range

To save a portion of your 3D spreadsheet, press

F10 **File Save_As**

Enable displays the Save As dialog box (see fig. 12.9).

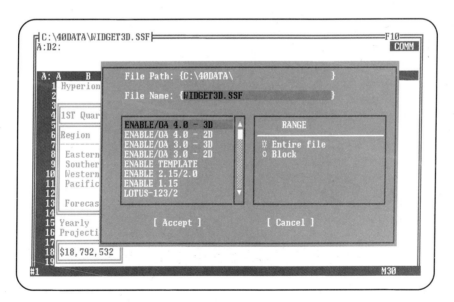

*Fig. 12.9. The Save As dialog box.*

Because you want to save only a portion of the 3D spreadsheet displayed on-screen, you should save the range to a different file name. Type an appropriate file name and press Enter. Enable uses the specified file name to save the range or cubic range to disk as a 3D spreadsheet.

Press Enter at the file name, choose `ENABLE/OA 4.0 - 3D`, and choose Block.

Enable then prompts you to enter the range you want to save. Type or point to the coordinates of the range or cubic range you want to save, and press Enter.

You also have the option to

    Relocate to Level A

Respond **Yes** if you want the range to begin in level A of the spreadsheet file saved to disk. Respond **No** to keep the range at its current level (higher levels are empty). Choose **Accept** to save the new spreadsheet.

## Saving a 3D Spreadsheet Level to a 2D Spreadsheet File

You may want to separate the levels of a 3D spreadsheet into one or more 2D spreadsheets. Enable provides the capability to save a portion or all of one level of a 3D spreadsheet to a 2D spreadsheet file. To save a 3D spreadsheet level to a 2D spreadsheet file, move the pointer to the level you want to save, and then press

    F10 **File Save_As**

Enable displays the Save As dialog box (again see fig. 12.9). This time, however, you choose `Enable/OA 4.0 - 2D` in the file format section.

Choose the range you want to save. Enable uses the specified file name to save the level or portion of a level to disk as a 2D spreadsheet.

# Using 3D Spreadsheet Functions

You can use any of Enable's spreadsheet functions in a 3D spreadsheet (refer to Chapter 10, "Using Spreadsheet Functions"). Enable provides several more functions specifically intended for use with 3D spreadsheets. The following paragraphs describe how to use these functions.

# @CURLEVEL

*Example:* @CURLEVEL

This function returns a value that corresponds to the current spreadsheet level. For example, when the pointer is in level A, the function @CURLEVEL returns the value 1; when the pointer is in level B, @CURLEVEL returns the value 2, and so on.

# @LEVELS

*Example:* @LEVELS(A:D7..E:F12)

The @LEVELS function returns the number of levels in a cubic range. In the example, the cubic range A:D7..E:F12 returns the value 5 because it includes five levels: A, B, C, D, and E.

# @LOOKUP3D

*Example:* @LOOKUP3D(A:I1,A:I2,A:A3..A:F6,1)

The spreadsheet function @LOOKUP3D combines the capabilities of the @VLOOKUP and @HLOOKUP functions by using three dimensions (refer to "@HLOOKUP and @VLOOKUP" in Chapter 10). Although the @VLOOKUP function uses a key column, and the @HLOOKUP function uses a key row, @LOOKUP3D uses a two-dimensional *key table* (also known as a *comparison range*), which you list as the third argument of the function. In the example, the key table is the range A:A3..A:F6.

The key table can consist of a two-dimensional range within one level or a cubic range that includes a portion of a single column in several levels. @VLOOKUP and @HLOOKUP use one *key value*, but @LOOKUP3D uses two key values—the first two arguments of the function. For @LOOKUP3D, @VLOOKUP, and @HLOOKUP, the last argument is the offset.

The method of operation of the function @LOOKUP3D depends on whether the key table is all in one level or covers multiple levels. The spreadsheet LOOKUP3D.SSF (see fig. 12.10) calculates personal income tax based on the Tax Rate Schedules X, Y, and Z. (Schedule X is filing status 1 and computes tax for single taxpayers. Schedule Y consists of two tables, one for filing status 2, married taxpayers filing a joint return; and one for filing status 3, married taxpayers filing separate returns. Schedule Z, filing status 4, is for individuals who qualify as heads of their households. A similar spreadsheet can be constructed from the tax rate schedules from any tax year.) The key table in this spreadsheet is contained entirely in level A, specifically A:A3..A:F6.

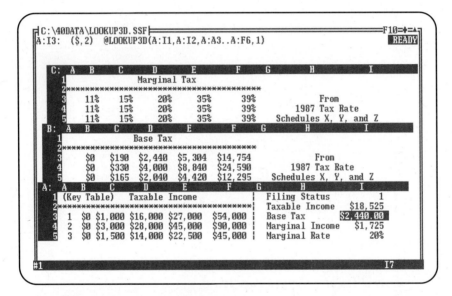

*Fig. 12.10. The spreadsheet LOOKUP3D.SSF.*

Suppose that a taxpayer qualifies for filing status 1 (single) and has taxable income of $18,525. Placing the filing status in cell A:I1 and the taxable income in cell A:I2, the following @LOOKUP3D formula in cell A:I3 calculates the base tax: @LOOKUP3D(A:I1,A:I2,A:A3..A:F6,1). The function @LOOKUP3D uses the first key value, the filing status, to search in the first column of the key table for the largest value not exceeding the key value. Because the first key value is 1, and the value in the first cell of the column is 1, the function stops at the first row of the key table (row 3 in level A).

Next, the function searches across this row, from left to right, for the largest value not exceeding the second key value-taxable income value of $18,525 found in cell A:I2. The function finds the proper tax bracket. Because the largest value in the first row of the key table that is less than $18,525 is $16,000, the function stops in the fourth column of the key table, cell A:D3. Finally, the function uses the offset value of 1 to move down one level to cell B:D3, and it retrieves the base tax amount $2,440 (again see fig. 12.10). In LOOKUP3D.SSF, the following formulas calculate marginal income, retrieve the marginal tax rate, and compute the income tax, respectively:

Cell A:I4:  +A:I2–@LOOKUP3D(A:I1,A:I2,A:A3..A:F6,0)

Cell A:I5:  @LOOKUP3D(A:I1,A:I2,A:A3..A:F6,2)

Cell A:I6:  +A:I3+A:I4*A:I5

The 3D spreadsheet LKUP3D2.SSF shown in figure 12.11 and figure 12.12 demonstrates an alternate way of using the @LOOKUP3D function.

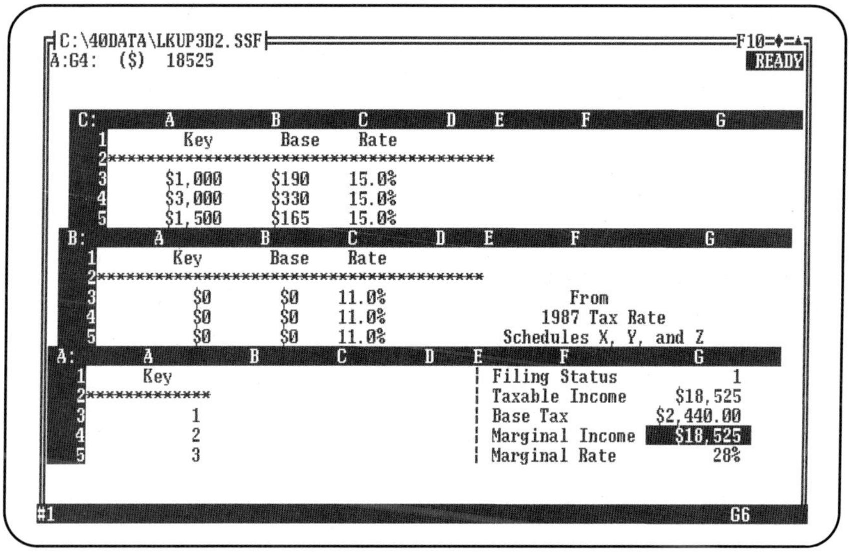

*Fig. 12.11. The first three levels of LKUP3D2.SSF.*

Again, the function @LOOKUP3D computes personal income tax. The key table is A:A3..F:A6 and extends over six levels, A through F. The following formula in cell A:G3 computes the base tax: @LOOKUP3D(A:G1, A:G2, A:A3..F:A6, 1). The function uses the first key value, the filing status 1, in cell A:G1 to search the first column. The function searches column A for the largest value not greater than the key value, 1. The function stops in the first row of the key table at cell A:A3 (again see fig. 12.11).

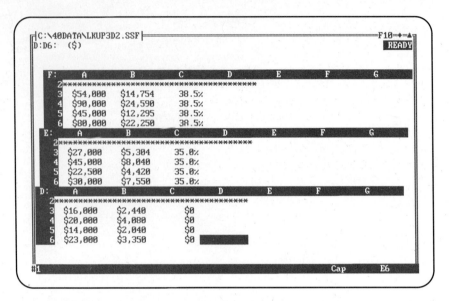

**Fig. 12.12.** *The last three levels of LKUP3D2.SSF.*

Next, the function uses the taxable income value in cell A:G2, $18,525, to search through the key table's levels, looking at cell A3 in each level. The function searches for the largest value not larger than $18,525 and stops searching in cell D:A3, which contains the value $16,000 (again see fig. 12.12). The function uses the offset value 1 to retrieve the base tax amount from cell D:B3, one column to the right of the key table. In LKUP3D2.SSF, the following formulas calculate marginal income, retrieve the marginal tax rate, and compute the income tax, respectively:

Cell A:G4: +A:G2−@LOOKUP3D(A:G1,A:G2,A:A3..F:A6,0)

Cell A:G5: @LOOKUP3D(A:G1,A:G2,A:A3..F:A6,2)

Cell A:G6: +A:G3+A:G4*A:G5

# Summary

This chapter explains how to use the features specific to Enable's 3D spreadsheets. You are now familiar with creating, changing the view of, and using ranges in a 3D spreadsheet. This chapter also explains how to use 3D spreadsheet commands, print and save a 3D spreadsheet, and use functions specifically designed for 3D spreadsheets. When you become comfortable with Enable's three-dimensional spreadsheets, you may wonder how you previously managed with only two-dimensional spreadsheets.

# Part V

# The Database Management Module

## Includes

**Quick Start V: Creating a Database**

**Understanding Database Management System Basics**

**Using Database Management System Power Features**

**Using Enable's Procedural Language**

# Quick Start V

# Creating a Database

---

This quick-start lesson gives a brief overview of Enable's Database Management System (DBMS) module. In this lesson, you define a simple database, use a built-in input form to enter data, display the data, and then print a report. The assumption in this lesson is that you properly have installed Enable/OA 4.0 and that your screen is at Enable's Main Menu. If not, refer to Appendix A and Quick Start I for information on getting started.

## Defining the Database

A *database* is an organized collection of information about a particular subject. Mailing lists, personnel files, telephone directories, and even Christmas card lists are databases. You probably are familiar with a "manual" system of keeping track of this information—paper files, manila folders, and so on. This section helps you understand Enable's way of keeping track of such information.

You are going to create a database to compile a list of your company's employees. Before you can enter information into the database, you must define the database, or create a "structure," to provide a blueprint of the data to be entered into the database and descriptive information about the data—its size, type, and so on. Your file will include name, address, telephone number, date hired, and salary for each employee.

1. From the Main Menu, press

   **Use_System Database Database**

   to create a new database definition file. Enable displays the DBMS Open File dialog box, which prompts you to give the database a file name. Because the database is an employee file, type **EMPLOYEE** as the file name, and press Enter.

2. Enable provides a space for entering an optional description of your database, which is strictly for your information and has no effect on the function of the database. Type **Quick Start Employee database** and press Enter. Press Enter two more times to bypass the following two questions. Enable displays a Field Definition screen (see fig. QSV.1).

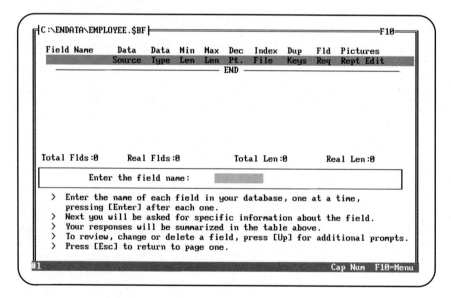

**Fig. QSV.1.** *The Field Definition Screen.*

The Field Definition screen prompts you to enter a field name. A *field* is the term used for each category of information contained in the database. Each field must be identified for later use. Just as you must assign file names, you must assign field names. Field names can be up to 10 characters in length. You start by defining the fields for an employee's first name, middle initial, and last name.

3. At the prompt `Enter the field name:`, type **FNAME** to assign a field name for the field for employees' first names and press Enter. Enable displays the initial Field Definition screen (see fig. QSV.2).

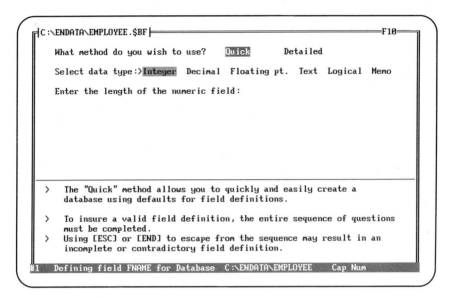

```
┌─C:\ENDATA\EMPLOYEE.$BF├──────────────────────────────────F10─┐
│                                                              │
│    What method do you wish to use?      Quick      Detailed  │
│                                                              │
│    Select data type:>Integer  Decimal  Floating pt.  Text  Logical  Memo │
│                                                              │
│    Enter the length of the numeric field:                    │
│                                                              │
│                                                              │
│                                                              │
│                                                              │
│    >  The "Quick" method allows you to quickly and easily create a │
│       database using defaults for field definitions.         │
│                                                              │
│    >  To insure a valid field definition, the entire sequence of questions │
│       must be completed.                                     │
│    >  Using [ESC] or [END] to escape from the sequence may result in an │
│       incomplete or contradictory field definition.         │
│                                                              │
│#1  Defining field FNAME for Database  C:\ENDATA\EMPLOYEE    Cap Num │
```

**Fig. QSV.2.** *The initial Field Definition screen.*

As you move through the ensuing Field Definition screens, Enable prompts you to provide information. Based on the choices you make at each prompt, Enable displays more prompts (for a detailed explanation of each prompt, refer to "Defining Fields" in Chapter 13).

To specify the definition method and the data type for the field for an employee's first name, press

**Quick Text**

Type **10** as the maximum length of the field and press Enter.

You successfully have defined the first field. Enable again prompts you to enter a field name (see fig. QSV.3). Notice that the program also displays the field FNAME you defined.

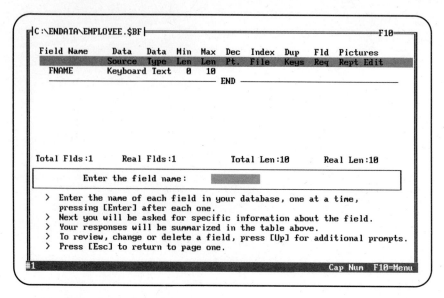

**Fig. QSV.3.** *The field FNAME defined.*

Use the procedures in Step 3 to define fields for employees' middle initials and last names. Name the middle-initial field MI, choose the Quick method, and define the field as Text with a maximum length of 2 characters. Name the last-name field LNAME, choose the Quick method, and define the field as Text with a maximum length of 15 characters. When you finish, your screen should look like the one in figure QSV.4.

You can split the address entry into several fields: street address, city, state, and zip code.

4. Use the Quick method to define the following fields:

| Field Name | Data Type | Length |
|------------|-----------|--------|
| ADDRESS    | Text      | 25     |
| CITY       | Text      | 20     |

You now are ready to define the state and zip code fields. Enable provides special options for choosing the data type of a state or zip code field, options that have several built-in advantages over the data type Text. When you use these special options, State-Code and Zip-Code, Enable automatically checks for a valid, two-letter state code, and it checks the zip code against the state code to make sure the zip code is valid for that state.

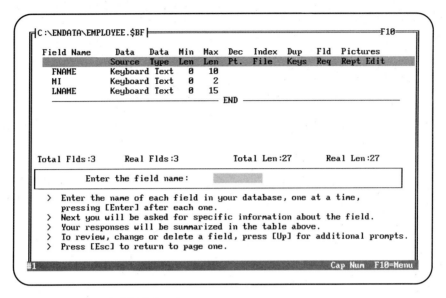

**Fig. QSV.4.** *Three fields defined.*

5. To define the state field, type **STATE** as the field name. This time, however, choose the **D**etailed method. Press Enter four times to bypass the next four options (see Chapter 13, "Understanding Database Management System Basics," for more information on these options) and to skip to the prompt Select the data type (see fig. QSV.5).

Press

   **O**ther **S**tate-Code

Press Enter twice to return to the initial Field Definition screen.

6. To define the zip code field, type **ZIP** as the field name and press Enter. Choose **D**etailed and press Enter four times. Press

   **O**ther **Z**ip-Code

and press **5** to indicate that you want exactly five numbers in each zip code, instead of a nine-digit zip code that uses the four-digit extension. Press Enter twice. Your screen should look like figure QSV.6. Notice that Enable displays the seven fields that you defined.

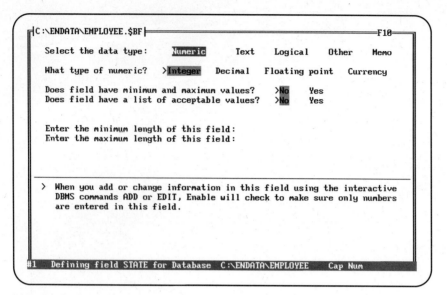

**Fig. QSV.5.** *The data type option.*

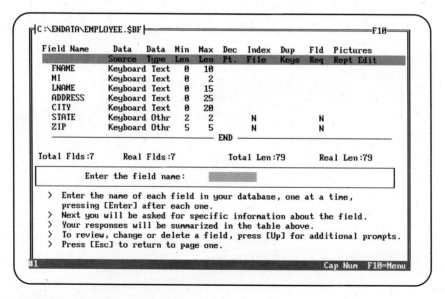

**Fig. QSV.6.** *The initial Field Definition screen, with seven fields defined.*

Next, you are going to define a field for an employee's hire date. Instead of choosing Text as the data type for a date field, you usually should choose Enable's special option **Date**.

7.  To define the date field, type **HIREDATE** as the field name and press Enter. As you did for the state and zip code fields, choose **Detailed** and press Enter four times. Next, press

    **Other Date**

8.  You need to specify the format you want to use later when you enter the employee hire dates. You must use the format YY/MM/DD if you want to sort employee names in the order of their hire date. At the prompt, type the *edit picture* **YY/MM/DD**, and press Enter five times to return to the initial Field Definition screen.

The next field to define is the salary field. Again, you use the Detailed method, but this time you choose the data type Numeric.

9.  First type **SALARY** as the field name and press Enter. Then choose **Detailed**, and press Enter four times to skip to the prompt Select Data type. To choose the data type, press

    **Numeric Currency**

    Type **0** as the number of decimal places, and press Enter three times. Indicate a minimum length of 0 and a maximum length of 8. Press Enter after each number, and then press Enter three more times to return to the initial Field Definition screen.

10. To define a field for the employee's telephone number, type **PHONE** as the field name and press Enter. Again choose the Detailed method and press Enter four times. Then choose

    **Other Phone-No.**

    At the prompt, type the following edit picture:

    **(AAA) NNN-NNNN**

    and press Enter five times to return to the initial Field Definition screen (see fig. QSV.7). Notice that although you have defined ten fields, Enable can display only eight fields at one time.

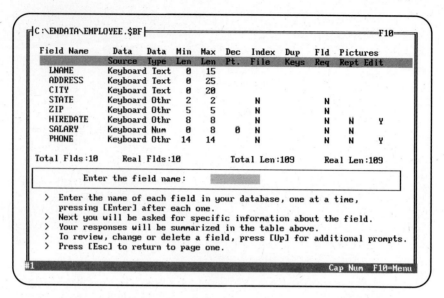

**Fig. QSV.7.** *The initial Field Definition screen, with all fields defined.*

11. To save the definition and return to the Main Menu, press

F10 **File Save**

and then press

F10 **File Exit Yes**

# Entering Data into the Database

After you create a database definition, you're ready to begin building, or adding information to, your database. To enter data, you must use an *input form*—the form Enable uses to prompt you for information, much like the forms you fill out to apply for a job or to participate in a survey. In this lesson, you use Enable's built-in standard input form to build your database.

1. To use the standard input form to add data to the EMPLOYEE database, press

Use_System **Database Interact**

Enable displays the DBMS Open File dialog box. Type the file name **EMPLOYEE** and press Enter. After Enable displays the DBMS Top Line menu, press

　**Modify Add**

Enable displays the DBMS Add screen (see fig. QSV.8). Enable does not know that EMPLOYEE is the database to which you want to add data, even though that file is the one you just opened; therefore, the program again prompts you for the database name. Press Enter to accept EMPLOYEE as the database name. The *pointer* (high-lighted bar indicating your position on-screen) jumps to the Using_form line. Read the message at the bottom half of the screen for more information, and then, without typing anything, press Enter. Enable displays the Standard Input Form (see fig. QSV.9) for the EMPLOYEE database.

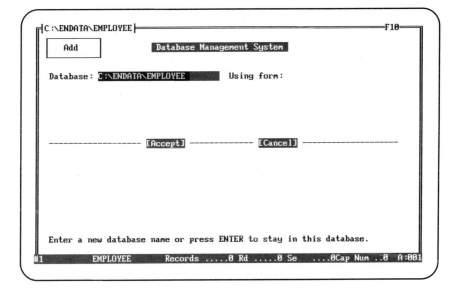

**Fig. QSV.8.** *The Add screen.*

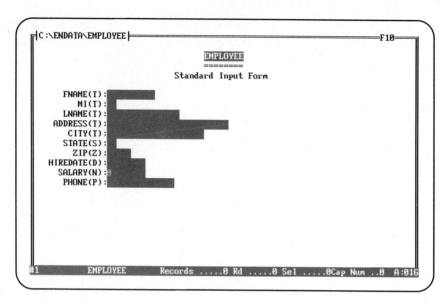

*Fig. QSV.9. The Standard Input Form.*

2. At the appropriate prompts, enter the following employee information in the input form. Do not type any symbols in numeric fields, such as diagonals (/) in the HIREDATE field or parentheses and hyphens in the PHONE field. Type only numbers. Press Enter to leave a field you do not fill completely.

| | |
|---|---|
| **Robert M. Harrison** | (FNAME, MI, and LNAME) |
| **213 Main Street** | (ADDRESS) |
| **Springfield VA 22151** | (CITY, STATE, and ZIP) |
| **87/03/08** | (HIREDATE) |
| **18000** | (SALARY) |
| **(703) 555-1234** | (PHONE) |

A *record* is a unit of data fields pertaining to a subject, in this case, the fields pertaining to an employee. Press F5 to save the first record and display a second, empty input form.

Do not press F5 when the input form is completely blank. If you press F5 from a blank input form, Enable saves a blank record.

3. Use the procedures from Step 2 to add the following records, pressing F5 after you complete each record:

> **William S. Allbright**
> **9321 Southside Blvd.**
> **Burke VA 22152**
> **86/09/21**
> **19500**
> **(703) 555-4422**

> **Allison V. Williams**
> **376 Fox Lane, Apt 16B**
> **Springfield VA 22150**
> **88/10/18**
> **17700**
> **(703) 555-7612**

> **Heather M. Millberg**
> **847 Raleigh Way**
> **Fairfax VA 22149**
> **88/07/05**
> **17700**
> **(703) 555-5437**

After you save the final record, press Alt-End from the blank input form to exit the DBMS module and return to the Main Menu.

# Displaying the Database

Now you learn how to display, or look at, the contents of your database.

1. To display the data you added to your database file EMPLOYEE, press

   **Use_System Database Interact**

   Enable displays the DBMS Open File dialog box. Type the file name **EMPLOYEE** and press Enter. Enable displays the DBMS Top Line menu, from which you press

   **Display Display**

   Enable displays the Display screen (see fig. QSV.10).

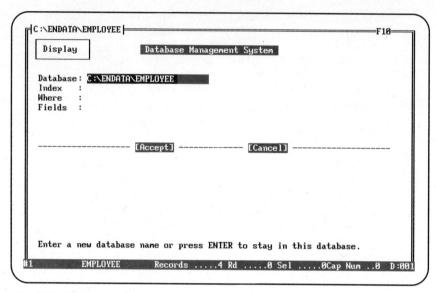

*Fig. QSV.10. The Display screen.*

2. From the Database line, press the End key to accept the file name EMPLOYEE and bypass the other three prompts. Enable displays the contents of your database file (see fig. QSV.11).

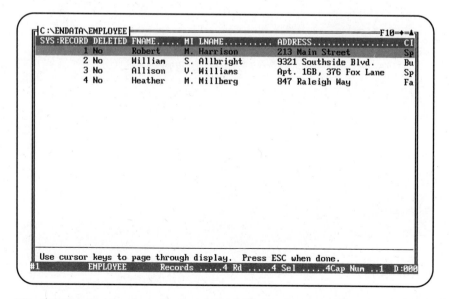

*Fig. QSV.11. The database displayed using the Display command.*

3. Use the arrow keys to move right, left, up, and down through the data.

   Notice that Enable adds dollar signs and commas to the figures in the SALARY field. The program also adds two additional fields, SYS:RECORD and DELETED. The SYS:RECORD field shows the *system record number*, assigned in the order in which you entered the data. You use the DELETED field if you decide to remove records from the database.

4. Press Alt-End to return to the Main Menu.

# Printing the Database

The ultimate goal of any DBMS project is to produce a printout from the information you entered into your database. This printout usually is called a *report*.

1. To print a report, press

   **Use_System Database**

   Enable displays the DBMS Open File dialog box. Type **EMPLOYEE** as the file name and press Enter. After Enable displays the DBMS Top Line menu, press **Display Report**. The program then displays the Report screen (see fig. QSV.12).

2. At the Database line, press Enter to accept EMPLOYEE as the database name. Read the message at the bottom half of the screen for more information. Press Enter twice to bypass the Using_form line and the Index line. Press **Printer** to send the report to the printer instead of the screen, and then press Enter to bypass the Where line.

3. In the Fields line, you specify which fields you want printed in the report. Type the following field names (be sure to include the commas):

   **FNAME,MI,LNAME,SALARY{s}**

   The {s} following the SALARY field name causes the report to total (sum) the salaries. Press Enter after typing the Fields line.

```
┌─┤C:\ENDATA\EMPLOYEE├──────────────────────────────────────────────F10─┐
│  ┌─────────┐                                                           │
│  │ Report  │         ┌─────────────────────────┐                      │
│  └─────────┘         │ Database Management System │                   │
│                      └─────────────────────────┘                      │
│  Database : ┌─────────────────────┐   Using form:                     │
│  Index    : │ C:\ENDATA\EMPLOYEE  │   To: ▓Screen▓  Disk  Printer  ASCII │
│             └─────────────────────┘                                   │
│  Where    :                                                           │
│  Fields   :                                                           │
│  Title    :                                                           │
│                                                                       │
│  ─────────────────── [Accept] ───────────── [Cancel] ──────────────── │
│                                                                       │
│                                                                       │
│                                                                       │
│                                                                       │
│                                                                       │
│   Enter a new database name or press ENTER to stay in this database.  │
│ #1       EMPLOYEE        Records .....4 Rd .....4 Se    ....4Cap Num ..1  9:001 │
└───────────────────────────────────────────────────────────────────────┘
```

***Fig. QSV.12.*** *The Report screen.*

4. At the Title line, type

   **Employee Salaries**

   Enable prints this title, or header, at the top of each page. Press
   Enter. Enable displays the Print form.

5. Verify that you have chosen your printer on the Print form, check to
   see that your printer is on-line, and then press Alt-F2 to print your
   report (refer to Chapter 5, "Understanding Word Processing
   Basics," for details on printing).

# 13

# Understanding Database Management System Basics

**E** nable's Database Management System (DBMS) provides all the tools needed to develop and maintain a collection of data. Unlike personal computer database programs that require you to become a programmer to create and supervise even a simple database, Enable's DBMS is fully menu-driven. With each step—from creating a database, through everyday maintenance and manipulation, to producing reports—Enable provides you with messages, prompts, and on-line help to guide you.

Enable's integrated nature enables you to share the data in your databases with other modules—word processing, spreadsheet, and graphics. You also can create a database with data from an existing spreadsheet, from a list of items in a word processing document, or from an external program or data file.

This chapter explains database basics and concepts—the generic characteristics of a database, and how to define, build, edit, and print your own Enable databases. The many commands used to manage and manipulate your data are discussed in the following chapter, "Using Database Management System Power Features."

467

# Understanding a Database

The term *database management system* is best broken into two parts: the *database* and the *management system*. The organization and storage of raw data is the database. The management system is the means by which you manipulate and control the raw data.

Using a database is not as foreign to your experience as you may think. Anytime you use index cards to collect information—card files, library card catalogs, recipe cards—you are using a database.

Just as with index cards, you can rearrange electronic database records in any order you want and as often as you want. You can separate your records into groups and sort, count, add to, and destroy them. If you run out of space for your index cards, you can throw out some cards or buy a bigger shoe box; if you run out of room for your database records, you can destroy some records or buy a bigger hard disk.

Every "electronic index card" in a database, called a *record*, has spaces available for data entries, called *fields*. You must predefine the size and type of data that can be entered into each field.

An important advantage of Enable is its capability to display, use, and change data in several databases at once. With an electronic database, you can perform the following six fundamental database management activities:

- Create a database and input form
- Enter data into records
- Manipulate the entered data
- Sort the records
- Select and manipulate subsets of records
- Generate database reports

# Designing the Database

Although the procedure may seem backward, your analysis of a potential database application should begin with the last of the fundamental database management activities. What do you want at the end of the process? If you don't have all the information you need at the beginning, you won't have it at the end either. The most critical decision, therefore, is deciding what data to collect in your database; this decision is based on what you want the final product to look like. The following two rules sum up your task:

1. Collect all the data you need.

2. Don't collect any data you don't need.

The assumption of this chapter and the following one is that you know which pieces of information you need and how they should be arranged on a final report. Your pieces of data are the database fields. All the fields relating to one person, place, thing, or event make up one record. All the records constitute the database.

## Defining a Database Definition

Before building your database, you must create a structure, or definition. To begin defining a database file from the Main Menu, press

Use_System **Database Database**

Enable displays the Open File dialog box (see fig. 13.1).

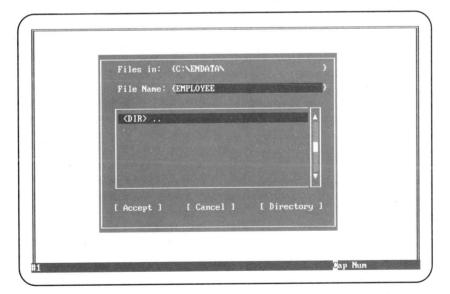

*Fig. 13.1.* The Open File dialog box.

To give the new database file a name, enter any valid file name beginning with a letter or a number, such as EMPLOYEE, and press Enter.

Enable creates two files for every database. The *definition file* is the file containing the definition, or database structure. Enable gives the definition file the extension *$BF*. When you enter records into the database, Enable creates a second file, the *database file*, with the same root file name, but with the extension *DBF*. For example, EMPLOYEE.$BF is the database definition, and EMPLOYEE.DBF is the database file, which contains the records.

After you enter a new database file name, Enable displays another screen (see fig 13.2). Responses to the questions on this screen are optional. On the first line you can type a short description of the database file you are creating.

The second line asks whether you intend to use a particular *input form* the majority of the time. When you initially define a database you probably do not yet have a name for your input form, so you can leave this line blank; Enable automatically creates a default input form, or *standard input form*, discussed in more detail later in this chapter.

The final line asks for the name of your *report form*. Leave this line blank until you create a report form. After you develop one, come back to this screen and enter the full name of the report file, including the file extension.

After you finish answering the questions, press Enter. Enable displays the Field Definition screen.

# Defining Fields

As you build your database definition, Enable displays in the Field Definition screen a summary of each field (see fig. 13.3). This screen can display as many as eight field definitions at once. Because you can define up to 254 fields for each database, many of the field definitions do not display every time you look at this screen. The word END marks the end of the field definitions. Press the up-arrow key to access the summary area, and then use the arrow keys to scroll through the list of fields.

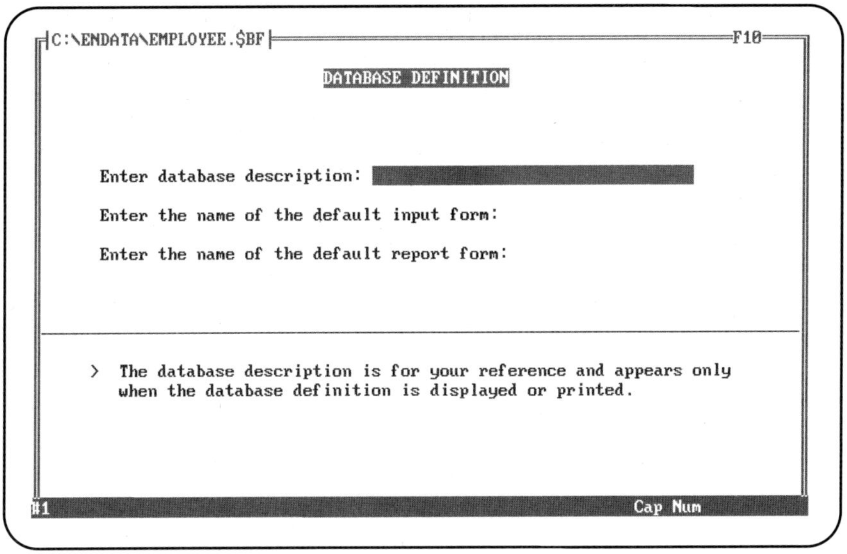

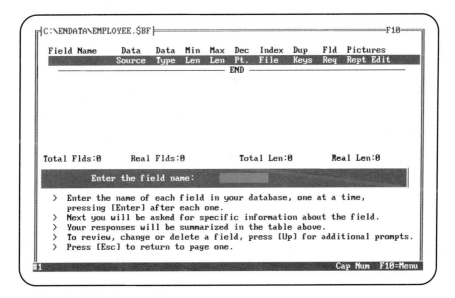

*Fig. 13.2. The first Database Definition screen.*

**Fig. 13.3.** *The Field Definition screen.*

For each field definition, you must provide the field name, the data type, and the maximum length of the field. To create a field definition, at the prompt

```
Enter the field name
```

type a field name of up to 10 characters, such as LASTNAME. The name can include letters, numbers, the underscore ( _ ), and the colon (:), but cannot begin with a number and cannot include spaces. Then press Enter.

Next, you choose either the Quick or the Detailed definition method.

## Using the Quick Definition Method

Use the Quick field definition method when you want to create a keyboard-entered integer, decimal, floating point, text, logical, or memo field without any other special features, such as validation criteria or editing criteria. When you use the Quick method, you have to specify only the type of data and the field length—the minimum information necessary to define a database field. For memo fields, you don't even have to specify the length because Enable automatically assigns a field length of 10. (You learn more about memo fields later.)

## Using the Detailed Definition Method

Choose the option Detailed when you need to create an *indexed*, *derived* (calculated), *external* (looked up from another database), or *system* (date, time) field, or if you want to set up editing or validation criteria.

- *Do you wish to copy an existing field definition?* Choose **Yes** if a field in another database has the same characteristics you want for the current field.

- *Is this an indexed field?* To answer this question, you first need a better idea of what an index does.

When you pick up a book to look for a particular topic, you usually turn to the index. A *database index file* is identical in concept to the index in the back of this book. When you tell Enable to maintain an index file for a particular field, it compiles a set of *pointers* to the data in that field and keeps the pointers in an index file in sorted order, just like the index of a book. Then, when you use this index file in a search, Enable does not have to begin its search with the first record; instead, it searches through the index, finds the pointer to the right record or group of records, and goes directly to the first one that matches.

If you want to create an index during the definition process, you can use the Detailed definition method and do the following:

1. Answer **Yes** in the third line on-screen to indicate that the field you are defining is indexed (see fig. 13.4). (If you do not index a field while defining it, you still can index it later by using the Index command on the DBMS command chart.)

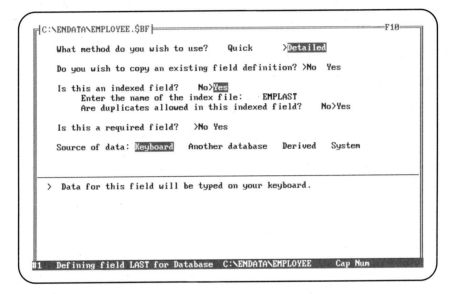

```
C:\ENDATA\EMPLOYEE.$BF                                        F10
       What method do you wish to use?    Quick      >Detailed

       Do you wish to copy an existing field definition? >No   Yes

       Is this an indexed field?    No>Yes
            Enter the name of the index file:    EMPLAST
            Are duplicates allowed in this indexed field?    No>Yes

       Is this a required field?   >No Yes

       Source of data: Keyboard   Another database   Derived   System


    >  Data for this field will be typed on your keyboard.



#1   Defining field LAST for Database   C:\ENDATA\EMPLOYEE      Cap Num
```

**Fig. 13.4.** *The index question.*

2. Enter the index file name. This name must be unique; you can use the name only once in a given data directory.

> When you create index file names, use a standard convention to help you avoid duplicates and remember which index files go with which database files. One such convention is to combine the first two letters of the database name with the first six letters of the field name, such as EMPLAST.

**TIP**

3. Decide whether duplicates should be allowed in the indexed field. If the field is a unique identifier, like a social security number, answer **No**. Enable prevents accidental reuse of the data in this field if you disallow duplicates. You allow duplicates, however, in fields

that are not unique. For example, you would answer **Yes** to the LASTNAME field because several records may have identical entries, such as Smith or Jones.

**TIP**

Fields you use as the link to provide external (looked-up) data to another database must be indexed and unique.

In addition to creating an index, you can use the Detailed definition method to provide several other special criteria that help in either the entry or display of data as follows:

- *Required field.* One of the questions on the screen shown in figure 13.4 asks you whether the field is required. Choose **Yes** if something always should be entered in this field in every record in the database. The minimum length of a required field is 1 character.

- *Source of data.* You enter most data used in a database from the Keyboard, but sometimes the data already exists in Another database, where you can look it up; sometimes new data can be calculated, or Derived, from already existing data in the same record; and sometimes the System can provide the desired data, such as the date and time of data entry or data edit. Use the Source of data line to choose any of these options.

- *Report picture.* Depending on the data type, Enable has various options for controlling the output of data to the screen and printer. For example, you can direct the output of a text field always to print in uppercase. You can define a date field so that it always prints in month-day-year format, even if the date entered is in a different format.

- *Columnar report heading.* In a Display command columnar listing, Enable's default heading is the name of the field, and in a standard columnar report, Enable prints the field name as the default column heading. Use this option (see fig. 13.5) to create a columnar report heading that is not the default, or field name, heading.

- *Error message.* Enable displays a default error message when an entry fails one of the edit or validation criteria. With this option, you can provide a customized error message.

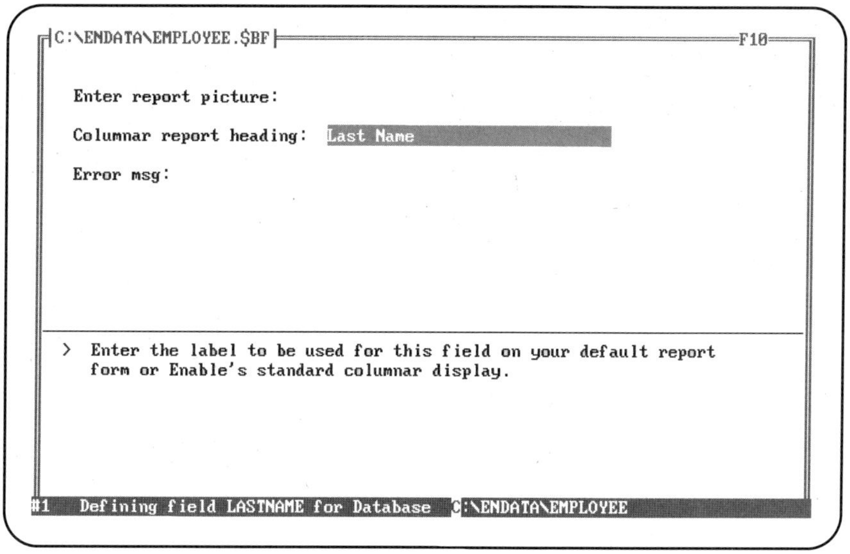

**Fig. 13.5.** *The columnar report heading option.*

## Selecting the Field Data Type

The most fundamental question you must answer about each field is its *data type*. The data type is the kind of data you plan on entering in a field. Enable handles four basic data types—text, numeric, logical, and memo—and five variations of the option "Other," resulting in nine distinct field data types available as follows:

- **Numeric.** You always define numeric fields as either integer (whole numbers with no decimals), decimal, or floating point. If you choose the Detailed definition method, you also can define the special numeric field type, currency, a quick way to define a special report format that includes a dollar sign and commas. *Note:* The default value of a numeric field is zero.

- **Text.** Standard text fields can contain any valid keyboard character. When using the Detailed definition method, you can limit valid characters in a particular field to only letters, only numbers and letters, or a specific edit picture. If you do not enter any text, Enable leaves the text field blank.

- **Logical.** You can use either the Quick or the Detailed definition method to create a logical field. Choose between true/false or yes/no. For example, you can choose yes/no for a U.S. citizenship field (then answer **Yes** if the person is a U.S. citizen and **No** if the person is not). The automatic field DELETED is a logical Y/N field. Logical fields have a default value of false (or no).

- **Other.** Use this option when you want to select one of the following data variations: Date, Time, State-Code, Zip-Code, or Phone-No. (See the next list for explanations of these variations.)

- **Memo.** This data type is not really a field at all, but associates an ASCII file of unlimited length with the database. This feature is equivalent to and fully compatible with dBASE III Plus memo fields.

If you select the Other option you can choose from the following data-type variations (see fig 13.6):

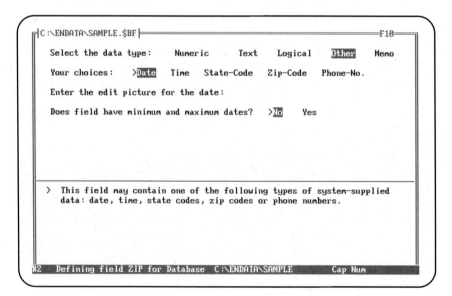

*Fig. 13.6. The Other data type options.*

- **Date.** A date field is a special field that acts like text on-screen but has features unique to entering a date. After you choose this option, you must enter an *edit picture*, which determines the format Enable uses when you enter data into the field. Based on this edit picture, Enable creates a template in the input form entry space, to enter the slashes (/) automatically. *Note:* You always should use the format YY/MM/DD in the date field edit picture so that Enable can sort the field or search on the field. (The format YYYY/MM/DD also is acceptable but requires more typing).

From the last field definition screen, you can specify a *report picture* that is different from the edit picture. For example, you can specify the report picture MONTH(MM) DD, YYYY. Then, even though you enter the date 89/02/03 to match the edit picture, Enable displays and prints it in the report picture format February 03, 1989.

- **Time.** The time field variation has requirements similar to the date field variation. Once again, you must enter an edit picture; in this case, you always should use either the military format (HM) or the standard format (HH:MM). If you want to differentiate between a.m. and p.m., precede the HH:MM with the symbol for a.m. (X) or p.m. (p). For example, X HH:MM.

- **State-Code.** Enable automatically checks data entered into the State-Code field against a built-in list of two-letter state codes recognized by the U.S. Postal Service. Enable also checks State-Code entries against Zip-Code and Phone-No. entries in the same record. If you enter a correct state code, such as PR for Puerto Rico, that is not in the system, you can override any resulting error message with the Tab key.

- **Zip-Code.** As with the State-Code field, Enable checks Zip-Code field data against the U.S. Postal Service list of approved ZIP codes. You can use either five- or nine-digit codes. Enable checks entries in this field against State-Code entries and the area code of Phone-No. entries in the same record. You can override any error message with the Tab key.

- **Phone-No.** You can design phone number fields to accept numbers up to 23 characters long, as well as the special characters normally used in phone numbers, such as ( ) - and /. Enable creates a template in the input form entry space based on the edit picture you created. Enable checks a phone number that includes an area code against State-Code and Zip-Code fields in the same record. The Tab key overrides validation errors.

## Specifying Field Lengths

In addition to specifying the data type, you must specify a length, or maximum number of characters, for each field (except memo fields, in which Enable automatically specifies 10 as the length, but has an unlimited actual length). The maximum length for each field type is shown in Table 13.1.

**Table 13.1**
**Enable DBMS Maximum Field Lengths**

| Data Type | Maximum Length |
|-----------|----------------|
| Integer | 16 |
| Decimal | 16 |
| Text | 254 |
| Logical | 1 |
| Date | 11 |
| Time | 16 |
| State-Code | 2 |
| Zip-Code | 10 |
| Phone-No. | 23 |

# Saving the Definition File

When you complete the steps for defining a database, to save the definition press

F10 **File Save**

To return to the Main Menu, press

F10 **File Exit Yes**

## Printing the Definition File

Keep a hard copy of the definition file so that if anything happens to the original, you do not have to re-create the file from memory. Before you can begin printing, you must copy the file DBMSDEF.$RF from the C:\EN400 directory (or the directory containing Enable's system files) into the directory containing your data.

To print the database definition, select

   Use_System **Database** Interact

Enable displays the Open File dialog box. Choose the database definition file you want to print and press Enter. From the DBMS Top Line menu, press

   **File** Print **Definition**

Press Enter to accept the database name specified in the Open File dialog box.

You also can print out the definition by pressing the following commands from the Database Definition screen. First, to access the Database Definition screen, select Use_System **Database** **Database**. In the Open File dialog box, specify the file name, then press

   F10 **File** **Print**

# Entering Data Using the Standard Input Form

Now that you have learned to create a database definition file—define the field names, field lengths, and field types—you're ready to begin building your database, a process known as *data entry*. Most likely, you enter your database information from your keyboard.

Enable offers two different formats for data entry. In the first method, Enable creates the input form for you. In the second method, you design your own data-entry screen, or *custom input form*. You learn more about the custom input form in Chapter 14, "Using Database Management System Power Features." This section shows you how to use the built-in standard input form.

Many organizations ask you to fill out a form that provides them with specific information, such as the card you fill out to subscribe to a magazine. Such organizations use the information from these forms to build their database. In the same way, Enable provides you with a form that you use to enter data into your database. Because you must have an input form to receive data, Enable creates a standard input form for you if you already do not have one. To display the Standard Input Form screen, start from Enable's Main Menu and press

> Use_System Database Interact

The Open File dialog box appears. At the File Name prompt, enter the name of the database file in which you want to enter data. You can either type in the file name or press the down-arrow key to highlight the file name from the displayed list. Press Enter to confirm your choice of the specified file. Enable displays the database Top Line menu. Press

> Modify Add

The program displays the Add screen (see fig. 13.7). When you build your database, you are adding records. Before you can start adding records, you must indicate the database to which you want to add records. Press Enter to accept the file name currently listed in the Database line, which you previously specified in the Open File dialog box. To use the standard input form, leave the Using_form line blank. Enable automatically creates and displays the Standard Input Form screen (see fig. 13.8).

To create the standard input form, Enable internally reads the definition of the database you want to build. Using the field name to prompt you and a one-character code to indicate the type of field, Enable lists the fields in the order in which you defined them, one below another (see fig. 13.8). For example, LNAME(T) is a text field, HIREDATE is a date field, and SALARY(N) is a numeric field. *Note:* Derived fields, external fields, and system fields do not appear on the Standard Input Form screen.

Now you can begin entering information, one field at a time. After you enter the information for the first field, press Tab or Enter to move to the next field. Repeat the process for all fields in the record.

When your data fills a field completely, Enable automatically moves the pointer to the following field without waiting for you to press Enter or Tab. If this occurs, and you press Enter or Tab anyway, the pointer skips a field, possibly resulting in incorrect data entry.

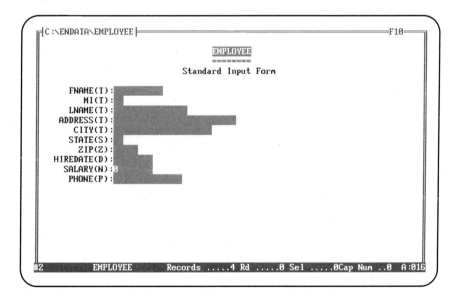

```
┌─C:\ENDATA\EMPLOYEE├══════════════════════════════════════════════════════F10═┐
│                                                                              │
│   ┌─────────┐                ┌─────────────────────────────┐                 │
│   │  Add    │                │ Database Management System   │                 │
│   └─────────┘                └─────────────────────────────┘                 │
│                                                                              │
│   Database: ┌─────────────────────────┐    Using form:                       │
│            │ C:\ENDATA\EMPLOYEE       │                                       │
│            └─────────────────────────┘                                       │
│                                                                              │
│                                                                              │
│                                                                              │
│   ──────────────────── [Accept] ──────────── [Cancel] ──────────────────     │
│                                                                              │
│                                                                              │
│                                                                              │
│                                                                              │
│   Enter a new database name or press ENTER to stay in this database.          │
│#2         EMPLOYEE        Records .....4 Rd .....0 Se    ...0Cap Num ..0 A:001│
└──────────────────────────────────────────────────────────────────────────────┘
```

**Fig. 13.7.** *The Add screen.*

```
┌─C:\ENDATA\EMPLOYEE├══════════════════════════════════════════════════════F10═┐
│                                                                              │
│                              ┌──────────┐                                     │
│                              │ EMPLOYEE │                                     │
│                              └──────────┘                                     │
│                               =========                                       │
│                           Standard Input Form                                 │
│                                                                              │
│            FNAME(T):                                                          │
│               MI(T):                                                          │
│            LNAME(T):                                                          │
│         ADDRESS(T):                                                           │
│            CITY(T):                                                           │
│           STATE(S):                                                           │
│             ZIP(Z):                                                           │
│        HIREDATE(D):                                                           │
│          SALARY(N):0                                                          │
│           PHONE(P):                                                           │
│                                                                              │
│#2         EMPLOYEE        Records .....4 Rd .....0 Sel ....0Cap Num ..0 A:016│
└──────────────────────────────────────────────────────────────────────────────┘
```

**Fig. 13.8.** *The Standard Input Form screen.*

After you finish entering data in a record, press F5 to save the record and advance to a new, blank input form. When you finish adding records, press F5 to save your final addition, and then press Alt-End to quit and return to the Main Menu. Enable assigns a *system record number* to each record you save. The first record number is 1, the tenth record number is 10, and so on.

# Displaying Data

To display the data you entered into a database, you first must open a database window. Then you can access the various DBMS command screens and use the Display command in the following two ways:

- Through the DBMS Top Line menu
- Through quick commands

After you get used to the DBMS Top Line menu, you find the expert and quick commands easier to use.

To use the Display command through the DBMS Top Line menu (see fig. 13.9), press

       **Use_System D**atabase **I**nteract

Choose the database file you want to display and press Enter.

To choose Display from the Top Line menu (see fig. 13.10), press

       **D**isplay **D**isplay

> To invoke any commands listed on the Top Line menu, press Esc to return to the menu, and then press the first letter of the command. If a command has a highlighted letter, press the indicated letter instead of the first letter.

To use quick commands to display database data, bypassing the menus, press

       **F9 Command D**isplay

Enable displays the Display screen (see fig. 13.10).

Press Enter to accept the database file currently shown in the Database line of the Display screen. If you want to display a different database file, press the question mark (?) on the first character of the current file name, and then press Enter. Enable displays a list of available database files.

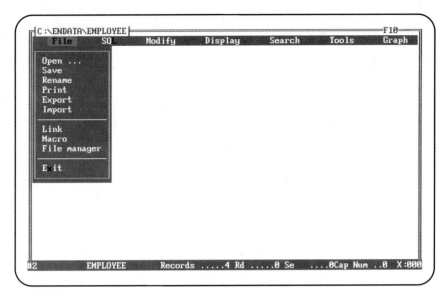

**Fig. 13.9.** *The DBMS Top Line menu.*

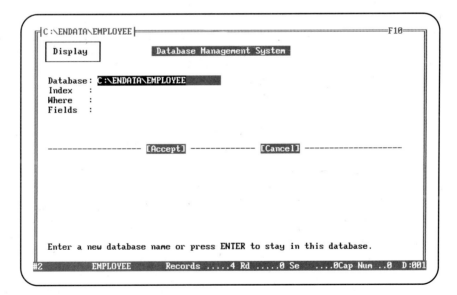

**Fig. 13.10.** *The Display screen.*

When Enable displays the directory showing the list of available DBMS files, you can choose either the definition file (extension $BF) or the database file (extension DBF).

When you use the Display command, Enable finds and displays records that match the search criteria you supply. Instead of displaying every record and field in the database, you can use the Index and Where lines of the Display screen to *select* specific records, and the Fields line to select specific fields.

## Using the Index Line to Select Records

You can use the Index line of the Display screen only if you have indexed one or more fields in the database you want to display. In a box on-screen, Enable displays a list of all indexed fields in the specified database file (see fig. 13.11). You can use the Index line to alphabetically or chronologically display the records or to quickly select records for display.

```
┌─┤C:\ENDATA\EMPLOYEE├──────────────────────────────────F10─┐
│                                                           │
│  ┌─────────┐         ┌───────────────────────────┐        │
│  │ Display │         │ Database Management System │        │
│  └─────────┘         └───────────────────────────┘        │
│                                                           │
│   Database: C:\ENDATA\EMPLOYEE                             │
│   Index   : ███████████████████████████████████████       │
│   Where   :                                               │
│   Fields  :                                               │
│                                                           │
│                                                           │
│   ────────────────── [Accept] ──────────── [Cancel] ───── │
│   Index choices for this database are:                    │
│  ┌──────────────────────────────────────────────────┐     │
│  │ SYS:RECORD   LNAME                                │     │
│  │                                                   │     │
│  └──────────────────────────────────────────────────┘     │
│   ▓Press PgDn to select from above▓            [PGDN]      │
│   Enter Index Name or Index Search Statement if desired.   │
│     Examples:                                             │
│       Index Name: LASTNAME                               │
│       Index Search Statement: LASTNAME = "Smith$"        │
│       Index Search Statement: ACCTNO = 123, 127, 130..139, 145 │
│ #2       EMPLOYEE      Records .....4 Rd .....0 Sel .....0Cap Num ..0  D:002 │
└───────────────────────────────────────────────────────────┘
```

*Fig. 13.11.* *The Index line of the Display screen.*

To display data arranged in order by field, type the name of the indexed field in the Index line. You also can press the PgDn key to move the pointer (cursor) to the box containing the indexed field names, use the arrow keys to choose the name you want, and press Enter. Enable displays the field definition information in the status line as you move the pointer from field to field.

The Index line provides the fastest possible search of the database. Type the name of the indexed field, followed by an equal sign and the search criteria. For example, if the LNAME field in the EMPLOYEE database is an indexed field, you can search for a particular employee whose last name is Allbright by typing the following index line search criteria:

**LNAME="Allbright"**

You must enclose text-field data in quotation marks; number field data does not require quotation marks. The Index search is case sensitive, which is why you need to be consistent with upper- and lowercase when you enter data into an indexed field.

# Using the Where Line to Select Records

At the Where line, you can specify the database records you want to display. To specify a condition, or selection criteria, you enter the field name and then the condition for selection of the records. The Where line is not case sensitive.

You use logical operators and either numeric values or text strings to define the conditions. Table 13.2 lists the operators and their meanings. In addition to logical operators, you also can use the following math operators (see "Using Operators in Formulas" in Chapter 9 for a discussion of Enable's math operators):

+ – * / ** ( )

**Table 13.2**
**DBMS Where-Line Logical Operators**

| Operator | Synonym | Meaning |
|----------|---------|---------|
| = | EQ | Equal to |
| > | GT | Greater than |
| >= | GE | Greater than or equal to |
| < | LT | Less than |
| <= | LE | Less than or equal to |
| <> | NE | Not equal to |
| & | | Concatenate (link two fields) |
| &– | | Concatenate, trim extra spaces |
| &+ | | Concatenate, one space between fields |

Multiple conditions can be tested by combining search expressions with the logical (Boolean) operators *NOT*, *AND*, and *OR*.

When you place the pointer on the Where line, Enable lists the names of all fields in a box near the bottom of the Display screen. Just above this box, Enable lists the available operators. You can enter the field names and search conditions in the Where line more simply by pressing the PgDn key, which drops the highlighted pointer into the field name list box. Use the arrow keys to move the pointer to the desired field name (note the field definition information in the status line), and then choose an operator by pressing its key. The pointer returns to the Where line, which displays the field name and the operator you selected. Complete the search condition and press Enter.

For example, to search a database for all records in which the field called FIRST contains the name Martha, and in which the field called LAST contains the name Bower, type the following clause in the Where line:

**FIRST="Martha" AND LAST="Bower"**

By default, the Where line is not case sensitive. If you want to search for an exact match, turn on case sensitivity, from the Top Line menu, by selecting

**Search Case_sensitive**

or by using the F9 command

F9 K E

Turn off case sensitivity by selecting **S**earch Case_**in**sensitive from the Top Line menu or by using the expert command F9 K D.

## Using the Fields Line to Select Fields

Instead of displaying all the fields, you can use the Fields line to display only certain fields in any order. When you place the pointer in the Fields line, Enable lists in the bottom half of the screen all fields available for display (see fig. 13.12). If you leave the Fields line blank, Enable displays the fields in the order in which you defined them. To display only those fields you want to view in the order you want to view them, enter each field name in the Fields line, in order, separating each with a comma.

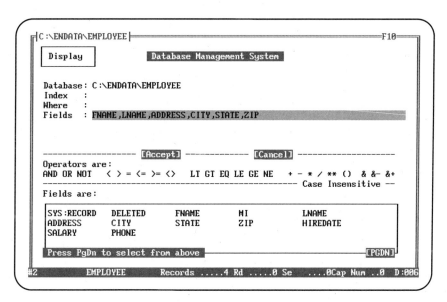

**Fig. 13.12.** *The Fields line in the Display screen.*

You can use the direction keys to enter field names in the Fields line. Press PgDn to move the pointer to the field name list box at the bottom of the screen; then use the arrow keys to highlight the field you want to display. Press a comma or one of the valid operators (see fig. 13.13). When you finish your list of fields, press Enter to confirm your choices and return the pointer to the Fields line. Press Enter to display the data.

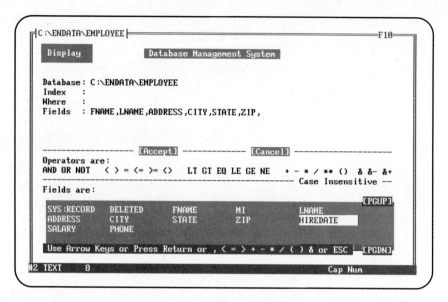

*Fig. 13.13. The Fields list box in the Display screen.*

After Enable displays the records you specify, you can use the up- and down-arrow keys to move from record to record. The right- and left-arrow keys move the screen horizontally, bringing additional fields into view, one at a time. The PgUp and PgDn keys move you up and down one screen—or 20 records—at a time. The Tab and Shift-Tab keys shift the fields horizontally one screen.

# Editing Data

Enable provides two methods of modifying data after you enter it into the database. The better method is to use the Edit command because Enable continues to do all normal-edit and validation-criteria checking, such as checking state and zip codes and phone numbers; however, you may find that editing data in the columnar Display screen is convenient.

## Using the Edit Screen to Modify Data

You access the Edit screen in much the same way as you access the Display screen—through menus or quick commands.

To access the Edit screen through the menus, from the Main Menu, select

Use_System **Database Interact**

Specify the name of the database file that you want to modify and press Enter. From the Top Line menu, choose

**Modify Edit**

To use the quick command, from any command screen in the DBMS window you can press

**F9 Command Edit**

> You also can modify records as you add them to the database. You already have learned that after you finish adding data to an input form, you press F5 to save the record and display a blank screen. If you want to modify the record that you just saved, press F6 from the blank screen. Enable returns you to the preceding record in the Edit screen so that you can make changes. To continue adding records, choose F10 **Record Add**.

**TIP**

In the Edit screen, if you do not see the name of the file you want to edit displayed in the Database line, type the name of the database file you want to edit and press Enter. To use the Standard Input Form screen for editing, press Enter at the Using_form line. Type a form name if you want to use a custom-designed form.

Like the Display screen, the Edit screen contains the lines Index and Where. Use these lines to select the record or records you want to edit. Enable displays the records in the input form you specified. You type, delete, and modify data the same way you initially entered the data.

To save the changes made to an edited record and go to the next record that meets your search criteria, press F5. When you finish editing and want to return to the Main Menu, press Alt-End.

## Using the Display Screen to Modify Data

When Enable displays the records you specify, if you notice that a particular field is incorrect or needs modification, you can edit in the Display screen. Use the left- and right-arrow keys to position against the left margin the field you want to modify. Use the up- and down-arrow keys to place the pointer on the incorrect record. When you press F4, Enable displays the current field value at the bottom of the screen. Edit the data, and then press Enter to save the change to the database.

> Enable does not check the edit and validation criteria when you edit in the Display screen. For example, while you are in the Display screen, if you change an entry in a State-Code field to an incorrect abbreviation, Enable does not catch the error.

# Using Enable's Query By Example

Enable's *Query By Example* (QBE) feature effectively combines the concepts of selecting data for display and for modification. You actually use the Edit screen and associated input form as a platform for retrieving data. Instead of using the Where or Index lines to select records, you use a blank input form

When you're in either the Add or the Edit screen and want to access the QBE feature, press

F10 **Search Query**

> If you want to access the QBE feature from the Add screen, make sure you save any data on-screen with F5 or F10 **R**ecord **S**ave. Otherwise, you lose the data in the current record.

Enable displays a blank Standard Input Form, used as the query form, that you use to build a Query By Example. By filling in the form, you can search for the specific records you want to edit or view. For example, to search the records for all employees who have the last name Williams, you type the value **Williams** in the LNAME field. You can fill in as many fields as necessary to create a search or *query example*.

After you fill in your query example, press F5. Pressing F5 creates a Where clause based on the fields and values you filled in on the query form. Because a Where clause is not case sensitive, you do not need to be careful about typing upper- or lowercase letters with this query method.

Enable searches the database, using the Where clause formulated from the query form. After Enable finds the records that meet the query example, it displays the first record of the matching group in the input form. If Enable does not find any records that match the search condition, you see the message No record found. Press Enter to display a new blank query form. You then can enter a new Query By Example.

If you want to change the current Index or Where clause without returning to the Edit Command screen, press F10 to display the DBMS Edit Top Line menu (see fig. 13.14). Then press **S**earch to choose QBE, display an Index line, or display a Where line.

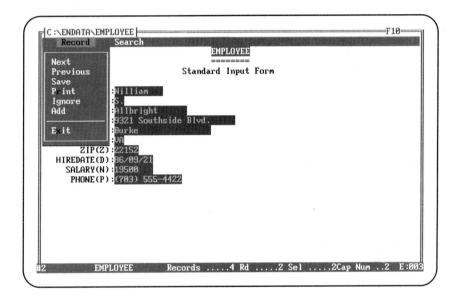

***Fig. 13.14.** The DBMS Edit Top Line menu.*

From the Top Line menu, press

Search Index

to display a blank Index line at the bottom of the screen. To invoke an Index search, enter an Index condition and press Enter. Enable displays any records, one at a time, that meet the Index condition. If Enable doesn't find any records that match the Index condition, it redisplays the Index line so that you can enter a new Index search condition. Press the Esc key to return to the current record.

You can select Where from the Search option of the Top Line menu to display a Where line at the bottom of the screen. If you previously issued a Query By Example, Enable displays the Where line already filled in, and you can modify the search pattern to suit your needs or press Alt-F3 to delete it. If you did not issue a Query By Example, enter a Where condition and press Enter. Enable displays any records, one at a time, that meet the Where condition. If Enable doesn't find any records that match the Where condition, it redisplays the Where line so that you can enter a new Where search condition. Press the Esc key to return to the current record.

# Printing a Report

The ultimate goal of any DBMS project is to produce some sort of output. Sometimes, just displaying information on-screen is sufficient. For example, with the Query By Example method, you can find and display data one record at a time. More often, however, you want to print some or all of your data in a particular format. This printout usually is called a *report*.

Enable's DBMS module can create reports in several ways. The easiest way is the standard columnar report. Enable arranges data from a database in columns, in a manner similar to the Display screen. Running page headers are a standard feature in columnar reports, and fairly sophisticated summary computations are available. Headers and summary computations are discussed in this section.

You also can create reports that are more customized—the "Put It Here!" report, mail merge report, and the procedural language report. You learn about these reports in Chapter 14, "Using Database Management System Power Features," and Chapter 15, "Using Enable's Procedural Language."

## Creating and Printing a Columnar Report

To create a report that displays your data in columns, from the Main Menu press

Use_System Database Perform_report

At the Open File dialog box, specify the name of the database file that you want to print; then press Enter.

Enable displays the Report screen (see fig. 13.15). Press Enter at the Database line to accept the current file name. Leave the Using_form line blank. You use this line to create a customized report form for either the "Put It Here!" report or a procedural language report. By default, Enable uses the standard columnar form when you leave the Using_form line blank.

┌─C:\ENDATA\EMPLOYEE┤════════════════════════════════════════════════════F10═

```
    Report                Database Management System

    Database: C:\ENDATA\EMPLOYEE        Using form:
    Index    :                          To: Screen  Disk   Printer   ASCII

    Where    :
    Fields   :
    Title    :

    ──────────────────── [Accept] ──────────── [Cancel] ────────────────────




    Enter a new database name or press ENTER to stay in this database.
#2          EMPLOYEE          Records .....4 Rd .....0 Sel .....0Cap Num ..0  9:001
```

**Fig. 13.15.** *The Report screen.*

After you press Enter to accept the default form, Enable moves the pointer to the Index line, which you can use to put records in order and select records for printing. Refer to the previous section "Using the Index Line to Select Records" in this chapter for a description of how to use the Index line.

The next prompt displays four choices:

    Screen   Disk   Printer   ASCII

- Choose **Screen** to send the report to the screen so that you can preview your report before you print it. Enable shows you 20 lines at a time; you can use the arrow keys to move to columns that aren't displayed in the 79-column screen. You can use PgDn or Enter to page through reports of more than 20 lines, but you cannot scroll back up through the report.

TIP

As good practice, always send your report to the screen at least once before printing so that you can proofread for changes you need to make before you print the report. You save a great deal of paper and time this way.

- Choose **Disk** to send the report to a word processing file on the disk instead of printing it. With this method, you can use the word processing features to spruce up the report. Enable prompts you for a file name and assigns the extension WPF.

- Choose **Printer** to send your report to the printer. After the report begins to print, you can press Ctrl-F2 to cancel printing.

TIP

Unless you have a severe shortage of disk space, don't choose the Print_Immediately report printing option in the system profile. Choose the Spool_Report option instead. This choice works nicely with the System_Print_Queue profile option to enable you to send a report to the printer and then forget about it.

- Choose ASCII, the last option on the To line, to create a word processing file in ASCII code rather than in Enable word processing format. Using this option to create an ASCII file is similar to using the Export command to create a fixed-field ASCII file (see the section "Using the Export Command" in Chapter 14 for more information).

After you choose an output device, Enable moves the pointer to the Where line, where you can specify records that you want processed in the report. After you press Enter, Enable moves the pointer to the Fields line, where you can select fields that you want shown in the report. Refer to the section "Displaying Data" in this chapter for a discussion of using the Where line and the Fields line to select records and fields.

The last line on the Report screen, the Title line, is a one-line header, exactly like a header in a word processing file. Any text you type in this line appears at the top of every page of the report. The automatic date feature (%DATE) and page-numbering feature (#) work in the Title line the same way they work in word processing. (See "Using Headers and Footers" in Chapter 7 for a discussion of these features.)

When you press Enter at the Title line, Enable generates your report. If the output device is the screen, Enable almost immediately displays the first 20 lines of the report; with the other devices, however, Enable first shows you the Hardware Setup screen. Make any necessary adjustments, and press Alt-F2. Enable then sends the report to the device you specify.

# Creating and Printing Summary Computations

Reports are more informative if they do more than just restate data. Summary computations such as totals, averages, maximums, and minimums are common, even in simple reports. Enable provides an easy method of generating computations in columnar reports.

To compute data in a numeric field, such as total salaries, include in braces ({ }) one or more of the computation codes listed in Table 13.3. This code must immediately follow the field name in the Fields line of the Report screen. When you use more than one code for the same field, separate them with commas, as shown in figure 13.16.

**Table 13.3**
**Enable DBMS Columnar Report Fields Line Computation Codes**

| Code | Meaning |
|------|---------|
| {a} | Average |
| {c} | Count |
| {h} | Highest (maximum) |
| {l} | Lowest (minimum) |
| {s} | Sum |
| {t} | Tally |

Enable also has a feature with which you can subtotal figures. Enable's subtotaling capability is discussed in "Creating Columnar Reports with Breaks and Subtotals" in the following chapter.

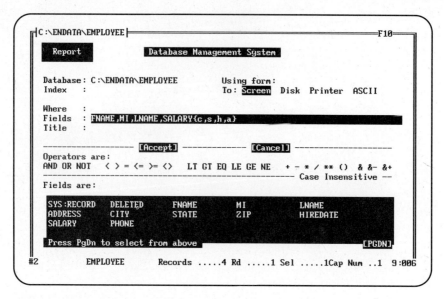

*Fig. 13.16. Computation codes in the Fields line.*

# Summary

In this chapter you learn how to create, add to, edit, and print a simple database using Enable's DBMS module. You can build and maintain a file of anything you formerly maintained on index cards. The following chapter, "Using Database Management System Power Features," provides a more in-depth discussion of the many DBMS commands that manipulate data and create new database files. Chapter 15 presents a brief discussion of Enable's procedural language for generating intricately customized reports.

# 14

# Using Database
# Management System
# Power Features

**D**atabase management as a concept is probably more difficult to understand than word processing or spreadsheets. After you have created, displayed, and printed a few simple files using the procedures presented in Chapter 13, "Understanding Database Management System Basics," you should be comfortable enough to move on to more powerful features and commands.

This chapter introduces you to the more advanced features of Enable's DBMS module. This chapter first describes how to change the definition of a database after you have begun to add data. This procedure always presents potential problems, whatever DBMS program you use.

A major function of a database management system is to manipulate the data in the database. This chapter discusses several of Enable's DBMS commands that give you great flexibility in selecting and rearranging records for further processing. The chapter also discusses methods of combining several database files, including how to use files from other Enable modules and from other database programs.

Just as important as how you use data is how you protect it. You already have seen how to enter data using the built-in Standard Input Form screen. Enable's custom-designed input form screens provide an amazing array of data entry enhancements that help prevent entry of invalid data and that insert data automatically. This chapter covers many of these *special processing options*. Enable's data archiving, backup, and removal commands also are covered here. The final portion of this chapter explains how to create output with your data: columnar reports with subtotals, word processing and spreadsheet files, and data formatted for use in other programs.

# Revising a Database Definition

After you have created a database, added records, and worked with your data for a while, you may need to revise the database definition. Perhaps you forgot to define a crucial field, or perhaps a field is not long enough for the data you need to store. You need to modify the database definition to accommodate these requirements.

The procedure for making such a change before you add data is identical to the procedure described in Chapter 13 for the initial definition. After you add records, however, Enable must reconcile the data of existing records with the new definition. Before taking the following steps, first copy your database and definition as they exist. Use the Copy command, the Backup command, or the File Manager screen to make a complete copy, and then continue.

The initial steps for changing the definition are the same as for creating a new database definition. From the Main Menu, press

   **Use_System Database Database**

At the Open File dialog box, specify the database file name, and press Enter.

The first screen should be familiar to you. It shows the optional database description and names of default input and report forms. Make any needed changes or additions to this screen, and advance to the next. The second screen displays two warnings you should not ignore. First, any existing input forms, including the Standard Input Form, also must be revised to conform with the new database definition. Second, if you change field type, length, number of decimal positions, or field order, you must reconcile the existing data and the new definition. After reading this screen, press Enter. Make any changes to the database description, default input, or report form prompts.

> When you use the Add or Edit command, Enable always asks whether the Standard Input form should be re-created. The following message appears in the dialog box in the middle of the screen:
>
> ```
> Form already exists.
> Use existing form or create new standard form?
> ```
>
> Simply press **Create** for Enable to rebuild the form. This rebuilding conforms the input form with the current database definition, whether or not the database definition changed since the form was created. Enable always gives this standard form the name of the current database; therefore, you should never use the database name as the name of a customized input form. Enable replaces the customized input form with the Standard Input form when you press **Create**.

When you get to the Field Definition screen, make your changes—increase or decrease the length of a field, add a new field, or delete an obsolete field. When you finish, save the new definition by pressing

F10 **File Save**

After Enable saves the new definition, you are ready to quit. Press

F10 **File Exit Yes**

Enable displays the following message in the dialog box (see fig 14.1):

```
Definition and database are NOT compatible.

Perform COPY command to make existing records compatible?
```

If you attempt to use a database whose DBF and $BF files do not match, Enable will give you a message similar to the one shown in figure 14.2.

Choosing **Yes** invokes the automatic data reconciliation process. Enable executes an internal macro for a few seconds and then displays the Copy Transfer Form screen (discussed in the section "Copying from a Word Processing Window").

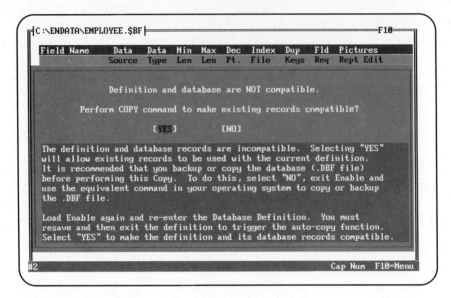

*Fig. 14.1. The screen used to conform existing data with a new database definition.*

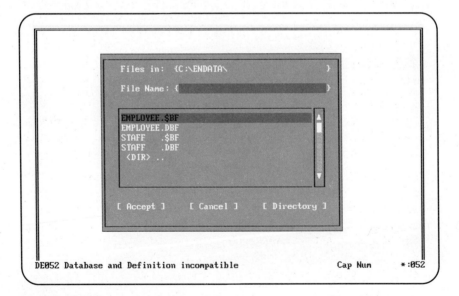

*Fig. 14.2. Message displayed when database and data are incompatible.*

Enable displays this screen here so that you can *initialize* any new field you may have created (that is, give every record the same value). To initialize a field, enter a value (or a text string within quotation marks) after the equal sign (=). *Note:* If you change a field name, be sure to enter the old name to the right of the equal sign or the data will be lost. When you are ready, press

> Shift-F9 Copy

to invoke the copy. When the copy is complete, Enable asks,

`Copy terminated...Do you wish to accept the new database?`

Choose **Yes**, because your new definition and your existing data files are fully compatible. Enable returns to the Main Menu (or to another open window). Remember to revise any input or report forms associated with the revised database to reflect the new field definitions. Delete (by pressing the space bar) the Shift-F9 fields for any "Put It Here!" input or report forms, and then enter the fields again.

# Manipulating Data

After you have built a database, you may want to rearrange it for printing or display, or you may want to work with only certain records. Chapter 13 describes how to use the Index line in DBMS command screens to put records in order and how to use both the Index line and the Where line to select records for processing. The following sections explain how to index an additional field so that you can use it in the Index line.

The following sections also discuss the methods of rearranging records and of selecting records for processing. The Find, Sort, Display, and Browse commands all are useful for selecting records for further processing. (Because Display is covered in Chapter 13, it is not covered here.)

All these commands provide a method of selecting records, but Sort and Find create a special type of file called a *select set*: a file made up only of the records that meet the criteria you specify in the Index and Where lines. Don't confuse this special file category with a full database; a select set is purely secondary to the database with which you are working and cannot stand on its own. Any changes you make to a select set, however, Enable automatically makes to the original database.

When Enable creates a select set, the program uses the current database name and adds a file name extension SS (for select set). For example, if you sort your EMPLOYEE database, you have both an EMPLOYEE.DBF file (the complete database) and an EMPLOYEE.SS file (the sorted select set). The SS file is not a separate database but merely a file with pointers to the selected records (in their sorted order). Keep in mind that any changes to this subset affect the selected records in the DBF file.

Enable keeps only one SS file for any database. Whenever you create a new select set of records, Enable creates a new SS file to reflect the new sort or find operation, writing over any earlier SS file on your disk. This process gives you the opportunity to sort a 5,000-record database on Friday afternoon, and then wait until Monday morning to manipulate the sorted database by typing **?.SS** to any DBMS command database prompt, to display a list of all available SS files on your disk.

The following sections give more detailed information about the commands that select subsets of information. You can choose each command option discussed in this chapter from the database Top Line menu or through the equivalent F9 command. Notice that if you create a select set using one of these commands and then issue a second command, you still are working with the select set created by the preceding command. Also notice that you can choose any of the options listed in this chapter from the Command Chart menu.

# Using the Index Command

As with all DBMS commands, you can access the Index command through the DBMS Top Line menu. Access the DBMS module from the Main Menu by pressing

Use_System **Database Interact**

Choose a database and press Enter.

From the Top Line menu press

**Tools Create_index**

If you already are in a DBMS window, you can use the F9 command

**F9 Command Index**

Press Enter to accept the database name and then enter a field name on the line provided (see fig. 14.3). At the Index File Name prompt, enter a unique file name. Finally, indicate whether to allow duplicates; choose No if this field always will have a unique value in each record. (Refer to Chapter 13 for a discussion of when and why you should index a field.)

You also use the Index command to reindex a field that already has been indexed. You may have to reindex a field if Enable ever gives you an error message that an index file is incompatible or corrupt.

```
┌─C:\ENDATA\EMPLOYEE├─────────────────────────────────────────F10─┐
│  ┌─────────┐        ┌───────────────────────────────┐          │
│  │  Index  │        │  Database Management System    │          │
│  └─────────┘        └───────────────────────────────┘          │
│                                                                 │
│   Database: C:\ENDATA\EMPLOYEE                                   │
│                                                                 │
│   Fieldname:  SALARY            Index File Name:  EMPSALRY       │
│                                                                 │
│   Allow Duplicates?        ▒Yes▒     No                          │
│                                                                 │
│   ─────────────────── [Accept] ──────────── [Cancel] ─────────  │
│                                                                 │
│                                                                 │
│                                                                 │
│                                                                 │
│                                                                 │
│                                                                 │
│   Duplicates are allowed in the field.                          │
│#2        EMPLOYEE        Records .....4 Rd .....0 Sel .....0Cap  ..0  I:008│
└─────────────────────────────────────────────────────────────────┘
```

**Fig. 14.3.** *An Index command screen.*

A corrupt index file often results in failed queries when you use the indexed field to search for data. Suspect a corrupt index if Enable returns the message No Record Found after searching for data you know exists in the database.

**TIP**

# Using the Find Command

To choose the Find command, from the DBMS Top Line menu, press

> **Search Find**

or use the expert command

> **F9 Command Find**

Enable displays the Find screen, shown in figure 14.4.

The Find command creates a select set. This command does not display any data; use Display or Report for that purpose. Notice that after you execute Find, Enable adds the file extension SS to the name on the Database line. You can execute the command again, but this time any new criteria applies to the first select set, thus creating a subset of the original subset.

Use Find to narrow your search in this step-by-step fashion so that you need not enter lengthy compound search statements in the Where line.

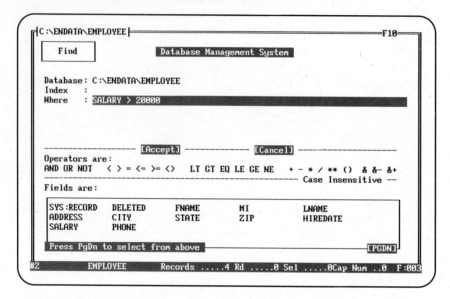

*Fig. 14.4. The Find screen.*

# Using the Sort Command

To display the Sort command screen, use the DBMS Top Line menu and choose

    **Tools Sort**

or use the expert command

    **F9 Command Sort**

Enable displays the Sort screen (see fig. 14.5).

You can use the Sort command to arrange database records alphabetically or numerically, in ascending or descending order. In the lines provided, type field names followed by a comma and then an A or D for ascending or descending order (ascending is the default). Enable executes the sort as soon as you press Enter at a blank Field line. You can sort on up to ten fields at once.

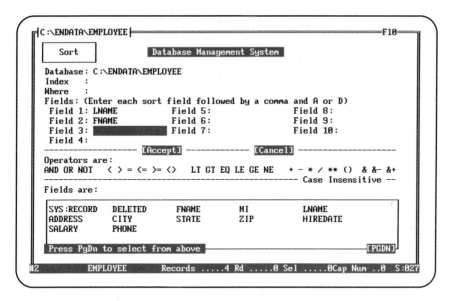

**Fig. 14.5.** *The Sort screen.*

After Enable completes the sort routine, the program creates a select set. You can have only one select set at a time per database. Use the Index and Where lines to select specific records you want included in the sort. Sort is used most often to put data in the proper order for use in a report.

# Using the Browse Command

To display the Browse command screen, use the DBMS Top Line menu and choose

> **Search Browse_index**

or use the expert command

> **F9 Command Browse**

Enable displays the Browse screen, shown in figure 14.6. You must make an entry in the Index line, but the Where line is optional.

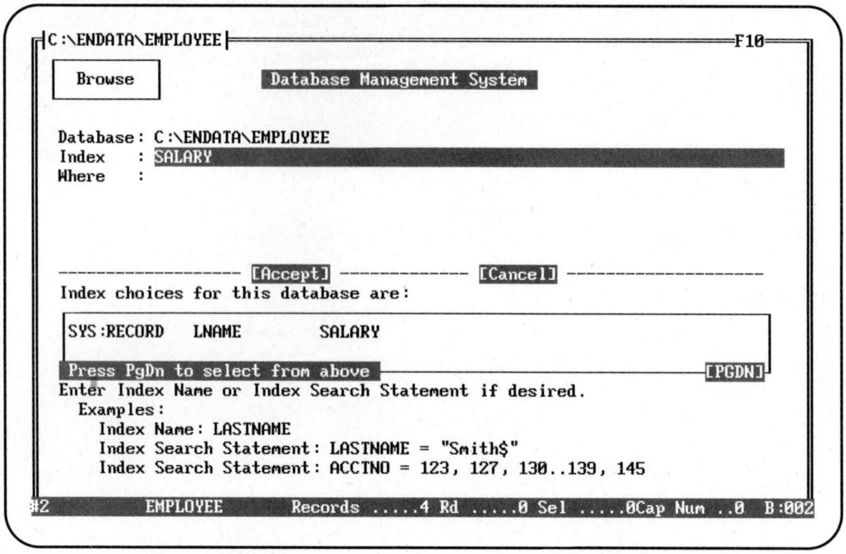

```
┌─┤C:\ENDATA\EMPLOYEE├══════════════════════════════════════F10═┐
│ ┌──────────┐                                                  │
│ │ Browse   │        ╔══════════════════════════════════╗     │
│ └──────────┘        ║ Database Management System        ║     │
│                     ╚══════════════════════════════════╝     │
│                                                               │
│    Database: C:\ENDATA\EMPLOYEE                                │
│    Index   : SALARY                                           │
│    Where   :                                                  │
│                                                               │
│                                                               │
│                                                               │
│    ─────────────────── [Accept] ───────────── [Cancel] ─────────│
│    Index choices for this database are:                       │
│   ┌───────────────────────────────────────────────────────┐  │
│   │ SYS:RECORD    LNAME          SALARY                     │  │
│   │                                                         │  │
│   ├─ Press PgDn to select from above ──────────────[PGDN]──┘  │
│    Enter Index Name or Index Search Statement if desired.     │
│      Examples:                                                │
│        Index Name: LASTNAME                                   │
│        Index Search Statement: LASTNAME = "Smith$"            │
│        Index Search Statement: ACCTNO = 123, 127, 130..139, 145│
│                                                               │
│ #2       EMPLOYEE       Records .....4 Rd .....0 Sel .....0Cap Num ..0  B:002│
└───────────────────────────────────────────────────────────────┘
```

*Fig. 14.6. The Browse screen.*

The Browse command displays only one indexed field at a time. Next to the field column, Browse displays a Count column that indicates the number of matches of a particular value for the indexed field (see fig. 14.7).

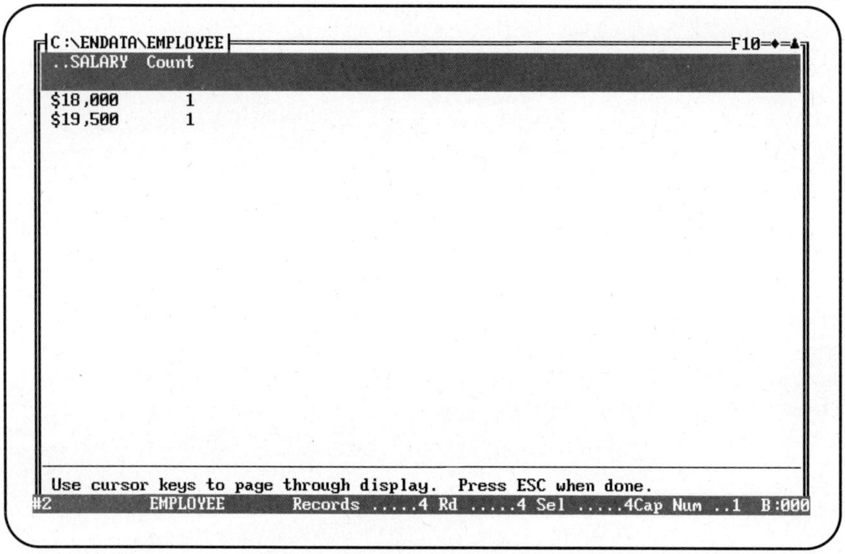

```
┌─┤C:\ENDATA\EMPLOYEE├══════════════════════════════════F10═◆═▲─┐
│  ..SALARY   Count                                             │
│                                                               │
│  $18,000       1                                              │
│  $19,500       1                                              │
│                                                               │
│                                                               │
│                                                               │
│                                                               │
│                                                               │
│                                                               │
│                                                               │
│                                                               │
│                                                               │
│                                                               │
│                                                               │
│                                                               │
│   Use cursor keys to page through display.  Press ESC when done.│
│ #2       EMPLOYEE       Records .....4 Rd .....4 Sel .....4Cap Num ..1  B:000│
└───────────────────────────────────────────────────────────────┘
```

*Fig. 14.7. A display generated by the Browse command.*

As in the Display screen, you can mark records in the display generated by the Browse command. You can mark all records that have a certain index value by moving the cursor to that value and pressing Alt-M. To mark a group of index values, position the cursor on the first entry, press F7, move to the last entry, and press F7 again. Records marked in Browse remain marked in Display and can be used in a report.

Enable treats marked records much like a select set; however, after you complete the current DBMS session by closing the window (choose **File Exit** from the Top Line menu), Enable unmarks the marked records and you must mark them again during the next session. In addition, if you use either the Index line or the Where line in any DBMS command screen, Enable automatically cancels the current marking.

# Modifying Data

In Chapter 13, "Understanding Database Management System Basics," you examine the Edit command that provides the most direct way to modify data. Using the Edit command, you can make changes to any keyboard field, in any database record—but always one record at a time. Two other commands, Replace and Update, provide ways to change many records in one step.

## Using the Replace Command

To display the Replace command screen (see fig. 14.8), use the DBMS Top Line menu and select choose

> **M**odify **R**eplace

or use the expert command

> F9 **C**ommand **R**eplace

This command is similar to a search and replace operation in word processing. You can replace every entry in a particular field with a new value, or use the Index line and Where line to choose particular records. Always enter the name of only one field in the Field line, and enter a value in the With line. Text data must be enclosed in quotations. You can use operators to create a derived (calculated) value for replacement. In the example shown in figure 14.8, the salary for all employees increases by 10%; the original value in the SALARY field is multiplied by 1.10, and the new value replaces the original value.

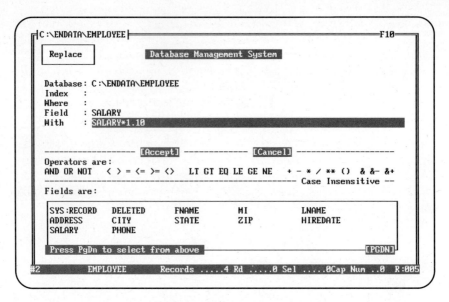

**Fig. 14.8.** *The Replace command screen.*

**TIP**

Because Replace does not preview the records to be affected and gives you no way to undo any modifications, a good practice is to use **D**isplay to select the records to be modified before you execute **R**eplace. Create the search criteria in the Index line or Where line, and display the target field and records to be modified. When the proper records are selected, return to the Replace screen. The correct Index and Where lines are carried over, and you can continue with confidence.

# Using the Update Command

To display the Update command screen, use the DBMS Top Line menu to choose

> **M**odify **U**pdate

or use the expert command

> F9 **C**ommand **U**pdate

A fairly common practice is to create copies of database files to be used and perhaps modified on more than one machine at a time. This practice quickly results in multiple versions of the database. The Update command is one tool you can use to consolidate these several files back into one master file without manually reentering the changes. You also can use Update to "post" multiple transactions to a master database, in much the same way that a bank "posts" the transactions of the day to individual accounts.

This command works properly only if you can identify a unique indexed field in the *master* (original) file that can be used to link the *transaction* (altered) file. In the example shown in figure 14.9, a field called *NAME* has been indexed with no duplicates allowed. The data for this new field is derived using the formula

FNAME&+MI&+LNAME

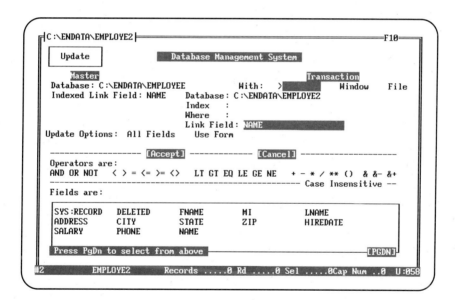

*Fig. 14.9. An Update command screen.*

The definitions for EMPLOYEE and EMPLOYE2 are identical (except that each has its own index files). The original records in EMPLOYE2 were copies of records in EMPLOYEE; you make changes and add new records to the original records in EMPLOYE2. Now you must add these additions and modifications to the master database, EMPLOYEE.

To use Update, enter the master database name, the master link field, the transaction database, and the transaction link field. You can use the Index line and Where line to select specific records or groups of records to update; these lines are optional. You also can use data from a word processing window, spreadsheet file (Enable or Lotus), or ASCII file as the transaction file. Refer to the section "Using the Copy Command" in this chapter for more information on using one of these other sources as a database.

Finally, you must indicate whether you want Enable to update all fields or only selected fields. To update all fields, choose the All_Fields option. Updating all fields in the example shown in figure 14.9 causes any modified data in any EMPLOYE2 field to replace the original data in the corresponding record in EMPLOYEE (where the NAME field in both databases match). Enable adds New records that don't yet exist in EMPLOYEE (that is, where NAME does not exist) to the end of the master database.

To update only certain fields, choose Use_Form to display the Using_form line. The first time you use this command for a particular database, just press Enter to leave this line blank. Enable displays a screen similar to figure 14.10, called an Update Transfer Form screen.

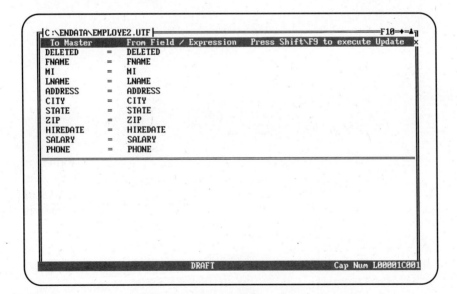

*Fig. 14.10. An Update Transfer Form screen.*

If you want Enable to ignore any field or fields, do one of the following:

1. Type a semicolon (;) at the start of the line with the field that should not be updated. If you change your mind, you can include the field simply by deleting the semicolon.

2. Use the word processing command Alt-F3 to delete a line.

The Update Transfer Form screen also serves two other purposes. Use it to match field names when the transaction file field names do not match the master file field names. You also can use any valid database operators to manipulate data values on this screen.

To save the form for future use, press

>F9 **S**ave **N**ew_name

Change the current file name to something unique and press Enter. Be sure to include the file name extension UTF (for update transfer form). The next time you use the Update command to perform this same task, enter this file name in the Using form line.

To complete the Update process, press

>Shift-F9 **U**pdate

Enable displays a message in the status line telling you the number of updates the program has applied to the master database. Return to the Main Menu by pressing Alt-End.

# Combining Database Files

Eventually you may have to move data from one database to another or from a word processing or spreadsheet file to a database. You may have downloaded the data from another type of computer into generic ASCII format. This section discusses how to use the Copy and Export commands to move this data to and from Enable, and how to use the Merge command to create a new database from two related database files.

**TIP**

You need not convert database files created with dBASE II, dBASE III, or CONDOR3 before you use them with Enable/OA. Enable keeps the existing format of a database from one of these programs, but uses the data as if the database had been created with Enable.

You also can export data to one of these programs. You can use the Database creation format of the database profile options to instruct Enable to format DBF files to be compatible with either dBASE II or dBASE III (see Appendix B for a discussion of profile options). The better choice is dBASE III format unless you routinely work with dBASE II. To export data to CONDOR3, create the database definition in CONDOR3 and then use Enable's Copy command to copy data from an Enable database to the CONDOR3 database definition.

Enable can read but not modify files created with PC-File III.

## Using the Copy Command

To display the Copy command screen, use the DBMS Top Line menu to choose

    **M**odify **C**opy

or use the expert command

    F9 Command Copy

The Copy command operates much like the Update command, discussed in the section "Using the Update Command"; however, instead of asking for a master file and a transaction file, the Copy screen asks for the destination (on the To_Database line) and the source (on the From line) (see fig. 14.11). The following paragraphs explain the use of this command.

### Copying from an Existing Database File

You can copy data from an existing database file to a new database file. To create a new database file, specify a new file name on the To_ Database line. Choose **D**atabase on the From line, and then, at the `database name` prompt, enter the name of an existing database. Enable creates a database definition for the new file; however, no derived or external fields can be copied.

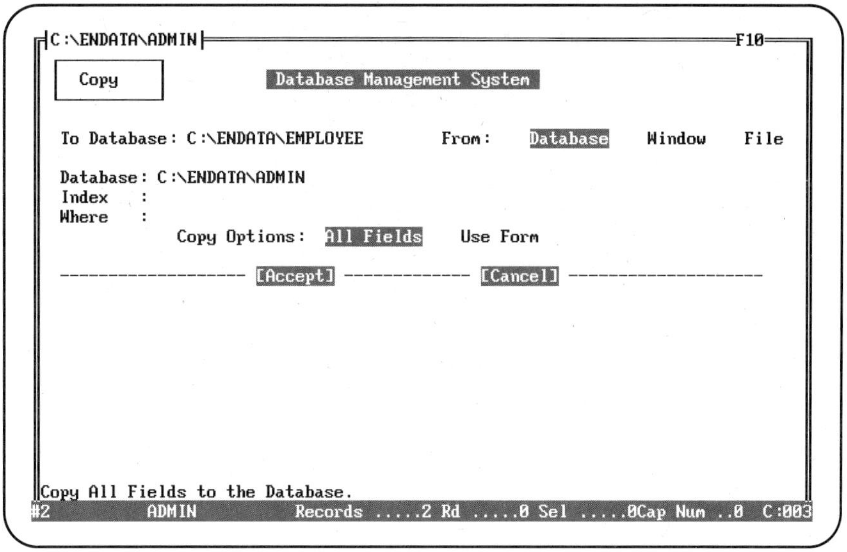

```
┌─┤C:\ENDATA\ADMIN├─────────────────────────────────────F10─┐
│ ┌──────────┐         ┌─────────────────────────────┐      │
│ │   Copy   │         │ Database Management System  │      │
│ └──────────┘         └─────────────────────────────┘      │
│                                                           │
│   To Database: C:\ENDATA\EMPLOYEE      From:  ┌────────┐ Window   File │
│                                               │Database│               │
│   Database: C:\ENDATA\ADMIN                   └────────┘               │
│   Index   :                                                            │
│   Where   :                                                            │
│              Copy Options: ┌──────────┐  Use Form                      │
│                            │All Fields│                                │
│   ─────────────── ┌──────┐ └──────────┘ ┌──────┐ ──────────────────   │
│                   │Accept│ ──────────── │Cancel│                       │
│                   └──────┘              └──────┘                       │
│                                                                        │
│                                                                        │
│                                                                        │
│ Copy All Fields to the Database.                                       │
│ #2        ADMIN          Records .....2 Rd .....0 Sel .....0Cap Num ..0 C:003 │
└────────────────────────────────────────────────────────────────────┘
```

*Fig. 14.11. A Copy command screen to copy from database to database.*

You also can add all or part of an existing Enable database file to the end of another existing database file. Specify the appropriate file names on the Database lines. Then, use the index or where prompts to select specific records for copying.

## Copying from a Word Processing Window

You can copy data from a word processing window to a new or existing database. Assume that the data is arranged in columns in a word processing file. First, display the data in a word processing window, and open a DBMS window to the Copy command screen. To copy the data to the end of an existing database file or to create a new database, specify the name of the database in the To_Database line. Choose Window on the From line.

Enable displays the standard Interwindow Copy Options screen. Choose the word processing window. Position the cursor at the top left corner of the data, and press F7. Move the cursor to the bottom right corner of the data, and again press F7. Next, press Alt-F5 . Enable displays a screen similar to the one shown in figure 14.12. Press Enter to use the displayed file name. The window number included the file name is the number of the word processing window. Choose Create to create a field definition file.

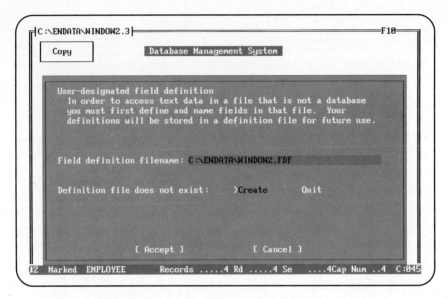

**Fig. 14.12.** *A dialog box for creating field definition.*

A second dialog box appears. The Field Definition screen, similar to figure 14.13, displays the first line of the word processing file's data. Enable assigns the field type and length of the data based on the order of the text. Verify and edit the field type and length by indicating the field type under each field: enter **C**haracter, **N**umber, **L**ogical, or **I**gnore under the last character in each field. For comma-separated fields, place the field type under the comma that separates each field. Use the space bar to delete an unwanted field type code. After you define the last field, press Enter.

Enable highlights the first field and display a `Field name` prompt (see fig. 14.14). Enter the field name for the designated field, then press Enter. Enter the correct number of decimal positions when prompted during the definition of a numeric field. Comma-separated fields display the default length; press Enter to accept. After the last field is defined, Enable returns to the DBMS Copy Command screen.

Bypass the Index and Where clauses by pressing Enter. Choose **U**se_Form, and press Enter at the Using_form line (see fig. 14.15). Enable displays the Copy Transfer Form screen with the field names from the destination database on the left and field names you defined on the right (see fig 14.16). Check the accuracy of the right side of the equations in the Copy Transfer Form screen.

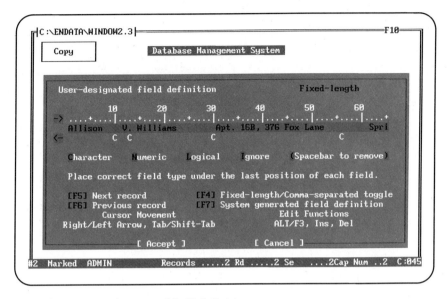

**Fig. 14.13.** *A user-designated field definition screen.*

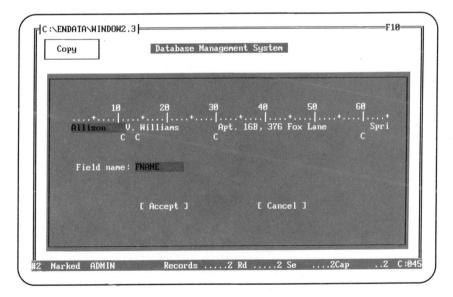

**Fig. 14.14.** *A Copy command screen for defining field names.*

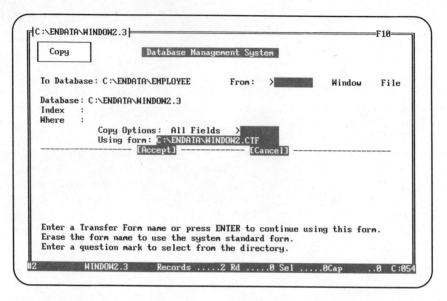

**Fig. 14.15.** *A Copy command screen to copy from a word processing window to a database.*

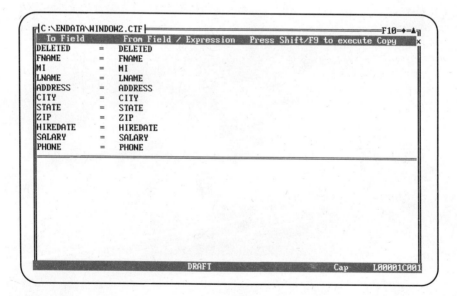

**Fig. 14.16.** *A Copy Transfer Form screen for copying from word processing to database.*

After you have verified all the fields, press the following command to copy the data:

Shift-F9 **Copy**

## Copying from a Spreadsheet File or Window

You also can copy data from a spreadsheet file or window to a new or existing database. The simplest way to make this type of data transfer is from a file to an existing database. You first must set up the spreadsheet file so that the first three rows contain a basic database definition, consisting of field name, data type, and maximum length. This is similar to the quick method of defining a field. Create a label column heading for each field in row 1 of the spreadsheet, beginning at cell A1. When you copy the data to an existing database, use the same field names as you used in the spreadsheet file. The second row must contain an *N*, *C*, or *L*, to indicate that the field is *numeric*, *character* (text), or *logical*, respectively. The final row of the definition area specifies the maximum length of each field. The remaining rows of the spreadsheet can contain data, arranged in columns beneath the field names. Save this spreadsheet to disk, and close the spreadsheet window.

In the Copy command screen, indicate the destination (To) database, and on the From line, choose **File**. Then choose **Enable_Spreadsheet**. Type the name of the spreadsheet file on the File_Name line and press Enter. Your screen should look like figure 14.17. This screen has a Where line where you can enter a condition statement to select specific records to be copied from the spreadsheet file. Finally, you can copy **All_Fields** or choose Use_Form to copy only some fields.

The procedure for converting a 1-2-3 database into an Enable DBMS file is the same except that you choose Lotus_1-2-3 as the file type.

## Copying from an ASCII File

To copy a comma-separated ASCII database into an Enable database, choose File on the From line of the Copy command screen (see fig. 14.18). Then choose ASCII, and enter the file name of the ASCII file. The file name should have the extension ASC.

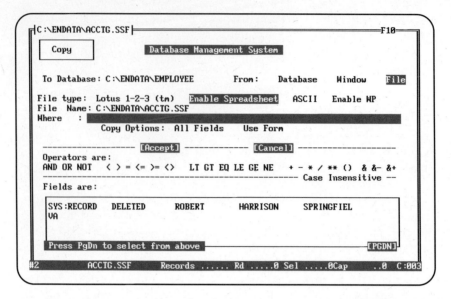

**Fig. 14.17.** *A Copy command screen to copy data from a spreadsheet to a database.*

```
┌─C:\ENDATA\SALES.ASC├─────────────────────────────────────F10─┐
│  ┌───────┐                                                    │
│  │ Copy  │        Database Management System                  │
│  └───────┘                                                    │
│                                                               │
│   To Database: C:\ENDATA\EMPLOYEE     From:   Database  Window  File │
│                                                               │
│   File type: Lotus 1-2-3 (tm)  Enable Spreadsheet  ASCII   Enable WP │
│   File  Name: C:\ENDATA\SALES.ASC                             │
│   Where   :                                                   │
│           Copy Options:  All Fields   Use Form                │
│   ─────────────────── [Accept] ───────────── [Cancel] ──────────────│
│                                                               │
│                                                               │
│                                                               │
│                                                               │
│                                                               │
│                                                               │
│                                                               │
│                                                               │
│                                                               │
│                                                               │
│ Copy fields Based on a New or Existing Form.                  │
│#2       SALES.ASC       Records ...... Rd .....0 Sel .....0Cap    ..0  C:003 │
└───────────────────────────────────────────────────────────────┘
```

**Fig. 14.18.** *A Copy command screen to copy from an ASCII file to a database.*

After you enter the ASCII file name, Enable displays the Field Definition screen. Define the ASCII file exactly as described in the section "Copying from a Word Processing Window." After you complete the definition, Enable returns you to the DBMS Copy Command screen.

Choose Use_Form to display the Copy Transfer Form screen. After you have verified the right side of the equations, press the following command to copy the data:

Shift-F9 Copy

# Using the Export Command

Occasionally you may need to convert an Enable database to ASCII format for use in another program. Use the Export command for this purpose. To display the Export command screen, use the DBMS Top Line menu to choose

**File Export**

or use the expert command

F9 Command 0=Export

The Export command creates an ASCII file, in fixed-field or comma-delimited format, that other programs can read and manipulate. You can select all or some of the fields and records to be exported.

# Using the Merge Command

To display the Merge command screen, use the DBMS Top Line menu to choose

**Modify Merge**

or use the expert command

F9 Command Merge

Unlike the Update and Copy commands that modify an existing database, the Merge command creates an entirely new database, consisting of some or all of the data from two source files. Enable combines these source database files according to criteria you set and according to the relationship between them. The files must have in common a field that can be used as a link, usually an identification code of some type. The source files remain unchanged after the merge.

For example, you can create a payroll listing that combines salary and commission by merging the database EMPLOYEE with a database COMMIS, whose Field Definition screen is shown in figure 14.19. You add a linking field IDNO (a three-digit employee ID number) to the EMPLOYEE database, as shown in figure 14.20. Each month, you enter the employees' commissions into COMMIS. Then you merge the two files using the Merge command screen shown in figure 14.21 and the Merge Transfer Form screen shown in figure 14.22. Enable merges each record from COMMIS with the record from EMPLOYEE that has a matching IDNO.

Notice that the field names listed in the Merge Transfer Form screen include all the real data fields (no external or derived fields) from the files EMPLOYEE and COMMIS. As with the Update command, you can exclude fields by typing a semicolon (;) at the beginning of the line or by deleting the line. In this example, create two new fields, called NAME and PAY, with the following formulas:

NAME = FNAME&+MI&+LNAME

PAY = SALARY/12+COMMISSION

Figure 14.23 shows some of the fields and records from the resulting database, PAYROLL. The PAYROLL database is now available so that you can give checks to the employees, and you can copy PAYROLL to a database with previous payrolls, as a permanent record.

The link field (such as IDNO) for the With_database section of the Merge command screen must be indexed. For the merge to work correctly, the values in this link field also must be unique. In the Merge example, you make the link unique by specifying the PAYDAY in the Where line (refer to fig. 14.21). The COMMIS database has one record for each employee ID number for each payday. If the link is not unique, Enable uses data from the first record in the With_database section with a match in the link field, which may not be what you intend.

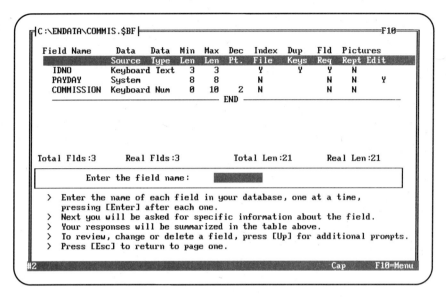

**Fig. 14.19.** *The COMMIS database definition.*

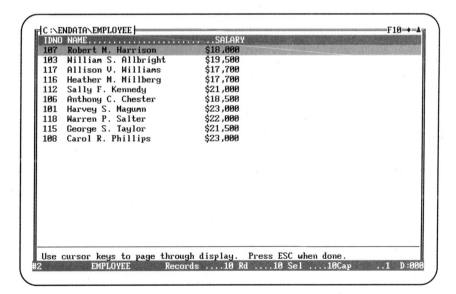

**Fig. 14.20.** *The EMPLOYEE database.*

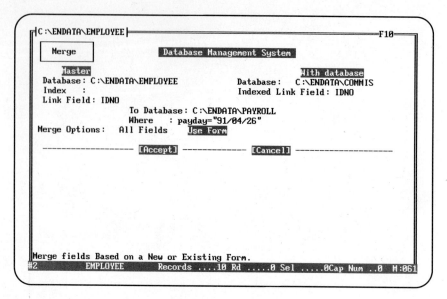

*Fig. 14.21. A Merge command screen.*

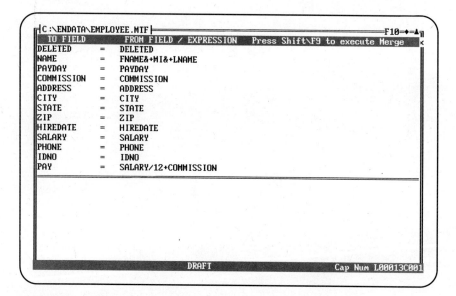

*Fig. 14.22. A Merge Transfer Form screen.*

```
┌┤C:\ENDATA\PAYROLL├════════════════════════════════════════════F10─◆═▲┐
│ IDNO NAME.................... ..SALARY COMMISSION .......PAY PAYDAY.. │
│ ┌──────────────────────────────────────────────────────────────────┐ │
│ │107  Robert M. Harrison        $18,000    $500.00  $1,500.00  91/04/26│ │
│ └──────────────────────────────────────────────────────────────────┘ │
│  103  William S. Allbright     $19,500    $250.00  $1,625.00  91/04/26 │
│  117  Allison V. Williams      $17,700    $150.00  $1,475.00  91/04/26 │
│  116  Heather M. Millberg      $17,700    $375.00  $1,475.00  91/04/26 │
│  112  Sally F. Kennedy         $21,000    $425.00  $1,750.00  91/04/26 │
│  106  Anthony C. Chester       $18,500    $420.00  $1,541.67  91/04/26 │
│  101  Harvey S. Magumn         $23,000    $250.00  $1,916.67  91/04/26 │
│  118  Warren P. Salter         $22,000    $325.00  $1,833.33  91/04/26 │
│  115  George S. Taylor         $21,500    $125.00  $1,791.67  91/04/26 │
│  108  Carol R. Phillips        $23,000    $245.00  $1,916.67  91/04/26 │
│                                                                        │
│                                                                        │
│                                                                        │
│                                                                        │
│                                                                        │
│                                                                        │
│                                                                        │
│                                                                        │
│                                                                        │
│ Use cursor keys to page through display.  Press ESC when done.         │
│#2       PAYROLL        Records ....10 Rd ....10 Sel ....10Cap Num ..1  D:000│
└────────────────────────────────────────────────────────────────────────┘
```

*Fig. 14.23. The result of Merge.*

# Validating Data Entry with Custom Input Forms

"Garbage in, garbage out!" is a common saying, but it is all too true. If you don't enter valid data into a database, then you cannot generate valid output. This section discusses several tools in Enable which help ensure that you enter only valid data.

## Creating Custom Input Forms

The standard input form, discussed in Chapter 13, is easy to create. If your database contains only a few fields, or if you are the only person who uses the input form, the standard input form may be the only form you need. A well-organized data entry screen, however, with clear on-screen instructions, helps greatly to ensure valid data entry. Transforming the fill-in-the-blank paper forms you already use into a custom input form is actually quite easy. Enable also has a few special options that help you validate data much more than a paper form ever can.

To create a custom input form, begin at the Main Menu and select

> **Use_System Database Add/Edit_forms**

Specify an input form file name at the Open File dialog box, then press Enter.

Enable then displays the first Input Form Definition screen (see fig. 14.24). On this screen, enter the database with which this input form will be associated. Enable then displays the second Input Form Definition screen (see fig. 14.25.). You can enter a description of the form or leave the screen blank. After you respond to the screens, you can design the form, as explained in the following sections.

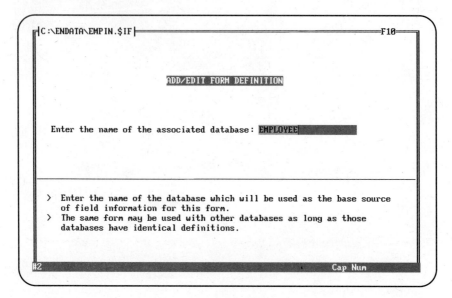

*Fig. 14.24. The first Input Form Definition screen.*

**TIP**

If you create a custom input form with the same name as the database, you destroy your efforts when you later tell Enable to create a standard input form for the database. One way to name a custom input form is to use the first few letters of the database name plus the letters IN to designate the file as an input form (for example, PERSONIN for a personnel database or VENDORIN for a vendor database).

You may not need to start from scratch with an input form. Perhaps the standard input form is almost good enough, but you want to add a few special validation options or change a field prompt. Use the File Manager screen to rename the standard input form (for example, from EMPLOYEE.$IF to EMPIN.$IF), then follow the instructions in this section to make the needed refinements.

**TIP**

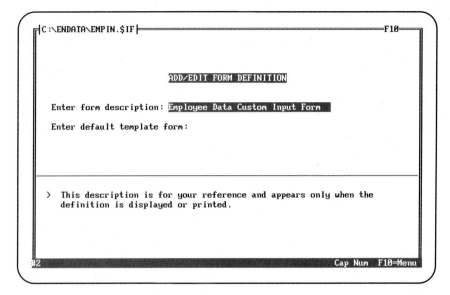

*Fig. 14.25. The second Input Form Definition screen.*

## Creating Screen Prompts

When you first begin defining the input form, it is simply a blank word processing screen. Think of the screen as a fill-in-the-blank paper form. You can move around in this screen and type just as you do in any Enable word processing window. All standard word processing features are available. To create this on-screen form, you must type everything but the blanks. The messages you type, referred to as *screen prompts* or *labels*, should clearly identify what information is to be entered in each blank. Figure 14.26 shows a sample data entry form with brief, clear labels. Access the standard word processing Top Line menu by pressing

F10 File Word_Processing_Options

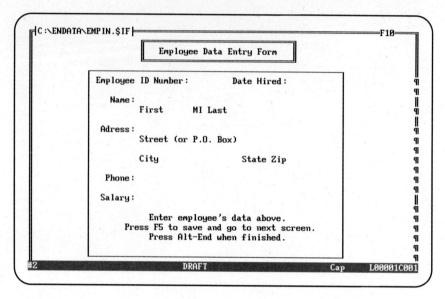

**Fig. 14.26.** *Sample data entry form with prompts.*

## Creating Data Entry Fields

Helpful prompts are important, but the purpose of the form is to enter data. To create the fields for the data entry form, position the cursor where you want to enter data in the data entry form, and press Shift-F9. Enable prompts Enter field name. Type a field name, and press Enter. If you are unsure how you spelled the name of the field you want at this position, type a question mark (?) to display a list of available fields. Move the pointer to the name of the field you want located at this position, and press Enter.

Enable displays the prompt

Do you wish to select special processing options?

Choose **Yes** to use one or more of the following options:

• Should this field be verified? Use this option in conjunction with the Verify command. (This option has no effect when data is added initially.) When you use the input form with the Verify command, this field is blank so that you can reenter the data, thus providing verification.

- Should this field be copied to the next ADD screen? **If you choose this option, Enable copies data from one input screen to the next screen when you use this form to add data to the database. You must enter a value in the field in the first screen in each Add session, but all subsequent screens automatically display this value.**

- Should this field be protected from being updated? **Another way to state this question is, "Should this field be protected from being edited?" This option prevents anyone from making changes to the field through the Edit command.**

- Does this field require an [Enter]? **Use this option at a field to prevent the cursor from jumping to the next field as soon as the current field is filled with data. You may want to use this option on every field to make cursor movement in the form easier to follow.**

- Do you want to provide default data for this field? **Use this option to supply a standard entry in the field, thus speeding data entry. The person who enters the data still can modify the data for a particular record.**

- Is there a special message if invalid data is entered? **This message overrides any system-supplied error message and any error message specified in the database definition for this field.**

- Does this field have a "GO TO field IF" condition? **Choose this option to cause the cursor to jump to a specific field on-screen when a certain condition is met. You can use this option to jump over irrelevant fields, saving keystrokes and decreasing the chances of entering data in the wrong field.**

- Suppress printing of this field. **During data entry, you print the current record to a template or preprinted form. Use this option to keep Enable from printing the field data.**

- Field placement on preprinted form. **Use this option to specify where on a preprinted form you want the field printed. You need to measure (in inches) down from the top and from the left margin exactly where the data will print on the form.**

- Field placement on template form. **If the data is to be used with a template, you need to specify how many inches down from the top and character spaces over from the left margin to print the data on the form.**

- Does this field have a macro procedure? The most powerful special processing option is also the most complicated. Each field can have up to ten associated macros: five when used with the Add command, and five when used with Edit. Use the F8 key to copy a macro from the Add list to the Edit list. You can use system macro codes and the database procedural language in these macros. You must enclose each procedural language command in brackets.

  Macro codes not enclosed in brackets execute first. Five types of macros are available:

  1. A *Shift-F9 macro* executes when you press Shift-F9 from the field during an Add or Edit operation.

  2. A *prefield macro* executes automatically whenever you move the cursor into the field.

  3. A *postfield macro* executes automatically after you move out of the field.

  4. A *prerec macro* executes while you are adding or editing records, when the record form appears on-screen.

  5. A *postrec macro* executes whenever you exit from a record.

After you indicate whether you want to use special processing options, Enable displays the data entry area as a highlighted space that begins with a diamond. The length of the highlighted space is the field length specified in the database definition. When you repeat this process for every field, your input form screen for the EMPLOYEE database should look similar to figure 14.27.

After you define the input form, save it by pressing

  Alt-F10 Same_name

To return to the Main Menu, press

  Alt-End Yes

## Using the Verify Command

To display the Verify command screen, use the DBMS Top Line menu and choose

  Modify Verify

or use the expert command

  F9 Command Verify

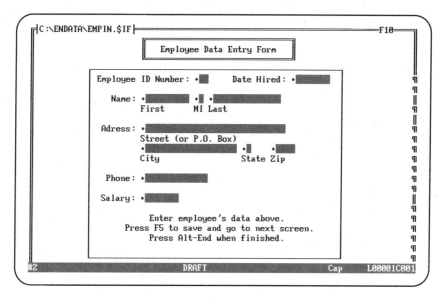

**Fig. 14.27.** *The input form screen for the EMPLOYEE database, showing the data entry fields.*

Enter the database name, and enter the name of the custom input form that contains a field or fields where you responded **Yes** to the prompt Should this field be verified? An Index line and a Where line are available so that you can select particular records. Enable displays the custom input form screen.

In this screen, any fields you defined with the Verify option are blank. Enter the data in the empty spaces. Enable does not accept an entry that varies from the initial data. Press F8 to see the current value and to make any necessary corrections.

Do not use the Verify command to verify every field. Verify is most suitable for long character strings, such as ID numbers, where reversed and misaligned letters are difficult to detect visually.

## Saving Records to Disk

Each time you press F5 (or F6 in Edit mode) to save a record, Enable saves the record to a memory buffer. Enable writes the records to disk only when you close the DBMS window or when the memory buffer is filled.

From the DBMS profile options, you can specify the number of record transactions (add or edit) to occur before Enable writes them to disk. From the DBMS Top Line menu, select

File Save Save_buffers_to_disk

to save the current records in the memory buffer. You also can choose **1** to disable the autosave feature or choose **2**, **3** or **4** to save after every record, after 10 records, or after 50 record transactions, respectively.

## Creating Passthru Fields

One of the database profile options asks whether to enable the Passthru feature (see Appendix B for a discussion of profile options). If you answer **Yes** to this option, you can enter data into more than one database from the same screen. For example, whenever you enter an employee's monthly commission into the COMMIS database (described in the section "Using the Merge Command"), you will also enter the employee's ID number. If you enter the COMMIS and EMPLOYEE data on the same form, you can see the name of the employee with that ID number to verify that you typed the number correctly; make corrections to employee data and add the commission all on the same screen, making your data entry very convenient; and, if the employee is new (not yet in the EMPLOYEE database), but you have entered a COMMIS record, you will be able to create a new EMPLOYEE record from a COMMIS input form. All these capabilities are possible with Enable's Passthru feature.

To define a field from another database in an input form, type a prompt for the field as usual, position the cursor where the field should begin, and press Shift-F9. When Enable asks for the field name, type the field name from the other database. For example, if you are working with the input form shown in figure 14.26, associated with the database COMMIS, you can define the field to be looked up as FNAME from the EMPLOYEE database. Enable then asks, Source of data. Choose **Another_database**, and answer the following prompts:

- From what database. Specify the name of the lookup database (in this example, EMPLOYEE).

- Name of lookup field in other database. Type the name of the field you want to display from the other database (FNAME in this example).

- `Name of indexed linking field in referenced database.` For Passthru to work, the other database must have an indexed field that links to a field in this database. Define this field with no duplicates allowed.

- `Name of linking field in this database.` **Enter the field in** this database you want used to link to the other database. In the EMPLOYEE and COMMIS example, the link field in both databases is the IDNO field.

- `Can this field be keyed over?` **Answer Yes to be able to pass** through changes to the other database. When a link value is entered that does not yet have a corresponding record in the lookup database, the Passthru feature creates a new record and adds it to the end of the database.

You also can enter three special processing options: the "GO TO field IF" condition, printing specifications, and macro procedures (see "Creating Data Entry Fields").

Enable provides three other options for choosing other source fields: Derived, Local, and System. Derived (calculated) fields can be used to combine text fields on-screen and to display the results of certain calculations. Local fields are usually used to trigger a macro—for example, to quit and return to the Main Menu. System fields use the system date or time.

# Maintaining the Database

If a bad experience is necessary to teach you to make backup copies of your data, then you have one bad experience too many. You should develop a practice of making backups, and stick with it.

The following paragraphs explain the use the Backup command to make copies easily of an entire database and its related files. Backups are intended as insurance against catastrophe, but you also may need to make copies of data for the more mundane purpose of creating an archive. You can use several related commands together to make archive copies and then purge the database. This section covers these commands as well. Finally, this section explains how to use the Rename command to change the name of a database.

# Using the Backup Command

To display the Backup command screen, use the DBMS Top Line menu to choose

>   **Tools Maintenance Backup**

or use the F9 command

>   F9 Command 4=Backup

This command creates a complete duplicate of your database, including definition, data, index files, archive files, and error sets. This copy helps ensure against accidental data loss; the command is available only on hard disk systems. Use a clean formatted disk, place it in the floppy disk drive, and continue with the Backup command. To back up more than one database at once onto the same floppy disk, be careful not to return to the DBMS Command Chart or the Main Menu before you have made all backups. If Enable runs out of room on one disk, the program prompts you to insert another.

If the original data is lost, use the **R**estore command to place the database back on the hard disk.

# Archiving and Purging the Database

The commands for archiving and purging the database are easiest to understand when studied as a group. Normally, records are active, and the value of a field called DELETED is *No*. Enable automatically creates the DELETED field for each database. The DELETED field's data type is logical (Yes/No). The Delete command can switch a record to inactive by changing the value of DELETED to *Yes*. You can reactivate an inactive record, changing the value of DELETED back to No, through the Undelete command. Normally, only active records are included in screen displays, sorts, and reports. Records must be inactive for you to archive them with the Archive command or to remove them permanently from the database with the Destroy command.

# Using the Delete Command

To display the Delete command screen, use the DBMS Top Line menu to choose

> **Modify Delete**

or use the F9 command

> **F9 Command 1**=Delete

Specify the records to be deactivated through a condition in the Index line or the Where line. Leaving both these lines blank deactivates the entire database.

You normally do not see the deleted (deactivated) records displayed on-screen or in reports; however, you can work with just the inactive records by using the criteria DELETED = YES in the Where line. To include all records, active as well as inactive, place the condition

> **DELETED OR NOT DELETED**

in the Where line.

# Using the Undelete Command

To display the Undelete command screen, use the DBMS Top Line menu to choose

> **Modify Undelete**

or use the expert command

> **F9 Command 2**=Undelete

Undelete is the opposite of Delete. This command reactivates records by changing the value of the DELETED field to No.

# Using the Archive Command

To display the Archive command screen, use the DBMS Top Line menu to choose

> **Tools Maintenance Archive**

or use the F9 command

> **F9 Command 3**=Archive

The Archive command copies all inactive records into a special database file called an *archive* file. This file is not a regular database file and cannot be used alone.

As its name implies, the Archive command is normally used as a safety feature to create archive copies of your data. This feature is especially important if you are going to use the Destroy command to destroy data permanently. Enable always creates the archive copy on your default directory.

**TIP**

Make sure you follow the same procedure every time you use the Archive command. Enable asks you whether it should destroy the old archive file before adding the current set of inactive (deleted) records to the archive. Your answer depends on what you did last time. If your practice is to destroy (remove from the database) all inactive records after archiving, then you should answer No to this question. The only copy of the old archived data is then in the old archive file. If, however, you leave inactive records in the database even after making an archive file, then you should instruct Enable to destroy the old archive before adding the new records, to prevent duplicating data in the archive.

## Using the Destroy Command

To use the Destroy command screen to purge the database, use the DBMS Top Line menu to choose

**Tools Maintenance Destroy**

or use the F9 command

**F9 Command 6=Destroy Records Enter**

Enable permanently removes all inactive records from the database.

This command is useful for removing indexing from an indexed field and for destroying an entire database, including the definition, indexes, and so on.

## Using the Restore Command

To display the Restore command screen, use the DBMS Top Line menu to choose

**T**ools **M**aintenance **R**estore

or use the F9 command

F9 Command **5**=Restore

This command has two options: Archive and Backup. The first option retrieves records from the archives and puts them in the inactive set of records; the second retrieves records from a backup file and reinstates those records in the active database.

## Using the Rename Command

To display the Rename command screen, use the DBMS Top Line menu to choose

**F**ile **R**ename

or use the F9 command

F9 Command **7**=Rename

Use this command when you want to change the database name for some reason. Issuing Rename is easier than using the File Manager screen because Rename renames both the DBF file and the $BF file in one step.

# Creating Custom Reports

Chapter 13 discusses creating simple reports and columnar reports. The following sections describe how to create more complex columnar reports for summarizing the data at intermediate levels and how to create a "Put It Here!" report, which does not limit you to the columnar format. (The procedural language and mail merge are covered in Chapter 15, "Using Enable's Procedural Language.")

# Creating Columnar Reports with Breaks and Subtotals

In Chapter 13, you learn how to use the Report command and the default report form to create columnar reports and how to generate summary computations at the end of the report. Creating a summary computation at an intermediate level (a subtotal, for example) involves using a *break*: a blank line between records, generated whenever the value in a field changes from one record to the next.

The first step is to sort the data. Use the Sort command to group the data in the order you want. For example, assume that your company has three departments: Sales, Production, and Administration. Each department has two groups. To generate a report that subtotals salaries for each group and each department, first sort the data by DEPT and GROUP, as shown in figure 14.28. The sorted fields often are called the *key fields*. Use the resulting select set in the Database line of the Report command screen.

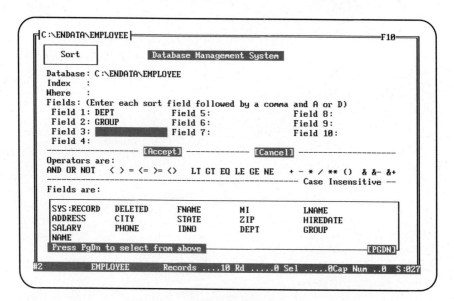

**Fig. 14.28.** *A Sort screen for sorting data for a report with breaks.*

The next step in creating a report with subtotals is to add breaks. Issue the Report command to display the Report command screen. In the Fields line of the screen, type the names of the fields, separated by commas, to be included in the report. To cause a break at the most "significant" key field (DEPT in the example), type the code {B1} between the field name and the next comma on the Fields line (refer to fig. 14.29).

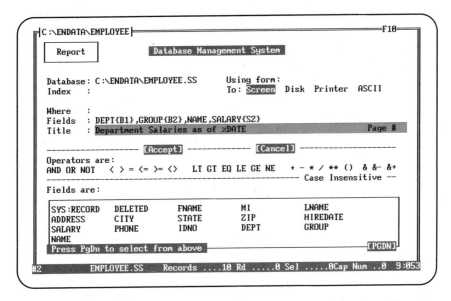

*Fig. 14.29. A Report command screen to create a report with breaks and intermediate-level summary computations.*

You can cause a second-level break by typing the code {B2} after the next most significant key field (GROUP in the example). You can have up to 16 break levels, but you first must have sorted the data to 16 levels (if that sort is ever necessary).

Creating summary computations at each break is now easy. To begin the subtotals at the second break level, type the code {S2} after the field to be computed (SALARY in the example). You also can use any of the other computation codes discussed in Chapter 13, followed by a break level number. The complete Fields line for the EMPLOYEE example shown in figure 14.29 is as follows:

    DEPT{B1},GROUP{B2},NAME,SALARY{S2}

The report created by this Fields line is shown in figure 14.30.

```
┌─┤C:\ENDATA\EMPLOYEE├───────────────────────────────────────F10═┐
│Header and Page Break════════════════════════════════════════════│
│Department Salaries as of %DATE                   Page #          │
│DEPT..........  GROUP  NAME...............   SALARY..             │
│                                                                  │
│Administration     1   Heather M. Millberg   $17,700             │
│Administration     1   Harvey S. Magumn      $23,000             │
│                      ─────                   ──────────          │
│                   1                          $40,700 S           │
│                                                                  │
│Administration     2   Allison V. Williams   $17,700             │
│Administration     2   Carol R. Phillips     $23,000             │
│                      ─────                   ──────────          │
│                   2                          $40,700 S           │
│                                                                  │
│─────────────────────                        ──────────          │
│Administration                               $81,400 S           │
│                                                                  │
│Production         1   Sally F. Kennedy      $21,000             │
│Production         1   Warren P. Salter      $22,000             │
│Production         1   George S. Taylor      $21,500             │
│                                                                  │
│ Arrow keys to scroll sideways, PGDN or RETURN to continue, or ESC to cancel.│
│                                                                  │
│#2        EMPLOYEE.SS    Records ....10 Rd .....7 Sel ....7Cap Num ..7  9:053│
└──────────────────────────────────────────────────────────────────┘
```

*Fig. 14.30. A report with breaks created by codes entered on the Fields line.*

# Creating "Put It Here!" Reports

*"Put It Here!"* reports are really the same fill-in-the-blank forms discussed in "Creating Custom Input Forms" in this chapter, except that you use "Put It Here!" reports to format output rather than input. In fact, you can use any custom input form you have created as a report form.

**TIP**

If you intend to use an input form as a report, make a copy of the input form using the File Manager screen, and change the file name extension from $IF to $RF. In Enable, "Put It Here!" report forms should have the $RF extension.

To create a "Put It Here!" report, from the Main Menu press

**Use_System Database Report_forms**

Enter a file name for the report at the Open File dialog box, then press Enter.

At the prompt `Enter the name of the associated database:`, Enter the name of the database you plan to use with this report form. At the prompt `Enter form description:`, you can enter a brief description of the report form.

The next screen outlines the steps to create a customized report form. Press Enter to continue.

The blank report form screen appears. Build the report form exactly as you built a customized input form. Refer to the section "Validating Data Entry with Custom Input Forms" in this chapter.

# Setting Database Environment Defaults

You can specify the environment under which the current database is controlled by changing the default environment settings. You choose most of these options through the database profile selections (see Appendix B for a discussion of profiles). You can override these settings by selecting from the menu

> **Tools Defaults**

Enable displays the Database Environment dialog box (see fig. 14.31), with the following options:

- *Database format is 3.0 or greater.* Choose this option if databases are to be created in Enable/OA format. If you don't choose this option, the database will be created in the Enable version 2.0 format.

- *Passthru data is linked to database.* Choose this option so that you can modify data and write the new data to the lookup field in the linked field.

- *Left justify numbers in ADD/EDIT.* Choose this option to left-justify numeric values in a field on an input form.

- *Stop on all database errors.* Choose this option to cause the system to stop whenever an error occurs and wait for user response. If you do not choose this option, Enable continues processing when it encounters an error.

- *Display records when page is full.* Choose this option to cause Enable to retrieve 20 records before displaying any records on-screen. If you remove the check mark in front of this option, Enable displays each record as it is retrieved during Display.

- *Display SYS:RECORD AND DELETED fields.* If you remove the check mark in front of this option, Enable does not display the SYS:RECORD and DELETED fields.

- *Make Where clause case sensitive.* Choose this option to make a Where clause search statement case sensitive.

- *INDEX prompt at end of Edit on select set.* If you choose this option, then when an Index prompt is used to select records for editing, after you have finished editing the last record in the select set, Enable displays an Index prompt so that a new select set can be created for editing.

- *Autolock records on LAN.* Choose this option to prevent another user from accessing records you are editing on a LAN.

- *Set maximum buffering.* Choose this option to increase the performance of certain database operations that take place in memory, such as Sort and Index. If you choose this option, then during database operations, Enable uses the maximum number of buffers your system has available. If no check mark appears in front of this option, Enable uses up to 50 buffers during database operations.

- *Database buffer size.* Choose the memory buffer that meets your needs. The higher the buffer size, the more Enable can process in memory before accessing the disk. The default memory size is 512K.

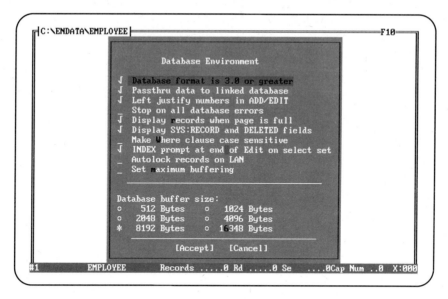

*Fig. 14.31. The Database Environment dialog box.*

# Summary

Enable's database management system is a powerful tool for storing, retrieving, manipulating, and reporting data on virtually any subject. Use the discussion in this chapter as a starting point for fully exploring Enable's DBMS capabilities. The next chapter introduces you to Enable's procedural language. After you learn to use the tools in this chapter and the procedural language, you may find that Enable is the only DBMS program you ever need.

# 15

# Using Enable's Procedural Language

E nable's DBMS commands give you the basic tools you need to create, maintain, and generate straightforward reports from a database without programming. System macros are available to help keep repetition to a minimum. Sooner or later, however, you will want to design reports that are beyond the capability of a standard columnar report. The "Put It Here!" report method discussed in Chapter 14 gives you some flexibility, but to produce more complex reports, you need to learn about *Enable's Procedural Language*.

Enable's Procedural Language is a simple programming language specifically designed for generating reports from Enable database files. The Procedural Language isn't a general-purpose programming language like BASIC, Pascal, or C. You can use the Procedural Language to produce sophisticated results, however, including reports with user interaction and direct data manipulation. Programming is beyond the scope of this book, but this chapter explains some of the Procedural Language fundamentals. For additional information on the Procedural Language, see the DBMS manual of the Enable/OA documentation.

This chapter also explains how to use the mail-merge feature on the Word Processing menu. The model letter and model mailing label formats you use to create form letters and mailing labels both use the Procedural Language.

Finally, this chapter gives you a brief explanation of *Structured Query Language* (SQL) and how to use Enable's SQL interactive and embedded command features.

# Creating Procedural Language Reports

Reports that use Procedural Language commands are generated with the Report command (from the DBMS command chart). Fill in the full file name of the report in the Using_form line of the Report command screen.

You can create Procedural Language reports either in the word processing module of Enable/OA or in the DBMS Report design screen (the "Put It Here!" method introduced in Chapter 14). The Report design screen is nearly identical to that of a word processing file, and with the Report design screen, you can use the Shift-F9 field definition method, explained in Chapter 14, as well.

**TIP**

If you use a report created in the word processing module, be sure that you include the file name extension WPF in the Using_form line of the Report command screen. Otherwise, Enable looks for a report with the file name extension $RF.

All Procedural Language commands must begin with a period (.) and should appear on a line by themselves. In Enable/OA, you can indent command lines. Indented command lines are easier to read and help you understand Enable's Procedural Language programming procedures, such as .if and .do case (see "Using Conditional Processing" in this chapter). You can use either upper- or lowercase to type Procedural Language commands; however, following your program is easier if you decide on a case convention, and then stay with that convention. This book shows Procedural Language commands in lowercase and shows field names and file names in uppercase.

Serious programmers use extensive internal documentation so that they can return to a program months later and immediately understand the program's purpose and logic. For the same reason, you should document liberally your Procedural Language programs. Precede all your internal documentation by a pair of semicolons; when Enable processes the report form, it does not process anything preceded by a pair of semicolons (;;).

When Enable processes a Procedural Language report that you create in the word processing module, the program turns on the automatic reformatting feature. This feature normally is turned off when you use the Report definition screen (the "Put It Here" method) to create a report. The .reformat_off command turns off automatic reformatting, and the

.reformat_on command turns it on. Use the .reformat_off command to align your data in columns; use the .reformat_on command to eliminate extra spaces between data values.

You can use the .report division command at the beginning of a report to distinguish the report from your other word processing files, but the command isn't required.

Enable prints the current value of a field whenever it finds the field name typed in brackets ([ ]). Don't put a Procedural Language command on the same line as a field to be printed, and use only one Procedural Language command per line.

You can align field values within the bracketed space by typing inside the brackets one of the following codes within braces:

| Character | Alignment |
|-----------|-----------|
| ^ | Center |
| < | Left |
| > | Right |

To center the value of the field DEPT, for example, use the following syntax:

[DEPT { ^ }]

A Procedural Language report has four main sections: *definitions*, *introduction*, *body*, and *conclusion*, explained in the following sections.

# Creating the Definitions Section

Enable opens any database you specify in the Report command screen. This database is called the *associated database*. You then can refer in your report to any field name in this database without further explanation, but you must define in your report any fields that are not defined in the associated database. Refer to a field from the associated database by its field name. Define these fields in the first section of the report, called the *definitions section*.

Begin the definitions section of your report with the .definitions command, which signals to Enable that you have begun the definitions section. Use the .define command to define one of the following kinds of fields in this area:

- A field from another database.

- A *derived field*. A field whose value derives from some calculation or combination of data from one or more other fields.

- A *system field*: time and date.

- A *memo* field.

- A field whose value is supplied during running of the report, often called a *local field*. You also can define the local field as a single dimension numeric or character string variable array.

To define a field from another database (the *external database*), you must specify a link that selects the correct record from the other database. Use the format

```
.define FIELDNAME=lookup in DATABASE2 link LINK1—LINK2
```

where *FIELDNAME* is the name you are using in the report. The data is in the field LOOKUP in DATABASE2. LINK1 is the key field in the associated database; LINK2 is the key field in the external database.

You also can open other database files with the .open command and point to specified records with the .read commands. See "Using Data from an External Database" in this chapter. After you open a database with the .open or .read command, or by some other means, you don't have to define all the database fields specifically before you can use them in the report. Instead, use the format

```
database.fieldname
```

where *database* is the name of the database and *fieldname* is the name of the field.

You can use the Detailed field definition method to define a new report picture, which specifies the appearance of data, for a field in the associated database. For example, if you defined a decimal field named BALANCE with the Quick field definition method (explained in Chapter 13) and want the output of the field to display in currency format, include the following command in the definitions section of your report form:

```
.define BALANCE using "$NNN,NNN.NN"
```

When Enable processes the report, Enable displays a BALANCE value of 5500.00 as $5,500.00. Be sure that you include enough spaces within the brackets surrounding the field name BALANCE to include the dollar sign and commas.

You can use arrays to define a group of subcategories belonging to one variable. Instead of defining 31 local fields for the days of the month, define one field, with 31 parts as follows:

```
.define DAYS[31] as integer n
```

The .map section command identifies the end of the definitions section and marks the beginning of the part of the report that determines where data prints. The .map section command is not a required command, but dividing the report into the appropriate sections is helpful.

# Creating the Introduction Section

The introduction section follows the definitions section and begins with the .intro command. Enable processes commands in this section before processing any records. Use the introduction area to include a title or a header or footer in your report, or to initialize local variables, such as setting counters to 0. You specify in this section most of the fields that are in your report.

# Creating the Body Section

The .body command begins the portion of the report that processes once for every record in the report. This section is the *body* of the report. If you don't specify any report sections, Enable considers that everything is in the body section.

# Creating the Conclusion Section

The conclusion section begins with the .conclusion command. Enable processes the commands in this section once at the end of the report after processing all the records. This section is a good place to include report summaries such as grand totals.

# Creating the Break Section

You can use breaks to print column headings, to force a page break, insert blank lines or descriptive lines of text, and to calculate summary values.

You can insert breaks in standard columnar reports by using the code {b*n*}, where *n* is the number of the break. A typical break procedure has the following structure:

```
.break nn procedure
    .break on condition or fieldname
```

```
.break heading
.break summary
.break end
```

You can place the break procedure in the .intro section.

The *nn* designates the number of the break procedure (you can have up to 16 breaks per report form). The condition determines when Enable invokes a break. If you use a field name in a break, Enable processes the break heading and summary when the value of the specified field changes from one record to the next.

Enable processes all break headings once before processing the body for the first record. When a break is triggered, Enable processes its break summary, using data from the record that caused the break, and then processes its break heading, using data from the next record. Only then does Enable process the body again. When the conditions that trigger more than one break occur at the same time, Enable first processes the break summary with the highest break number. Break headings are processed in reverse order, from lowest to highest break number.

**TIP**

> If you include a break or several breaks in your reports, be sure to sort the database in the same order as you designed the break procedures before you run the report.

# Using Conditional Processing

If you want a report to perform a certain calculation or take some other action based on the value of one or more fields in the database, Enable's Procedural Language has two programming constructions you can use: the .if and the .do case commands.

With the .if command, you can design reports that take one of several paths depending on the values in your database. The .if command uses the following format:

```
.if condition1
   (command(s))
   .elseif condition2
       (alternate command(s)
       .else
           (more alternate command(s))
 .endif
```

where *condition1* and *condition2* are expressions that can be evaluated to true or false. If the value of condition1 is true, Enable executes the first set of commands. If the value of condition1 is false, Enable checks the second condition. When the first condition is false and the second condition is true, Enable executes the alternate set of commands that follow the first .elseif command. When both condition1 and condition2 are false, Enable executes the second set of more alternate commands.

> You can use as many .elseif commands as you want; however, a report that "nests" conditional processing too deeply is difficult to follow. Be sure to end each .if construction with the .endif command.

The following example calculates commission (COMMIS) based on the value of sales (SALES) on a graduated scale; it is a typical .if construction:

```
.if SALES<10000
    .let COMMIS=SALES*.01
    .elseif SALES<50000
        .let COMMIS=100+((SALES-10000)*.02)
        .elseif SALES<100000
            .let COMMIS=900+((SALES-50000)*.03)
            .else
                .let COMMIS=2400+((SALES-100000)*.04)
.endif
```

The .do_case construction is often a clearer method than the .if construction to check a series of contingencies, setting forth more explicitly each condition that triggers a distinct action. The normal order of commands is as follows:

```
.do case
    .case condition1
        (command(s))
    .case condition2
        (alternate command(s))
    .case condition3
        (more alternate commands)
.endcase
```

You can express the sales commission example using .do_case as follows:

```
.do case
    .case SALES<10000
```

```
         .let COMMIS=SALES*.01
   .case SALES>=10000 and SALES<50000
         .let COMMIS=100+((SALES-10000)*.02)
   .case SALES>=50000 and SALES<100000
         .let COMMIS=900+((SALES-50000)*.03)
   .case SALES>=100000
         .let COMMIS=2400+((SALES-100000)*.04)
.endcase
```

The .let command assigns a new value to a field. For example, to give a five percent commission only to those salespeople with sales over $100,000, use the .let command in the following way:

```
.if SALES > 100000
    .let COMMIS=SALES*.05
.else
    .let COMMIS=0
.endif
```

You usually use the .let command to assign a value to a locally defined field or to assign a new value to any field in response to a conditional statement. Using the .let command to assign a new value to a field in an existing database is equivalent to typing the value in an input form data-entry space. Enable does not save the value until the .add, .update, or .write command passes it to a database record.

# Using Program Control Commands

A fundamental feature of any programming language is the capability of controlling the sequence of program execution. Enable's Procedural Language has a number of commands you can use to control the order of command processing in the report.

## Creating Branches

You may want the processing of the report to move or skip over a particular section of commands. First, use the .label command to label in the report the line to which processing should jump. Use the following format:

```
.label labelname
```

The label name must be a single word and cannot contain spaces or punctuation marks; however, a label name can include the underline character. Use a descriptive name to make the program easier to follow and understand.

Use the .goto command to cause processing to branch to the labeled line. The syntax of the .goto command is as follows:

```
.goto labelname
```

You use the .goto command most often in a conditional statement, where it redirects the processing depending on whether the .if condition is true or false. Here is an example:

```
.read DATABASE first LINKFIELD1 = LINKFIELD2
.label loop
.if SYS:RECORD = 0
    .goto end_loop
.endif
(commands)
.read DATABASE next LINKFIELD1 = LINKFIELD2
.goto loop
.label end_loop
(more commands)
```

When SYS:RECORD is not equal to zero, Enable repeatedly processes the commands between the loop label and the end_loop label. When SYS:RECORD is equal to zero, Enable skips those commands, branching out of the loop.

## Creating Loops

Use the .while and .endwhile commands to cause Enable to execute a group of commands repeatedly as long as a stated condition is true. This construction is clearer than using multiple .goto commands to create a loop. The normal order of commands is as follows:

```
.while condition
    (commands to be repeated)
.endwhile
```

You can use the .while command to rewrite the .goto loop described in the preceding section as follows:

```
.read DATABASE first LINKFIELD1 = LINKFIELD2
.while SYS:RECORD<>0
```

```
    (commands)
    .read DATABASE next LINKFIELD1 = LINKFIELD2
.endwhile
(more commands)
```

# Calling Subroutines

The .subroutines command identifies the beginning of the subroutine section of the report. This section appears at the end of the report and contains one or more blocks of commands, called *subroutines*, that the Procedural Language program executes many times.

A subroutine helps divide a large report into smaller segments that you can write, read, and manage. Each subroutine contains lines of code that the report uses again and again. Instead of rewriting the same lines of code, you write the code once, name your subroutine with the .label command, and call the section of code when you need it by referring to the label.

To direct processing to the subroutine, use the following format:

```
.gosub labelname
```

The processing of the report jumps to the label name and Enable executes the lines in the subroutine. When Enable encounters the .return command, processing returns to the line immediately after the .gosub command that called the subroutine.

You can have as many subroutines as necessary. Each subroutine must begin with the .label command and end with the .return command. Use the following format:

```
.subroutines
    .label ROUTINE1
        (commands)
    .return
    .label ROUTINE2
        (commands)
    .return
    .label ROUTINE3
        (commands)
    .return
```

For example, to call a subroutine that calculates sales commission (COMMIS) based on total sales (SALES), you can use the following command sequence:

```
.intro
    (introduction)
.body
    (commands)
.gosub get_commission
    (more commands)
.conclusion
    (conclusion)
;;
.subroutines
;;
.label get_commission
    .do case
        .case SALES<10000
            .let COMMIS=SALES*.01
        .case SALES>=10000 and SALES<50000
            .let COMMIS=100+((SALES-10000)*.02)
        .case SALES>=50000 and SALES<100000
            .let COMMIS=900+((SALES-50000)*.03)
        .case SALES>=100000
            .let COMMIS=2400+((SALES-100000)*.04)
    .endcase
.return
```

# Calling Procedures

Whenever you find that two or more reports have sections that do the same thing, you can replace these sections with a .perform command that calls a Procedural Language report containing the common procedure. Portions of reports that print data, however, cannot be handled through a procedure.

A procedure, called a *perform file* in Enable's documentation, is similar to a subroutine. A subroutine always must appear in the report that calls it; a procedure (perform file), however, is a separate file on the disk.

Use the following syntax to call a procedure:

```
.perform filename VAR1 VAR2 VAR3 ... VAR9
```

where *filename* is the name of a the procedure file and VAR1 through VAR9 are variables. The variables are represented in the procedure by %1 through %9 and are referred to as *replaceable variables*. When Enable processes the procedure commands, processing returns to the line immediately after the calling line.

If you convert the subroutine in the preceding section to a procedure file with replaceable variables, it looks like the following:

```
.do case
     .case SALES<%1
           .let COMMIS=SALES*%2
     .case SALES>=%1 and SALES<%3
           .let COMMIS=%1*%2$pl(SALES-%1)*%4
     .case SALES>=%3 and SALES<%5
           .let COMMIS=%1*%2$pl(%3-%1)*%4$pl(SALES-%3)*%6
     .case SALES>=%5
           .let COMMIS=%1*%2$pl(%3-%1)*%4$pl(%5-
%3)*%6$pl(SALES-%5)*%7
     .endcase
```

If you give this procedure the file name COMMIS.WPF, you can duplicate the effect of the subroutine with the command

```
.perform COMMIS.WPF 10000 .01 50000 .02 10000 .03 .04
```

You can use this COMMIS procedure in more than one report. Changing the values of the variables changes the commission scale.

**TIP** You don't need to include section commands (.intro, .body, .conclusion) in a procedure because they have no effect.

## Executing Keystrokes

Use the .macro command to execute keystrokes during the report processing. The syntax for the command is as follows:

```
.macro macrocodes
```

where *macrocodes* are the macro codes for the desired keystrokes (see Chapter 4 for Enable's macro codes). Enable replaces field names enclosed in brackets with the current value of the field and executes Procedural Language commands enclosed in brackets.

## Terminating the Report

Use the .exit command to terminate a report before it would normally finish processing. You use this command most often with an .if or .do case construct to abort processing when an error condition occurs.

# Accepting User Interaction

Normally, you use an input form and the Add command to enter the majority of data in your database. Sometimes, however, user input is necessary during report processing. For example, you may want the person running the report to enter a user name so that it can be used within the report (in a line such as `Prepared by User Name`). The .input and .getchar commands give you the capability to accept user input. Use the .escape_off command to prevent the user from terminating a report by pressing the Esc key. These commands usually are placed in the .intro section.

The .input command gives you a method for accepting input from the user during report processing. This command prompts you to enter data directly into a local field. You can specify a message to display at the bottom of the screen next to the data entry space. Use the following syntax

```
.input "message" FIELDNAME
```

where *message* is text and *FIELDNAME* is the field that holds the data.

Use the .getchar statement to pause processing of the report until you press a key. When you press any key, the report continues, but Enable stores the key's scan code value in the variable called *sys:1char*. Enable/OA's DBMS documentation lists scan codes. This command differs from .input in that no data is written to a local variable and no message displays in the status line.

To prevent the user from terminating the report by pressing the Esc key, use the .escape_off command. You can reactivate the Esc key with the .escape_on command. The syntax of these commands is simply

```
.escape off
.escape on
```

# Manipulating Data

Procedural Language reports have the capability to manipulate data directly in database files—a major advantage over standard columnar reports. You can use columnar reports to generate summary computations—sum, average, maximum, and so on—but you cannot use them to store these computations for future reference.

You can use the Procedural Language commands discussed in this section to pass the results of calculations to fields in existing records of the associated database and other database files and to create new records.

# Using Data from an External Database

A database that is not the associated database is called an *external database*. Other discussions in the DBMS part of this book have referred to external fields and files as well. The concept here is the same. To access data in an external file during a report, you need to use one or more of the commands discussed in this section.

To open the external database named DATABASE, use the following command:

```
.open DATABASE
```

Enable finds the file and prepares to read it.

The .read command tells Enable to read a record from the database. If the file has not yet been opened, Enable finds it, opens the database, and reads the record specified in the command. You can specify the record to be read by constructing a search criterion within the .read command. If you don't specify a criterion, Enable reads the next available record in SYS:RECORD order.

The syntax for the .read command is as follows:

```
.read DATABASE first search_criteria
.read DATABASE next search_criteria
.read DATABASE prior search_criteria
```

When Enable reads a record, it positions a pointer at the first, next, or prior record in the database that matches the search criterion. Enable makes all the fields in that record available for use in the report. The search criterion operates in the same way and with the same available operators as the Where line in a DBMS command screen, but your report has access to one record at a time, not a group of records. You can use the same operators and wild cards available in a Where line for the search criteria.

**TIP**

Enable sets the SYS:RECORD fields to the value zero when it finds no match in a .read search. Your report therefore can use the .if or .do case construction to read and process records until SYS:RECORD = 0.

You also can instruct Enable to read records in index file order. As with DBMS commands, this method is faster than using a normal search statement, which is equivalent to a Where clause.

Use the syntax

```
.read DATABASE index FIELDNAME = expression
```

or

```
.read DATABASE index FIELDNAME >= expression
```

When you use the > = operator, Enable stops at a match or at the first record greater than the criterion expression if no exact match exists. Subsequent .read commands, such as

```
.read DATABASE next
```

access the database in index file order.

> You need to specify a search criterion for an indexed search, but if you want to step through the entire database in index order, begin with the command
>
> ```
> .read DATABASE index FIELDNAME = "$"
> ```
>
> **Each time you need to read another record, use the command**
>
> ```
> .read DATABASE next
> ```

Enable/OA also has a .position command that you can use to locate data. You use this command with the .read command to determine whether Enable reads records in record-order sequence or in index-order sequence. The syntax for the record-order sequence is as follows:

```
.position DATABASE seq SYS:RECORD = expression
```

The next .read command, for example,

```
.read DATABASE next
```

reads the record with the next SYS:RECORD number in order.

The syntax to use the .position command for sequencing in index order is as follows:

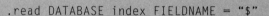

```
.position DATABASE index = FIELDNAME SYS:RECORD = expression
```

Subsequent .read commands read the records in the order of the *FIELDNAME*'s index file.

When you close a DBMS window, Enable automatically closes all opened DATABASE files in the window. To close a particular file to ensure that it's written to disk, and to free RAM without closing the window, issue the following command:

```
.close DATABASE
```

## Writing Data to a Database File

The .add command adds the current field values of the specified database to the end of the database as a new record. The Procedural Language .add command has the same effect the DBMS Add command has if you enter the data into an input form, and then save the record. Use the following syntax

```
.add DATABASE
```

The .update command changes the values of the fields in the current record of the specified database. The .update command is equivalent to the DBMS Edit command. The syntax is as follows:

```
.update DATABASE
```

The .write command is a combination of the .add and .update commands. This command first compares the value of SYS:RECORD to zero to see whether any previously executed .read command found a match. If the command finds no match (SYS:RECORD=0), Enable adds a new record to the database. Otherwise, the .write command updates the fields in the current record. The syntax is as follows:

```
.write DATABASE
```

# Using Procedural Language in Input Form Macros

You can use Procedural Language commands in input form macros. You must enclose each command in brackets ([ ]). You have a limit of 135 characters in each input form macro, and you cannot print these macros. You can eliminate both of these drawbacks when you use the .perform command to call a procedure in another file.

If, in some input form macros, you combine regular macro codes with Procedural Language commands, be sure to enclose the macro codes in brackets. Inside the brackets, precede the macro codes with the .macro command. Otherwise, all macro codes outside the brackets execute after any Procedural Language commands execute.

# Using Procedural Language in DBMS Command Screens

You can use Procedural Language commands in any DBMS command screen that has a Where line or a Fields line. Type the desired command in the command screen line and press Enter. For example, you can create a temporary field FULLNAME from two existing fields, FIRST and LAST, by typing the following .define command on a Where line or a Fields line:

```
.define FULLNAME = FIRST&+LAST
```

After you press Enter, Enable displays the message READY in the status line. The Procedural Language command still displays just as you typed it. Enable adds the FULLNAME field to the list of available fields.

Be sure to delete the Procedural Language command before you press Enter again or Enable creates another new field with the same name. Press Alt-F3 to delete the line, and then continue as usual with the command screen.

# Using Advanced Commands

As explained at the beginning of this chapter, programming is beyond the scope of this book. For those readers interested in more advanced commands, however, additional Procedural Language commands are available. Table 15.1 lists these commands along with a brief explanation.

**Table 15.1**
**Advanced Programming Commands**

| Command | Meaning |
|---|---|
| *LAN commands:* | |
| .autolock | Activates record locking in a specified database |
| .noautolock | Removes record locking on a specified database |
| .lockwait | Locks a specified record and protects it from update |
| .unlock | Removes the lock from a record previously locked with .lockwait |
| *Diagnostic commands:* | |
| .echo on | Placed at the beginning of a report, displays or prints commands as the report is run |
| .echo off | Turns off the display of report commands |
| .debug on | Turns on Enable's Interactive Report Debugger |
| .debug off | Turns off Enable's Interactive Report Debugger |
| .debug break | When you use this command, you can press Ctrl-Break to activate Enable's Interactive Report Debugger |
| *Screen Commands:* | |
| .maxscreen | Gives you access to the full 22 lines of the screen |
| .screenpos | Controls the placement of fields on the screen |
| .clrscreen | Clears a specified portion (all or part) of the screen |
| .clrmouse | Clears a rectangular area, defined by .setmouse, on which you click the mouse during report execution |
| .setmouse | Specifies row and column coordinates that define an area on which you click the mouse during reporting |

| Command | Meaning |
|---------|---------|
| .status | Displays specified information on the line above the status line |
| .color | Assigns character and background colors to the screen |

*Memo Field Commands:*

| Command | Meaning |
|---------|---------|
| .mconcat | Concatenates two memo fields or string statements to create a new memo field |
| .mshiftl | Removes a specified number of characters from the *beginning* of a memo field and places them in a second memo field |
| .mshiftr | Removes a specified number of characters from the *end* of a memo field and places them in a second memo field |
| .mtriml | Removes blank spaces from the *beginning* of a specified memo field and places the result in a second memo field |
| .mtrimr | Removes blank spaces from the *end* of a specified memo field and places the result in a second memo field |

*Executing DOS commands:*

| Command | Meaning |
|---------|---------|
| .exec_dos | Temporarily halts the reporting process and exits to DOS; type **exit** to return to reporting; if you add a DOS statement to the command, Enable temporarily halts reporting to execute the command, and then returns to the report processing |

*Input Form Commands:*

| Command | Meaning |
|---------|---------|
| .error | Used on Add/Edit macros to display a system error message during processing |
| .passthru on | Sends changes made to an external field back to the lookup field in the linked database |
| .passthru off | If you use this command, Enable cannot pass changes back to the linked database |

# Using Mail Merge

When you use mail merge, you use a database (usually a mailing list) to convert form letters into letters that appear to be individually typed. Although the largest portion of the letter repeats, the address block, salutation, and perhaps small portions of the body of the letter change from letter to letter.

To use mail merge in Enable, use the form letter as a Procedural Language report. The variable portions are fields in the associated database. Type the field names in brackets at the proper position in the word processing letter.

To assist Enable users who want to use mail merge but who don't want to become DBMS experts, a generic mail-merge letter, mail-merge database, and mailing label form are distributed with Enable/OA. After installation, Enable stores these files in the specified data directory or in the \EN400 directory. Copy the following files to your default data disk directory:

| File Name | Purpose |
| --- | --- |
| MAIL.$BF | Mailing list database definition |
| MAIL.DBF | Mailing list database data |
| MAILIN.$IF | Input form for mailing list |
| LETTER.TSG | Sample mail-merge letter |
| LABEL.TSG | Sample mailing label form |

You can treat these files as normal database, input form, and report form files, and use them through a DBMS window. You also can access these files through the Main Menu. To get to the Mail Merge menu from the Main Menu, press

Use_System **M**ail_merge

Enable displays the screen shown in figure 15.1.

## Building the Mailing List

To add records to the mailing list database, MAIL, access the Mail Merge menu and press Build_**DB**. Choose the MAIL database at the Open File dialog box and press Enter. Choose MAILIN as the input form name and press Enter. Enable displays the input form shown in figure 15.2. If this generic database does not have the fields you need, refer to Chapter 13,

"Understanding Database Management System Basics," and Chapter 14, "Using Database Management System Power Features," for instructions on changing the database definition and input form.

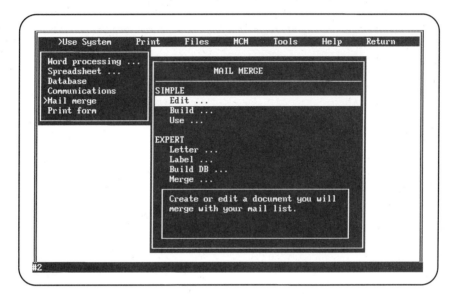

**Fig. 15.1.** *The Mail Merge menu.*

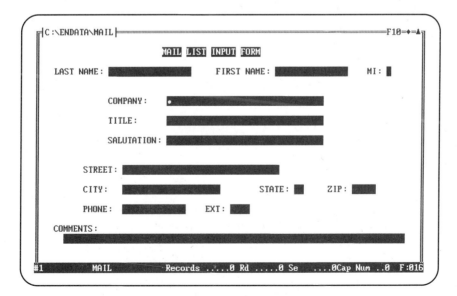

**Fig. 15.2.** *The Mail List Input form.*

Enter your mailing list record in the blanks. Press F5 to save the record and to go to the next screen. After you enter and save all your records, press Alt-End to return to the Main Menu.

# Creating and Revising a Letter

The easiest way to create a mail-merge letter is to start with the generic template or model letter, and then customize it as necessary. First, copy the file LETTER.TSG to a new file name (use the file name extension WPF) and access it for customization from the Mail Merge menu by pressing

Letter

Select the file name and press Enter. Enable opens a word processing window and displays the generic form letter (see fig. 15.3). Because this letter is a Procedural Language report form designed to work with the MAIL database, it contains many Procedural Language commands—all the commands that begin with dots (.).

```
┌─C:\ENDATA\NEWLTR.WPF────────────────────────────────F10─♦─▲─┐
 L──────────────────────────────┼─────────────────────────R
 .body                                                        ¶
                                                             ¶
                                                             ¶
                                                             ¶
                                                             ¶
                                                             ¶
                                                             ¶
 .reformat on                                                ¶
 .if initial=" "                                             ¶
 [FIRSTNAME] [LASTNAME]                                      ¶
 .else                                                       ¶
 [FIRSTNAME] [INITIAL]. [LASTNAME]                           ¶
 .endif                                                      ¶
 .if title>" "                                               ¶
 [TITLE]                                                     ¶
 .endif                                                      ¶
 .if company=" "                                             ¶
 [STREET]                                                    ¶
 [CITY], [STATE{2}]  [ZIP]                                   ¶
                                                             ¶
 .else                                                       ¶
 [COMPANY]                                                   ¶
 #2    REF/B              DRAFT          Cap Num L00001C001
```

*Fig. 15.3. The model mail-merge letter.*

Because this report form is a template, you must modify the form to use it. Before you make any changes to this letter, however, you may want to review the effect of the Procedural Language commands contained in it. The first six blank lines below the .body command create six blank lines at the top of each letter. This space is for your return address block; you type the return address into this area. The lines from the .reformat command down to the third .endif command print the address block of the recipient. Figures 15.3 and 15.4 together show the model form letter. The SALUTATION field prints to the right of Dear. Delete the rest of the model letter (the message box). Next, type the text you want to appear in all the form letters.

```
┌─C:\ENDATA\NEWLTR.WPF────────────────────────────────────F10─◆═▲┐
│[COMPANY]                                                        ¶
│[STREET]                                                         ¶
│[CITY], [STATE{2}]  [ZIP]                                        ¶
│.endif                                                           ¶
│                                                                 ¶
│                                                                 ¶
│                                                                 ¶
│Dear [SALUTATION]:                                               ¶
│                                                                 ¶
│                                                                 ¶
│                                                                 ¶
│                                                                 ¶
│                                                                 ¶
│                 ██████████████████████████████                 ¶
│                 █ Use this document as the starting █           ¶
│                 █ point for creating your mail merge █          ¶
│                 █ letter.   Delete this box before █            ¶
│                 █ creating your letter.            █            ¶
│                 ██████████████████████████████                 ¶
│                                                                 ¶
│                                                                 ¶
│Page Break (User Defined)════════════════════════════════════════
│#2    REF/B                    DRAFT              Cap Num L00022C001
```

*Fig. 15.4. The salutation field of the model mail-merge letter.*

After you make any necessary changes, deletions, and additions, to save the letter press

Alt-F10

To return to the Main Menu, press

Alt-End

# Creating and Revising the Label Layout

The preceding section shows you how to use the LETTER.TSG file as a template or model for a mail-merge letter. This section shows you how to use the LABEL.TSG file as a template or model for a mailing label form. LABEL.TSG is designed to work with the MAIL database.

Copy the file LETTER.TSG to a new file name with the extension WPF. Then, from the Mail Merge menu, press

> Label

Select the file name and press Enter. Enable opens a word processing window and displays the generic label form (see fig. 15.5). As you did with the mail-merge letter, modify this Procedural Language report to fit your needs. Delete the lines between the .intro command and the .body command. Without further modification, this form prints properly on a single column of 1 1/2-inch-by-6-inch labels. Use the word processing multicolumn feature to print labels one up, two up, and so on. Change the length and width settings on the Page form for labels of a different size.

**TIP**

Make sure that you delete any blank lines above the .intro command and below the user-defined page break. A set of double lines, the end-of-file marker, moves up to the user-defined page break marker after you delete all the blank lines below it. Do not introduce any blank lines between the last .endif command and the user-defined page break. Follow these tips to keep proper line spacing on your labels.

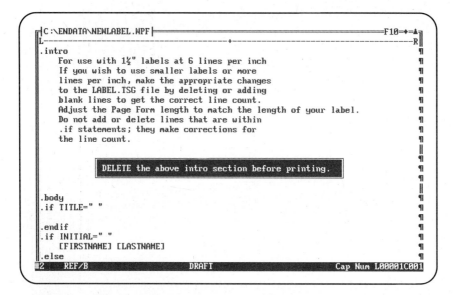

**Fig. 15.5.** *The model mailing label form.*

After you customize the labels form, to save it press

>Alt-F10

To return to the Main Menu, press

>Alt-End

## Printing Letters and Labels

To merge your mailing list data with the form letter, from the Mail Merge menu press

>**Merge**

Choose MAIL as the database and press Enter. Choose the name of the mail-merge letter file you created and press Enter. Enable then displays a Report command screen that is filled in to the Index line.

You can use the Index line as well as the Where line to limit the mail merge only to some of the records in your mailing list. Refer to Chapter 13, for a full discussion of the Index and Where lines.

To print the letter for all records, press Enter at a blank Index line and press **Printer**. Press Enter at the Where line (leaving it blank to print letters for all records). Check the Hardware and Page Setup forms, make sure that your printer is ready, and press Alt-F2. Each record in your MAIL database merges with a separate copy of the form letter. Press Alt-End to return to the Main Menu.

You use the same procedure to print the mailing labels, except enter the file name of the label form when Enable prompts you to enter the name of the letter or label layout.

# Using Structured Query Language (SQL)

Structured Query Language (SQL), new to Enable/OA 4.0, is a language used with relational databases. When you use Enable's Procedural Language, you specify which data is retrieved and how to retrieve it. When you use SQL, however, you specify only the retrieved data.

You must have Expanded Memory Specification (EMS) to use SQL on a DOS-based computer. Because SQL programming is beyond the scope of this book, this section gives you only a brief overview of SQL and how to access it in Enable.

Enable's SQL is based on the standards of the American National Standard for Information Systems (ANSI). SQL is based on the use of a database system, or *dbsystem*, which is equivalent to a database application in Enable. An individual database file in Enable is a *table* in SQL. A personnel dbsystem, for example, can include tables on general information, payroll, insurance, education, and so on. Within each table, a *row* is equivalent to an Enable record and a *column* is equivalent to an Enable field.

Although you can use SQL for ad-hoc queries in its *interactive* form, you also can use it for *embedded* commands in a Procedural Language report.

To access SQL's interactive mode, from the Main Menu choose

> Use_System Database SQL

or from the DBMS Top Line menu choose

> SQL SQL_command_screen

With either method, Enable displays a blank SQL Query Command Screen. Type SQL commands directly on the screen, and then press F5 to execute the statement. You can enter up to 140 characters on one line. Separate multiple statements with a semicolon(;).

To access the SQL Interactive menu, press F10. Enable displays a menu similar to the one shown in figure 15.6. Use this menu to perform simple SQL commands without typing the statements yourself. *Note:* You cannot access all the SQL commands from the menu.

You can use embedded SQL commands on a DBMS Where line or within a Procedural Language report. The .SQL command precedes a single SQL command on the Where line. The command to open a dbsystem called STAFF on the Where line is as follows:

```
.sql connect@STAFF
```

If you are using a multiline SQL statement in a Procedural Language report, precede the statement with EXEC SQL. Specify the end of the SQL statement with a semicolon or the command END-EXEC.

```
EXEC SQL
SELECT FNAME,LNAME,HIREDATE,SALARY FROM EMPLOYEE
WHERE HIREDATE >88/01/01
END EXEC
```

or

```
EXEC SQL
SELECT FNAME,LNAME,HIREDATE,SALARY FROM EMPLOYEE
WHERE HIREDATE >88/01/01;
```

Precede a single line statement embedded in a Procedural Language report by **.SQL**.

For more information on SQL refer to *Using SQL*, by George T. Chou (QUE Corporation, 1990).

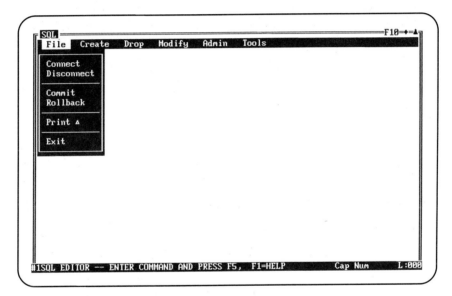

*Fig. 15.6. The SQL Top Line menu.*

# Summary

With the exception of the discussion of mail merge and SQL, this chapter is primarily a Procedural Language command reference, with the commands grouped according to their functions. Although this chapter doesn't teach you how to program, it shows you a few simple examples of how you can use Enable's Procedural Language commands to accomplish typical programming tasks. Keep this chapter in mind as you begin to experiment with custom-designed report forms. Use as many of these commands as you can; it's difficult to understand exactly what the commands accomplish until you actually use them.

# Part VI

# The Graphics Module

# Quick Start VI

# Creating a
# Pie Graph

---

This lesson is the sixth of seven quick-start lessons that appear at the beginning of each part of this book. This lesson provides an overview of Enable's graphics module. In this lesson, you create a pie graph from the spreadsheet you created in Quick Start IV, display the graph on-screen, and print it. To perform this exercise, you first must complete Quick Start IV, and you must use a system with a graphics display and graphics printer. The instructions in this exercise assume that you properly have installed Enable/OA 4.0 and that your screen is at Enable's Main Menu. If not, refer to Appendix A and Quick Start I for information on getting started.

## Creating the Graph

With Enable, you can generate graphs from spreadsheet data and from DBMS data. In this exercise, you use data from the spreadsheet QS4BUDGT.SSF, a simple family budget you created in Quick Start IV that shows income, expenses, and savings. You create a *pie graph* to display as a circle the six categories of expenses listed in the spreadsheet, and to emphasize the relative contribution of each expense item to the total family expenses. You display the largest expense, Rent, as an *exploded* slice of the pie—separated from the rest of the pie as emphasis. The first step is to open the spreadsheet, enter the graphics module, and create the graph by completing the following steps.

1. To open the QS4BUDGT.SSF spreadsheet, press

   **Use_System Spreadsheet**

Enable prompts you for a file name. Type **QS4BUDGT** and press Enter. Enable displays the Family Budget spreadsheet, QS4BUDGT.SSF (see fig. QSVI.1).

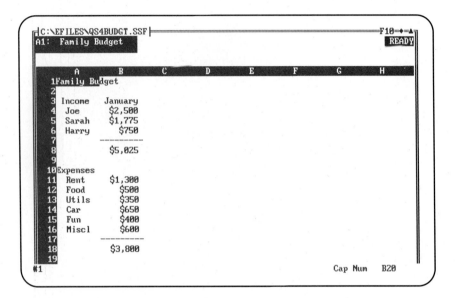

**Fig. QSVI.1** *The Family Budget spreadsheet, QS4BUDGT.SSF.*

2. Access the graphics module to begin creating a graph called PIE. Press

   F10 **Graph Create**

   Enable prompts you for the name of the new graph. Type **PIE** and press Enter. Enable displays the Global Options dialog box (see fig. QSVI.2), which contains all the Global options.

3. To choose the graph-type option Exploded, press the down-arrow key until the *pointer* (highlighted bar indicating your location on-screen) highlights Exploded, and then press Enter. Enable displays an asterisk (*) in front of the option.

4. Specify the data for graphing. Each of the six categories of expenses in the spreadsheet is a data group. You can define up to eight data groups. Press the PgDn key to obtain the Data Group dialog box, in which you enter pertinent information about the data being graphed. To define data group 1, type **B11..B11**—the cell range for

the rent expense—in the appropriate line. To offset the rent expense as the exploded pie slice, press Tab five times to move to the OPTION column. Press an uppercase **E** to indicate "exploded."

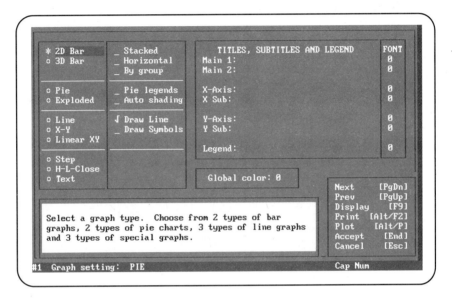

**Fig.** *QSVI.2. The Global Options dialog box.*

To define the second data group, press Shift-Tab to move back to the DATA GROUP DEFINITION column and press Enter. Type **B12..B12**, the cell range for the food expense and press Enter. Repeat these steps to define data groups 3, 4, 5, and 6 as the expenses for utilities, car, fun, and miscellaneous, respectively. Enter the following ranges for each group:

| Data Group | Data Range |
|---|---|
| 1 | **B11..B11** |
| 2 | **B12..B12** |
| 3 | **B13..B13** |
| 4 | **B14..B14** |
| 5 | **B15..B15** |
| 6 | **B16..B16** |

5.  Press F9 to display the graph as it looks so far (see fig. QSVI.3).
    Enable automatically calculates the percentage of the total expenses
    represented by each expense category—that is, each slice of pie.
    Notice that Enable offsets the largest slice of pie, Rent, in the ex-
    ploded pie graph. Press Esc to return to the Global Options dialog
    box after you finish viewing the graph. To retain the graph, press
    the End key to save your work, exit the graphics module, and re-
    turn to the spreadsheet.

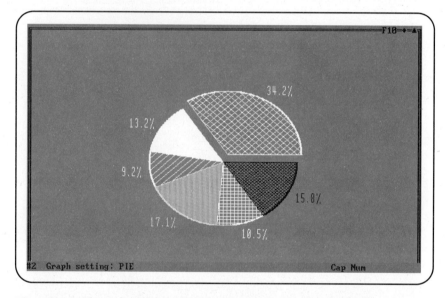

**Fig. QSVI.3.** *The pie graph with graph type and data groups defined.*

# Adding Descriptive Elements

You already have completed the most important steps in generating a graph
with Enable—specifying the graph type and defining the data groups. But
something is missing. You need labels to describe the information shown in
the pie graph. In this section of the lesson, you label the slices, add headings,
and assign special fonts to these descriptive elements.

1.  To return to the graph PIE, press

    F10 **Graph Select**

Move the pointer to the correct graph, and press Enter. Then press Enter twice to choose Edit. Enable returns you to the Global Options dialog box.

2.  You are going to use the expense labels in cells A11..A16 (Rent, Food, Utils, and so on) to label the slices of your pie graph. To specify the labels for each slice, press PgDn twice to display the Format and Layout dialog box (see Chapter 16, "Creating Graphs with Enable," for a detailed description of this dialog box). Press the Tab key twice to move to the X-Axis Data selection in the X-AXIS and TEXT DATA column. Press F7 to display the spreadsheet. Use the arrow keys to move the cell pointer to cell A11, and press the period (.) to anchor the cell range. Use the down-arrow key to move the cell pointer to cell A16. In the line just above your spreadsheet, Enable displays the range A11..A16. Press Enter to accept this data range.

3.  Press F9 to display your work to this point. Enable displays the exploded pie graph with the slices labeled (see fig. QSVI.4). Press Esc to return to the Global Options dialog box.

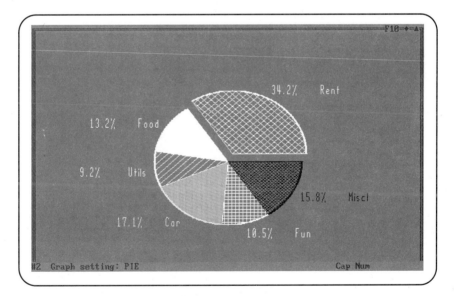

***Fig. QSVI.4.*** *The pie graph with the slices labeled.*

4. Now you are ready to add headings to your graph. You're going to add a main heading, "Monthly Family Expenses," and a main sub-heading, "($3,800)" (the total of all expenses). From the Global Options dialog box, press Tab twice to move to the TITLES, SUBTITLES AND LEGEND column.

To add the main heading, type **Monthly Family Expenses** on the Main_1 line and press Enter. To add the subheading, type **($3,800)** on the Main_2 line and press Enter.

5. Next, you're going to add fonts to these descriptive elements. Press Tab once to move to the FONT column. Press **4_=_Roman2** to choose the font Roman2 for your main heading, and press Enter. Press the down-arrow key once to move to the FONT column for the Main_2 heading. Press **3_=_Roman1** to choose the font Roman1 for your subheading, and press Enter.

Press F9 to display the final product, with headings and fonts added (see fig. QSVI.5). Press Esc to exit the graph, and press End to exit the Global Options dialog box and return to the spreadsheet.

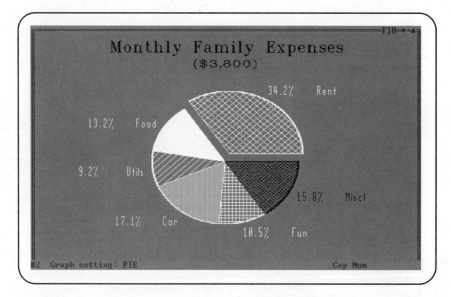

*Fig. QSVI.5. The pie graph with headings and fonts added.*

# Printing the Graph

Now you are ready to print the graph you designed. Before you begin, make sure your printer is on and loaded with paper.

1.  To return to the Global Options dialog box, press

    F10 **G**raph **S**elect

    Use the arrow keys to choose the graph PIE and press Enter. Press Enter two more times to choose Edit and Accept.

2.  To print the graph, press the Tab key five times to move to the Utility menu in the lower right corner. Press **P**rint. Enable prints your graph just like the program displays it on-screen. Press End to return to the spreadsheet.

When you save your spreadsheet, Enable automatically saves the spreadsheet's graphs with it. Because a graph cannot exist without the data upon which it is based, and because that data is part of its corresponding spreadsheet, the graph always is part of the spreadsheet—not a separate file.

3.  To save the graph, press

    Alt-F10

    and then press

    Alt-End

    to return to Enable's Main Menu.

# 16

# Creating Graphs
# with Enable

You often have heard the expression "A picture is worth a thousand words." This saying is particularly true when you need to communicate numeric information to a boardroom full of business people. Graphs bring dry columns of numbers to life. Enable's graph-building capabilities always have been impressive when compared with other spreadsheet and integrated software packages. With Enable, placing these graphs into a word processing file is easy. In addition, Enable/OA has several enhancements, including the capabilities to copy graph settings, plot to a file, and create a different kind of X-Y line graph.

Enable has two separate graph generators—Enable's graphics module, discussed in this chapter, and the spectacular graphics program Perspective Junior, covered in Chapter 17, "Producing Graphs with Perspective Junior." Perspective Junior is an add-in program you can access within Enable/OA. Enable/OA's graphics module can generate vertical bar graphs, pie graphs, line graphs, X-Y graphs, linear fit graphs, open-high-low-close (HLC) graphs, and a new form called a *text graph*. The graphics module also can create vertical bar graphs that appear to have depth. Perspective, however, can generate graphs that appear to be truly three-dimensional. Chapter 17 discusses Enable/OA's capability to import graphics from other programs, including Perspective, into word processing.

To understand Enable graphics, you need to become familiar with the graphics menu system. More than any other Enable module, graphics relies on dialog box choices. Some of these choices work in conjunction with others. For example, you may choose a graph option with one choice, but to activate the option, you need to choose from another dialog box. This combination of choices may seem complicated at first. After you understand the procedures, however, you have the capability to create graphs that please you and your audience.

# Understanding Spreadsheet and DBMS Graphics

You can generate graphs from the spreadsheet module and the database management system modules. The capabilities of the graphics module are the same wherever the data is stored, but the graph settings created by the graphics module are stored in different locations. When you generate a graph from spreadsheet data, Enable stores the graph settings along with the spreadsheet file on the disk. When you generate a graph from data in a database file, however, Enable creates a separate file on the disk to hold the graph settings. With a database, therefore, you need to be sure that the database file and the corresponding graph settings file do not get separated. The graph settings file must be on your data disk or directory before you can use this file.

# Understanding the Graphics Dialog Boxes

The dialog box is the only way to operate in Enable's graphics module. Figures 16.1-16.5 represent the five dialog boxes that control the graphics module. These dialog boxes always appear in the order presented here. Enable's documentation refers to all these screens as the *graph design form*. This chapter refers to them as follows:

- *The Current Settings dialog box* holds all the current graph settings (see fig. 16.1).

- *The Global dialog box* holds all the global graphics options (see fig. 16.2).

- *The Data Groups dialog box* holds the data group options (see fig. 16.3).

- *The Format and Layout dialog box* holds the formatting and layout options (see fig. 16.4).

- *The Device dialog box* holds all the options for printing or plotting (see fig. 16.5).

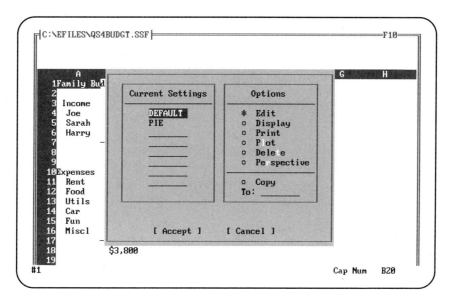

**Fig. 16.1.** *The Current Settings dialog box.*

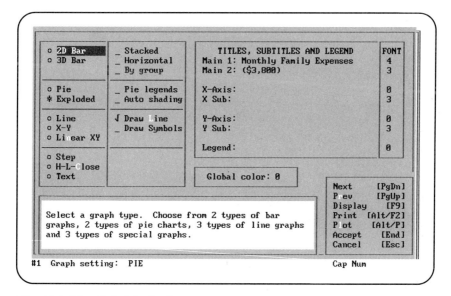

**Fig. 16.2.** *The Global dialog box.*

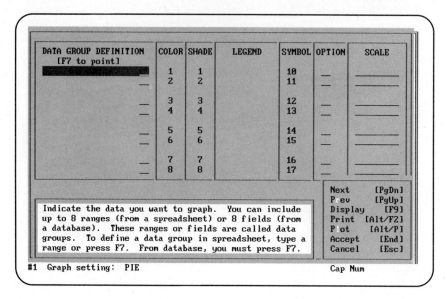

*Fig. 16.3. The Data Groups dialog box.*

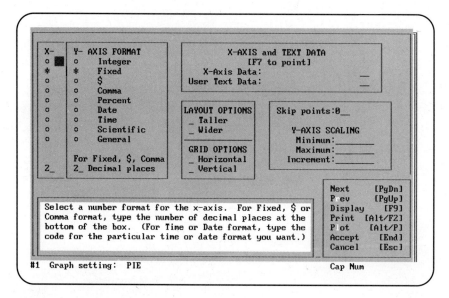

*Fig. 16.4. The Format and Layout dialog box.*

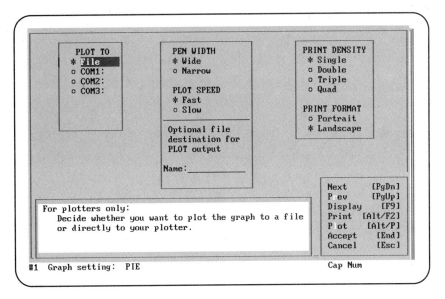

**Fig. 16.5.** *The Device dialog box.*

To access these dialog boxes from a spreadsheet, first press

F10 Graph

Enable displays the pull-down menu shown in figure 16.6. To create a new graph setting, type **Create**. Enable then prompts you for the name of the new graph. Press Enter. To select a previously established graph setting, type **Select**. Enable displays the first dialog box, the Current Settings dialog box. Use the arrow keys to highlight the graph you want and press Enter to select it.

To display the Graphics dialog boxes in a DBMS window, select Graph from the DBMS Top Line menu, or press

F9 Command Graph

Enable prompts

    Enter the name of the graph settings file:

Type the same name as your database, so that you can remember the file name easily. Enable assigns the file name extension GRF. After you press Enter, Enable displays the Current Settings dialog box. Select an existing graph name, or move to a blank line and type a new name. Press Enter.

From this point on, the only aspect of creating the graph that differs between the spreadsheet and the database is selecting the data groups.

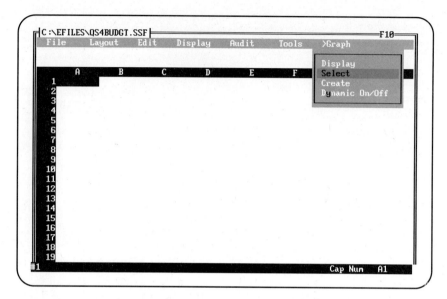

***Fig. 16.6.** The Graph pull-down menu.*

You can delete a graph setting only from the Current Settings dialog box (see figure 16.1). Use the arrow keys and the Enter key to select the name of the graph you want to delete. A greater than sign (>) appears in front of the selected graph name. Use the arrow keys and the Enter key to choose the Delete option. An asterisk (*) appears in front of the option. Press Enter to accept these actions. Enable prompts you to verify the deletion; press Enter to continue.

Enable/OA can copy a graph setting so that you do not have to start from scratch. To copy an existing graph setting, you need to be in the Current Settings dialog box (see figure 16.1). Use the arrow keys and the Enter key to select the graph setting to copy. A greater than sign (>) appears in front of the selected graph name. Use the arrow keys and the Enter key to choose the Copy option. An asterisk (*) appears in front of the option. At the To: prompt, type the name of the new graph setting. Press Enter. Press Enter again to accept these settings and create a new graph that has all the selections of the graph setting you copied.

You are now in the second dialog box of the graphics module, the Global dialog box. The following sections explain how to continue without getting lost.

# Selecting Essential Elements of an Enable Graph

Enable needs two pieces of information before displaying a graph: a *graph type* (vertical bar, pie, X-Y, and so on) and one or more *data groups* to graph. The other settings are important, but secondary. The next two sections explain these two crucial graph elements.

## Selecting the Graph Type

The graph type is an essential element of every Enable graph. You see an area for selecting the graph type in the upper left corner of the dialog box. To choose a graph type, use the arrow keys to highlight a graph type from the following choices:

- **2D Bar** or **3D Bar.** Enable has four kinds of vertical bar graphs: two-dimensional standard-bar, three-dimensional standard-bar, two-dimensional stacked-bar, and three-dimensional stacked-bar. Enable also offers these four graph styles in a new horizontal fashion as well as the vertical format.

  All vertical and horizontal standard-bar graphs can display data by set, which is the default viewing mode (see fig. 16.7) or by group (see fig. 16.8). Figure 16.9 shows the same data in a two-dimensional vertical or horizontal stacked-bar graph.

- **Pie** or **Exploded.** Enable has two types of pie graphs: standard and exploded. Standard is the default when you choose the pie graph. An *exploded* pie graph has one or more pieces moved away from the whole. Choosing **Exploded** does not by itself separate the pieces of the pie. You also must specify in the corresponding Data Group dialog box which piece or pieces to explode.

  The pie graph you create in the quick-start lesson uses x-axis data to label the slices of the pie. This option is the default. You also can choose **Pie_legends**; however, you must specify the legend for each data group from the Data Group dialog box.

  Enable automatically assigns a different shading pattern and color to each data group (up to eight) when the graph displays. Leave the **Auto_Shading** setting off to control which shading patterns and colors Enable assigns to which areas. Turn the setting on only for automatic assignment of colors as well as shading.

- **Line.** A line graph uses lines, symbols, or both to show the data's trends over time. The default line graph uses lines only. The lines go through the data points specified in the Data Group dialog box. The same data graphed as vertical bars in figures 16.7, 16.8, and 16.9 shows as a line graph in figure 16.10. To display symbols at the graphed points, highlight Draw_Symbols and press Enter. A check mark appears in front of the Draw_Symbols option to indicate that the option is active.

- **X-Y.** An X-Y graph also displays lines, but instead of showing trends over time, it shows the correlation between the rise or fall of one category of data to the rise or fall of some related data category. For example, the spreadsheet shown in figure 16.11 shows the average number of widgets sold per month at various prices. When you choose **X-Y,** Enable connects the data points with a line. The X-Y graph in figure 16.12 shows the relationship between the price of widgets and sales by Hyperion Widgets Corp. This graph also shows symbols (the open squares at each point on the graph) used with a line. The y-axis has been scaled to show only the range 60-75.

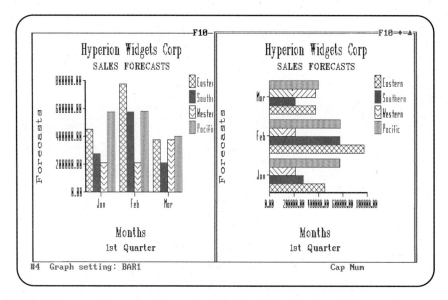

**Fig. 16.7.** *A two-dimensional vertical and horizontal standard-bar graph displaying data by set.*

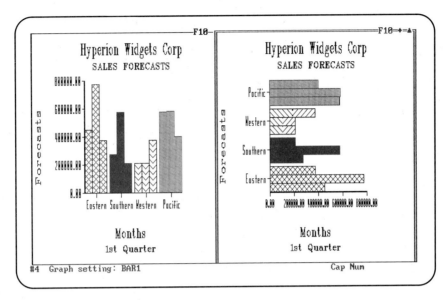

**Fig. 16.8.** *A two-dimensional vertical and horizontal standard-bar graph displaying data by group.*

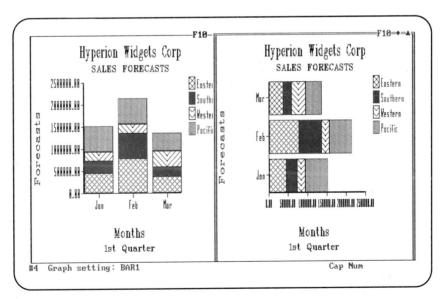

**Fig. 16.9.** *A two-dimensional vertical and horizontal stacked-bar graph.*

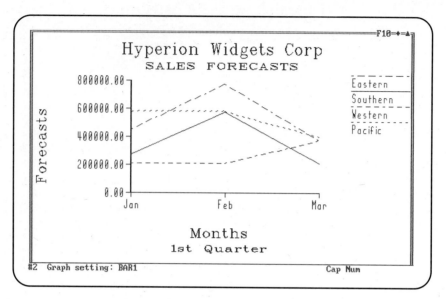

*Fig. 16.10. A line graph.*

| | A | B | C | D | E |
|---|---|---|---|---|---|
| 1 | PRICE | AVG MONTHLY SALES (K WIDGETS) | | | |
| 2 | $22.50 | 73 | | | |
| 3 | $23.00 | 70 | | | |
| 4 | $26.00 | 69 | | | |
| 5 | $30.00 | 65 | | | |
| 6 | $32.00 | 66 | | | |

C:\EFILES\WIDGET.SSF     F10=◆=▲
B2:   (C)  73     READY

#1     Cap Num    B6

*Fig. 16.11. Spreadsheet to correlate price with average monthly sales, in thousands of widgets.*

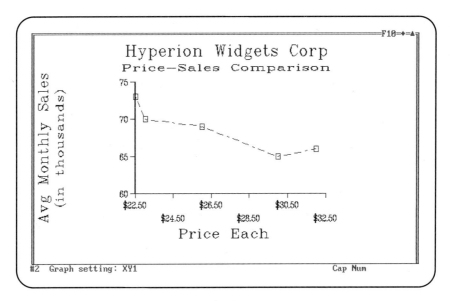

**Fig. 16.12.** *An X-Y graph connecting the data points.*

- **Linear_XY.** This option uses the *least-squares linear fit* method to draw a straight line between the points, but without necessarily connecting them. The graph in figure 16.13 uses the same data as the graph in figure 16.12, but was drawn with the Linear_XY option.

- **Step.** This option is based on the same principal as the line graphs. Instead of showing a straight line between points, this graph shows each point as a "step" from the preceding one. Figure 16.14 shows the Hyperion Widget sales data drawn as a step graph.

- **H-L-Close.** The open-high-low-close graph shows daily opening, high, low, and closing market prices. Figure 16.16 graphs the prices listed in figure 16.15.

After you highlight a graph type, press Enter to make the selection.

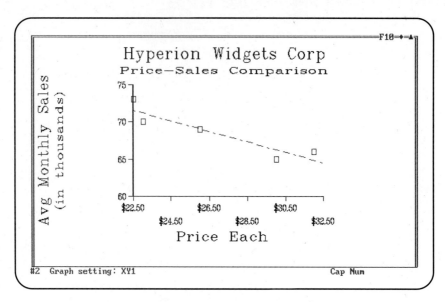

**Fig. 16.13.** *An X-Y graph using least-squares linear fit.*

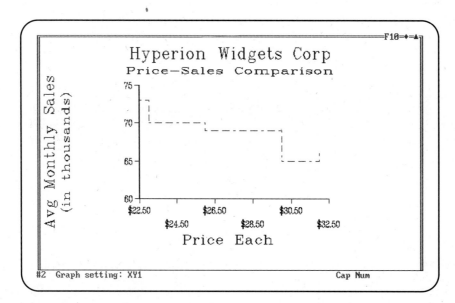

**Fig. 16.14.** *A step graph.*

```
┌┤C:\EFILES\WIDGET.SSF├══════════════════════════════════════F10=◆=▲┐
│A1:  Hyperion                                                  READY │
│                                                                     │
│          A          B          C          D          E        F     │
│   1  Hyperion    03-Oct-90  04-Oct-90  05-Oct-90  06-Oct-90         │
│   2 ----------------------------------------------------------------│
│   3      Open     $12.45     $13.00     $12.50     $13.50           │
│   4      High     $13.15     $13.50     $14.00     $14.25           │
│   5      Low      $12.40     $12.10     $12.50     $13.50           │
│   6      Close    $13.00     $12.50     $13.50     $14.00           │
│   7                                                                 │
│   8                                                                 │
│   9                                                                 │
│  10                                                                 │
│  11                                                                 │
│  12                                                                 │
│  13                                                                 │
│  14                                                                 │
│  15                                                                 │
│  16                                                                 │
│  17                                                                 │
│  18                                                                 │
│  19                                                                 │
│#1                                              Cap Num    E6        │
└─────────────────────────────────────────────────────────────────────┘
```

**Fig. 16.15.** *A spreadsheet showing stock quotes for four days.*

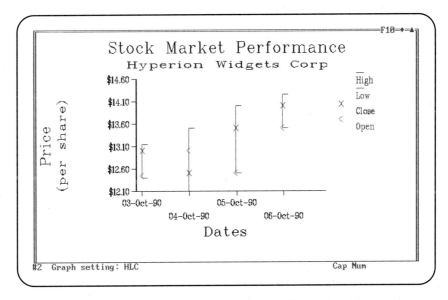

**Fig. 16.16.** *An HLC graph showing stock market performance of one stock over a four-day period.*

# Assigning Data Groups

The other graph element you need to define is the data. For the program to build vertical bars, cut pie slices, or draw lines, you must provide the numbers through the Data Group dialog box. To call up the Data Group dialog box, press PgDn from the Global dialog box. You can list up to eight data groups in the Data Group dialog box.

Enable generates all graph types except the pie graph in a two-dimensional coordinate system with an x-axis (horizontal) and a y-axis (vertical). For convenience, Enable keeps this terminology even when you specify data for a pie graph. Enable treats the slices of a pie graph as y-axis data and treats the words that label each slice as x-axis data.

You can assign only y-axis data, including data for the slices of a pie, through the Data Group dialog box. This data is always numeric. To assign x-axis data, access the X-Axis Data option from the Format and Layout dialog box. X-axis data is almost always text—the only exception is x-axis data for the X-Y graph, which is always numeric.

Most people naturally arrange data in clearly labeled columns and rows. WIDGET.SSF, shown in figure 16.17, and WIDGET.SS, shown in figure 16.18, are examples. The numbers in such tables become y-axis data, and the labels become x-axis data.

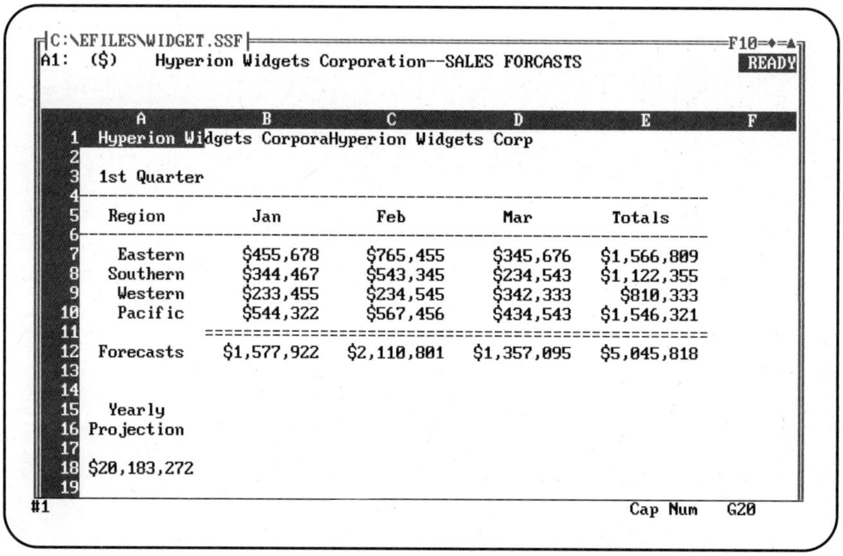

```
┌C:\EFILES\WIDGET.SSF├──────────────────────────────────────F10=◆=▲┐
│A1:  ($)    Hyperion Widgets Corporation--SALES FORCASTS      READY│
│                                                                    │
│        A           B           C           D           E       F   │
│  1  Hyperion Widgets CorporaHyperion Widgets Corp                 │
│  2                                                                 │
│  3  1st Quarter                                                    │
│  4 ──────────────────────────────────────────────────────────────│
│  5  Region      Jan         Feb         Mar         Totals        │
│  6 ──────────────────────────────────────────────────────────────│
│  7  Eastern    $455,678    $765,455    $345,676    $1,566,809     │
│  8  Southern   $344,467    $543,345    $234,543    $1,122,355     │
│  9  Western    $233,455    $234,545    $342,333      $810,333     │
│ 10  Pacific    $544,322    $567,456    $434,543    $1,546,321     │
│ 11             ====================================================│
│ 12  Forecasts  $1,577,922  $2,110,801  $1,357,095  $5,045,818     │
│ 13                                                                │
│ 14                                                                │
│ 15  Yearly                                                        │
│ 16 Projection                                                     │
│ 17                                                                │
│ 18 $20,183,272                                                    │
│ 19                                                                │
│#1                                              Cap Num   G20      │
└──────────────────────────────────────────────────────────────────┘
```

*Fig. 16.17. A spreadsheet, WIDGET.SSF, with data for creating graphs.*

To compare graphically the data from one row to the data in the other rows, define the data in each row as a separate data group (y-axis data). The first row then becomes data group 1, the second row becomes data group 2, and so on. The column that contains the row labels is the x-axis data. To compare the columns, define the numbers in each column as a data group, and define the column labels as the x-axis data.

Enable can create a graph from a spreadsheet or from a database. The procedures for assigning data groups are different, depending on the data source, but the concepts are the same.

```
┌─C:\EFILES\WIDGET────────────────────────────────────F10=◆=▲┐
│REGION....... DISTRICT.. MONTH ....FORECAST                  │
│Eastern      Alpha      FEB       $277,582                   │
│Eastern      Alpha      JAN       $123,421                   │
│Eastern      Alpha      MAR        $88,049                   │
│Eastern      Beta       FEB       $197,037                   │
│Eastern      Beta       JAN       $104,556                   │
│Eastern      Beta       MAR        $59,742                   │
│Eastern      Delta      FEB       $205,780                   │
│Eastern      Delta      JAN       $115,356                   │
│Eastern      Delta      MAR       $110,685                   │
│Pacific      Alpha      FEB       $205,780                   │
│Pacific      Alpha      JAN       $157,191                   │
│Pacific      Alpha      MAR       $110,685                   │
│Pacific      Beta       FEB       $146,069                   │
│Pacific      Beta       JAN       $118,827                   │
│Pacific      Beta       MAR        $75,100                   │
│Pacific      Delta      FEB       $152,551                   │
│Pacific      Delta      JAN       $187,770                   │
│Pacific      Delta      MAR       $871,985                   │
│                                                             │
│                                                             │
║ Use cursor keys to page through display.  Press ESC when done.║
║#1         WIDGET.SS      Records ....18 Rd ....18 Sel ....18Cap Num ..1  D:000║
```

**Fig. 16.18.** *A database, WIDGET.SS (select set from WIDGET.DBF), with data for creating graphs.*

## Assigning Data Groups in a Spreadsheet

Assign data groups in the same order as the rows or columns appear in the spreadsheet. In the WIDGET.SSF spreadsheet shown in figure 16.17, rows 7, 8, 9, and 10 become data groups 1, 2, 3, and 4. From the Data Group dialog box, type or point out (using F7) the cell range that includes the data group. In the WIDGET.SSF example, assign the four data groups as follows:

| Data Group | Cell Range |
|---|---|
| 1 | B7..D7 |
| 2 | B8..D8 |
| 3 | B9..D9 |
| 4 | B10..D10 |

After you define the data group, press Enter to accept it. To display the graph as it currently appears, press F9.

For a pie graph, assign only one point to each data group. You are limited to eight pie slices, but the graph will be less cluttered and therefore easier to understand than if you assign more than one point to each data group.

Now that you have defined the essential elements, the graph type and the data groups, Enable can display a graph. All the other elements of the graphics module are secondary to these first two.

## Assigning Data Groups in a Database

The easiest way to group data in a database is first to use the DBMS Sort command (to learn more about sorting the database, see "Using the Sort Command" in Chapter 14). Figure 16.18 shows the WIDGET database sorted by REGION, DISTRICT, and MONTH. After you sort the database, use the resulting select set to generate the graph. In this example, a three-dimensional vertical stacked-bar graph compares the first-quarter sales forecasts of the three districts in the Eastern region. Another graph does the same for the Pacific region. Two other graphs compare district sales figures for the Southern and Western regions.

To assign a data group, press F7 from the Data Group dialog box to begin pointing.

If you just sorted the database, the name of the select set already appears on the Database line. Otherwise, enter the name of the database (or the database select set) on the Database line. Use the Index line and the Where line to select the data group. In the WIDGET.SS example, the first data group is the three monthly sales forecasts for the Alpha District, Eastern Region; in the Where line, type

**REGION="Eastern" AND DISTRICT="Beta"**

In the Fields line, type the name of the field that contains the data to be graphed: in this case, type **FORECAST**. Figure 16.19 shows the completed Data Selection screen.

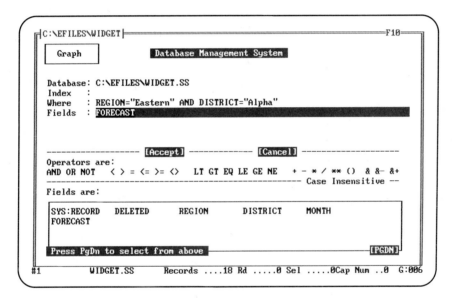

**Fig. 16.19.** *The Data Selection screen for data group 1.*

Group 2 for the Eastern Region's first-quarter forecast graph consists of the three monthly forecasts for the Beta district. The only change in the data selection screen is in the Where line; type

**REGION="Eastern" AND DISTRICT="Beta"**

For data group 3, type the following in the Where line:

**REGION="Eastern" AND DISTRICT="Gamma"**

For data group 4, type the following in the Where line:

**REGION="Eastern" AND DISTRICT="Delta"**

To display the graph as it appears thus far, press F9.

Because you have defined the essential elements—the graph type and the data groups—Enable displays a graph. All the other elements of the graphics module are secondary to these first two.

# Selecting Descriptive Elements

Enable can display a graph with only the graph type and the data defined. With no other descriptive elements, however, such a graph is almost impossible to understand. A graph that clouds the information it presents is worse than no graph at all.

Fortunately, Enable/OA has many descriptive elements that help to explain and enhance the initially dry display of your raw data. These options fall into two major groups: *global* options, which apply to the entire graph, and *data group* options, which affect only individual data groups.

## Enhancing the Graph with Global Options

To access the Global descriptive element options, you must be in either the Global dialog box or the Format and Layout dialog box. Because both contain global options, you can press the PgDn or PgUp key until you are in the box that contains the selections you want to change.

You already have learned how to select the graph type. The following sections discuss the other options available through these screens.

### Adding a Grid

All graph types except the pie can accept a grid. A *grid* consists of horizontal and vertical lines that act as a background for the bars, lines, or symbols of your graph. To choose this option, you must be in the Format and Layout dialog box. Tab to the GRID OPTIONS section; highlight the desired grid (Horizontal or Vertical). Press Enter. A check mark should appear to indicate that the grid is now active. You can activate one or both grid selections.

## Scaling the Y-Axis Data

All graphs except the pie graph display a scale along the y-axis. Enable normally assigns the beginning and ending points of this scale for you: zero (unless the data contains a negative value) and a value large enough to accommodate the largest number in the data.

Sometimes Enable's automatic scaling is not appropriate for your graph. Because Enable uses the highest and lowest values to create the scale, one unusually large or small number can create problems. Limiting the scale to the range actually used enlarges the critical area of the graph.

You adjust the y-axis scaling from the Format and Layout dialog box. Type the lower limit of the y-axis scale, and press Enter; then type the upper limit, and press Enter. Finally, type the increment at which you want Enable to place scale marks and values. The lower limit, upper limit, and increment used to generate the graphs in figures 16.13 and 16.14 are 60, 75, and 5, respectively.

## Specifying the X-Axis Data

X-axis data, except in an X-Y graph, is usually text data. The x-axis is the horizontal axis of the two-dimensional coordinate system in which Enable generates its graphs. For line graphs, bar graphs, and HLC graphs, each piece of data along the x-axis is a label for one or more data points graphed against the y-axis. For example, the x-axis data for the graph shown in figure 16.20 is the cell range B5..D5, the first-quarter months of the spreadsheet shown in figure 16.17. You also can use x-axis data to label the slices of a pie graph.

Like the procedures for selecting y-axis data, the procedures for selecting x-axis data differ slightly between a spreadsheet and a database. To select x-axis data from either a spreadsheet or a database, use the arrow keys to move to the prompt X-Axis Data: in the X-AXIS and TEXT DATA section of the Format and Layout dialog box.

For a spreadsheet, either point to (using F7) or type the appropriate cell range.

For a database, specify an Index line or Where line (or both) to select the records that contain the proper data. In the Fields line, type the name of the field that contains the x-axis data, and press Enter. As shown in figure 16.21, the Fields line can include complicated formulas. The formula in figure 16.21 converts the text stings 01, 02, and 03 to the strings JAN, FEB, and MAR, for use as x-axis data.

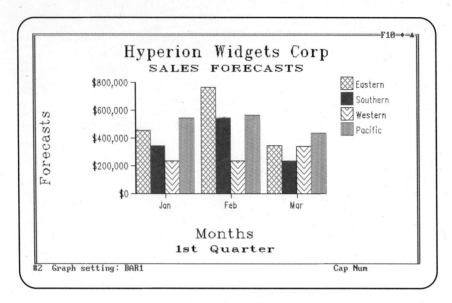

*Fig. 16.20. A graph using data from WIDGET.SSF.*

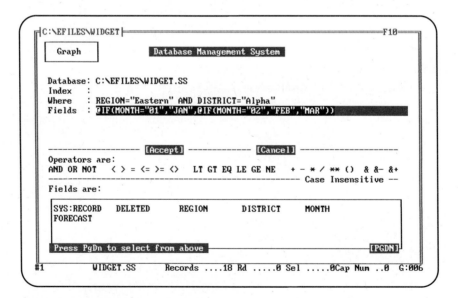

*Fig. 16.21. The x-axis Data Selection screen.*

# Formatting the Axes

Just as you can format values in an Enable spreadsheet to look like currency, percentages, dates, and so on, you also can format values plotted along the x- or y-axis in a graph.

To format y-axis data, move to the Y-AXIS FORMAT section in the Format and Layout dialog box. Use the arrow keys to highlight the desired format. Press Enter. An asterisk (*) should appear in front of the selection.

Refer to Chapter 9, "Understanding Spreadsheet Basics," for more information on these formatting options.

You also can format the x-axis data. You almost certainly need to format the x-axis data for X-Y graphs. You also need to format the x-axis data if you use numeric data for labels along the x-axis of line graphs, bar graphs, or HLC graphs, or for pie-slice labels.

# Adding Headings

Virtually every graph needs clear headings to be understandable. To add headings to your graph, move to the TITLES, SUBTITLES, AND LEGEND section of the Global dialog box. Move to the appropriate heading and type the heading as you want it to appear in the space provided. The following is a list of the available titles, subtitles, and legends:

- *Main 1*. Enable centers the main title at the top of the graph in the largest-size print. Figure 16.20 shows a graph with the main heading *Hyperion Widgets Corp*.

- *X-Axis*. The x-axis heading appears below the horizontal x-axis. *Months* is the x-axis heading in figure 16.20.

- *Y-Axis*. The y-axis heading appears in landscape (sideways) print along the vertical y-axis. The y-axis heading in figure 16.20 is *Forecasts*.

- *Main 2, X Sub, and Y Sub*. Subheadings appear just below their corresponding headings, in smaller type. In figure 16.20, the main heading and the x-axis heading have subheadings.

- *Legend*. Choose this dialog box option to assign a legend heading for use with Perspective Junior *Legend* has no effect in Enable/OA's native graphics.

## Assigning Fonts

A *font* is a collection of letters and characters of the same size and style. Enable's Default font is plain but functional. Use this font to develop your graphs; Enable can display headings much more quickly without having to look up font definitions. You can assign different fonts after you have added headings.

Move to the FONT section of the Global dialog box. In the lower left corner of the screen, Enable displays a list of fonts from which you can choose. In addition to the default font, Enable has the following fonts: *italic*, *roman*, *block*, and *script*. Each of these fonts has two styles: the second font style is slightly more heavily boldface. Figure 16.19 uses Roman2 for the main heading and Roman1 for x- and y-axis headings and all subheadings. Type in the corresponding number of the font you want after the heading to which it is to be applied.

Before you can use any of these fonts, the corresponding *font file* (the file with the same root name and file extension FNT) must be in the data directory or the directory that contains the Enable/OA program (usually C:\EN400). The Enable installation program copies these files into the program directory.

**TIP**

Different situations call for different fonts. The script fonts look good on a plotter but often are difficult to read on-screen or when printed with a graphics printer. (A *plotter* is a type of output device that uses pens of different colors to draw the output, unlike a printer, which uses a print-head to type the material, or a laser to burn the image onto the paper.) Because the block fonts are easiest to read, use them for the smaller labels (the Labels-and-legends option). Only the default font can include the foreign and special characters in the ASCII character set (press Alt and the decimal ASCII code to display the characters).

## Adding Color

Choose Color from the Global dialog box to assign pen colors (on a multipen plotter) and the screen color (on EGA and VGA systems) to the axes and all labels except legends. Enable/OA normally plots your graph with one pen and displays your graph in high resolution and in one color. Whether you can add more colors depends largely on your plotter and your display system.

The colors that a multipen plotter can plot are determined by the color of the ink in the pens you use. The Enable graphics module distinguishes 10 different colors. You therefore can plot in up to 10 colors; however, they may not be the same colors listed in the Global dialog box. For example, to get the same colors that appear on a VGA screen, you need to use pens with the same color ink and place them in the plotter's pen holders in the same order as the colors are shown on-screen.

To choose the same color for the axes, the main heading, x- and y-axis headings, subheadings, and x- and y-axis labels, move to the Global Color section on the Global dialog box and type in the appropriate number. Enable gives you a choice from these colors: black, red, green, blue, brown, violet, gold, lime, turquoise, and orange.

Assign colors for bars, lines, pie slices, and legends through the Data Group dialog box. (For more information, see the section "Enhancing the Graph with Data Group Options" in this chapter.)

## Choosing between Lines and Symbols

X-Y graphs and line graphs normally depict data as lines drawn through the data coordinates. However, you can also display the data with symbols added at the coordinates, or only with symbols. To select one or both of these formats, move to the area on the Global dialog box containing the Draw_Line and Draw_Symbols prompts. Highlight the option you want, and press Enter. A check mark should appear. Follow similar steps to activate the other option.

The check mark is a toggle switch. To deactivate an option, simplyB highlight it again and press Enter. The check mark disappears.

## Skipping X-Axis Labels

Choose the Skip_points option (ignore points) to skip a selected number of points on an x-axis, thus making your graph easier to read. For example, suppose that you create a line graph of the sine curve. To generate a smooth curve, you provide data points in 1-degree increments, from 0-360 degrees, producing 361 data points. The x-axis is too small to display 361 labels; however, you can ignore some labels by moving to the Skip_points option on the Format and Layout dialog box.

Enable prompts you to enter a number between 1 and 256. For the sine curve graph, type **90** and press Enter. Enable displays an x-axis label for every 90th data point.

## Changing a Graph's Layout

The Layout option gives you additional control of your graph display, so that you can change the percentage of the graphics screen devoted to different parts of the output. You can reduce the space for the main title and x-axis, making the graph taller, or decrease the y-axis space, making the graph wider; or you can do both at once.

To choose this option on the Format and Layout dialog box, move to the LAYOUT OPTIONS section. To make the graph either taller, wider, or both, highlight the Taller or Wider option, or both, and press Enter. The check mark appears beside the option(s).

Figure 16.22 shows a graph after you have widened and lengthened it.

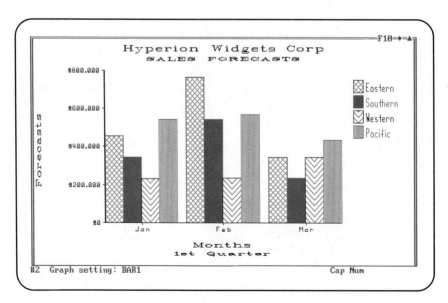

*Fig. 16.22. A graph after choosing the layout options Taller and Wider.*

# Enhancing the Graph with Data Group Options

Graphs almost always make the raw data more interesting and more understandable. However, when you include more than one data group in a graph, you must make sure that you distinguish each group clearly. Enable/ OA's Data Group options give several descriptive elements to assist you with this distinction. One Data Group dialog box appears for all data groups.

## Adjusting the Scale of an Individual Data Group

This option has a different purpose than the Scale option on the Global dialog box. The Scale option on the Data Group dialog box is best explained through an example.

Suppose that you are creating a bar graph to display the first-quarter sales totals for each of four salespersons. Enable automatically scales the y-axis to accommodate the highest and lowest sales values, starting at zero. But what if three salespersons are "rookies" and sold between $5,000 and $15,000 each, and the fourth, an "old pro," sold $950,000? The bars on the graph depicting the sales of the three rookies would be squeezed at the bottom, and you would have trouble seeing them (see fig. 16.23).

To show all the sales data, you can adjust the bar representing your superstar's sales. Move to the SCALE section of the Data Group dialog box. Move to the space provided for the data group you want to scale. Then enter a scaling factor—in this case *.10*—by which the $950,000 figure can be multiplied. Now Enable has to show values only between 5,000 and 95,000 along the y-axis. The top salesperson still has the largest bar, but the bars for the other three salespersons are larger and easier to compare with one another. To remind yourself (and others) of the change in scale, add a legend explaining that the large bar is shown in 1/10 scale (see fig. 16.24).

## Assigning Colors

Use the COLOR section on the Data Group dialog box to assign a color to the graphic that depicts the data group. This option's primary purpose is to assign pen colors for plotting; however, on EGA and VGA systems, this option also affects colors that appear on-screen.

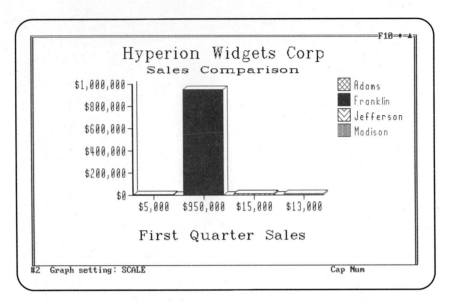

**Fig. 16.23.** *An unadjusted graph of a sales comparison.*

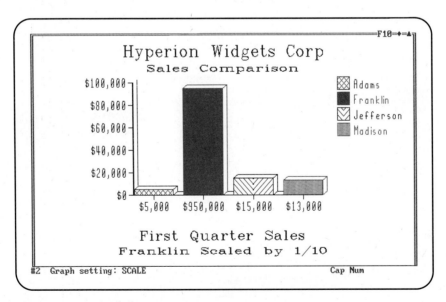

**Fig. 16.24.** *A graph of a sales comparison with one value scaled by 1/10.*

Enable supports up to 10 colors for plotting your graph. When you choose the Color option, the selections are black, red, green, blue, brown, violet, gold, lime, turquoise, and orange.

As noted in the section "Adding Color" in this chapter, the colors that actually plot are determined by the pens you use and the holder in which you place them.

## Assigning Shading and Line Patterns

The Shade option does more than its name implies. With Shade, you can change the default assignments for the shading pattern of data group bars or pie slices. In addition, you can change the line design of each data group line in a line graph.

To change the shading or line style for a data group, move to the SHADE section of the Data Group dialog box.

Move to the space next to the data group you want to adjust. Type a number from 1 to 8. The number represents one of the eight shading or line styles shown in figures 16.25 and 16.26.

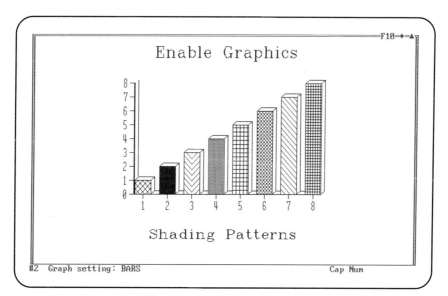

*Fig. 16.25. Enable's shading patterns.*

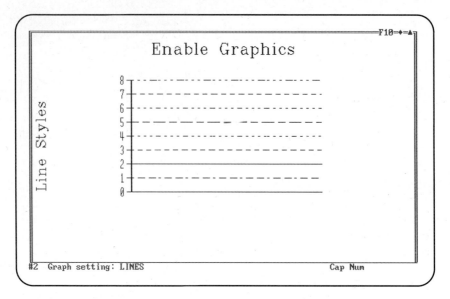

*Fig. 16.26. Enable's line styles.*

Enable usually assigns these shading patterns and line styles in the sequence shown in these figures. Like the Color option, the Shade option works for pie graphs only when the graph's Auto shading option is off (the default setting).

**TIP**

For Global Options Color to be effective for a pie graph, make sure that the graph's Auto shading setting is off.

## Adding Legends

All the shaded bar graphs in the world do not inform your audience if the graphs do not show what the bars stand for. You usually should assign a legend to describe the data for each data group in a bar, line, step, X-Y, and HLC graph. Occasionally labels on the x-axis are sufficient, particularly when you are using a vertical bar graph that displays the data by group. For pie graphs, you may prefer to label the slices with x-axis data rather than with legends.

To specify a legend for a data group, move to the space provided for the appropriate group in the Data Group dialog box. Type the text of the legend next to the shading or line style assigned to the group. Enable reserves the right side of the screen for legends. Most figures in this chapter show graphs with legends.

> The Legend option in the Headings section of the Global dialog box is for use with Perspective and has no effect in Enable's native graphics.

## Eliminating a Data Group

To eliminate a data group from the graph, move to the appropriate data range in the Data Group dialog box and press Alt-F3. This option doesn't reset the other settings for the group, but without data, Enable ignores the settings. This technique is different from changing the data range, which does not eliminate the group.

## Exploding Pie Graphs

You can use an exploded pie graph to highlight the value of one or more slices by pulling them out slightly from the center (see fig. 16.27).

The section "Selecting the Graph Type" in this chapter points out that creating an exploded pie graph is a two-step process. First, you select the exploded pie graph on the Global dialog box. Next, you indicate through the OPTION section on the Data Group dialog box which piece(s) to explode.

If you selected the exploded pie as the graph type, explode a pie slice by typing a capital **E** in the space provided for the slice.

## Selecting Symbols To Mark
## Points on a Graph

From the SYMBOL section of the Data Group dialog box, you can choose the type of symbol that marks points on a line graph or an X-Y graph. You can assign a different symbol to each line. From the Data Group dialog box, move to the space provided for the appropriate group. Figure 16.28 shows the default symbol set. If you do not choose another symbol, Enable assigns one in the following order: square, triangle, *x*, less-than sign, plus sign, greater-than sign, diamond, and block. You also can assign eight keyboard characters for use as symbols, one for each data group. Some examples are shown in figure 16.29. The special characters shown in figure 16.30 are available for use as symbols. These characters and more appear in a list at the bottom left corner of the screen, along with their assigned numbers.

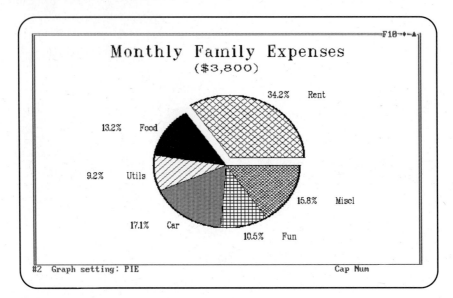

*Fig. 16.27. An exploded pie graph.*

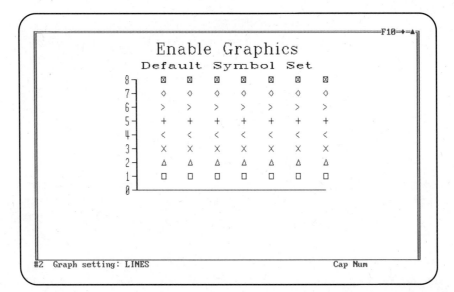

*Fig. 16.28. The default symbol set.*

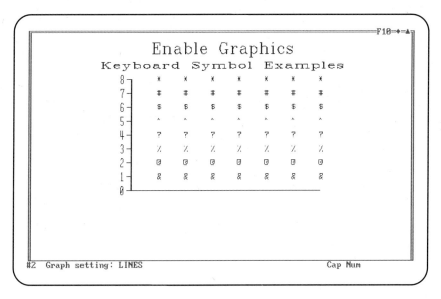

***Fig. 16.29.*** *Examples of keyboard symbols.*

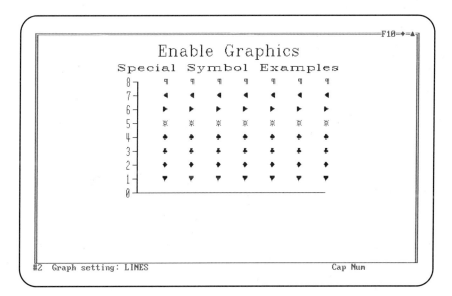

***Fig. 16.30.*** *Examples of the Special symbols.*

Enable uses the symbol you choose here only if you also make an appropriate choice from the Global Options dialog box. You must set the **XYL**-format option from the Global Options dialog box to **Symbols** or to **Both**. In other words, XYL-format enables you to choose whether to use only symbols or both a line and symbols for each data group.

# Using Text Graphs

Enable/OA has a graph known as a *text graph* in its graphics module. You can use a text graph to choose from a wide selection of existing artwork (known as *symbols*) stored in the *Symbol Library*. You then can copy these images into your word processing documents to enhance their appearance.

To create a text graph, you first must establish the spreadsheet data on which the graph is built. Create a separate spreadsheet to hold the symbol specifications and use it as a template. Whenever you want a different symbol, simply change the numbers.

The recommended layout is a spreadsheet containing descriptive labels in one column and the actual figures in the next column, as shown in figure 16.31.

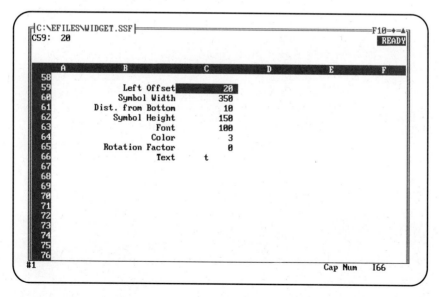

*Fig. 16.31. Text graph specifications.*

Each text graph contains the following eight items of information:

- *Left offset*. This number is the distance the graph should be from the left side of the screen, expressed as a pixel coordinate. (A *pixel*, usually expressed in *dpi*, or *dots per inch*, is the smallest element of an on-screen image.)

- *Symbol Width*. This number, expressed as a pixel coordinate, represents the width of the graph.

- *Distance from Bottom*. This number, expressed as a pixel coordinate, represents the distance of the graph from the bottom of the screen.

- *Symbol Height*. This number, expressed as a pixel coordinate, represents the height of the graph.

- *Font*. The font always should be 100 when you use the Symbol Library. The number 100 is the library extension number and enables you to gain entry to the library.

- *Color*. To choose the color of the graph, enter any of the 10 color numbers discussed in the section "Adding Color" in this chapter.

- *Rotation Factor*. This number represents the amount of rotation of the graph. The graph can be rotated clockwise from 0 degrees to 359 degrees (if you want to see the graph upside down, type **359**).

- *Text*. The symbol number you want to graph. Enter the corresponding library number from the list of the images contained in the section "Using Symbol Art" in Chapter 6 of your Enable graphics documentation.

After you have set up the spreadsheet, create a graph following the normal steps. On the Global dialog box, choose Text as the graph type. Use PgDn to go to the Format and Layout dialog box. Move to the X-AXIS and TEXT DATA section. At the prompt for `User Text Data`, type or point to the range where the symbol specifications are in the spreadsheet. Display the graph as usual (see fig. 16.32).

> Because of the flexibility involved with using symbol art, no single, set method will give you the "perfect" result. The best way to get the proper result is to experiment: change a setting, display the graph; change another setting, display the graph again. Eventually you will get the output you desire.

**TIP**

*Fig. 16.32. Text graph displayed.*

# Selecting and Modifying Graphic Output Devices

After you design your graph and master the graphics dialog boxes, you probably want to create a permanent record of your work by printing the graph. Enable can send its graphics to three types of output device: the screen, a printer, and a plotter. You probably have already found these choices and are displaying your graphs as you go through this chapter. The output choices are on the Device dialog box.

TIP

If your graph doesn't print or plot when you choose the appropriate option, first check that you have defined your graph properly. If the graph appears on-screen, it should print or plot. Next, check the Print Form or Hardware Profile options. Make sure that the driver for your printer or plotter is installed and selected properly.

# Changing Printer Options

You access the printer options from the Device dialog box. Enable displays the following choices:

- *Print_Density.* This option gives you a choice of densities: Single, Double, Triple, or Quad. The term *density* is used here to describe the quality of printed output. The higher the density, the more detailed the graph looks. The drawback is that higher-density output takes much longer to print.

- *Print_Format.* The default orientation, or *format*, of an Enable graph is Landscape (sideways), which creates the largest graph possible on normal letter-size paper. The other available format is Portrait. In this format the graph comes out of the printer top side up, but it occupies only half the page.

# Changing Plotter Options

You access the plotter options from the Device dialog box. Enable displays the following options:

- *Pen_Width.* Use this option to choose Narrow (P.3 size) or Wide (P.7 or worn) pens. Use Wide for transparencies. The default choice is Wide.

- *Plot_Speed.* This option changes the plotting speed. The default is Fast. Choose Slow to get the smoothest and widest lines when you are preparing transparencies.

- *Plot_To.* You can use this profile setting to set a default COM port, to which your plotter normally is attached. Use this option to switch temporarily to another port (COM1, COM2, or COM3). Enable/OA also can send plotter output to a file. The file then can be imported into a word processing file. (Enable/OA automatically adds the file extension PLT to a plotter file.)

# Integrating Graphics with Word Processing

One of the best uses of graphs is to add them to reports and other documents. Integrating graphics with text is one of Enable's strong features. Continuing in that tradition, Enable/OA has the capability to import graphics from other programs into word processing. This section discusses how to copy Enable's native graphics into a word processing file.

Because you do not want your graphs to overwhelm your document, you often shrink a graph before you copy it to a word processing file. Only a few details distinguish this process from the process of copying text from a word processing window.

## Shrinking a Graph

To reduce the size of a graph, display the graph and press

> F10 Window **Modify**

or

> F9 Window **Locate_and_size**

The spreadsheet screen appears with a highlighted border and the following message listed in the status line:

```
Press M(move) or S(shrink) or E(expand).
```

To shrink the screen, press **Shrink**, and then use the arrow keys.

A fourth option, not listed in the status line, is *R* for *rapid*. To shrink the graphics window quickly from all sides at once, after you press **Shrink**, press R repeatedly until the screen border is the size you want. The graph is redrawn in the new smaller size. Now you can copy the smaller version of the graph to a word processing file.

## Copying a Graph to Word Processing

To copy a graph into a document, you must display the graph in one window and open a word processing file in another window. Move the cursor in the word processing window to the position in your document where the top left corner of the graph should be.

To begin the copy process, press Alt-F5. Enable displays the Interwindow Copy Options screen. Press the number of the window that contains the graph. Then press Alt-F5 again. Enable copies the graph. The result may look strange, however. Enable normally displays word processing in text mode (medium resolution), but the program displays graphics in graphics mode (high resolution). Because you started the copy from within the word processing window, Enable displays the graph inside that window as a solid mass.

To switch the screen to graphics mode, press

> F10 **D**isplay **V**ideo_Mode **G**raphics

and press Enter.

You now can scroll through your document and see both graphics and text. You even can type text around and on top of your graph. Keep in mind, however, that text entered on top of a portion of your graph replaces that portion. The text is *not* superimposed on the graph.

To return to text mode, press

> F10 **D**isplay Video_Mode Color_80x25

(or F10 **D**isplay Video_Mode *B*/W80x25 for monochrome graphics users)

and press Enter.

# Displaying a Graph and a Spreadsheet Simultaneously

When you produce graphs from a spreadsheet, you can display your graph and the underlying data at the same time. This procedure works best after you design the graph and want to use it in some "what if" analysis. Each time you change an assumption (some number in the spreadsheet), the graph repaints immediately.

To display a graph alongside your spreadsheet data, position the spreadsheet pointer in the area of the spreadsheet you want to be able to see. Access the graphics dialog boxes and select the proper graph, but do not display it yet. Press Esc until you return to ready mode (no dialog box). You are ready to display the graph.

Press

F10 **G**raph **D**ynamic_On/Off

or

Shift-F7

The screen splits vertically in the center, with the spreadsheet on the left. The graph appears in the right half of the screen (see fig. 16.33). You still control the spreadsheet cell pointer. Whenever you change a number in the spreadsheet, the graph repaints. Return to the normal spreadsheet display by pressing F10 **G**raph **D**ynamic_On/Off, or Shift-F7 again.

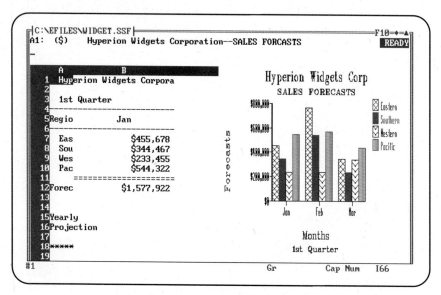

*Fig. 16.33. A simultaneous display of a spreadsheet and a graph.*

To expedite graph repainting, don't use special fonts that require disk access; Enable's default font does not require disk access. The default font also is more legible when squeezed to half-screen size. Figure 16.33 shows a graph in the default font.

# Saving the Graph Settings

When you create graph settings in a spreadsheet, be sure to save the spreadsheet before quitting that file. Saving the spreadsheet also saves the graph settings. Enable has no separate graph settings file.

On the other hand, Enable does keep a graph setting file when you graph DBMS data. At the beginning, Enable asks for a file name. When you are ready to quit from the Graphics dialog box, press Esc. Enable asks if you want to save the settings to the file you initially specified. Unless you want to redo all your work the next time, answer this question **Yes**. The next time you want to display the DBMS graph, enter the same file name. Enable retrieves the graph settings you saved.

# Summary

Like its other modules, Enable's graphics module is full-featured. Of course, that means that the module takes some time to learn. At first, several of the many dialog boxes seem to do almost the same thing. Follow the steps outlined in this chapter, and you develop a nearly foolproof method for creating graphs from spreadsheet or DBMS data.

# 17

# Producing Graphs with Perspective Junior

C hapter 16 explains how to use Enable's graphics module to create graphs from Enable spreadsheets and database files. In addition to the graphics module, as early as Enable Version 2.0, Enable Software included with the software package a graphics program called Perspective that enables you to create advanced two-dimensional and three-dimensional graphs. Enable/OA 4.0 includes Perspective Junior, a significantly modified version of this three-dimensional graphics program.

Like its predecessors, Perspective Junior helps you develop and print astonishing graphs directly from Enable spreadsheets and database files, and yet Perspective remains a separate program from Enable. You automatically can transfer data from Enable to Perspective Junior; however, if you make changes to your data while in Perspective, you cannot transfer it back to Enable as easily (see the section "Saving Files" in this chapter).

With Perspective Junior, you can display, print, and plot graphics in color, and send output to a file you, in turn, can import into Enable's word processing module.

Perspective Junior is a powerful presentation graphics program that easily could be the subject of an entire book, especially if all of its most intriguing features were fully explored. In the context of a book about Enable, however, this chapter cannot cover every detail. This chapter gives you enough information and assistance to create printouts and plots to wow your friends and employers, but exploring the full depth of Perspective's power, using this chapter as a starting point, is up to you.

# Understanding Three-Dimensional Graphs

Before you comfortably can make the leap into the third dimension, you need to get your bearings and clearly understand the meaning of the term *two-dimensional*.

When Enable displays a vertical-bar graph of Hyperion Widgets Corporation's Sales Forecasts (see fig. 17.1), for example, the height of each bar represents total sales. Dollars are scaled along the y-axis (the vertical axis). The y-axis is the first dimension. Because you want to compare total sales in January with total sales in each of the months February and March, the x-axis (horizontal axis) is labeled with the month names. The x-axis is the second dimension. Dollars and time, therefore, are the two dimensions.

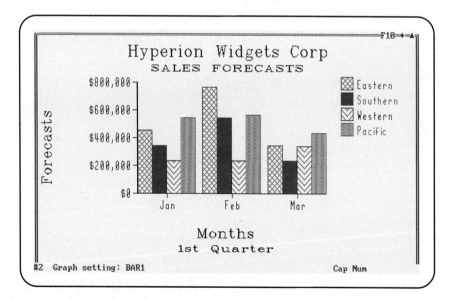

*Fig. 17.1. An Enable vertical-bar graph.*

You also want to compare sales over the three-month period in the four regions, which adds a third dimension to the data. The three dimensions, therefore, are dollars, time, and regions. Enable's vertical-bar graph accomplishes this three-dimensional comparison with distinctive shading patterns and legends to distinguish the regions. Although the graph in figure 17.1 depicts three dimensions, the graph doesn't "look" three-dimensional.

Perspective displays the same data in a way that looks three-dimensional by adding a second horizontal axis, the z-axis. The y-axis still is vertical and is scaled in dollars. The x-axis still is horizontal and is scaled in months (time). But Perspective gives the third dimension, regions, its own axis (see fig. 17.2). Shading is no longer needed.

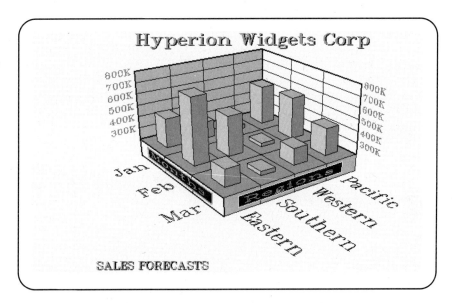

**Fig. 17.2.** *A Perspective 3-D bar graph.*

As you read and then apply the procedures and techniques presented in this chapter, try to keep this concept of data *dimensions* in mind. Never lose sight of your ultimate goal of presenting data in a more understandable format. If you overshadow the information you want to present with the novelty of 3-D graphics, you completely defeat your purpose. If your data has three dimensions, Perspective may well be the tool you need, but two-dimensional data usually is best presented in a two-dimensional graph. A three-dimensional graph looks great but often is not easy to understand. Tread carefully in this territory or risk losing your audience.

# Preparing To Use Perspective Junior

This chapter assumes that you properly have installed Perspective Junior on your system. The Perspective Junior files were copied to your hard disk when you installed Enable. If these files were not copied, you need to reinstall Enable and answer **Yes** when asked whether you want to install Perspective.

## Getting Started

Perspective Junior is included with Enable/OA 4.0 as a *bound-in*, or *add-in*, product, which is an accessory program designed to work with an applications program, such as Enable, and extend its capabilities. Although actually a separate program, Perspective Junior is accessed from within Enable. The command to start Perspective is an option in Enable's graphics module. You first must go through several of the steps necessary to create an Enable graph.

Start by creating or revising an Enable spreadsheet or database file that holds data you want to graph. Access Enable's graphics module. To create a Perspective graph, you first must complete the procedures described in Chapter 16 for specifying data groups and corresponding titles to create an Enable graph, although with several subtle variations described in the following few sections. The graph type you specify in Enable does not matter because Perspective automatically starts with a three-dimensional bar graph.

When you transport Enable data to Perspective Junior, the data you specified as x-axis data for your Enable graph appears as row headers in Perspective, and the x-axis title you assigned appears as the row title. The text you specified as legend text for your Enable graph appears as column headers, and the legend title you assigned appears as the column title in Perspective.

Use as an example the information taken from the Enable spreadsheet WIDGET.SSF (see fig. 17.3). The x-axis data, month names Jan, Feb, and Mar, appear as row headers in Perspective (again see fig. 17.2). The legend data, region names Eastern, Southern, Western, and Pacific, appear as column headers in the Perspective graph. The x-axis title, Month, from the

Enable graph appears as the row title in Perspective. The legend title, Regions, appears as the column title in the Perspective graph. Each data group is the sales forecast for a region. Notice that the main title and main subtitle in both graphs are the same. (Refer to Chapter 16, "Creating Graphs with Enable," for a discussion of establishing graphs.)

```
┌─C:\EFILES\WIDGET.SSF────────────────────────────────F10=◆=▲┐
│A9:  ($)    Western                                    READY │
│                                                             │
│        A           B           C           D           E    │
│ 1  Hyperion Widgets Corporation--SHyperion Widgets Corp     │
│ 2                                                           │
│ 3  1st Quarter                                             │
│ 4  ──────────────────────────────────────────────────────  │
│ 5  Region        Jan         Feb         Mar       Totals   │
│ 6  ──────────────────────────────────────────────────────  │
│ 7  Eastern      $455,678    $765,455    $345,676  $1,566,809 │
│ 8  Southern     $344,467    $543,345    $234,543  $1,122,355 │
│ 9  Western      $233,455    $234,545    $342,333    $810,333 │
│10  Pacific      $544,322    $567,456    $434,543  $1,546,321 │
│11             ============================================== │
│12  Forecasts  $1,577,922  $2,110,801  $1,357,095  $5,045,818 │
│13                                                           │
│14                                                           │
│15   Yearly                                                  │
│16  Projection                                              │
│17                                                           │
│18  $20,183,272                                             │
│19                                                           │
│#1                                        Cap Num    I66     │
└─────────────────────────────────────────────────────────────┘
```

*Fig. 17.3. The Enable spreadsheet WIDGET.SSF.*

# Accessing Perspective Junior

After assigning data groups and titles, you are ready to access Perspective. From the spreadsheet, press

F10 **Graph Select**

Enable displays the initial Current Settings dialog box. Choose the graph setting you want to transport into Perspective, choose the option Perspective, and then press either the Enter key or the End key to proceed into Perspective.

Perspective displays an introductory screen while it loads the graph setting, and then the program uses the default settings for graph type, color, and title location to display the graph in three dimensions. The first level of the menu system, the Main Menu, also appears with the graph (see fig. 17.4).

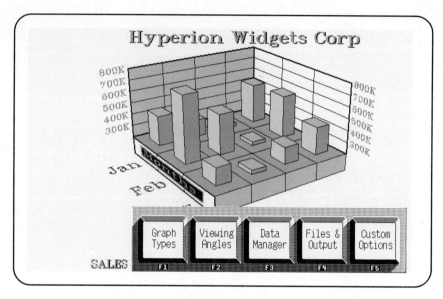

*Fig. 17.4. The Perspective Junior Main Menu.*

**TIP**

You can enter Perspective Junior without first creating an Enable graph—something you may want to do if you plan to use a data file from another program, or even an Enable file saved in 1-2-3 format. Access the Enable graphics module and create a single data group, using blank cells (or fields in a database) as the data range. Then access Perspective Junior. The program displays a graph with no data, and you can use the Data Manager to load the file you want to use. (For a detailed discussion of the Data Manager, refer to "Customizing Data with the Data Manager," in this chapter.)

# Understanding Perspective Junior's Menus

Perspective Junior displays the Main Menu along the edge of your screen, with the menu choices on the tops of five function keys (again see fig. 17.4). Perspective displays the keys on the bottom right side of your screen, corresponding to keys F1, F2, F3, F4, and F5 on your keyboard.

You use these five function keys to make selections from all Perspective menus. You cannot use either of the familiar Enable methods—first-letter or point-and-shoot—to choose Perspective's menu options. You select options by pressing the function key in the corresponding position on your keyboard. For example, to select the option Data Manager from the Main Menu (again see fig. 17.4), press F3 on your keyboard.

Like Enable's graphics menus, these menus have many levels. Making one menu choice usually leads to a display of other menus, each of which leads to the display of even more choices. (The menus Graph_Types and Viewing_Angles are exceptions; they have no submenus. When you select these menus, the program prompts you to choose a graph type and viewing angle, respectively.) F10 is the standard key for backing out of a choice and moving back down the menu tree. Perspective Junior's menu tree is included in this section.

When you start Perspective, you automatically are at the Main Menu. Although this initial menu is called the Main Menu, it is not at the root of the tree. If you press the F10 key at the Main Menu, Perspective displays the Exit menu (see fig. 17.5).

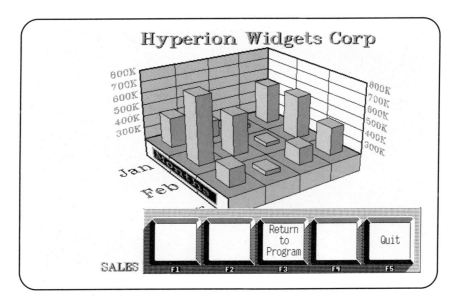

*Fig. 17.5. The Exit menu.*
*Perspective Junior Menu Tree*

**Perspective Junior Menu Tree**

*GRAPH TYPES*

*VIEWING ANGLES*

*DATA MANAGER*

EDIT PARAMS
   Data Range
   Titles
   R/C Titles
   R/C Headers
OPTIONS
   Graph Range
FILEMANAGER
   Load File
   Merge File
   Save ASCII
   Save 3DT
   Data Protect
BLOCK OP'Sl
ROW/COL OP'S
   Row Op's
   Col Op's
   Sort Rows
   Sort Col's
OPTIONS
   Show Range
   Zero Float
   Clear All
   Transpose
   Exec. Math

*FILES & OUTPUT*

FILEMANAGER
   Load Graph
   Load Image
   Save Graph
   Save Image
SLIDE SHOW MANAGER
   Load Show
   New Show
   Run Show
   Save Show
   Options
PRINT MANAGER
   Print
   Preview
      Change Box
      Pattern
      Set #1
      Set #2
      Set #3
      Set #4
      Set #5
      Change Riser
      Pattern
      Set #1
      Set #2
      Set #3
      Set #4
      Set #5

**Perspective Junior Menu Tree** *(continued)*

Change 2D
Pattern
   Set #1
   Set #2
   Set #3
   Set #4
   Set #5
Page Setup
  Size
  Position
  Border On/Off
  Portrait or Landscape
  Paper Size
Printer Options
  Select Printer
  Resolution
  Color
  Port
  Serial
PLOT MANAGER
Plot
Preview
  Gridline Color
  Graph Outline Color
  Base Text Color
  2D Text Color
  Title & Subtitle Color
Page Setup
  Size
  Position
  Border On/Off
  Portrait or Landscape
  Paper Size

Plotter Options
  Select Plotter
  Quality
  Options
  Port
  Serial

*CUSTOM OPTIONS*

COLOR OPTIONS
  Color Mixer
  Color By Row
  Color By Column
DATA REVERSAL OPTIONS
  Normal Sequence
  Exchange Rows & Columns
  Reverse Row Order
  Reverse Column Order
CYCLE TITLES
WALLS, GRIDS, RISERS
  Left Wall On/Off
  Right Wall On/Off
  Wall Grid Control
  Base Grid Control
  Riser Sizing
CUSTOM VIEWING ANGLES
  Rotate in 3D
  Zoom  Pan  Distort
  Box Sizing
  Hide Show/Graph
  Step Size

To turn off the menu display so that you can see the entire graph, press the space bar. If you press the space bar again, the menu returns. You also can use the cursor-movement keys—Home, End, PgUp, and PgDn—to move the function-key display around the screen so that you can see the portion of the graph you are interested in and still see the menus. To reduce the distance that the program moves the menu each time, press and hold the Ctrl key and then press one of the following keys: right arrow, left arrow, PgUp, or PgDn.

The five remaining function keys—F6, F7, F8, F9, and F10—always perform the following functions:

- *Redraw.* Press F6 to redraw the entire screen.

- *Draw Box.* Press F7 to redraw only the graph.

- *Draw Text.* Press F8 to redraw only the text of the graph, including all labels, headers, the title, and the subtitle.

- *Help.* Press F9 to access context-sensitive on-line documentation, which provides a brief explanation of each option on the current menu.

- *Exit.* Press F10 (on either type of keyboard) to back up, or exit, one menu level. You can back up as far as the Exit menu. The function of F10 in Perspective's menus is similar to the function of Esc in Enable's menus. (In the Data Manager, you press F10 to accept changes made to parameters, as explained in "Customizing Data with the Data Manager," in this chapter.) You also can use the Esc key to back up one menu level in Perspective; however, the function of this key is not consistent.

To effectively use Perspective, you also can press the following keys:

- *Esc.* Press Esc to halt graph drawing immediately.

- *Enter.* Press Enter to accept an option. In the Data Manager, however, you press Enter when you want to edit a worksheet cell.

# Quitting Perspective Junior

You can quit Perspective Junior in two ways. Normally, you should use the F10 key to go back to the Exit menu, and press the appropriate function key to choose Quit. If Perspective prompts you to save the graph, press either **Y** to save or **N** to exit without saving. Perspective returns you to Enable's graphics module and to the spreadsheet or database you were using when you started Perspective.

You can use the second method of quitting Perspective from anywhere in the program. Just press Ctrl-C, and Perspective returns you to Enable.

# Customizing Data with the Data Manager

Now that you know how to move through Perspective's menus, you can begin to look at the menu options. From the Main Menu, you can access the Data Manager, Perspective's built-in worksheet for entering and modifying data. When you start Perspective Junior from Enable, Enable passes data from your Enable spreadsheet or database into the Data Manager.

The Data Manager worksheet is similar in appearance to Enable's spreadsheet module, but you use a different cell-address convention to reference each cell. Enable uses numbers to label spreadsheet rows, and letters to label spreadsheet columns; however, Perspective uses numbers to label both columns and rows. The intersection of row 3 and column 2, for example, is referred to as R3C2, where R represents row and C represents column. You can use the arrow keys to move the reverse-video cell pointer from cell to cell, and then you can enter data into a cell by typing numbers or text and pressing Enter.

Like a spreadsheet, Perspective's Data Manager has the capacity to calculate mathematical formulas based on values in worksheet cells. When compared with the power of Enable's spreadsheet module, however, the Data Manager's power is weak. Think of the Data Manager mainly as a table in which you enter and store graphing data. Do your heavy-duty calculating in Enable and then transfer the data to the Data Manager for use in Perspective Junior

The Data Manager worksheet holds all the numbers and text displayed in a Perspective graph, including header and title data. You must access the Data Manager whenever you want manually to change or add to this data.

## Examining the Data Manager Worksheet

The Data Manager worksheet (see fig. 17.6) has six parts: the top line, the message line, the menu, the status area, the entry line, and the worksheet area.

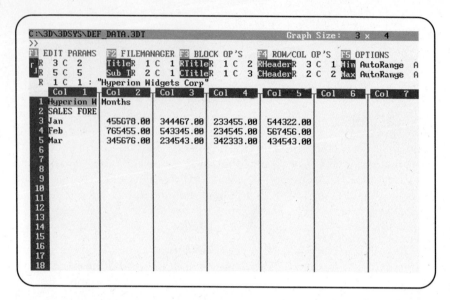

**Fig. 17.6.** *The Data Manager worksheet.*

## Interpreting the Top Line

The *top line*, which Perspective displays at the top of the screen, shows the full DOS path of the file with which you are working. When you first start Perspective Junior, the file path is

        C:\3D\3DSYS\DEF_DATA.3DT

Enable passes data to Perspective through the file DEF_DATA.3DT. If you load a different file later, the top line shows its path.

At the right end of the top line, Perspective shows the graph size. The first dimension (3 in fig. 17.6) indicates the number of rows of data. The second dimension (4 in fig. 17.6) is the number of columns that corresponds to the number of data groups chosen in Enable's graphics module.

## Interpreting the Message Line

The second line from the top of the screen (beginning with >>) is the *message line* that Perspective uses to display messages to you at appropriate times. Sometimes the message only informs you, and other times the message instructs you to take some action.

When you first access the Data Manager, the message line is empty.

## Interpreting the Menu

The third line of the Data Manager screen is the *menu*. The first five options are the following:

EDIT PARAMS  FILEMANAGER  BLOCK OP'S  ROW/COL OP'S  OPTIONS

This menu is the main Data Manager menu. As with all Perspective menus, you use the function keys to access the multiple levels of this menu. The function key number listed next to each option indicates the key you use to select the option and is determined by the orientation of the function keys on your keyboard. The menu in figure 17.6, for example, reflects the use of a keyboard with horizontal function keys.

## Interpreting the Status Area

The next two lines of the Data Manager worksheet (the fourth and fifth lines) inform you of the location of the data to be graphed, the locations of the titles and headers, and the location of the data range to be graphed.

Figure 17.6, for example, shows that the top left data cell, indicated by the box-drawing character, is R3C2 (row 3, column 2). When Perspective draws the graph, it depicts the value of this cell in the first row and first column of the graph. The bottom right data cell is R5C5 (row 5, column 5). Perspective graphs all cells between those two corner cells. The main title is in cell R1C1. The subtitle is in cell R2C1. The row title and column title are in cells R1C2 and R1C3, respectively. Row headers begin in cell R3C1, and column headers begin in cell R2C2. Perspective Junior automatically determines both minimum and maximum graph ranges, based on the data in cells R3C2 through R5C5.

## Interpreting the Entry Line

Much the same as in an Enable spreadsheet, you don't enter data directly into the worksheet. Instead you move the cell pointer to the cell into which you want to enter data. As you type numbers or text, Perspective displays the characters in the *entry line*, the sixth line from the top of the screen. You can edit the data you type in the entry line before you enter it in the cell. *Note:* Perspective is always in insert mode, which means that typing a character pushes the character at the cursor's location to the right to insert the new character.

After you correctly type data in the entry line, press Enter, the up-arrow key, or the down-arrow key to enter the data into the cell (the right- and left-arrow keys do not enter data).

You also can edit data that already exists in a cell. Move the cell pointer to the cell you want to edit, and press Enter. Perspective displays the cell data in the entry line so that you can edit it. After you make your changes, press Enter, the up-arrow key, or the down-arrow key to replace the original cell data with the revised data.

### Interpreting the Worksheet Area

The remainder of the screen is the worksheet area, which is labeled at the top with column numbers and at the left with row numbers. You must enter into the worksheet area all the numeric and textual data you want Perspective Junior to graph.

## Leaving the Data Manager

To exit the Data Manager and redraw the graph, return to the main Data Manager menu (again see fig. 17.6) and press F10. Press Esc to return to your graph without redrawing it. Either method returns you to the menu from which you accessed the Data Manager.

## Changing Graph Parameters

You use the Data Manager to enter and specify all data you want to display in your graph. Entering the data is a straightforward process, nearly identical to entering data in Enable. Although Enable enters data for you when you start Perspective Junior, you may want to add data as you customize the graph. If you add data, you may need to modify some of the *parameters* (the data range, titles, headers, and graph range) listed in the status area.

To make changes to parameters in the status area, choose EDIT_PARAMS by pressing the appropriate function key indicated in the main Data Manager menu. Perspective displays the EDIT_PARAMS menu (see fig. 17.7).

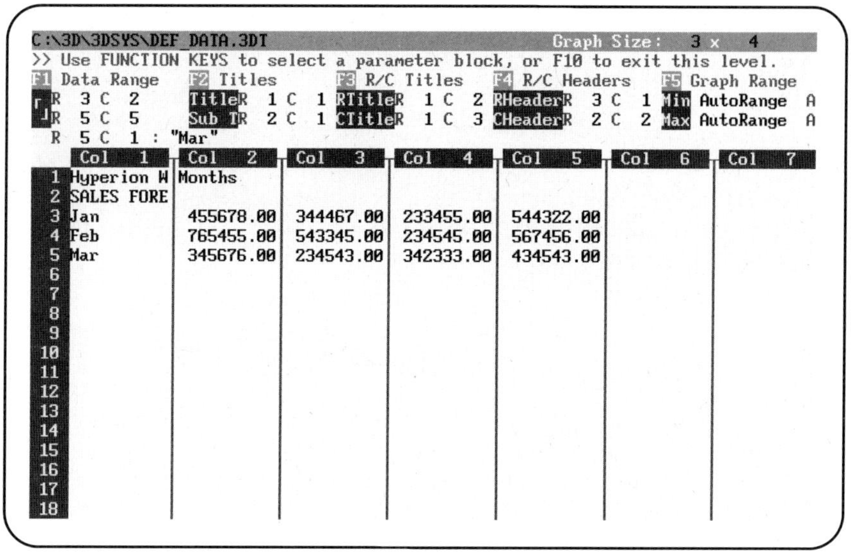

```
C:\3D\3DSYS\DEF_DATA.3DT                          Graph Size:   3 x   4
>> Use FUNCTION KEYS to select a parameter block, or F10 to exit this level.
F1 Data Range    F2 Titles        F3 R/C Titles     F4 R/C Headers    F5 Graph Range
 R  3 C  2      Title R  1 C  1  RTitle R  1 C  2  RHeader R  3 C  1  Min AutoRange  A
 R  5 C  5      Sub T R  2 C  1  CTitle R  1 C  3  CHeader R  2 C  2  Max AutoRange  A
 R  5 C  1 : "Mar"
       Col   1      Col   2      Col   3      Col   4      Col   5      Col   6      Col   7
  1  Hyperion W Months
  2  SALES FORE
  3  Jan          455678.00   344467.00   233455.00   544322.00
  4  Feb          765455.00   543345.00   234545.00   567456.00
  5  Mar          345676.00   234543.00   342333.00   434543.00
  6
  7
  8
  9
 10
 11
 12
 13
 14
 15
 16
 17
 18
```

*Fig. 17.7. The EDIT_PARAMS menu.*

The following sections explain the five menu choices from the EDIT_PARAMS menu.

## Specifying the Data Range

The *data range* is the block of data that Perspective uses to display a graph. Based on the data you transport from Enable, Perspective Junior automatically calculates the data range and displays in the status line the cell addresses of the top left and bottom right data cells (see the previous section "The Status Area" for more information about this display). These two cell addresses, top left and bottom right, are the *data range parameters*.

Although Perspective sets the data range for you, if you manually add or delete data, you must adjust the data range parameters. Such adjustments change not only the amount of data in the graph, but also the graph size indicated in the top line. You can adjust the parameters in two ways: from the status area or from the worksheet area. Before you can adjust the data range parameters, however, you must choose Data_Range from the EDIT_PARAMS menu. In the message line, Perspective specifies the two methods of adjusting the data range (see fig. 17.8).

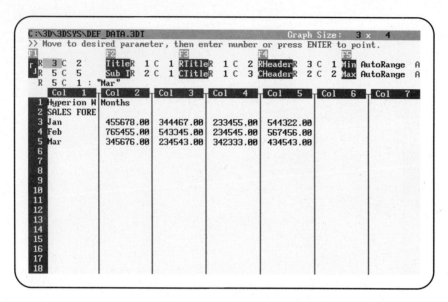

**Fig. 17.8.** *The message line after you choose Data_Range.*

To adjust the data range parameters from the status area, use the arrow keys to move the cursor to the data range row or column parameter (in the status area) you want to modify. Type the correct row or column number, and press Enter.

To adjust the data range parameters from the worksheet area, use the arrow keys to move the cursor to the data range row or column parameter (in the status line) you want to modify. Instead of typing a number, you press Enter. Perspective displays the data range as a reverse-video block. Use the arrow keys to expand or contract this area. After you make your changes, press Enter to accept the new data range parameters. This method of using the worksheet area to "point" to the data range you want is the better and easier method.

After you finish specifying the new data range, press F10.

## Entering Titles and Subtitles: The Title and Sub_T Parameters

To specify or modify the title or subtitle, press F10 to return to the main Data Manager menu, and simply move the cell pointer to the cell indicated in the status area. For example, the title in figure 17.7 is in cell R1C1, and the subtitle is in R2C1. To edit the title or subtitle, move the cursor to cell R1C1 or R2C1 in the worksheet area, type the new title or subtitle, and press Enter to confirm your changes.

In contrast, if you want to change the location of the title cell or subtitle cell, choose Titles from the EDIT_PARAMS menu by pressing the appropriate function key.

The Title and Sub T parameters define the cell locations for the graph's title and subtitle, respectively. To change the cell location, enter a new cell address. Or, as with the data range, you also can use the point method. To point out the current cell location, press Enter to highlight the title or subtitle data block in the worksheet area, and use the arrow keys to move the cursor to the cell containing the new title or subtitle. Again, press Enter to confirm the new cell location.

## Entering Row and Column Titles: The RTitle and CTitle Parameters

The RTitle and CTitle parameters specify the cell addresses of the row title and column title, respectively, that appear on the base of a 3-D graph. Perspective does not display row or column titles in a 2-D graph (see fig. 17.9).

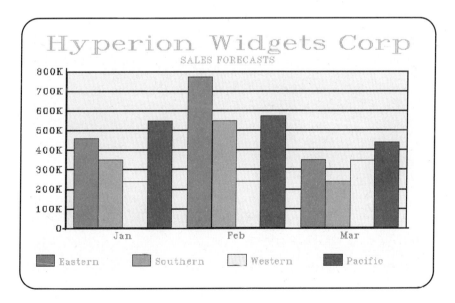

***Fig. 17.9.*** *A 2-D vertical-bar graph in Perspective Junior.*

As explained in the preceding section, "Entering Titles and Subtitles: The Title and Sub_T Parameters," Enable transports these two parameters to Perspective. Enable's x-axis title becomes the row title in a Perspective graph, and Perspective specifies the row title's cell address in the RTitle parameter of the Data Manager's status area. A legend heading specified in Enable becomes the column title in Perspective, and its cell address appears in the CTitle parameter. (The only purpose of the legend heading in Enable is to create a column title in Perspective; Enable graphs do not display legend headings.)

To modify a row or column title, you can either change the text without changing the cell reference or change the cell reference so that it points to different data. Use one or more of the methods described in the preceding sections to make these changes. If you want no title for a particular location, erase the data or change the cell address to an empty cell.

## Entering Row and Column Headers: The RHeader and CHeader Parameters

The RHeader and CHeader parameters specify the cell addresses of the data that Perspective uses to label the rows and columns, respectively, in a 3-D graph and the x-axis data and legend data, respectively, in a 2-D graph.

The cell address listed in each parameter is the starting cell for the headers. Perspective automatically matches the remaining headers with the corresponding rows or columns of data.

## Entering the Graph Range: The Min and Max Parameters

The graph range parameter enables you to scale the vertical axis, or y-axis, of your Perspective graph. By default, Perspective automatically scales the vertical axis, using the lowest and highest values from the data being graphed as the beginning (Min) and ending (Max) points, respectively, for the *scaling factor* (the y-axis increments).

For example, when Perspective automatically scales the y-axis for the data from the spreadsheet WIDGET.SSF (again see fig. 17.8), the program determines that the data ranges from a value of 234,543 to a value of 765,455. Consequently, the graph shown in figure 17.10 is scaled so that the y-axis goes from 300K to 800K.

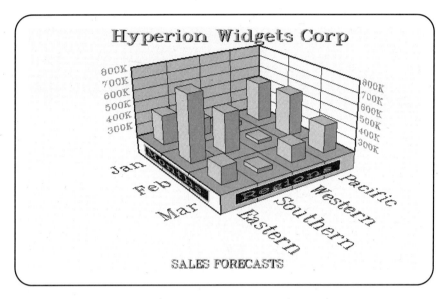

*Fig. 17.10.* A 3-D graph with the graph range automatically scaled.

To manually scale the graph range, choose Graph_Range from the EDIT_PARAMS menu.

Use the right-arrow key to move the pointer to the letter A (Automatic) in the status area, following the word AutoRange in the Min parameter. Press Enter and notice that the A changes to M (Manual). Move the pointer back to the left, to the Min parameter, and enter the minimum range value. Move the pointer down to the Max parameter and, if you want, change its value. Finally, press F10 to accept the changes.

In the example, changing the value in the Min parameter to 0 (see fig. 17.11) results in the graph shown in figure 17.12.

# Using the Option FILEMANAGER

The second option on the main Data Manager menu is FILEMANAGER. Choosing this option displays another menu:

Load File  Merge File  Save ASCII  Save 3DT  Data Protect

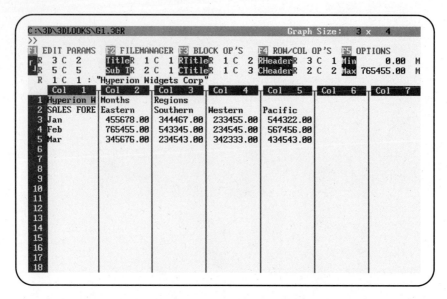

**Fig. 17.11.** *The graph range minimum scaled to the value 0.*

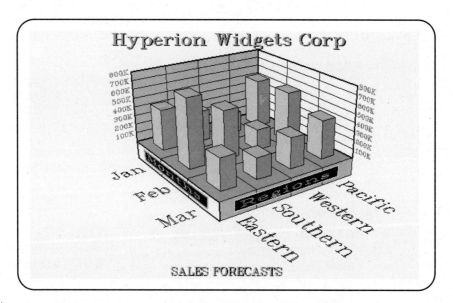

**Fig. 17.12.** *A 3-D graph with the graph range manually scaled.*

## Loading Files

The Load_File option prompts you to highlight the file you want from the list available in the default path, C:\3D\3DDATA. If you want to change the path and extension, press Tab and type in the new information. After you highlight the file, press Enter to accept it. You can press Esc to cancel at any time.

Perspective can load data, or bring in data from a disk file, in any of the following formats:

Perspective 3DT
DIF (Data Interchange Format—VisiCalc)
SYLK (Multiplan)
Boeing Calc (ASC file)
Lotus 1-2-3 Release 1A
Lotus 1-2-3 Release 2
ASCII Files

To use a 3DF file created with an earlier version of Perspective, use that version to create either a DIF file or a DAT (ASCII) file. Then load the newly created file into Perspective Junior. Because Enable can save a spreadsheet in 1-2-3 format, you easily can send an entire spreadsheet of data to Perspective outside of the standard Enable-to-Perspective transfer. Save the file in one of the 1-2-3 formats, and then use the FILEMANAGER option to load the file into Perspective.

When you indicate a file to load, Perspective clears the worksheet and status area and loads the new file. Any previous data on the worksheet disappears. The program automatically assigns the status area parameters for your newly loaded data file, but you usually will want to reassign the parameters manually.

## Merging Files

The Merge_File choice on the FILEMANAGER menu works the same way as the Load_File option, except that Merge_File does not first erase existing data. The file being merged destroys existing data only if the incoming file contains data in identical cell locations. This option works much the same as the Combine-Copy feature in Enable's spreadsheet module.

## Saving Files

Perspective Junior can save files in two different ways.

- *Save_ASCII.* This option saves the current page in ASCII format.

- *Save_3DT.* This method, the preferred method of saving files, saves all Data Manager pages in a special Perspective format with the file name extension 3DT. This special format, the quickest and most disk-efficient of the available formats, is Perspective's native format and requires no conversion.

Recall from Chapter 9 that Enable can read spreadsheets in DIF, SYLK, and ASCII format. If you need to transfer data back to Enable from Perspective, save the Data Manager worksheet in one of these formats. Then use Enable to retrieve it.

## Protecting Data

When loading a graph file (see the section "Using the Files_&_Output Option" in this chapter), Perspective Junior, by default, replaces the information in the Data Manager with the newly loaded file. If you choose Data_Protect, the program prevents this loss of data. Perspective loads the formatting information (its type, colors, viewing angle, and so on), but the data it graphs remains what is currently in the Data Manager.

# Copying, Moving, and Clearing Blocks of Data: Using Block Options

The choices on the Data Manager Block Options menu (BLOCK_OP'S) are analogous to the Enable spreadsheet commands Copy, Move, and Range Erase. You can use Perspective's block options to copy, move, or erase a rectangular block of data—as small as one cell or as large as an entire page of the Data Manager worksheet.

Whichever operation you want to perform—copy, move, or clear (erase)—you always begin by specifying the target block. From the main Data Manager menu, press

    BLOCK_OP'S

Perspective then displays a message telling you to

```
Position cursor to starting corner. ENTER to accept, ESC to cancel.
```

Use the arrow keys to move the cursor to either the top left or bottom right corner of the target group of cells (the cells you want to block), and press Enter. Then follow the instructions in Perspective's next message:

```
Put the cursor on the opposite corner and press ENTER.
```

Perspective displays a menu with these choices:

Copy Block   Move Block   Clear Block

The difference between the first two options, Copy_Block and Move_Block, is the same as in Enable's spreadsheet and word processing modules. When you copy a block of cells to another location in the worksheet, the original block is not affected. The Move_Block command places a copy of the data at a new location and erases the original block. To use either option, choose Copy_Block or Move_Block from the menu, position the cursor at the upper left corner of the block destination, and press Enter. After you press Enter, Perspective places the target block of cells at the new location. If you use the Move_Block command, Perspective erases the data from the original block of cells.

The Clear_Block command erases the data in the target block. Because this option is destructive, when you choose this option, Perspective displays the message

```
Do you really want to delete this [Y/N]?
```

Answer Y to erase the contents of the target block of cells.

# Using Row and Column Options

Use the ROW/COL_OP'S choice from the main Data Manager menu to copy, move, delete, exchange, insert, and sort entire rows or columns at a time. After you choose ROW/COL_OP'S, Perspective displays the following menu:

Row Op's   Column Op's   Sort Rows   Sort Col's

The following two sections explain these four options.

## Manipulating Rows and Columns

Choosing Row_Op's from the ROW/COL_OP'S menu provides the following row command choices:

Copy Row   Move Row   Delete Row   Exchange Rows   Insert Row

To use any of these options, place the cursor in the row to be affected (the source row), and press the appropriate function key. The Insert_Row option works immediately, inserting a blank row at the cursor and pushing all rows following the cursor down one row. The Delete_Row option takes effect after you confirm the deletion by pressing Y and then Enter. The other three options—Move_Row, Copy_Row, and Exchange_Rows—require you to point out a destination row. As with Copy_Block and Move_Block, the Copy_Row command does not erase data from the source row, but the Move_Row command does. Both Copy_Row and Move_Row place a copy of the contents of the source row at the destination row, replacing any existing data in the destination row. The Exchange_Rows command switches the contents of the source row with the contents of the destination row.

For example, to copy a row of data to another location in the worksheet, position the cursor in the row to be copied and choose

ROW/COL_OP'S
Row_Op's
Copy_Row

Column commands work in the same manner as row commands. To copy, move, delete, exchange, or insert columns, choose Column_Op's from the ROW/COL_OP'S menu, and then choose from the following menu:

Copy Col   Move Col   Delete Col   Exchange Cols   Insert Col

Perspective Junior displays the row in reverse video. Move the cursor to the destination row, and press Enter to copy the row to the new location.

## Sorting Rows and Columns

Perspective enables you to alphabetically or numerically sort rows according to the data in one of the columns, or vice versa. To sort a row of data, choose Sort_Rows from the ROW/COL_OP'S menu. Perspective highlights in reverse video the column containing the cursor. Use the cursor-movement keys to move this highlight to the column that you want to use as the key column for sorting. Then choose one of the following menu options that Perspective displays:

Alpha Down  Alpha Up  Numeric Down  Numeric Up

Alpha_Down and Alpha_Up enable you to sort the rows alphabetically, down (A to Z) or up (Z to A), respectively, according to the data in the specified column. Similarly, Numeric_Down and Numeric_Up numerically sort the rows in descending (9 to 0) or ascending (0 to 9) order, based on the data in the specified column.

You accomplish column sorting in the same manner. After you choose Sort_Col's from the ROW/COL_OP'S menu, the steps are identical except that Perspective sorts the data by column, based on the value in a specified row.

## Using Miscellaneous Options

If you choose OPTIONS from the main Data Manager menu, Perspective displays the following menu:

Show Range  Float Zero  Clear All  Transpose  Exec. Math

The following five sections explain these options.

### Using Show_Range

The Show_Range option works with the y-axis minimum and maximum ranges set in the Graph Range parameter. Show_Range acts as a toggle switch. The first time you choose the Show_Range option, Perspective displays the following message:

`Values outside the current data range will NOT be displayed.`

This message means you have turned off the Show_Range option so that Perspective does not display in the graph any worksheet data outside the minimum or maximum range you establish. If you choose the Show_Range option again, however, the message changes:

`Values outside the current data range WILL be displayed.`

You have turned on the Show_Range option, which is the default setting.

## Using the Float_Zero Option

Perspective normally graphs negative numbers below the zero plane (the graph's imaginary floor, located at the zero on the scale). To cause Perspective to graph negative numbers from the floor upward, choose

Float_Zero

Like the option Show_Range, Float_Zero is a toggle switch. Choose the option again to turn off Float_Zero, which is the default condition.

## Erasing All Cells with the Clear_All Option

The quickest way to erase all data in the entire worksheet is to choose Clear_All from the OPTIONS menu. Because this command is destructive, Perspective asks you to confirm it. At the message

```
Erase all cells [Y/N]?
```

press Y, and then press Enter.

## Switching Rows and Columns: Using the Transpose Option

To switch rows and columns, which, in effect, switches x- and z-axes, choose the Transpose option from the OPTIONS menu. For example, the graphs in figures 17.13 and 17.14 are based on the same data but with rows and columns transposed.

## Executing Math Equations with the Exec._Math Option

Perspective can perform a limited number of mathematical operations and functions. The standard arithmetic operators are

+ − * / **

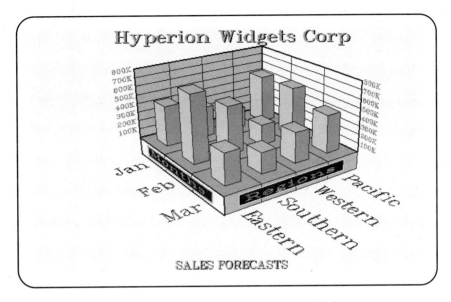

*Fig. 17.13. A 3-D graph before transposition of rows and columns.*

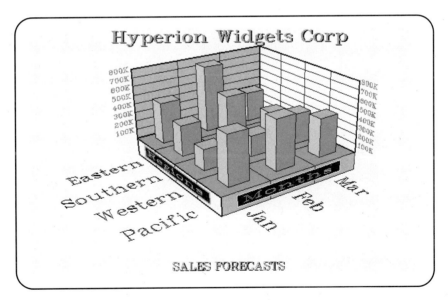

*Fig. 17.14. A 3-D graph after transposition of rows and columns.*

These operators have the same effect as they have in Enable's spreadsheet and DBMS modules. The syntax for typing a formula, however, is quite different.

In an Enable spreadsheet, for example, you can type the formula +A1+A2 into the cell A3. Enable places in cell A3 the sum of the values in the cells A1 and A2. In the Perspective worksheet, however, you must type formulas in a different cell from the destination cell. Therefore, to arrive at the same result—to place the sum of cells R1C1 and R2C1 into cell R3C1—you must type the formula

@r3c1=r1c1+r2c1

and press Enter. The @ sign identifies the entry as a formula, and the cell address indicated to the left of the equal sign identifies the destination of the answer.

Another distinction is Perspective's use of the terms *absolute* and *relative* cell reference. In Enable, a cell address designation in a formula always refers to the contents of that cell. A *relative* cell address in Enable takes on significance only if you copy a formula to another location. As you may expect, in Perspective the address r3c1 (lowercase r and c) refers to the contents of the cell in the third row and first column of the worksheet: an *absolute* reference; however, a deceptively similar reference, R3C1, a *relative* reference, does not always refer to the same cell. R3C1 refers to the cell located at the first column of the third row from the top of the data range specified through the EDIT_PARAMS menu.

The Data Manager does not automatically calculate a formula as soon as you enter it. To cause formulas to be calculated, choose Exec._Math from the OPTIONS menu. Perspective scans the worksheet from left to right and from top to bottom, calculates all the formulas, and places the answers in the cells indicated in the formula. After you add a formula, you must choose the Exec._Math option again to calculate the new formula and to recalculate all other formulas.

# Creating 3-D and 2-D Graphs

After you transfer data to Perspective Junior from Enable, or use the Data Manager to enter data, you are ready to build your graph.

With Perspective Junior, you can create 13 preset 3-D graph types and 8 preset 2-D graph types—probably more types of graphs than you ever may use. After you choose a graph type, you can choose from nine preset viewing angles and customize the graph with a number of different options. The following two sections explain selecting preset graph types and viewing angles.

## Selecting Preset Graph Types

When you first start Perspective, the Main Menu displays the following options:

Graph Types   Viewing Angles   Data Manager   Files & Output   Custom Options

To choose one of the preset graph types, choose

>   Graph_Types

Perspective displays a "honeycomb" menu of 13 3-D graph types and 8 2-D graph types (see fig. 17.15). To select a new graph, use the cursor-movement keys to move the blinking border to the graph type you want. Then press Enter. Don't be afraid to experiment. Perspective draws so quickly that trying each of the graph types takes little effort.

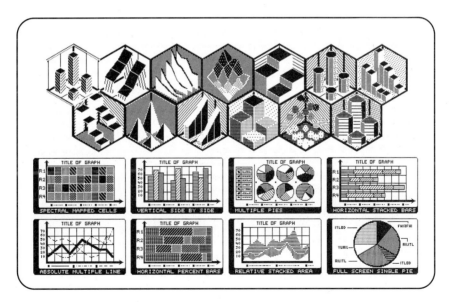

***Fig. 17.15.*** *Preset 3-D and 2-D graph types.*

All of Perspective's 3-D graph types are variations of one idea: *risers*, the bars or other shapes that graph a cell value. However, the graph types range from a simple 3-D bar graph to a continuously flowing surface designed to graph elevation figures (longitude and latitude) or recreate a surface. One graph type may be so exotic that you never use it, and another may be perfect for your particular data. Several of the graph types use *spectral mapping*, which causes the graph's risers to change patterns (or colors on a color system) as they increase in height. This shading or coloring makes your graph appear dynamic. Figure 17.16 shows an example of a spectral-mapped graph.

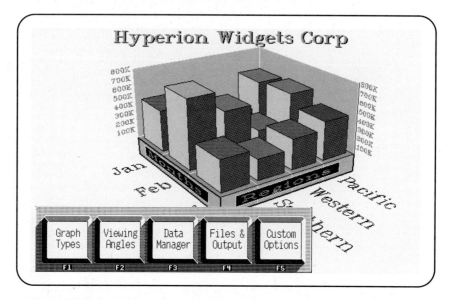

**Fig. 17.16.** *A spectral-mapped 3-D graph.*

Sometimes you need to choose a particular graph type that makes your data easier to see. For example, graph type 9 displays triangles that are especially useful for revealing data otherwise blocked behind thick bars. Compare figures 17.17 and 17.16; both are based on the same data.

## Selecting Preset Viewing Angles

Because Perspective draws a 3-D graph in true perspective, you can depict the data on-screen from any angle or side. For ease of use, Perspective provides nine preset viewing angles, shown in figure 17.18. To access this screen, choose the following option from the Main Menu:

Viewing_Angles

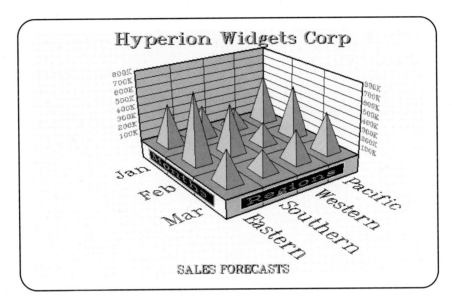

**Fig. 17.17.** *A triangle graph.*

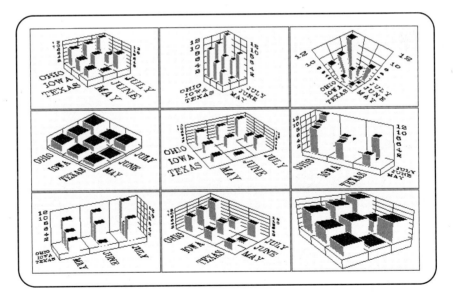

**Fig. 17.18.** *Preset viewing angles.*

To specify a viewing angle, press the arrow keys until the blinking border surrounds the viewing angle you want. Press Enter or F10 to redisplay your graph. Notice that if you change the graph type from the default, Perspective continues to display the graph type from the newly specified viewing angle.

Experiment with the preset graph types and viewing angles. Change the graph type, then change the angle. Go back and forth between graph types and viewing angles until the result satisfies you.

> If you use a color system, you can use the left- and right-arrow keys to cycle, or browse, through the various color patterns available for the parameters (walls, background, and so on), and the up- and down-arrow keys to cycle through the graph colors. Press Enter or F10 to accept the changes.

# Customizing Your Graph

After you choose the graph type and viewing angle, look at your graph. If you are not satisfied with the result, you can use the customizing features described in this section to fine tune it. Although Perspective provides many preset graph styles, you may want to add, delete, or adjust some features to suit your particular needs. You should make sure, however, that you don't get carried away. Remember that the purpose of using a graph is to clearly and accurately inform your audience, not dazzle them.

## Adjusting the Color

Perspective provides three basic color options. To access each option, select Custom_Options and then Color_Options. Choose one of the following options:

- *Color_Mixer*. This option enables you manually to mix colors on-screen to suit your taste—like an artist mixing paints on a palette. By mixing red, green, and blue in different proportions, you change the colors on-screen. Use the arrow keys to adjust the colors, and the PgUp and PgDn keys to cycle among the graph elements. A small box appears in the corner of the screen and shows the currently displayed proportions of color. Use the Home and End keys to move this box to either the top left or bottom left corner of the screen.

- *Color_by_Row*. This option enables you to make each row a separate color to help you identify which data belongs to which data group.

- *Color_by_Column*. This option enables you to make each column a separate color to help you identify which data belongs to which data group.

# Reversing the Data

Data_Reversal_Options enable you to transpose data between axes or to reverse the order of the rows or columns. This feature is similar to the Data Manager's Transpose option; however, Sequence Options is temporary, affecting only the immediate display of the graph—not the data stored on disk.

Select Custom_Options and then Data_Reversal_Options. Choose one of the following reversal options:Normal_Sequence, Exchange_Rows_&_Columns, Reverse_Row_Order, and Reverse_Column_Order.

# Arranging Titles and Subtitles

Every time you choose the Cycle_Titles option, Perspective moves the main titles and subtitles to different positions on-screen, enabling you to position them exactly where you want them.

# Adjusting Walls, Grids, and Risers

The Walls_Grids_Risers option consists of a series of toggles that enable you to display or hide the left and right walls and the horizontal and vertical grid lines, and enables you to adjust the width and height of the risers. (To reveal data hidden by large risers, make your risers thinner.) To access these options, select Custom_Options and then Walls_Grids_Risers. Then choose one of the following options: Left_Wall_On/Off, Right_Wall_On/Off, Wall_Grid_Control, Base_Grid_Control, and Riser_Sizing.

# Customizing the Viewing Angle

A previous section of this chapter, "Selecting Preset Viewing Angles," discusses Perspective's preset viewing angles. Although Perspective has many preset angles, you can customize the viewing angle to your satisfaction. By using the options from the Custom_Viewing_Angles menu, accessed from the Custom_Options menu, you can rotate and move the graph along any of its three axes, and you can "pan" the graph on-screen, zoom in and out, change the cube proportions, and distort the perspective of an angle.

When you choose Custom_Viewing_Angles, your graph disappears and Perspective displays a "wire frame" outline of the graph (see fig. 17.19). Use this wire frame to set the new viewing angle of your graph.

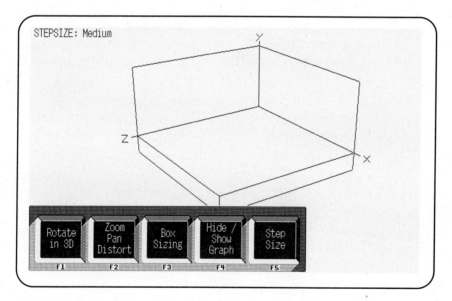

*Fig. 17.19. A wire frame outline of a graph.*

The Custom_Viewing_Angles menu provides the following options:

- *Rotate_in_3-D.* Use this option to rotate the box in three dimensions along any axis (x, y, or z). Perspective also provides stepping options that speed or slow the rotation.

- *Zoom_Pan_Distort.* Use this option to move the entire graph right or left (pan_x), move it up or down (pan_y), make it bigger or smaller (zoom), or change the perspective (distort).

- *Box_Sizing*. Change the x-wall width (Width), the box height (Height), the z-wall width (Length), and the base height through this option.

- *Hide/Show_Graph*. Because Perspective does not display the graph as you make adjustments to the viewing angle, you quickly can forget the graph's original position as you rotate, pan, and zoom the wire frame. Toggle on this option to display the graph as it was last drawn. Perspective superimposes the wire frame over the graph.

- *Step_Size*. You can adjust the wire frame in small, medium, or large increments. Use this option to toggle between these three "steps."

# Using the Files_&_Output Option

The Data Manager, discussed in a previous section of this chapter, provides the means for saving and retrieving the raw data used to create a Perspective graph. It also assigns all labels. All adjustments you make outside of the Data Manager (graph type, viewing angle, color, size, and so on), however, are not saved when you save the Data Manager worksheet.

The Files_&_Output option assumes this duty. With this option, you also can save the entire graph as a picture in several formats compatible with other programs.

Another task you can accomplish using the Files_&_Output option is really a culmination of everything else: *output*. You use the Files_&_Output option to control where you send the graph, whether to a printer or to a plotter or to a film recording device.

## Saving and Loading Graph Files

With Perspective, you can generate spectacular graphics, but as you probably have discovered, wading through the menus and waiting, time after time, for Perspective to redraw your graph requires effort on your part. When your graph finally is perfect, you probably do not want to have to do it all over again tomorrow. Saving your graph at this point, therefore, is a good idea.

Perspective saves graph settings in a type of file called a *graph file*. To save a graph setting, choose the following options from the Main Menu:

> Files_&_Output
> File_Manager
> Save_Graph

Perspective displays the prompt

    Save under what name?

Type the name you want to give the file. If the file already exists, Perspective displays the prompt

    File already exists. Overwrite it [Y/N]?

If you want to replace the old file on the disk with the new file in memory, press Yes. Press No if you do not want to overwrite the old file. The file name extension is 3GR. By default, Perspective stores graph files in the subdirectory \3D\3DLOOKS.

Later, when you again want to use this *look file* (the graph settings for graph type, color, title locations, and so on) with the same data or other data, choose the following option from the File_Manager menu:

> Load_Graph

Perspective displays a list of look files from which you can choose. Use the cursor-movement keys to move to the file you want to use, and then press Enter. Perspective applies the graph settings saved in the look file. (To apply the graph settings to the data currently loaded in the Data Manager worksheet, you first must set Data Protection in the Data Manager; otherwise, Perspective uses the data stored in the graph file.)

# Saving and Loading Image Files

An *image file* is a snapshot of the screen and is much different from a graph file. An image file does not save the actual data or graph settings. Rather, it saves the exact image you see on-screen when the graph is displayed.

Because picture (image) files are bit-mapped images, they take a relatively large amount of disk space—at least when compared to graph files—and you cannot change them in any way. You mainly use them to store an image you want to use later in drawing multiple graphs or in another program.

Perspective saves image files in the format called GEM, which works with Ventura Publisher and any other program that uses GEM-formatted image files. Perspective assigns the extension IMG to these files.

To save an image file, from the File_Manager menu, choose

> Save_Image

At the prompt, type the name under which you want to save the image file, and press Enter.

Loading a picture file is just as easy. From the File_Manager menu, choose

> Load_Image

Choose the proper image file from the menu, and press Enter.

# Printing and Plotting a Perspective Graph

Perspective provides several output methods, or methods of printing, that essentially fall into two categories: to a printer and to a plotter. Each of these methods in turn has options. This section discusses the most fundamental output options.

## Sending Output to a Printer

From the Files_&_Output menu, choose Print_Manager.

From this menu, many different options are available to help you improve the output.

- *Preview*. Use this option to set the pattern for the walls, floor, and base of the box. You can choose from five selected patterns. First press the function key that corresponds to the wall, floor, or base on which you want to use the pattern, and then press the function key that corresponds to the pattern you want to use.

- *Page_Setup*. From this menu, you can adjust the size, position, and orientation (landscape or portrait) of the graph; you can adjust the paper size; and you can turn on the border option that prints a border around the graph.

- *Printer_Options*. From this menu you can specify a printer; change the resolution of the output; adjust the color scheme (if you use a color printer); change the printer port; and select a serial port.

After you establish the printing options to your satisfaction, choose Print from the Print_Manager menu to print the graph.

## Sending Output to a Plotter

Plotting a graph is quite similar to printing a graph, except for the difference in hardware. From the Files_&_Output menu, choose

Plot_Manager

Before sending a graph to the plotter, make desired choices from the following options:

- *Preview*. Use this option to set the colors for the various gridlines, outlines, and text of the graph. When you press the selected function key, Perspective prompts you to enter a pen number. Eight different pens are available. (A plotter identifies each colored pen by its number. By assigning a pen number, you specify the pen on the plotter that matches the color on-screen.)

- *Page_Setup*. This option enables you to adjust the size, position, and orientation (landscape or portrait) of the graph; adjust the paper size; and turn on the border option that prints a border around the graph.

- *Plotter_Options*. From this menu of options, you can specify a plotter; change the quality of the output; set the number of pens, pen width, bleed percentage, and media; change the plotter port; and choose a serial port.

After you adjust the plotter settings, choose Plot from the Plot_Manager menu to send the graph to the plotter.

TIP

To use a Perspective graph in an Enable word processing file, you must save the graph as a *plot file*, which is the output sent to a disk file by way of the plotter options. From the Plotter_Options menu, choose

Select_Plotter

Highlight the plotter IBM Model 6180, and press Enter. Then press the function key corresponding to Port until you select the option Disk. Press F10 to return to the Plot_Manager menu.

Finally, choose Plot from the Plot_Manager menu to send the plot to disk.

Specify the desired file name and press Enter. Later, use the File_Copy option in Enable's word processing module to import the file into a word processing file.

# Using the Slide Show Manager

The Slide Show Manager, new in Perspective Junior, is a full-featured presentation instrument that works like a slide projector, complete with transition and timing effects. Instead of taking pictures, however, you use Perspective Junior to create slides and combine them into an organized presentation. After you develop a slide show, you can save it and play back, at any time, what you saved.

A slide show consists of two main components: screen images (see section on "Saving and Loading Image Files") that make up the "slides," and a list of presentation effects.

From the Slide_Show_Manager menu, you can choose from the following options:

- *Load_Show*. If you want to use an existing slide show, use this option to load it. Perspective stores each slide show in the default directory C:\3D\3DPICS and assigns the extension LST. After you load a show, you can highlight a slide and use the Enter, Ins, and Del keys to add slides, move slides from one slot to another, and delete slides. You can use the Dissolve and Time columns to alter the transition from one slide to the next. From the Dissolve column, you can choose Switch, Overlay, Venetian, LeftRite, UpDown, or Dissolve, and in the Time column, you can specify a time interval of between 0 and 99 seconds.

- *New_Show*. Use this option to create a new slide show. This feature has the same features as the option Load_Show.

- *Run_Show*. Choose this option to run a show. Before you can run a show, however, you first must load an existing slide show or create a new one.

- *Save_Show*. Choose this option to save a slide show. Perspective prompts you to enter a file name; you also can change the directory path at this prompt. Type a file name and press Enter. Perspective automatically adds the extension LST.

- *Options*. With this option, you specify whether you want to run the slide show manually (Manual) or unattended (Auto). You also specify whether you want the show to run continuously (Loop) or only once (No_Loop).

To save your changes and exit the Slide_Show_Manager menu, press F10. Perspective returns you to the Files_&_Output menu.

# Summary

Although Perspective Junior still is not completely integrated into Enable, the program does enable you to create remarkable graphics and copy them into Enable files. More than likely, you may use the graphs you create with Perspective as stand-alone products. This chapter has left unexplored several other, more complicated features. When you think you have mastered all the features covered in this chapter, go exploring to discover even greater treasures.

# Part VII

# The Telecommunications Module

---

### Includes

---

**Quick Start VII: Using the
Telecommunications Module**

**Telecommunicating with Enable**

# Quick Start VII

# Using the Telecommunications Module

This lesson, the last of the quick-start lessons, gives a brief overview of Enable's telecommunications module. The telecommunications module enables you to transmit information through your telephone system; you can *upload* (send) data from your computer to another, and you can *download* (receive, or "capture") data from another computer system, called the *host system*. The host system with which you exchange data in this lesson is an *information service*, which is a computer system that offers PC users information through *electronic mail*, *bulletin boards*, and so on. You learn more about information services in the following chapter, "Telecommunicating with Enable."

To "connect" your computer with a host system, you must have a *modem*, a device that converts your computer's signals to the signals required by telephone lines, and vice versa. To complete this lesson, you must have an *autodial modem* connected to your computer system. An autodial modem generates tones that enable it to dial another computer system, and the modem answers incoming calls to establish a connection with your computer. For more information on hooking up your modem, and to find out whether you have an autodial modem, see your owner's manual.

To connect your computer with a host system, you also must have the telephone number of a bulletin board system (BBS) or an electronic mail service. Enable Software, Inc. maintains a bulletin board, ESI-BBS, that you can call by dialing: (518) 877-6316; however, you must subscribe to one of the company's technical support plans to upload a message or file to this BBS. For a list of other available information services, see Appendix B of your Enable/OA 4.0 Communications documentation. If you want to avoid long-distance charges, you can dial a local BBS (see "Using Bulletin Boards" in the following chapter to find out about dialing local bulletin boards).

With this telephone number ready, your modem properly connected, and Enable properly installed, you are ready to begin this lesson. You learn how to connect your computer system to another system, and you learn how to send and receive a file. You also learn how to disconnect from the host system and save the captured data to a file for later reference.

# Initializing the System

Before you can use your modem to call another system, you must *initialize*, or prepare for use, the modem and the *communications port* (COMM port or serial port—these terms all mean the mechanism that governs the connection between your computer and modem). Initializing your modem and port means you "alert" them to "pay attention" when Enable gives them a command. The following steps explain the process of initializing your modem and communications port.

1. From Enable's Main Menu, choose

   **Use_System Communications Quick-Connect**

   Enable displays the Quick Connection form (see fig QSVII.1). The settings you choose for BAUD, PARITY, WORD_SIZE, STOP_BITS, and DUPLEX must match the settings of the computer system you are calling. (Contact someone who is familiar with the host system or refer to your Enable documentation to match these settings.) If your first attempt at connecting to the host system fails, or if you connect and see nothing but gibberish on your screen, you probably have a mismatch of one or more of the settings on the Quick Connection form. The following chapter, "Telecommunicating with Enable," discusses each of these settings in detail.

2. Choose the following settings—the most commonly used settings. Press End if you don't need to make any changes.

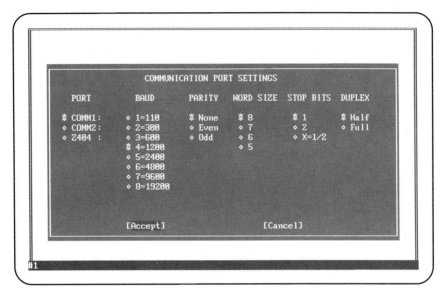

**Fig. QSVII.1.** *The Quick Connection form.*

- *PORT:* Choose COMM1. If you use an internal modem that is connected to a serial port, you may need to choose COMM2 instead.

- *BAUD:* Choose 4=1200.

- *PARITY:* Choose **None**.

- *WORD_SIZE:* Choose **8**.

- *STOP_BITS:* Choose **1** stop bit.

- *DUPLEX:* Choose **Full**.

3. After you make your choices, choose **Accept**. Enable displays a new screen to prompt you for a file name (see fig. QSVII.2). Type the file name **QS7LTR** and press Enter to establish a file in which Enable can place text captured while *on-line* (successfully connected) with the host system. (If Enable does not prompt you for a file name, the program uses a default file to capture text. If you want Enable to display this prompt, refer to Appendix B, "Using Profiles to Customize Enable," to adjust the telecommunications settings.)

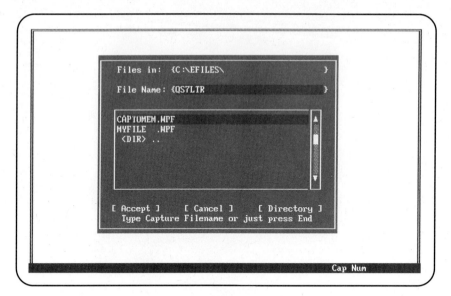

***Fig. QSVII.2.*** *The prompt for a capture file name.*

4. Next, Enable displays a third screen (see fig. QSVII.3) to indicate that the program is initializing the communications port and the modem.

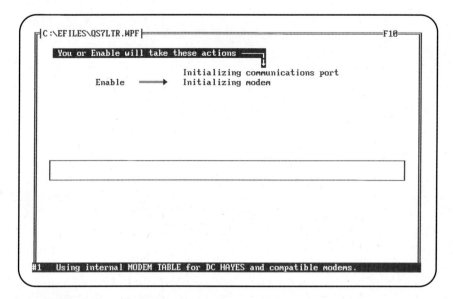

***Fig. QSVII.3.*** *Message displayed as Enable initializes the communications port and modem.*

5. After initializing your hardware, Enable displays a blank screen, called the *Telecom screen* (see fig.QSVII.4), from which all communications take place.

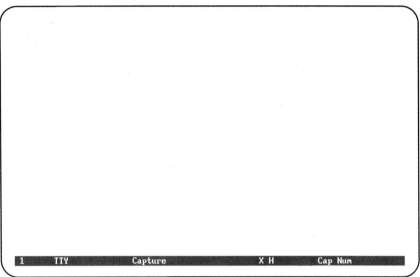

| 1 | TTY | Capture | X H | Cap Num |

***Fig. QSVII.4.*** *The Telecom screen.*

Now that Enable has initialized your modem and communications port, you are ready to send a mail message to a host system; however, you first must prepare the message.

# Typing a Mail Message

Although you usually can type your message while on-line with the host system, composing and typing your message *off-line* (before you connect) is more economical if you must pay a connect charge or a long-distance toll. You then can highlight, or *mark*, the text you want to send. The following steps outline the process of typing and marking a message.

1. To use the Telecom screen for word processing, press PgUp. Enable displays a word processing screen. The status line looks like a normal word processing status line, but Enable displays a second line below it at the bottom of the screen (see fig. QSVII.5) to remind you that you still are in telecommunications, not word processing.

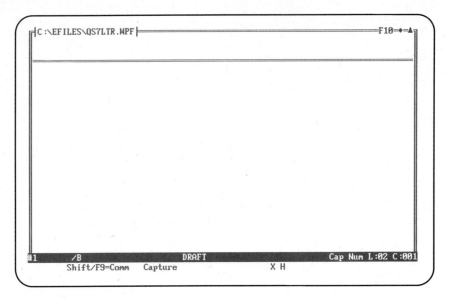

*Fig. QSVII.5. The word processing screen from the Telecom screen.*

2. Type the following message:

   **MESSAGE TO ME:**
   **This paragraph is an example of a message you can send to an**
   **electronic mail system. You can type it while your computer is**
   **on-line, but typing it before you connect is more economical.**
   **BYE.**

3. To mark your message, use the arrow keys to move the cursor to
   the first character of your message. Press F7. Move the cursor to the
   end of your message and press F7 again. Your entire message
   should appear in reverse video.

4. Press Shift-F9 to return to the Telecom screen. The message remains in memory in the word processing window; press PgUp to
   return to your message.

# Calling Another System

Now that you have initialized your modem and COMM port and have typed
your message, you are ready to call a host system.

1. To place the call, press

   F10 **Modem Call**

   Enable prompts you to enter the telephone number of the host system (see fig. QSVII.6).

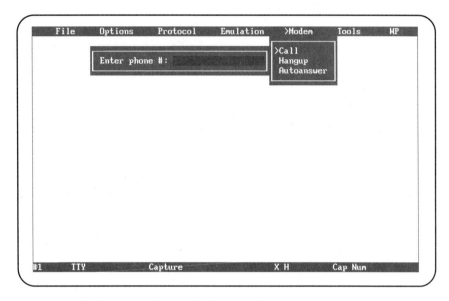

***Fig. QSVII.6.*** *The prompt for a telephone number.*

2. Before typing the telephone number, press **T** if you use a touch-tone phone or **P** for a rotary phone. Then type the telephone number and press Enter.

3. You hear a dial tone, and then you hear the modem dial the telephone number. After you hear a ring or two, the host system answers the call, and the two systems "shake hands" to connect. Enable may display the speed at which you are connected, such as 1200 baud in this example. The host system then prompts you to sign on, discussed in the following section.

# Signing On

The steps required to sign on to the host system vary from system to system. Most bulletin boards prompt you to type your name, and then your password. When you call a BBS for the first time, the host system gives you the opportunity to register. After you register, you have an opportunity to type a password to use the next time you sign on. Electronic mail systems, however, often require you to preregister, and they assign you a user ID and a password.

1. Sign on to the host system you called. The host system greets you with its opening messages.

2. Follow the steps required by the host system to access its message or mail area. Figure QSVII.7 shows the mail menu from General Electric's GEnie Information Service (see fig. QSVII.7).

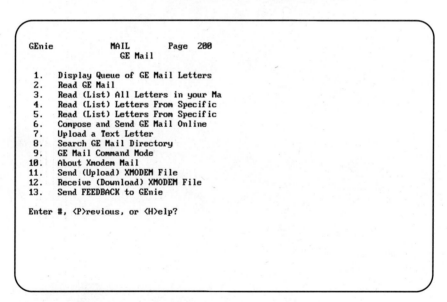

```
GEnie           MAIL         Page  200
                 GE Mail

    1.   Display Queue of GE Mail Letters
    2.   Read GE Mail
    3.   Read (List) All Letters in your Ma
    4.   Read (List) Letters From Specific
    5.   Read (List) Letters From Specific
    6.   Compose and Send GE Mail Online
    7.   Upload a Text Letter
    8.   Search GE Mail Directory
    9.   GE Mail Command Mode
    10.  About Xmodem Mail
    11.  Send (Upload) XMODEM File
    12.  Receive (Download) XMODEM File
    13.  Send FEEDBACK to GEnie

    Enter #, <P>revious, or <H>elp?
```

*Fig. QSVII.7. GEnie's mail menu.*

# Sending a Text File

For practice, you are going to send to yourself the message you previously typed and marked.

1. Follow the steps required by the host system to send or upload a text file or message. For example, if you were using GEnie, you would choose option 7, `Upload a Text Letter`, from the GEnie MAIL menu (again see fig. QSVII.8).

2. When the host system prompts you for the name of the person to whom you want to send the message (often indicated by TO:), enter your own name or ID (whichever is appropriate for the host system) and press Enter.

3. Press F8 when the host system prompts you to send or upload the file or message. Enable copies your marked message to the location of the cursor and sends it to the host system. Because transferring data takes several seconds, Enable displays the following message in the status line while it sends the file:

   `Transfer in process. Press ESC to stop transmission.`

4. After Enable finishes the transmission, enter the host system's code to send the letter. Check your electronic mail messages. You should have a message from yourself. Read the message, and then exit from the host system's message or mail area.

# Disconnecting

The final step in this exercise is disconnecting from the host system and returning to Enable's Main Menu.

1. Each electronic mail or bulletin board system has its own preferred method of disconnection. Don't disconnect without using this preferred method of signing off, or of saying "good-bye." When you issue the appropriate command, the host system drops the connection, and Enable displays the message

   `NO CARRIER`

2.  To exit the telecommunications module and return to the Main
    Menu, press

    Alt-End

or

    F10 **File Exit** (Disconnect)

When Enable asks you whether you want to save the data you captured, answer

    **Yes**

Enable saves the session to the word processing file QS7LTR.WPF,
and then displays the Main Menu.

# Telecommunicating with Enable

T alking is the most basic form of communication. Communicating with computers is an electronic extension of talking. With Enable, you can use your computer to talk to other people who have computers.

This chapter describes how you can use your computer to exchange information with other computers. The chapter also shows you how to communicate with information services, mainframe computers, and public networks. You learn how to use Enable's two telecommunications methods: Quick-Connect for "quick-and-dirty" communications, and Setup for more complex communications. In addition, the chapter shows you how to upload files to and download files from other systems and how to "capture" data from other systems.

## Taking Advantage of Telecommunications

The process of communicating with another computer is called *telecommunications* because you usually use a telephone. Most telephone signals are *analog*—audible sounds represented by continuous waves that reflect the differences in amplitude (loudness) and frequency (pitch), used to represent data. In contrast, the electronic signals of a computer generally are *digital*: all data is represented by separate off and on signals that stand for the binary digits 0 and 1. To convert the computer's digital format to the telephone line's analog format at the sending end of a transmission, and to convert the format back again at the receiving end, you need a device called a *modem* at each end. The name is short for *modulate-demodulate*, the name for the conversion process.

With your PC, Enable, and a modem, you can telecommunicate with a variety of other computers: mainframe computers, other PCs, and computers that provide information services. You also can use networks to reduce the cost of telecommunications. This section discusses the major advantages of using telecommunications.

## Using Information Services

Several companies offer electronic information services to personal computer users. You can access these services through your computer's telecommunications capability. Some features of such information services include the following:

- *Electronic mail.* You can use this feature to send private notes to another computer user.

- *Bulletin boards.* This feature provides public notes, usually organized by topic and posted to a group of computer users.

- *Public domain software and shareware.* With this feature, you can obtain programs written by someone who is willing to distribute them free of charge or for a small fee.

- *News services.* Use this feature to gain access to general or specific news, such as business news.

- *Databases.* When connected to another system, this feature enables you to obtain large amounts of information on almost every conceivable topic.

Information services can be tremendously helpful. You can discuss your computing problems with sympathetic users who probably can offer helpful advice. Information services also can transmit (or *download*) to your PC hundreds of free or low-cost programs ranging from utilities to games. With information services, you can get current business or financial news, communicate with people all over the world without playing "telephone tag," and electronically search through dozens of databases in the same amount of time you need to drive to the library.

Sometimes a single service provides more than one feature. For example, CompuServe Information Service has electronic mail, bulletin boards, shareware, and several news services, including Associated Press. Similar services include The Source, GEnie, Delphi, and BYTE's Information Exchange (BIX). Members of PRODIGY can receive information on topics such as shopping, travel, electronic mail, financial services, and entertainment. You can take advantage of the Enable Product Support Roundtable, available on GEnie, to leave technical questions, get sample files, and receive on-line hints about using Enable.

You easily can find information services; Enable's telecommunications documentation (Appendix B) lists several services. The cost of most information services ranges from $3 to $50 per hour. Information services that specialize in a certain topic usually cost more than other services. Some services have minimum monthly charges or yearly subscription fees. Generally, you pay by entering your credit card number or bank card number the first time you log on to the network.

You may discover that the information service you want requires a long-distance telephone call. Those long-distance charges quickly add up. Although you may never talk for an hour long distance, you find that communicating with an information service for an hour is not unusual. For this reason, several companies have set up public networks, which are less expensive ways to call a distant computer. In the United States, the two main public network services are Telenet and Tymnet.

## Using Bulletin Boards

The most abundant source of good public domain software and interesting conversation on technical problems is the microcomputer bulletin board community. A microcomputer *bulletin board* is simply a microcomputer set up as a host system. A *SYSOP* (system operator) operates the bulletin board and usually is a private hobbyist who supports the system out of his or her own personal funds. Because the costs of such an operation can become significant, more and more microcomputer bulletin boards charge a registration fee to cover expenses.

Computer newspapers, local PC users groups, and other computer bulletin boards are all good sources for lists of bulletin boards in your area. Computer magazines often feature lists of bulletin boards. *BYTE* magazine advertises its own BIX service, and *PC Magazine* now has a bulletin board accessible through CompuServe.

Enable Software, Inc. also maintains a PC bulletin board. You can use your computer to call the bulletin board, read messages, and download files; however, only subscribers to one of Enable Software, Inc.'s technical support plans can upload messages or files. The telephone number (as of this writing) for this bulletin board is (518) 877-6316.

## Using Terminal Emulation

*Mainframe computers* are the large central computers where you find company information such as the annual budget, personnel records, and so on. People usually communicate with a mainframe computer through a *terminal*, which is a simpler, "lobotomized" PC that can manage only input and output; they do not "think" on their own. Consequently, to communicate with a mainframe, a PC must pretend to be a terminal—a function called *terminal emulation*.

Enable contains built-in terminal *emulators*—programs that enable one device to imitate another, such as enabling a microcomputer to imitate a terminal. Enable can imitate, or emulate, five types of terminals: VT320, VT220, VT-52, VT-100/102, and ANSI (x3.64-79).

When emulating one of these terminals, your PC doesn't work the same way that it usually does. For example, the up-arrow key switches telecommunications to word processing, but when Enable emulates a VT-100 terminal, the PgUp key switches to word processing. This feature, *snapshot capture*, sends any data on-screen to word processing where you can edit it. Each time you press PgUp, Enable sends a picture of whatever is displayed on-screen to word processing.

If you want to learn to communicate with your company's mainframe, ask your MIS department or information center for assistance.

## Using PC-to-PC Telecommunication

Enable provides your PC the capability of communicating with other PCs, even if those PCs do not use Enable. While your computer is connected to another PC, you can exchange information such as data files and programs.

You also can send typewritten messages to other PCs. For example, you can type a message that appears on the other PC's screen. This type of communication, however, is generally useful only for short messages, such as "Okay, send the file now," because typing messages is slower than simply talking on the telephone.

# Setting Up Your Hardware

Telecommunication requires that your system have a *serial port*, often referred to as the *communications port*, or COMM1, which is where the modem plugs into the computer. You may have more than one communications port. Enable also supports COMM2 and the Z404 board in Zenith Data Systems computers (in Setup, use COMM3).

You also must have a modem to use Enable's telecommunications. If you have an external modem, connect it to the communications port with a cable. Then plug in a telephone RJ11 jack (modular) to the modem. An *internal modem*, an integrated circuit board specially designed to plug into a slot inside your PC, includes the communications port. Plug the telephone line into the internal modem card in the back of the PC.

Just as PCs by IBM have become a standard for other companies, modems by Hayes Microcomputer Products have become a standard. Many communications programs, including Enable, assume that the modem you are using is 100% Hayes-compatible. If you purchase a modem, you probably should buy one that is Hayes-compatible. (Some modem manufacturers advertise their modems as compatible with the AT command set rather than as Hayes-compatible. Both descriptions mean the same thing.)

See your Enable communications manual (Appendix A, "Enable-Supported Modem Tables") for a list of the modems that Enable supports. If your modem is not on the list, it still may work if it recognizes the AT command set. If not, Enable provides a method of building an *external modem table*, an advanced procedure that is beyond the scope of this book; check your Enable communications documentation for instructions on creating this table if you need it.

Modems can transmit data at rates ranging from 300 to more than 50,000 bits per second (bps). A *bit* is the smallest piece of information your computer can understand. A character, such as a number or letter, usually requires 8 bits to represent it. Certain speeds, such as 300, 1200, and 2400 bps, are the most common modem speeds. You cannot find a modem that transmits at 373 bps, for example. The transmission speed is sometimes expressed as *baud*. Baud is roughly equal to bits per second; therefore, 1200 baud and 1200 bps are equivalent.

Unless you plan to transmit extremely large volumes of data, you don't need a modem faster than 2400 bps; although Enable can handle speeds of up to 19,200 bps (with the proper hardware). High-speed modems are expensive because complex error checking is required to deal with small bursts of noise (static) on the telephone line. (At 2400 bps, a 1-second burst corrupts 2400 bits. At 9600 bps, 4 times as many bits are corrupted.) Furthermore, information services such as CompuServe do not transmit faster than 2400 bps and charge more for 2400 bps than for slower speeds.

**TIP**

Try to reserve telecommunicating for a telephone line without features such as call waiting and call parking. The clicking noise you hear when you get another call wreaks havoc with computer connections and usually disconnects you. If you must use such a line, check with your telephone service company for the procedure for temporarily disabling these features. In some areas, for example, you can shut off call waiting for one call by pressing *70 before dialing the number. In addition, you do not need an expensive data-only line. A voice-quality line is sufficient.

# Communicating with Another Computer System

To communicate with another system, from the Enable Main Menu choose

    Use_System Communications

Enable has two ways to communicate with other systems: Quick-Connect and Setup. Quick-Connect is useful for one-time use, when you don't expect to call the other system again soon. Quick-Connect, however, doesn't provide some of the more technical options that the other method, Setup, provides.

Setup enables you to choose more options than Quick-Connect and enables you to save those options in a file, also called a *Setup*. If you plan to communicate often with a certain computer or service, or if novice users are going to use your Enable system to communicate with other systems, defining a Setup is worth the effort. To use a setup after you establish it, all you do is choose the name of the setup you want to activate from a list of setups. You do not have to choose the setup options each time; you simply choose the setup you want and let the setup do all the work.

In this section, you learn to use both communication methods: Quick-Connect and Setup.

# Using Quick-Connect

As its name implies, Quick-Connect provides a quick way to use your computer and modem to connect to another system. This method requires that you answer only the minimum number of questions to make a connection. After you are connected, you still can capture data and transfer and receive files through the telephone line.

To use Quick-Connect, after selecting Communications from the Main Menu, choose

> Quick-Connect

Enable displays the Quick-Connect Form (see fig. 18.1).

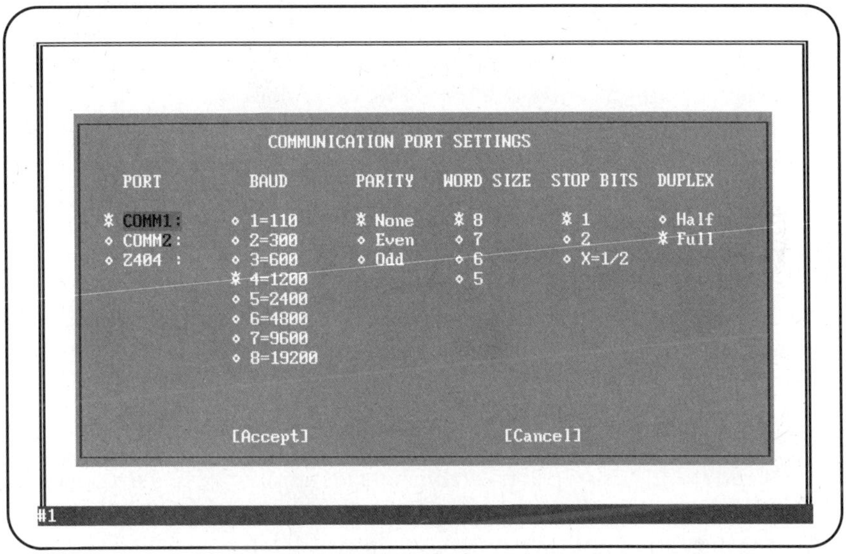

```
              COMMUNICATION PORT SETTINGS

      PORT        BAUD       PARITY   WORD SIZE   STOP BITS   DUPLEX

   ✳ COMM1:    ◇ 1=110    ✳ None    ✳ 8       ✳ 1        ◇ Half
   ◇ COMM2:    ◇ 2=300    ◇ Even    ◇ 7       ◇ 2        ✳ Full
   ◇ 2404 :    ◇ 3=600    ◇ Odd     ◇ 6       ◇ X=1/2
                ✳ 4=1200              ◇ 5
                ◇ 5=2400
                ◇ 6=4800
                ◇ 7=9600
                ◇ 8=19200


            [Accept]                    [Cancel]
```

*Fig. 18.1. The Quick-Connect Form.*

# Defining the Communication Parameters

The Quick-Connect Form, shown in figure 18.1, displays six communication parameter settings. If the default choices are correct, press End; Enable goes to the next screen. (You can change the default choices in the profile.)

Otherwise, Quick-Connect requires that you set the following six parameters before you communicate with another system. Use the up- or down-arrow keys to highlight the option you want to change, and press Enter to confirm your choice.

- *PORT*. The port is the area, usually in the back of your computer, where you plug in the modem to the computer. If the modem cable is plugged into your COMM1 port, choose COMM1. Otherwise, choose COMM2. If you have only one port, choose COMM1. The Z404 option is designed for use with Zenith computers that have a third port.

- *BAUD*. Most likely, you can choose from 300, 1200, and 2400. If you don't know how fast the information service or other computer transmits, first try 1200, the most common setting.

- *PARITY*. This parameter is used to determine whether any errors have occurred during data transmission. Parity often is not used when communicating at a baud rate of 1200 or more. Both computers must use the same parity.

  ° *None*. Choose this option to disable error checking.

  ° *Even*. The sending computer counts the number of bits it sends, and the receiving computer counts the number of bits it receives. When the data transmission is complete, both computers compare numbers. Choosing this option means that if both numbers are not even numbers, Enable reports an error.

  ° *Odd*. Choosing this option means that if both numbers are not odd after data transmission is complete, Enable reports an error.

- *WORD SIZE*. This option establishes the number of bits that make up a character. The number of bits in a character is sometimes referred to as "word length." In most cases, 8 bits make up a character; however, some older computers use a different number for word size.

- *STOP BITS*. This option determines the number of bits that the sending computer uses to let the receiving computer know that a character has been transmitted. The setting you usually use is 1.

- *DUPLEX*. This option determines how the data flows between the sending and receiving computer. *Full duplex* enables both computers to simultaneously "talk," like communication by telephone. *Half duplex* enables one computer to talk while the other listens, like communicating by CB radio.

This parameter also determines whether the text you type echoes back to you, causing you to see double characters when you type. If you see double characters as you type, you are in full duplex and should switch to half. If you see nothing as you type, you are in half duplex and should switch to full. Both computers should use the same duplex. While your system is connected to another, you can press the following command to toggle between the duplex settings. Enable displays H (half) or F (full) in the status line.

F10 **O**ptions **D**uplex change

TIP

If you already have defined your communications port with the DOS MODE command, Enable overrides these settings. If you are using another program or piece of hardware that requires different settings, you must reenter the DOS MODE command.

## Capturing Data with Quick-Connect

Unless you are a speed reader, reading on-line data that streams in at 1200 bps—about 1800 words per minute—is difficult. In addition, if you are downloading data to use in a report or to study, you want to save this data. Enable offers three ways to save the data.

After you answer the questions on the Quick-Connect Form, Enable offers you the chance to specify a new name for a data-capture file or choose an existing file (see fig. 18.2). By "capturing" data, you can save the information that is on-screen for future use. Enable immediately starts capturing data to memory, indicated by the word CAPTURE in the status line.

Enable establishes a file for the captured data and assigns the file name extension WPF. If you press Enter without specifying a data-capture file, Enable provides the file name TPNONAME.WPF but does not save the data in memory. Data that scrolls off-screen, therefore, is lost. If you choose a file name that already exists, Enable displays the prompt:

```
File exists:   Add to end of file   Re-use file.
```

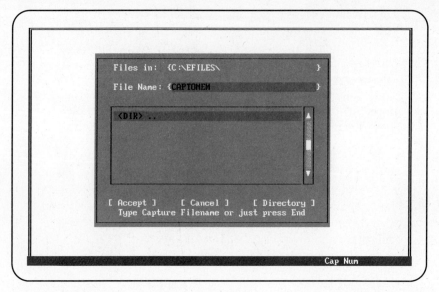

**Fig. 18.2.** *The prompt for a capture file name.*

Understanding the significance of a data-capture file requires a little explanation. With Enable, you can use three distinct methods to save data
transmitted to your computer:

- *Disk_Capture*. Choose this option to save the captured data directly
  to disk. Enable continuously saves data to disk as it receives data,
  but you cannot scroll through the data on-screen while connected
  to the other system. Enable saves the data captured in this manner
  in a file in ASCII format.

- *Memory_Capture*. With most telecommunications programs, data
  that scrolls off the top of the screen is gone forever. This option
  enables you to retrieve that information and save it in a word processing file. Enable saves the data in RAM until you retrieve it and
  save it as a word processing file. When you type a file name at the
  screen shown in figure 18.2, Enable automatically places the system
  in memory capture mode and establishes a file to receive the data
  captured to memory. You must take further action to save the captured data to the specified file. The program reminds you to do so
  when you disconnect or attempt to return to the Main Menu.

- *Print_Capture*. Choose this option to send data directly to your
  printer. For this method to work, you must be running Enable in a
  DOS environment.

These three methods are not mutually exclusive. You simultaneously can capture data to disk, to memory, and to the printer.

You can toggle on and off the memory capture mode during a communications session; press

F10 **F**ile **C**apture_settings **M**emory_Capture **A**ccept

or press

F7

> Communicating with other systems usually is a line-by-line operation, during which the cursor-movement keys on your PC don't work properly. If you press the PgUp key while you are communicating with the other system, Enable suspends transmission and switches to the word processing module with your captured data. To return to the telecommunications module and continue with your transmission, press Shift-F9.

**TIP**

During a communications session, you can capture incoming data directly to disk in ASCII format; press

F10 **F**ile **D**isk_capture_**o**pen

Type a file name or select an existing file name, then press Enter. If the file exists, Enable appends the new data to the end of the existing data (the file must be in ASCII format). If you specify a new file, Enable adds the extension TPF to the file name.

While disk capture is active, your system sends all the data received to disk as ASCII characters, and the status line displays the message `Disk Capt.`

To deactivate disk capture, press

F10 **F**ile **D**isk_capture_**c**lose

When you activate both memory capture and disk capture, the status line message is `Capt(W+D)`, which means, "Capture to window (memory) and disk."

To send data directly to the printer, first press

F10 **F**ile **P**rint_capture_device

Then select the port to which the printer is connected.

After you choose the printer port, you must turn on the print capture option (see figure 18.3); press

F10 **File** Capture_settings **Print_capture Accept**

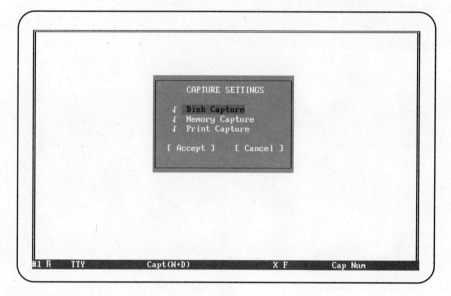

**CAPTURE SETTINGS**

√  Disk Capture
√  Memory Capture
√  Print Capture

[ Accept ]    [ Cancel ]

#1 R    TTY        Capt(M+D)              X F        Cap Num

***Fig. 18.3.*** *The Capture Settings screen.*

The second method of starting and stopping print capture is to press Shift-F2.

When the print capture option is active, Enable displays the message Pt in the Status line.

## Using an Autodial Modem

What you do now depends on whether Enable and your modem "speak the same language" and whether your modem is "smart" enough to dial a telephone number. Three possibilities exist: you have a Hayes-compatible modem, which can dial a telephone number and "understand" Enable's commands; you have a non-Hayes-compatible modem that can dial a telephone number; or you have an acoustic coupler or a modem that cannot dial a telephone number.

The recommended modem is an *autodial modem*, which is capable of responding to software commands for carrying out tasks such as dialing another system's telephone number. The standard software command set for modems used with PCs is usually called the *Hayes* or the *AT command set*. Unless you specify otherwise, Enable assumes that your autodial modem understands this command set.

If your modem understands a command language that is different from Enable's, you can create an *external modem table*, which translates the AT command set into your modem's native command language. To create this modem table, refer to your Enable communications documentation for instructions about using the Forms option from the communications module.

Even though an autodial modem "automatically" dials, you still must instruct Enable when to dial and which telephone number to dial. In addition, you can instruct Enable to wait for another modem to call, and then to answer the ring to connect with the incoming call. Occasionally, you also may want to switch from a voice call to computer telecommunications. In this section, you learn how to use Enable and an autodial modem to accomplish these tasks.

## Using Quick-Connect to Dial Another System

After you choose the capture settings you want, you are ready to dial another system. To use a Hayes-compatible modem to call another system, press

> F10 **Modem Call**

Enable displays the following prompt:

```
Enter phone #:
```

Press **T** if you have a touch-tone telephone line, or **P** if you have a pulse (rotary) line. Then type the number you want to dial.

> To turn off features such as call waiting or call parking, type the appropriate digits after you press the T and before you type the phone number.

TIP

Remember to include digits needed to switch to an outside line and to access long-distance services such as MCI or Sprint. If you want to include a pause in the dialing, perhaps to ensure enough time for an outside line to clear or for the long-distance service to engage, add a comma for each two-second pause that you want.

After you correctly enter the telephone number and commas, press Enter. You hear a dial tone, and then the number being dialed. The modem on the other end answers the call (perhaps after several rings), and the two modems connect.

## Selecting Auto-Answer Mode

To set your modem so that it automatically answers the phone and connects with an incoming call from another computer's modem, from the Telecom screen press

F10 Modem Autoanswer

Enable sends a command to your modem instructing it to answer the phone at the third ring. You can specify the number of rings at which you want the modem to answer the phone by typing the following command, where $n$ is the number of rings:

ATS0=$n$

## Using the Line on Which You Are Talking

Occasionally you may be talking to someone on the same telephone line that your modem uses, and you discover that you need to transmit a file over the line. You can hang up, and then use your computer to call the other computer, or vice versa; however, Enable offers another way—an alternative that is useful if you don't want to make a second long-distance call or if you need to help the other individual through the steps.

You both should start Enable and proceed to the Telecom screen by way of Quick-Connect. Your communication parameters must match, including choosing half duplex.

The other individual should type **ATA** (it must be in uppercase letters; don't worry that it echoes as AATTAA) and press Enter. As soon as the other person hears the carrier tone from the modem, he or she should hang up. When you hear the tone, type **ATD** (in uppercase), press Enter, and hang up.

The modems connect, enabling you to send or receive files (see "Transferring Files" in this chapter).

## Using an Acoustic Coupler or a Modem without Autodial

To use an acoustic coupler to call another system, press the Enter key a couple times to clear any line noise, and then put the acoustic cups on your telephone. Press the receiver button to hang up the phone. Then release the receiver button and dial the number.

When using a nonautodial modem, press the Enter key and dial the phone number of the other computer system. When you hear a carrier tone, press the data button (or some other switch to signal your modem to connect with the modem on the other end). The modems connect.

# Using Setup

Setup offers several advantages over Quick-Connect for communicating with another system. With Setup, you can specify more options than you can with Quick-Connect. Setup also enables you to save these options in a file so that you don't have to specify them each time you call another system.

With Enable you can create and store up to 256 Setups. Enable saves these Setups in the file TPSETUP.$TP from your Enable installation disks. This file contains sample Setup files for communicating with LEXIS/NEXIS through MeadNet and for communicating with LEXIS/NEXIS, NewsNet, and Official Airline Guide: Electronic Edition through Telenet and Enable's bulletin board system. If you have a hard disk system, the TPSETUP.$TP file already is copied to C:\EN400; however, you cannot use any of the services until you acquire an account and a password. Enable's installation program retains any existing Setup file, inserting the default response for any new Setup options.

## Defining a Setup

To define a Setup, from the Main Menu press

Use_System Communications Forms Setup

Enable displays the initial Setup screen (see fig. 18.4), which shows the six Setups that Enable already has defined.

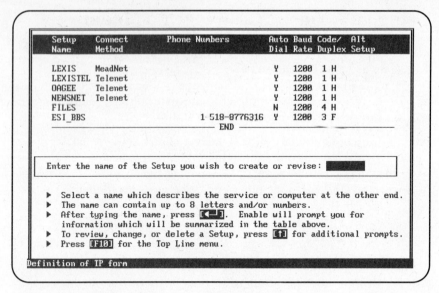

```
     Setup     Connect          Phone Numbers       Auto Baud Code/ Alt
     Name      Method                               Dial Rate Duplex Setup

     LEXIS     MeadNet                               Y    1200  1 H
     LEXISTEL  Telenet                               Y    1200  1 H
     OAGEE     Telenet                               Y    1200  1 H
     NEWSNET   Telenet                               Y    1200  1 H
     FILES                                           N    1200  4 H
     ESI_BBS                        1 518-8776316    Y    1200  3 F
     ─────────────────────────── END ───────────────────────────


    ┌─────────────────────────────────────────────────────────────┐
    │ Enter the name of the Setup you wish to create or revise: ███ │
    └─────────────────────────────────────────────────────────────┘

      ▶  Select a name which describes the service or computer at the other end.
      ▶  The name can contain up to 8 letters and/or numbers.
      ▶  After typing the name, press [◀┘].  Enable will prompt you for
         information which will be summarized in the table above.
      ▶  To review, change, or delete a Setup, press [↑] for additional prompts.
      ▶  Press [F10] for the Top Line menu.

    Definition of TP form
```

*Fig. 18.4. The initial Setup screen.*

To create a new Setup, type a name of up to eight letters, and press Enter. Enable displays a screen with the following Setup options:

- Are special digits required to get an outside line? **If** you need to dial a number (for example, 9) to get an outside line, answer **Yes** and enter the required numbers.

- Will you use an alternative telephone system? **Answer Yes** to this question if you are using a long-distance service, such as MCI or Sprint, that requires you to dial another telephone number or an authorization code. Enable asks you for the numbers.

- Will you use a telecommunications network? These networks are low-cost ways to call computers, instead of a long-distance phone call. The major networks—including Telenet, Tymnet, and Uninet—have local phone numbers in most major U.S. cities and in many foreign cities. Enable asks for the type of network, the network's telephone number, your terminal identifier, and the network address of the system to which you want to connect.

- Enter the computer's telephone number. **Enter the telephone** number of the system to which you want to connect, and press Enter. Enable bypasses this option if you indicate that you will call through a telecommunications network.

In the second Setup screen you answer the following questions:

- `Will you use an autodial modem?` **Answer Yes** if you have a Hayes-compatible modem or another type of autodial modem for which you have built an external modem table. Without an autodial modem, you manually must dial the other computer. Answer **No** if your modem is acoustic.

- `Select type automatic dial`. If you answered **Yes** to the preceding prompt, choose between **T**one (push button) and **P**ulse (rotary) here.

The following three prompts are similar to the prompts in Quick-Connect:

- `Baud rate`. You probably can choose 300, 1200, or 2400. If you don't know how fast the information service or other computer transmits, first try 1200, the most common rate. Both computers must be communicating at the same baud rate.

- `Select one of the options described below`. Use this option to set the parity, word size, and stop bit combination. The information service or the other computer often tells you which combination you should use. For example, if a listing for a bulletin board contains the phrase 8-N-1 (8-bit word size, no parity, and 1 stop bit), you should choose option 3. (Many services use the term *data bits* instead of *word size*.) Option 4 enables you to specify a different combination of parity, word size, and stop bits. Few systems require you to use this option because most systems use one of the first three combinations.

- `Select type of duplex`. Choose **F**ull or **H**alf (see previous section "Defining the Communication Parameters" for a discussion of duplex options). To toggle the duplex setting while you are on-line, press

    F10 **O**ptions **D**uplex change

On the third Setup screen you answer the following questions:

- `Inter-character transmission delay`. This option enables you to establish a pause between each transmission of data. Most systems don't require this delay. If you do not have this requirement, or you are not sure of the requirement, choose zero (0).

- `Flow control characters`. This option enables the two computers to tell each other to stop if data comes too quickly. You need to choose the type of flow control the other system uses (None, Xon/Xoff, ETX/ACK, or User Defined). Most systems support Xon/Xoff.

Enable asks the following two questions only if the system you are calling does not support Xon/Xoff, ETX/ACK, or User Defined:

- `Does the system at the other end use turnaround character(s)?` If the other system doesn't support Xon/Xoff, the system may use a *turnaround character*, which tells your system that it's ready to receive data. Answer **Yes** or **No**.

- `Pause time`. This option enables you to specify the number of seconds you want Enable to wait between data transmissions. Unless the information service's manual or the other computer operator tells you otherwise, enter **0** as the pause time.

The last two questions on this screen ask for the following information:

- `Enter the password or first response`. Enter the information that you first must type after you connect to the other system. After you are connected, Enable informs you to press Enter whenever it should send this *first response*—for example, your user ID number, your name, or your password. You can enter up to 120 characters on this line. Follow the first response with a tilde (~) if you want Enable to press Enter after it sends the response. Whatever you enter here normally appears on-screen when Enable sends it online. To prevent Enable from displaying your password on-screen, precede the entry with the code {echo off}.

- `Enter the second response`. Many times, signing on to another system involves typing an ID number, pressing Enter, and then typing a password. This Setup option stores the second response that needs to be typed. After you press Enter to send the first response, Enable waits for you to press Enter again before it sends the second response to the host. This entry can be up to 130 characters. The tilde (~) and the {echo off} code have the same purpose in this option as in the first response.

Enable then displays the fourth screen of Setup prompts, requesting the following information:

- `Do you wish to see the approximate cost on the Status Line?` Information services can be interesting and expensive. Spending hours exploring such a service is easy. With this option, Enable can keep a rough running total of the money you are spending; however, the total does not include telecommunications charges, such as with Telenet, or any additional charges. If you answer **Yes**, Enable asks you to specify the cost per hour that the service charges.

- `Do you wish to see the approximate time of the connec-tion?` **If you answer Yes to this question,** Enable displays in the status line approximately how many minutes you have been logged on to the system.

- `Which of your computer's COMM-PORTs are you using?` **If the** modem cable is plugged into your COMM1 port, choose COMM1. Otherwise, choose another communications port. If you have only one port or are unsure of which port you are using, choose COMM1.

- `Enter number of times to retry this Setup.` **Sometimes the** line is busy or doesn't answer. Enter here how many times you want Enable to try this Setup again.

- `Enter name of Setup to try if this one fails.` **Sometimes** one telephone line to an information service malfunctions. This option enables you to specify a second setup to try.

- `Terminal emulation?` **This option enables your personal com-**puter to simulate a mainframe terminal. Options available are VT100/102, VT52, VT220, VT320, and ANSI. When using terminal emulation, the PgUp key switches to word processing mode. Shift-F9 switches back to telecommunications mode.

The final Setup screen displays only one prompt as follows:

- `Do you wish to select any of the options listed below?` These options are for advanced telecommunications users and are not discussed in this book. Refer to Chapter 2 of your Enable communications manual for more information on these options.

After you answer the final question, Enable returns to the initial Setup screen and displays the new Setup that you defined: the telephone number; autodial; the baud rate; the code for parity, word size, and data bit; and the duplex (see fig. 18.5).

Whenever you are at this Setup screen, you can modify any Setup by typing its name and going through the prompts as before. To save the new Setup, press

F10 **File Save**

You also can use Enable's *quick edit* feature to change any of the Setup options that appear on this screen. To use quick edit, press the up-arrow key to highlight the Setup you want to revise, and use the left- or right-arrow keys to highlight the appropriate Setup option. Press the space bar at the option you want to change. Enable displays the prompt for that option so that you can make a change. Press Esc when finished. Remember to save the Setup (F10 **F S**) if you make any changes.

To exit the Setup screen, press

F10 **File Exit**

Enable returns to the Main Menu. You now are ready to use your new Setup. In the following section, you learn how to use a Setup.

```
Setup      Connect       Phone Numbers      Auto Baud Code/ Alt
Name       Method                           Dial Rate Duplex Setup

LEXIS      MeadNet                           Y   1200  1 H
LEXISTEL   Telenet                           Y   1200  1 H
OAGEE      Telenet                           Y   1200  1 H
NEWSNET    Telenet                           Y   1200  1 H
FILES                                        N   1200  4 H
ESI_BBS                  1-518-8776316       Y   1200  3 F
PRACTICE                 555-1212            Y   1200  3 F
  ───────────────────────  END  ───────────────────────

 Enter the name of the Setup you wish to create or revise: ▊

  ▶  Select a name which describes the service or computer at the other end.
  ▶  The name can contain up to 8 letters and/or numbers.
  ▶  After typing the name, press [◄─┘]. Enable will prompt you for
     information which will be summarized in the table above.
  ▶  To review, change, or delete a Setup, press [↑] for additional prompts.
  ▶  Press [F10] for the Top Line menu.
Definition of TP form
```

*Fig. 18.5. The initial Setup screen with a new Setup.*

# Using a Setup to Dial Another System

To use a defined Setup, go to Enable's Main Menu and press

**Use_System Communications Use_Setup**

Enable displays the list of Setups that you already have defined (see fig. 18.6). Choose the Setup you want to use by typing its name at the prompt, or by using the down-arrow key to highlight the appropriate Setup. Press Enter to confirm your choice.

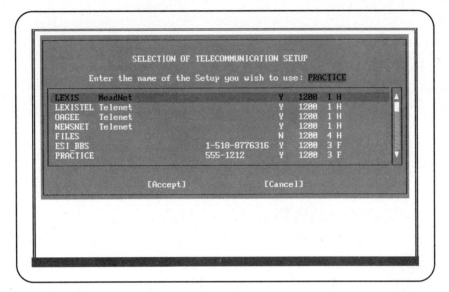

```
            SELECTION OF TELECOMMUNICATION SETUP
        Enter the name of the Setup you wish to use: PRACTICE

LEXIS     MeadNet                           Y   1200  1 H
LEXISTEL  Telenet                           Y   1200  1 H
OAGEE     Telenet                           Y   1200  1 H
NEWSNET   Telenet                           Y   1200  1 H
FILES                                       N   1200  4 H
ESI_BBS                    1-518-8776316    Y   1200  3 F
PRACTICE                   555-1212         Y   1200  3 F


            [Accept]                [Cancel]
```

**Fig. 18.6.** *The prompt for a setup name.*

Enable then asks whether you want to specify a data-capture file name and start capturing data right away. The procedure for capturing data with a Setup is the same as the procedure for capturing data with Quick-Connect. Refer to the previous section "Capturing Data with Quick-Connect" for more information on this option. You should type a file name here anyway; otherwise, you cannot recover the text that scrolls off-screen. This procedure starts memory capture. After you connect with the other computer, you can turn on disk or printer capture as discussed in "Capturing Data with Quick-Connect."

Next, Enable checks the port and modem and dials the number. Enable presents a status report of steps it takes to connect with the other system, as shown in figure 18.7 (when you connect through a network, Enable displays a longer list). When you see the appropriate prompt from the host system, press Enter to send the first response that you specified in the Setup. Enable displays only an x on-screen if you used the {echo off} code for the response. Enable sends access code #2 (the second response in the Setup) the second time you press Enter after connecting with the host. You should then be connected with the other system.

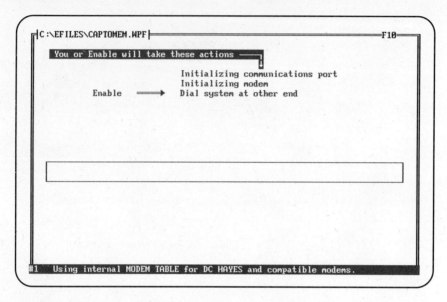

**Fig. 18.7.** *The status report for establishing a connection.*

**TIP**

If your modem isn't plugged in, turned on, and connected to the telephone system, or if you selected an incorrect communications port, Enable returns you to the Main Menu about 30 seconds after dialing. Enable does not display an error message. If your Setup doesn't work, check your modem connections.

# Transferring Files

To enable you to transmit data to and receive data from other computers, Enable supports eight protocols. A *protocol* is an agreed-upon set of rules that both computers follow to communicate. The protocols have different instructions for breaking the file into pieces, transmitting the pieces, and reassembling them at the receiving computer. Both computers must use the same protocol. If both computers use Enable, choose ENABLE-1; otherwise, choose a protocol that both systems have in common. Most systems support Ymodem or Kermit.

Enable supports the following eight protocols:

- *None*. This protocol actually is Xon/Xoff.

- *ENABLE-1*. Use this protocol to communicate with another PC that is running Enable

- *Xmodem-Checksum*. This protocol is an error-checking file transfer protocol that is generally used by other systems.

- *CRC-Xmodem*. This protocol also is an error-checking file transfer protocol, but it is more reliable than Xmodem-Checksum.

- *1K-Xmodem*. Also an error-checking file transfer protocol, 1K-Xmodem can handle larger portions of data than the previous Xmodem protocols.

- *Ymodem-Batch*. This protocol, an error-checking file transfer protocol and an enhanced version of Xmodem, is convenient when transferring several files at one time or if your line has a lot of static.

- *Kermit*. Used by many mainframe systems and PCs, this error-correcting protocol can transfer several files.

- *B+ Compuserv*. CompuServe Information Service uses this protocol.

Many computers and information systems support the Xmodem protocols and Kermit. Some systems support one or the other; some support both or all. Whenever possible, you should use Xmodem or Kermit rather than the None protocol. The None protocol supports the transfer of only ASCII text files; therefore, to transmit or receive a program or binary file, including any Enable file (word processing, spreadsheet, or database), you must use Xmodem or Kermit.

# Setting Up Enable for File Transfer

If you use an Xmodem protocol or the Enable protocol, you must configure your system for an 8-bit word size, no parity, and 1 stop bit (option 3 for Setup). If you use a Setup, Enable automatically changes your Setup options to option 3, and then reverts them to the original options after you finish transmitting or receiving data. If you choose the Ymodem-Batch protocol but the other computer does not support it, the system tries the other Xmodem protocols until it finds a compatible protocol.

# Receiving a File with Xmodem, Ymodem, or Kermit Protocols

To receive a file using the Xmodem protocol or the Ymodem or Kermit protocols, first use Quick-Connect or Setup to start communicating with the other computer or information service. You need to find out which protocol is supported. Nearly all computers and services support one or the other. You also need to know how to start the protocol program on the other system. Unfortunately, each system is different. In fact, if you are communicating with a PC that is running Enable, a knowledgeable operator has to be at the other end to start transmission in the proper protocol at the proper time.

The other system must be ready to transmit the file to your computer. When the other system is ready, press

F10 **P**rotocol

Then choose the appropriate protocol, depending on which one you are using (see fig. 18.8).

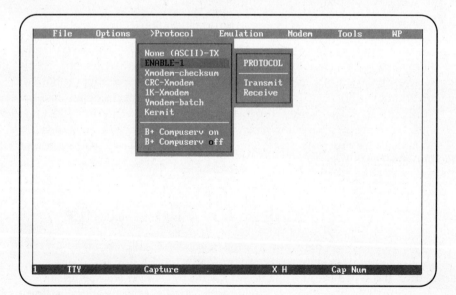

**Fig. 18.8.** *Enable's protocol list.*

After you choose the appropriate protocol, choose **R**eceive. Enable then prompts you for the name of the file to be received. If you specify a file that already exists on the disk, Enable gives you the option to destroy the existing file. If you are using the Kermit protocol, the sending computer specifies the file name—just press Enter at the Enter filename prompt.

Using the specified protocol, Enable then starts receiving data from the other computer. Enable also displays a status screen that tells you how many blocks it has received and how many errors it has corrected (see fig. 18.9). If a transmission error occurs, Xmodem or Kermit retransmits that piece of the file. When the transmission is complete, Enable displays a message and returns you to the telecommunications window, where you can resume communicating with the bulletin board or host system.

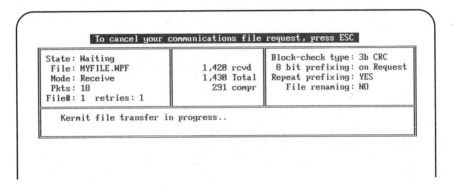

*Fig. 18.9. The status screen displayed when receiving data.*

# Transmitting a File with Xmodem or Kermit Protocols

Transmitting a file from your PC to another computer requires a procedure similar to the one for receiving a file. First, find out how to run the protocol program on the other computer. Then start communicating with the other computer, and prepare it to accept your file. Press

    F10 **P**rotocol

Then choose the protocol you are using (again see fig. 18.8).

After you choose the protocol, press **Transmit**. The system prompts you for the name of the file you are sending. If you are sending multiple files, you can use wild cards (* or ?). Press Enter. You can watch the progression of the transmission on Enable's status screen (see fig. 18.10). If a transmission error occurs, Xmodem or Kermit retransmits that piece of the file. After the transmission is complete, Enable returns you to the remote session.

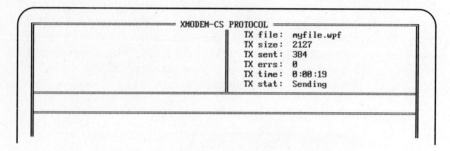

**Fig. 18.10.** *The status screen displayed when transmitting data.*

# Using ENABLE-1 and None Protocols

The ENABLE-1 protocol, which you can use only when communicating with a computer that also is running Enable, is an enhanced version of Xmodem.

If the system with which you are communicating does not support any of the error-checking protocols, such as Kermit or Xmodem, then you should use the None protocol; however, None should be your last choice because it does not support any error checking. When you use the None protocol, you should save your file in ASCII format. The None protocol cannot handle binary files, such as a file in the normal Enable word processing format.

The steps for transferring files using ENABLE-1 or None protocol are the same as outlined in the preceding section, "Transmitting a File with Xmodem or Kermit Protocols."

# Disconnecting Telecommunications

To stop your communications session and return to Enable's Main Menu, first exit the other computer or information service with whatever command it uses—such as Quit, Exit, or Bye; otherwise, the computer may not realize that you have logged off and continues to charge you for computer time. (Before you begin the session, find out how to exit the other system by checking with the bulletin board, service manual, system personnel, or Customer Service department.)

Then press either

> F10 **File Exit_**(Disconnect)

or

> Alt-End

Enable prompts you to save your memory capture file (see fig. 18.11).

To save the captured data, press

> **Yes**

Enable saves the captured information in its word processing format with the name you specified when you started the communications session. Enable then displays the Main Menu.

If you want to finish the current call but remain in telecommunications, first exit the other system with the proper command, and then press

> F10 **Modem Hang-up**

This command disconnects your call but leaves you in communications so that you can use the steps outlined in the previous sections of this chapter to initiate or receive another call.

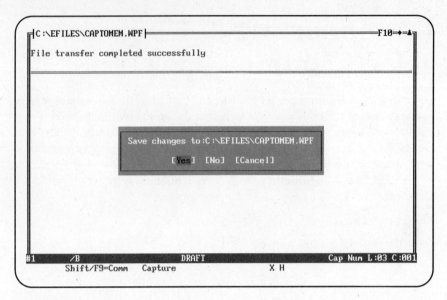

**Fig. 18.11.** *The prompt to save the memory capture file.*

# Writing Scripts for Unattended Telecommunications

Enable telecommunications goes one step further than Setups with its script language called *Unattended File Transfer*. This pseudo-programming language enables you to automate the process of dialing and logging on to any system that you routinely use. This feature gets its name from its capability to dial, sign on, transmit files, receive files, and execute other commands without user intervention.

A complete discussion of writing script files is beyond the scope of this book; however, if you want to create an unattended script file, press

    Use_System Communications Forms Scripts

Enter the name that you want to assign to the script file, then create the contents of the file.

# Summary

As in the preceding chapters, this final chapter of *Que's Using Enable* gives you a good look at fundamental concepts and techniques—of telecommunications in this case. Some of the technical terms may confuse you at first, but you become used to them with time. The key to learning the telecommunications module is practice. Practice using Quick-Connect. Create a few Setups and practice using them. Use the error-checking protocols to send files. Using the steps outlined in this chapter, you quickly can become a telecommunications wizard.

# Installing and Starting Enable

This appendix covers installing and starting Enable for the DOS operating system. If you need to install and start Enable for the UNIX operating system, refer to the Enable/OA 4.0 documentation, "Getting Started."

This appendix explains how to install your copy of Enable and run it for the first time. The text also explains how to start the tutorial, and gives you a number of suggestions for using DOS batch files and special Enable start-up commands. The computer you use determines how you install Enable and which start-up commands you should use, and the organization of the various procedures in this appendix is by system.

## Understanding the System Requirements

To use Enable/OA, you must have an IBM AT, PS/2, or compatible, and DOS 2.0 or higher. Your computer must have at least 640K of RAM to use all of Enable's features under DOS (PC DOS or MS-DOS). *Note:* Previous versions of Enable do not work properly in the DOS compatibility box.

To use Enable's graphics module, you must have a graphics display adapter and a compatible monitor. The three-dimensional graphics program, Perspective Junior, is more demanding and works with only the more limited group of display adapters listed as follows:

- IBM AT with EGA monochrome card, or compatible
- IBM AT with EGA (Enhanced Graphics Adapter) Card, or compatible, with 256K memory
- IBM AT with Sigma Color 400 Graphics Card
- IBM PS/2 with VGA Card
- AT&T 6300/6300+
- NEC APC III
- Cordata (formerly Corona Data Systems) AT/ATP
- Corona PC-400/PPC-400
- Epson QX-16
- Hewlett-Packard Vectra Systems
- TANDY Deluxe Graphics Display Adapter
- Toshiba 3100 "Super EGA"

Enable's telecommunications module needs an asynchronous communications port (serial port) and modem. Although the standard modem command table assumes that your modem recognizes the AT command set made popular by Hayes modems, Enable/OA includes a facility for modifying this table to match other command sets. You also can use a manual-dial modem. *Note:* You need an asynchronous communications port and an RS-232 cable if you have only an external modem.

In Enable/OA, the spreadsheet is 1,024 columns by 9,999 rows. To handle such large files under DOS, Enable/OA has added support for LIM/EMS 3.2 and 4.0. You don't have to do anything special at start-up; however, you need to install a LIM/EMS 3.2 and 4.0 compatible memory board before start-up. (This installation is also necessary if you intend to use SQL.)

# Configuring a DOS System

For DOS, you need to prepare a CONFIG.SYS file so that you can change the default number of files and memory buffers that your computer opens at once. The CONFIG.SYS file also loads into RAM other files known as device drivers whenever you turn on or warm boot your computer. DOS does not automatically create the CONFIG.SYS file; you must create it yourself. If you are using DOS 3.1 or higher, the following line must appear in your CONFIG.SYS file:

**FILES=40**

If you later use Enable's new spreadsheet-linking feature, you may need to edit this line to increase the number of files. (An error message instructs you to edit this line.)

AT users should add the line

**BUFFERS=40**

If you plan to use Enable/OA's capability to shrink and move a DOS window, you need to add the line

**DEVICE=C:\EN400\ANSITSG.SYS**

This line loads into memory a special screen driver so that your computer can shrink and move the display of any DOS program you run from Enable's DOS window.

Keep in mind that the CONFIG.SYS file must be in the root directory of your hard disk or on the floppy from which you boot DOS; otherwise, you won't be able to boot Enable successfully. The file ANSITSG.SYS must be in the C:\EN400 directory.

You can create your CONFIG.SYS file with the DOS line editor EDLIN, any word processing program that can save files in ASCII, or the DOS COPY CON command. This last method is the most readily available.

Before you create you CONFIG.SYS file, however, type

**DIR C:\ /W**

to see whether a CONFIG.SYS file already exists. If you see this file listed, type

**TYPE C:\CONFIG.SYS**

If your existing CONFIG.SYS file contains lines other than the lines mentioned in the steps that follow, be sure that you add the existing lines to the end of the CONFIG.SYS file you are going to create. Add these lines before you press F6.

Press Enter at the end of each of the following lines; press F6 and Enter at the end of the last line (pressing F6 displays ^Z on the screen). At the DOS prompt, type

**COPY CON CONFIG.SYS**

**FILES=40**

**BUFFERS=40**

**DEVICE=C:\EN400\ANSITSG.SYS**

After you create your CONFIG.SYS file, reboot your computer by pressing Ctrl-Alt-Del. When you return to the DOS prompt, you can install Enable.

# Installing Enable on a Hard Disk System

Depending on whether you purchased Enable for a 3 1/2- or 5 1/4-inch disk system computer, you should have 12 low-density or 9 high-density 3 1/2-inch program disks, or 22 low-density or 10 high density 5 1/4-inch program disks.

Enable is exactly the same program in each format. Make sure that you make a back-up copy of your original disks through the install procedure and put them away in a safe place.

The procedure for installing Enable on a hard-disk-based PC is the same whether you have a 5 1/4- or 3 1/2-inch disk drive. Enable prompts you through the entire procedure, asking you to insert the appropriate disk at the appropriate time. The following discussion assumes that you are using 5 1/4-inch disks.

To begin the procedure, boot your computer with DOS. At the C> prompt:

1. Place the disk labeled *Install* into drive A of your computer. Type **a:install** and press Enter.

2. Choose Install at the first screen. Next, because this is the first time you are installing the program, choose **Complete**. Later, if you want to change printers or monitor drivers, you may need to do a **Partial** installation.

3. The next screen asks whether you are installing Enable/OA on a Local Area Network (LAN) server. If you answer **Yes**, the installation program copies to the hard disk special files necessary for multiple user access to Enable/OA.

4. Enable asks if you want to install Perspective Junior and displays a list of the hardware requirements. If you choose to install Perspective Junior, you need almost 2M of disk space more than you need for Enable alone, which is almost 4M—a total of about 6M.

5. If you answer **Yes** on the next screen, the program copies all the video drivers to the hard disk. If you're installing Enable on a LAN server, the program copies all video drivers, even if you don't answer **Yes** on the screen.

6. If you answer **Yes** on the next screen, the program copies all the printer drivers to the hard disk.

7. Decide whether to install tutorials now or later. You don't have to repeat the entire installation process later just to install tutorials. Instead, you choose **Partial** at the second installation screen.

8. At the next screen, accept the default path (C:\EN400) by pressing Enter. Answer **Yes** on the next screen to confirm this decision.

9. The program now prompts you for the name of the directory to establish as a default to use with Enable/OA. Type in the complete path and press Enter. Answer **Yes** on the next screen to confirm this choice. *Note:* Never choose A: or B: as your default data directory at the installation.

10. Answer **Yes** on the next screen so that the program automatically creates a start-up batch file for you. If you do not want the program to create one for you, you can create your own later on. (See the section "Using a Batch File" later in this appendix.) The program creates the file and places it in the \EN400 directory, with a name of EN.BAT.

11. The next procedure installs video drivers. Follow the instructions on the screen to select a driver for your type of graphics system.

12. If you answered **No** to the question

```
Do you wish to install all of printer drivers
```

the next procedure installs individual print drivers. Follow the instructions on the screen to choose a driver for each printer you want to use.

13. The program now begins the installation. After each disk, the system beeps and prompts you for the next disk in the series. Remove the disk, place the next disk in the drive, and press Enter.

Follow instructions on the screen, placing disks in your drive when the program prompts you. When the process finishes, the Enable installation on your hard disk is complete.

# Starting Enable on a Hard Disk System Using DOS

The procedure for starting Enable on a hard disk system is the same whether you have a 5 1/4- or 3 1/2-inch disk drive. Turn on your computer and, if necessary, enter the correct date and time. If you choose to bypass the date and time prompts, you later can enter the correct date and time on Enable's Sign-On screen. This information is necessary if you want the system to keep track of when you create and revise your files and if you want to use Enable's built-in system date features.

You may want to set a path to the directory that contains your Enable program files so that DOS can find them from any place on the hard disk. (See the "Using a Batch File" section of this appendix for instructions on how to include the path in a batch file.) To set the path, at the DOS prompt type

**PATH C:\;C:\DOS;C:\EN400**

and press Enter. (If you included C:\EN400 in a PATH command in AUTOEXEC.BAT, you can skip this step. Refer to the section "Using a Batch File" in this appendix.) This example assumes that the directory C:\DOS stores the DOS external program files.

If you created a start-up batch file during the installation procedure, type the start-up command **EN** and press Enter. The PATH command tells DOS where to find Enable. (If you bypassed this step in the installation, you can start Enable manually by typing the command **ENABLE** at the prompt and pressing Enter. See "Using Batch Files" for more information.)

Enable's Sign-On screen appears. See the next section, "Completing the Sign-On Screen," for instructions on how to answer the prompts on this screen.

# Completing the Sign-On Screen

After starting Enable, the first screen you encounter is the Sign-On screen (see fig. A.1). You usually press the End key to bypass the options on this screen, but you also should understand these options.

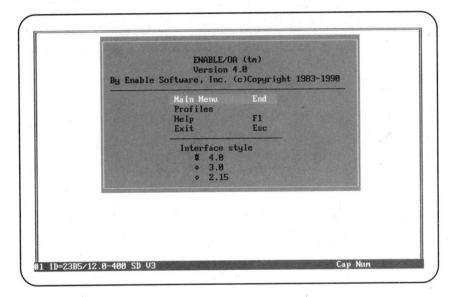

*Fig. A.1. The Enable Sign-On screen.*

The first option is **Profiles**. A *profile* is a collection of choices (usually called *defaults*) that you make about what hardware you are going to use (printer, plotter, modem) and how certain features should operate. Appendix B, "Customizing Enable: Profiles," explains how to create and change profiles. To use a different collection of default choices, choose this option. Enable displays a second menu. Choose **Select**. Enable displays a list of profiles. To choose a profile, type its name and press Enter.

The second option is **Help**. Choose this option (press **H** or F1) to access Enable's on-line help before you enter the system.

Choose the third option to exit Enable. You simply press **X** or Esc, or highlight the option and press Enter.

Enable also has a selection of Interface styles from which you can choose before you enter the system. These styles control the style of menu system Enable uses. You can choose from the 4.0, 3.0, and 2.15 menu styles.

If you press the End key to bypass these prompts, Enable uses the profile named DEFAULT with a 4.0 menu style.

After you respond to any prompts that appear, Enable displays the Main Menu, shown in figure A.2. (See Chapter 2, "Understanding the Keyboard and Enable's Screens, Menus, and Keyboard Commands," for a discussion of the Main Menu.)

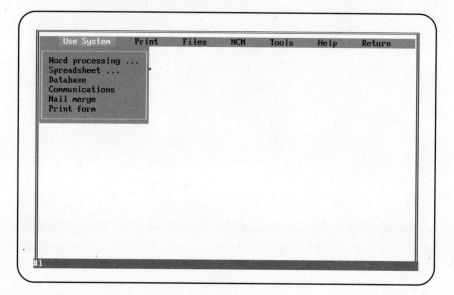

*Fig. A.2.* *The Enable Main Menu.*

# Accessing the Tutorials

Enable Software includes a computer-aided tutorial with Enable/OA. To access the tutorial, however, you must start Enable with a special batch file, TUTOR.BAT, that copies onto your disk during installation.

On a hard disk system, start DOS and, at the C> prompt, type

**CD\EN400**

If you told the Enable installation program to copy the tutorial files to the hard disk, type **TUTOR C** at the C> prompt. If you didn't copy the tutorial files to your hard disk, insert the Tutorial disk into drive A and type **TUTOR A**.

Enable displays the Sign-On screen. You don't need to respond to the questions and prompts; Enable responds automatically in the tutorials. Enable displays the Tutorial menu. Follow the on-screen instructions.

# Enhancing Enable's Performance

You can add parameters to your commands to enhance the performance of Enable. The sections that follow discuss these enhancements and explain how you can streamline the start-up procedure by using batch files.

## Adding Parameters to the Start-Up Command

To start Enable from DOS, you normally type **ENABLE**. You can add *parameters*—special start-up options—to this command. These parameters can help you use memory more efficiently, control the speed at which text is scrolled, initiate a macro on start-up, reduce the disk swapping involved in some procedures on a two-floppy disk system, or allocate memory for the Hypertext documentation.

To use one of these start-up parameters, just leave a space and type the appropriate code after the **ENABLE** command (If you want to alter the **EN** batch file, simply add the parameters *after* the end parenthesis). Separate multiple parameters with commas. For example, typing the start-up command

  **ENABLE 512,V9,@0**

reserves all RAM over 384K bytes for a DOS window, uses the fastest video scroll speed, and runs a start-up macro named 0 (zero). The following sections explain these parameters in further detail.

# Allocating Memory

When you start Enable in DOS, you can instruct Enable to reserve some memory for a DOS window. You use a DOS window to leave Enable temporarily to execute DOS commands, and then return to the program. Refer to Chapter 3, "Understanding the Master Control Module," for more information on how and when to use a DOS window. To reserve RAM for a DOS window, add to the start-up command the total K amount of RAM you want allocated to the following:

- The operating system

- Any memory resident (TSR) programs loaded before Enable

- Virtual or RAM disks

- DOS buffers

- Enable

- Enable data

Any remaining memory is available for a DOS window. If your system has 384K of RAM, then the start-up command **ENABLE 320** leaves 64K for use in a DOS window. The recommended minimum of RAM for using a DOS window, however, is 512K.

# Increasing Scrolling Speed

To increase scrolling speed, you need to experiment a little. You can set the scrolling speed from V1 (slowest) to V9 (fastest). If, however, you set the scroll faster than your microprocessor and video display monitor can handle, you see snow or some other distortion on the screen when text scrolls. Try increasing scrolling speed to the maximum by typing **ENABLE V9**. If that speed causes problems, work your way down through lower speeds until you arrive at the maximum speed your system can handle without snow.

# Using Start-Up Macros

As discussed in Chapter 4, "Using the Master Control Module's Advanced Features," you can use Enable to create macros that store a sequence of keystrokes in a file and execute the whole sequence at your command. Macros named with a single digit between 0 and 9 can be preceded with an @ sign and included in the start-up command, for example, **ENABLE @1**.

The macro begins executing as soon as the Sign-On screen displays. A handy macro to use this way is one that activates the End key at the Sign-On screen, automatically taking you to Enable's Main Menu.

## Reducing Disk Swapping

The parameters described in this section load parts of Enable into memory and keep them there for fast access. Use these parameters only if your computer has 640K RAM or more. When you start Enable with these parameters, the program prompts you to insert disks containing the programs you want to load.

The command **ENABLE R=(T1)** holds terminal emulation programs in memory so that they are readily available during a telecommunications session. **ENABLE R=(T2)** holds file transfer programs in memory so that you can transmit or receive disk files during a telecommunications session without having to swap files in memory. The parameter **ENABLE R=(G)** holds graphics programs in memory so that you can create graphs through the DBMS without swapping files in memory.

Many of Enable's special features are not always loaded in RAM. For this reason, Enable can do so much while using so little memory, but it also means that the program has to read the disk whenever you request one of these "non-resident" features.

One way to speed up the operation is for Enable to keep any non-resident routine in memory until it needs the RAM for something else. Enable needs to read the disk for the first use of the feature, but not for any subsequent uses. To use this option, enter **ENABLE M**.

## Using the Print Routines Memory

Sometimes you need to have available as much memory as possible, for example, to work on a large spreadsheet. You can free the 2K to 6K bytes of RAM, otherwise being used by Enable's print routines, by using the parameter **ENABLE N**.

# Parameters for Special Hardware

If you have an LIM/EMS board, but you don't want Enable to access it, use the parameter **ENABLE E**.

To use an internal modem in DATA GENERAL/One, use **ENABLE C2**, and to use an external modem with DATA GENERAL/One, use **ENABLE C3**.

If you use telecommunications on an IBM convertible, you need to use the parameter **ENABLE C4**. Because a Leading Edge Model D initializes its hardware in a special way, use the parameter **ENABLE A**.

# Using a Batch File

As discussed in a previous section of this appendix, starting Enable on a hard disk system in DOS requires several commands on the command line. For example, the following commands start Enable on a system operating DOS with the data files in the directory C:\MYDATA:

> PATH C:\;C:\DOS;C:\EN400
>
> CD \MYDATA
>
> ENABLE

Instead of entering these commands each time you want to start the program, you can use a *batch file* to make DOS handle start-up. A batch file is a file that contains a sequence of operating system commands that execute one after another when you invoke the file name. Batch files are generic text files (ASCII) and must have the file name extension BAT. You can think of a batch file as a computer program made up of consecutive DOS commands.

A useful batch file in DOS is the AUTOEXEC.BAT. If it exists on the root directory of the boot disk, this file automatically executes each time you boot your system. For example, you can create an AUTOEXEC.BAT file including the following line:

> **PATH C:\;C:\DOS;C:\EN400**

The AUTOEXEC.BAT sets the path automatically each time you start the computer.

Some computer programs come with an AUTOEXEC.BAT file already created. To see whether you have an AUTOEXEC.BAT file in your root directory, ask DOS to show you the directory of files in the root directory in alphabetical order. Enter the following commands at the DOS prompt in the root directory:

**DIR | SORT**

If an AUTOEXEC.BAT file does not exist, and if you want Enable to load every time you boot the system, create the file with Enable by following these steps:

1. At the Main Menu, choose

   Use_System Word_Processing

2. Name the file

   **C:\AUTOEXEC.BAT**

3. Type

   **PATH C:\;C:\DOS;C:\EN400**

   **CD\MYDATA**

   **ENABLE**

4. Save the file in ASCII format by pressing

   F10 File Save_As

Press Enter at the file name; highlight **ASCII** and press Enter; highlight **Entire_File** and press Enter; press Enter on **Accept**.

Every time you turn on your computer, DOS automatically enters the path command, switches to the ENABLE directory, and loads the program.

Suppose that you don't want Enable to begin every time you turn on your system. You still don't have to type these commands every time. Just create a file with the same contents as before, but give it some other valid file name with the extension BAT. For example, you can follow the same exact steps, but give the file the name EN.BAT. (This is what the Enable installation program does.) Then, to start Enable from the C> prompt, you only have to type **EN** (the name of this batch file) and press Enter.

The more common practice is to include the PATH command in AUTOEXEC.BAT, and then leave it out of the batch file to start Enable. Either way works fine.

The instructions in this appendix help you configure your computer for Enable, install Enable, and run the program. Appendix B shows you how to create and change your profiles to customize the program's operation further.

# B

# Using Profiles to Customize Enable

I n Enable, a *profile* is a collection of settings that specifies how the program operates. These settings tell Enable whether and how you plan to use certain features of the program. The many features affected by profiles fall into the following eight categories:

- *Hardware*: printer and plotter options

- *Page form*: options for paper size; font; margins; line spacing; and header, footer, and footnote options

- *Special text*: screen-color options and display of text attributes (boldface, italic, and so on)

- *Word processing*: print and format options

- *Communications*: Quick-Connect and terminal emulation options

- *Database*: options for automatic modification of lookup data, error handling, database display, and the database format

- *Spreadsheet*: options for cell protection, automatic backup, and 1-2-3's cell macro conversion

- *System*: options specifying key operations (such as how the backspace key operates) and the print queue

With profiles, not only can you customize Enable for your own use, but several users of the same computer also can customize Enable without interfering with others, who may have different preferences. This appendix explains how to rename profiles and how to customize Enable by modifying its many profile settings.

Enable comes with several built-in profiles, including one named DEFAULT and one named COLOR. COLOR displays the text on your screen in color, whereas DEFAULT displays text in white on black (monochrome). Each time you start an Enable session, the program first displays the Sign-On screen. To use the DEFAULT profile, you simply press the End key at the Sign-On screen. To use a profile with a name other than DEFAULT, select **P**rofiles from the Sign-On screen. You then have the option to **S**elect, **C**reate, or **R**evise. Choose **S**elect. Enable displays a list of available profiles, as in figure B.1.

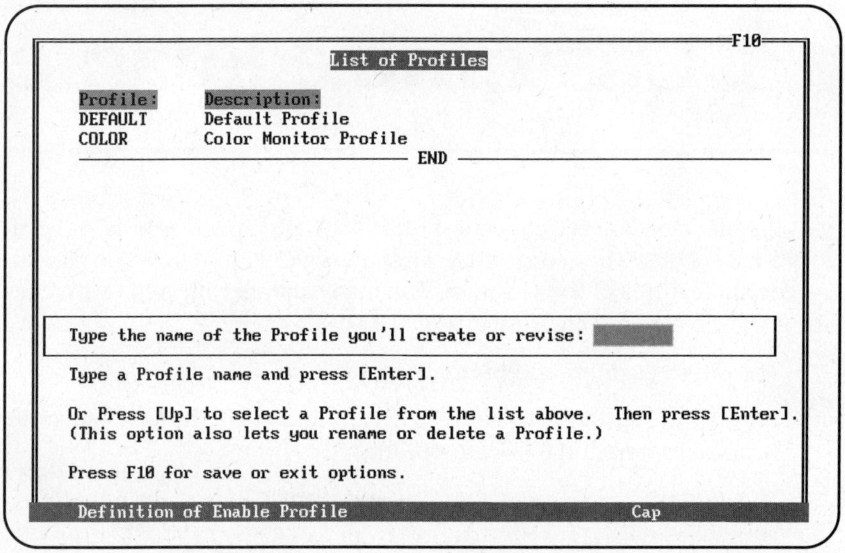

```
┌────────────────────────────────────────────────────F10═══╗
│                                                           │
│                      ▓List of Profiles▓                   │
│                                                           │
│         ▓Profile:▓    ▓Description:▓                       │
│         DEFAULT       Default Profile                      │
│         COLOR         Color Monitor Profile                │
│         ─────────────────────── END ──────────────        │
│                                                           │
│                                                           │
│                                                           │
│                                                           │
│   ┌─────────────────────────────────────────────────┐    │
│   │ Type the name of the Profile you'll create or revise: ▓▓▓│
│   └─────────────────────────────────────────────────┘    │
│   Type a Profile name and press [Enter].                  │
│                                                           │
│   Or Press [Up] to select a Profile from the list above.  Then press [Enter].│
│   (This option also lets you rename or delete a Profile.)  │
│                                                           │
│   Press F10 for save or exit options.                     │
│                                                           │
│   ▓Definition of Enable Profile▓                 Cap      │
└───────────────────────────────────────────────────────────┘
```

*Fig. B.1. The Profile Summary screen.*

Type the name of the profile you intend to invoke and press Enter, or use your cursor keys to highlight the desired profile and press Enter.

As you can see, the DEFAULT profile is much easier to use; you probably want to set it up the way you want to use Enable. If you have a color screen, you may want to rename COLOR so that it becomes the DEFAULT profile (see "Renaming a Profile" in this appendix).

# Using Profiles

Enable's installation program installs the file containing the profiles into the program directory on the hard disk (C:\EN400). The name of this file is PROFILE.$PR. If, however, you also copy this file to your data directory or disk, Enable uses this second copy instead of the one in the program directory. If you use several different data directories or disks, you can have DEFAULT profiles in each of the data directories or disks. Then, if you use the appropriate start-up command to establish the data directory (see Appendix A), you always can choose the DEFAULT profile by pressing End.

Each user on the network can have an individual profile. Whenever a user saves a profile, Enable saves the file as PROF*ID*.$PR, where *ID* is that user's Enable identification. You also can store this profile in the data directory and in Enable's program directory.

Whenever Enable gives you a list of options, choose an option by pressing the first letter (or number) of the option instead of using the arrow keys to highlight the choice and pressing Enter. Pressing the first letter is quicker and usually more accurate. To encourage you to get into this habit, this appendix does not mention the arrow-key method of selecting a profile option, unless it is the only workable method.

To make any changes, additions, or deletions to profiles, you first must close all open Enable windows. Then, at the Main Menu, press **MCM Profile_options**. As at sign-on, you have the option to **S**elect, **R**evise, or **C**reate. After you choose an option, Enable displays the Profile Summary Screen, shown in figure B.1.

You can access the profiles through two routes. Use one route when you first enter Enable by pressing **P**rofiles at the Start-up menu. Use the second route at any time from within Enable by pressing F10 **MCM Profile_options**.

# Renaming a Profile

If you have a color screen and are using Enable for the first time after installation, rename the built-in profiles so that the original COLOR profile becomes the new DEFAULT profile. (If you have a monochrome screen, you can skip this section unless you want to know how to rename a profile.)

To rename the built-in DEFAULT profile, press the up-arrow key to move the highlighted bar into the list of available profiles to the profile named DEFAULT. Next, press **Rename** (which appears as an option in a menu in the bottom third of the screen); at the prompt `Enter new Profile name:`, type **OLDDEF** and press Enter. The name of the original DEFAULT profile changes to OLDDEF. If you someday want to use the original DEFAULT profile, you simply can rename OLDDEF as DEFAULT.

You now are ready to rename COLOR. Again, press the up-arrow key to highlight COLOR. Press **Rename**; at the prompt, type **DEFAULT** and press Enter. The name of the original COLOR profile changes to DEFAULT.

For Enable to use these new names, you need to save the new profiles. To save the profiles, press

> F10 **F**ile **S**ave

To use the new DEFAULT profile, which displays text in color, you must leave the Profile Summary screen and select that profile. Press F10 **F**ile **E**xit to return to the Main Menu. Select a new profile by pressing **M**C**M** **P**rofile_options **S**elect. Then, enter the name of the profile, or use your cursor keys to select a profile, and press Enter.

Enable displays the Main Menu in color. Special text attributes such as underlining, italic, and boldface appear in a variety of different colors. You can change this color scheme by following the steps described in the section "Setting Special Text Options" in this appendix.

# Changing a Profile

After installing Enable, you need to modify the DEFAULT profile to match your computer system. Until you do, Enable probably will not work properly with your printer. (If you have a color system, rename the COLOR profile to DEFAULT, as described in "Renaming a Profile," before you make any of the changes described in this section.)

To change the DEFAULT profile, close all open Enable windows. At the Main Menu, press **MCM** **P**rofile_options **R**evise. Enable displays the Profile Summary screen (refer to fig. B.1).

Type **DEFAULT** or press the up-arrow key to move the highlighted bar to the profile named DEFAULT; then press Enter. Enable displays the Profile Definition menu (see fig. B.2).

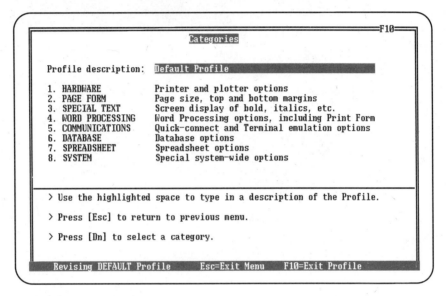

```
                                                                    ═F10═
                          ┌─────────────┐
                          │ Categories  │
                          └─────────────┘

   Profile description:  ▐ Default Profile                        ▌

   1. HARDWARE            Printer and plotter options
   2. PAGE FORM           Page size, top and bottom margins
   3. SPECIAL TEXT        Screen display of bold, italics, etc.
   4. WORD PROCESSING     Word Processing options, including Print Form
   5. COMMUNICATIONS      Quick-connect and Terminal emulation options
   6. DATABASE            Database options
   7. SPREADSHEET         Spreadsheet options
   8. SYSTEM              Special system-wide options


   > Use the highlighted space to type in a description of the Profile.

   > Press [Esc] to return to previous menu.

   > Press [Dn] to select a category.


    Revising DEFAULT Profile      Esc=Exit Menu     F10=Exit Profile
```

*Fig. B.2. The Profile Definition menu.*

The first line of this menu is an optional description you can use to remind yourself of the settings that make this profile different from others you may have created. On this line, you can list the type of printer you choose as the default—for example, you can type **Default Profile**. This description also appears in the Profile Summary screen next to the profile name DEFAULT. After you type a description, press Enter or the down-arrow key. Press the number of the category you want to change. Refer to the following discussions for setting feature options in each category.

# Setting Hardware Options

To set hardware options at the Profile Definition menu, press

        **1**. HARDWARE

The first screen (see fig. B.3) displays a series of questions about your printer. The first question is

```
Do you want to change the printer options?
```

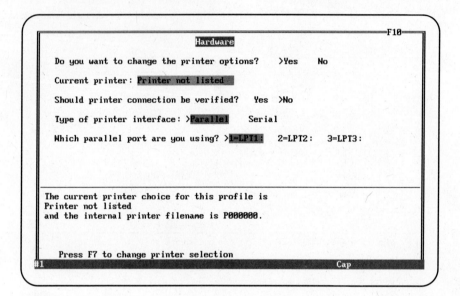

**Fig. B.3.** *The Printer profile choices.*

If you are modifying the DEFAULT profile for the first time, you should answer this question **Yes**. At the next line, press F7. Enable/OA then lists at the bottom of the screen the printers whose drivers you chose during installation. Use the arrow keys to move the highlighted bar to the name of the printer you want to use and press Enter. If necessary, you can choose another printer at print time. If your printer (or one your printer can emulate) isn't listed, see Appendix A for instructions on installing the appropriate printer driver. Press Enter or the down-arrow key to continue.

The next question on the screen is

```
Should printer connection be verified?
```

If you have a laser jet, and you always get a printer error, you should answer **No** to this prompt; otherwise, answer **Yes** so that Enable does not attempt to send a print job to a disconnected printer.

The next prompt on this screen is `Type of printer interface`. If you are unsure which type of printer interface your printer uses, check the printer manual. Some laser printers, for instance, use a serial printer interface. For most printers, however, you should choose **P**arallel. If you choose **P**arallel, you also need to indicate the printer port: LPT1, LPT2, or LPT3. Again, you may have to check your hardware manuals for the answer to this question. For most computers, you choose 1=LPT1.

If you have a serial printer, you need to answer several other questions. The first question is `Which serial port are you using?` At this question, indicate the serial port (COMM1 or COMM2) to which you have connected your printer. If you have only one serial port, it is probably COMM1. If you have a modem or mouse connected to your computer, your printer may be connected to COMM2. The second question is for the *baud rate*, the speed at which data transmits from your computer to the serial printer. The default setting of 9,600 bytes per second probably works for most printers. The last question asks you to specify a *protocol* (set of rules) for transmitting data from your computer to your printer. The protocol includes word size (the length in bits of a character), the number of *stop bits* (the additional bits that must follow each character to signal its end), and *parity* (the computer's error checking, if any, of data). Most printers work with option number 3, which specifies eight-bit word size, one stop bit, and no parity.

After you answer the last question on the Printer Options screen, Enable displays the Plotter Options screen. You must provide information for a plotter if your system has one. Answer **N**o to the first prompt `Do you wish to change plotter options?` to bypass this screen and return to the Printer Options screen. The questions on the Plotter Options screen are similar to the questions on the Printer Options screen. Refer to your plotter manual for the answer to the question about the Xon/Xoff protocol.

After you define the hardware options, press the Esc key to return to the main Profile Definition screen.

TIP

You don't have to go through every screen if you later make changes to a profile choice. Find the screen you need by pressing the down-arrow key, make the change, and then press Esc. Be careful: if you press Esc without first either pressing the first letter (or number) of that choice or highlighting the choice and pressing Enter (or the down arrow), the choice does not register. The same is true if you type an answer and then forget to press Enter before pressing Esc.

# Setting Page Form Options

To set Enable for paper size, line spacing, margin settings, character spacing, and print quality, start at the Profile Definition menu and press

 **2.** PAGE FORM

This category of options includes two screens. Enable uses the settings established here during printing in each of its modules; however, you can change all these settings at print time.

You may not need to change the first screen until you have used Enable for a time and find yourself frequently changing the settings at print time. Now, however, you may want to add a left margin offset of 10, which automatically adds a one-inch margin to the left of anything printed. The last item on the first screen, `Line spacing`, sets the number of blank lines between each line of text. For double spacing, set the number of blank lines to 1, not 2. Similarly, the header and footer settings determine the number of blank lines between a running header and the first line of text or between the last line of text and a running footer.

The second screen of the Page Form category has questions about page numbering, date format, pitch, proportional spacing, microjustification, letter quality, and graph print color and shading. You probably don't need to change these options until later, if you find yourself often changing them at print time.

After you customize the page form settings, press Esc to return to the Profile Definition menu.

# Setting Special Text Options

To set screen text colors, at the Profile Definition menu press

 **3.** SPECIAL TEXT

Enable supports three types of monitors. After you select your monitor type—**M**onochrome, **N**on-color graphics, or **C**olor graphics—you can use a separate screen to customize your monitor's text display.

If you use a monochrome monitor, you can choose different intensities for special text. If you have a color monitor, make sure that you have renamed the built-in COLOR profile to DEFAULT (see the section "Renaming a Profile" in this appendix). If you don't like the color scheme of the built-in

COLOR profile, experiment with the available colors shown at the bottom of the screen until you find color settings you like.

After you customize the screen display, press the Esc key until you return to the Profile Definition menu.

# Setting Word Processing Options

The word processing category of the profile options contains an assortment of choices that relate to many different word processing features. Because the chapters on word processing cover these features, this section does not cover them in detail.

With few exceptions, the supplied DEFAULT and COLOR profiles are already set as you probably want to use these options in word processing. If you do decide to change any of the word processing options, at the Profile Definition menu press

4. WORD PROCESSING

The options on the first screen, shown in figure B.4, determine whether the listed parts of a word processing document appear on-screen when they are created. If you change any of these options to No, that part of the document (header, footer, and so on), if created, does not appear on-screen when you open the file. For example, if you don't want to clutter your screen with table of contents entries, choose No for that option on this screen. When you later work on the file, any table of contents entries do not appear on-screen, but do appear when you compile the table of contents. One change from the original settings you may find helpful is to display the ruler at the top of the screen and within the body of the text at all times. (The default is to display it only at the top of the document.)

To view the second screen of word processing settings choices, move the cursor to `Display paper clips` and press the down-arrow key. Enable displays the screen shown in figure B.5.

You can set the text deletion feature in Enable/OA to ask for verification for deletion of blocks as well as lines, paragraphs, and larger segments of text. Answer Yes to the prompt

    Do you wish to be prompted to verify text deletion

to have a chance to change your mind before you delete large amounts of text from a word processing document.

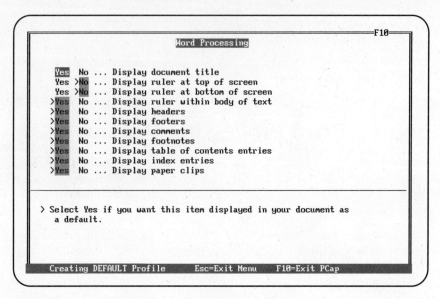

**Fig. B.4.** *The first Word Processing settings profile screen.*

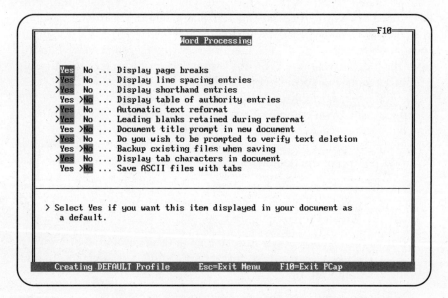

**Fig. B.5.** *The second Word Processing settings profile screen.*

Automatic backup is another protection feature. If you want Enable automatically to make a copy of the preceding version of a file whenever you save a new version, answer Yes to the option

```
Backup existing files when saving
```

Backup files have the same root name as the original file, but Enable changes the extension to WP@.

Enable/OA handles tabs in word processing much differently than previous versions of the program. Refer to Chapter 7, "Using Formatting Features," for a discussion of this feature. You may find keeping track of these new document tabs easier by displaying special tab characters in the document; to activate this feature, answer Yes to the option

```
Display tab characters in document
```

The final setting on this screen concerns files saved to disk in ASCII format. If you choose this option, when you save files in ASCII format, Enable uses tab markers rather than spaces, preserving more room on disk. Files in this format may not be compatible with some programs into which you want to import the ASCII files; therefore, the safest choice for now is No.

> ASCII (American Standard Code for Information Interchange) was developed by the American Standards Institute to standardize the codes used to represent letters, numbers, and special characters in computer systems. Look for additional information about saving files in ASCII format in Chapter 5, "Understanding Word Processing Basics."

After you finish with the second screen of prompts, press the down-arrow key, and the next Profile Definition screen appears. This third screen and the next two screens ask how and where to print footnotes. Because many people never use footnotes, and because Chapter 7 covers this topic, no further discussion of these options is necessary in this section.

You can use the next screen, the sixth word processing screen, to set a default margin and tab settings for the default ruler (see fig. B.6). New in Enable/OA 4.0 is the capability to use either a quick or detailed definition of the ruler. If you select Quick, the initial default ruler is set at a line length of 78 characters with 5 tab settings 8 spaces apart. If you print documents at 12 characters per inch (in Elite font), the original margin settings are fine. Just remember to set the Page Form profile to a one-inch left margin offset. If you print at 10 characters per inch (Pica), change the right margin to column 65. If you select Detailed, Enable displays an actual ruler that you can modify. Refer to the section "Using Rulers" in Chapter 7.

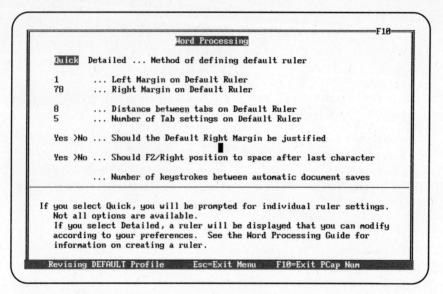

```
╔════════════════════════════════════════════════════════════F10══╗
║                      ▌Word Processing▐                           ║
║                                                                  ║
║     ▐Quick▌ Detailed ... Method of defining default ruler       ║
║                                                                  ║
║     1        ... Left Margin on Default Ruler                    ║
║     78       ... Right Margin on Default Ruler                   ║
║                                                                  ║
║     8        ... Distance between tabs on Default Ruler          ║
║     5        ... Number of Tab settings on Default Ruler         ║
║                                                                  ║
║     Yes >No ... Should the Default Right Margin be justified     ║
║                                    ▮                             ║
║     Yes >No ... Should F2/Right position to space after last character ║
║                                                                  ║
║              ... Number of keystrokes between automatic document saves ║
║  ──────────────────────────────────────────────────────────────║
║   If you select Quick, you will be prompted for individual ruler settings. ║
║   Not all options are available.                                 ║
║   If you select Detailed, a ruler will be displayed that you can modify ║
║   according to your preferences.  See the Word Processing Guide for ║
║   information on creating a ruler.                               ║
║                                                                  ║
║  ▐ Revising DEFAULT Profile      Esc=Exit Menu    F10=Exit PCap Num▌ ║
╚══════════════════════════════════════════════════════════════════╝
```

**Fig. B.6.** *The sixth Word Processing settings profile screen.*

You can choose how you want the F2-right arrow combination to work. The default setting causes the word processing cursor to move to the far-right character in a line of text when you press F2-right arrow in sequence. Try this setting now before you change this option.

Another feature you can choose is automatic save. In answer to the last question on this screen, you can specify how often, in terms of number of keystrokes, you want Enable automatically to save a document to disk. You probably want to use this option. The file name, unlike Automatic Backup discussed earlier, is TMPWP00X.WPF, or TMPWP00X.WP@. The X refers to the window in which you are editing the word processing file. If a file TMPWP00X.WPF exists, Enable renames it with the WP@ extension, and the current file saves with the WPF extension.

If you are concerned that you may write over an earlier version of the file prematurely, you also should choose the automatic backup feature.

After responding to each line on the screen, press the down-arrow key, and another screen of questions appears (see fig B.7).

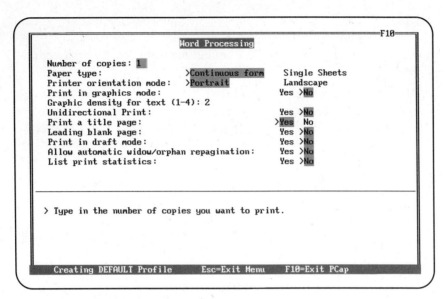

*Fig. B.7. The seventh Word Processing settings profile screen.*

The first question on this screen asks how many copies of each document you normally want to print. Most people enter **1** here; you can change this setting at print time. The next line of the screen asks about the type of printer paper. If you select **S**ingle Sheets, the printer pauses at the end of each page for you to feed the next sheet of paper. If you select **C**ontinuous form, the printer does not pause between pages.

Next, choose whether you normally plan to print in **P**ortrait or **L**andscape ("sideways") mode. Most printers always print in portrait mode. Many laser printers, and a few other types of printers, can print in landscape. You should choose **P**ortrait, because you can change this option at print time.

All printers will print "sideways" when you use the graphical interface; however, printing this way is much slower than "true" landscape printing.

Next, choose whether you normally plan to print in graphics mode. Most printers always print in character mode. If you answer Yes to this question, you also must specify a density for the text. You have a choice of 1-4. The higher the number, the darker the image and the finer the resolution.

The next question refers to unidirectional printing. If your printer can print in two directions, you may want to experiment before you answer this question to determine whether the higher-quality output of unidirectional printing is worth the reduced printer speed that results.

If you answer **Yes** to the next item, `Print a title page:`, Enable prints on a separate page information entered as the document title. In Enable, you enter title information in a special space on-screen at the beginning of each document. A leading blank page is useful as a cover sheet for printed documents or as a divider between copies.

Draft and final mode, as well as widows and orphans, are discussed in Chapter 7. Refer to that chapter for information on when and how to best use these options.

If you choose **Yes** for the final option, `List print statistics:`, Enable produces a printed summary of information about your document. This summary includes the number of words, the number of pages, and other similar data about your document, and prints on a separate page at the end of your document.

If you continue to press the down-arrow key, Enable displays another screen of questions. You can answer these prompts about the arrangement of the table of contents and which dictionary to use after you have some experience with Enable.

The next, and last, screen has two questions concerning the spelling checker. At the first prompt,

`Select master dictionary: Standard  Legal/Medical`

select your default dictionary. For most users, Standard is the correct response.

Finally, Enable prompts you to enter a user dictionary path. Enter a path at this prompt if you want to use the same user dictionary regardless of your data directory.

After you finish this screen of word processing prompts, press the Esc key to return to the Profile Definition menu.

# Setting Telecommunications Options

To customize the telecommunications options, at the Profile Definition menu press

**5**. COMMUNICATIONS

Refer to Chapter 18, "Telecommunicating with Enable," for discussions of the terminology used in these screens and for information about when and why you may want to change one or more of these defaults.

Press the Esc key to return to the Profile Definition menu.

# Setting Database Options

The next category of settings you can customize concerns the database module (see fig. B.8). To access the Database profile screen, at the Profile Definition menu press

6. DATABASE

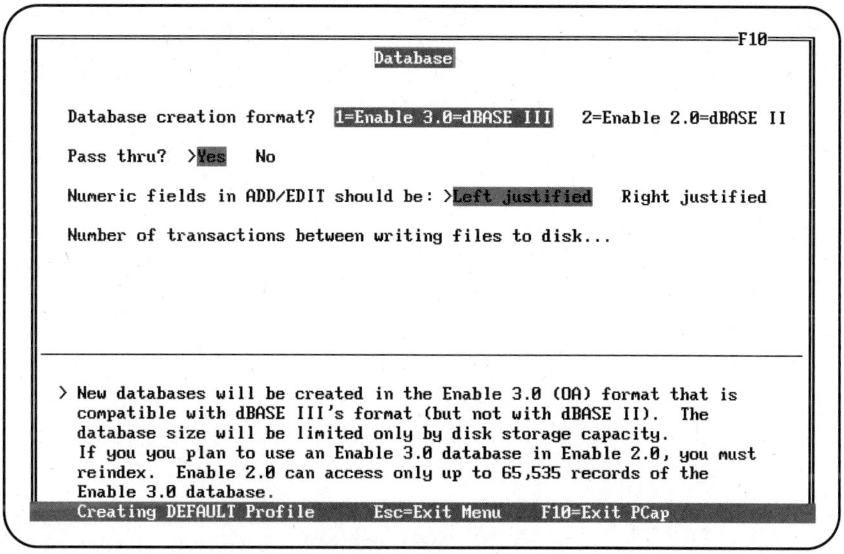

```
┌───────────────────────────────────────────────────────────────F10══┐
│                                                                     │
│                          ▨Database▨                                 │
│                                                                     │
│   Database creation format?  ▨1=Enable 3.0=dBASE III▨   2=Enable 2.0=dBASE II │
│                                                                     │
│   Pass thru?  >▨Yes▨   No                                           │
│                                                                     │
│   Numeric fields in ADD/EDIT should be: >▨Left justified▨   Right justified │
│                                                                     │
│   Number of transactions between writing files to disk...          │
│                                                                     │
│                                                                     │
│  ──────────────────────────────────────────────────────────────    │
│   > New databases will be created in the Enable 3.0 (OA) format that is │
│     compatible with dBASE III's format (but not with dBASE II).  The │
│     database size will be limited only by disk storage capacity.    │
│     If you you plan to use an Enable 3.0 database in Enable 2.0, you must │
│     reindex.  Enable 2.0 can access only up to 65,535 records of the │
│     Enable 3.0 database.                                            │
│   ▨Creating DEFAULT Profile      Esc=Exit Menu    F10=Exit PCap▨    │
└─────────────────────────────────────────────────────────────────────┘
```

***Fig. B.8.*** *The first Database settings profile screen.*

A significant feature of Enable/OA is full compatibility with dBASE III PLUS, including memo fields. This database format, however, is not compatible with Enable 2.0 and dBASE II. Choose option **1** on this screen unless you know you must exchange data frequently with Enable 2.0 and dBASE II. Option **1** only refers to all *new* databases creatcd with Enable/OA 4.0.

`Pass thru` means that data looked up from another database can be modified, and then automatically replaced in the database from which it came. Leave this option set at **Yes**.

At the third option, you can choose **Right_justified** to make numeric fields right-justified in a database input form. You should not change this answer (the default is **Left_justified**) until you have used the Database module for a while.

The last option on this screen is a much needed automatic save feature for Enable's Database module. Enter a number here (for example, **10**) to instruct Enable how often, in terms of number of records accessed, you want Enable to save to disk the data you have entered into RAM (memory).

The next screen has three more questions. For now, leave the answer to `Stop on all database errors` set at **No**. Choosing **Yes** forces you to press Enter repeatedly to continue past even minor database errors.

Change the `REPORT print option` to `Spool report` so that you can continue to work on a database even while printing a report from it.

The `DISPLAY records option` has advantages and disadvantages no matter which way you set it. For now, leave the option set at **Full-Page**.

Press the Esc key to return to the Profile Definition menu.

# Setting Spreadsheet Options

The next selection on the Profile Definition menu is for the spreadsheet module options. At the Profile Definition menu, press

> 7. SPREADSHEET

The options on the first page are shown in figure B.9

If you plan to exchange spreadsheet files with 1-2-3, you probably should change the protection default from **No** to **Yes**. The reason for this setting becomes clear when you read the discussion about protecting spreadsheet cells in Chapter 11, "Using Spreadsheet Advanced Features."

Set `Convert Lotus 1-2-3 macros` according to your preference. Use this option if you want Enable to convert Lotus 1-2-3 macros to equivalent Enable macros. Choose **No** if you want to use the macros only in 1-2-3, and **Yes** if you want to use the macros in Enable. If you routinely import 1-2-3 worksheets into Enable, you probably know whether you want the macros converted.

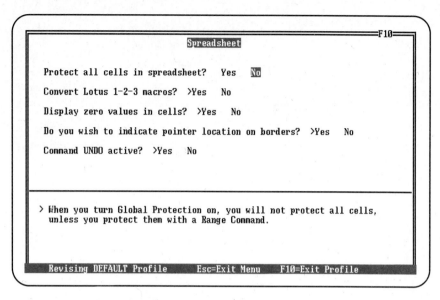

```
                                                                    =F10=
                            Spreadsheet

    Protect all cells in spreadsheet?    Yes    No

    Convert Lotus 1-2-3 macros?  >Yes   No

    Display zero values in cells?  >Yes   No

    Do you wish to indicate pointer location on borders?   >Yes    No

    Command UNDO active?  >Yes   No



   ──────────────────────────────────────────────────────────────────

   > When you turn Global Protection on, you will not protect all cells,
     unless you protect them with a Range Command.



    Revising DEFAULT Profile     Esc=Exit Menu    F10=Exit Profile
```

**Fig. B.9.** *The first Spreadsheet settings profile screen.*

Use the next choice on the spreadsheet profile screen in Enable/OA to choose whether zero values should be displayed in cells in a spreadsheet. You can decide how to answer this question after you gain experience with the spreadsheet.

Use the next choice to indicate whether you want your pointer location reverse highlighted on the borders. Try this option to see whether you like it (the default answer is **No**).

The last choice on this screen is `Command UNDO active`. **Answer Yes** so that you can undo the last command you made in a spreadsheet. Be aware that this option uses extra memory. Refer to the section "Using the Undo Command" in Chapter 9 for more information about the Undo command.

Press the down arrow after the last prompt, and Enable displays the second spreadsheet screen, shown in figure B.10.

The first option, `Check contents of referenced cells`, is a toggle that, if activated, warns you when you enter a formula that references a cell containing nonnumeric data. This feature is useful to lessen the number of data entry errors.

The second option asks

`Backup existing spreadsheet files when saving`

Change this feature to **Yes** only if you want Enable to make an extra copy of a spreadsheet on disk before replacing the copy on disk with the one on-screen. Enable saves the file with the extension SS@.

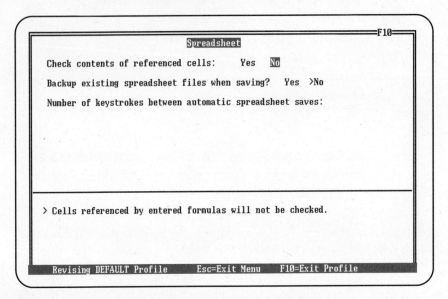

*Fig. B.10. The second Spreadsheet settings profile screen.*

The next feature is the same as the automatic save in the Word Processing section. In answer to the last question on this screen, specify how often, in terms of number of keystrokes, you want Enable automatically to save a spreadsheet to disk. You probably want to use this option. If you are concerned that you may prematurely write over an earlier version of the file, you also should choose the automatic backup feature discussed in the preceding paragraph.

Press Esc to return to the Profile Definition menu.

# Setting System Options

The final group of options to set on your profile is system options (see fig. B.11). Choose

9. SYSTEM

You need to make only five choices here. First, choose what action should occur when you press the backspace key. You probably want to choose **4**, which causes the backspace key to delete the character to the left and pull over the remaining text from the right.

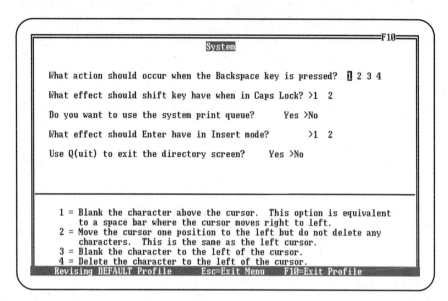

**Fig. B.11.** *The System Options settings profile screen.*

The next choice on this screen concerns the relationship of the Shift key and the Caps Lock key. You probably want to choose **2** so that you can type lowercase letters when the Caps Lock key is on by pressing Shift and the letter you want.

Choose the next option to turn off the system print queue. Choosing **Yes** leaves the print queue on and gives you the most flexibility during printing. Be sure, however, that you read the entire printing section in Chapter 5, "Understanding Word Processing Basics," to understand fully the operation of the print queue.

The option you choose for the effect of the Enter key depends on your preference. Choose **1** to insert a paragraph and move the cursor to the left margin of the next line; choose **2** to split the line and begin a new paragraph.

The last option concerns the File Manager screen discussed in Chapter 3, "Understanding the Master Control Module." If you choose **Yes** in answer to this option, before you leave the File Manager screen, a new feature of Enable/OA 4.0 automatically prompts you if you have any marked files.

After you change the profile, press the following keys to save your changes:

F10 **File Save** F10 **File Exit**

Remember that whenever you modify the default profile, the changes do not take effect until you select that profile again, even if you currently are using the same profile. You must select that profile from the list of profile names by pressing **MCM Profile_options Select**. Either type the name or highlight the DEFAULT profile and press Enter.

# Creating a Profile

If you use Enable on a single-user computer at your home or office, you may not have to worry about which feature option settings someone else may prefer; you can customize and use only the DEFAULT profile. However, if you share Enable at the office or at home, others who use the system may have different preferences about screen color, margin settings, the print font, and so on. To accommodate different needs and tastes, you can create several profiles with Enable, one to suit each user.

To create a new profile, close all open Enable windows. At the Main Menu, press **MCM Profile_options Create**. The Profile Summary screen appears.

Type the name you want to give this profile (up to eight letters) and press Enter. The Profile Definition screen appears.

The first line of this menu is an optional description line you can use to remind yourself of the settings that make this profile unique. You can name the printer you choose as the default—for example, you can type **HP Laser Jet II Printer**. This description also appears in the Profile Summary screen next to the profile name. When you finish on this line, press Enter or the down arrow. Then press the number that precedes the feature category you want to change. You need not start from scratch when you create a profile in this manner. When you begin defining the new profile, all the settings are identical to the current DEFAULT profile settings. Refer to the discussions that follow the "Changing a Profile" section to learn about setting feature options in each category.

# Deleting a Profile

You may decide to remove one of the profiles from the list on the Profile Summary screen. To delete a profile, you first need to close all open Enable windows. At the Main Menu, press **MCM Profile_options Revise**. Enable displays the Profile Summary screen.

Press the up arrow to move the highlighted bar up into the list of profiles, and then use the arrow keys to move the highlighted bar to the name of the profile you want to remove. To delete this profile, press **Delete**. Enable displays the following prompt:

```
Are you sure this profile should be deleted?  Yes  No
```

Press **Yes** to remove the profile name from the list. To complete the deletion, you must save the new, shorter profile list, and then quit from the Profile Summary screen by pressing

F10 **File Save** F10 **File Exit**

# Summary

Now that you have set up Enable the way you want it, you are ready to learn about the basic structure and organization of the program, covered in Chapter 1, "Using Enable's Modules."

# Index

## X-Z